11⁹⁵

D0938030

WORD PICTURES
IN THE
NEW TESTAMENT

BOOKS BY PROFESSOR A. T. ROBERTSON

The English New Testament as a Whole:
SYLLABUS FOR NEW TESTAMENT STUDY
THE STUDENT'S CHRONOLOGICAL NEW TESTAMENT
STUDIES IN THE NEW TESTAMENT
NEW TESTAMENT HISTORY (AIRPLANE VIEW)

The Greek New Testament:
WORD PICTURES IN THE NEW TESTAMENT (IN SIX VOLS.)
A NEW SHORT GRAMMAR OF THE GREEK TESTAMENT
A GRAMMAR OF THE GREEK NEW TESTAMENT IN THE LIGHT OF HISTORICAL RESEARCH
THE MINISTER AND HIS GREEK NEW TESTAMENT
AN INTRODUCTION TO THE TEXTUAL CRITICISM OF THE NEW TESTAMENT
STUDIES IN THE TEXT OF THE NEW TESTAMENT

The Gospels and Jesus:
A HARMONY OF THE GOSPELS FOR STUDENTS OF THE LIFE OF CHRIST
A COMMENTARY ON MATTHEW
STUDIES IN MARK'S GOSPEL
LUKE THE HISTORIAN IN THE LIGHT OF RESEARCH
A TRANSLATION OF LUKE'S GOSPEL
THE DIVINITY OF CHRIST IN THE GOSPEL OF JOHN
JOHN THE LOYAL (THE MINISTRY OF THE BAPTIST)
THE PHARISEES AND JESUS (STONE LECTURES FOR 1916)
EPOCHS IN THE LIFE OF JESUS
KEYWORDS IN THE TEACHING OF JESUS
THE TEACHING OF JESUS CONCERNING GOD THE FATHER
THE CHRIST OF THE LOGIA (PORTRAITS OF CHRIST IN Q AND THE GOSPELS)
THE MOTHER OF JESUS: HER PROBLEMS AND HER GLORY

Paul:
PAUL AND THE INTELLECTUALS (EPISTLE TO THE COLOSSIANS)
EPOCHS IN THE LIFE OF PAUL
PAUL THE INTERPRETER OF CHRIST
PAUL'S JOY IN CHRIST (EPISTLE TO THE PHILIPPIANS)
THE GLORY OF THE MINISTRY (II COR. 2:12–6:10)
THE NEW CITIZENSHIP

Other Studies in the New Testament:
SOME MINOR CHARACTERS IN THE NEW TESTAMENT
STUDIES IN THE EPISTLE OF JAMES
MAKING GOOD IN THE MINISTRY (SKETCH OF JOHN MARK)
TYPES OF PREACHERS IN THE NEW TESTAMENT

Biography:
LIFE AND LETTERS OF JOHN ALBERT BROADUS

WORD PICTURES
IN THE
NEW TESTAMENT

BY

ARCHIBALD THOMAS ROBERTSON
A. M., D. D., LL. D., Litt. D.

PROFESSOR OF NEW TESTAMENT INTERPRETATION
IN THE
SOUTHERN BAPTIST THEOLOGICAL SEMINARY
OF
LOUISVILLE, KENTUCKY

VOLUME IV
THE EPISTLES OF PAUL

BROADMAN PRESS
NASHVILLE, TENNESSEE

PRINTED IN THE UNITED STATES OF AMERICA

CONTENTS

THE EPISTLES OF PAUL

FIRST THESSALONIANS
PAGE

CHAPTER I 5
CHAPTER II 15
CHAPTER III 25
CHAPTER IV 28
CHAPTER V 34

SECOND THESSALONIANS
CHAPTER I 41
CHAPTER II 47
CHAPTER III 56

FIRST CORINTHIANS
CHAPTER I 68
CHAPTER II 82
CHAPTER III 92
CHAPTER IV 102
CHAPTER V 111
CHAPTER VI 117
CHAPTER VII 124
CHAPTER VIII 137
CHAPTER IX 142
CHAPTER X 151
CHAPTER XI 159
CHAPTER XII 167
CHAPTER XIII 176
CHAPTER XIV 181
CHAPTER XV 186
CHAPTER XVI 200

SECOND CORINTHIANS PAGE
CHAPTER I 208
CHAPTER II 215
CHAPTER III 220
CHAPTER IV 224
CHAPTER V 228
CHAPTER VI 234
CHAPTER VII 238
CHAPTER VIII 243
CHAPTER IX 247
CHAPTER X 251
CHAPTER XI 257
CHAPTER XII 264
CHAPTER XIII 270

GALATIANS
CHAPTER I 275
CHAPTER II 282
CHAPTER III 291
CHAPTER IV 300
CHAPTER V 309
CHAPTER VI 315

ROMANS
CHAPTER I 323
CHAPTER II 334
CHAPTER III 341
CHAPTER IV 350
CHAPTER V 355
CHAPTER VI 361
CHAPTER VII 366
CHAPTER VIII 372
CHAPTER IX 380
CHAPTER X 387
CHAPTER XI 392

ROMANS—*Continued*   PAGE
CHAPTER XII 402
CHAPTER XIII 407
CHAPTER XIV 412
CHAPTER XV 417
CHAPTER XVI 425

PHILIPPIANS
CHAPTER I 435
CHAPTER II 443
CHAPTER III 451
CHAPTER IV 458

PHILEMON 464

COLOSSIANS
CHAPTER I 473
CHAPTER II 487
CHAPTER III 500
CHAPTER IV 509

EPHESIANS
CHAPTER I 516
CHAPTER II 523
CHAPTER III 530
CHAPTER IV 535
CHAPTER V 542
CHAPTER VI 548

FIRST TIMOTHY
CHAPTER I 560
CHAPTER II 567
CHAPTER III 572
CHAPTER IV 578
CHAPTER V 583
CHAPTER VI 591

TITUS
                                                        PAGE
    CHAPTER   I   597
    CHAPTER   II   602
    CHAPTER   III 606

SECOND TIMOTHY
    CHAPTER   I   610
    CHAPTER   II   616
    CHAPTER   III 623
    CHAPTER   IV   629

THE EPISTLES OF PAUL

BY WAY OF INTRODUCTION

IMPORTANCE OF PAUL'S WORK

It is impossible to put too much emphasis on the life and work of Paul as the great interpreter of Christ. He has been misunderstood in modern times as he was during his career. Some accuse him of perverting the pure gospel of Christ about the Kingdom of God into a theological and ecclesiastical system. He has been accused of rabbinizing the gospel by carrying over his Pharisaism, while others denounce him for Hellenizing the gospel with Greek philosophy and the Greek mystery-religions. But out of all the welter of attacks Paul's Epistles stand as the marvellous expression of his own conception of Christ and the application of the gospel to the life of the Christians in the Graeco-Roman world in which they lived by eternal principles that apply to us today. In order to understand Paul's Epistles one must know the Acts of the Apostles in which Luke has drawn with graphic power the sudden change of the foremost opponent of Christ into the chief expounder and proclaimer of the gospel of the Risen Christ. The Acts and the Epistles supplement each other in a marvellous way, though chiefly in an incidental fashion. It is by no means certain that Luke had access to any of Paul's Epistles before he wrote the Acts, though that was quite possible for the early Epistles. It does not greatly matter for Luke had access to Paul himself both in Caesarea and in Rome. The best life of Paul one can get comes by combining the Acts with the Epistles if he knows how to do it. Paul is Luke's hero, but he has not overdrawn the picture in the Acts as is made clear by the Epistles themselves which reveal his own grasp and growth. The literature on Paul is vast and constantly growing. He possesses a fascination for students of the New Testament and of Christianity. It is impossible here to allude even to the most important in so vast a field. Conybeare and Howson's *Life and Epistles of St. Paul* still has value. Sir W. M. Ramsay has a small library on Paul and his Epistles. Stalker's masterful little book on Paul still grips men as does the work of Sabatier. Deissmann's *St. Paul* continues to throw light on the great Apostle to the Gentiles. Those who wish my own view at greater length will find them in my various books on Paul (*Epochs in the Life of Paul, Paul the Interpreter of Christ, etc.*).

THE REASON FOR HIS EPISTLES

In a real sense Paul's Epistles are tracts for the times, not for the age in general, but to meet real emergencies. He wrote to a particular church or group of churches or persons to meet immediate needs brought to his attention by messengers or letters. Dr. Deissmann contends strongly for the idea of calling Paul's Epistles "letters" rather than "Epistles." He gives a studied literary character to "epistles" as more or less artificial and written for the public eye rather than for definite effect. Four of Paul's Epistles are personal (those to Philemon, Titus, and Timothy) beyond a doubt, but in these which can properly be termed personal letters there are the principles of the gospel applied to personal, social, and ecclesiastical problems in such a pungent fashion that they possess permanent value. In the earliest group of Paul's Epistles, he reminds the Thessalonians of the official character of the Epistle which was meant for the church as a whole (I Thess. 5:27). He says also: "But if any one does not obey our word by the epistle, mark this one, not to associate with him, that he may be put to shame" (II Thess. 3:14). He calls attention to his signature as proof of the genuineness of every epistle (II Thess. 3:17). He gave directions for the public reading of his epistles (Col. 4:16). He regarded them as the expression of God's will through the life of the churches and he put his whole heart into them. Two great controversies stirred Paul's life. That with the Judaizers called forth the great doctrinal group (I Corinthians, II Corinthians, Galatians, Romans). That with the Gnostics occasioned the Epistles to the Colossians and the Ephesians (Laodiceans) and this controversy ran on into the Pastoral Epistles. Each Epistle had its particular occasion which will be pointed out in due season. But even in the short ones like Philippians, Colossians and Ephesians Paul deals with the sublimest of all themes, the Person of Christ, with a masterfulness never equalled elsewhere. Even in I Corinthians, which deals so largely with church problems in Corinth, two great chapters rise to the heights of real eloquence (Chapter 13 on Love and Chapter 15 on the Resurrection). Romans, the greatest of his Epistles, has the fullest discussion of Paul's gospel of grace and Chapter 8 has a sweep of imagination and a grasp of faith unsurpassed. Hence, while denying to Paul the artificial rules of the rhetoricians attributed to him by Blass, I cannot agree that Paul's church Epistles are mere incidental letters. It is not a question whether Paul was writing for posterity or for the present emergency. He wrote for the present emergency in the most effective possible way. He brought the whole gospel message to bear upon the varied and pressing problems of the early Christians in the power of the Holy Spirit with the eloquence of a mind all ablaze with the truth and with a heart that yearned for their souls for Christ. They are not literary epistles, but they are more than personal letters. They are thunderbolts of passion and power that struck centre and that strike fire now for all who will take the trouble to come to them for the mind of Christ that is here.

DATES OF HIS EPISTLES

Unfortunately there is not complete agreement among scholars as to the dates of some of Paul's Epistles. Baur denied the Pauline authorship of all the Epistles save I and II Corinthians, Galatians, Romans. Today some deny that Paul wrote the Pastoral Epistles, though admitting the others. Some admit Pauline fragments even in the Pastoral Epistles, but more about this when these Epistles are reached. There is more doubt about the date of Galatians than any of the others. Lightfoot put it just before Romans, while Ramsay now makes it the earliest of all. The Epistle itself has no notes of place or time. The Epistles to the Thessalonians were written from Corinth after Timothy had been sent from Athens by Paul to Thessalonica (I Thess. 3:1f.) and had just returned to Paul (I Thess. 3:6) which we know was in Corinth (Acts 18:5) shortly before Gallio came as Proconsul of Achaia (Acts 18:12). We can now feel certain from the new "acclamation" of Claudius in the inscription at Delphi recently explained by Deissmann in

his *St. Paul* that the Thessalonian Epistles were written
50 to 51 A.D. We know also that he wrote I Corinthians
while in Ephesus (I Cor. 16:8) and before pentecost, though
the precise year is not given. But he spent three years at
Ephesus in round numbers (Acts 19:8, 10; 20:31) and he
wrote just before he left, probably spring of A.D. 54 or 55.
He wrote II Corinthians from Macedonia shortly after leaving Ephesus (II Cor. 2:12) apparently the same year. Romans
was written from Corinth and sent by Phoebe of Cenchreae
(Rom. 16:1f.) unless Rom. 16 be considered a separate
Epistle to Ephesus as some hold, a view that does not commend itself to me. Deissmann (*New Testament in the Light
of Modern Research*, p. 33) accepts a modern theory that
Ephesus was the place of the writing of the first prison
Epistles (Philippians, Philemon, Colossians, Ephesians) as
well as I Corinthians and Galatians and dates them all
between A.D. 52 and 55. But we shall find that these prison
Epistles most naturally fall to Rome between A.D. 61 and 63.
If the Pastoral Epistles are genuine, as I hold, they come
between A.D. 65 and 68. Bartlet argues for a date before
A.D. 64, accepting the view that Paul was put to death then.
But it is still far more probable that Paul met his death in
Rome in A.D. 68 shortly before Nero's death which was
June 8, A.D. 68. It will thus be seen that the dates of several
of the Epistles are fairly clear, while some remain quite
uncertain. In a broad outlook they must all come between
A.D. 50 and 68.

Four Groups of Pauline Epistles

I. First Thessalonians. ⎫
   Second Thessalonians. ⎬ A.D. 50 to 51.

 Chief topic Eschatology. To correct misconceptions
 in Thessalonica.

II. First Corinthians. ⎫
  Second Corinthians. ⎪
  Galatians. ⎬ A.D. 54 to 57.
  Romans. ⎭

 Chief topic Justification by Faith. Defence against
 the Judaizers.

III. Philippians.
Philemon.
Colossians.   } A.D. 61 to 63.
Ephesians (Laodiceans).

Chief topic Christology. Defence against the Gnostic perversions of the Person of Christ.

IV. First Timothy.
Titus.   } A.D. 65 to 68.
Second Timothy.

Ecclesiastical Problems to the fore.

DEVELOPMENT IN PAUL'S THEOLOGY

The study of Paul's Epistles in the order of their writing is the best possible way of seeing his own growth as a theologian and interpreter of Christ. Sabatier long ago laid emphasis on this point in his book *The Apostle Paul* as did Matheson in *The Spiritual Development of Paul*. It is a tragedy to have to read Paul's Epistles as printed in the usual Greek text of Westcott and Hort and the English translations, beginning with Romans and ending with Philemon. In the manuscripts that give Paul's Epistles Romans comes first as the largest and most important, but Titus and Philemon come after II Timothy (the last just before his death). We know something of Paul's early preaching how he laid emphasis on the Messiahship of Jesus proven by his resurrection, Paul himself having seen the Risen Christ (Acts 9:22). This conviction and experience lay at the foundation of all his work and he never faltered concerning it (Acts 17:3). In the earliest sermon of which we have a full report Paul proclaims justification by faith in Christ with forgiveness of sins (Acts 13:38f.), blessings not obtained by the law of Moses. In the unfolding life of Paul he grappled with great problems of Jewish rabbinism and Greek philosophy and mystery-religions and Paul himself grew in stature as he courageously and victoriously faced Judaizer and Gnostic. There are scholars who claim that Paul surrendered to the appeal of Gnostic sacramentarianism and so went back on his great doctrine of justification by faith, not by works. It will be shown at the proper time that this view misinterprets Paul's attitude. The events given by Luke in the Acts fit in with the self-revelation of Paul in his own Epistles as we read them. Each one of the four groups of Epistles has a slightly different style and vocabulary as is natural when one comes to think of it. The same thing is true of the plays of Shakespeare and the poems of Milton. Style is the man, Buffon says. Yes, but style is also a function of the subject. Particularly is this true of vocabulary which has to vary with the different topics treated. But style in the same man varies with different ages. Ripened old age mellows the exuberance of youth and the passionate vehemence of manhood. We shall see Paul himself in his Epistles, letting himself go in various ways and in different moods. But in all the changing phases of his life and work there is the same masterful man who glories in being the slave of Jesus Christ and the Apostle to the Gentiles. The passion of Paul is Christ and one can feel the throb of the heart of the chief of sinners who became the chief of saints in all his Epistles. There is the Pauline glow and glory in them all.

SOME BOOKS ON THE PAULINE EPISTLES

Bate, *As a Whole Guide to the Epistles of St. Paul* (1927).
Bonnet-Schroeder, *Epîtres de Paul* (4 ed. 1912).
Champlain, *The Epistles of Paul* (1906).
Clemen, *Einheitlichkeit d. paul. Briefe* (1894).
Conybeare and Howson, *Life and Epistles of St. Paul.*
Drummond, *The Epistles of Paul the Apostle* (1899).
Hayes, *Paul and His Epistles* (1915).
Heinrici, *Die Forschungen über die paul. Briefe* (1886).
Lake, *The Earlier Epistles of St. Paul* (1915).
Lewin, *Life and Epistles of St. Paul.* (1875).
Neil, *The Pauline Epistles* (1906).
Scott, *The Pauline Epistles* (1909).
Shaw, *The Pauline Epistles* (1903).
Vischer, *Die Paulusbriefe* (1910).
Voelter, *Die Composition der paul. Haupt Briefe* (1890).
Voelter, *Paulus und seine Briefe* (1905).
Way, *The Letters of Paul to Seven Churches and Three Friends* (1906).

Weinel, *Die Echtheit der paul. Hauptbriefe* (1920).

Weiss, B., *Present Status of the Inquiry Concerning the Genuineness of the Pauline Epistles* (1901).

Weiss, B., *Die Paulinische Briefe* (1902).

Wood, *Life, Letters, and Religion of St. Paul* (1925).

THE FIRST GROUP:
First Thessalonians
Second Thessalonians
A.D. 50 TO 51

FIRST THESSALONIANS
From Corinth a.d. 50 to 51

BY WAY OF INTRODUCTION

We cannot say that this is Paul's first letter to a church, for in II Thess. 2:2 he speaks of some as palming off letters as his and in II Thess. 3:17 he says that he appends his own signature to every letter after dictating it to an amanuensis (Rom. 16:22). We know of one lost letter (I Cor. 5:11) and perhaps another (II Cor. 2:3). But this is the earliest one that has come down to us and it may even be the earliest New Testament book, unless the Epistle of James antedates it or even Mark's Gospel. We know, as already shown, that Paul was in Corinth and that Timothy and Silas had just arrived from Thessalonica (I Thess. 3:6; Acts 18:5). They had brought supplies from the Macedonian churches to supply Paul's need (II Cor. 11:9), as the church in Philippi did once and again while Paul was in Thessalonica (Phil. 4:15f.). Before Timothy and Silas came to Corinth Paul had to work steadily at his trade as tent-maker with Aquila and Priscilla (Acts 18:3) and could only preach in the synagogue on sabbaths, but the rich stores from Macedonia released his hands and "Paul devoted himself to the word" (*suneicheto tōi logōi Paulos*). He gave himself wholly to preaching now. But Timothy and Silas brought news of serious trouble in the church in Thessalonica. Some of the disciples there had misunderstood Paul's preaching about the second coming of Christ and had quit work and were making a decided disturbance on the subject. Undoubtedly Paul had touched upon eschatological matters while in Thessalonica. The Jewish leaders at Thessalonica charged it against Paul and Silas to the politarchs that they had preached another king, Jesus, in place of Caesar. Paul had preached Jesus as King of the spiritual kingdom which the Jews misrepresented to the politarchs as treason against

3

Caesar as the Sanhedrin had done to Pilate about Jesus. Clearly Paul had said also that Jesus was going to come again according to his own promise before his ascension. Some asserted that Paul said Jesus was going to come right away and drew their own inferences for idleness and fanaticism as some do today. Strange as it may seem, there are scholars today who say that Paul did believe and say that Jesus was going to come back right away. They say this in spite of II Thess. 2:1f. where Paul denies having ever said it. Undoubtedly Paul hoped for the early return of Jesus as most of the early Christians did, but that is a very different thing from setting a time for his coming. It is open to us all to hope for the speedy return of Christ, but times and seasons are with God and not with us. It is not open to us to excuse our negligence and idleness as Christians because of such a hope. That hope should serve as a spur to increased activity for Christ in order to hasten his coming. So Paul writes this group of Epistles to correct gross misapprehension and misrepresentation of his preaching about last things (eschatology). It is a rare preacher who has never been misunderstood or misrepresented.

There are excellent commentaries on the Thessalonian Epistles.

On the Greek text one may note those by
Dibelius, *Handbuch zum N. T. Zweite Auflage* (1925);
Dobschütz, *Meyer-Kommentar* (1909);
Ellicott, *Crit. and Grammat. Comm.* (1884);
Findlay, *Cambridge Gk. Test.* (1904);
Frame, *Intern. Critical Comm.* (1912);
Lightfoot, *Notes on Epistles of Paul* (1895);
Mayer, *Die Thessalonischerbriefe* (1908);
Milligan, *St. Paul's Epistles to the Thess.* (1908);
Moffatt, *Expos. Gk. Test.* (1910);
Plummer, *First Thess.* (1908), *Second Thess.* (1908);
Wohlenberg, *Zahn-Komm. 2 aufl.* (1908).
On the English text note those by
Adeney, *New Century Bible* (1907);
Denney, *Expos. Bible* (1892);
Findlay, *Cambridge Bible* (1891);
Hutchinson, *Lectures on I & II Thess.* (1883).

CHAPTER I

1. *Paul, and Silvanus, and Timothy (Paulos kai Silouanos kai Timotheos)*. Nominative absolute as customary in letters. Paul associates with himself Silvanus (Silas of Acts, spelled *Silbanos* in D and the papyri), a Jew and Roman citizen, and Timothy, son of Jewish mother and Greek father, one of Paul's converts at Lystra on the first tour. They had both been with Paul at Thessalonica, though Timothy is not mentioned by Luke in Acts in Macedonia till Beroea (Acts 17:14f.). Timothy had joined Paul in Athens (I Thess. 3:1f.), had been sent back to Thessalonica, and with Silas had rejoined Paul in Corinth (I Thess. 3:5; Acts 18:5, II Cor. 1:19). Silas is the elder and is mentioned first, but neither is in any sense the author of the Epistle any more than Sosthenes is co-author of I Corinthians or Timothy of II Corinthians, though Paul may sometimes have them in mind when he uses "we" in the Epistle. Paul does not here call himself "apostle" as in the later Epistles, perhaps because his position has not been so vigorously attacked as it was later. Ellicott sees in the absence of the word here a mark of the affectionate relations existing between Paul and the Thessalonians. *Unto the church of the Thessalonians (tēi ekklēsiāi Thessalonikeōn)*. The dative case in address. Note absence of the article with *Thessalonikeōn* because a proper name and so definite without it. This is the common use of *ekklēsia* for a local body (church). The word originally meant "assembly" as in Acts 19:39, but it came to mean an organization for worship whether assembled or unassembled (cf. Acts 8:3). The only superscription in the oldest Greek manuscripts (Aleph B A) is *Pros Thessalonikeis A (To the Thessalonians First)*. But probably Paul wrote no superscription and certainly he would not write A to it before he had written II Thessalonians (B). His signature at the close was the proof of genuineness (II Thess. 3:17) against all spurious claimants (II Thess. 2:2). Unfortunately the brittle papyrus on which he wrote easily perished outside of the sand heaps and tombs of Egypt or the lava covered ruins

5

of Herculaneum. What a treasure that autograph would be! *In God the Father and the Lord Jesus Christ (en theōi patri kai kuriōi Jēsou Christōi).* This church is grounded *in* (*en*, with the locative case) and exists in the sphere and power of *God the Father and the Lord Jesus Christ.* No article in the Greek, for both *theōi patri* and *kuriōi Jēsou Christōi* are treated as proper names. In the very beginning of this first Epistle of Paul we meet his Christology. He at once uses the full title, "Lord Jesus Christ," with all the theological content of each word. The name "Jesus" (Saviour, Matt. 1:21) he knew, as the "Jesus of history," the personal name of the Man of Galilee, whom he had once persecuted (Acts 9:5), but whom he at once, after his conversion, proclaimed to be "the Messiah," (*ho Christos,* Acts 9:22). This position Paul never changed. In the great sermon at Antioch in Pisidia which Luke has preserved (Acts 13:23) Paul proved that God fulfilled his promise to Israel by raising up "Jesus as Saviour" (*sōtēra Iēsoun*). Now Paul follows the Christian custom by adding *Christos* (verbal from *chriō,* to anoint) as a proper name to Jesus (Jesus Christ) as later he will often say "Christ Jesus" (Col. 1:1). And he dares also to apply *kurios* (Lord) to "Jesus Christ," the word appropriated by Claudius (*Dominus, Kurios*) and other emperors in the emperor-worship, and also common in the Septuagint for God as in Psa. 32:1f. (quoted by Paul in Rom. 4:8). Paul uses *Kurios* of God (I Cor. 3:5) or of Jesus Christ as here. In fact, he more frequently applies it to Christ when not quoting the Old Testament as in Rom. 4:8. And here he places "the Lord Jesus Christ" in the same category and on the same plane with "God the father." There will be growth in Paul's Christology and he will never attain all the knowledge of Christ for which he longs (Phil. 3:10-12), but it is patent that here in his first Epistle there is no "reduced Christ" for Paul. He took Jesus as "Lord" when he surrendered to Jesus on the Damascus Road: "And I said, What shall I do, Lord? And the Lord said to me" (Acts 22:10). It is impossible to understand Paul without seeing clearly this first and final stand for the Lord Jesus Christ. Paul did not get this view of Jesus from current views of Mithra or of Isis or any other alien faith. The Risen Christ became at once for Paul the Lord of his life. *Grace to you*

and peace (*charis humin kai eirēnē*). These words, common
in Paul's Epistles, bear "the stamp of Paul's experience"
(Milligan). They are not commonplace salutations, but the
old words "deepened and spiritualised" (Frame). The infinitive (*chairein*) so common in the papyri letters and seen
in the New Testament also (Acts 15:23; 23:26; James 1:1)
here gives place to *charis*, one of the great words of the New
Testament (cf. John 1:16f.) and particularly of the Pauline
Epistles. Perhaps no one word carries more meaning for
Paul's messages than this word *charis* (from *chairō*, rejoice)
from which *charizomai* comes. *Peace* (*eirēnē*) is more than
the Hebrew *shalōm* so common in salutations. One recalls
the "peace" that Christ leaves to us (John 14:27) and the
peace of God that passes all understanding (Phil. 4:7). This
introduction is brief, but rich and gracious and pitches the
letter at once on a high plane.

2. *We give thanks* (*eucharistoumen*). Late denominative
verb *eucharisteō* from *eucharistos* (grateful) and that from *eu*,
well and *charizomai*, to show oneself kind. See *charis* in
verse 1. "The plural implies that all three missionaries
prayed together" (Moffatt). *Always* (*pantote*). Late word,
rare in LXX. So with *eucharisteō* in II Thess. 1:3; 2:13; I
Cor. 1:4; Eph. 5:20; Phil. 1:3. Moffatt takes it to mean
"whenever Paul was at his prayers." Of course, he did not
make audible prayer always, but he was always in the spirit
of prayer, "a constant attitude" (Milligan), "in tune with
the Infinite." *For you all* (*peri pantōn humōn*). Paul "en-
circled (*peri*, around) them all," including every one of
them and the church as a whole. Distance lends enchant-
ment to the memory of slight drawbacks. Paul is fond of
this phrase "you all," particularly in Phil. (1:3, 7). *Making
mention* (*mneian poioumenoi*). Paul uses this very idiom in
Rom. 1:9; Eph. 1:16; Philemon 4. Milligan cites a papyrus
example of *mneian poioumenoi* in prayer (B. Y. U. 652, 5).
Did Paul have a prayer list of the Thessalonian disciples
which he read over with Silas and Timothy? *In* here is
epi="in the time of our prayers." "Each time that they
are engaged in prayers the writers mention the names of
the converts" (Frame).

3. *Remembering* (*mnēmoneuontes*). Present active participle of old verb from adjective *mnēmōn* (mindful) and so

to call to mind, to be mindful of, used either with the accusative as in I Thess. 2:9 or the genitive as here. *Without ceasing* (*adialeiptōs*). Double compound adverb of the *Koinē* (Polybius, Diodorus, Strabo, papyri) from the verbal adjective *a-dia-leiptos* (*a* privative and *dia-leipō*, to leave off). In the N.T. alone by Paul and always connected with prayer. Milligan prefers to connect this adverb (amphibolous in position) with the preceding participle *poioumenoi* rather than with *mnēmoneuontes* as Revised Version and Westcott and Hort rightly do. *Your work of faith* (*humōn tou ergou tēs pisteōs*). Note article with both *ergou* and *pisteōs* (correlation of the article, both abstract substantives). *Ergou* is genitive case the object of *mnēmoneuontes* as is common with verbs of emotion (Robertson, *Grammar*, pp. 508f.), though the accusative *kopon* occurs in I Thess. 2:9 according to common Greek idiom allowing either case. *Ergou* is the general term for work or business, employment, task. Note two genitives with *ergou*. *Humōn* is the usual possessive genitive, *your work*, while *tēs pisteōs* is the descriptive genitive, marked by, characterized by, faith, "the activity that faith inspires" (Frame). It is interesting to note this sharp conjunction of these two words by Paul. We are justified by faith, but faith produces works (Rom. 6–8) as the Baptist taught and as Jesus taught and as James does in James 2. *Labour of love* (*tou kopou tēs agapēs*). Note article with both substantives. Here again *tou kopou* is the genitive the object of *mnēmoneuontes* while *tēs agapēs* is the descriptive genitive characterizing the "labour" or "toil" more exactly. *Kopos* is from *koptō*, to cut, to lash, to beat the bread, to toil. In Rev. 14:13 the distinction is drawn between *kopou* (toil) from which the saints rest and *erga* (works, activities) which follow with them into heaven. So here it is the labour that love prompts, assuming gladly the toil. *Agapē* is one of the great words of the N.T. (Milligan) and no certain example has yet been found in the early papyri or the inscriptions. It occurs in the Septuagint in the higher sense as with the sensuous associations. The Epistle of Aristeas calls love (*agapē*) God's gift and Philo uses *agapē* in describing love for God. "When Christianity first began to think and speak in Greek, it took up *agapē* and its group of terms more freely, investing them with the new glow with which the N.T. writings make us familiar, a content which is invariably religious" (Moffatt, *Love in the New Testament*, p. 40). The New Testament never uses the word *erōs* (lust). *Patience of hope (tēs hupomonēs tēs elpidos)*. Note the two articles again and the descriptive genitive *tēs elpidos*. It is patience marked by hope, "the endurance inspired by hope" (Frame), yes, and sustained by hope in spite of delays and set-backs. *Hupomonē* is an old word (*hupo, menō*, to remain under), but it "has come like *agapē* to be closely associated with a distinctively Christian virtue" (Milligan). The same order as here (*ergou, kopos, hupomonē*) appears in Rev. 2:2 and Lightfoot considers it "an ascending scale as practical proofs of self-sacrifice." The church in Thessalonica was not old, but already they were called upon to exercise the sanctifying grace of hope (Denney). *In our Lord Jesus Christ (tou Kuriou hēmōn Iēsou Christou)*. The objective genitive with *elpidos* (hope) and so translated by "in" here (Robertson, *Grammar*, pp. 499f.). Jesus is the object of this hope, the hope of his second coming which is still open to us. Note "Lord Jesus Christ" as in verse 1. *Before our God and Father (emprosthen tou theou kai patros hēmōn)*. The one article with both substantives precisely as in Gal. 1:4, not "before God and our Father," both article and possessive genitive going with both substantives as in II Peter 1:1, 11; Titus 2:13 (Robertson, *Grammar*, pp. 785f.). The phrase is probably connected with *elpidos*. *Emprosthen* in the N.T. occurs only of place, but it is common in the papyri of time. The picture here is the day of judgment when all shall appear before God.

4. *Knowing (eidotes)*. Second perfect active participle of *oida (eidon)*, a so-called causal participle = since we know, the third participle with the principal verb *eucharistoumen*, the Greek being fond of the circumstantial participle and lengthening sentences thereby (Robertson, *Grammar*, p. 1128). *Beloved by God (ēgapēmenoi hupo [tou] theou)*. Perfect passive participle of *agapaō*, the verb so common in the N.T. for the highest kind of love. Paul is not content, with the use of *adelphoi* here (often in this Epistle as 2:1 14, 17; 3:7; 4:1, 10), but adds this affectionate phrase nowhere else in the N.T. in this form (cf. Jude 1) though in

Sirach 45:1 and on the Rosetta Stone. But in II Thess. 2:13 he quotes "beloved by the Lord" from Deut. 33:12. The use of *adelphoi* for members of the same brotherhood can be derived from the Jewish custom (Acts 2:29, 37) and the habit of Jesus (Matt. 12:48) and is amply illustrated in the papyri for burial clubs and other orders and guilds (Moulton and Milligan's *Vocabulary*). *Your election* (*tēn eklogēn humōn*). That is the election of you by God. It is an old word from *eklegomai* used by Jesus of his choice of the twelve disciples (John 15:16) and by Paul of God's eternal selection (Eph. 1:4). The word *eklogē* is not in the LXX and only seven times in the N.T. and always of God's choice of men (Acts 9:15; I Thess. 1:4; Rom. 9:11; 11:5, 7, 58; II Peter 1:10). The divine *eklogē* was manifested in the Christian qualities of verse 3 (Moffatt).

5. *How that* (*hoti*). It is not certain whether *hoti* here means "because" (*quia*) as in II Thess. 3:7; I Cor. 2:14; Rom. 8:27 or declarative *hoti* "how that," knowing the circumstances of your election (Lightfoot) or explanatory, as in Acts 16:3; I Thess. 2:1; I Cor. 16:15; II Cor. 12:3f.; Rom. 13:11. *Our gospel* (*to euaggelion hēmōn*). The gospel (see on Matt. 4:23; Mark 1:1, 15 for *euaggelion*) which we preach, Paul's phrase also in II Thess. 2:14; II Cor. 4:3; Rom. 2:16; 16:25; II Tim. 2:8. Paul had a definite, clear-cut message of grace that he preached everywhere including Thessalonica. This message is to be interpreted in the light of Paul's own sermons in Acts and Epistles, not by reading backward into them the later perversions of Gnostics and sacramentarians. This very word was later applied to the books about Jesus, but Paul is not so using the term here or anywhere else. In its origin Paul's gospel is of God (I Thess. 2:2, 8, 9), in its substance it is Christ's (3:2; II Thess. 1:8), and Paul is only the bearer of it (I Thess. 2:4, 9; II Thess. 2:14) as Milligan points out. Paul and his associates have been entrusted with this gospel (I Thess. 2:4) and preach it (Gal. 2:2). Elsewhere Paul calls it God's gospel (II Cor. 11:7; Rom. 1:1; 15:16) or Christ's (I Cor. 9:12; II Cor. 2:12; 9:13; 10:14; Gal. 1:7; Rom. 15:19; Phil. 1:27). In both instances it is the subjective genitive. *Came unto you* (*egenēthē eis humās*). First aorist passive indicative of *ginomai* in practically same sense as *egeneto* (second aorist middle in-

dicative as in the late Greek generally). So also *eis humās* like the *Koiné* is little more than the dative *humin* (Robertson, *Grammar*, p. 594). *Not only—but also (ouk—monon, alla kai)*. Sharp contrast, negatively and positively. The contrast between *logos* (word) and *dunamis* (power) is seen also in I Cor. 2:4; 4:20. Paul does not refer to miracles by *dunamis*. *In the Holy Spirit and much assurance (en pneumati hagiōi kai plērophoriāi pollēi)*. Preposition *en* repeated with *logōi, dunamei*, but only once here thus uniting closely *Holy Spirit* and *much assurance*. No article with either word. The word *plērophoriāi* is not found in ancient Greek or the LXX. It appears once in Clement of Rome and one broken papyrus example. For the verb *plērophoreō* see on Luke 1:1. The substantive in the N.T. only here and Col. 2:2; Heb. 6:11; 10:22. It means the full confidence which comes from the Holy Spirit. *Even as ye know (kathōs oidate)*. Paul appeals to the Thessalonians themselves as witnesses to the character of his preaching and life among them. *What manner of men we showed ourselves toward you (hoioi egenēthēmen humin)*. Literally, *What sort of men we became to you*. Qualitative relative *hoioi* and dative *humin* and first aorist passive indicative *egenēthēmen*, (not *emetha*, we were). An epexegetical comment with *for your sake (di' humās)* added. It was all in their interest and for their advantage, however it may have seemed otherwise at the time.

6. *Imitators of us and of the Lord (mimētai hēmōn kai tou kuriou)*. *Mimētēs (-tēs* expresses the agent) is from *mimeomai*, to imitate and that from *mimos (mimic,* actor). Old word, more than "followers," in the N.T. only six times (I Thess. 1:6; 2:14; I Cor. 4:16; 11:1; Eph. 5:1; Heb. 6:12). Again Paul uses *ginomai*, to become, not *eimi*, to be. It is a daring thing to expect people to "imitate" the preacher, but Paul adds "and of the Lord," for he only expected or desired "imitation" as he himself imitated the Lord Jesus, as he expressly says in I Cor. 11:1. The peril of it all is that people so easily and so readily imitate the preacher when he does not imitate the Lord. The fact of the "election" of the Thessalonians was shown by the character of the message given them and by this sincere acceptance of it (Lightfoot). *Having received the word (dexamenoi ton logon)*.

First aorist middle participle of *dechomai*, probably simultaneous action (receiving), not antecedent. *In much affliction (en thlipsei pollēi)*. Late word, pressure. Tribulation (Latin *tribulum*) from *thlibō*, to press hard on. Christianity has glorified this word. It occurs in some Christian papyrus letters in this same sense. Runs all through the N.T. (II Thess. 1:4; Rom. 5:3). Paul had his share of them (Col. 1:24; II Cor. 2:4) and so he understands how to sympathize with the Thessalonians (I Thess. 3:3f.). They suffered after Paul left Thessalonica (I Thess. 2:14). *With joy of the Holy Spirit (meta charas pneumatos hagiou)*. The Holy Spirit gives the joy in the midst of the tribulations as Paul learned (Rom. 5:3). "This paradox of experience" (Moffatt) shines along the pathway of martyrs and saints of Christ.

7. *So that ye became (hōste genesthai humās)*. Definite result expressed by *hōste* and the infinitive *genesthai* (second aorist middle of *ginomai*) as is common in the *Koiné*. *An ensample (tupon)*. So B D, but Aleph A C have *tupous* (plural). The singular looks at the church as a whole, the plural as individuals like *humās*. *Tupos* is an old word from *tuptō*, to strike, and so the mark of a blow, print as in John 20:25. Then the figure formed by the blow, image as in Acts 7:43. Then the mould or form (Rom. 6:17; Acts 23:25). Then an example or pattern as in Acts 7:44, to be imitated as here, Phil. 3:17, etc. It was a great compliment for the church in Thessalonica to be already a model for believers in Macedonia and Achaia. Our word *type* for printers is this same word with one of its meanings. Note separate article with both Macedonia (*tēi Makedoniāi*) and Achaia (*tēi Achaiāi*) treated as separate provinces as they were.

8. *From you hath sounded forth (aph' humōn exēchētai)*. Perfect passive indicative of *exēcheō*, late compound verb (*ex, ēchos, ēchō, ēchē*, our echo) to sound out of a trumpet or of thunder, to reverberate like our echo. Nowhere else in the N.T. So "from you" as a sounding board or radio transmitting station (to use a modern figure). It marks forcibly "both the clear and the persuasive nature of the *logos tou Kuriou*" (Ellicott). This phrase, the word of the Lord, may be subjective with the Lord as its author or objective with the Lord as the object. It is both. It is a graphic picture with a pardonable touch of hyperbole (Moffatt) for Thes-

salonica was a great commercial and political centre for disseminating the news of salvation (on the Egnation Way). *But in every place (all' en panti topōi).* In contrast to Macedonia and Achaia. The sentence would naturally stop here, but Paul is dictating rapidly and earnestly and goes on. *Your faith to God-ward (hē pistis humōn hē pros ton theon).* Literally, *the faith of you that toward the God.* The repeated article makes clear that their faith is now directed toward the true God and not toward the idols from which they had turned (verse 10). *Is gone forth (exelēluthen).* Second perfect active indicative of old verb *exerchomai,* to go out, state of completion like *exēchētai* above. *So that we need not to speak anything (hōste mē chreian echein hēmās lalein ti).* *Hōste* with the infinitive for actual result as in verse 7. No vital distinction between *lalein* (originally to chatter as of birds) and *legein,* both being used in the *Koiné* for speaking and preaching (in the N.T.).

9. *They themselves (autoi).* The men of Macedonia, voluntarily. *Report (apaggellousin).* Linear present active indicative, keep on reporting. *What manner of entering in (hopoian eisodon).* What sort of entrance, qualitative relative in an indirect question. *We had (eschomen).* Second aorist active (ingressive) indicative of the common verb *echō.* *And how (kai pōs).* Here the interrogative adverb *pōs* in this part of the indirect question. This part about "them" (you) as the first part about Paul. The verb *epistrephō* is an old verb for turning and is common in the Acts for Gentiles turning to God, as here from idols, though not by Paul again in this sense. In Gal. 4:9 Paul uses it for turning to the weak and beggarly elements of Judaism. *From idols (apo tōn eidolōn).* Old word from *eidos* (figure) for image or likeness and then for the image of a heathen god (our *idol).* Common in the LXX in this sense. In Acts 14:15 Paul at Lystra urged the people *to turn from these vain things to the living God (apo toutōn tōn mataiōn epistrephein epi theon zōnta),* using the same verb *epistrephein.* Here also Paul has a like idea, *to serve a living and true God (douleuein theōi zōnti kai alēthinōi).* No article, it is true, but should be translated "the living and true God" (cf. Acts 14:15). Not "dead" like the idols from which they turned, but alive and genuine (*alēthinos,* not *alēthēs).*

10. *To wait for his Son from heaven (anamenein ton huion autou ek tōn ouranōn).* Present infinitive, like *douleuein,* and so linear, to keep on waiting for. The hope of the second coming of Christ was real and powerful with Paul as it should be with us. It was subject to abuse then as now as Paul will have to show in this very letter. He alludes to this hope at the close of each chapter in this Epistle. *Whom he raised from the dead (hon ēgeiren ek [tōn] nekrōn).* Paul gloried in the fact of the resurrection of Jesus from the dead of which fact he was himself a personal witness. This fact is the foundation stone for all his theology and it comes out in this first chapter. *Jesus which delivereth us from the wrath to come (Iēsoun ton ruomenon hēmās ek tēs orgēs tēs erchomenēs).* It is the historic, crucified, risen, and ascended Jesus Christ, God's Son, who delivers from the coming wrath. He is our Saviour (Matt. 1:21) true to his name Jesus. He is our Rescuer (Rom. 11:26, *ho ruomenos,* from Isa. 59:20). It is eschatological language, this coming wrath of God for sin (I Thess. 2:16; Rom. 3:5; 5:9; 9:22; 13:5). It was Paul's allusion to the day of judgment with Jesus as Judge whom God had raised from the dead that made the Athenians mock and leave him (Acts 17:31f.). But Paul did not change his belief or his preaching because of the conduct of the Athenians. He is certain that God's wrath in due time will punish sin. Surely this is a needed lesson for our day. It was coming then and it is coming now.

CHAPTER II

1. *For yourselves know* (*autoi gar oidate*). This explanatory *gar* takes up in verses 1 to 12 the allusion in 1:9 about the "report" concerning the entrance (*eisodon*, way in, *eis, hodon*), *unto you* (*tēn pros humās*). Note repeated article to sharpen the point. This proleptic accusative is common enough. It is expanded by the epexegetic use of the *hoti* clause *that it hath not been found vain* (*hoti ou kenē gegonen*). Literally, *that it has not become empty*. Second perfect active (completed state) of *ginomai*. Every pastor watches wistfully to see what will be the outcome of his work. Bengel says: *Non inanis, sed plena virtutis*. Cf. 1:5. *Kenos* is hollow, empty, while *mataios* is fruitless, ineffective. In I Cor. 15:14, 17 Paul speaks of *kenon to kērugma* (*empty the preaching*) and *mataia hē pistis* (*vain the faith*). One easily leads to the other.

2. *But having suffered before* (*alla propathontes*). Strong adversative *alla*, antithesis to *kenē*. Appeal to his personal experiences in Thessalonica known to them (*as ye know, kathōs oidate*). Second aorist active participle of *propaschō*, old compound verb, but here alone in the N.T. The force of *pro-* (before) is carried over to the next verb. The participle may be regarded as temporal (Ellicott) or concessive (Moffatt). *And been shamefully entreated in Philippi* (*kai hubristhentes en Philippois*). First aorist passive participle of *hubrizō*, old verb, to treat insolently. "More than the bodily suffering it was the personal indignity that had been offered to him as a Roman citizen" (Milligan), for which account see Acts 16:16–40, an interesting example of how Acts and the Epistles throw light on each other. Luke tells how Paul resented the treatment accorded to him as a Roman citizen and here Paul shows that the memory still rankled in his bosom. *We waxed bold in our God* (*eparrēsiasametha en tōi theōi hēmōn*). Ingressive first aorist middle of *parrēsiazomai*, old deponent verb from *parrēsia* (full story, *pan-, rēsia*). In his reply to Festus (Acts 26:26) Paul uses *parrēsiazomenos lalō, being bold I speak*, while here he has *we*

15

waxed bold to speak (eparrēsiasametha lalēsai). The insult in Philippi did not close Paul's mouth, but had precisely the opposite effect "in our God." It was not wild fanaticism, but determined courage and confidence in God that spurred Paul to still greater boldness in Thessalonica, *unto you (pros humās)*, be the consequences what they might, *the gospel of God in much conflict, (to euaggelion tou theou en polloi agōni)*. This figure of the athletic games *(agōn)* may refer to outward conflict like Phil. 1:30 or inward anxiety (Col. 2:1). He had both in Thessalonica.

3. *Exhortation (paraklēsis)*. Persuasive discourse, calling to one's side, for admonition, encouragement, or comfort. *Not of error (ouk ek planēs)*. This word is same as *planaō*, to lead astray (II Tim. 3:13) like Latin *errare*. Passive idea of *error* here rather than deceit. That is seen in *nor in guile (oude en doloi)* from *delo*, to catch with bait. Paul is keenly sensitive against charges against the correctness of his message and the purity of his life. *Nor of uncleanness (oude ex akatharsias)*. "This disclaimer, startling as it may seem, was not unneeded amidst the impurities consecrated by the religions of the day" (Lightfoot). There was no necessary connection in the popular mind between religion and morals. The ecstatic initiations in some of the popular religions were grossly sensual.

4. *But even as we have been approved by God (alla kathōs dedokimasmetha hupo tou theou)*. Perfect passive indicative of *dokimazō*, old verb to put to the test, but here the tense for completed state means tested and proved and so approved by God. Paul here claims the call of God for his ministry and the seal of God's blessing on his work and also for that of Silas and Timothy. *To be entrusted with the gospel (pisteuthēnai to euaggelion)*. First aorist passive infinitive of *pisteuō*, common verb for believing, from *pistis* (faith), but here to entrust rather than to trust. The accusative of the thing is retained in the passive according to regular Greek idiom as in I Cor. 9:17; Gal. 2:7; Rom. 3:2; I Tim. 1:11; Titus 1:3, though the active had the dative of the person. *So we speak (houtōs laloumen)*. Simple, yet confident claim of loyalty to God's call and message. Surely this should be the ambition of every preacher of the gospel of God. *Not as pleasing men (ouch hōs anthrōpois areskontes)*.

Dative case with *areskō* as in Gal. 1:10. Few temptations assail the preacher more strongly than this one to please men, even if God is not pleased, though with the dim hope that God will after all condone or overlook. Nothing but experience will convince some preachers how fickle is popular favour and how often it is at the cost of failure to please God. And yet the preacher wishes to win men to Christ. It is all as subtle as it is deceptive. God tests our hearts (the very verb *dokimazō* used in the beginning of this verse) and he is the only one whose approval matters in the end of the day (I Cor. 4:5).

5. *Using words of flattery (en logōi kolakeias)*. Literally, *in speech of flattery or fawning*. Old word, only here in N.T., from *kolaks*, a flatterer. An Epicurean, Philodemus, wrote a work *Peri Kolakeias* (Concerning Flattery). Milligan (*Vocabulary*, etc.) speaks of "the selfish conduct of too many of the rhetoricians of the day," conduct extremely repugnant to Paul. The third time (verses 1, 2, 5) he appeals to their knowledge of his work in Thessalonica. Frame suggests "cajolery." *Nor a cloke of covetousness (oute prophasei pleonexias)*. Pretext (*prophasis* from *prophainō*, to show forth, or perhaps from *pro-phēmi*, to speak forth). This is the charge of self-interest rather than the mere desire to please people. Pretext of greediness is Frame's translation. *Pleonexia* is merely "having more" from *pleonektēs*, one eager for more, and *pleonekteō*, to have more, then to over-reach, all old words, all with bad meaning as the result of the desire for more. In a preacher this sin is especially fatal. Paul feels so strongly his innocence of this charge that he calls God as witness as in II Cor. 1:23; Rom. 9:1; Phil. 1:8, a solemn oath for his own veracity.

6. *Nor seeking glory of men (oute zētountes ex anthrōpōn doxan)*. "Upon the repudiation of covetousness follows naturally the repudiation of worldly ambition" (Milligan). See Acts 20:19; II Cor. 4:5; Eph. 4:2. This third disclaimer is as strong as the other two. Paul and his associates had not tried to extract praise or glory out of (*ex*) men. *Neither from you nor from others (oute aph' humōn oute aph' allōn)*. He widens the negation to include those outside of the church circles and changes the preposition from *ex* (out of) to *apo* (from). *When we might have been burdensome, as apostles of*

Christ (*dunamenoi en barei einai hōs Christou apostoloi*).
Westcott and Hort put this clause in verse 7. Probably
a concessive participle, *though being able to be in a position of
weight* (either in matter of finance or of dignity, or a burden
on your funds or "men of weight" as Moffatt suggests).
Milligan suggests that Paul "plays here on the double sense
of the phrase" like the Latin proverb: *Honos propter onus*.
So he adds, including Silas and Timothy, *as Christ's apostles*,
as missionaries clearly, whether in the technical sense or
not (cf. Acts 14:4, 14; II Cor. 8:23; 11:13; Rom. 16:7; Phil.
2:25; Rev. 2:2). They were entitled to pay as "Christ's
apostles" (cf. I Cor. 9 and II Cor. 11:7ff.), though they
had not asked for it.

7. *But we were gentle in the midst of you* (*alla egenēthēmen
nēpioi en mesōi humōn*). Note *egenēthēmen* (became), not
ēmetha (were). This rendering follows *ēpioi* instead of *nēpioi*
(Aleph B D C Vulg. Boh.) which is clearly correct, though
Dibelius, Moffatt, Ellicott, Weiss prefer *ēpioi* as making
better sense. Dibelius terms *nēpioi unmöglich* (impossible),
but surely that is too strong. Paul is fond of the word *nēpioi*
(babes). Lightfoot admits that he here works the metaphor
to the limit in his passion, but does not mar it as Ellicott
holds. *As when a nurse cherishes her own children* (*hōs ean
trophos thalpēi ta heautēs tekna*). This comparative clause
with *hōs ean* (Mark 4:26; Gal. 6:10 without *ean* or *an*) and
the subjunctive (Robertson, *Grammar*, p. 968) has a sudden
change of the metaphor, as is common with Paul (I Tim.
5:24; II Cor. 3:13ff.) from *babes* to *nurse* (*trophos*), old word,
here only in the N.T., from *trephō*, to nourish, *trophē*, nourish-
ment. It is really the mother-nurse "who suckles and nurses
her own children" (Lightfoot), a use found in Sophocles,
and a picture of Paul's tender affection for the Thessalonians.
Thalpō is an old word to keep warm, to cherish with tender
love, to foster. In N.T. only here and Eph. 5:29.

8. *Even so, being affectionately desirous of you* (*houtōs
omeiromenoi humōn*). Clearly the correct text rather than
himeiromenoi from *himeirō*, old verb to long for. But the
verb *homeiromai* (Westcott and Hort *om.*, smooth breathing)
occurs nowhere else except MSS. in Job 3:21 and Psa. 62:2
(Symmachus) and the Lycaonian sepulchral inscription
(4th cent. A.D.) about the sorrowing parents *homeiromenoi*

peri paidos, greatly desiring their son (Moulton and Milligan, *Vocabulary*). Moulton suggests that it comes from a root *smer*, remember, and that *o-* is a derelict preposition *o* like *o-duromai, o-kellō, ō-keanos*. Wohlenberg (Zahn, *Kommentar*) calls the word "a term of endearment," "derived from the language of the nursery" (Milligan). *We were well pleased* (*ēudokoumen*). Imperfect active of *eudokeō*, common verb in later Greek and in N.T. (see on Matt. 3:17), picturing Paul's idea of their attitude while in Thessalonica. Paul often has it with the infinitive as here. *To impart* (*metadounai*). Second aorist active infinitive of *metadidōmi*, old verb to share with (see on Luke 3:11). Possible zeugma with *souls* (*psuchas*), though Lightfoot renders "lives." Paul and his associates held nothing back. *Because ye were become very dear to us* (*dioti agapētoi hēmin egenēthēte*). Note *dioti* (double cause, *dia, hoti*, for that), use of *ginomai* again for become, and dative *hēmin* with verbal *agapētoi*, beloved and so dear. A beautiful picture of the growth of Paul's affection for them as should be true with every pastor.

9. *Travail* (*mochthon*). Old word for difficult labour, harder than *kopos* (toil). In the N.T. only here, II Thess. 3:8; II Cor. 11:27. Note accusative case here though genitive with *mnēmoneuō* in 1:3. *Night and day* (*nuktos kai hēmeras*). Genitive case, both by day and by night, perhaps beginning before dawn and working after dark. So in 3:10. *That we might not burden any of you* (*pros to mē epibarēsai tina humōn*). Use of *pros* with the articular infinitive to express purpose (only four times by Paul). The verb *epibareō* is late, but in the papyri and inscriptions for laying a burden (*baros*) on (*epi-*) one. In N.T. only here and II Thess. 3:8; II Cor. 2:5. Paul boasted of his financial independence where he was misunderstood as in Thessalonica and Corinth (II Cor. 9 to 12), though he vindicated his right to remuneration. *We preached* (*ekēruxamen*). *We heralded* (from *kērux*, herald) to you, common verb for preach.

10. *How holily and righteously and unblameably* (*hōs hosiōs kai dikaiōs kai amemptōs*). Paul calls the Thessalonians and God as witnesses (*martures*) to his life toward you the believers (*humin tois pisteuousin*) dative of personal interest. He employs three common adverbs that show how holily toward God and how righteously toward men so that they

did not blame him and his associates in either respect. So there is a reason for each adverb. All this argues that Paul spent a considerable time in Thessalonica, more than the three sabbaths mentioned by Luke. The pastor ought to live so that his life will bear close inspection.

11. *As a father with his own children* (*hōs patēr tekna heautou*). Change from the figure of the mother-nurse in verse 7. There is ellipse of a principal verb with the participles *parakalountes, paramuthoumenoi, marturoumenoi.* Lightfoot suggests *enouthetoumen* (we admonished) or *egenēthēmen* (we became). The three participles give three phases of the minister's preaching (exhorting, encouraging or consoling, witnessing or testifying). They are all old verbs, but only the first (*parakaleō*) is common in the N.T.

12. *To the end that* (*eis to*). Final use of *eis* and the articular infinitive, common idiom in the papyri and Paul uses *eis to* and the infinitive fifty times (see again in 3:2), some final, some sub-final, some result (Robertson, *Grammar*, pp. 989–91). *Walk worthily of God* (*peripatein axiōs tou theou*). Present infinitive (linear action), and genitive case with adverb *axiōs* as in Col. 1:10 (cf. Phil. 1:27; Eph. 4:1), like a preposition. *Calleth* (*kalountos*). Present active participle, keeps on calling. Some MSS. have *kalesantos*, called. *Kingdom* (*basileian*) here is the future consummation because of glory (*doxan*) as in II Thess. 1:5; I Cor. 6:9; 15:50; Gal. 5:21; II Tim. 4:1, 18), but Paul uses it for the present kingdom of grace also as in I Cor. 4:20; Rom. 14:17; Col. 1:13.

13. *And for this cause we also* (*kai dia touto kai hēmeis*). Note *kai* twice. We as well as you are grateful for the way the gospel was received in Thessalonica. *Without ceasing* (*adialeiptōs*). Late adverb for which see on 1:2 and for *eucharistoumen* see on 1:2. *The word of the message* (*logon akoēs*). Literally, *the word of* hearing, as in Sir. 42:1 and Heb. 4:2 *ho logos tēs akoēs*, the word marked by hearing (genitive case), the word which you heard. Here with *tou theou* (of God) added as a second descriptive genitive which Paul expands and justifies. *Ye received it so* (*paralabontes*) and *accepted or welcomed it* (*edexasthe*) so, *not as the word of men* (*ou logou anthrōpōn*), *but as the word of God* (*alla logon theou*), *as it is in truth* (*kathōs alēthōs estin*). This last clause is literally, *as it truly is.* Paul had not a doubt that he was

proclaiming God's message Should any preacher preach his doubts if he has any? God's message can be found and Paul found it. *Worketh in you (energeitai en humin)*. Perhaps middle voice of *energeō (en, ergon,* work) late verb, not in ancient Greek or LXX, but in papyri and late writers (Polybius, etc.) and in N.T. only by Paul and James. If it is passive, as Milligan thinks, it means "is set in operation," as Polybius has it. The idea then is that the word of God is set in operation in you that believe.

14. *Imitators of the churches of God which are in Judea (mimētai tōn ekklēsiōn tou theou tōn ousōn en tēi Ioudaiāi).* On *mimētai* see on 1:5. "This passage, implying an affectionate admiration of the Jewish churches on the part of St. Paul, and thus entirely bearing out the impression produced by the narrative in the Acts, is entirely subversive of the theory maintained by some and based on a misconception of Gal. ii, and by the fiction of the Pseudo-Clementines, of the feud existing between St. Paul and the Twelve" (Lightfoot). *In Christ Jesus (en Christōi Iēsou).* It takes this to make a *Christian* church of God. Note order here *Christ Jesus* as compared with *Jesus Christ* in 1:1, 3. *Ye also—even as they (kai humeis—kai autoi).* Note *kai* twice (correlative use of *kai*). *Countrymen (sumphuletōn).* Fellow-countrymen or tribesmen. Late word that refers primarily to Gentiles who no doubt joined the Jews in Thessalonica who instigated the attacks on Paul and Silas so that it "was taken up by the native population, without whose co-operation it would have been powerless" (Lightfoot). *Own (idiōn)* here has apparently a weakened force. Note *hupo* here with the ablative both with *sumphuletōn* and *Ioudaiōn* after the intransitive *epathete* (suffered). The persecution of the Christians by the Jews in Judea was known everywhere.

15. *Who both killed the Lord Jesus and the prophets (tōn kai ton Kurion apokteinantōn Iēsoun kai tous prophētas).* First aorist active participle of *apokteinō.* Vivid justification of his praise of the churches in Judea. The Jews killed the prophets before the Lord Jesus who reminded them of their guilt (Matt. 23:29). Paul, as Peter (Acts 2:23), lays the guilt of the death of Christ on the Jews. *And drove us out (kai hēmās ekdiōxantōn).* An old verb to drive out or banish, to

chase out as if a wild beast. Only here in N.T. It is Paul's
vivid description of the scene told in Acts 17:5ff. when the
rabbis and the hoodlums from the agora chased him out of
Thessalonica by the help of the politarchs. *Please not God*
(*Theōi mē areskontōn*). The rabbis and Jews thought that
they were pleasing God by so doing as Paul did when he
ravaged the young church in Jerusalem. But Paul knows
better now. *And are contrary to all men* (*kai pasin anthrōpois enantiōn*). Dative case with the adjective *enantiōn*
(old and common word, face to face, opposite). It seems
like a bitter word about Paul's countrymen whom he really
loved (Rom. 9:1-5; 10:1-6), but Paul knew only too well
the middle wall of partition between Jew and Gentile as
he shows in Eph. 2 and which only the Cross of Christ can
break down. Tacitus (*Hist.* V. 5) says that the Jews are
adversus omnes alios hostile odium.

16. *Forbidding us* (*kōluontōn hēmās*). Explanatory participle of the idea in *enantiōn*. They show their hostility to
Paul at every turn. Right here in Corinth, where Paul is
when he writes, they had already shown venomous hostility
toward Paul as Luke makes plain (Acts 18:6ff.). They not
simply oppose his work among the Jews, but also to the
Gentiles (*ethnesi*, nations outside of the Abrahamic covenant
as they understood it). *That they may be saved* (*hina sōthōsin*).
Final use of *hina* with first aorist passive subjunctive of *sōzō*
old verb to save. It was the only hope of the Gentiles, Christ
alone and not the mystery-religions offered any real hope.
To fill up their sins alway (*eis to anaplērōsai autōn tas hamartias pantote*). Another example of *eis to* and the infinitive
as in verse 12. It may either be God's conceived plan to
allow the Jews to go on and fill up (*anaplērōsai*, note *ana*,
fill up full, old verb) or it may be the natural result from the
continual (*pantote*) sins of the Jews. *Is come* (*ephthasen*).
First aorist (timeless aorist) active indicative of *phthanō*
which no longer means to come before as in I Thess. 4:15
where alone in the N.T. it retains the old idea of coming
before. Some MSS. have the perfect active *ephthaken*,
prophetic perfect of realization already. Frame translates
it: "But the wrath has come upon them at last." This is
the most likely meaning of *eis telos*. Paul vividly foresees
and foretells the final outcome of this attitude of hate on

the part of the Jews. *Tristis exitus,* Bengel calls it. Paul speaks out of a sad experience.

17. *Being bereaved of you (aporphanisthentes aph' humōn).* First aorist passive participle of the rare compound verb (*aporphanizō,* in Aeschylus, but nowhere else in N.T.). Literally, *being orphaned from you (aph' humōn,* ablative case). Paul changes the figure again (*trophos* or mother nurse in verse 7, *nēpios* or babe in verse 7, *patēr* or father in verse 11) to *orphan (orphanos).* He refers to the period of separation from them, *for a short season (pros kairon hōras) for a season of an hour.* This idiom only here in N.T., but *pros kairon* in Luke 8:13 and *pros hōran* in II Cor. 7:8. But it has seemed long to Paul. Precisely how long he had been gone we do not know, some months at any rate. *In presence, not in heart (prosōpōi ou kardiāi).* Locative case. *Prosōpon,* old word (*pros, ops,* in front of the eye, face) for face, look, person. Literally, *in face or person.* His heart was with them, though they no longer saw his face. Heart, originally *kardia,* is the inner man, the seat of the affections and purposes, not always in contrast with intellect (*nous*). "Out of sight, not out of mind" (Rutherford). *Endeavoured the more exceedingly (perissoterōs espoudasamen).* Ingressive aorist active indicative of *spoudazō,* old word to hasten (from *spoudē, speudō*). *We became zealous.* Comparative adverb *perissoterōs* from *perisson,* more abundantly than before being orphaned from you. *Your face (to prosōpon humōn).* Cf. his *face* above. *With great desire (en pollēi epithumiāi). In much longing (epithumia* from *epi* and *thumos, epithumeō,* to run after, to yearn after, whether good or bad).

18. *Because (dioti).* As in 2:8. *We would fain have come to you (ethelēsamen elthein pros humas).* First aorist active indicative of *thelō.* Literally, *we desired to come to you. I Paul (egō men Paulos).* Clear example of literary plural *ethelēsamen* with singular pronoun *ego.* Paul uses his own name elsewhere also as in II Cor. 10:1; Gal. 5:2; Col. 1:23; Eph. 3:1; Philemon 19. *Once and again (kai hapax kai dis). Both once and twice* as in Phil. 4:16. Old idiom in Plato. *And Satan hindered us (kai enekopsen hēmas ho Satanas).* Adversative use of *kai=* but or and yet. First aorist active indicative of *enkoptō,* late word to cut in, to hinder. Milligan quotes papyrus example of third century, B.C. Verb used to cut

in a road, to make a road impassable. So Paul charges
Satan with cutting in on his path. Used by Paul in Acts
24:4; Gal. 5:7 and passive *enekoptomēn* in Rom. 15:22 and
I Peter 3:7. This hindrance may have been illness, opposition of the Jews in Corinth, what not.

19. *Crown of glorying* (*stephanos kauchēseōs*). When a
king or conqueror came on a visit he was given a chaplet of
glorying. Paul is answering the insinuation that he did not
really wish to come. *At his coming* (*en tēi autou parousiāi*).
This word *parousia* is untechnical (just *presence* from *pareimi*) in II Thess. 2:9; I Cor. 16:17; II Cor. 7:6f.; 10:10;
Phil. 1:26; 2:12. But here (also I Thess. 3:13; 4:15; 5:23;
II Thess. 2:1, 8; I Cor. 15:23) we have the technical sense
of the second coming of Christ. Deissmann (*Light from the
Ancient East*, pp. 372ff.) notes that the word in the papyri
is almost technical for the arrival of a king or ruler who
expects to receive his "crown of coming." The Thessalonians, Paul says, will be his crown, glory, joy when Jesus
comes.

CHAPTER III

1. *When we could no longer forbear* (*mēketi stegontes*). *Stegō* is old verb to cover from *stegē*, roof (Mark 2:4), to cover with silence, to conceal, to keep off, to endure as here and I Cor. 9:12; 13:7. In the papyri in this sense (Moulton and Milligan's *Vocabulary*). *Mēketi* usual negative with participle in the *Koiné* rather than *ouketi*. *We thought it good* (*eudokēsamen*). Either literary plural as in 2:18 or Paul and Silas as more likely. If so, both Timothy and Silas came to Athens (Acts 17:15f.), but Timothy was sent (*we sent, epempsamen*, verse 2) right back to Thessalonica and later Paul sent Silas on to Beroea or Thessalonica (verse 5, *I sent, epempsa*). Then both Silas and Timothy came from Macedonia to Corinth (Acts 18:5). *Alone* (*monoi*). Including Silas. *God's minister* (*diakonon tou theou*). See on Matt. 22:13 for this interesting word, here in general sense not technical sense of deacon. Some MSS. have *fellow*-worker (*sunergon*). Already *apostle* in 2:7 and now *brother, minister* (and possibly *fellow-worker*).

3. *That no man be moved* (*to mēdena sainesthai*). Epexegetical articular infinitive in accusative case of general reference. *Sainō* is old word to wag the tail, to flatter, beguile and this sense suits here (only N.T. example). The sense of "moved" or troubled or disheartened is from *siainesthai* the reading of F G and found in the papyri. *We are appointed* (*keimetha*). Present middle, used here as passive of *tithēmi*. We Christians are set *hereunto* (*eis touto*) to be beguiled by tribulations. We must resist.

4. *We told you beforehand* (*proelegomen humin*). Imperfect active, we used to tell you beforehand. Old verb, rare in N.T. (only in Paul). *That we are to suffer persecution* (*hoti mellomen thlibesthai*). *Mellō* and present passive infinitive. Not mere prediction, but God's appointed will as it turned out in Thessalonica.

5. *That I might know* (*eis to gnōnai*). Paul's common idiom (verse 2), *eis to* and the infinitive of purpose (second aorist ingressive active of *ginōskō*, come to know). *Lest by*

25

any means the tempter had tempted you (mē pōs epeirasen humās ho peirazōn). Findlay takes this as a question with negative answer, but most likely negative final clause with *mē pōs* about a past action with aorist indicative according to the classic idiom as in Gal. 2:2 *(mē pōs—edramon)* and Gal. 4:11 after verb of fearing (Robertson, *Grammar*, p. 988). It is a fear that the thing may turn out to be so about the past. *Should be (genētai).* Here the usual construction appears (aorist subjunctive with *mē pōs*) about the future.

6. *Even now (arti).* Just now, Timothy having come *(elthontos Timotheou,* genitive absolute). Why Silas is not named is not clear, unless he had come from Beroea or elsewhere in Macedonia. *Glad tidings of (euaggelisamenou).* First aorist middle participle of the verb for evangelizing (gospelizing). *Good remembrance (mneian).* Same word used by Paul 1:2. *Longing to see us (epipothountes hēmās idein).* Old and strong verb, *epi-,* directive, to long after. Mutual longing that pleased Paul ("we also you").

7. *Over you (eph' humin).* *Epi* with the locative, the basis on which the "comfort" rests. *In (epi).* Locative case again with *epi.* *Distress (anagkēi).* *Physical necessity,* common sense in late Greek, choking *(agchō, angor),* and *crushing* trouble *(thlipsis, thlibō).*

8 *If ye stand fast (ean humeis stēkete).* Condition of first class, *ean* and present active indicative (correct text, not *stēkēte* subj.) of *stēkō,* late form from perfect *hestēka* of *histēmi,* to place.

9. *Render again unto God (tōi theōi antapodounai).* Second aorist active infinitive of double compound verb *ant-apodidōmi,* to give back *(apo)* in return for *(anti).* Old verb rare in N.T., but again in II Thess. 1:6. *For you (peri humōn).* Around (concerning) you, while in verse 2 *huper* (over is used for "concerning your faith." *For (epi).* Basis again as cause or ground for the joy. *Wherewith we joy (hēi chairomen).* Probably cognate accusative *hēn* with *chairomen* attracted to locative *charāi* (Matt. 2:10).

10. *Exceedingly (huperekperissou).* Double compound adverb, only in I Thess. 3:10; 5:13 (some MSS. -ōs). Like piling Ossa on Pelion, *perissōs,* abundantly, *ek perissou,* out of bounds, *huperekperissou,* more than out of bounds (overflowing all bounds). *And perfect (kai katartisai).* First aorist

active articular infinitive of purpose (*eis to idein*—*kai*) of *katartizō*, to mend nets (Matt. 4:21) or men (Gal. 6:1) repair. Chiefly late. *That which is lacking in* (*ta husterēmata*). The shortcomings, the lacks or left-overs (Col. 1:24). From *hustereō* ʼ(*husteron*), to be late.

11. *Our God and Father himself* (*autos ho theos kai patēr hēmōn*). Note one article with both substantives for one person. *And our Lord Jesus* (*kai ho Kurios hēmōn Iēsous*). Separate article here with *Iēsous*. In Titus 2:13 and II Peter 1:1 only one article (not two) treating "our God and Saviour Jesus Christ" as one just like "our Lord and Saviour Jesus Christ" in II Peter 1:11; 2:20; 3:18. *Direct our way* (*kateuthunai tēn hodon hēmōn*). First aorist optative (acute accent on penult, not circumflex first aorist active infinitive) of *kateuthunō*, old verb to make straight path. Singular verb also, though both God and Christ mentioned as subject (unity in the Godhead). Apart from *mē genoito* (*may it not come to pass*) the optative in a wish of the third person is found in N.T. only in I Thess. 3:11, 12; 5:23; II Thess. 2:17; 3:5, 16; Rom. 15:5, 13.

12. *The Lord* (*ho Kurios*). The Lord Jesus. Paul prays to Christ. *Make you to increase* (*humas pleonasai*). First aorist active optative (wish for future) of *pleonazō*, late verb from *pleon* (more), *to superabound*. *And abound* (*perisseusai*). First aorist active optative (wish for future) of *perisseuō* from *perissos*, old verb, to be over (common in N.T.). It is hard to see much difference between the two verbs.

13. *To the end he may stablish* (*eis to stērixai*). Another example of *eis* and the articular infinitive of purpose. Same idiom in 3:2. From *stērizō*, from *stērigx*, a support. *Unblameable* (*amemptous*). Old compound adjective (*a* privative and verbal of *memphomai*, to blame). Rare in N.T. Predicate position here. Second coming of Christ again.

CHAPTER IV

1. *Finally (loipon)*. Accusative of general reference of *loipos*, as for the rest. It does not mean actual conclusion, but merely a colloquial expression pointing towards the end (Milligan) as in II Cor. 13:11; II Tim. 4:8. So *to loipon* in II Thess. 3:1; Phil. 3:1; 4:8. *We beseech (erōtōmen)*. Not "question" as in ancient Greek, but as often in N.T. (I Thess. 5:12; II Thess. 2:1; Phil. 4:3) and also in papyri to make urgent request of one. *How ye ought (to pōs dei humās)*. Literally, explanatory articular indirect question (*to pōs*) after *parelabēte* according to common classic idiom in Luke (1:62; 22:2, 4, 23, 24) and Paul (Rom. 8:26). *That ye abound (hina perisseuēte)*. Loose construction of the *hina* clause with present subjunctive after two subordinate clauses with *kathōs* (as, even as) to be connected with "beseech and exhort." *More and more (mallon)*. Simply *more*, but added to same idea in *perisseuēte*. See also verse 11.

2. *What charge (tinas paraggelias)*. Plural, charges or precepts, command (Acts 16:24), prohibition (Acts 5:28), right living (I Tim. 1:5). Military term in Xenophon and Polybius.

3. *Your sanctification (ho hagiasmos humōn)*. Found only in the Greek Bible and ecclesiastical writers from *hagiazō* and both to take the place of the old words *hagizō, hagismos* with their technical ideas of consecration to a god or goddess that did not include holiness in life. So Paul makes a sharp and pointed stand here for the Christian idea of sanctification as being "the will of God" (apposition) and as further explained by the epexegetic infinitive *that ye abstain from fornication (apechesthai humas apo tēs porneias)*. Pagan religion did not demand sexual purity of its devotees, the gods and goddesses being grossly immoral. Priestesses were in the temples for the service of the men who came.

4. *That each one of you know how (eidenai hekaston humōn)*. Further epexegetic infinitive (second perfect active), learn how and so know how (learn the habit of purity). *To possess*

himself of his own vessel (to heautou skeuos ktasthai). Present middle infinitive of *ktaomai*, to acquire, not *kektēsthai*, to possess. But what does Paul mean by "his own vessel"? It can only mean his own body or his own wife. Objections are raised against either view, but perhaps he means that the man shall acquire his own wife "in sanctification and honour," words that elevate the wife and make it plain that Paul demands sexual purity on the part of men (married as well as unmarried). There is no double standard here. When the husband comes to the marriage bed, he should come as a chaste man to a chaste wife.

5. *Not in the passion of lust (mē en pathei epithumias)*. Plain picture of the wrong way for the husband to come to marriage. *That know not God (ta mē eidota ton theon)*. Second perfect participle of *oida*. The heathen knew gods as licentious as they are themselves, but not God. One of the reasons for the revival of paganism in modern life is professedly this very thing that men wish to get rid of the inhibitions against licentiousness by God.

6. *That no man transgress (to mē huperbainein)*. Old verb to go beyond. Final use of *to* (accusative of general reference) and the infinitive (negative *mē*), parallel to *apechesthai* and *eidenai ktasthai* above. *And wrong his brother (kai pleonektein ton adelphon autou)*. To take more, to overreach, to take advantage of, to defraud. *In the matter (en tōi pragmati)*. The delicacy of Paul makes him refrain from plainer terms and the context makes it clear enough as in II Cor. 7:11 (*tōi pragmati*). *An avenger (ekdikos)*. Regular term in the papyri for legal avenger. Modern men and women need to remember that God is the avenger for sexual wrongs both in this life and the next.

7. *Not for uncleanness, but in sanctification (epi akatharsiāi all' en hagiasmōi)*. Sharp contrast made still sharper by the two prepositions *epi* (on the basis of) and *en* (in the sphere of). God has "called" us all for a decent sex life consonant with his aims and purposes. It was necessary for Paul to place this lofty ideal before the Thessalonian Christians living in a pagan world. It is equally important now.

8. *Therefore (toigaroun)*. This old triple compound particle (*toi, gar, oun*) is in the N.T. only here and Heb. 12:1.

Paul applies the logic of the case. *He that rejecteth (ho athetōn).* This late verb (Polybius and LXX) is from *a-thetos (a* privative and verbal of *tithēmi,* to proscribe a thing, to annul it. *But God (alla ton theon).* Paul sees this clearly and modern atheists see it also. In order to justify their licentiousness they do not hesitate to set aside God.

9. *Concerning love of the brethren (peri tēs philadelphias).* Late word, love of brothers or sisters. In profane Greek (one papyrus example) and LXX the word means love of those actually kin by blood, but in the N.T. it is the kinship in the love of Christ as here. *Are taught by God (theodidaktoi este).* Only here and ecclesiastical writers. Passive verbal adjective in *-tos* from *didaskō* as if *theo-* in ablative case like *didaktoi theou* (John 6:45). *To love one another (eis to agapāin allēlous).* Another example of *eis to* and the infinitive. Only those taught of God keep on loving one another, love neighbours and even enemies as Jesus taught (Matt. 5:44). Note the use of *agapaō,* not *phileō.*

10. *Ye do it (poieite auto).* The *auto* refers to *to agapāin allēlous* (to love one another). Delicate praise.

11. *That ye study to be quiet (philotimeisthai hēsuchazein).* First infinitive dependent on *parakaloumen* (verse 10, we exhort you), the second on *philotimeisthai* (old verb from *philotimos,* fond of honour, *philos, timē*). The notion of ambition appears in each of the three N.T. examples (I Thess. 4:11; II Cor. 5:9; Rom. 5:20), but it is ambition to do good, not evil. The word ambition is Latin *(ambitio* from *ambo, ire,* to go on both sides to accomplish one's aims and often evil). A preacher devoid of ambition lacks power. There was a restless spirit in Thessalonica because of the misapprehension of the second coming. So Paul urges an ambition to be quiet or calm, to lead a quiet life, including silence (Acts 11:18). *To do your own business (prassein ta idia).* Present infinitive like the others, to have the habit of attending to their own affairs *(ta idia).* This restless meddlesomeness here condèmned Paul alludes to again in II Thess. 3:11 in plainer terms. It is amazing how much wisdom people have about other people's affairs and so little interest in their own. *To work with your own hands (ergazesthai tais chersin humōn).* Instrumental case *(chersin).* Paul gave a new dignity to manual labour by precept and example.

There were "pious" idlers in the church in Thessalonica who were promoting trouble. He had commanded them when with them.

12. *That ye may walk honestly (hina peripatēte euschēmonōs)*. Present subjunctive (linear action). Old adverb from *euschēmōn (eu, schēma,* Latin *habitus,* graceful figure), becomingly, decently. In N.T. only here and Rom. 13:13. This idea includes honest financial transactions, but a good deal more. People outside the churches have a right to watch the conduct of professing Christians in business, domestic life, social life, politics.

13. *We would not have (ou thelomen)*. We do not wish. *You ignorant (humas agnoein)*. Old word, not to know (*a* privative, *gno-,* root of *ginōskō*). No advantage in ignorance of itself. *Concerning them that fall asleep (peri tōn koimōmenōn)*. Present passive (or middle) participle (Aleph B) rather than the perfect passive *kekoimēmenōn* of many later MSS. From old *koimaō,* to put to sleep. Present tense gives idea of repetition, from time to time fall asleep. Greeks and Romans used this figure of sleep for death as Jesus does (John 11:11) and N.T. generally (cf. our word *cemetery*). Somehow the Thessalonians had a false notion about the dead in relation to the second coming. *Even as the rest which have no hope (kathōs hoi loipoi hoi mē echontes elpida)*. This picture of the hopelessness of the pagan world about the future life is amply illustrated in ancient writings and particularly by inscriptions on tombs (Milligan). Some few pagans clung to this hope, but most had none.

14. *For if we believe (ei gar pisteuomen)*. Condition of first class, assuming the death and resurrection of Jesus to be true. *In Jesus (dia tou Iēsou)*. Literally, through or by means of Jesus. It is amphibolous in position and can be taken either with *tous koimēthentas* (that are fallen asleep in or through Jesus) like *hoi koimēthentes en Christōi* in I Cor. 15:18 and probably correct or with *axei* (through Jesus with God). *With him (sun autōi)*. Together with Jesus. Jesus is the connecting link (*dia*) for those that sleep (*koimēthentas* first aorist passive, but with middle sense) and their resurrection.

15. *By the word of the Lord (en logōi Kuriou)*. We do not know to what word of the Lord Jesus Paul refers, probably

Paul meaning only the point in the teaching of Christ rather than a quotation. He may be claiming a direct revelation on this important matter as about the Lord's Supper in I Cor. 11:23. Jesus may have spoken on this subject though it has not been preserved to us (cf. Mark 9:1). *We that are alive* (*hēmeis hoi zōntes*). Paul here includes himself, but this by no means shows that Paul knew that he would be alive at the Parousia of Christ. He was alive, not dead, when he wrote. *Shall in no wise precede* (*ou mē phthasōmen*). Second aorist active subjunctive of *phthanō*, to come before, to anticipate. This strong negative with *ou mē* (double negative) and the subjunctive is the regular idiom (Robertson, *Grammar*, p. 929). Hence there was no ground for uneasiness about the dead in Christ.

16. *With a shout* (*en keleusmati*). Note this so-called instrumental use of *en*. Old word, here only in N.T., from *keleuō*, to order, command (military command). Christ will come as Conqueror. *With the voice of the archangel* (*en phōnēi archaggelou*). Further explanation of *keleusmati* (command). The only archangel mentioned in N.T. is Michael in Jude 9. But note absence of article with both *phōnēi* and *archaggelou*. The reference may be thus indefinite. *With the trump of God* (*en salpiggi theou*). Trumpet. See same figure in I Cor. 15:52. *The dead in Christ shall rise first* (*hoi nekroi en Christōi anastēsontai prōton*). *First* here refers plainly to the fact that, so far from the dead in Christ having no share in the Parousia, they will rise before those still alive are changed.

17. *Then* (*epeita*). The next step, not the identical time (*tote*), but immediately afterwards. *Together with them* (*hama sun autois*). Note both *hama* (at the same time) and *sun* (together with) with the associative instrumental case *autois* (the risen saints). *Shall be caught up* (*harpagēsometha*). Second future passive indicative of *harpazō*, old verb to seize, to carry off like Latin *rapio*. *To meet the Lord in the air* (*eis apantēsin tou Kuriou eis aera*). This special Greek idiom is common in the LXX like the Hebrew, but Polybius has it also and it occurs in the papyri (Moulton, *Proleg.*, p. 14, n. 3). This rapture of the saints (both risen and changed) is a glorious climax to Paul's argument of consolation. *And so* (*kai houtōs*). This is the outcome, to be forever with the

Lord, whether with a return to earth or with an immediate departure for heaven Paul does not say. To be with Christ is the chief hope of Paul's life (I Thess. 5:10; Phil. 1:23; Col. 3:4; II Cor. 5:8).

18. *With these words* (*en tois logois toutois*). In these words. They were a comfort to the Thessalonians as they still comfort the people of God.

CHAPTER V

1. *But concerning the times and the seasons* (*peri de tōn chronōn kai tōn kairōn*). See both words used also in Titus 1:2f. *Chronos* is rather an extended period and *kairos* a definite space of time.

2. *Know perfectly* (*akribōs oidate*). Accurately know, not "the times and the seasons," but their own ignorance. *As a thief in the night* (*hōs kleptēs en nukti*). As a thief at night, suddenly and unexpectedly. Reminiscence of the word of Jesus (Matt. 24:43 = Luke 12:39), used also in II Pet. 3:10; Rev. 3:3; 16:15. *Cometh* (*erchetai*). Prophetic or futuristic present tense.

3. *When they are saying* (*hotan legōsin*). Present active subjunctive picturing these false prophets of *peace and safety* like Ezek. 13:10 (Peace, and there is no peace). *Asphaleia* only in N.T. in Luke 1:4 (which see); Acts 5:23 and here. *Sudden destruction* (*aiphnidios olethros*). *Olethros* old word from *ollumi*, to destroy. See also II Thess. 1:9. *Aiphnidios*, old adjective akin to *aphnō* and in N.T. only here and Luke 21:34 where Westcott and Hort spell it *ephnidios*. *Cometh upon them* (*autois epistatai*). Unaspirated form instead of the usual *ephistatai* (present middle indicative) from *ephistēmi* perhaps due to confusion with *epistamai*. *As travail upon a woman with child* (*hōsper hē ōdin tēi en gastri echousēi*). Earlier form *ōdis* for birth-pang used also by Jesus (Mark 13:8; Matt. 24:8). Technical phrase for pregnancy, *to the one who has it in belly* (cf. Matt. 1:18 of Mary). *They shall in no wise escape* (*ou mē ekphugōsin*). Strong negative like that in 4:15 *ou mē* (double negative) and the second aorist active subjunctive.

4. *As a thief* (*hōs kleptēs*). As in verse 2, but A B Bohairic have *kleptas* (thieves), turning the metaphor round.

5. *Sons of light* (*huioi phōtos*), *sons of day* (*huioi hēmeras*). Chiefly a translation Hebraism (Deissmann, *Bible Studies*, pp. 161ff.). Cf. words of Jesus in Luke 16:8 and Paul in Eph. 5:9. He repeats the same idea in turning from "ye"

34

to "we" and using *nuktos* (night) and *skotous* (darkness), predicate genitives.

6. *So then* (*ara oun*). Two inferential particles, accordingly therefore, as in II Thess. 2:15 and only in Paul in N.T. *Let us not sleep* (*mē katheudōmen*). Present active subjunctive (volitive), let us not go on sleeping. *Let us watch* (*grēgorōmen*). Present active subj. (volitive) again, let us keep awake (late verb *grēgoreō* from perfect *egrēgora*). *Be sober* (*nēphōmen*). Present active subjunctive (volitive). Old verb not to be drunk. In N.T. only in figurative sense, to be calm, sober-minded. Also in verse 8 with the metaphor of drunkenness in contrast.

7. *They that be drunken are drunken in the night* (*hoi methuskomenoi nuktos methuousin*). No need of "be" here, they that are drunken. No real difference in meaning between *methuskō* and *methuō*, to be drunk, except that *methuskō* (inceptive verb in *-skō*) means to get drunk. *Night* (*nuktos*, genitive by night) is the favourite time for drunken revelries.

8. *Putting on the breastplate of faith and love* (*endusamenoi thōraka pisteōs kai agapēs*). First aorist (ingressive) middle participle of *enduō*. The same figure of breastplate in Eph. 6:14, only there "of righteousness." The idea of watchfulness brings the figure of a sentry on guard and armed to Paul's mind as in Rom. 13:12 "the weapons of light." The word *thōrax* (breastplate) is common in the LXX. *For a helmet, the hope of salvation* (*perikephalaian elpida sōtērias*). Same figure in Eph. 6:17 and both like Isa. 59:17. Late word meaning around (*peri*) the head (*kephale*) and in Polybius, LXX, and in the papyri. *Sōtērias* is objective genitive.

9. *But unto the obtaining of salvation through our Lord Jesus Christ* (*alla eis peripoiēsin sōtērias dia tou Kuriou hēmōn Iēsou Christou*). The difficult word here is *peripoiēsin* which may be passive, God's possession as in I Peter 2:9, or active, obtaining, as in II Thess. 2:14. The latter is probably the idea here. We are to keep awake so as to fulfil God's purpose (*etheto*, appointed, second aorist middle indicative of *tithēmi*) in calling us. That is our hope of final victory (salvation in this sense).

10. *For us* (*peri hēmōn*). *Around us.* So Westcott and Hort, but *huper* (over, in behalf of) as in many MSS. These

prepositions often interchanged in N.T. MSS. *Whether we wake or sleep (eite grēgorōmen eite katheudōmen).* Alternative condition of third class with present subjunctive, though *eante—eante* more usual conjunction (Robertson, *Grammar,* p. 1017). Used here of life and death, not as metaphor. *That we should live together with him (hina hama sun autōi zēsōmen).* First aorist active subjunctive constative aorist covering all life (now and hereafter) together with (*hama sun* as in 5:17) Jesus.

11. *Build each other up (oikodomeite heis ton hena).* Literally, build ye, one the one (*heis* nominative in partitive apposition with unexpressed *humeis* subject of *oikodomeite.* Then *ton hena* the accusative in partitive apposition with the unexpressed *heautous* or *allēlous.* See the same idiom in I Cor. 4:6 *one in behalf of the one, heis huper tou henos.* Build is a favourite Pauline metaphor.

12. *Them that labour among you (tous kopiōntas en humin).* Old word for toil even if weary. *And are over you in the Lord (kai proistamenous humōn en Kuriōi).* Same article with this participle. Literally, those who stand in front of you, your leaders in the Lord, the presbyters or bishops and deacons. Get acquainted with them and follow them. *And admonish you (kai nouthetountas humas).* Old verb from *nouthetēs* and this from *nous* (mind) and *tithēmi,* to put. Putting sense into the heads of people. A thankless, but a necessary, task. The same article connects all three participles, different functions of the same leaders in the church.

13. *And to esteem them (kai hēgeisthai).* Get acquainted with them and esteem the leaders. The idlers in Thessalonica had evidently refused to follow their leaders in church activities. We need wise leadership today, but still more wise following. An army of captains and colonels never won a battle.

14. *Admonish the disorderly (noutheteite tous ataktous).* Put sense into the unruly mob who break ranks (*a* privative and *taktos,* verbal adjective of *tassō,* to keep military order). Recall the idlers from the market-place used against Paul (Acts 17:5). This is a challenging task for any leader. *Encourage the fainthearted (paramutheisthe tous oligopsuchous).* Old verb to encourage or console as in John 11:31, though not so common in N.T. as *parakaleō,* the compound adjective

(*oligos*, little or small, *psuchē*, soul), small-souled, little-souled, late word in LXX. The verb *oligopsucheō* occurs in the papyri. Local conditions often cause some to lose heart and wish to drop out, be quitters. These must be held in line. *Support the weak* (*antechesthe tōn asthenōn*). Middle voice with genitive of *antechō*, old verb, in N.T. only in middle, to cling to, to hold on to (with genitive). The weak are those tempted to sin (immorality, for instance). *Be long-suffering toward all* (*makrothumeite pros pantas*). These disorderly elements try the patience of the leaders. Hold out with them. What a wonderful ideal Paul here holds up for church leaders!

15. *See to it that no one render unto any one evil for evil* (*horate mē tis kakon anti kakou apodōi*). Note *mē* with the aorist subjunctive (negative purpose) *apodōi* from *apodidōmi*, to give back. Retaliation, condemned by Jesus (Matt. 5:38–42) and by Paul in Rom. 12:17, usually takes the form of "evil for evil," rather than "good for good" (*kalon anti kalou*). Note idea of exchange in *anti*. *Follow after* (*diōkete*). Keep up the chase (*diōkō*) after the good.

18. *In everything give thanks* (*en panti eucharisteite*). There is a silver lining to every cloud. God is with us whatever befalls us. It is God's will that we find joy in prayer in Christ Jesus in every condition of life.

19. *Quench not the spirit* (*to pneuma mē sbennute*). *Mē* with the present imperative means to stop doing it or not to have the habit of doing it. It is a bold figure. Some of them were trying to put out the fire of the Holy Spirit, probably the special gifts of the Holy Spirit as verse 20 means. But even so the exercise of these special gifts (I Cor. 12–14; II Cor. 12:2–4; Rom. 12:6–9) was to be decently (*euschēmonōs*, I Thess. 4:12) and in order (*kata taxin*, I Cor. 14:40) and for edification (*pros oikodomēn*, I Cor. 14:26). Today, as then, there are two extremes about spiritual gifts (cold indifference or wild excess). It is not hard to put out the fire of spiritual fervor and power.

20. *Despise not prophesyings* (*prophēteias mē exoutheneite*). Same construction, stop counting as nothing (*exoutheneō*, *outhen = ouden*), late form in LXX. Plutarch has *exoudenizō*. Plural form *prophēteias* (accusative). Word means *forthtelling* (*pro-phēmi*) rather than *fore-telling* and is the chief

of the spiritual gifts (I Cor. 14) and evidently depreciated in Thessalonica as in Corinth later. 21. *Prove all things* (*panta [de] dokimazete*). Probably *de* (but) is genuine. Even the gift of prophecy has to be tested (I Cor. 12:10; 14:29) to avoid error. Paul shows fine balance here. *Hold fast that which is good* (*to kalon katechete*). Keep on holding down the beautiful (noble, morally beautiful). Present imperative *kat-echō* (perfective use of *kata-* here). 22. *Abstain from every form of evil* (*apo pantos eidous ponērou apechesthe*). Present middle (direct) imperative of *ap-echō* (contrast with *kat-echō*) and preposition *apo* repeated with ablative as in I Thess. 4:3. Note use of *ponērou* here for evil without the article, common enough idiom. *Eidos* (from *eidon*) naturally means look or appearance as in Luke 3:23; 9:29; John 5:37; II Cor. 5:7. But, if so taken, it is not semblance as opposed to reality (Milligan). The papyri give several examples of *eidos* in the sense of class or kind and that idea suits best here. Evil had a way of showing itself even in the spiritual gifts including prophecy. 23. *The God of peace* (*ho theos tēs eirēnēs*). The God characterized by peace in his nature, who gladly bestows it also. Common phrase (Milligan) at close of Paul's Epistles (II Cor. 13:11; Rom. 15:33; 16:20; Phil. 4:9) and *the Lord of peace* in II Thess. 3:6. *Sanctify you* (*hagiasai humās*). First aorist active optative in a wish for the future. New verb in LXX and N.T. for the old *hagizō*, to render or to declare holy (*hagios*), to consecrate, to separate from things profane. *Wholly* (*holoteleis*). Predicate adjective in plural (*holos*, whole, *telos*, end), not adverb *holotelōs*. Late word in Plutarch, Hexapla, and in inscription A.D. 67 (Moulton and Milligan, *Vocabulary*). Here alone in N.T. Here it means the whole of each of you, every part of each of you, "through and through" (Luther), qualitatively rather than quantitatively. *Your spirit and soul and body* (*humōn to pneuma kai hē psuchē kai to sōma*). Not necessarily trichotomy as opposed to dichotomy as elsewhere in Paul's Epistles. Both believers and unbelievers have an inner man (soul *psuchē*, mind *nous*, heart *kardia*, the inward man *ho esō anthrōpos*) and the outer man (*sōma*, *ho exō anthrōpos*). But the believer has the Holy Spirit of God, the renewed spirit of man (I Cor. 2:11; Rom. 8:9–11). *Be preserved entire* (*holoklēron tērētheiē*). First aorist passive optative in wish for the future. Note singular verb and singular adjective (neuter) showing that Paul conceives of the man as "an undivided whole" (Frame), prayer for the consecration of both body and soul (cf. I Cor. 6). The adjective *holoklēron* is in predicate and is an old form and means complete in all its parts (*holos*, whole, *klēros*, lot or part). There is to be no deficiency in any part. *Teleios* (from *telos*, end) means final perfection. *Without blame* (*amemptōs*). Old adverb (*a* privative, *memptos*, verbal of *memphomai*, to blame) only in I Thess. in N.T. (2:10; 3:13?; 5:23). Milligan notes it in certain sepulchral inscriptions discovered in Thessalonica. *At the coming* (*en tēi parousiāi*). The Second Coming which was a sustaining hope to Paul as it should be to us and mentioned often in this Epistle (see on 2:19).

24. *Faithful* (*pistos*). God, he means, who calls and will carry through (Phil. 1:6).

25. *Pray for us* (*proseuchesthe* [*kai*] *peri hēmōn*). He has made his prayer for them. He adds this "human touch" (Frame) and pleads for the prayers of his converts (II Thess. 3:1; Col. 4:2f.). Probably *kai* also is genuine (B D).

26. *With a holy kiss* (*en philēmati hagiōi*). With a kiss that is holy (Milligan) a token of friendship and brotherly love (I Cor. 16:20; II Cor. 13:12; Rom. 16:16). In I Peter 5:14 it is "with a kiss of love." This was the customary salutation for rabbis.

27. *I adjure you by the Lord* (*enorkizō humas ton Kurion*). Late compound for old *horkizō* (Mark 5:7), to put one on oath, with two accusatives (Robertson, *Grammar*, pp. 483f.). Occurs in inscriptions. *That this epistle be read unto all the brethren* (*anagnōsthēnai tēn epistolēn pasin tois adelphois*). First aorist passive infinitive of *anaginōskō* with accusative of general reference in an indirect command. Clearly Paul wrote for the church as a whole and wished the epistles read aloud at a public meeting. In this first epistle we see the importance that he attaches to his epistles.

28. *The grace* (*hē charis*). Paul prefers this noble word to the customary *errōsthe* (Farewell, Be strong). See II Thess. 3:18 for identical close save added *pantōn* (all). A bit shorter form in I Cor. 16:23; Rom. 16:20 and still shorter in Col. 4:18; I Tim. 6:21; Titus 3:15; II Tim. 4:22. The full Trinitarian benediction we find in II Cor. 13:13.

SECOND THESSALONIANS
From Corinth a.d. 50 or 51

BY WAY OF INTRODUCTION

It is plain that First Thessalonians did not settle all the difficulties in Thessalonica. With some there was precisely the opposite result. There was some opposition to Paul's authority and even defiance. So Paul repeats his "command" for discipline (II Thess. 3:6) as he had done when with them (3:10). He makes this Epistle a test of obedience (3:14) and finds it necessary to warn the Thessalonians against the zeal of some deceivers who even invent epistles in Paul's name to carry their point in the church (2:1f.), an early instance of pseudepigraphic "Pauline" epistles, but not for a "pious" purpose. Paul's keen resentment against the practise should make us slow to accept the pseudepigraphic theory about other Pauline Epistles. He calls attention to his own signature at the close of each genuine letter. As a rule he dictated the epistle, but signed it with his own hand (3:17). Paul writes to calm excitement (Ellicott) and to make it plain that he had not said that the Second Coming was to be right away.

This Epistle is a bit sharper in tone than the First and also briefer. It has been suggested that there were two churches in Thessalonica, a Gentile Church to which First Thessalonians was sent, and a Jewish Church to which Second Thessalonians was addressed. There is no real evidence for such a gratuitous hypothesis. It assumes a difficulty about his sending a second letter to the same church that does not exist. The bearer of the first letter brought back news that made a second necessary. It was probably sent within the same year as the first.

CHAPTER I

1. *Paul, etc. (Paulos, etc.).* This address or superscription is identical with that in I Thess. 1:1 save that our (*hēmōn*) is added after *Father (patri).*

2. *From God the Father and the Lord Jesus Christ (apo theou patros kai Kuriou Iēsou Christou).* These words are not genuine in I Thess. 1:1, but are here and they appear in all the other Pauline Epistles. Note absence of article both after *en* and *apo*, though both God and Lord Jesus Christ are definite. In both cases Jesus Christ is put on a par with God, though not identical. See on I Thess. 1:1 for discussion of words, but note difference between *en*, in the sphere of, by the power of, and *apo*, from, as the fountain head and source of grace and peace.

3. *We are bound (opheilomen).* Paul feels a sense of obligation to keep on giving thanks to God (*eucharistein tōi theōi*, present infinitive with dative case) because of God's continued blessings on the Thessalonians. He uses the same idiom again in 2:13 and nowhere else in his thanksgivings. It is not necessity (*dei*) that Paul here notes, but a sense of personal obligation as in I John 2:6 (Milligan). *Even as it is meet (kathōs axion estin).* *Opheilomen* points to the divine, *axion* to the human side of the obligation (Lightfoot), perhaps to cheer the fainthearted in a possible letter to him in reply to Paul's First Thessalonian epistle (Milligan). This adjective *axios* is from *agō*, to drag down the scales, and so weighty, worthy, worthwhile, old word and appropriate here. *For that your faith groweth exceedingly (hoti huperauxanei hē pistis humōn).* Causal use of *hoti* referring to the obligation stated in *opheilomen.* The verb *huperauxanō* is one of Paul's frequent compounds in *huper* (*huper-bainō*, I Thess. 4:6; *huper-ek-teinō*, II Cor. 10:14; *huper-en-tugchanō*, Rom. 8:26; *huper-nikaō*, Rom. 8:37; *huper-pleonazō*, I Tim. 1:14) and occurs only here in N.T. and rare elsewhere (Galen, Dio Cass.). Figure of the tree of faith growing above (*huper*) measure. Cf. parable of Jesus about faith like a grain of

41

mustard seed (Matt. 13:31f.). *Aboundeth* (*pleonazei*). Same verb in I Thess. 3:12, here a fulfilment of the prayer made there. Milligan finds *diffusive* growth of love in this word because of "each one" (*henos hekastou*). Frame finds in this fulfilment of the prayer of I Thess. 3:12 one proof that II Thessalonians is later than I Thessalonians. 4. *So that* (*hōste*). Another example of *hōste* and the infinitive (*enkauchāsthai*) for result as in I Thess. 1:7 which see. *We ourselves* (*autous hēmās*). Accusative of general reference with the infinitive, but not merely *hēmās* (or *heautous*), perhaps in contrast with *en humin* (in you), as much as to say, "so that we ourselves, contrary to your expectations, are boasting" (Frame). *Enkauchaomai* occurs here alone in N.T., but is found in the LXX and in *Aesop's Fables*, proof enough of its vernacular use. Paul was not above praising one church to other churches, to provoke them to good works. Here he is boasting of Thessalonica in Macedonia to the Corinthians as he did later to the Corinthians about the collection (II Cor. 8:1–15) after having first boasted to the Macedonians about the Corinthians (II Cor. 9:1–5). There were other churches in Achaia besides Corinth (II Cor. 1:1). *For* (*huper*). Over, about, like *peri* (I Thess. 1:2). *In all your persecutions* (*en pasin tois diōgmois humōn*). Their patience and faith had already attracted Paul's attention (I Thess. 1:3) and their tribulations *thlipsesin* (I Thess. 1:6). Here Paul adds the more specific term *diōgmos*, old word from *diōkō*, to chase, to pursue, a word used by Paul of his treatment in Corinth (II Cor. 12:10). *Which ye endure* (*hais anechesthe*). B here reads *enechesthe*, to be entangled in, to be held in as in Gal. 5:1, but *anechesthe* is probably correct and the *hais* is probably attracted to locative case of *thlipsesin* from the ablative *hōn* after *anechesthe*, *from which ye hold yourselves back* (cf. Col. 3:13). 5. *A manifest token of the righteous judgment of God* (*endeigma tēs dikaias kriseōs tou theou*). Old word from *endeiknumi*, to point out, result reached (-*ma*), a thing proved. It is either in the accusative of general reference in apposition with the preceding clause as in Rom. 8:3; 12:1, or in the nominative absolute when *ho estin*, if supplied, would explain it as in Phil. 1:28. This righteous judgment is future and final (verses 6–10). *To the end that you may be counted worthy (eis to kataxiōthēnai humas).* Another example of *eis to* for purpose with first aorist passive infinitive from *kataxioō*, old verb, with accusative of general reference *humas* and followed by the genitive *tēs basileias* (kingdom of God). See I Thess. 2:12 for *kingdom of God. For which ye also suffer (huper hēs kai paschete).* Ye *also* as well as we and the present tense means that it is still going on.

6. *If so be that it is a righteous thing with God (eiper dikaion para theōi).* Condition of first class, determined as fulfilled, assumed as true, but with *eiper* (if on the whole, provided that) as in Rom. 8:9 and 17, and with no copula expressed. A righteous thing "with God" means by the side of God *(para theōi)* and so from God's standpoint. This is as near to the idea of absolute right as it is possible to attain. Note the phrase in verse 5. *To recompense affliction to them that afflict you (antapodounai tois thlibousin hēmās thlipsin).* Second aorist active infinitive of double compound *ant-apo-didōmi*, old verb, either in good sense as in I Thess. 3:9 or in bad sense as here. Paul is certain of this principle, though he puts it conditionally.

7. *Rest with us (anesin meth' hēmōn).* Let up, release. Old word from *aniēmi*, from troubles here (II Cor. 2:13; 7:5; 8:13), and hereafter as in this verse. Vivid word. They shared suffering with Paul (verse 5) and so they will share *(meth')* the *rest. At the revelation of the Lord Jesus (en tēi apokalupsei tou Kuriou Iēsou).* Here the *Parousia* (I Thess. 2:19; 3:13; 5:23) is pictured as a *Revelation* (Un-veiling, *apo-kalupsis*) of the Messiah as in I Cor. 1:7, I Peter 1:7, 13 (cf. Luke 17:30). At this Unveiling of the Messiah there will come the *recompense* (verse 6) to the persecutors and the *rest* from the persecutions. This Revelation will be *from heaven (ap' ouranou)* as to place and *with the angels of his power (met' aggelōn dunameōs autou)* as the retinue and *in flaming fire (en puri phlogos,* in a fire of flame, fire characterized by flame). In Acts 7:30 the text is *flame of fire* where *puros* is genitive (like Isa. 66:15) rather than *phlogos* as here (Ex. 3:2).

8. *Rendering (didontos).* Genitive of present active participle of *didōmi,* to give, agreeing with *Iēsou. Vengeance (ekdikēsin).* Late word from *ekdikeō,* to vindicate, in Polybius and LXX. *To them that know not God (tois mē eidosin theon).* Dative plural of perfect active participle *eidōs.* Apparently

chiefly Gentiles in mind (I Thess. 4:3; Gal. 4:8; Rom. 1:28;
Eph. 2:12), though Jews are also guilty of wilful ignorance
of God (Rom. 2:14). *And to them that obey not the gospel of
our Lord Jesus* (*kai tois mē hupakouousin tōi euaggeliōi tou
kuriou hēmōn Iēsou*). Repetition of the article looks like
another class and so Jews (Rom. 10:16). Both Jews as in-
stigators and Gentiles as officials (*politarchs*) were involved
in the persecution in Thessalonica (Acts 17:5–9; II Thess.
1:6). Note the use of "gospel" here as in Mark 1:15 " believe in the gospel."
    9. *Who* (*hoitines*). Qualitative use, such as. Vanishing in
papyri though surviving in Paul (I Cor. 3:17; Rom. 1:25;
Gal. 4:26; Phil. 4:3). *Shall suffer punishment* (*dikēn tisousin*).
Future active of old verb *tinō*, to pay penalty (*dikēn*, right,
justice), here only in N.T., but *apotinō* once also to repay
Philemon 19. In the papyri *dikē* is used for a case or process
in law. This is the regular phrase in classic writers for paying
the penalty. *Eternal destruction* (*olethron aiōnion*). Accusative case in apposition with *dikēn* (penalty). This phrase
does not appear elsewhere in the N.T., but is in IV Macc.
10:15 *ton aiōnion tou turannou olethron* the eternal destruction of the tyrant (Antiochus Epiphanes). Destruction
(cf. I Thess. 5:3) does not mean here annihilation, but, as
Paul proceeds to show, separation *from the face of the Lord*
(*apo prosōpou tou kuriou*) and from the *glory of his might*
(*kai apo tēs doxēs tēs ischuos autou*), an eternity of woe such
as befell Antiochus Epiphanes. *Aiōnios* in itself only means
age-long and papyri and inscriptions give it in the weakened
sense of a Caesar's life (Milligan), but Paul means by age-
long *the coming age* in contrast with *this age*, as *eternal* as
the New Testament knows how to make it. See on Matt.
25:46 for use of *aiōnios* both with *zōēn*, life, and *kolasin*,
punishment.
    10. *When he shall come* (*hotan elthēi*). Second aorist active
subjunctive with *hotan*, future and indefinite temporal clause
(Robertson, *Grammar*, pp. 971ff.) coincident with *en tēi
apokalupsei* in verse 7. *To be glorified* (*endoxasthēnai*). First
aorist passive infinitive (purpose) of *endoxazō*, late verb, in
N.T. only here and verse 12, in LXX and papyri. *In his
saints* (*en tois hagiois autou*). The sphere in which Christ
will find his glory at the Revelation. *And to be marvelled at*

(*kai thaumasthēnai*). First aorist passive infinitive (purpose), common verb *thaumazō*. *That believed* (*tois pisteusasin*). Why aorist active participle instead of present active *pisteuousin* (that believe)? Frame thinks that Paul thus reassures those who believed his message when there (I Thess. 1:6ff.; 2:13f.). The parenthetical clause, though difficult, falls in with this idea: *Because our testimony unto you was believed* (*hoti episteuthē to marturion hēmōn eph' humas*). Moffatt calls it an anti-climax. *On that day* (*en tēi hēmerāi ekeinēi*). The day of Christ's coming (II Tim. 1:12, 18; 4:8). 11. *To which end* (*eis ho*). So Col. 1:29. Probably purpose with reference to the contents of verses 5 to 10. We have had the Thanksgiving (verses 3 to 10) in a long, complicated, but rich period or sentence. Now he makes a brief Prayer (verses 11 and 12) that God will fulfil all their hopes and endeavours. Paul and his colleagues can still pray for them though no longer with them (Moffatt). *That* (*hina*). Common after *proseuchomai* (Col. 4:3; Eph. 1:17; Phil. 1:9) when the content of the prayer blends with the purpose (purport and purpose). *Count you worthy* (*humas axiōsēi*). Causative verb (aorist active subjunctive) like *kataxioō* in verse 5 with genitive. *Of your calling* (*tēs klēseōs*). *Klēsis* can apply to the beginning as in I Cor. 1:26; Rom. 11:29, but it can also apply to the final issue as in Phil. 3:14; Heb. 3:1. Both ideas may be here. It is God's calling of the Thessalonians. *And fulfil every desire of goodness* (*kai plērōsēi pasan eudokian agathōsunēs*). "Whom he counts worthy he first makes worthy" (Lillie). Yes, in purpose, but the wonder and the glory of it all is that God begins to count us worthy in Christ before the process is completed in Christ (Rom. 8:29f.). But God will see it through and so Paul prays to God. *Eudokia* (cf. Luke 2:14) is more than mere desire, rather good pleasure, God's purpose of goodness, not in ancient Greek, only in LXX and N.T. *Agathōsunē* like a dozen other words in *-sunē* occurs only in late Greek. This word occurs only in LXX, N.T., writings based on them. It is made from *agathos*, good, akin to *agamai*, to admire. May the Thessalonians find delight in goodness, a worthy and pertinent prayer. *Work of faith* (*ergon pisteōs*). The same phrase in I Thess. 1:3. Paul prays for rich fruition of what he had seen in the beginning. Work marked by faith, springs from faith, sustained by faith. *With power* (*en dunamei*). In power. Connect with *plērōsei* (fulfil), God's power (Rom. 1:29; Col. 1:4) in Christ (I Cor. 1:24) through the Holy Spirit (I Thess. 1:5).

12. *That* (*hopōs*). Rare with Paul compared with *hina* (I Cor. 1:29; II Cor. 8:14). Perhaps here for variety (dependent on *hina* clause in verse 11). *The name* (*to onoma*). The Old Testament (LXX) uses *onoma* embodying the revealed character of Jehovah. So here the *Name* of our Lord Jesus means the Messiahship and Lordship of Jesus. The common Greek idiom of *onoma* for title or dignity as in the papyri (Milligan) is not quite this idiom. The papyri also give examples of *onoma* for person as in O.T. and Acts 1:15 (Deissmann, *Bible Studies*, pp. 196ff.). *In you, and ye in him* (*en humin, kai humeis en autōi*). This reciprocal glorying is Pauline, but it is also like Christ's figure of the vine and the branches in John 15:1–11. *According to the grace* (*kata tēn charin*). Not merely standard, but also aim (Robertson, *Grammar*, p. 609). *Of our God and the Lord Jesus Christ* (*tou theou hēmōn kai kuriou Iēsou Christou*). Here strict syntax requires, since there is only one article with *theou* and *kuriou* that one person be meant, Jesus Christ, as is certainly true in Titus 2:13; II Peter 1:1 (Robertson, *Grammar*, p. 786). This otherwise conclusive syntactical argument, admitted by Schmiedel, is weakened a bit by the fact that *Kurios* is often employed as a proper name without the article, a thing not true of *sōtēr* in Titus 2:13 and II Peter 1:1. So in Eph. 5:5 *en tēi basileiāi tou Christou kai theou* the natural meaning is *in the Kingdom of Christ and God* regarded as one, but here again *theos*, like *Kurios*, often occurs as a proper name without the article. So it has to be admitted that here Paul may mean "according to the grace of our God and the Lord Jesus Christ," though he may also mean "according to the grace of our God and Lord, Jesus Christ."

CHAPTER II

1. *Touching the coming of our Lord Jesus Christ* (*huper tēs parousias tou Kuriou* (*hēmōn*) *Iēsou Christou*). For *erōtōmen*, to beseech, see on I Thess. 4:1; 4:12. *Huper* originally meant over, in behalf of, instead of, but here it is used like *peri*, around, concerning as in 1:4; I Thess. 3:2; 5:10, common in the papyri (Robertson, *Grammar*, p. 632). For the distinction between *Parousia, Epiphaneia* (Epiphany), and *Apokalupsis* (Revelation) as applied to the Second Coming of Christ see Milligan on *Thessalonian Epistles*, pp. 145 to 151, in the light of the papyri. *Parousia* lays emphasis on the *presence* of the Lord with his people, *epiphaneia* on his *manifestation* of the power and love of God, *apokalupsis* on the *revelation* of God's purpose and plan in the Second Coming of the Lord Jesus. *And our gathering together unto him* (*kai hēmōn episunagōgēs ep' auton*). A late word found only in II Macc. 2:7; II Thess. 2:1; Heb. 10:25 till Deissmann (*Light from the Ancient East*, p. 103) found it on a stele in the island of Syme, off Caria, meaning "collection." Paul is referring to the rapture, mentioned in I Thess. 4:15–17, and the being forever with the Lord thereafter. Cf. also Matt. 24:31 = Mark 13:27.

2. *To the end that* (*eis to*). One of Paul's favourite idioms for purpose, *eis to* and the infinitive. *Ye be not quickly shaken* (*mē tacheōs saleuthēnai humas*). First aorist passive infinitive of *saleuō*, old verb to agitate, to cause to totter like a reed (Matt. 11:7), the earth (Heb. 12:26). Usual negative *mē* and accusative of general reference *humas* with the infinitive. *From your mind* (*apo tou noos*). Ablative case of *nous*, mind, reason, sober sense, "from your witte" (Wyclif), to "keep their heads." *Nor yet be troubled* (*mēde throeisthai*). Old verb *throeō*, to cry aloud (from *throos*, clamour, tumult), to be in a state of nervous excitement (present passive infinitive, as if it were going on), "a continued state of agitation following the definite shock received (*saleuthēnai*)" (Milligan). *Either by spirit* (*mēte dia pneumatos*). By ecstatic utterance (I Thess. 5:10). The nervous fear that

47

the coming was to be at once prohibited by *mēde* Paul
divides into three sources by *mēte, mēte, mēte.* No individual
claim to divine revelation (the gift of prophecy) can justify
the statement. *Or by word* (*mēte dia logou*). Oral statement
of a conversation with Paul (Lightfoot) to this effect *as
from us.* An easy way to set aside Paul's first Epistle by
report of a private remark from Paul. *Or by epistle as from
us* (*mēte di' epistolēs hōs di' hēmōn*). In I Thess. 4:13–5:3
Paul had plainly said that Jesus would come as a thief in
the night and had shown that the dead would not be left
out in the rapture. But evidently some one claimed to have
a private epistle from Paul which supported the view that
Jesus was coming at once, *as that the day of the Lord is now
present* (*hōs hoti enestēken hē hēmera tou kuriou*). Perfect
active indicative of *enistēmi*, old verb, to place in, but intransitive in this tense to stand in or at or near. So "is
imminent" (Lightfoot). The verb is common in the papyri.
In I Cor. 3:22 and Rom. 8:38 we have a contrast between
ta enestōta, the things present, and *ta mellonta,* the things
future (to come). The use of *hōs hoti* may be disparaging
here, though that is not true in II Cor. 5:19. In the *Koiné*
it comes in the vernacular to mean simply "that" (Moulton,
Proleg., p. 212), but that hardly seems the case in the N.T.
(Robertson, *Grammar,* p. 1033). Here it means "to wit
that," though "as that" or "as if" does not miss it much.
Certainly it flatly denies that by conversation or by letter
he had stated that the second coming was immediately
at hand. "It is this misleading assertion that accounts both
for the increased discouragement of the faint-hearted to
encourage whom Paul writes 1:3–2:17, and for the increased
meddlesomeness of the idle brethren to warn whom Paul
writes 3:1–18" (Frame). It is enough to give one pause to
note Paul's indignation over this use of his name by one
of the over-zealous advocates of the view that Christ was
coming at once. It is true that Paul was still alive, but, if
such a "pious fraud" was so common and easily condoned
as some today argue, it is difficult to explain Paul's evident
anger. Moreover, Paul's words should make us hesitate to
affirm that Paul definitely proclaimed the early return of
Jesus. He hoped for it undoubtedly, but he did not specifically proclaim it as so many today assert and accuse him

of misleading the early Christians with a false presentation.

3. *Let no man beguile you in any wise* (*mē tis humas exapatēsei kata mēdena tropon*). First aorist active subjunctive of *exapataō* (old verb, to deceive, strengthened form of simple verb *apataō*) with double negative (*mē tis, mēdena*) in accord with regular Greek idiom as in I Cor. 16:11 rather than the aorist imperative which does occur sometimes in the third person as in Mark 13:15 (*mē katabatō*). Paul broadens the warning to go beyond conversation and letter. He includes "tricks" of any kind. It is amazing how gullible some of the saints are when a new deceiver pulls off some stunts in religion. *For it will not be* (*hoti*). There is an ellipse here of *ouk estai* (or *genēsetai*) to be supplied after *hoti*. Westcott and Hort make an anacoluthon at the end of verse 4. The meaning is clear. *Hoti* is causal, because, but the verb is understood. The second coming not only is not "imminent," but will not take place before certain important things take place, a definite rebuff to the false enthusiasts of verse 2. *Except the falling away come first* (*ean mē elthēi hē apostasia prōton*). Negative condition of the third class, undetermined with prospect of determination and the aorist subjunctive. *Apostasia* is the late form of *apostasis* and is our word apostasy. Plutarch uses it of political revolt and it occurs in I Macc. 2:15 about Antiochus Epiphanes who was enforcing the apostasy from Judaism to Hellenism. In Josh. 22:22 it occurs for rebellion against the Lord. It seems clear that the word here means a religious revolt and the use of the definite article (*hē*) seems to mean that Paul had spoken to the Thessalonians about it. The only other New Testament use of the word is in Acts 21:21 where it means apostasy from Moses. It is not clear whether Paul means revolt of the Jews from God, of Gentiles from God, of Christians from God, or of the apostasy that includes all classes within and without the body of Christians. But it is to be *first* (*prōton*) before Christ comes again. Note this adverb when only two events are compared (cf. Acts 1:1). *And the man of sin be revealed, the son of perdition* (*kai apokaluphthēi ho anthrōpos tēs anomias, ho huios tēs apōleias*). First aorist passive subjunctive after *ean mē* and same condition as with *elthēi*. The use of this verb *apokaluptō*, like

apokalupsin of the second coming in 1:7, seems to note the superhuman character (Milligan) of the event and the same verb is repeated in verses 6 and 8. The implication is that *the man of sin* is hidden somewhere who will be suddenly manifested just as false apostles pose as angels of light (II Cor. 11:13ff.), whether the crowning event of the apostasy or another name for the same event. Lightfoot notes the parallel between the man of sin, of whom sin is the special characteristic (genitive case, a Hebraism for the lawless one in verse 8) and Christ. Both Christ and the adversary of Christ are revealed, there is mystery about each, both make divine claims (verse 4). He seems to be the Antichrist of I John 2:18. The terrible phrase, the son of perdition, is applied to Judas in John 17:12 (like Judas doomed to perdition), but here to the lawless one (*ho anomos*, verse 8), who is not Satan, but some one definite person who is doing the work of Satan. Note the definite article each time.

4. *He that opposeth and exalteth himself* (*ho antikeimenos kai huperairomenos*). Like John's Antichrist this one opposes (*anti-*) Christ and exalts himself (direct middle of *huperairō*, old verb to lift oneself up *above* others, only here and II Cor. 12:7 in N.T.), but not Satan, but an agent of Satan. This participial clause is in apposition with the two preceding phrases, the man of sin, the son of perdition. Note I Cor. 8:5 about one called God and Acts 17:23 for *sebasma* (from *sebazomai*), object of worship, late word, in N.T. only in these two passages. *So that he sitteth in the temple of God* (*hōste auton eis ton naon tou theou kathisai*). Another example of the infinitive with *hōste* for result. Caius Caligula had made a desperate attempt to have his statue set up for worship in the Temple in Jerusalem. This incident may lie behind Paul's language here. *Setting himself forth as God* (*apodeiknunta heauton hoti estin theos*). Present active participle (*mi* form) of *apodeiknumi*, agreeing in case with *auton*, *showing himself that he is God*. Caligula claimed to be God. Moffatt doubts if Paul is identifying this deception with the imperial cultus at this stage. Lightfoot thinks that the deification of the Roman emperor supplied Paul's language here. Wetstein notes a coin of Julius with *theos* on one side and *Thessalonikeōn* on the other. In I John 2:18 we are told of "many antichrists" some of whom had already

come. Hence it is not clear that Paul has in mind only one individual or even individuals at all rather than evil principles, for in verse 6 he speaks of *to katechon* (that which restraineth) while in verse 7 it is *ho katechōn* (the one that restraineth). Frame argues for a combination of Belial and Antichrist as the explanation of Paul's language. But the whole subject is left by Paul in such a vague form that we can hardly hope to clear it up. It is possible that his own preaching while with them gave his readers a clue that we do not possess.

5. *When I was yet with you (eti ōn pros humas).* The present participle takes the time of the verb *elegon* (imperfect active), *I used to tell you these things.* So Paul recalls their memory of his words and leaves us without the clue to his idea. We know that one of the charges against him was that Jesus was another king, a rival to Caesar (Acts 17:7). That leads one to wonder how far Paul went when there in contrasting the kingdom of the world of which Rome was ruler and the kingdom of God of which Christ is king. Frame notes Paul's abrupt question here "with an unfinished sentence behind him" (verses 3f.), even "with a trace of impatience."

6. *That which restraineth (to katechon). And now you know (kai nun oidate),* says Paul in this cryptic apocalyptic passage. Unfortunately we do not know what Paul means by *that which restrains* (holds back, *katechon*), neuter here and masculine in verse 7 *ho katechōn.* "This impersonal principle or power is capable also of manifesting itself under a personal form" (Milligan). "He is Satan's messiah, an infernal caricature of the true Messiah" (Moffatt). Warfield (*Expositor*, III, iv, pp. 30ff.) suggested that the man of lawlessness is the imperial line with its rage for deification and that the Jewish state was the restraining power. But God overrules all human history and his ultimate purpose is wrought out. *To the end that (eis to).* Another example of *eis to* and the infinitive for purpose. *In his own season (en tōi autou kairōi).* Note *autou* (his), not *heautou* (his own), *revealed in his time*, in the time set him by God.

7. *For the mystery of lawlessness doth already work (to gar mustērion ēdē energeitai tēs anomias).* See I Thess. 2:13 for *energeitai.* The genitive *tēs anomias* (lawlessness) describes

to mustērion (note emphatic position of both). This mystery (*mustērion* secret, from *mustēs*, an initiate, *mueō*, to wink or blink) means here the secret purpose of lawlessness already at work, the only instance of this usage in the N.T. where it is used of the kingdom of God (Matt. 13:11), of God (I Cor. 2:1) and God's will (Eph. 1:9), of Christ (Eph. 3:4), of the gospel (Eph. 6:9), of faith (I Tim. 3:9), of godliness (I Tim. 3:16), of the seven stars (Rev. 1:20), of the woman (Rev. 17:7). But this secret will be "revealed" and then we shall understand clearly what Paul's meaning is here. *Until he be taken out of the way* (*heōs ek mesou genētai*). Usual construction with *heōs* for the future (aorist middle subjunctive, *genētai*). Note absence of *an* as often in N.T. and the *Koinē*. Paul uses *heōs* only here and I Cor. 4:5. When the obstacle is removed then the mystery of lawlessness will be revealed in plain outline.

8. *And then* (*kai tote*). Emphatic note of time, *then* when the restraining one (*ho katechōn*) is taken out of the way, then *the lawless one* (*ho anomos*), the man of sin, the man of perdition, will be revealed. *Whom the Lord [Jesus] shall slay* (*hon ho kurios [Iēsous] anelei*). Whether Jesus is genuine or not, he is meant by Lord. *Anelei* is a late future from *anaireō*, in place of *anairēsei*. Paul uses Isa. 11:4 (combining *by the word of his mouth* with *in breath through lips*) to picture the triumph of Christ over this adversary. It is a powerful picture how the mere breath of the Lord will destroy this arch-enemy (Milligan). *And bring to naught by the manifestation of his coming* (*kai katargēsei tēi epiphaneiāi tēs parousias autou*). This verb *katargeō* (*kata, argos*) to render useless, rare in ancient Greek, appears 25 times in Paul and has a variety of renderings. In the papyri it has a weakened sense of hinder. It will be a grand fiasco, this advent of the man of sin. Paul here uses both *epiphaneia* (*epiphany*, elsewhere in N.T. in the Pastorals, familiar to the Greek mind for a visit of a god) and *parousia* (more familiar to the Jewish mind, but common in the papyri) of the second coming of Christ. "The apparition of Jesus heralds his doom" (Moffatt). The mere appearance of Christ destroys the adversary (Vincent).

9. *Whose coming is* (*hou estin hē parousia*). Refers to *hon* in verse 8. The Antichrist has his *parousia* also. Deissmann

(*Light from the Ancient East*, pp. 374, 378) notes an inscription at Epidaurus in which "Asclepius manifested his *Parousia*." Antiochus Epiphanes is called *the manifest god* (III Macc. 5:35). So the two Epiphanies coincide. *Lying wonders* (*terasin pseudous*). "In wonders of a lie." Note here the three words for the miracles of Christ (Heb. 2:4), power (*dunamis*), signs (*sēmeia*), wonders (*terata*), but all according to the working of Satan (*kata energeian tou Satana*, the energy of Satan) just as Jesus had foretold (Matt. 24:24), wonders that would almost lead astray the very elect.

10. *With all deceit of unrighteousness* (*en pasēi apatēi adikias*). This pastmaster of trickery will have at his command all the energy and skill of Satan to mislead and deceive. How many illustrations lie along the pathway of Christian history. *For them that are perishing* (*tois apollumenois*). Dative case of personal interest. Note this very phrase in II Cor. 2:15 and 4:3. Present middle participle of *appollumi*, to destroy, the dreadful process goes on. *Because* (*anth' hōn*). In return for which things (*anti* and the genitive of the relative pronoun). Same idiom in Luke 1:20; 12:3; 19:44; Acts 12:23 and very common in the LXX. *The love of the truth* (*tēn agapēn tēs alētheias*). That is the gospel in contrast with *lying* and *deceit*. *That they might be saved* (*eis to sōthēnai autous*). First aorist passive infinitive of *sōzō* with *eis to*, again, epexegetic purpose of *the truth* if they had heeded it.

11. *And for this reason God sendeth them* (*kai dia touto pempei autois ho theos*). Futuristic (prophetic) present of the time when the lawless one is revealed. Here is the definite judicial act of God (Milligan) who gives the wicked over to the evil which they have deliberately chosen (Rom. 1:24, 26, 28). *A working of error* (*energeian planēs*). Terrible result of wilful rejection of the truth of God. *That they should believe a lie* (*eis to pisteusai autous tōi pseudei*). Note *eis to* again and *tōi pseudei* (the lie, the falsehood already described), a contemplated result. Note Rom. 1:25 "who changed the truth of God into the lie."

12. *That they all might be judged* (*hina krithōsin pantes*). First aorist passive subjunctive of *krinō*, to sift, to judge, with *hina*. Ultimate purpose, almost result, of the preceding

obstinate resistance to the truth and "the judicial infatua-
tion which overtakes them" (Lightfoot), now final punishment. Condemnation is involved in the fatal choice made.
These victims of the man of sin did not believe the truth
and found pleasure in unrighteousness.
13. See 1:3 for same beginning. *Beloved of the Lord* (*ēgapēmenoi hupo kuriou*). Perfect passive participle of *agapaō*
with *hupo* and the ablative as in I Thess. 1:4, only here
kuriou instead of *theou*, the Lord Jesus rather than God the
Father. *Because that God chose you* (*hoti heilato humas ho
theos*). First aorist middle indicative of *haireō*, to take, old
verb, but uncompounded only in N.T. here, Phil. 1:22; Heb.
11:25, and here only in sense of *choose*, that being usually
exaireomai or *proorizō*. *From the beginning* (*ap' archēs*).
Probably the correct text (Aleph D L) and not *aparchēn*
(first fruits, B G P), though here alone in Paul's writings
and a hard reading, the eternal choice or purpose of God
(I Cor. 2:7; Eph. 1:4; II Tim. 1:9), while *aparchēn* is a favourite idea with Paul (I Cor. 15:20, 23; 16:15; Rom. 8:23; 11:16;
16:5). *Unto salvation* (*eis sōtērian*). The ultimate goal, final
salvation. *In sanctification of the Spirit* (*en hagiasmōi pneumatos*). Subjective genitive *pneumatos*, sanctification
wrought by the Holy Spirit. *And belief of the truth* (*kai pistei
alētheias*). Objective genitive *alētheias*, belief in the truth.
14. *Whereunto* (*eis ho*). The goal, that is the final salvation (*sōtēria*). *Through our gospel* (*dia tou euaggeliou hēmōn*).
God called the Thessalonians through Paul's preaching as
he calls men now through the heralds of the Cross as God
chose (cf. I Thess. 2:12; 5:24). *To the obtaining* (*eis peripoiēsin*). Probably correct translation rather than possession. See on I Thess. 5:9, there *of salvation*, here *of glory*
(the *shekinah*, glory of Jesus).
15. *So then* (*ara oun*). Accordingly then. The illative
ara is supported (Ellicott) by the collective *oun* as in I Thess.
5:6; Gal. 6:10, etc. Here is the practical conclusion from
God's elective purpose in such a world crisis. *Stand fast*
(*stēkete*). Present imperative active of the late present
stēkō from *hestēka* (perfect active of *histēmi*). See on I Thess.
3:8. *Hold the traditions* (*krateite tas paradoseis*). Present
imperative of *krateō*, old verb, to have masterful grip on a
thing, either with genitive (Mark 1:31) or usually the accusa-

tive as here. *Paradosis* (tradition) is an old word for what is handed over to one. Dibelius thinks that Paul reveals his Jewish training in the use of this word (Gal. 1:14), but the word is a perfectly legitimate one for teaching whether oral, *by word* (*dia logou*), or written, *by epistle of ours* (*di' epistolēs hēmōn*). Paul draws here no distinction between oral tradition and written tradition as was done later. The worth of the tradition lies not in the form but in the source and the quality of the content. Paul in I Cor. 11:23 says: "I received from the Lord what I also handed over (*paredōka*) unto you." He praises them because ye "hold fast the traditions even as I delivered them unto you." The *tradition* may be merely that of men and so worthless and harmful in place of the word of God (Mark 7:8; Col. 2:6–8). It all depends. It is easy to scoff at truth as mere tradition. But human progress in all fields is made by use of the old, found to be true, in connection with the new if found to be true. In Thessalonica the saints were already the victims of theological charlatans with their half-baked theories about the second coming of Christ and about social duties and relations. *Which ye were taught* (*has edidachthēte*). First aorist passive indicative of *didaskō*, to teach, retaining the accusative of the thing in the passive as is common with this verb like *doceō* in Latin and teach in English.

16. *And God our Father* (*kai [ho] theos ho patēr hēmōn*). It is uncertain whether the first article *ho* is genuine as it is absent in B D. Usually Paul has the Father before Christ except here, II Cor. 13:13; Gal. 1:1. *Which loved us* (*ho agapēsas hēmas*). This singular articular participle refers to *ho patēr*, "though it is difficult to see how St. Paul could otherwise have expressed his thought, if he had intended to refer to the Son, as well as to the Father. There is probably no instance in St. Paul of a plural adjective or verb, when the two Persons of the Godhead are mentioned" (Lightfoot). *Eternal comfort* (*paraklēsin aiōnian*). Distinct feminine form of *aiōnios* here instead of masculine as in Matt. 25:46.

17. *Comfort and stablish* (*parakalesai kai stērixai*). First aorist active optative of wish for the future of two common verbs *parakaleō* (see on I Thess. 3:7; 4:18; 5:14) and *sterizō* (see on I Thess. 3:2, 13). God is the God of *comfort* (II Cor. 1:3–7) and strength (Rom. 1:11; 16:25).

CHAPTER III

1. *Finally (to loipon).* Accusative of general reference. Cf. *loipon* I Thess. 4:1. *Pray (proseuchesthe).* Present middle, keep on praying. Note *peri* as in I Thess. 5:25. *That the word of the Lord may run and be glorified (hina ho logos tou kuriou trechēi kai doxazētai).* Usual construction of *hina* after *proseuchomai*, sub-final use, content and purpose combined. Note present subjunctive with both verbs rather than aorist, may keep on running and being glorified, two verbs joined together nowhere else in the N.T. Paul probably derived this metaphor from the stadium as in I Cor. 9:24ff.; Gal. 2:2; Rom. 9:16; Phil. 2:16; II Tim. 4:7. Lightfoot translates "may have a triumphant career." On the word of the Lord see on I Thess. 1:8. Paul recognizes the close relation between himself and the readers. He needs their prayers and sympathy and he rejoices in their reception of the word of the Lord already, *even as also it is with you (kathōs kai pros humas).* "As it does in your case" (Frame).

2. *And that we may be delivered (kai hina rusthōmen).* A second and more personal petition (Milligan). First aorist passive subjunctive of *ruomai*, old verb to rescue. Note change in tense from present to aorist (effective aorist). *From unreasonable and evil men (apo tōn atopōn kai ponērōn anthrōpōn).* Ablative case with *apo*. Originally in the old Greek *atopos (a* privative and *topos)* is out of place, odd, unbecoming, perverse, outrageous, both of things and persons. *Ponēros* is from *poneō*, to work *(ponos)*, looking on labour as an annoyance, bad, evil. Paul had a plague of such men in Corinth as he had in Thessalonica. *For all have not faith (ou gar pantōn hē pistis).* Copula *estin* not expressed. *Pantōn* is predicate possessive genitive, faith (article with abstract substantive) does not belong to all. Hence their evil conduct.

3. *But the Lord is faithful (pistos de estin ho kurios).* But *faithful is the Lord* (correct rendition), with a play (paronomasia) on *pistis* by *pistos* as in Rom. 3:3 we have a word-play on *apisteō* and *apistia.* The Lord can be counted on, however perverse men may be. *From the evil one (apo tou*

56

ponērou). Apparently a reminiscence of the Lord's Prayer in Matt. 6:13 *rusai hēmas apo tou ponērou*. But here as there it is not certain whether *tou ponērou* is neuter (evil) like *to ponēron* in Rom. 12:9 or masculine (the evil one). But we have *ho ponēros* (the evil one) in I John 5:18 and *tou ponērou* is clearly masculine in Eph. 6:16.' If masculine here, as is probable, is it "the Evil One" (Ellicott) or merely the evil man like those mentioned in verse 2? Perhaps Paul has in mind the representative of Satan, the man of sin, pictured in 2:1–12, by the phrase here without trying to be too definite.

4. *And we have confidence* (*pepoithomen*). Second perfect indicative of *peithō*, to persuade, intransitive in this tense, we are in a state of trust. *In the Lord touching you* (*en kuriōi eph' humas*). Note the two prepositions, *en* in the sphere of the Lord (I Thess. 4:1) as the *ground* of Paul's confident trust, *eph'* (*epi*) with the accusative (towards you) where the dative could have been used (cf. II Cor. 2:3). *Ye both do and will do* ([*kai*] *poieite kai poiēsete*). Compliment and also appeal, present and future tenses of *poieō*. *The things which we command* (*ha paraggellomen*). Note of apostolic authority here, not advice or urging, but command.

5. *Direct* (*kateuthunai*). First aorist active optative of wish for the future as in 2:17 and I Thess. 5:23 from *kateuthunō*, old verb, as in I Thess. 3:11 (there *way*, here *hearts*) and Luke 1:79 of *feet* (*podas*). Perfective use of *kata*. Bold figure for making smooth and direct road. The Lord here is the Lord Jesus. *Into the love of God* (*eis tēn agapēn tou theou*). Either subjective or objective genitive makes sense and Lightfoot pleads for both, "not only as an objective attribute of deity, but as a ruling principle in our hearts," holding that it is "seldom possible to separate the one from the other." Most scholars take it here as subjective, the characteristic of God. *Into the patience of Christ* (*eis tēn hupomnēn tou Christou*). There is the same ambiguity here, though the subjective idea, the patience shown by Christ, is the one usually accepted rather than "the patient waiting for Christ" (objective genitive).

6. *Now we command you* (*paraggellomen de humin*). Paul puts into practice the confidence expressed on their obedience to his commands in verse 4. *In the name of the Lord*

Jesus Christ (en onomati tou kuriou Iēsou Christou). *Name*
(*onoma*) here for authority of Jesus Christ with which
compare *through the Lord Jesus (dia tou kuriou Iēsou)* in I
Thess. 4:2. For a full discussion of the phrase see the mono-
graph of W. Heitmüller, *Im Namen Jesu*. Paul wishes his
readers to realize the responsibility on them for their obedience to his command. *That ye withdraw yourselves (stel-
lesthai humas)*. Present middle (direct) infinitive of *stellō*,
old verb to place, arrange, make compact or shorten as
sails, to move oneself from or to withdraw oneself from
(with *apo* and the ablative). In II Cor. 8:20 the middle voice
(*stellomenoi*) means taking care. *From every brother that
walketh disorderly (apo pantos adelphou ataktōs peripatountos)*.
He calls him "brother" still. The adverb *ataktōs* is common
in Plato and is here and verse 11 alone in the N.T., though
the adjective *ataktos*, equally common in Plato we had in
1 Thess. 5:14 which see. Military term, out of ranks. *And
not after the tradition (kai mē kata tēn paradosin)*. See
on 2:15 for *paradosin*. *Which they received of us (hēn parela-
bosan par hēmōn)*. Westcott and Hort put this form of the
verb (second aorist indicative third person plural of *paralambanō*, the *-osan* form instead of *-on*, with slight support
from the papyri, but in the LXX and the Boeotian dialect,
Robertson, *Grammar*, pp. 335f.) in the margin with *parelabete* (ye received) in the text. There are five different read-
ings of the verb here, the others being *parelabon, parelabe,
elabosan*.

7. *How ye ought to imitate us (pōs dei mimeisthai hēmas)*.
Literally, how it is necessary to imitate us. The infinitive
mimeisthai is the old verb *mimeomai* from *mimos* (actor,
mimic), but in N.T. only here (and verse 9), Heb. 13:7;
III John 11. It is a daring thing to say, but Paul knew
that he had to set the new Christians in the midst of Jews
and Gentiles a model for their imitation (Phil. 3:17). *For
we behaved not ourselves disorderly among you (hoti ouk ētak-
tēsamen en humin)*. First aorist active indicative of old verb
atakteō, to be out of ranks of soldiers. Specific denial on
Paul's part in contrast to verse 6 and verse 17.

8. *For nought (dōrean)*. Adverbial accusative, as a gift,
gift-wise (*dōrea*, gift, from *didōmi*). Same claim made to the
Corinthians (II Cor. 11:7), old word, in LXX, and papyri.

He lodged with Jason, but did not receive his meals *gratis*, for he paid for them. Apparently he received no invitations to meals. Paul had to make his financial independence clear to avoid false charges which were made in spite of all his efforts. To eat bread is merely a Hebraism for eat (verse 10). See I Thess. 2:9 for labour and· travail, and night and day (*nuktos kai hēmeras*, genitive of time, by night and by day). See I Thess. 2:9 for rest of the verse in precisely the same words.

9. *Not because we have not the right* (*ouch hoti ouk echomen exousian*). Paul is sensitive on his *right* to receive adequate support (I Thess. 2:6 and I Cor. 9:4 where he uses the same word *exousian* in the long defence of this *right*, I Cor. 9:1–27). So he here puts in this limitation to avoid misapprehension. He did allow churches to help him where he would not be misunderstood (II Cor. 11:7–11; Phil. 4:45f.). Paul uses *ouch hoti* elsewhere to avoid misunderstanding (II Cor. 1:24; 3:5; Phil. 4:17). *But to make ourselves an ensample unto you* (*all' hina heautous tupon dōmen humin*). Literally, *but that we might give ourselves a type to you*. Purpose with *hina* and second aorist active subjunctive of *didōmi*. On *tupon* see on I Thess. 1:7.

10. *This* (*touto*). What he proceeds to give. *If any will not work, neither let him eat* (*hoti ei tis ou thelei ergazesthai mēde esthietō*). Recitative *hoti* here not to be translated, like our modern quotation marks. Apparently a Jewish proverb based on Gen. 3:19. Wetstein quotes several parallels. Moffatt gives this from Carlyle's *Chartism:* "He that will not work according to his faculty, let him perish according to his necessity." Deissmann (*Light from the Ancient East*, p. 314) sees Paul borrowing a piece of workshop morality. It was needed, as is plain. This is a condition of the first class (note negative *ou*) with the negative imperative in the conclusion.

11. *For we hear* (*akouomen gar*). Fresh news from Thessalonica evidently. For the present tense compare I Cor. 11:18. The accusative and the participle is a regular idiom for indirect discourse with this verb (Robertson, *Grammar*, pp. 1040–2). Three picturesque present participles, the first a general description, *peripatountas ataktōs*, the other two specifying with a vivid word-play, *that work not at all,*

but are busy-bodies (mēden ergazomenous alla periergazomen-ous). Literally, *doing nothing but doing around.* Ellicott suggests, *doing no business but being busy bodies.* "The first persecution at Thessalonica had been fostered by a number of fanatical loungers (Acts 17:5)" (Moffatt). These theological dead-beats were too pious to work, but perfectly willing to eat at the hands of their neighbours while they piddled and frittered away the time in idleness.

12. *We command and exhort (paraggellomen kai parakaloumen).* Paul asserts his authority as an apostle and pleads as a man and minister. *That with quietness they work, and eat their own bread (hina meta hēsuchias ergazomenoi ton heautōn arton esthiōsin).* Substance of the command and exhortation by *hina* and the present subjunctive *esthiōsin.* Literally, *that working with quietness they keep on eating their own bread.* The precise opposite of their conduct in verse 11.

13. *But ye, brethren, be not weary in well-doing (humeis de, adelphoi, mē enkakēsēte kalopoiountes).* Emphatic position of *humeis* in contrast to these piddlers. *Mē* and the aorist subjunctive is a prohibition against beginning an act (Robertson, *Grammar,* pp. 851-4). It is a late verb and means to behave badly in, to be cowardly, to lose courage, to flag, to faint, *(en, kakos)* and outside of Luke 18:1 in the N.T. is only in Paul's Epistles (II Thess. 3:13; II Cor. 4:1, 16; Gal. 6:9; Eph. 3:13). It occurs in Polybius. The late verb *kalopoieō,* to do the fair *(kalos)* or honourable thing occurs nowhere else in the N.T., but is in the LXX and a late papyrus. Paul uses *to kalon poiein* in II Cor. 13:7; Gal. 6:9; Rom. 7:21 with the same idea. He has *agathopoieō,* to do good, in I Tim. 6:18.

14. *And if any one obeyeth not our word by this epistle (ei de tis ouch hupakouei tōi logōi hēmōn dia tēs epistolēs).* Paul sums up the issue bluntly with this ultimatum. Condition of the first class, with negative *ou,* assuming it to be true. *Note that man (touton sēmeiousthe).* Late verb *sēmeioō,* from *sēmeion,* sign, mark, token. Put a tag on that man. Here only in N.T. "The verb is regularly used for the signature to a receipt or formal notice in the papyri and the ostraca of the Imperial period" (Moulton & Milligan's *Vocabulary*). How this is to be done (by letter or in public meeting) Paul does not say. *That ye have no company with him (mē sun-*

anamignusthai autōi). The MSS. are divided between the present middle infinitive as above in a command like Rom. 12:15; Phil. 3:16 or the present middle imperative *sunanamignusthe* (-*ai* and -*e* often being pronounced alike in the *Koinē*). The infinitive can also be explained as an indirect command. This double compound verb is late, in LXX and Plutarch, in N.T. only here and I Cor. 5:9, 11. *Autōi* is in associative instrumental case. *To the end that he may be ashamed* (*hina entrapēi*). Purpose clause with *hina*. Second aorist passive subjunctive of *entrepō*, to turn on, middle to turn on oneself or to put to shame, passive to be made ashamed. The idea is to have one's thoughts turned in on oneself.

15. *Not as an enemy* (*mē hōs echthron*). This is always the problem in such ostracism as discipline, however necessary it is at times. Few things in our churches are more difficult of wise execution than the discipline of erring members. The word *echthros* is an adjective, hateful, from *echthos*, hate. It can be passive, *hated*, as in Rom. 11:28, but is usually active *hostile*, enemy, foe.

16. *The Lord of peace himself* (*autos ho kurios tēs eirēnēs*). See I Thess. 5:23 for *the God of peace himself*. *Give you peace* (*doiē humin tēn eirēnēn*). Second aorist active optative (*Koinē*) of *didōmi*, not *dōei* (subjunctive). So also Rom. 15:5; II Tim. 1:16, 18. The Lord Jesus whose characteristic is peace, can alone give real peace to the heart and to the world. (John 14:27).

17. *Of me Paul with mine own hand* (*tēi emēi cheiri Paulou*). Instrumental case *cheiri*. Note genitive *Paulou* in apposition with possessive idea in the possessive pronoun *emēi*. Paul had dictated the letter, but now wrote the salutation in his hand. *The token in every epistle* (*sēmeion en pasēi epistolēi*). Mark (verse 14) and proof of the genuineness of each epistle, Paul's signature. Already there were spurious forgeries (II Thess. 2:2). Thus each church was enabled to know that Paul wrote the letter. If only the autograph copy could be found!

18. Salutation just like that in I Thess. 5:28 with the addition of *pantōn* (all).

THE SECOND GROUP

First Corinthians
Second Corinthians
Galatians
Romans
A.D. 54 TO 57

FIRST CORINTHIANS
From Ephesus a.d. 54 or 55

BY WAY OF INTRODUCTION

It would be a hard-boiled critic today who would dare deny the genuineness of I Corinthians. The Dutch wild man, Van Manen, did indeed argue that Paul wrote no epistles if indeed he ever lived. Such intellectual banality is well answered by Whateley's *Historic Doubts about Napolean Bonaparte* which was so cleverly done that some readers were actually convinced that no such man ever existed, but is the product of myth and legend. Even Baur was compelled to acknowledge the genuineness of I and II Corinthians, Galatians and Romans (the Big Four of Pauline criticism). It is a waste of time now to prove what all admit to be true. Paul of Tarsus, the Apostle to the Gentiles, wrote I Corinthians.

We know where Paul was when he wrote the letter for he tells us in I Cor. 16:8: "But I will tarry at Ephesus until Pentecost." That was, indeed, his plan, but the uproar in Ephesus at the hands of Demetrius caused his departure sooner than he expected (Acts 18:21–20:1; II Cor. 2:12f.). But he is in Ephesus when he writes.

We know also the time of the year when he writes, in the spring before pentecost. Unfortunately we do not know the precise year, though it was at the close of his stay of three years (in round numbers) at Ephesus (Acts 20:31). Like all the years in Paul's ministry we have to allow a sliding scale in relation to his other engagements. One may guess the early spring of a.d. 54 or 55.

The occasion of the Epistle is made plain by numerous allusions personal and otherwise. Paul had arrived in Ephesus from Antioch shortly after the departure of Apollos for Corinth with letters of commendation from Priscilla and Aquila (Acts 18:28–19:1). It is not clear how long Apollos remained in Corinth, but he is back in Ephesus when Paul writes the letter and he has declined Paul's request to go back to Corinth (I Cor. 16:12). Some of the household of

Chloe had heard or come from Corinth with full details of the factions in the church over Apollos and Paul, clearly the reason why Apollos left (I Cor. 1:10–12). Even Cephas nominally was drawn into it, though there is no evidence that Peter himself had come to Corinth. Paul had sent Timothy over to Corinth to put an end to the factions (4:17), though he was uneasy over the outcome (16:10f.). This disturbance was enough of itself to call forth a letter from Paul. But it was by no means the whole story. Paul had already written a letter, now lost to us, concerning a peculiarly disgusting case of incest in the membership (5:9). They were having lawsuits with one another before heathen judges. Members of the church had written Paul a letter about marriage whether any or all should marry (7:1). They were troubled also whether it was right to eat meat that had been offered to idols in the heathen temples (8:1). Spiritual gifts of an unusual nature were manifested in Corinth and these were the occasion of a deal of trouble (12:1). The doctrine of the resurrection gave much trouble in Corinth (15:12). Paul was interested in the collection for the poor saints in Jerusalem (16:1) and in their share in it. The church in Corinth had sent a committee (Stephanas, Fortunatus, Achaicus) to Paul in Ephesus. He hopes to come himself after passing through Macedonia (16:5f.). It is possible that he had made a short visit before this letter (II Cor. 13:1), though not certain as he may have intended to go one time without going as he certainly once changed his plans on the subject (II Cor. 1:15–22). Whether Titus took the letter on his visit or it was sent on after the return of Timothy is not perfectly clear. Probably Timothy returned to Ephesus from Corinth shortly after the epistle was sent on, possibly by the committee who returned to Corinth (I Cor. 16:17), for Timothy and Erastus were sent on from Ephesus to Macedonia before the outbreak at the hands of Demetrius (Acts 19:22). Apparently Timothy had not fully succeeded in reconciling the factions in Corinth for Paul dispatched Titus who was to meet him at Troas as he went on to Macedonia. Paul's hurried departure from Ephesus (Acts 20:1) took him to Troas before Titus arrived and Paul's impatience there brought him to Macedonia where he did meet Titus on his return from Corinth (II Cor. 2:12f.).

It is clear therefore that Paul wrote what we call I Corinthians in a disturbed state of mind. He had founded the church there, had spent two years there (Acts 18), and took pardonable pride in his work there as a wise architect (I Cor. 3:10) for he had built the church on Christ as the foundation. He was anxious that his work should abide. It is plain that the disturbances in the church in Corinth were fomented from without by the Judaizers whom Paul had defeated at the Jerusalem Conference (Acts 15:1–35; Gal. 2:1–10). They were overwhelmed there, but renewed their attacks in Antioch (Gal. 2:11–21). Henceforth throughout the second mission tour they are a disturbing element in Galatia, in Corinth, in Jerusalem. While Paul is winning the Gentiles in the Roman Empire to Christ, these Judaizers are trying to win Paul's converts to Judaism. Nowhere do we see the conflict at so white a heat as in Corinth. Paul finally will expose them with withering sarcasm (II Cor. 10–13) as Jesus did the Pharisees in Matthew 23 on that last day in the temple. Factional strife, immorality, perverted ideas about marriage, spiritual gifts, and the resurrection, these complicated problems are a vivid picture of church life in our cities today. The discussion of them shows Paul's manysidedness and also the powerful grasp that he has upon the realities of the gospel. Questions of casuistry are faced fairly and serious ethical issues are met squarely. But along with the treatment of these vexed matters Paul sings the noblest song of the ages on love (chapter 13) and writes the classic discussion on the resurrection (chapter 15). If one knows clearly and fully the Corinthian Epistles and Paul's dealings with Corinth, he has an understanding of a large section of his life and ministry. No church caused him more anxiety than did Corinth (II Cor. 11:28).

Some good commentaries on I Corinthians are the following: On the Greek Bachmann in the *Zahn Kommentar*, Edwards, Ellicott, Findlay (Expositor's Greek Testament), Godet, Goudge, Lietzmann (*Handbuch zum N.T.*), Lightfoot (chs. 1–7), Parry, Robertson and Plummer (*Int. Crit.*), Stanley, J. Weiss (*Meyer Kommentar*); on the English Dods (*Exp. Bible*), McFadyen, Parry, Ramsay, Rendall, F. W. Robertson, Walker (*Reader's Comm.*).

CHAPTER I

1. *Called to be an apostle* (*klētos apostolos*). Verbal adjective *klētos* from *kaleō*, without *einai*, to be. Literally, *a called apostle* (Rom. 1:1), not so-called, but one whose apostleship is due not to himself or to men (Gal. 1:1), but to God, *through the will of God* (*dia thelēmatos tou theou*). The intermediate (*dia, duo,* two) agent between Paul's not being Christ's apostle and becoming one was God's will (*thelēma,* something willed of God), God's command (I Tim. 1:1). Paul knows that he is not one of the twelve apostles, but he is on a par with them because, like them, he is chosen by God. He is an apostle of Jesus Christ or Christ Jesus (MSS. vary here, later epistles usually Christ Jesus). The refusal of the Judaizers to recognize Paul as equal to the twelve made him the more careful to claim his position. Bengel sees here Paul's denial of mere human authority in his position and also of personal merit: *Namque mentione Dei excluditur auctoramentum humanum, mentione Voluntatis Dei, meritum Pauli.* *Our brother* (*ho adelphos*). Literally, the brother, but regular Greek idiom for our brother. This Sosthenes, now with Paul in Ephesus, is probably the same Sosthenes who received the beating meant for Paul in Corinth (Acts 18:17). If so, the beating did him good for he is now a follower of Christ. He is in no sense a co-author of the Epistle, but merely associated with Paul because they knew him in Corinth. He may have been compelled by the Jews to leave Corinth when he, a ruler of the synagogue, became a Christian. See I Thess. 1:1 for the mention of Silas and Timothy in the salutation. Sosthenes could have been Paul's amanuensis for this letter, but there is no proof of it.

2. *The church of God* (*tēi ekklēsiāi tou theou*). Belonging to God, not to any individual or faction, as this genitive case shows. In I Thess. 1:1 Paul wrote "the church of the Thessalonians in God" (*en theōi*), but "the churches of God" in 2:14. See same idiom in I Cor. 10:32; 11:16, 22; 15:9; II Cor. 1:1; Gal. 1:13, etc. *Which is in Corinth* (*tēi*

ousēi en Korinthōi). See on Acts 13:1 for idiom. It is God's church even in Corinth, "*laetum et ingens paradoxon*" (Bengel). This city, destroyed by Mummius B.C. 146, had been restored by Julius Caesar a hundred years later, B.C. 44, and now after another hundred years has become very rich and very corrupt. The very word "to Corinthianize" meant to practise vile immoralities in the worship of Aphrodite (Venus). It was located on the narrow Isthmus of the Peloponnesus with two harbours (Lechaeum and Cenchreae). It had schools of rhetoric and philosophy and made a flashy imitation of the real culture of Athens. See Acts 18 for the story of Paul's work here and now the later developments and divisions in this church will give Paul grave concern as is shown in detail in I and II Corinthians. All the problems of a modern city church come to the front in Corinth. They call for all the wisdom and statesmanship in Paul. *That are sanctified* (*hēgiasmenois*). Perfect passive participle of *hagiazō*, late form for *hagizō*, so far found only in the Greek Bible and in ecclesiastical writers. It means to make or to declare *hagion* (from *hagos*, awe, reverence, and this from *hazō*, to venerate). It is significant that Paul uses this word concerning the *called saints* or *called to be saints* (*klētois hagiois*) in Corinth. Cf. *klētos apostolos* in 1:1. It is because they are sanctified *in Christ Jesus* (*en Christōi Iēsou*). He is the sphere in which this act of consecration takes place. Note plural, construction according to sense, because *ekklēsia* is a collective substantive. *With all that call upon* (*sun pāsin tois epikaloumenois*). Associative instrumental case with *sun* rather than *kai* (*and*), making a close connection with "saints" just before and so giving the Corinthian Christians a picture of their close unity with the brotherhood everywhere through the common bond of faith. This phrase occurs in the LXX (Gen. 12:8; Zech. 13:9) and is applied to Christ as to Jehovah (II Thess. 1:7, 9, 12; Phil. 2:9, 10). Paul heard Stephen pray to Christ as Lord (Acts 7:59). Here "with a plain and direct reference to the Divinity of our Lord" (Ellicott). *Their Lord and ours* (*autōn kai hēmōn*). This is the interpretation of the Greek commentators and is the correct one, an afterthought and expansion (*epanorthōsis*) of the previous "our," showing the universality of Christ.

3. Identical language of II Thess. 1:2 save absence of *hēmōn* (our), Paul's usual greeting. See on I Thess. 1:1.

4. *I thank my God* (*eucharistō tōi theōi*). Singular as in Rom. 1:8; Phil. 1:3; Philemon 4, but plural in I Thess. 1:2; Col. 1:3. The grounds of Paul's thanksgivings in his Epistles are worthy of study. Even in the church in Corinth he finds something to thank God for, though in II Cor. there is no expression of thanksgiving because of the acute crisis in Corinth nor is there any in Galatians. But Paul is gracious here and allows his general attitude (always, *pantote*) concerning (*peri*, around) the Corinthians to override the specific causes of irritation. *For the grace of God which was given to you in Christ Jesus* (*epi tēi chariti tou theou tēi dotheisēi humin en Christōi Iēsou*). Upon the basis of (*epi*) God's grace, not in general, but specifically given (*dotheisēi*, first aorist passive participle of *didōmi*), in the sphere of (*en* as in verse 2) Christ Jesus.

5. *That* (*hoti*). Explicit specification of this grace of God given to the Corinthians. Paul points out in detail the unusual spiritual gifts which were their glory and became their peril (chapters 12 to 14). *Ye were enriched in him* (*eploutisthēte en autōi*). First aorist passive indicative of *ploutizō*, old causative verb from *ploutos*, wealth, common in Attic writers, dropped out for centuries, reappeared in LXX. In N.T. only three times and alone in Paul (I Cor. 1:5; II Cor. 6:10, 11). The Christian finds his real riches in Christ, one of Paul's pregnant phrases full of the truest mysticism. *In all utterance and all knowledge* (*en panti logōi kai pasēi gnōsei*). One detail in explanation of the riches in Christ. The outward expression (*logōi*) here is put before the inward knowledge (*gnōsei*) which should precede all speech. But we get at one's knowledge by means of his speech. Chapters 12 to 14 throw much light on this element in the spiritual gifts of the Corinthians (the gift of tongues, interpreting tongues, discernment) as summed up in I Cor. 13:1 and 2, the greater gifts of 12:31. It was a marvellously endowed church in spite of their perversions.

6. *Even as* (*kathōs*). In proportion as (I Thess. 1:5) and so inasmuch as (Phil. 1:7; Eph. 1:4). *The testimony of Christ* (*to marturion tou Christou*). Objective genitive, the testimony to or concerning Christ, the witness of Paul's preach-

ing. *Was confirmed in you* (*ebebaiōthē en humin*). First aorist passive of *bebaioō*, old verb from *bebaios* and that from *bainō*, to make to stand, to make stable. These special gifts of the Holy Spirit which they had so lavishly received (ch. 12) were for that very purpose.

7. *So that ye come behind in no gift* (*hōste humas mē hustereisthai en mēdeni charismati*). Consecutive clause with *hōste* and the infinitive and the double negative. Come behind (*hustereisthai*) is to be late (*husteros*), old verb seen already in Mark 10:21; Matt. 19:20. It is a wonderful record here recorded. But in II Cor. 8:7-11 and 9:1-7 Paul will have to complain that they have not paid their pledges for the collection, pledges made over a year before, a very modern complaint. *Waiting for the revelation* (*apekdechomenous tēn apokalupsin*). This double compound is late and rare outside of Paul (I Cor. 1:7; Gal. 5:5; Rom. 8:19, 23, 25; Phil. 3:20), I Peter 3:20; Heb. 9:28. It is an eager expectancy of the second coming of Christ here termed revelation like the eagerness in *prosdechomenoi* in Titus 2:13 for the same event. "As if that attitude of expectation were the highest posture that can be attained here by the Christian" (F. W. Robertson).

8. *Shall confirm* (*bebaiōsei*). Direct reference to the same word in verse 6. The relative *hos* (who) points to Christ. *Unto the end* (*heōs telous*). End of the age till Jesus comes, final preservation of the saints. *That ye be unreproveable* (*anegklētous*). Alpha privative and *egkaleō*, to accuse, old verbal, only in Paul in N.T. Proleptic adjective in the predicate accusative agreeing with *humas* (you) without *hōste* and the infinitive as in I Thess. 3:13; 5:23; Phil. 3:21. "Unimpeachable, for none will have the right to impeach" (Robertson and Plummer) as Paul shows in Rom. 8:33; Col. 1:22, 28.

9. *God is faithful* (*pistos ho theos*). This is the ground of Paul's confidence as he loves to say (I Thess. 5:24; I Cor. 10:13; Rom. 8:36; Phil. 1:16). God will do what he has promised. *Through whom* (*di' hou*). God is the agent (*di'*) of their call as in Rom. 11:36 and also the ground or reason for their call (*di' hon*) in Heb. 2:10. *Into the fellowship* (*eis koinōnian*). Old word from *koinōnos*, partner for partnership, participation as here and II Cor. 13:13f.; Phil. 2:1; 3:10.

Then it means fellowship or intimacy as in Acts 2:42; Gal. 2:9; II Cor. 6:14; I John 1:3, 7. And particularly as shown by contribution as in II Cor. 8:4; 9:13; Phil. 1:5. It is high fellowship with Christ both here and hereafter.

10. *Now I beseech you* (*parakalō de humas*). Old and common verb, over 100 times in N.T., to call to one's side. Corresponds here to *eucharistō, I thank*, in verse 4. Direct appeal after the thanksgiving. *Through the name* (*dia tou onomatos*). Genitive, not accusative (cause or reason), as the medium or instrument of the appeal (II Cor. 10:1; Rom. 12:1; 15:30). *That* (*hina*). Purport (sub-final) rather than direct purpose, common idiom in *Koiné* (Robertson, *Grammar*, pp. 991–4) like Matt. 14:36. Used here with *legēte, ēi, ēte katērtismenoi*, though expressed only once. *All speak* (*legēte pantes*). Present active subjunctive, that ye all keep on speaking.· With the divisions in mind. An idiom from Greek political life (Lightfoot). This touch of the classical writers argues for Paul's acquaintance with Greek culture. *There be no divisions among you* (*mē ēi en humin schismata*). Present subjunctive, that divisions may not continue to be (they already had them). Negative statement of preceding idea. *Schisma* is from *schizō*, old word to split or rend, and so means a rent (Matt. 9:16; Mark 2:21). Papyri use it for a splinter of wood and for ploughing. Here we have the earliest instance of its use in a moral sense of division, dissension, see also I Cor. 11:18 where a less complete change than *haireseis;* 12:25; John 7:43 (discord); 9:16; 10:19. "Here, faction, for which the classical word is *stasis:* division within the Christian community" (Vincent). These divisions were over the preachers (1:12–4:21), immorality (5:1–13), going to law before the heathen (6:1–11), marriage (7:1–40), meats offered to idols (8 to 10), conduct of women in church (11:1–16), the Lord's Supper (11:17–34), spiritual gifts (12–14), the resurrection (ch. 15). *But that ye be perfected together* (*ēte de katērtismenoi*). Periphrastic perfect passive subjunctive. See this verb in Matt. 4:21 (=Mark 1:19) for mending torn nets and in moral sense already in I Thess. 3:10. Galen uses it for a surgeon's mending a joint and Herodotus for composing factions. See II Cor. 13:11; Gal. 6:1. *Mind* (*noi*), *judgment* (*gnōmēi*). "Of these words *nous* denotes the frame or state of mind, *gnōmē* the

judgment, opinion or sentiment, which is the outcome of *nous*" (Lightfoot).

11. *For it hath been signified unto me* (*edēlōthē gar moi*). First aorist passive indicative of *dēloō* and difficult to render into English. Literally, It was signified to me. *By them of Chloe* (*hupo tōn Chloēs*). Ablative case of the masculine plural article *tōn*, by the (folks) of Chloe (genitive case). The words "which are of the household" are not in the Greek, though they correctly interpret the Greek, "those of Chloe." Whether the children, the kinspeople, or the servants of Chloe we do not know. It is uncertain also whether Chloe lived in Corinth or Ephesus, probably Ephesus because to name her if in Corinth might get her into trouble (Heinrici). Already Christianity was working a social revolution in the position of women and slaves. The name *Chloe* means tender verdure and was one of the epithets of Demeter the goddess of agriculture and for that reason Lightfoot thinks that she was a member of the freedman class like Phoebe (Rom. 16:1), Hermes (Rom. 16:14), Nereus (Rom. 16:15). It is even possible that Stephanas, Fortunatus, Achaicus (I Cor. 16:17) may have been those who brought Chloe the news of the schisms in Corinth. *Contentions* (*erides*). Unseemly wranglings (as opposed to discussing, *dialegomai*) that were leading to the *schisms*. Listed in works of the flesh (Gal. 5:19f.) and the catalogues of vices (II Cor. 12:20; Rom. 1:19f.; I Tim. 6:4).

12. *Now this I mean* (*legō de touto*). Explanatory use of *legō*. Each has his party leader. *Apollō* is genitive of *Apollōs* (Acts 18:24), probably abbreviation of *Apollōnius* as seen in Codex Bezae for Acts 18:24. See on Acts for discussion of this "eloquent Alexandrian" (Ellicott), whose philosophical and oratorical preaching was in contrast "with the studied plainness" of Paul (I Cor. 2:1; II Cor. 10:10). People naturally have different tastes about styles of preaching and that is well, but Apollos refused to be a party to this strife and soon returned to Ephesus and refused to go back to Corinth (I Cor. 16:12). *Cēphā* is the genitive of *Cēphās*, the Aramaic name given Simon by Jesus (John 1:42), *Petros* in Greek. Except in Gal 2:7, 8 Paul calls him Cephas. He had already taken his stand with Paul in the Jerusalem Conference (Acts 15:7-11; Gal. 2:7-10). Paul had to rebuke

him at Antioch for his timidity because of the Judaizers (Gal. 2:11-14), but, in spite of Baur's theory, there is no evidence of a schism in doctrine between Paul and Peter. If II Peter 3:15f. be accepted as genuine, as I do, there is proof of cordial relations between them and I Cor. 9:5 points in the same direction. But there is no evidence that Peter himself visited Corinth. Judaizers came and pitted Peter against Paul to the Corinthian Church on the basis of Paul's rebuke of Peter in Antioch. These Judaizers made bitter personal attacks on Paul in return for their defeat at the Jerusalem Conference. So a third faction was formed by the use of Peter's name as the really orthodox wing of the church, the gospel of the circumcision. *And I of Christ* (*egō de Christou*). Still a fourth faction in recoil from the partisan use of Paul, Apollos, Cephas, with "a spiritually proud utterance" (Ellicott) that assumes a relation to Christ not true of the others. "Those who used this cry arrogated the common watchword as their *peculium*" (Findlay). This partisan use of the name of Christ may have been made in the name of unity against the other three factions, but it merely added another party to those existing. In scouting the names of the other leaders they lowered the name and rank of Christ to their level.

13. *Is Christ divided?* (*memeristai ho Christos;*). Perfect passive indicative, Does Christ stand divided? It is not certain, though probable, that this is interrogative like the following clauses. Hofmann calls the assertory form a "rhetorical impossibility." The absence of *mē* here merely allows an affirmative answer which is true. The fourth or Christ party claimed to possess Christ in a sense not true of the others. Perhaps the leaders of this Christ party with their arrogant assumptions of superiority are the false apostles, ministers of Satan posing as angels of light (II Cor. 11:12-15). *Was Paul crucified for you?* (*Mē Paulos estaurōthē huper humōn;*). An indignant "No" is demanded by *mē*. Paul shows his tact by employing himself as the illustration, rather than Apollos or Cephas. Probably *huper*, over, in behalf of, rather than *peri* (concerning, around) is genuine, though either makes good sense here. In the *Koinē huper* encroaches on *peri* as in II Thess. 2:1. *Were ye baptized into the name of Paul?* (*eis to onoma Paulou ebaptis-*

thēte;). It is unnecessary to say *into* for *eis* rather than *in* since *eis* is the same preposition originally as *en* and both are used with *baptizō* as in Acts 8:16 and 10:48 with no difference in idea (Robertson, *Grammar*, p. 592). Paul evidently knows the idea in Matt. 28:19 and scouts the notion of being put on a par with Christ or the Trinity. He is no rival of Christ. This use of *onoma* for the person is not only in the LXX, but the papyri, ostraca, and inscriptions give numerous examples of the name of the king or the god for the power and authority of the king or god (Deissmann, *Bible Studies*, pp. 146ff., 196ff.; *Light from the Ancient East*, p. 121).

14. *I thank God (eucharistō tōi theōi).* See verse 4, though uncertain if *tōi theōi* is genuine here. *Save Crispus and Gaius (ei mē Krispon kai Gaion).* Crispus was the ruler of the synagogue in Corinth before his conversion (Acts 18:8), a Roman cognomen, and Gaius a Roman praenomen, probably the host of Paul and of the whole church in Corinth (Rom. 16:23), possibly though not clearly the hospitable Gaius of III John 5, 6. The prominence and importance of these two may explain why Paul baptized them.

15. *Lest any man should say (hina mē tis eipēi).* Certainly sub-final *hina* again or contemplated result as in 7:29; John 9:2. Ellicott thinks that already some in Corinth were laying emphasis on the person of the baptizer whether Peter or some one else. It is to be recalled that Jesus himself baptized no one (John 4:2) to avoid this very kind of controversy. And yet there are those today who claim Paul as a sacramentalist, an impossible claim in the light of his words here.

16. *Also the household of Stephanas (kai ton Stephanā oikon).* Mentioned as an afterthought. Robertson and Plummer suggest that Paul's amanuensis reminded him of this case. Paul calls him a first-fruit of Achaia (I Cor. 16:15) and so earlier than Crispus and he was one of the three who came to Paul from Corinth (16:17), clearly a family that justified Paul's personal attention about baptism. *Besides (loipon).* Accusative of general reference, "as for anything else." Added to make clear that he is not meaning to omit any one who deserves mention. See also I Thess. 4:1; I Cor. 4:2; II Cor. 13:11; and II Tim. 4:8. Ellicott insists on

a sharp distinction from *to loipon* "as for the rest" (II Thess. 3:1; Phil. 3:1; 4:8; Eph. 6:10). Paul casts no reflection on baptism, for he could not with his conception of it as the picture òf the new life in Christ (Rom. 6:2–6), but he clearly denies here that he considers baptism essential to the remission of sin or the means of obtaining forgiveness.

17. *For Christ sent me not to baptize* (*ou gar apesteilen me Christos baptizein*). The negative *ou* goes not with the infinitive, but with *apesteilen* (from *apostellō, apostolos,* apostle). *For Christ did not send me to be a baptizer* (present active infinitive, linear action) like John the Baptist. *But to preach the gospel* (*alla euaggelizesthai*). This is Paul's idea of his mission from Christ, as Christ's apostle, to be *a gospelizer.* This led, of course, to baptism, as a result, but Paul usually had it done by others as Peter at Caesarea ordered the baptism to be done, apparently by the six brethren with him (Acts 10:48). Paul is fond of this late Greek verb from *euaggelion* and sometimes uses both verb and substantive as in I Cor. 15:1 "the gospel which I gospelized unto you." *Not in wisdom of words* (*ouk en sophiāi logou*). Note *ou*, not *mē* (the subjective negative), construed with *apesteilen* rather than the infinitive. Not in wisdom of speech (singular). Preaching was Paul's forte, but it was not as a pretentious philosopher or professional rhetorician that Paul appeared before the Corinthians (I Cor. 2:1–5). Some who followed Apollos may have been guilty of a fancy for external show, though Apollos was not a mere performer and juggler with words. But the Alexandrian method as in Philo did run to dialectic subtleties and luxuriant rhetoric (Lightfoot). *Lest the cross of Christ should be made void* (*hina mē kenōthēi ho stauros tou Christou*). Negative purpose (*hina mē*) with first aorist passive subjunctive, effective aorist, of *kenoō*, old verb from *kenos*, to make empty. In Paul's preaching the Cross of Christ is the central theme. Hence Paul did not fall into the snare of too much emphasis on baptism nor into too little on the death of Christ. "This expression shows clearly the stress which St. Paul laid on the death of Christ, not merely as a great moral spectacle, and so the crowning point of a life of self-renunciation, but as in itself the ordained instrument of salvation" (Lightfoot).

18. *For the word of the cross* (*ho logos gar ho tou staurou*).

Literally, "for the preaching (with which I am concerned as the opposite of *wisdom of word* in verse 17) that (repeated article *ho*, almost demonstrative) of the cross." "Through this incidental allusion to preaching St. Paul passes to a new subject. The discussions in the Corinthian Church are for a time forgotten, and he takes the opportunity of correcting his converts for their undue exaltation of human eloquence and wisdom" (Lightfoot). *To them that are perishing (tois men apollumenois).* Dative of disadvantage (personal interest). Present middle participle is here timeless, those in the path to destruction (not annihilation. See II Thess. 2:10). Cf. II Cor. 4:3. *Foolishness (mōria).* Folly. Old word from *mōros*, foolish. In N.T. only in I Cor. 1:18, 21, 23; 2:14; 3:19. *But unto us which are being saved (tois sōzomenois hēmin).* Sharp contrast to those that are perishing and same construction with the articular participle. No reason for the change of pronouns in English. This present passive participle is again timeless. Salvation is described by Paul as a thing done in the past, "we were saved" (Rom. 8:24), as a present state, "ye have been saved" (Eph. 2:5), as a process, "ye are being saved" (I Cor. 15:2), as a future result, "thou shalt be saved" (Rom. 10:9). *The power of God (dunamis theou).* So in Rom. 1:16. No other message has this dynamite of God (I Cor. 4:20). God's power is shown in the preaching of the Cross of Christ through all the ages, now as always. No other preaching wins men and women from sin to holiness or can save them. The judgment of Paul here is the verdict of every soul winner through all time.

19. *I will destroy (apolō).* Future active indicative of *apollumi.* Attic future for *apolesō.* Quotation from Isa. 29:14 (LXX). The failure of worldly statesmanship in the presence of Assyrian invasion Paul applies to his argument with force. The wisdom of the wise is often folly, the understanding of the understanding is often rejected. There is such a thing as the ignorance of the learned, the wisdom of the simple-minded. God's wisdom rises in the Cross sheer above human philosophizing which is still scoffing at the Cross of Christ, the consummation of God's power.

20. *Where is the wise? Where is the scribe? Where is the disputer of this world? (Pou sophos; pou grammateus; pou sunzētētēs tou aiōnos toutou;).* Paul makes use of Isa. 33:18

without exact quotation. The sudden retreat of Sennacherib with the annihilation of his officers. "On the tablet of Shalmaneser in the Assyrian Gallery of the British Museum there is a surprisingly exact picture of the scene described by Isaiah" (Robertson and Plummer). Note the absence of the Greek article in each of these rhetorical questions though the idea is clearly definite. Probably *sophos* refers to the Greek philosopher, *grammateus* to the Jewish scribe and *sunzētētēs* suits both the Greek and the Jewish disputant and doubter (Acts 6:9; 9:29; 17:18; 28:29). There is a note of triumph in these questions. The word *sunzētētēs* occurs here alone in the N.T. and elsewhere only in Ignatius, *Eph.* 18 quoting this passage, but the papyri give the verb *sunzēteō* for disputing (questioning together). *Hath not God made foolish?* (*ouchi emōranen ho theos;*). Strong negative form with aorist active indicative difficult of precise translation, "Did not God make foolish?" The old verb *mōrainō* from *mōros*, foolish, was to be foolish, to act foolish, then to prove one foolish as here or to make foolish as in Rom. 1:22. In Matt. 5:13 and Luke 14:34 it is used of salt that is tasteless. *World* (*kosmou*). Synonymous with *aiōn* (age), orderly arrangement, then the non-Christian cosmos.

21. *Seeing that* (*epeidē*). Since (*epei* and *dē*) with explanatory *gar. Through its wisdom* (*dia tēs sophias*). Article here as possessive. The two wisdoms contrasted. *Knew not God* (*ouk egnō*). Failed to know, second aorist (effective) active indicative of *ginōskō*, solemn dirge of doom on both Greek philosophy and Jewish theology that failed to know God. Has modern philosophy done better? There is today even a godless theology (Humanism). "Now that God's wisdom has reduced the self-wise world to ignorance" (Findlay). *Through the foolishness of the preaching (dia tēs mōrias tou kērugmatos).* Perhaps "proclamation" is the idea, for it is not *kēruxis*, the act of heralding, but *kērugma*, the message heralded or the proclamation as in verse 23. The metaphor is that of the herald proclaiming the approach of the king (Matt. 3:1; 4:17). See also *kērugma* in I Cor. 2:4; II Tim. 4:17. The proclamation of the Cross seemed foolishness to the wiseacres then (and now), but it is consummate wisdom, God's wisdom and good-pleasure (*eudokēsan*). The foolishness of preaching is not the preaching of foolishness.

To save them that believe (*sōsai tous pisteuontas*). This is the heart of God's plan of redemption, the proclamation of salvation for all those who trust Jesus Christ on the basis of his death for sin on the Cross. The mystery-religions all offered salvation by initiation and ritual as the Pharisees did by ceremonialism. Christianity reaches the heart directly by trust in Christ as the Saviour. It is God's wisdom.

22. *Seeing that* (*epeidē*). Resumes from verse 21. The structure is not clear, but probably verses 23 and 24 form a sort of conclusion or apodosis to verse 22 the protasis. The resumptive, almost inferential, use of *de* like *alla* in the apodosis is not unusual. *Ask for signs* (*sēmeia aitousin*). The Jews often came to Jesus asking for signs (Matt. 12:38; 16:1; John 6:30). *Seek after wisdom* (*sophian zētousin*). "The Jews claimed to *possess* the truth: the Greeks were *seekers, speculators*" (Vincent) as in Acts 17:23.

23. *But we preach Christ crucified* (*hēmeis de kērussomen Christon estaurōmenon*). Grammatically stated as a partial result (*de*) of the folly of both Jews and Greeks, actually in sharp contrast. We proclaim, "we do not discuss or dispute" (Lightfoot). Christ (Messiah) as crucified, as in 2:2 and Gal. 3:1, "not a sign-shower nor a philosopher" (Vincent). Perfect passive participle of *stauroō*. *Stumbling-block* (*skandalon*). Papyri examples mean trap or snare which here tripped the Jews who wanted a conquering Messiah with a world empire, not a condemned and crucified one (Matt. 27:42; Luke 24:21). *Foolishness* (*mōrian*). Folly as shown by their conduct in Athens (Acts 17:32).

24. *But to them that are called* (*autois de tois klētois*). Dative case, to the called themselves. *Christ* (*Christon*). Accusative case repeated, object of *kērussomen*, both *the power of God* (*theou dunamin*) and *the wisdom of God* (*theou sophian*). No article, but made definite by the genitive. Christ crucified is God's answer to both Jew and Greek and the answer is understood by those with open minds.

25. *The foolishness of God* (*to mōron tou theou*). Abstract neuter singular with the article, the foolish act of God (the Cross as regarded by the world). *Wiser than men* (*sophōteron tōn anthrōpōn*). Condensed comparison, wiser than the wisdom of men. Common Greek idiom (Matt. 5:20; John 5:36) and quite forcible, brushes all men aside. *The weakness*

of God (to asthenes tou theou). Same idiom here, *the weak act of God,* as men think, *is stronger (ischuroteron).* The Cross seemed God's defeat. It is conquering the world and is the mightiest force on earth.

26. *Behold (blepete).* Same form for imperative present active plural and indicative. Either makes sense as in John 5:39 *eraunate* and 14:1 *pisteuete. Calling (klēsin).* The act of calling by God, based not on the external condition of those called *(klētoi,* verse 2), but on God's sovereign love. It is a clinching illustration of Paul's argument, an *argumentum ad hominen. How that (hoti).* Explanatory apposition to *klēsin. After the flesh (kata sarka).* According to the standards of the flesh and to be used not only with *sophoi* (wise, philosophers), but also *dunatoi* (men of dignity and power), *eugeneis* (noble, high birth), the three claims to aristocracy (culture, power, birth). *Are called.* Not in the Greek, but probably to be supplied from the idea in *klēsin.*

27. *God chose (exelexato ho theos).* First aorist middle of *eklegō,* old verb to pick out, to choose, the middle for oneself. It expands the idea in *klēsin* (verse 26). Three times this solemn verb occurs here with the purpose stated each time. Twice the same purpose is expressed, *that he might put to shame (hina kataischunēi,* first aorist active subjunctive with *hina* of old verb *kataischunō,* perfective use of *kata).* The purpose in the third example is *that he might bring to naught (hina katargēsēi,* make idle, *argos,* rare in old Greek, but frequent in Paul). The contrast is complete in each paradox: *the foolish things (ta mōra), the wise men (tous sophous); the weak things (ta asthenē), the strong things (ta ischura); the things that are not (ta mē onta), and that are despised (ta exouthenēmena,* considered nothing, perfect passive participle of *exoutheneō), the things that are (ta onta).* It is a studied piece of rhetoric and powerfully put.

29. *That no flesh should glory before God (hopōs mē kauchēsētai pāsa sarx enōpion tou theou).* This is the further purpose expressed by *hopōs* for variety and appeals to God's ultimate choice in all three instances. The first aorist middle of the old verb *kauchaomai,* to boast, brings out sharply that not a single boast is to be made. The papyri give numerous examples of *enōpion* as a preposition in the vernacular, from

adjective *en-ōpios*, in the eye of God. One should turn to II Cor. 4:7 for Paul's further statement about our having this treasure in earthern vessels that the excellency of the power may be of God and not of us. 30. *Of him (ex autou)*. Out of God. He chose you. *In Christ Jesus (en Christōi Iēsou)*. In the sphere of Christ Jesus the choice was made. This is God's wisdom. *Who was made unto us wisdom from God (hos egenēthē sophia hēmin apo theou)*. Note *egenēthē*, became (first aorist passive and indicative), not *ēn*, was, the Incarnation, Cross, and Resurrection. Christ is the wisdom of God (Col. 2:2f.) "both righteousness and sanctification and redemption" (*dikaiosunē te kai hagiasmos kai apolutrōsis*), as is made plain by the use of *te — kai — kai*. The three words (*dikaiosunē, hagiasmos, apolutrōsis*) are thus shown to be an epexegesis of *sophia* (Lightfoot). All the treasures of wisdom and knowledge in Christ Jesus. We are made righteous, holy, and redeemed in Christ Jesus. Redemption comes here last for emphasis though the foundation of the other two. In Rom. 1:17 we see clearly Paul's idea of the God kind of righteousness (*dikaiosunē*) in Christ. In Rom. 3:24 we have Paul's conception of redemption (*apolutrōsis*, setting free as a ransomed slave) in Christ. In Rom. 6:19 we have Paul's notion of holiness or sanctification (*hagiasmos*) in Christ. These great theological terms will call for full discussion in Romans, but they must not be overlooked here. See also Acts 10:35; 24:25; I Thess. 4:3-7; I Cor. 1:2.

31. *That (hina)*. Probably ellipse (*genētai* to be supplied) as is common in Paul's Epistles (II Thess. 2:3; II Cor. 8:13; Gal. 1:20; 2:9; Rom. 4:16; 13:1; 15:3). Some explain the imperative *kauchasthō* as an anacoluthon. The shortened quotation is from Jer. 9:24. Deissmann notes the importance of these closing verses concerning the origin of Paul's congregations from the lower classes in the large towns as "one of the most important historical witnesses to Primitive Christianity" (*New Light on the N.T.*, p. 7; *Light from the Ancient East*, pp. 7, 14, 60, 142).

CHAPTER II

1. *Not with excellency of speech or of wisdom (ou kath'* *huperochēn logou ē sophias)*. *Huperochē* is an old word from the verb *huperechō* (Phil. 4:7) and means preëminence, rising above. In N.T. only here and I Tim. 2:2 of magistrates. It occurs in inscriptions of Pergamum for persons of position (Deissmann, *Bible Studies*, p. 255). Here it means excess or superfluity, "not in excellence of rhetorical display or of philosophical subtlety" (Lightfoot). *The mystery of God* *(to mustērion tou theou)*. So Aleph A C Copt. like 2:7, but B D L P read *marturion* like 1:6. Probably *mystery* is correct. Christ crucified is the mystery of God (Col. 2:2). Paul did not hesitate to appropriate this word in common use among the mystery religions, but he puts into it his ideas, not those in current use. It is an old word from *mueō*, to close, to shut, to initiate (Phil. 4:12). This mystery was once hidden from the ages (Col. 1:26), but is now made plain in Christ (I Cor. 2:7; Rom. 16:25f.). The papyri give many illustrations of the use of the word for secret doctrines known only to the initiated (Moulton and Milligan's *Vocabulary*).

2. *For I determined not to know anything among you (ou* *gar ekrina ti eidenai en humin)*. Literally, "For I did not decide to know anything among you." The negative goes with *ekrina*, not with *ti*. Paul means that he did not think it fit or his business to know anything for his message beyond this "mystery of God." *Save Jesus Christ (ei mē* *Iēsoun Christon)*. Both the person and the office (Lightfoot). I had no intent to go beyond him and in particular, *and him* *crucified (kai touton estaurōmenon)*. Literally, *and this one* *as crucified* (perfect passive participle). This phase in particular (1:18) was selected by Paul from the start as the centre of his gospel message. He decided to stick to it even after Athens where he was practically laughed out of court. The Cross added to the *scandalon* of the Incarnation, but Paul kept to the main track on coming to Corinth.

3. *I was with you (egenomēn pros humas)*. Rather, "I came to you" (not *ēn*, was). "I not only eschewed all af-

fectation of cleverness or grandiloquence, but I went to the opposite extreme of diffidence and nervous self-effacement" (Robertson and Plummer). Paul had been in prison in Philippi, driven out of Thessalonica and Beroea, politely bowed out of Athens. It is a human touch to see this shrinking as he faced the hard conditions in Corinth. It is a common feeling of the most effective preachers. Cool complacency is not the mood of the finest preaching. See *phobos* (fear) and *tromos* (trembling) combined in II Cor. 7:15; Phil. 2:12; Eph. 6:5.

4. *Not in persuasive words of wisdom* (*ouk en pithois sophias logois*). This looks like a false disclaimer or mock modesty, for surely the preacher desires to be persuasive. This adjective *pithos* (MSS. *peithos*) has not yet been found elsewhere. It seems to be formed directly from *peithō*, to persuade, as *pheidos* (*phidos*) is from *pheidomai*, to spare. The old Greek form *pithanos* is common enough and is used by Josephus (*Ant.* VIII. 9. 1) of "the plausible words of the lying prophet" in I Kings. 13. The kindred word *pithanologia* occurs in Col. 2:4 for the specious and plausible Gnostic philosophers. And gullible people are easy marks for these plausible pulpiteers. Corinth put a premium on the veneer of false rhetoric and thin thinking. *But in demonstration* (*all' en apodeixei*). In contrast with the *plausibility* just mentioned. This word, though an old one from *apodeiknumi*, to show forth, occurs nowhere else in the New Testament. *Spirit* (*pneuma*) here can be the Holy Spirit or inward spirit as opposed to superficial expression and *power* (*dunamis*) is moral power rather than intellectual acuteness (cf. 1:18).

5. *That your faith should not stand* (*hina hē pistis humōn mē ēi*). Purpose of God, but *mē ēi* is "not be" merely. The only secure place for faith to find a rest is in God's power, not in the wisdom of men. One has only to instance the changing theories of men about science, philosophy, religion, politics to see this. A sure word from God can be depended on.

6. *Among the perfect* (*en tois teleiois*). Paul is not here drawing a distinction between exoteric and esoteric wisdom as the Gnostics did for their initiates, but simply to the necessary difference in teaching for babes (3:1) and adults or grown men (common use of *teleios* for relative perfection,

for adults, as is in I Cor. 14:20; Phil. 3:15; Eph. 4:13; Heb.
5:14). Some were simply old babes and unable in spite of
their years to digest solid spiritual food, "the ample teaching
as to the Person of Christ and the eternal purpose of God.
Such 'wisdom' we have in the Epistles to the Ephesians
and the Colossians especially, and in a less degree in the
Epistle to the Romans. This 'wisdom' is discerned in the
Gospel of John, as compared with the other Evangelists"
(Lightfoot). These imperfect disciples Paul wishes to de-
velop into spiritual maturity. *Of this world* (*tou aiōnos
toutou*). This age, more exactly, as in 1:20. This wisdom
does not belong to the passing age of fleeting things, but
to the enduring and eternal (Ellicott). *Which are coming to
naught* (*tōn katargoumenōn*). See on 1:28. Present passive
participle genitive plural of *katargeō*. The gradual nullifica-
tion of these "rulers" before the final and certain triumph
of the power of Christ in his kingdom.

7. *God's wisdom in a mystery* (*theou sophian en mustēriōi*).
Two points are here sharply made. It is God's wisdom (note
emphatic position of the genitive *theou*) in contrast to the
wisdom of this age. Every age of the world has a conceit of
its own and it is particularly true of this twentieth century,
but God's wisdom is eternal and superior to the wisdom of
any age or time. God's wisdom is alone absolute. See on
2:1 for *mystery*. It is not certain whether *in a mystery* is
to be taken with *wisdom* or *we speak*. The result does not
differ greatly, probably with *wisdom*, so long a secret and
now at last revealed (Col. 1:26; II Thess. 2:7). *That hath
been hidden* (*tēn apokekrummenēn*). See Rom. 16:25; Col.
1:26; Eph. 3:5. Articular perfect passive participle of *apokruptō*, more precisely defining the indefinite *sophian* (wisdom). *Foreordained before the worlds* (*proōrisen pro tōn aiōnōn*).
This relative clause (*hēn*) defines still more closely God's
wisdom. Note *pro* with both verb and substantive (*aiōnōn*).
Constative aorist of God's elective purpose as shown in
Christ crucified (I Cor. 1:18–24). "It was no afterthought
or change of plan" (Robertson and Plummer). *Unto our
glory* (*eis doxan hēmōn*). "The glory of inward enlighten-
ment as well as of outward exaltation" (Lightfoot).

8. *Knoweth* (*egnōken*). Has known, has discerned, perfect
active indicative of *ginōskō*. They have shown amazing ig-

norance of God's wisdom. *For had they known it* (*ei gar egnōsan*). Condition of the second class, determined as unfulfilled, with aorist active indicative in both condition (*egnōsan*) and conclusion with an (*ouk an estaurōsan*). Peter in the great sermon at Pentecost commented on the "ignorance" (*kata agnoian*) of the Jews in crucifying Christ (Acts 3:17) as the only hope for repentance on their part (Acts 3:19). *The Lord of glory* (*ton Kurion tēs doxēs*). Genitive case *doxēs*, means characterized by glory, "bringing out the contrast between the indignity of the Cross (Heb. 12:2) and the majesty of the Victim (Luke 22:69; 23:43)" (Robertson and Plummer). See James 2:1; Acts 7:2; Eph. 1:17; Heb. 9:5.

9. *But as it is written* (*alla kathōs gegraptai*). Elliptical sentence like Rom. 15:3 where *gegonen* (*it has happened*) can be supplied. It is not certain where Paul derives this quotation as Scripture. Origen thought it a quotation from the *Apocalypse of Elias* and Jerome finds it also in the *Ascension of Isaiah*. But these books appear to be post-Pauline, and Jerome denies that Paul obtained it from these late apocryphal books. Clement of Rome finds it in the LXX text of Isa. 64:4 and cites it as a Christian saying. It is likely that Paul here combines freely Isa. 64:4; 65:17; and 52:15 in a sort of catena or free chain of quotations as he does in Rom. 3:10–18. There is also an anacoluthon for *ha* (which things) occurs as the direct object (accusative) with *eiden* (saw) and *ēkousan* (heard), but as the subject (nominative) with *anebē* (entered, second aorist active indicative of *anabainō*, to go up). *Whatsoever* (*hosa*). A climax to the preceding relative clause (Findlay). *Prepared* (*hētoimasen*). First aorist active indicative of *hetoimazō*. The only instance where Paul uses this verb of God, though it occurs of final glory (Luke 2:31; Matt. 20:23; 25:34; Mark 10:40; Heb. 11:16) and of final misery (Matt. 25:41). But here undoubtedly the dominant idea is the present blessing to these who love God (I Cor. 1:5–7). *Heart* (*kardian*) here as in Rom. 1:21 is more than emotion. The Gnostics used this passage to support their teaching of esoteric doctrine as Hegesippus shows. Lightfoot thinks that probably the apocryphal *Ascension of Isaiah* and *Apocalypse of Elias* were Gnostic and so quoted this passage of Paul to support their

position. But the next verse shows that Paul uses it of what is now *revealed* and made plain, not of mysteries still unknown.

10. *But unto us God revealed them* (*hēmin gar apekalupsen ho theos*). So with *gar* B 37 Sah Cop read instead of *de* of Aleph A C D. "*De* is superficially easier; *gar* intrinsically better" (Findlay). Paul explains why this is no longer hidden, "for God revealed unto us" the wonders of grace pictured in verse 9. We do not have to wait for heaven to see them. Hence we can utter those things hidden from the eye, the ear, the heart of man. This revelation (*apekalupsen,* first aorist active indicative) took place, at "the entry of the Gospel into the world," not "when we were admitted into the Church, when we were baptized" as Lightfoot interprets it. *Through the Spirit* (*dia tou pneumatos*). The Holy Spirit is the agent of this definite revelation of grace, a revelation with a definite beginning or advent (constative aorist), an unveiling by the Spirit where "human ability and research would not have sufficed" (Robertson and Plummer), "according to the revelation of the mystery" (Rom. 16:25), "the revelation given to Christians as an event that began a new epoch in the world's history " (Edwards). *Searcheth all things* (*panta eraunāi*). This is the usual form from A.D. 1 on rather than the old *ereunaō.* The word occurs (Moulton and Milligan's *Vocabulary*) for a professional searcher's report and *eraunētai*, searchers for customs officials. "The Spirit is the organ of understanding between man and God" (Findlay). So in Rom. 8:27 we have this very verb *eraunaō* again of God's searching our hearts. The Holy Spirit not merely investigates us, but he searches "even the deep things of God" (*kai ta bathē tou theou*). *Profunda Dei* (Vulgate). Cf. "the deep things of Satan" (Rev. 2:24) and Paul's language in Rom. 11:33 "Oh the depth of the riches and wisdom and knowledge of God." Paul's point is simply that the Holy Spirit fully comprehends the depth of God's nature and his plans of grace and so is fully competent to make the revelation here claimed.

11. *Knoweth* (*oiden, egnōken*). Second perfect of root *id-,* to see and so know, first perfect of *ginōskō,* to know by personal experience, has come to know and still knows. See First John for a clear distinction in the use of *oida* and

ginōskō. *The spirit of man that is in him* (*to pneuma tou anthrōpou to en autōi*). The self-consciousness of man that resides in the man or woman (generic term for mankind, *anthrōpos*). *The Spirit of God* (*to pneuma tou theou*). Note the absence of *to en autōi*. It is not the mere self-consciousness of God, but the personal Holy Spirit in his relation to God the Father. Paul's analogy between the spirit of man and the Spirit of God does not hold clear through and he guards it at this vital point as he does elsewhere as in Rom. 8:26 and in the full Trinitarian benediction in II Cor. 13:13. *Pneuma* in itself merely means breath or wind as in John 3:8. To know accurately Paul's use of the word in every instance calls for an adequate knowledge of his theology, and psychology. But the point here is plain. God's Holy Spirit is amply qualified to make the revelation claimed here in verses 6–10.

12. *But we* (*hēmeis de*). We Christians like *us* (*hēmin*) in verse 10 of the revelation, but particularly Paul and the other apostles. *Received* (*elabomen*). Second aorist active indicative of *lambanō* and so a definite event, though the constative aorist may include various stages. *Not the spirit of the world* (*ou to pneuma tou kosmou*). Probably a reference to the wisdom of this age in verse 6. See also Rom. 8:4, 6, 7; II Cor. 11:4 (the *pneuma heteron*). *But the spirit which is of God* (*alla to pneuma to ek theou*). Rather, "from God" (*ek*), which proceeds from God. *That we might know* (*hina eidōmen*). Second perfect subjunctive with *hina* to express purpose. Here is a distinct claim of the Holy Spirit for understanding (Illumination) the Revelation received. It is not a senseless rhapsody or secret mystery, but God expects us to understand "the things that are freely given us by God" (*ta hupo tou theou charisthenta hēmin*). First aorist passive neuter plural articular participle of *charizomai*, to bestow. God gave the revelation through the Holy Spirit and he gives us the illumination of the Holy Spirit to understand the mind of the Spirit. The tragic failures of men to understand clearly God's revealed will is but a commentary on the weakness and limitation of the human intellect even when enlightened by the Holy Spirit.

13. *Which things also we speak* (*ha kai laloumen*). This onomatopoetic verb *laleō* (from *la-la*), to utter sounds. In the

papyri the word calls more attention to the form of utterance while *legō* refers more to the substance. But *laleō* in the N.T. as here is used of the highest and holiest speech. Undoubtedly Paul employs the word purposely for the utterance of the revelation which he has understood. That is to say, there is revelation (verse 10), illumination (verse 12), and inspiration (verse 13). Paul claims therefore the help of the Holy Spirit for the reception of the revelation, for the understanding of it, for the expression of it. Paul claimed this authority for his preaching (I Thess. 4:2) and for his epistles (II Thess. 3:14). *Not in words which man's wisdom teacheth* (*ouk en didaktois anthrōpinēs sophias logois*). Literally, "not in words taught by human wisdom." The verbal adjective *didaktois* (from *didaskō*, to teach) is here passive in idea and is followed by the ablative case of origin or source as in John 6:45, *esontai pantes didaktoi theou* (from Isa. 54: 13), "They shall all be taught by God." The ablative in Greek, as is well known, has the same form as the genitive, though quite different in idea (Robertson, *Grammar*, p. 516). So then Paul claims the help of the Holy Spirit in the utterance (*laloumen*) of the words, "which the Spirit teacheth (*en didaktois pneumatos*), "in words taught by the Spirit" (ablative *pneumatos* as above). Clearly Paul means that the help of the Holy Spirit in the utterance of the revelation extends to the words. No theory of inspiration is here stated, but it is not *mere* human wisdom. Paul's own Epistles bear eloquent witness to the lofty claim here made. They remain today after nearly nineteen centuries throbbing with the power of the Spirit of God, dynamic with life for the problems of today as when Paul wrote them for the needs of the believers in his time, the greatest epistles of all time, surcharged with the energy oi God. *Comparing spiritual things with spiritual* (*pneumatikois pneumatika sunkrinontes*). Each of these words is in dispute. The verb *sunkrinō*, originally meant to combine, to join together fitly. In the LXX it means to interpret dreams (Gen. 40:8, 22; 41:12) possibly by comparison. In the later Greek it may mean to compare as in II Cor. 10:12. In the papyri Moulton and Milligan (*Vocabulary*) give it only for "decide," probably after comparing. But "comparing," in spite of the translations, does not suit well here. So it is best to follow the original meaning to combine as do Lightfoot and Ellicott. But what gender is *pneumatikois?* Is it masculine or neuter like *pneumatika?* If masculine, the idea would be "interpreting (like LXX) spiritual truths to spiritual persons" or "matching spiritual truths with spiritual persons." This is a possible rendering and makes good sense in harmony with verse 14. If *pneumatikois* be taken as neuter plural (associative instrumental case after *sun* in *sunkrinontes*), the idea most naturally would be, "combining spiritual ideas (*pneumatika*) with spiritual words" (*pneumatikois*). This again makes good sense in harmony with the first part of verse 13. On the whole this is the most natural way to take it, though various other possibilities exist.

14. *Now the natural man* (*psuchikos de anthrōpos*). Note absence of article here, "A natural man" (an unregenerate man). Paul does not employ modern psychological terms and he exercises variety in his use of all the terms here present as *pneuma* and *pneumatikos, psuchē* and *psuchikos, sarx* and *sarkinos* and *sarkikos.* A helpful discussion of the various uses of these words in the New Testament is given by Burton in his *New Testament Word Studies,* pp. 62–68, and in his *Spirit, Soul, and Flesh.* The papyri furnish so many examples of *sarx, pneuma,* and *psuchē* that Moulton and Milligan make no attempt at an exhaustive treatment, but give a few miscellaneous examples to illustrate the varied uses that parallel the New Testament. *Psuchikos* is a qualitative adjective from *psuchē* (breath of life like *anima,* life, soul). Here the Vulgate renders it by *animalis* and the German by *sinnlich,* the original sense of animal life as in Jude 19; James 3:15. In I Cor. 15:44, 46 there is the same contrast between *psuchikos* and *pneumatikos* as here. The *psuchikos* man is the unregenerate man while the *pneumatikos* man is the renewed man, born again of the Spirit of God. *Receiveth not* (*ou dechetai*). Does not accept, rejects, refuses to accept. In Rom. 8:7 Paul definitely states the inability (*oude gar dunatai*) of the mind of the flesh to receive the things of the Spirit untouched by the Holy Spirit. Certainly the initiative comes from God whose Holy Spirit makes it possible for us to accept the things of the Spirit of God. They are no longer "foolishness" (*mōria*) to us as was once the case (1:23). Today one notes certain of the *intelligentsia*

who sneer at Christ and Christianity in their own blinded ignorance. *He cannot know them (ou dunatai gnōnai).* He is not able to get a knowledge (ingressive second aorist active infinitive of *ginōskō*). His helpless condition calls for pity in place of impatience on our part, though such an one usually poses as a paragon of wisdom and commiserates the deluded followers of Christ. *They are spiritually judged (pneumatikōs anakrinetai).* Paul and Luke are fond of this verb, though nowhere else in the N.T. Paul uses it only in I Corinthians. The word means a sifting process to get at the truth by investigation as of a judge. In Acts 17:11 the Beroeans scrutinized the Scriptures. These *psuchikoi* men are incapable of rendering a decision for they are unable to recognize the facts. They judge by the *psuchē* (mere animal nature) rather than by the *pneuma* (the renewed spirit).

15. *Judgeth all things (anakrinei panta).* The spiritual man *(ho pneumatikos)* is qualified to sift, to examine, to decide rightly, because he has the eyes of his heart enlightened (Eph. 1:18) and is no longer blinded by the god of this world (II Cor. 4:4). There is a great lesson for Christians who know by personal experience the things of the Spirit of God. Men of intellectual gifts who are ignorant of the things of Christ talk learnedly and patronizingly about things of which they are grossly ignorant. The spiritual man is superior to all this false knowledge. *He himself is judged of no man (autos de hup' oudenos anakrinetai).* Men will pass judgment on him, but the spiritual man refuses to accept the decision of his ignorant judges. He stands superior to them all as Polycarp did when he preferred to be burnt to saying, "Lord Caesar" in place of "Lord Jesus." He was unwilling to save his earthly life by the worship of Caesar in place of the Lord Jesus. Polycarp was a *pneumatikos* man.

16. *For who hath known the mind of the Lord (Tis gar egnō noun Kuriou;).* Quotation from Isa. 40:13. *That he should instruct him (hos sunbibasei auton).* This use of *hos* (relative *who*) is almost consecutive (result). The *pneumatikos* man is superior to others who attempt even to instruct God himself. See on Acts 9:22 and 16:10 for *sunbibazō*, to make go together. *But we have the mind of Christ (hēmeis de noun Christou echomen).* As he has already shown (verses 6 to

13). Thus with the mind (*nous*. Cf. Phil. 2:5 and Rom. 8:9, 27). Hence Paul and all *pneumatikoi* men are superior to those who try to shake their faith in Christ, the mystery of God. Paul can say, "I know him whom I have believed." "I believe; therefore I have spoken."

CHAPTER III

1. *But as unto carnal(all' hōs sarkinois).* Latin *carneus.*
"As men o' flesh," Braid Scots; "as worldlings," Moffatt.
This form in *-inos* like *lithinos* in II Cor.
3:3 means the material of flesh, "not on tablets of stone, but on fleshen tablets on hearts." So in Heb. 7:16. But in Rom. 7:14 Paul says, "I am fleshen (*sarkinos*) sold under sin," as if *sarkinos* represented the extreme power of the *sarx*. Which does Paul mean here? He wanted to speak the wisdom of God among the adults (I Cor. 2:6), the spiritual (*hoi pneumatikoi*, 2:15), but he was unable to treat them as *pneumatikoi* in reality because of their seditions and immoralities. It is not wrong to be *sarkinos*, for we all live in the flesh (*en sarki*, Gal. 2:20), but we are not to live according to the flesh (*kata sarka*, Rom. 8:12). It is not culpable to a babe in Christ (*nēpios*, I Cor. 13:11), unless unduly prolonged (I Cor. 14:20; Heb. 5:13f.). It is one of the tragedies of the minister's life that he has to keep on speaking to the church members "as unto babes in Christ" (*hōs nēpiois en Christōi*), who actually glory in their long babyhood whereas they ought to be teachers of the gospel instead of belonging to the cradle roll. Paul's goal was for all the babes to become adults (Col. 1:28).

2. *I fed you with milk, not with meat (gala humas epotisa, ou brōma).* Note two accusatives with the verb, *epotisa*, first aorist active indicative of *potizō*, as with other causative verbs, that of the person and of the thing. In the LXX and the papyri the verb often means to irrigate. *Brōma* does not mean meat (flesh) as opposed to bread, but all solid food as in "meats and drinks" (Heb. 9:7). It is a zeugma to use *epotisa* with *brōma*. Paul did not glory in making his sermons thin and watery. Simplicity does not require lack of ideas or dulness. It is pathetic to think how the preacher has to clip the wings of thought and imagination because the hearers cannot go with him. But nothing hinders great preaching like the dulness caused by sin on the part of

auditors who are impatient with the high demands of the gospel.

3. *For ye are yet carnal* (*eti gar sarkikoi este*). *Sarkikos*, unlike *sarkinos*, like- *ikos* formations, means adapted to, fitted for the flesh (*sarx*), one who lives according to the flesh (*kata sarka*). Paul by *psuchikos* describes the unregenerate man, by *pneumatikos* the regenerate man. Both classes are *sarkinoi* made in flesh, and both may be *sarkikoi* though the *pneumatikoi* should not be. The *pneumatikoi* who continue to be *sarkinoi* are still babes (*nēpioi*), not adults (*teleioi*), while those who are still *sarkikoi* (carnal) have given way to the flesh as if they were still *psuchikoi* (unregenerate). It is a bold and cutting figure, not without sarcasm, but necessary to reveal the Corinthians to themselves. *Jealousy and strife* (*zēlos kai eris*). Zeal (*zēlos* from *zeō*, to boil) is not necessarily evil, but good if under control. It may be not according to knowledge (Rom. 10:2) and easily becomes jealousy (same root through the French *jaloux*) as zeal. Ardour may be like the jealousy of God (II Cor. 11:2) or the envy of men (Acts 5:17). *Eris* is an old word, but used only by Paul in N.T. (see on I Cor. 1:11). Wrangling follows jealousy. These two voices of the spirit are to Paul proof that the Corinthians are still *sarkikoi* and walking according to men, not according to the Spirit of Christ.

4. *For when one saith* (*hotan gar legēi tis*). Indefinite temporal clause with the present subjunctive of repetition (Robertson, *Grammar*, p. 972). Each instance is a case in point and proof abundant of the strife. *Of Paul* (*Paulou*). Predicate genitive, belong to Paul, on Paul's side. *Of Apollos* (*Apollō*). Same genitive, but the form is the so-called Attic second declension. See the nominative *Apollōs* in verse 5. *Men* (*anthrōpoi*). Just mere human creatures (*anthrōpoi*, generic term for mankind), in the flesh (*sarkinoi*), acting like the flesh (*sarkikoi*), not *pneumatikoi*, as if still *psuchikoi*. It was a home-thrust. Paul would not even defend his own partisans.

5. *What then?* (*ti oun;*). He does not say *tis* (who), but *ti* (what), neuter singular interrogative pronoun. *Ministers* (*diakonoi*). Not leaders of parties or sects, but merely servants through whom ye believed. The etymology of the word Thayer gives as *dia* and *konis* "raising dust by hastening."

In the Gospels it is the servant (Matt. 20:26) or waiter (John 2:5). Paul so describes himself as a minister (Col. 1:23, 25). The technical sense of deacon comes later (Phil. 1:1; I Tim. 3:8, 12). *As the Lord gave to him* (*hōs ho Kurios edōken*). Hence no minister of the Lord like Apollos and Paul has any basis for pride or conceit nor should be made the occasion for faction and strife. This idea Paul enlarges upon through chapters 3 and 4 and it is made plain in chapter 12.

6. *I planted* (*egō ephuteusa*). First aorist active indicative of old verb *phuteuō*. This Paul did as Luke tells us in Acts 18:1–18. *Apollos watered* (*Apollōs epotisen*). Apollos irrigated the church there as is seen in Acts 18:24–19:1. Another aorist tense as in verse 2. *But God gave the increase* (*alla ho theos ēuxanen*). Imperfect tense here (active indicative) for the continuous blessing of God both on the work of Paul and Apollos, co-labourers with God in God's field (verse 9). Reports of revivals sometimes give the glory to the evangelist or to both evangelist and pastor. Paul gives it all to God. He and Apollos coöperated as successive pastors.

7. *So then neither—neither—but* (*Hōste oute—oute—all'*). Paul applies his logic relentlessly to the facts. He had asked *what* (*ti*) is Apollos or Paul (verse 5). The answer is here. *Neither is anything* (*ti*) *the one who plants nor the one who waters.* God is the whole and we are not anything.

8. *Are one* (*hen eisin*). The neuter singular again (*hen,* not *heis*) as with the interrogative *ti* and the indefinite *ti.* By this bold metaphor which Paul expands he shows how the planter and the waterer work together. If no one planted, the watering would be useless. If no one watered, the planting would come to naught as the dreadful drouth of 1930 testifies while these words are written. *According to his own labour* (*kata ton idion kopon*). God will bestow to each the reward that his labour deserves. That is the pay that the preacher is sure to receive. He may get too little or too much here from men. But the due reward from God is certain and it will be adequate however ungrateful men may be.

9. *God's fellow-workers* (*theou sunergoi*). This old word (co-workers of God) has a new dignity here. God is the

major partner in the enterprise of each life, but he lets us work with him. Witness the mother and God with the baby as the product. *God's husbandry* (*theou georgion*). God's tilled land (*ge*, *ergon*). The farmer works with God in God's field. Without the sun, the rains, the seasons the farmer is helpless. *God's building* (*theou oikodome*). God is the Great Architect. We work under him and carry out the plans of the Architect. It is building (*oikos*, house, *demo*, to build). Let us never forget that God sees and cares what we do in the part of the building where we work for him.

10. *As a wise masterbuilder* (*hos sophos architekton*). Paul does not shirk his share in the work at Corinth with all the sad outcome there. He absolves Apollos from responsibility for the divisions. He denies that he himself is to blame. In doing so he has to praise himself because the Judaizers who fomented the trouble at Corinth had directly blamed Paul. It is not always wise for a preacher to defend himself against attack, but it is sometimes necessary. Factions in the church were now a fact and Paul went to the bottom of the matter. God gave Paul the grace to do what he did. This is the only New Testament example of the old and common word *architekton*, our architect. *Tekton* is from *tikto*, to beget, and means a begetter, then a worker in wood or stone, a carpenter or mason (Matt. 13:55; Mark 6:3). *Archi-* is an old inseparable prefix like *archaggelos* (archangel), *archepiscopos* (archbishop), *archiereus* (chiefpriest). *Architekton* occurs in the papyri and inscriptions in an even wider sense than our use of architect, sometimes of the chief engineers. But Paul means to claim primacy as pastor of the church in Corinth as is true of every pastor who is the architect of the whole church life and work. All the workmen (*tektones*, carpenters) work under the direction of the architect (Plato, *Statesman*, 259). "As a wise architect I laid a foundation" (*themelion etheka*). Much depends on the wisdom of the architect in laying the foundation. This is the technical phrase (Luke 6:48; 14:29), a cognate accusative for *themelion*. The substantive *themelion* is from the same root *the* as *etheka* (*ti-the-mi*). We cannot neatly reproduce the idiom in English. "I placed a placing" does only moderately well. Paul refers directly to the events described by Luke in Acts 18:1–18. The aorist *etheka* is the correct text, not the perfect *tetheika*.

Another buildeth thereon (allos epoikodomei). Note the preposition *epi* with the verb each time (10, 11, 12, 14). The successor to Paul did not have to lay a new foundation, but only to go on building on that already laid. It is a pity when the new pastor has to dig up the foundation and start all over again as if an earthquake had come. *Take heed how he buildeth thereon (blepetō pōs epoikodomei)*. The carpenters have need of caution how they carry out the plans of the original architect. Successive architects of great cathedrals carry on through centuries the original design. The result becomes the wonder of succeeding generations. There is no room for individual caprice in the superstructure.

11. *Other foundation (themelion allon)*. The gender of the adjective is here masculine as is shown by *allon*. If neuter, it would be *allo*. It is masculine because Paul has Christ in mind. It is not here *heteron* a different kind of gospel (*heteron euaggelion*, Gal. 1:6; II Cor. 11:4) which is not another (*allo*, Gal. 1:7) in reality. But another Jesus (II Cor. 11:4, *allon Iēsoun*) is a reflection on the one Lord Jesus. Hence there is no room on the platform with Jesus for another Saviour, whether Buddha, Mahomet, Dowie, Eddy, or what not. Jesus Christ is the one foundation and it is gratuitous impudence for another to assume the rôle of Foundation. *Than that which is laid, which is Christ Jesus (para ton keimenon, hos estin Iēsous Christos)*. Literally, "alongside (*para*) the one laid (*keimenon*)," already laid (present middle participle of *keimai*, used here as often as the perfect passive of *tithēmi* in place of *tetheimenon*). Paul scouts the suggestion that one even in the interest of so-called "new thought" will dare to lay beside Jesus another foundation for religion. And yet I have seen an article by a professor in a theological seminary in which he advocates regarding Jesus as a landmark, not as a goal, not as a foundation. Clearly Paul means that on this one true foundation, Jesus Christ, one must build only what is in full harmony with the Foundation which is Jesus Christ. If one accuses Paul of narrowness, it can be replied that the architect has to be narrow in the sense of building here and not there. A broad foundation will be too thin and unstable for a solid and abiding structure. It can be said also that Paul is here merely repeating the claim of Jesus himself on this very subject when he quoted

Psa. 118:22f. to the members of the Sanhedrin who challenged his authority (Mark 11:10f.=Matt. 21:42-45=Luke 20:17f.). Apostles and prophets go into this temple of God, but Christ Jesus is the chief corner stone (*akrogōnaios*, Eph. 2:20). All believers are living stones in this temple (I Peter 2:5). But there is only one foundation possible.

12. *Gold, silver, precious stones, wood, hay, stubble* (*chrusion, argurion, lithous timious, xula, chorton, kalamēn*). The durable materials are three (gold, silver, marble or precious stones), perishable materials (pieces of wood, hay, stubble), "of a palace on the one hand, of a mud hut on the other" (Lightfoot). Gold was freely used by the ancients in their palaces. Their marble and granite pillars are still the wonder and despair of modern men. The wooden huts had hay (*chortos*, grass, as in Mark 6:39) and stubble (*kalamē*, old word for stubble after the grain is cut, here alone in the N.T., though in LXX as Ex. 5:12) which were employed to hold the wood pieces together and to thatch the roof. It is not made clear whether Paul's metaphor refers to the persons as in God's building in verse 9 or to the character of the teaching as in verse 13. Probably both ideas are involved, for look at the penalty on shoddy work (verse 15) and shoddy men (verse 17). The teaching may not always be vicious and harmful. It may only be indifferent and worthless. A co-worker with God in this great temple should put in his very best effort.

13. *The day* (*hē hēmera*). The day of judgment as in I Thess. 5:4 (which see), Rom. 13:12; Heb. 10:25. The work (*ergon*) of each will be made manifest. There is no escape from this final testing. *It is revealed in fire* (*en puri apokaluptetai*). Apparently "the day" is the subject of the verb, not the work, not the Lord. See II Thess. 1:8; 2:8. This metaphor of fire was employed in the O.T. (Dan. 7:9f.; Mal. 4:1) and by John the Baptist (Matt. 3:12; Luke 3:16f.). It is a metaphor that must not be understood as purgatorial, but simple testing (Ellicott) as every fire tests (*the fire itself will test, to pur auto dokimasei*) the quality of the material used in the building, *of what sort it is* (*hopoion estin*), qualitative relative pronoun. Men today find, alas, that some of the fireproof buildings are not fireproof when the fire actually comes.

14. *If any man's work shall abide* (*ei tinos to ergon menei*). Condition of the first class with future indicative, determined as fulfilled, assumed as true. When the fire has done its work, what is left? That is the fiery test that the work of each of us must meet. Suitable reward (Matt. 20:8) will come for the work that stands this test (gold, silver, precious stones). 15. *Shall be burned* (*katakaēsetai*). First-class condition again, assumed as true. Second future (late form) passive indicative of *katakaiō*, to burn down, old verb. Note perfective use of preposition *kata*, shall be burned down. We usually say "burned up," and that is true also, burned up in smoke. *He shall suffer loss* (*zēmiōthēsetai*). First future passive indicative of *zēmiō*, old verb from *zēmia* (damage, loss), to suffer loss. In *Matt.* 16:26 = Mark 8:36 = Luke 9:25 the loss is stated to be the man's soul (*psuchēn*) or eternal life. But here there is no such total loss as that. The man's work (*ergon*) is burned up (sermons, lectures, books, teaching, all dry as dust). *But he himself shall be saved* (*autos de sōthēsetai*). Eternal salvation, but not by purgatory. His work is burned up completely and hopelessly, but he himself escapes destruction because he is really a saved man, a real believer in Christ. *Yet so as through fire* (*houtōs de hōs dia puros*). Clearly Paul means with his work burned down (verse 15). It is the tragedy of a fruitless life, of a minister who built so poorly on the true foundation that his work went up in smoke. His sermons were empty froth or windy words without edifying or building power. They left no mark in the lives of the hearers. It is the picture of a wasted life. The one who enters heaven by grace, as we all do who are saved, yet who brings no sheaves with him. There is no garnered grain the result of his labours in the harvest field. There are no souls in heaven as the result of his toil for Christ, no enrichment of character, no growth in grace.

16. *Ye are a temple of God* (*naos theou este*). Literally, a sanctuary (*naos*, not *hieron*, the sacred enclosure, but the holy place and the most holy place) of God. The same picture of building as in verse 9 (*oikodomē*), only here the sanctuary itself. *Dwelleth in you* (*en humin oikei*). The Spirit of God makes his home (*oikei*) in us, not in temples made with hands (Acts 7:48; 17:24).

17. *Destroyeth* (*phtheirei*). The outward temple is merely the symbol of God's presence, the Shechinah (the Glory). God makes his home in the hearts of his people or the church in any given place like Corinth. It is a terrible thing to tear down ruthlessly a church or temple of God like an earthquake that shatters a building in ruins. This old verb *phtheirō* means to corrupt, to deprave, to destroy. It is a gross sin to be a church-wrecker. There are actually a few preachers who leave behind them ruin like a tornado in their path. *Him shall God destroy* (*phtherei touton ho theos*). There is a solemn repetition of the same verb in the future active indicative. The condition is the first class and is assumed to be true. Then the punishment is certain and equally effective. The church-wrecker God will wreck. What does Paul mean by "will destroy"? Does he mean punishment here or hereafter? May it not be both? Certainly he does not mean annihilation of the man's soul, though it may well include eternal punishment. There is warning enough here to make every pastor pause before he tears a church to pieces in order to vindicate himself. *Holy* (*hagios*). Hence deserves reverential treatment. It is not the building or house of which Paul speaks as "the sanctuary of God" (*ton naon tou theou*), but the spiritual organization or organism of God's people in whom God dwells, "which temple ye are" (*hoitines este humeis*). The qualitative relative pronoun *hoitines* is plural to agree with *humeis* (*ye*) and refers to the holy temple just mentioned. The Corinthians themselves in their angry disputes had forgotten their holy heritage and calling, though this failing was no excuse for the ringleaders who had led them on. In 6:19 Paul reminds the Corinthians again that the body is the temple (*naos*, sanctuary) of the Holy Spirit, which fact they had forgotten in their immoralities.

18. *Let no man deceive himself* (*Mēdeis heauton exapatō*). A warning that implied that some of them were guilty of doing it (*mē* and the present imperative). Excited partisans can easily excite themselves to a pious phrenzy, hypnotize themselves with their own supposed devotion to truth. *Thinketh that he is wise* (*dokei sophos einai*). Condition of first class and assumed to be true. Predicate nominative *sophos* with the infinitive to agree with subject of *dokei*

(Robertson, *Grammar*, p. 1038). Paul claimed to be "wise" himself in verse 10 and he desires that the claimant to wisdom may become wise (*hina genētai sophos*, purpose clause with *hina* and subjunctive) by becoming a fool (*mōros genesthō*, second aorist middle imperative of *ginomai*) as this age looks at him. This false wisdom of the world (1:18-20, 23; 2:14), this self-conceit, has led to strife and wrangling. Cut it out.

19. *Foolishness with God* (*mōria para tōi theōi*). Whose standard does a church (temple) of God wish, that of this world or of God? The two standards are not the same. It is a pertinent inquiry with us all whose idea rules in our church. Paul quotes Job 5:13. *That taketh* (*ho drassomenos*). Old verb *drassomai*, to grasp with the hand, is used here for the less vivid word in the LXX *katalambanōn*. It occurs nowhere else in the N.T., but appears in the papyri to lay hands on. Job is quoted in the N.T. only here and in Rom. 11:35 and both times with variations from the LXX. This word occurs in Ecclesiasticus 26:7; 34:2. In Psa. 2:12 the LXX has *draxasthe paideias*, lay hold on instruction. *Craftiness* (*panourgiāi*). The *panourgos* man is ready for any or all work (if bad enough). So it means versatile cleverness (Robertson and Plummer), *astutia* (Vulgate).

20. *And again* (*kai palin*). Another confirmatory passage from Psa. 94:11. *Reasonings* (*dialogismous*). More than *cogitationes* (Vulgate), sometimes disputations (Phil. 2:14). Paul changes "men" of LXX to wise (*sophōn*) in harmony with the Hebrew context. *Vain* (*mataioi*). Useless, foolish, from *matē*, a futile attempt.

21. *Wherefore let no one glory in men* (*hōste mēdeis kauchasthō en anthrōpois*). The conclusion (*hōste*) from the self-conceit condemned. This particle here is merely inferential with no effect on the construction (*hōs* + *te* = and so) any more than *oun* would have, a paratactic conjunction. There are thirty such examples of *hōste* in the N.T., eleven with the imperative as here (Robertson, *Grammar*, p. 999). The spirit of glorying in party is a species of self-conceit and inconsistent with glorying in the Lord (1:31).

22. *Yours* (*humōn*). Predicate genitive, belong to you. All the words in this verse and 23 are anarthrous, though not indefinite, but definite. The English reproduces them

all properly without the definite article except *kosmos* (the world), and even here just world will answer. Proper names do not need the article to be definite nor do words for single objects like world, life, death. Things present (*enestōta*, second perfect participle of *enistēmi*) and things to come divide two classes. Few of the finer points of Greek syntax need more attention than the absence of the article. We must-not think of the article as "omitted" (Robertson, *Grammar*, p. 790). The wealth of the Christian includes all things, all leaders, past, present, future, Christ, and God. There is no room for partisan wrangling here.

CHAPTER IV

1. *Ministers of Christ* (*hupēretas Christou*). Paul and all ministers (*diakonous*) of the New Covenant (I Cor. 3:5) are under-rowers, subordinate rowers of Christ, only here in Paul's Epistles, though in the Gospels (Luke 4:20 the attendant in the synagogue) and the Acts (13:5) of John Mark. The *so* (*houtōs*) gathers up the preceding argument (3:5–23) and applies it directly by the *as* (*hōs*) that follows. *Stewards of the mysteries of God* (*oikonomous mustēriōn theou*). The steward or house manager (*oikos*, house, *nemō*, to manage, old word) was a slave (*doulos*) under his lord (*kurios*, Luke 12:42), but a master (Luke 16:1) over the other slaves in the house (menservants *paidas*, maidservants *paidiskas* Luke 12:45), an overseer (*epitropos*) over the rest (Matt. 20:8). Hence the under-rower (*hupēretēs*) of Christ has a position of great dignity as steward (*oikonomos*) of the mysteries of God. Jesus had expressly explained that the mysteries of the kingdom were open to the disciples (Matt. 13:11). They were entrusted with the knowledge of some of God's secrets, though the disciples were not such apt pupils as they claimed to be (Matt. 13:51; 16:8–12). As stewards Paul and other ministers are entrusted with the mysteries (see on I Cor. 2:7 for this word) of God and are expected to teach them. "The church is the *oikos* (I Tim. 3:15), God the *oikodespotēs* (Matt. 13:52), the members the *oikeioi* (Gal. 6:10; Eph. 2:19)" (Lightfoot). Paul had a vivid sense of the dignity of this stewardship (*oikonomia*) of God given to him (Col. 1:25; Eph. 1:10). The ministry is more than a mere profession or trade. It is a calling from God for stewardship.

2. *Here* (*hōde*). Either here on earth or in this matter. It is always local. *Moreover* (*loipon*). Like *loipon* in 1:16 which see, accusative of general reference, as for what is left, besides. *It is required* (*zēteitai*). It is sought. Many MSS. read *zēteite*, ye seek, an easy change as *ai* and *e* came to be pronounced alike (Robertson, *Grammar*, p. 186). *That a man be found faithful* (*hina pistos tis heurethēi*). Non-final use of *hina* with first aorist passive subjunctive of *heuriskō*,

the result of the seeking (*zēteō*). Fidelity is the essential requirement in all such human relationships, in other words, plain honesty in handling money like bank-clerks or in other positions of trust like public office. 3. *But with me* (*emoi de*). The ethical dative of personal relation and interest, "as I look at my own case." Cf. Phil. 1:21. *It is a very small thing* (*eis elachiston estin*). This predicate use of *eis* is like the Hebrew, but it occurs also in the papyri. The superlative *elachiston* is elative, very little, not the true superlative, least. "It counts for very little with me." *That I should be judged of you* (*hina huph' humōn anakrithō*). Same use of *hina* as in verse 2. For the verb (first aorist passive subjunctive of *anakrinō*) see on I Cor. 2:14f. Paul does not despise public opinion, but he denies "the competency of the tribunal" in Corinth (Robertson and Plummer) to pass on his credentials with Christ as his Lord. *Or of man's judgement* (*ē hupo anthrōpinēs hēmeras*). Or "by human day," in contrast to the Lord's Day (*der Tag*) in 3:13. "*That* is the tribunal which the Apostle recognizes; a *human* tribunal he does not care to satisfy" (Robertson and Plummer). *Yea, I judge not mine own self* (*all' oude emauton anakrinō*). *Alla* here is confirmatory, not adversative. "I have often wondered how it is that every man sets less value on his own opinion of himself than on the opinion of others" (M. Aurelius, xii. 4. Translated by Robertson and Plummer). Paul does not even set himself up as judge of himself.

4. *For I know nothing against myself* (*ouden gar emautōi sunoida*). Not a statement of fact, but an hypothesis to show the unreliability of mere complacent self-satisfaction. Note the use of *sunoida* (second perfect active indicative with dative (disadvantage) of the reflexive pronoun) for guilty knowledge against oneself (cf. Acts 5:2; 12:12; 14:6). *Yet* (*all'*). Adversative use of *alla*. *Am I not hereby justified* (*ouk en toutōi dedikaiōmai*). Perfect passive indicative of state of completion. Failure to be conscious of one's own sins does not mean that one is innocent. Most prisoners plead "not guilty." Who is the judge of the steward of the mysteries of God? It is the Lord "that judgeth me" (*ho anakrinōn me*). Probably, who examines me and then passes on my fidelity (*pistos* in verse 2).

5. *Wherefore* (*hōste*). As in 3:21 which see. *Judge nothing* (*mē ti krinete*). Stop passing judgment, stop criticizing as they were doing. See the words of Jesus in Matt. 7:1. The censorious habit was ruining the Corinthian Church. *Before the time* (*pro kairou*). The day of the Lord in 3:13. "Do not therefore anticipate the great judgment (*krisis*) by any preliminary investigation (*anakrisis*) which must be futile and incomplete" (Lightfoot). *Until the Lord come* (*heōs an elthēi ho kurios*). Common idiom of *heōs* and the aorist subjunctive with or without *an* for a future event. Simple futurity, but held forth as a glorious hope, the Second Coming of the Lord Jesus as Judge. *Who will both bring to light* (*hos kai phōtisei*). Future indicative of this late verb (in papyri also) from *phōs* (light), to turn the light on the hidden things of darkness. *And make manifest* (*kai phanerōsei*). (Ionic and late) causative verb *phaneroō* from *phaneros*. By turning on the light the counsels of all hearts stand revealed. *His praise* (*ho epainos*). The praise (note article) due him from God (Rom. 2:29) will come to each then (*tote*) and not till then. Meanwhile Paul will carry on and wait for the praise from God.

6. *I have in a figure transferred* (*meteschēmatisa*). First aorist active (not perfect) indicative of *meta-schēmatizō*, used by Plato and Aristotle for changing the form of a thing (from *meta*, after, and *schēma*, form or habit, like Latin *habitus* from *echō* and so different from *morphē* as in Phil. 2:7; Rom. 12:2). For the idea of refashioning see Field, *Notes*, p. 169f. and Preisigke, *Fachwörter*). Both Greek and Latin writers (Quintilian, Martial) used *schēma* for a rhetorical artifice. Paul's use of the word (in Paul only in N.T.) appears also further in II Cor. 11:13-15 where the word occurs three times, twice of the false apostles posing and passing as apostles of Christ and ministers of righteousness, and once of Satan as an angel of light, twice with *eis* and once with *hōs*. In Phil. 3:21 the word is used for the change in the body of our humiliation to the body of glory. But here it is clearly the rhetorical figure for a veiled allusion to Paul and Apollos "for your sakes" (*dia humas*). *That in us ye may learn* (*hina en hēmin mathēte*). Final clause with *hina* and the second aorist active subjunctive of *manthanō*, to learn. As an object lesson in our cases (*en hēmin*). It is no

more true of Paul and Apollos than of other ministers, but the wrangles in Corinth started about them. So Paul boldly puts himself and Apollos to the fore in the discussion of the principles involved. *Not to go beyond the things which are written (to Mē huper ha gegraptai).* It is difficult to reproduce the Greek idiom in English. The article *to* is in the accusative case as the object of the verb *mathēte* (learn) and points at the words "*Mē huper ha gegraptai,*" apparently a proverb or rule, and elliptical in form with no principal verb expressed with *mē,* whether "think" (Auth.) or "go" (Revised). There was a constant tendency to smooth out Paul's ellipses as in II Thess. 2:3; I Cor. 1:26, 31. Lightfoot thinks that Paul may have in mind O.T. passages quoted in I Cor. 1:19, 31; 3:19, 20. *That ye be not puffed up (hina mē phusiousthe).* Sub-final use of *hina* (second use in this sentence) with notion of result. It is not certain whether *phusiousthe* (late verb form like *phusiaō, phusaō,* to blow up, to inflate, to puff up), used only by Paul in the N.T., is present indicative with *hina* like *zēloute* in Gal. 4:17 (cf. *hina ginōskomen* in I John 5:20) or the present subjunctive by irregular contraction (Robertson, *Grammar,* pp. 203, 342f.), probably the present indicative. *Phusioō* is from *phusis* (nature) and so meant to make natural, but it is used by Paul just like *phusaō* or *phusiaō* (from *phusa,* a pair of bellows), a vivid picture of self-conceit. *One for the one against the other (heis huper tou henos kata tou heterou).* This is the precise idea of this idiom of partitive apposition. This is the rule with partisans. They are "for" (*huper*) the one and "against" (*kata,* down on, the genitive case) the other (*tou heterou,* not merely another or a second, but the different sort, *heterodox*).

7. *Maketh thee to differ (se diakrinei).* Distinguishes thee, separates thee. *Diakrinō* means to sift or separate between (*dia*) as in Acts 15:9 (which see) where *metaxu* is added to make it plainer. All self-conceit rests on the notion of superiority of gifts and graces as if they were self-bestowed or self-acquired. *Which thou didst not receive (ho ouk elabes).* "Another home-thrust" (Robertson and Plummer). Pride of intellect, of blood, of race, of country, of religion, is thus shut out. *Dost thou glory (kauchasai).* The original second person singular middle ending -*sai* is here preserved with

variable vowel contraction, *kauchaesai=kauchasai* (Robertson, *Grammar*, p. 341). Paul is fond of this old and bold verb for boasting. *As if thou hadst not received it (hōs mē labōn).* This neat participial clause (second aorist active of *lambanō*) with *hōs* (assumption) and negative *mē* punctures effectually the inflated bag of false pride. What pungent questions Paul has asked. Robertson and Plummer say of Augustine, "Ten years before the challenge of Pelagius, the study of St. Paul's writings, and especially of this verse and of Rom. 9:16, had crystallized in his mind the distinctively Augustinian doctrines of man's total depravity, of irresistible grace, and of absolute predestination." Human responsibility does exist beyond a doubt, but there is no foundation for pride and conceit.

8. *Already are ye filled? (ēdē kekoresmenoi este?).* Perfect passive indicative, state of completion, of *korennumi*, old Greek verb to satiate, to satisfy. The only other example in N.T. is Acts 27:38 which see. Paul may refer to Deut. 31:20; 32:15. But it is keen irony, even sarcasm. Westcott and Hort make it a question and the rest of the sentence also. *Already ye are become rich (ēdē eploutēsate).* Note change to ingressive aorist indicative of *plouteō*, old verb to be rich (cf. II Cor. 8:9). "The aorists, used instead of perfects, imply indecent haste" (Lightfoot). "They have got a private millennium of their own" (Robertson & Plummer) with all the blessings of the Messianic Kingdom (Luke 22:29f.; I Thess. 2:12; II Tim. 2:12). *Ye have reigned without us (chōris hēmōn ebasileusate).* Withering sarcasm. Ye became kings without our company. Some think that Paul as in 3:21 is purposely employing Stoic phraseology though with his own meanings. If so, it is hardly consciously done. Paul was certainly familiar with much of the literature of his time, but it did not shape his ideas. *I would that ye did reign (kai ophelon ge ebasileusate).* More exactly, "And would at least that ye had come to reign (or become kings)." It is an unfulfilled wish about the past expressed by *ophelon* and the aorist indicative instead of *ei gar* and the aorist indicative (the ancient idiom). See Robertson, *Grammar*, p. 1003, for the construction with particle *ophelon* (an unaugmented second aorist form). *That we also might reign with you (hina kai hēmeis humin sunbasileusōmen).* Ironical con-

trast to *chōris hēmōn ebasileusate,* just before. Associative instrumental case of *humin* after *sun-.*

9. *Hath set forth us the apostles last* (*hēmas tous apostolous eschatous apedeixen*). The first aorist active indicative of *apodeiknumi,* old verb to show, to expose to view or exhibit (Herodotus), in technical sense (cf. II Thess. 2:4) for gladiatorial show as in *ethēriomachēsa* (I Cor. 15:32). In this grand pageant Paul and other apostles come last (*eschatous,* predicate accusative after *apedeixen*) as a grand finale. *As men doomed to die* (*hōs epithanatious*). Late word, here alone in N.T. The LXX (Bel and the Dragon 31) has it for those thrown daily to the lions. Dionysius of Halicarnassus (*A.R.* vii. 35) uses it of those thrown from the Tarpeian Rock. The gladiators would say *morituri salutamus.* All this in violent contrast to the kingly Messianic pretensions of the Corinthians. *A spectacle* (*theatron*). Cf. Heb. 11:33–40. The word, like our theatre, means the place of the show (Acts 19:29, 31). Then, it means the spectacle shown there (*theama* or *thea*), and, as here, the man exhibited as the show like the verb *theatrizomenoi,* made a spectacle (Heb. 10:33). Sometimes it refers to the spectators (*theatai*) like our "house" for the audience. Here the spectators include "the world, both to angels and men" (*tōi kosmōi kai aggelois kai anthrōpois*), dative case of personal interest.

10. *We—you* (*hēmeis—humeis*). Triple contrast in keenest ironical emphasis. "The three antitheses refer respectively to teaching, demeanour, and worldly position" (Robertson and Plummer). The apostles were fools for Christ's sake (II Cor. 4:11; Phil. 3:7). They made "union with Christ the basis of worldly wisdom" (Vincent). There is change of order (chiasm) in the third ironical contrast. They are over strong in pretension. *Endoxos,* illustrious, is one of the 103 words found only in Luke and Paul in the N.T. Notion of display and splendour.

11. *Even unto this present hour* (*achri tēs arti hōras*). *Arti* (just now, this very minute) accents the continuity of the contrast as applied to Paul. Ten verbs and four participles from 11 to 13 give a graphic picture of Paul's condition in Ephesus when he is writing this epistle. *We hunger* (*peinōmen*), *we thirst* (*dipsōmen*), *are naked* (*gumniteuomen*), late verb for scant clothing from *gumnētēs, are buffeted* (*kolaphizometha*), to strike a blow with the fist from *kolaphos* and

one of the few N.T. and ecclesiastical words and see on Matt. 26:67, *have no certain dwelling place* (*astatoumen*) from *astatos*, strolling about and only here save Anthol. Pal. and Aquila in Isa. 58:7. Field in *Notes*, p. 170 renders I Cor. 4:11 "and are vagabonds" or spiritual hobos.

12. *We toil* (*kopiōmen*). Common late verb for weariness in toil (Luke 5:5), *working with our own hands* (*ergazomenoi tais idiais chersin*) instrumental case *chersin* and not simply for himself but also for Aquila and Priscilla as he explains in Acts 20:34. This personal touch gives colour to the outline. Paul alludes to this fact often (I Thess. 2:9; II Thess. 3:8; I Cor. 9:6; II Cor. 11:7). "Greeks despised manual labour; St. Paul glories in it" (Robertson and Plummer). Cf. Deissmann, *Light, etc.*, p. 317. *Being reviled we bless* (*loidoroumenoi eulogoumen*). Almost the language of Peter about Jesus (I Peter 2:23) in harmony with the words of Jesus in Matt. 5:44; Luke 6:27. *Being persecuted we endure* (*diōkomenoi anechometha*). We hold back and do not retaliate. Turn to Paul's other picture of his experiences in the vivid contrasts in II Cor. 4:7–10; 6:3–10 for an interpretation of his language here.

13. *Being defamed we intreat* (*dusphēmoumenoi parakaloumen*). The participle *dusphēmoumenoi* is an old verb (in I Macc. 7:41) to use ill, from *dusphēmos*, but occurs here only in the N.T. Paul is opening his very heart now after the keen irony above. *As the filth of the world* (*hōs perikatharmata tou kosmou*). Literally, sweepings, rinsings, cleansings around, dust from the floor, from *perikathairō*, to cleanse all around (Plato and Aristotle) and so the refuse thrown off in cleansing. Here only in the N.T. and only twice elsewhere. *Katharma* was the refuse of a sacrifice. In Prov. 21:18 *perikatharma* occurs for the scapegoat. The other example is Epictetus iii. 22, 78, in the same sense of an expiatory offering of a worthless fellow. It was the custom in Athens during a plague to throw to the sea some wretch in the hope of appeasing the gods. One hesitates to take it so here in Paul, though Findlay thinks that possibly in Ephesus Paul may have heard some such cry like that in the later martyrdoms *Christiani ad leones*. At any rate in I Cor. 15:32 Paul says "I fought with wild beasts" and in II Cor. 1:9 "I had the answer of death." Some terrible experience may be alluded to here. The word

shows the contempt of the Ephesian populace for Paul as is shown in Acts 19:23–41 under the influence of Demetrius and the craftsmen. *The offscouring of all things (pantōn peripsēma).* Late word, here only in N.T., though in Tob. 5:18. The word was used in a formula at Athens when victims were flung into the sea, *peripsēma hēmōn genou* (Became a *peripsēma* for us), in the sense of expiation. The word merely means scraping around from *peripsaō*, offscrapings or refuse. That is probably the idea here as in Tob. 5:18. It came to have a complimentary sense for the Christians who in a plague gave their lives for the sick. But it is a bold figure here with Paul of a piece with *perikatharmata.*

14. *To shame you (entrepōn).* Literally, shaming you (present active participle of *entrepō*), old verb to turn one on himself either middle or with reflexive pronoun and active, but the reflexive *heautois* is not expressed here. See on II Thess. 3:14. The harsh tone has suddenly changed.

15. *To admonish (nouthetōn).* Literally, admonishing (present active participle of *noutheteō*). See on I Thess. 5:12, 14. *For though ye should have (ean gar echēte).* Third-class condition undetermined, but with prospect of being determined (*ean* and present subjunctive), "for if ye have." *Tutors (paidagōgous).* This old word (*pais*, boy, *agōgos*, leader) was used for the guide or attendant of the child who took him to school as in Gal. 3:24 (Christ being the schoolmaster) and also as a sort of tutor who had a care for the child when not in school. The papyri examples (Moulton and Milligan, *Vocabulary*) illustrate both aspects of the paedagogue. Here it is the "tutor in Christ" who is the Teacher. These are the only two N.T. examples of the common word. *I begot you (humas egennēsa).* Paul is their *spiritual father* in Christ, while Apollos and the rest are their *tutors* in Christ.

16. *Be ye imitators of me (mimētai mou ginesthe).* "Keep on becoming (present middle imperative) imitators of me (objective genitive)." *Mimētēs* is an old word from *mimeomai*, to copy, to mimic (*mimos*). Paul stands for his rights as their spiritual father against the pretensions of the Judaizers who have turned them against him by the use of the names of Apollos and Cephas.

17. *Have I sent (epempsa).* First aorist active indicative.

Probably Timothy had already gone as seems clear from 16:10f. Apparently Timothy came back to Ephesus and was sent on to Macedonia before the uproar in Ephesus (Acts 19:22). Probably also Titus was then despatched to Corinth, also before the uproar. *In every church* (*en pasēi ekklēsiāi*). Paul expects his teachings and practices to be followed in every church (I Cor. 14:33). Note his language here "my ways those in Christ Jesus." Timothy as Paul's spokesman *will remind* (*anamnēsei*) the Corinthians of Paul's teachings.

18. *Some are puffed up* (*ephusiōthēsan*). First aorist (effective) passive indicative of *phusioō* which see on verse 6. *As though I were not coming to you* (*hōs mē erchomenou mou pros humas*). Genitive absolute with particle (assuming it as so) with *mē* as negative.

19. *If the Lord will* (*ean ho kurios thelēsēi*). Third-class condition. See James 4:15; Acts 18:21; I Cor. 16:7 for the use of this phrase. It should represent one's constant attitude, though not always to be spoken aloud. *But the power* (*alla tēn dunamin*). The puffed up Judaizers did a deal of talking in Paul's absence. He will come and will know their real strength. II Corinthians gives many evidences of Paul's sensitiveness to their talk about his inconsistencies and cowardice (in particular chs. 1, 2, 10, 11, 12, 13). He changed his plans to spare them, not from timidity. It will become plain later that Timothy failed on this mission and that Titus succeeded.

21. *With a rod* (*en rabdōi*). The so-called instrumental use of *en* like the Hebrew (I Sam. 17:43). The shepherd leaned on his rod, staff, walking stick. The paedagogue had his rod also. *Shall I come?* (*elthō;*). Deliberative subjunctive. Paul gives them the choice. They can have him as their spiritual father or as their paedagogue with a rod.

CHAPTER V

1. *Actually* (*holōs*). Literally, wholly, altogether, like Latin *omnino* and Greek *pantōs* (I Cor. 9:22). So papyri have it for "really" and also for "generally" or "everywhere" as is possible here. See also 6:7. With a negative it has the sense of "not at all" aş in 15:29; Matt. 5:34 the only N.T. examples, though a common word. *It is reported* (*akouetai*). Present passive indicative of *akouō*, to hear; so literally, it is heard. "Fornication is heard of among you." Probably the household of Chloe (1:11) brought this sad news (Ellicott). *And such* (*kai toiautē*). Climactic qualitative pronoun showing the revolting character of this particular case of illicit sexual intercourse. *Porneia* is sometimes used (Acts 15:20, 29) of such sin in general and not merely of the unmarried whereas *moicheia* is technically adultery on the part of the married (Mark 7:21). *As is not even among the Gentiles* (*hētis oude en tois ethnesin*). Height of scorn. The Corinthian Christians were actually trying to win pagans to Christ and living more loosely than the Corinthian heathen among whom the very word "Corinthianize" meant to live in sexual wantonness and license. See Cicero *pro Cluentio*, v. 14. *That one of you hath his father's wife* (*hōste gunaika tina tou patros echein*). "So as (usual force of *hōste*) for one to go on having (*echein*, present infinitive) a wife of the (his) father." It was probably a permanent union (concubine or mistress) of some kind without formal marriage like John 4:8. The woman probably was not the offender's mother (step-mother) and the father may have been dead or divorced. The Jewish law prescribed stoning for this crime (Lev. 18:8; 22:11; Deut. 22:30). But the rabbis (Rabbi Akibah) invented a subterfuge in the case of a proselyte to permit such a relation. Perhaps the Corinthians had also learned how to split hairs over moral matters in such an evil atmosphere and so to condone this crime in one of their own members. Expulsion Paul had urged in II Thess. 3:6 for such offenders.

2. *And ye are puffed up* (*kai humeis pephusiōmenoi este*). Emphatic position of *humeis* (you). It may be understood as a question. Perfect passive periphrastic indicative of the same verb *phusioō* used already of the partisans in Corinth (4:6, 19, 20). Those of the same faction with this scoundrel justified his rascality. *Did not rather mourn* (*kai ouchi mallon epenthēsate*). Possibly question also and note strong negative form *ouchi*, which favours it. The very least that they could have done (*mallon* rather than be puffed up) was to mourn for shame (*pentheō*, old verb for lamentation) as if for one dead. *That he might be taken away* (*hina arthēi*). The subfinal use of *hina* of desired result (1:15) so common in the *Koiné*. First aorist passive subjunctive of *airō*, to lift up, to carry off. Decent self-respect should have compelled the instant expulsion of the man instead of pride in his rascality.

3. *For I verily* (*egō men gar*). Emphatic statement of Paul's own attitude of indignation, *egō* in contrast with *humeis*. He justifies his demand for the expulsion of the man. *Being absent* (*apōn*). Although absent (concessive participle) and so of *parōn* though present. Each with locative case (*tōi sōmati, tōi pneumati*). *Have already judged* (*ēdē kekrika*). Perfect active indicative of *krinō*. I have already decided or judged, as though present (*hōs parōn*). Paul felt compelled to reach a conclusion about the case and in a sentence of much difficulty seems to conceive an imaginary church court where the culprit has been tried and condemned. There are various ways of punctuating the clauses in this sentence in verses 3 to 5. It is not merely Paul's individual judgment. The genitive absolute clause in verse 4, *ye being gathered together* (*sunachthentōn humōn*, first aorist passive participle of *sunagō*, in regular assembly) *and my spirit* (*kai tou emou pneumatos*) with the assembly (he means) and meeting *in the name of our Lord Jesus* (*en tōi onomati tou Kuriou* [*hēmōn*] *Iēsou*) *with the power of the Lord Jesus* (*sun tēi dunamei tou Kuriou hēmōn Iēsou*), though this clause can be taken with the infinitive to deliver (*paradounai*). It makes good syntax and sense taken either way. The chief difference is that, if taken with "gathered together" (*sunachthentōn*) Paul assumes less apostolic prerogative to himself. But he did have such power and used it against Elymas (Acts 13:8ff.) as Peter did against Ananias and Sapphira (Acts 5:1ff.).

5. *To deliver such an one unto Satan (paradounai ton toiouton tōi Satanāi).* We have the same idiom in I Tim. 1:20 used of Hymenius and Alexander. In II Cor. 12:7 Paul speaks of his own physical suffering as a messenger *(aggelos)* of Satan. Paul certainly means expulsion from the church (verse 2) and regarding him as outside of the commonwealth of Israel (Eph. 2:11f.). But we are not to infer that expulsion from the local church means the damnation of the offender. The wilful offenders have to be expelled and not regarded as enemies, but admonished as brothers (II Thess. 3:14f.). *For the destruction of the flesh (eis olethron tēs sarkos).* Both for physical suffering as in the case of Job (Job 2:6) and for conquest of the fleshly sins, remedial punishment. *That the spirit may be saved (hina to pneuma sōthēi).* The ultimate purpose of the expulsion as discipline. Note the use of *to pneuma* in contrast with *sarx* as the seat of personality (cf. 3:15). Paul's motive is not merely vindictive, but the reformation of the offender who is not named here nor in II Cor. 2:5–11 if the same man is meant, which is very doubtful. The final salvation of the man in the day of Christ is the goal and this is to be attained not by condoning his sin.

6. *Not good (ou kalon).* Not beautiful, not seemly, in view of this plague spot, this cancer on the church. They needed a surgical operation at once instead of boasting and pride (puffed up). *Kauchēma* is the thing gloried in. *A little leaven leaveneth the whole lump (mikra zumē holon to phurama zumoi).* This proverb occurs *verbatim* in Gal. 5:9. *Zumē* (leaven) is a late word from *zeō*, to boil, as is *zumoō*, to leaven. The contraction is regular *(-oei = oi)* for the third person singular present indicative. See the parables of Jesus for the pervasive power of leaven (Matt. 13:33). Some of the members may have argued that one such case did not affect the church as a whole, a specious excuse for negligence that Paul here answers. The emphasis is on the "little" *(mikra*, note position). *Lump (phurama* from *phuraō*, to mix, late word, in the papyri mixing a medical prescription) is a substance mixed with water and kneaded like dough. Compare the pervasive power of germs of disease in the body as they spread through the body.

7. *Purge out (ekkatharate).* First aorist (effective) active imperative of *ekkathairō*, old verb to cleanse out *(ek)*, to

clean completely. Aorist tense of urgency, do it now and do it effectively before the whole church is contaminated. This turn to the metaphor is from the command to purge out the old (*palaian*, now old and decayed) leaven before the passover feast (Ex. 12:15f.; 13:7; Zeph. 1:12). Cf. modern methods of disinfection after a contagious disease. *A new lump* (*neon phurama*). Make a fresh start as a new community with the contamination removed. *Neos* is the root for *neaniskos*, a young man, not yet old (*gēraios*). So new wine (*oinon neon* Matt. 9:17). *Kainos* is fresh as compared with the ancient (*palaios*). See the distinction in Col. 3:10; Eph. 4:22ff.; II Cor. 5:17. *Unleavened* (*azumoi*). Without (*a* privative) leaven, the normal and ideal state of Christians. Rare word among the ancients (once in Plato). They are a new creation (*kainē ktisis*), "exemplifying Kant's maxim that you should treat a man as if he were what you would wish him to be" (Robertson and Plummer). *For our passover also hath been sacrificed, even Christ* (*kai gar to pascha hēmōn etuthē Christos*). First aorist passive indicative of *thuō*, old verb to sacrifice. Euphony of consonants, *th* to *t* because of *-thē*. Reference to the death of Christ on the Cross as the Paschal Lamb (common use of *pascha* as Mark 14:12; Luke 22:7), the figure used long before by the Baptist of Jesus (John 1:29). Paul means that the Lamb was already slain on Calvary and yet you have not gotten rid of the leaven.

8. *Wherefore let us keep the feast* (*hōste heortazōmen*). Present active subjunctive (volitive). Let us keep on keeping the feast, a perpetual feast (Lightfoot), and keep the leaven out. It is quite possible that Paul was writing about the time of the Jewish passover, since it was before pentecost (I Cor. 16:8). But, if so, that is merely incidental, and his language here is not a plea for the observance of Easter by Christians. *With the leaven of malice and wickedness* (*en zumēi kakias kai ponērias*). Vicious disposition and evil deed. *With the unleavened bread of sincerity and truth* (*en azumois eilikrinias kai alētheias*). No word for "bread." The plural of *azumois* may suggest "elements" or "loaves." *Eilikrinia* (sincerity) does not occur in the ancient Greek and is rare in the later Greek. In the papyri it means probity in one example. The etymology is uncertain. Boisacq in-

clines to the notion of *heilē* or *helē*, sunlight, and *krinō*, to judge by the light of the sun, holding up to the light. *Alētheia* (truth) is a common word from *alēthēs* (true) and this from a privative and *lēthō* (*lathein*, *lanthanō*, to conceal or hide) and so unconcealed, not hidden. The Greek idea of truth is out in the open. Note Rom. 1:18 where Paul pictures those who are holding down the truth in unrighteousness.

9. *I wrote unto you in my epistle* (*egrapsa humin en tēi epistolēi*). Not the epistolary aorist, but a reference to an epistle to the Corinthians earlier than this one (our First Corinthians), one not preserved to us. What a "find" it would be if a bundle of papyri in Egypt should give it back to us? *To have no company with fornicators* (*mē sunanamignusthai pornois*). Present middle infinitive with *mē* in an indirect command of a late double compound verb used in the papyri to mix up with (*sun-ana-mignusthai*, a *mi* verb). It is in the N.T. only here and verse 11 and II Thess. 3:14 which see. It is used here with the associative instrumental case (*pornois*, from *peraō*, *pernēmi*, to sell, men and women who sell their bodies for lust). It is a pertinent question today how far modern views try to put a veneer over the vice in men and women.

10. *Not altogether* (*ou pantos*). Not absolutely, not in all circumstances. Paul thus puts a limitation on his prohibition and confines it to members of the church. He has no jurisdiction over the outsiders (this world, *tou kosmou toutou*). *The covetous* (*tois pleonektais*). Old word for the overreachers, those avaricious for more and more (*pleon*, *echō*, to have more). In N.T. only here, 6:10; Eph. 5:5. It always comes in bad company (the licentious and the idolaters) like the modern gangsters who form a combination of liquor, lewdness, lawlessness for money and power. *Extortioners* (*harpaxin*). An old adjective with only one gender, rapacious (Matt. 7:15; Luke 18:11), and as a substantive robber or extortioner (here and 6:10). Bandits, hijackers, grafters they would be called today. *Idolaters* (*eidōlolatrais*). Late word for hirelings (*latris*) of the idols (*eidōlon*), so our very word idolater. See 6:9; 10:7; Eph. 5:5; Rev. 21:8; 22:15. Nägeli regards this word as a Christian formation. *For then must ye needs* (*epei ōpheilete oun*). This neat Greek idiom of *epei* with the imperfect indicative (*ōpheilete*, from *opheilō*,

to be under obligation) is really the conclusion of a second-class condition with the condition unexpressed (Robertson, *Grammar*, p. 965). Sometimes *an* is used also as in Heb. 10:2, but with verbs of obligation or necessity *an* is usually absent as here (cf. Heb. 9:20). The unexpressed condition here would be, "if that were true" (including fornicators, the covetous, extortioners, idolaters of the outside world). *Ara* means in that case.

11. *But now I write unto you* (*nun de egrapsa humin*). This is the epistolary aorist referring to this same epistle and not to a previous one as in verse 9. As it is (when you read it) I did write unto you. *If any man that is named a brother be* (*ean tis adelphos onomazomenos ēi*). Condition of the third class, a supposable case. *Or a reviler or a drunkard* (*ē loidoros ē methusos*). *Loidoros* occurs in Euripides as an adjective and in later writings. In N.T. only here and 6:10. For the verb see I Cor. 4:12. *Methusos* is an old Greek word for women and even men (cf. *paroinos*, of men, I Tim. 3:3). In N.T. only here and 6:10. Cf. Rom. 13:13. Deissmann (*Light from the Ancient East*, p. 316) gives a list of virtues and vices on counters for Roman games that correspond remarkably with Paul's list of vices here and in 6:10. Chrysostom noted that people in his day complained of the bad company given by Paul for revilers and drunkards as being men with more "respectable" vices! *With such a one, no, not to eat* (*tōi toioutōi mēde sunesthiein*). Associative instrumental case of *toioutōi* after *sunesthiein*, "not even to eat with such a one." Social contacts with such "a brother" are forbidden.

12. *For what have I to do?* (*ti gar moi;*). "For what is it to me (dative) to judge those without (*tous exo*)?" They are outside the church and not within Paul's jurisdiction. God passes judgment on them.

13. *Put away the wicked man* (*exarate ton ponēron*). By this quotation from Deut. 17:7 Paul clinches the case for the expulsion of the offender (5:2). Note *ex* twice and effective aorist tense.

CHAPTER VI

1. *Dare any of you?* (*tolmāi tis humōn;*). Does any one of you dare? Rhetorical question with present indicative of *tolmaō*, old verb from *tolma*, daring. Bengel: *grandi verbo notatur laesa majestas Christianorum.* "The word is an argument in itself" (Robertson and Plummer). Apparently Paul has an actual case in mind as in chapter 5 though no name is called. *Having a matter against his neighbour* (*pragma echōn pros ton heteron*). Forensic sense of *pragma* (from *prassō*, to do, to exact, to extort as in Luke 3:13), a case, a suit (Demosthenes 1020, 26), with the other or the neighbour as in 10:24; 14:17; Gal. 6:4; Rom. 2:1. *Go to law* (*krinesthai*). Present middle or passive (ch. Rom. 3:4) in the same forensic sense as *krithēnai* in Matt. 5:40. *Kritēs*, judge, is from this verb. *Before the unrighteous* (*epi tōn adikōn*). This use of *epi* with the genitive for "in the presence of" is idiomatic as in II Cor. 7:14, *epi Titou*, in the case of Titus. The Jews held that to bring a lawsuit before a court of idolaters was blasphemy against the law. But the Greeks were fond of disputatious lawsuits with each other. Probably the Greek Christians brought cases before pagan judges.

2. *Shall judge the world* (*ton kosmon krinousin*). Future active indicative. At the last day with the Lord Jesus (Matt. 19:28; Luke 22:30). *Are ye unworthy to judge the smallest matters?* (*anaxioi este kritēriōn elachistōn;*). *Anaxios* is an old word (*an* and *axios*), though only here in the N.T. There is dispute as to the meaning of *kritēria* here and in verse 4, old word, but nowhere else in N.T. save in James 2:6. Naturally, like other words in -*tērion* (*akroatērion*, auditorium, Acts 25:23), this word means the place where judgment is rendered, or court. It is common in the papyri in the sense of tribunal. In the *Apost. Const.* ii. 45 we have *mē erchesthō epi kritērion ethnikon* (Let him not come before a heathen tribunal). Hence here it would mean, "Are ye unworthy of the smallest tribunals?" That is, of sitting on the smallest tribunals, of forming courts yourselves to settle such things?

3. *How much more, things that pertain to this life?* (*Mēti ge biōtika;*). The question expects the answer no and *ge* adds sharp point to Paul's surprised tone, "Need I so much as say?" It can be understood also as ellipsis, "let me not say" (*mētige legō*), not to say. *Biōtika* occurs first in Aristotle, but is common afterwards. In the papyri it is used of business matters. It is from *bios* (manner of life in contrast to *zōē*, life principle).

4. *If then ye have to judge things pertaining to this life* (*biōtika men oun kritēria ean echēte*). Note emphatic position (proleptic) of *biōtika kritēria* (tribunals pertaining to this life, as above). "If ye have tribunals pertaining to this life" (condition of third class, *ean echēte*). If *kathizete* (do ye set) is indicative and interrogative, then by "who are of no account in the church" (*tous exouthenēmenous en tēi ekklēsiāi*) Paul means the heathen as in verse 1. If *kathizete* be imperative, then Paul means the least esteemed members of the church for such unwished for work. It is a harsh term for the heathen, but one of indignation toward Christians.

5. *I say this to move you to shame* (*pros entropēn humin legō*). Old word *entropē* from *entrepō*, to turn in (I Cor. 4:14 which see). In N.T. only here and 15:34. *One wise man* (*sophos*). From sarcasm to pathos Paul turns. ·*Does there not exist* (*eni*, short form for *enesti*)? With double negative *ouk—oudeis*, expecting the answer yes. Surely one such man exists in the church. *Who* (*hos*). Almost consecutive in idea, of such wisdom that he will be able. *To decide between his brethren* (*diakrinai ana meson tou adelphou autou*). *Krinai* is to judge or decide (first aorist active infinitive of *krinō* and *dia* (two) carries on the idea of between. Then *ana meson* makes it still plainer, in the midst as *arbitrator* between brother and brother like *ana meson emou kai sou* (Gen. 23:15). It is even so a condensed expression with part of it unexpressed (*ana meson kai tou adelphou autou*) between brother and his brother. The use of *adelphos* has a sharp reflection on them for their going to heathen judges to settle disputes between brothers in Christ.

6. *And that before unbelievers* (*kai touto epi apistōn*). Climactic force of *kai*. The accusative of general reference with *touto*. "That there should be disputes about *biōtika* is bad; that Christian should go to law with Christian is worse;

that Christians should do this before unbelievers is worst of all" (Robertson and Plummer).

7. *Nay, already it is altogether a defect among you (ēdē men oun holōs hēttēma humin estin).* "Indeed therefore there is to you already (to begin with, *ēdē*, before any question of courts) wholly defeat." *Hēttēma* (from *hēttaomai*) is only here, Rom. 11:12 and Isa. 31:8 and ecclesiastical writers. See *hēttaomai* (from *hēttōn*, less) in II Cor. 12:13 and II Peter 2:19f. *Nikē* was victory and *hētta* defeat with the Greeks. It is defeat for Christians to have lawsuits (*krimata*, usually decrees or judgments) with one another. This was proof of the failure of love and forgiveness (Col. 3:13). *Take wrong (adikeisthe).* Present middle indicative, of old verb *adikeō* (from *adikos*, not right). Better undergo wrong yourself than suffer *defeat* in the matter of love and forgiveness of a brother. *Be defrauded (apostereisthe).* Permissive middle again like *adikeisthe.* Allow yourselves to be robbed (old verb to deprive, to rob) rather than have a lawsuit.

8. *Nay, but ye yourselves do wrong and defraud (alla humeis adikeite kai apostereite).* "But (adversative *alla*, on the contrary) you (emphatic) do the wronging and the robbing" (active voices) "and that your brethren" (*kai touto adelphous*). Same idiom as at close of verse 6. The very climax of wrong-doings, to stoop to do this with one's brethren in Christ.

9. *The unrighteous (adikoi).* To remind them of the verb *adikeō* just used. *The Kingdom of God (theou basileian).* Precisely, God's kingdom. *Be not deceived (mē planāsthe).* Present passive imperative with negative *mē*. Do not be led astray by plausible talk to cover up sin as mere animal behaviourism. Paul has two lists in verses 9 and 10, one with repetition of *oute*, neither (fornicators, idolaters, adulterers, effeminate, or *malakoi*, abusers of themselves with men or *arsenokoitai* or sodomites as in I Tim. 1:10 a late word for this horrid vice, thieves, covetous), the other with *ou* not (drunkards, revilers, extortioners). All these will fall short of the kingdom of God. This was plain talk to a city like Corinth. It is needed today. It is a solemn roll call of the damned even if some of their names are on the church roll in Corinth whether officers or ordinary members.

11. *And such were some of you (kai tauta tines ēte).* A

sharp homethrust. Literally, "And these things (*tauta*, neuter plural) were ye (some of you)." The horror is shown by *tauta*, but by *tines* Paul narrows the picture to some, not all. But that was in the past (*ēte*, imperfect indicative) like Rom. 6:17. Thank God the blood of Jesus does cleanse from such sins as these. But do not go back to them. *But ye were washed (apelousasthe)*. First aorist middle indicative, not passive, of *apolouō*. Either direct middle, ye washed yourselves, or indirect middle, as in Acts 22:16, ye washed your sins away (force of *apo*). This was their own voluntary act in baptism which was the outward expression of the previous act of God in cleansing (*hēgiasthēte*, ye were sanctified or cleansed before the baptism) and justified (*edikaiōthēte*, ye were put right with God before the act of baptism). "These twin conceptions of the Christian state in its beginning appear commonly in the reverse order" (Findlay). The outward expression is usually mentioned before the inward change which precedes it. In this passage the Trinity appear as in the baptismal command in Matt. 28:19.

12. *Lawful (exestin)*. Apparently this proverb may have been used by Paul in Corinth (repeated in 10:23), but not in the sense now used by Paul's opponents. The "all things" do not include such matters as those condemned in chapter 5 and 6:1–11. Paul limits the proverb to things not immoral, things not wrong *per se*. But even here liberty is not license. *But not all things are expedient (all'ou panta sumpherei)*. Old word *sumpherei*, bears together for good and so worthwhile. Many things, harmless in themselves in the abstract, do harm to others in the concrete. We live in a world of social relations that circumscribe personal rights and liberties. *But I will not be brought under the power of any (all ouk egō exousiasthēsomai hupo tinos)*. Perhaps a conscious play on the verb *exestin* for *exousiazō* is from *exousia* and that from *exestin*. Verb from Aristotle on, though not common (Dion. of Hal., LXX and inscriptions). In N.T. only here, 7:4; Luke 22:25. Paul is determined not to be a slave to anything harmless in itself. He will maintain his self-control. He gives a wholesome hint to those who talk so much about personal liberty.

13. *But God shall bring to nought both it and them (ho de*

theos kai tautēn kai tauta katargēsei). Another proverb about the adaptation of the belly (*koilia*) and food (*brōmata*, not just flesh), which had apparently been used by some in Corinth to justify sexual license (fornication and adultery). These Gentiles mixed up matters not alike at all (questions of food and sensuality). "We have traces of this gross moral confusion in the circumstances which dictated the Apostolic Letter (Acts 15:23–29), where things wholly diverse are combined, as directions about meats to be avoided and a prohibition of fornication" (Lightfoot). Both the belly (*tautēn*) and the foods (*tauta*) God will bring to an end by death and change. *But the body is not for fornication, but for the Lord, and the Lord for the body (to de sōma ou tēi porneiāi alla tōi kuriōi, kai ho kurios tōi sōmati).* Paul here boldly shows the fallacy in the parallel about appetite of the belly for food. The human body has a higher mission than the mere gratification of sensual appetite. Sex is of God for the propagation of the race, not for prostitution. Paul had already stated that God dwells in us as the sanctuary of the Holy Spirit (3:16f.). This higher function of the body he here puts forward against the debased Greek philosophy of the time which ignored completely Paul's idea, "the body for the Lord and the Lord for the body" (dative of personal interest in both cases). "The Lord Jesus and *porneia* contested for the bodies of Christian men; loyal to him they must renounce *that*, yielding to *that* they renounce him" (Findlay).

14. *Will raise up us (hēmas exegerei).* Future active indicative of *exegeirō* though the MSS. vary greatly, some having the present and some even the aorist. But the resurrection of the body gives added weight to Paul's argument about the dignity and destiny of the body (*quanta dignitas,* Bengel) which should not be prostituted to sensuality.

15. *Members of Christ (melē Christou).* Old word for limbs, members. Even the Stoics held the body to be common with the animals (Epictetus, *Diss.* l. iii. 1) and only the reason like the gods. Without doubt some forms of modern evolution have contributed to the licentious views of animalistic sex indulgence, though the best teachers of biology show that in the higher animals monogamy is the rule. The

body is not only adapted for Christ (verse 13), but it is a part of Christ, in vital union with him. Paul will make much use of this figure further on (12:12–31; Eph. 4:11–16; 5:30). *Shall I then take away?* (*aras oun;*). First aorist active participle of *airō*, old verb to snatch, carry off like Latin *rapio* (our rape). *Make* (*poiēsō*). Can be either future active indicative or first aorist active subjunctive (deliberative). Either makes good sense. The horror of deliberately taking "members of Christ" and making them "members of a harlot" in an actual union staggers Paul and should stagger us. *God forbid* (*mē genoito*). Optative second aorist in a negative wish for the future. *May it not happen!* The word "God" is not here. The idiom is common in Epictetus, though rare in the LXX. Paul has it thirteen times and Luke once (Luke 20:16).

16. *One body* (*hen sōma*). With the harlot. That union is for the harlot the same as with the wife. The words, quoted from Gen. 2:24 describing the sexual union of husband and wife, are also quoted and explained by Jesus in Matt. 19:5f. which see for discussion of the translation Hebraism with use of *eis*. *Saith he* (*phēsin*). Supply either *ho theos* (God) or *hē graphē* (the Scripture).

17. *One spirit* (*hen pneuma*). With the Lord, the inner vital spiritual union with the Lord Jesus (Eph. 4:4; 5:30).

18. *Flee* (*pheugete*). Present imperative. Have the habit of fleeing without delay or parley. Note abruptness of the asyndeton with no connectives. Fornication violates Christ's rights in our bodies (verses 13–17) and also ruins the body itself. *Without the body* (*ektos tou sōmatos*). Even gluttony and drunkenness and the use of dope are sins wrought on the body, not "within the body" (*entos tou sōmatos*) in the same sense as fornication. Perhaps the dominant idea of Paul is that fornication, as already shown, breaks the mystic bond between the body and Christ and hence the fornicator (*ho porneuōn*) *sins against his own body* (*eis to idion sōma hamartanei*) in a sense not true of other dreadful sins. The fornicator takes his body which belongs to Christ and unites it with a harlot. In fornication the body is the instrument of sin and becomes the subject of the damage wrought. In another sense fornication brings on one's own body the two most terrible bodily diseases that are still incurable (gonor-

rhea and syphilis) that curse one's own body and transmit
the curse to the third and fourth generation.   Apart from
the high view given here by Paul of the relation of the body
to the Lord no possible father or mother has the right to lay
the hand of such terrible diseases and disaster on their
children and children's children.   The moral and physical
rottenness wrought by immorality defy one's imagination.
   19. *Your body is a temple (to sōma humōn naos estin)*.   A
sanctuary as in 3:16 which see.   Our spirits dwell in our
bodies and the Holy Spirit dwells in our spirits.   Some of the
Gnostics split hairs between the sins of the body and fellowship with God in the spirit.   Paul will have none of this subterfuge.   One's body is the very shrine for the Holy Spirit.
In Corinth was the temple to Aphrodite in which fornication
was regarded as consecration instead of desecration.   Pros-
titutes were there as priestesses of Aphrodite, to help men
worship the goddess by fornication.   *Ye are not your own
(ouk este heautōn)*.   Predicate genitive.   Ye do not belong to
yourselves, even if you could commit fornication without
personal contamination or self-violation.   Christianity makes
unchastity dishonour in both sexes.   There is no double
standard of morality.   Paul's plea here is primarily to men
to be clean as members of Christ's body.
   20. *For ye were bought with a price (ēgorasthēte gar timēs)*.
First aorist passive indicative of *agorazō*, old verb to buy in
the marketplace *(agora)*.   With genitive of price.   Paul does
not here state the price as Peter does in I Peter 1:19 (the
blood of Christ) and as Jesus does in Matt. 20:28 (his life a
ransom).   The Corinthians understood his meaning.   *Glorify
God therefore in your body (doxasate dē ton theon en tōi sōmati
humōn)*.   Passionate conclusion to his powerful argument
against sexual uncleanness.   *Dē* is a shortened form of *ēdē*
and is an urgent inferential particle.   See on Luke 2:15.
Paul holds to his high ideal of the destiny of the body and
urges glorifying God in it.   Some of the later Christians felt
that Paul's words could be lightened a bit by adding "and
in your spirits which are his," but these words are found
only in late MSS. and are clearly not genuine.   Paul's argument stands four-square for the dignity of the body as the
sanctuary of the Holy Spirit united to the Lord Jesus.

CHAPTER VII

1. *Now concerning the things whereof ye wrote (peri de hōn egrapsate)*. An ellipsis of *peri toutōn*, the antecedent of *peri hōn*, is easily supplied as in papyri. The church had written Paul a letter in which a number of specific problems about marriage were raised. He answers them *seriatim*. The questions must be clearly before one in order intelligently to interpret Paul's replies. The first is whether a single life is wrong. Paul pointedly says that it is not wrong, but good (*kalon*). One will get a one-sided view of Paul's teaching on marriage unless he keeps a proper perspective. One of the marks of certain heretics will be forbidding to marry (I Tim. 4:3). Paul uses marriage as a metaphor of our relation to Christ (II Cor. 11:2; Rom. 7:4; Eph. 5:28–33). Paul is not here opposing marriage. He is only arguing that celibacy may be good in certain limitations. The genitive case with *haptesthai* (touch) is the usual construction.

2. *Because of fornications (dia tas porneias)*. This is not the only reason for marriage, but it is a true one. The main purpose of marriage is children. Mutual love is another. The family is the basis of all civilization. Paul does not give a low view of marriage, but is merely answering questions put to him about life in Corinth.

3. *Render the due (tēn opheilēn apodidotō)*. Marriage is not simply not wrong, but for many a duty. Both husband and wife have a mutual obligation to the other. "This dictum defends marital intercourse against rigorists, as that of ver. 1 commends celibacy against sensualists" (Findlay).

4. *The wife (hē gunē)*. The wife is mentioned first, but the equality of the sexes in marriage is clearly presented as the way to keep marriage undefiled (Heb. 13:4). "In wedlock separate ownership of the person ceases" (Robertson and Plummer).

5. *Except it be by consent for a season (ei mēti [an] ek sumphōnou pros kairon)*. If *an* is genuine, it can either be regarded as like *ean* though without a verb or as loosely

124

THE EPISTLES OF PAUL 125

added after *ei mēti* and construed with it. *That ye may give yourselves unto prayer* (*hina scholasēte tēi proseuchēi*). First aorist active subjunctive of *scholazō*, late verb from *scholē*, leisure (our "school"), and so to have leisure (punctiliar act and not permanent) for prayer. Note private devotions here. *That Satan tempt you not* (*hina mē peirazēi*). Present subjunctive, that Satan may not keep on tempting you. *Because of your incontinency* (*dia tēn akrasian* [*humōn*]). A late word from Aristotle on for *akrateia* from *akratēs* (without self-control, *a* privative and *krateō*, to control, common old word). In N.T. only here and Matt. 23:25 which see.

6. *By way of permission* (*kata sungnōmēn*). Old word for pardon, concession, indulgence. *Secundum indulgentiam* (Vulgate). Only here in N.T., though in the papyri for pardon. The word means "knowing together," understanding, agreement, and so concession. *Not of commandment* (*ou kat' epitagēn*). Late word (in papyri) from *epitassō*, old word to enjoin. Paul has not commanded people to marry. He has left it an open question.

7. *Yet I would* (*thelō de*). "But I wish." Followed by accusative and infinitive (*anthrōpous einai*). This is Paul's personal preference under present conditions (7:26). *Even as I myself* (*hōs kai emauton*). This clearly means that Paul was not then married and it is confirmed by 9:5. Whether he had been married and was now a widower turns on the interpretation of Acts 26:10 "I cast my vote." If this is taken literally (the obvious way to take it) as a member of the Sanhedrin, Paul was married at that time. There is no way to decide. *His own gift from God* (*idion charisma ek theou*). So each must decide for himself. See on 1:7 for *charisma*, a late word from *charizomai*.

8. *To the unmarried and to the widows* (*tois agamois kai tais chērais*). It is possible that by "the unmarried" (masculine plural) the apostle means only men since widows are added and since virgins receive special treatment later (verse 25) and in verse 32 *ho agamos* is the unmarried man. It is hardly likely that Paul means only widowers and widows and means to call himself a widower by *hōs kagō* (even as I). After discussing marital relations in verses 2 to 7 he returns to the original question in verse 1 and repeats his own personal preference as in verse 7. He does not say that it is

better to be unmarried, but only that it is *good* (*kalon* as in verse 1) for them to remain unmarried. *Agamos* is an old word and in N.T. occurs only in this passage. In verses 11 and 34 it is used of women where the old Greeks would have used *anandros*, without a husband. 9. *But if they have not continency* (*ei de ouk egkrateuontai*). Condition of the first class, assumed as true. Direct middle voice *egkrateuontai*, hold themselves in, control themselves. *Let them marry* (*gamēsatōsan*). First aorist (ingressive) active imperative. Usual *Koiné* form in *-tōsan* for third plural. *Better* (*kreitton*). Marriage is better than continued sexual passion. Paul has not said that celibacy is *better* than marriage though he has justified it and expressed his own personal preference for it. The metaphorical use of *purousthai* (present middle infinitive) for sexual passion is common enough as also for grief (II Cor. 11:29).

10. *To the married* (*tois gamēkosin*). Perfect active participle of *gameō*, old verb, to marry, and still married as the tense shows. *I give charge* (*paraggellō*). Not mere wish as in verses 7 and 8. *Not I, but the Lord* (*ouk egō alla ho kurios*). Paul had no commands from Jesus to the unmarried (men or women), but Jesus had spoken to the married (husbands and wives) as in Matt. 5:31f.; 19:3–12; Mark 10:9–12; Luke 16:18. The Master had spoken plain words about divorce. Paul reënforces his own inspired command by the command of Jesus. In Mark 10:9 we have from Christ: "What therefore God joined together let not man put asunder" (*mē chorizetō*). *That the wife depart not from her husband* (*gunaika apo andros mē choristhēnai*). First aorist passive infinitive (indirect command after *paraggellō*) of *chorizō*, old verb from adverbial preposition *chōris*, separately, apart from, from. Here used of divorce by the wife which, though unusual then, yet did happen as in the case of Salome (sister of Herod the Great) and of Herodias before she married Herod Antipas. Jesus also spoke of it (Mark 10:12). Now most of the divorces are obtained by women. This passive infinitive is almost reflexive in force according to a constant tendency in the *Koiné* (Robertson, *Grammar*, p. 817).

11. *But and if she depart* (*ean de kai choristhēi*). Third class condition, undetermined. If, in spite of Christ's clear prohibition, she get separated (ingressive passive subjunc-

tive), *let her remain unmarried (menetō agamos).* Paul here
makes no allowance for remarriage of the innocent party as
Jesus does by implication. *Or else be reconciled to her husband
(ē tōi andri katallagētō).* Second aorist (ingressive) passive
imperative of *katallassō*, old compound verb to exchange
coins as of equal value, to reconcile. One of Paul's great
words for reconciliation with God (II Cor. 5:18–20; Rom.
5:10). *Diallassō* (Matt. 5:24 which see) was more common
in the older Greek, but *katallassō* in the later. The difference
in idea is very slight, *dia-* accents notion of exchange, *kat-*
the perfective idea (complete reconciliation). Dative of
personal interest is the case of *andri.* This sentence is a
parenthesis between the two infinitives *chōristhēnai* and
aphienai (both indirect commands after *paraggellō*). *And that
the husband leave not his wife (kai andra mē aphienai).* This
is also part of the Lord's command (Mark 10:11). *Apoluō*
occurs in Mark of the husband's act and *aphienai* here, both
meaning to send away. Bengel actually stresses the difference between *chōristhēnai* of the woman as like *separatur* in
Latin and calls the wife "pars ignobilior" and the husband
"nobilior." I doubt if Paul would stand for that extreme.

12. *But to the rest say I, not the Lord (tois de loipois legō
egō, ouch ho Kurios).* Paul has no word about marriage
from Jesus beyond the problem of divorce. This is no disclaimer of inspiration. He simply means that here he is not
quoting a command of Jesus. *An unbelieving wife (gunaika
apiston).* This is a new problem, the result of work among
the Gentiles, that did not arise in the time of Jesus. The
form *apiston* is the same as the masculine because a compound adjective. Paul has to deal with mixed marriages as
missionaries do today in heathen lands. The rest *(hoi loipoi)*
for Gentiles (Eph. 2:3) we have already had in I Thess. 4:13;
5:6 which see. The Christian husband married his wife when
he himself was an unbeliever. The word *apistos* sometimes
means unfaithful (Luke 12:46), but not here (cf. John 20:27).
She is content (suneudokei). Late compound verb to be
pleased together with, agree together. In the papyri. *Let
him not leave her (mē aphietō autēn).* Perhaps here and in
verses 11 and 13 *aphiēmi* should be translated "put away"
like *apoluō* in Mark 10:1. Some understand *aphiēmi* as
separation from bed and board, not divorce.

13. *Which hath an unbelieving husband* (*hētis echei andra apiston*). Relative clause here, while a conditional one in verse 12 (*ei tis*, if any one). Paul is perfectly fair in stating both sides of the problem of mixed marriages.

14. *Is sanctified in the wife* (*hēgiastai en tēi gunaiki*). Perfect passive indicative of *hagiazō*, to set apart, to hallow, to sanctify. Paul does not, of course, mean that the unbelieving husband is saved by the faith of the believing wife, though Hodge actually so interprets him. Clearly he only means that the marriage relation is sanctified so that there is no need of a divorce. If either husband or wife is a believer and the other agrees to remain, the marriage is holy and need not be set aside. This is so simple that one wonders at the ability of men to get confused over Paul's language. *Else were your children unclean* (*epei ara ta tekna akatharta*). The common ellipse of the condition with *epei:* "since, accordingly, if it is otherwise, your children are illegitimate (*akatharta*)." If the relations of the parents be holy, the child's birth must be holy also (not illegitimate). "He is not assuming that the child of a Christian parent would be baptized; that would spoil rather than help his argument, for it would imply that the child was not *hagios* till it was baptized. The verse throws no light on the question of infant baptism" (Robertson and Plummer).

15. *Is not under bondage* (*ou dedoulōtai*). Perfect passive indicative of *douloō*, to enslave, has been enslaved, does not remain a slave. The believing husband or wife is not at liberty to separate, unless the disbeliever or pagan insists on it. Wilful desertion of the unbeliever sets the other free, a case not contemplated in Christ's words in Matt. 5:32; 19:9. Luther argued that the Christian partner, thus released, may marry again. But that is by no means clear, unless the unbeliever marries first. *But God hath called us in peace* (*en de eirēnēi keklēken hēmas* or *humas*). Perfect active indicative of *kaleō*, permanent call in the sphere or atmosphere of peace. He does not desire enslavement in the marriage relation between the believer and the unbeliever.

16. *For how knowest thou?* (*ti gar oidas;*). But what does Paul mean? Is he giving an argument *against* the believer accepting divorce or *in favour* of doing so? The syntax allows

either interpretation with *ei* (*if*) after *oidas*. Is the idea in *ei* (if) *hope* of saving the other or *fear* of not saving and hence peril in continuing the slavery of such a bondage? The latter idea probably suits the context best and is adopted by most commentators. And yet one hesitates to interpret Paul as *advocating* divorce unless strongly insisted on by the unbeliever. There is no problem at all unless the unbeliever makes it. If it is a hopeless case, acquiescence is the only wise solution. But surely the believer ought to be sure that there is no hope before he agrees to break the bond. Paul raises the problem of the wife first as in verse 10.

17. *Only* (*ei mē*). This use of *ei mē* as an elliptical condition is very common (7:5; Gal. 1:7, 19; Rom. 14:14), "except that" like *plēn*. Paul gives a general principle as a limitation to what he has just said in verse 15. "It states the general principle which determines these questions about marriage, and this is afterwards illustrated by the cases of circumcision and slavery" (Robertson and Plummer). He has said that there is to be no compulsory slavery between the believer and the disbeliever (the Christian and the pagan). But on the other hand there is to be no reckless abuse of this liberty, no license. *As the Lord hath distributed to each man* (*hekastōi hōs memeriken ho kurios*). Perfect active indicative of *merizō*, old verb from *meros*, apart. Each has his lot from the Lord Jesus, has his call from God. He is not to seek a rupture of the marriage relation if the believer does not ask for it. *And so ordain I* (*kai houtōs diatassomai*). Military term, old word, to arrange in all the churches (distributed, *dia-*). Paul is conscious of authoritative leadership as the apostle of Christ to the Gentiles.

18. *Let him not become uncircumcized* (*mē epispasthō*). Present middle imperative of *epispaō*, old verb to draw on. In LXX (I Macc. 1:15) and Josephus (*Ant.* XII, V. 1) in this sense. Here only in N.T. The point is that a Jew is to remain a Jew, a Gentile to be a Gentile. Both stand on an equality in the Christian churches. This freedom about circumcision illustrates the freedom about Gentile mixed marriages.

19. *But the keeping of the commandments of God* (*alla tērēsis entolōn theou*). Old word in sense of watching (Acts 4:3). Paul's view of the worthlessness of circumcision or of

uncircumcision is stated again in Gal. 5:6; 6:15; Rom. 2:25–29 (only the inward or spiritual Jew counts).

20. *Wherein he was called* (*hēi eklēthē*). When he was called by God and saved, whether a Jew or a Gentile, a slave or a freeman.

21. *Wast thou called being a bondservant?* (*doulos eklēthēs;*). First aorist passive indicative. Wast thou, a slave, called? *Care not for it* (*mē soi meletō*). "Let it not be a care to thee." Third person singular (impersonal) of *melei*, old verb with dative *soi*. It was usually a fixed condition and a slave could be a good servant of Christ (Col. 3:22; Eph. 6:5; Titus 2:9), even with heathen masters. *Use it rather* (*mallon chrēsai*). Make use of what? There is no "it" in the Greek. Shall we supply *eleutheriāi* (instrumental case after *chrēsai* or *douleiāi?*) Most naturally *eleutheriāi*, freedom, from *eleutheros*, just before. In that case *ei kai* is not taken as although, but *kai* goes with *dunasai*, "But if thou canst also become free, the rather use your opportunity for freedom." On the whole this is probably Paul's idea and is in full harmony with the general principle above about mixed marriages with the heathen. *Chrēsai* is second person singular aorist middle imperative of *chraomai*, to use, old and common verb.

22. *The Lord's freedman* (*apeleutheros Kuriou*). *Apeleutheros* is an old word for a manumitted slave, *eleutheros* from *erchomai*, to go and so go free, *ap-* from bondage. Christ is now the owner of the Christian and Paul rejoices to call himself Christ's slave (*doulos*). But Christ set us free from sin by paying the ransom (*lutron*) of his life on the Cross (Matt. 20:28; Rom. 8:2; Gal. 5:1). Christ is thus the *patronus* of the *libertus* who owes everything to his *patronus*. He is no longer the slave of sin (Rom. 6:6, 18), but a slave to God (Rom. 6:22). *Likewise the freeman when called is Christ's slave* (*homoiōs ho eleutheros klētheis doulos estin Christou*). Those who were not slaves, but freemen, when converted, are as much slaves of Christ as those who were and still were slaves of men. All were slaves of sin and have been set free from sin by Christ who now owns them all.

23. *Ye were bought with a price* (*timēs ēgorasthēte*). See on 6:20 for this very phrase, here repeated. Both classes (slaves and freemen) were purchased by the blood of Christ. *Become not bondservants of men* (*mē ginesthe douloi anthrōpōn*).

Present middle imperative of *ginomai* with negative *mē*. Literally, stop becoming slaves of men. Paul here clearly defines his opposition to human slavery as an institution which comes out so powerfully in the Epistle to Philemon. Those already free from human slavery should not become enslaved.

24. *With God (para theōi).* There is comfort in that. Even a slave can have God at his side by remaining at God's side.

25. *I have no commandment of the Lord (epitagēn Kuriou ouk echō).* A late word from *epitassō,* old Greek verb to enjoin, to give orders to. Paul did have (verse 10) a command from the Lord as we have in Matthew and Mark. It was quite possible for Paul to know this command of Jesus as he did other sayings of Jesus (Acts 20:35) even if he had as yet no access to a written gospel or had received no direct revelation on the subject from Jesus (I Cor. 11:23). Sayings of Jesus were passed on among the believers. But Paul had no specific word from Jesus on the subject of virgins. They call for special treatment, young unmarried women only Paul means (7:25, 28, 34, 36–38) and not as in Rev. 14:4 (metaphor). It is probable that in the letter (7:1) the Corinthians had asked about this problem. *But I give my judgment (gnōmēn de didōmi).* About mixed marriages (12–16) Paul had the command of Jesus concerning divorce to guide him. Here he has nothing from Jesus at all. So he gives no "command," but only "a judgment," a deliberately formed decision from knowledge (II Cor. 8:10), not a mere passing fancy. *As one that hath obtained mercy of the Lord to be faithful (hōs ēleēmenos hupo kuriou pistos einai).* Perfect passive participle of *eleeō,* old verb to receive mercy (*eleos*). *Pistos* is predicate nominative with infinitive *einai.* This language, so far from being a disclaimer of inspiration, is an express claim to help from the Lord in the forming of this duly considered judgment, which is in no sense a command, but an inspired opinion.

26. *I think therefore (nomizō oun).* Paul proceeds to express therefore the previously mentioned judgment (*gnōmēn*) and calls it his opinion, not because he is uncertain, but simply because it is not a command, but advice. *By reason of the present distress (dia tēn enestōsan anagkēn).* The participle *enestōsan* is second perfect active of *enistēmi* and

means "standing on" or "present" (cf. Gal. 1:4; Heb. 9:9). It occurs in II Thess. 2:2 of the advent of Christ as not "present." Whether Paul has in mind the hoped for second coming of Jesus in this verse we do not certainly know, though probably so. Jesus had spoken of those calamities which would precede his coming (Matt. 24:8ff.) though Paul had denied saying that the advent was right at hand (II Thess. 2:2). *Anagkē* is a strong word (old and common), either for external circumstances or inward sense of duty. It occurs elsewhere for the woes preceding the second coming (Luke 21:23) and also for Paul's persecutions (I Thess. 3:7; II Cor. 6:4; 12:10). Perhaps there is a mingling of both ideas here. *Namely*. This word is not in the Greek. The infinitive of indirect discourse (*huparchein*) after *nomizō* is repeated with recitative *hoti*, "That the being so is good for a man" (*hoti kalon anthrōpōi to houtōs einai*). The use of the article *to* with *einai* compels this translation. Probably Paul means for one (*anthrōpōi*, generic term for man or woman) to remain as he is whether married or unmarried. The copula *estin* is not expressed. He uses *kalon* (good) as in 7:1.

27. *Art thou bound to a wife?* (*dedesai gunaiki;*). Perfect passive indicative of *deō*, to bind, with dative case *gunaiki*. Marriage bond as in Rom. 7:2. *Seek not to be loosed* (*mē zētei lusin*). Present active imperative with negative *mē*, "Do not be seeking release" (*lusin*) from the marriage bond, old word, here only in N.T. *Seek not a wife* (*mē zētei gunaika*). Same construction, Do not be seeking a wife. Bachelors as well as widowers are included in *lelusai* (loosed, perfect passive indicative of *luō*). This advice of Paul he only urges "because of the present necessity" (verse 26). Whether he held on to this opinion later one does not know. Certainly he gives the noblest view of marriage in Eph. 5:22-33. Paul does not present it as his opinion for all men at all times. Men feel it their duty to seek a wife.

28. *But and if thou marry* (*ean de kai gamēseis*). Condition of the third class, undetermined with prospect of being determined, with the ingressive first aorist (late form) active subjunctive with *ean*: "But if thou also commit matrimony or get married," in spite of Paul's advice to the contrary. *Thou hast not sinned* (*ouch hēmartes*). Second aorist active indicative of *hamartanō*, to sin, to miss a mark.

Here either Paul uses the timeless (gnomic) aorist indicative or by a swift transition he changes the standpoint (proleptic) in the conclusion from the future (in the condition) to the past. Such mixed conditions are common (Robertson, *Grammar*, pp. 1020, 1023). Precisely the same construction occurs with the case of the virgin (*parthenos*) except that the old form of the first aorist subjunctive (*gēmēi*) occurs in place of the late *gamēsēi* above. The MSS. interchange both examples. There is no special point in the difference in the forms. *Shall have tribulation in the flesh* (*thlipsin tēi sarki hexousin*). Emphatic position of *thlipsin* (pressure). See II Cor. 12:7 *skolops tēi sarki* (thorn in the flesh). *And I would spare you* (*egō de humōn pheidomai*). Possibly conative present middle indicative, I am trying to spare you like *agei* in Rom. 2:4 and *dikaiousthe* in Gal. 5:4.

29. *But this I say* (*touto de phēmi*). Note *phēmi* here rather than *legō* (verses 8, 12). A new turn is here given to the argument about the present necessity. *The time is shortened* (*ho kairos sunestalmenos estin*). Perfect periphrastic passive indicative of *sustellō*, old verb to place together, to draw together. Only twice in the N.T., here and Acts 5:6 which see. Found in the papyri for curtailing expenses. Calvin takes it for the shortness of human life, but apparently Paul pictures the foreshortening of time (opportunity) because of the possible nearness of and hope for the second coming. But in Philippians Paul faces death as his fate (Phil. 1:21–26), though still looking for the coming of Christ (3:20). *That henceforth* (*to loipon hina*). Proleptic position of *to loipon* before *hina* and in the accusative of general reference and *hina* has the notion of result rather than purpose (Robertson, *Grammar*, p. 997). *As though they had none* (*hōs mē echontes*). This use of *hōs* with the participle for an assumed condition is regular and *mē* in the *Koinē* is the normal negative of the participle. So the idiom runs on through verse 31.

30. *As though they possessed not* (*hōs mē katechontes*). See this use of *katechō*, old verb to hold down (Luke 14:9), to keep fast, to possess, in II Cor. 6:10. Paul means that all earthly relations are to hang loosely about us in view of the second coming.

31. *Those that use the world* (*hoi chrōmenoi ton kosmon*). Old verb *chraomai*, usually with the instrumental case, but

the accusative occurs in some Cretan inscriptions and in late writers according to a tendency of verbs to resume the use of the original accusative (Robertson, *Grammar*, p. 468). *As not abusing it (hōs mē katachrēmenoi)*. Perfective use of *kata* in composition, old verb, but here only in N.T., to use up, use to the full. Papyri give examples of this sense. This is more likely the idea than "abusing" it. *For the fashion of this world passeth away (paragei gar to schēma tou kosmou toutou)*. Cf. I John 2:17. *Schēma* is the *habitus*, the outward appearance, old word, in N.T. only here and Phil. 2:7f. *Paragei* (old word) means "passes along" like a moving panorama (movie show!). Used of Jesus passing by in Jericho (Matt. 20:30).

32. *Free from cares (amerimnous)*. Old compound adjective (*a* privative and *merimna*, anxiety). In N.T. only here and Matt. 28:14 which see. *The things of the Lord (ta tou Kuriou)*. The ideal state (so as to the widow and the virgin in verse 33), but even the unmarried do let the cares of the world choke the word (Mark 4:19). *How he may please the Lord (pōs aresēi tōi Kuriōi)*. Deliberative subjunctive with *pōs* retained in an indirect question. Dative case of *Kuriōi*. Same construction in verse 33 with *pōs aresēi tēi gunaiki* (his wife) and in 34 *pōs aresēi tōi andri* (her husband).

34. *And there is a difference also between the wife and the virgin (kai memeristai kai hē gunē kai hē parthenos)*. But the text here is very uncertain, almost hopelessly so. Westcott and Hort put *kai memeristai* in verse 33 and begin a new sentence with *kai hē gunē* and add *hē agamos* after *hē gunē*, meaning "the widow and the virgin each is anxious for the things of the Lord" like the unmarried man (*ho agamos*, bachelor or widow) in verse 32. Possibly so, but the MSS. vary greatly at every point. At any rate Paul's point is that the married woman is more disposed to care for the things of the world. But, alas, how many unmarried women (virgins and widows) are after the things of the world today and lead a fast and giddy life.

35. *For your own profit (pros to humōn autōn sumphoron)*. Old adjective, advantageous, with neuter article here as substantive, from verb *sumpherō*. In N.T. here only and 10:33. Note reflexive plural form *humōn autōn*. *Not that I*

may cast a snare upon you (ouch hina brochon humin epibalō).
Brochon is a noose or slip-knot used for lassoing animals,
old word, only here in N.T. Papyri have an example "hanged
by a noose." *Epibalō* is second aorist active subjunctive of
epiballō, old verb to cast upon. Paul does not wish to capture
the Corinthians by lasso and compel them to do what they
do not wish about getting married. *For that which is seemly*
(pros to euschēmon). Old adjective *(eu,* well, *schēmōn,* shapely,
comely, from *schēma,* figure). For the purpose of decorum.
Attend upon the Lord (euparedron). Adjective construed
with *pros to,* before, late word (Hesychius) from *eu,* well,
and *paredros,* sitting beside, "for the good position beside
the Lord" (associative instrumental case of *Kurioi).* Cf.
Mary sitting at the feet of Jesus (Luke 10:39). *Without*
distraction (aperispastōs). Late adverb (Polybius, Plutarch,
LXX) from the adjective *aperispastos* (common in the papyri) from *a* privative and *perispaō,* to draw around (Luke
10:40).
36. *That he behaveth himself unseemly (aschēmonein).* Old
verb, here only in N.T., from *aschēmōn* (I Cor. 12:23), from
a privative and *schēma.* Occurs in the papyri. Infinitive in
indirect discourse after *nomizei* (thinks) with *ei* (condition
of first class, assumed as true). *If she be past the flower of her*
age (ean ēi huperakmos). Old word, only here in N.T., from
huper (over) and *akmē* (prime or bloom of life), past the
bloom of youth, *superadultus* (Vulgate). Compound adjective with feminine form like masculine. Apparently the
Corinthians had asked Paul about the duty of a father towards his daughter old enough to marry. *If need so requireth*
(kai houtōs opheilei ginesthai). "And it ought to happen."
Paul has discussed the problem of marriage for virgins on
the grounds of expediency. Now he faces the question where
the daughter wishes to marry and there is no serious objection to it. The father is advised to consent. Roman and
Greek fathers had the control of the marriage of their daughters. "My marriage is my father's care; it is not for me to
decide about that" (Hermione in Euripides' *Andromache,*
987). *Let them marry (gameitōsan).* Present active plural
imperative (long form).
37. *To keep his own virgin daughter (tērein tēn heautou*
parthenon). This means the case when the virgin daughter

does not wish to marry and the father agrees with her, *he shall do well* (*kalōs poiēsei*).

38. *Doeth well* (*kalōs poiei*). So Paul commends the father who gives his daughter in marriage (*gamizei*). This verb *gamizō* has not been found outside the N.T. See on Matt. 22:30. *Shall do better* (*kreisson poiēsei*). In view of the present distress (7:26) and the shortened time (7:29). And yet, when all is said, Paul leaves the whole problem of getting married an open question to be settled by each individual case.

39. *For so long time as her husband liveth* (*eph' hoson chronon zēi ho anēr autēs.*) While he lives (*tōi zōnti andri*) Paul says in Rom. 7:2. This is the ideal and is pertinent today when husbands meet their ex-wives and wives meet their ex-husbands. There is a screw loose somewhere. Paul here treats as a sort of addendum the remarriage of widows. He will discuss it again in I Tim. 5:9–13 and then he will advise younger widows to marry. Paul leaves her free here also to be married again, "only in the Lord" (*monon en Kuriōi*). Every marriage ought to be "in the Lord." *To be married* (*gamēthēnai*) is first aorist passive infinitive followed by the dative relative *hōi* with unexpressed antecedent *toutōi*.

40. *Happier* (*makariōterā*). Comparative of *makarios* used in the Beatitudes (Matt. 5:3ff.). *After my judgment* (*kata tēn emēn gnōmēn*). The same word used in verse 25, not a command. *I think* (*dokō*). From *dokeō*, not *nomizō* of verse 26. But he insists that he has "the spirit of God" (*pneuma theou*) in the expression of his inspired judgment on this difficult, complicated, tangled problem of marriage. But he has discharged his duty and leaves each one to decide for himself.

CHAPTER VIII

1. *Now concerning things sacrificed to idols* (*peri de tōn eidōlothutōn*). Plainly the Corinthians had asked also about this problem in their letter to Paul (7:1). This compound adjective (*eidōlon*, idol, *thutos*, verbal adjective from *thuō*, to sacrifice) is still found only in the N.T. and ecclesiastical writers, not so far in the papyri. We have seen this problem mentioned in the decision of the Jerusalem Conference (Acts 15:29; 21:25). The connection between idolatry and impurity was very close, especially in Corinth. See both topics connected in Rev. 2:14, 20. By *eidōlothuta* was meant the portion of the flesh left over after the heathen sacrifices. The heathen called it *hierothuton* (I Cor. 10:28). This leftover part "was either eaten sacrificially, or taken home for private meals, or sold in the markets" (Robertson and Plummer). What were Christians to do about eating such portions either buying in the market or eating in the home of another or at the feast to the idol? Three questions are thus involved and Paul discusses them all. There was evidently difference of opinion on the subject among the Corinthian Christians. Aspects of the matter come forward not touched on in the Jerusalem Conference to which Paul does not here allude, though he does treat it in Gal. 2:1-10. There was the more enlightened group who acted on the basis of their superior knowledge about the non-existence of the gods represented by the idols. *We know that we all have knowledge* (*oidamen hoti pantes gnōsin echomen*). This may be a quotation from the letter (Moffatt, *Lit. of N.T.*, p. 112). Since their conversion to Christ, they know the emptiness of idol-worship. Paul admits that all Christians have this knowledge (personal experience, *gnōsis*), but this problem cannot be solved by knowledge.

2. *Puffeth up* (*phusioi*). From *phusioō* (present indicative active). See on 4:6. Pride may be the result, not edification (*oikodomei*) which comes from love. Note article (*hē*) with both *gnōsis* and *agapē*, making the contrast sharper. See on I Thess. 5:11 for the verb *oikodomeō*, to build up. Love is the

solution, not knowledge, in all social problems. *That he knoweth anything* (*egnōkenai ti*). Perfect active infinitive in indirect discourse after *dokei* (condition of first class with *ei*). So "has acquired knowledge" (cf. 3:18), has gone to the bottom of the subject. *He knoweth not yet* (*oupō egnō*). Second aorist active indicative, timeless aorist, summary (punctiliar) statement of his ignorance. *As he ought to know* (*kathōs dei gnōnai*). Second aorist active infinitive, ingressive aorist (come to know). Newton's remark that he was only gathering pebbles on the shore of the ocean of truth is pertinent. The really learned man knows his ignorance of what lies beyond. Shallow knowledge is like the depth of the mud hole, not of the crystal spring.

3. *The same is known of him* (*houtos egnōstai hup' autou*). Loving God (condition of first class again) is the way to come to know God. It is not certain whether *houtos* refers to the man who loves God or to God who is loved. Both are true. God knows those that are his (II Tim. 2:19; Ex. 33:12). Those who know God are known of God (Gal. 4:9). We love God because he first loved us (I John 4:19). But here Paul uses both ideas and both verbs. *Egnōstai* is perfect passive indicative of *ginōskō*, an abiding state of recognition by (*hup'*) God. No one is acquainted with God who does not love him (I John 4:8). God sets the seal of his favour on the one who loves him. So much for the principle.

4. *No idol is anything in the world* (*ouden eidōlon en kosmōi*). Probably correct translation, though no copula is expressed. On *eidōlon* (from *eidos*), old word, see on Acts 7:41; 15:20; I Thess. 1:9. The idol was a mere picture or symbol of a god. If the god has no existence, the idol is a non-entity. This Gentile Christians had come to know as Jews and Jewish Christians already knew. *No God but one* (*oudeis theos ei mē heis*). This Christians held as firmly as Jews. The worship of Jesus as God's Son and the Holy Spirit does not recognize three Gods, but one God in three Persons. It was the worship of Mary the Mother of Jesus that gave Mahomet his cry: "Allah is One." The cosmos, the ordered universe, can only be ruled by one God (Rom. 1:20).

5. *For though there be* (*kai gar eiper eisi*). Literally, "For even if indeed there are" (a concessive clause, condition of first class, assumed to be true for argument's sake). *Called*

gods (*legomenoi theoi*). So-called gods, reputed gods. Paul denied really the existence of these so-called gods and held that those who worshipped idols (non-entities) in reality worshipped demons or evil spirits, agents of Satan (I Cor. 10:19–21).

6. *Yet to us there is one God, the Father* (*all' hēmin heis theos ho patēr*.) B omits *all'* here, but the sense calls for it anyhow in this apodosis, a strong antithesis to the protasis (*even if at least, kai eiper*). *Of whom* (*ex hou*). As the source (*ex*) of the universe (*ta panta* as in Rom. 11:36; Col. 1:16f.) and also our goal is God (*eis auton*) as in Rom. 11:36 where *di' autou* is added whereas here *di' hou* (through whom) and *di' autou* (through him) point to Jesus Christ as the intermediate agent in creation as in Col. 1:15–20; John 1:3f. Here Paul calls Jesus *Lord* (*Kurios*) and not *God* (*theos*), though he does apply that word to him in Rom. 9:5; Tit. 2:13; Col. 2:9; Acts 20:28.

7. *Howbeit in all men there is not that knowledge* (*all' ouk en pasin hē gnōsis*). The knowledge (*hē gnōsis*) of which Paul is speaking. Knowledge has to overcome inheritance and environment, prejudice, fear, and many other hindrances. *Being used until now to the idol* (*tēi sunētheiāi heōs arti tou eidōlou*). Old word *sunētheia* from *sunēthēs* (*sun, ēthos*), accustomed to, like Latin *consuetudo*, intimacy. In N.T. only here and John 18:39; I Cor. 11:16. It is the force of habit that still grips them when they eat such meat. They eat it "as an idol sacrifice" (*hōs eidōlothuton*), though they no longer believe in idols. The idol-taint clings in their minds to this meat. *Being weak* (*asthenēs ousa*). "It is defiled, not by the partaking of polluted food, for food cannot pollute (Mark 7:18f.; Luke 11:41), but by the doing of something which the unenlightened conscience does not allow" (Robertson and Plummer). For this great word *suneidēsis* (conscientia, knowing together, conscience) see on Acts 23:1. It is important in Paul's Epistles, Peter's First Epistle, and Hebrews. Even if unenlightened, one must act according to his conscience, a sensitive gauge to one's spiritual condition. Knowledge breaks down as a guide with the weak or unenlightened conscience. For *asthenēs*, weak (lack of strength) see on Matt. 26:41. *Defiled* (*molunetai*). Old word *molunō*, to stain, pollute, rare in N.T. (I Tim. 3:9; Rev. 3:4).

8. *Will not commend (ou parastēsei)*. Future active indicative of *paristēmi*, old word to present as in Acts 1:3; Luke 2:22; Col. 1:28. Food (*brōma*) will not give us an entrée to God for commendation or condemnation, whether meat-eaters or vegetarians. *Are we the worse (husteroumetha)*. Are we left behind, do we fall short. Both conditions are of the third class (*ean mē, ean*) undetermined. *Are we the better (perisseuometha)*. Do we overflow, do we have excess of credit. Paul here disposes of the pride of knowledge (the enlightened ones) and the pride of prejudice (the unenlightened). Each was disposed to look down upon the other, the one in scorn of the other's ignorance, the other in horror of the other's heresy and daring.

9. *Take heed (blepete)*. A warning to the enlightened. *Lest by any means (mē pōs)*. Common construction after verbs of caution or fearing, *mē pōs* with aorist subjunctive *genētai*. *This liberty of yours (hē exousia humōn hautē)*. Exousia, from *exestin*, means a grant, allowance, authority, power, privilege, right, liberty. It shades off easily. It becomes a battle cry, personal liberty does, to those who wish to indulge their own whims and appetites regardless of the effect upon others. *A stumbling-block to the weak (proskomma tois asthenesin)*. Late word from *proskoptō*, to cut against, to stumble against. So an obstacle for the foot to strike. In Rom. 14:13 Paul uses *skandalon* as parallel with *proskomma*. We do not live alone. This principle applies to all social relations in matters of law, of health, of morals. *Noblesse oblige*. The enlightened must consider the welfare of the unenlightened, else he does not have love.

10. *If a man see thee which hast knowledge sitting at meat in an idol's temple (ean gar tis idēi [se] ton echonta gnōsin en eidōleiōi katakeimenon)*. Condition of third class, a possible case. Paul draws the picture of the enlightened brother exercising his "liberty" by eating in the idol's temple. Later he will discuss the peril to the man's own soul in this phase of the matter (10:14-22), but here he considers only the effect of such conduct on the unenlightened or weak brother. This bravado at a sacrificial banquet is in itself idolatrous as Paul will show. But our weak brother will be emboldened (*oikodomēthēsetai*, future passive indicative, will be built up) to go on and do what he still believes to be wrong, to eat

things sacrificed to idols (*eis to ta eidōlothuta esthiein*). Alas, how often that has happened. Defiance is flung in the face of the unenlightened brother instead of loving consideration.
11. *Through thy knowledge* (*en tēi sēi gnōsei*). Literally, in thy knowledge. Surely a poor use to put one's superior knowledge. *Perisheth* (*apollutai*). Present middle indicative of the common verb *apollumi*, to destroy. Ruin follows in the wake of such daredevil knowledge. *For whose sake Christ died* (*di' hon Christos apethanen*). Just as much as for the enlightened brother with his selfish pride. The accusative (*hon*) with *di'* gives the reason, not the agent as with the genitive in 8:6 (*di' hou*). The appeal to the death (*apethanen*, second aorist active indicative of *apothnēskō*) of Christ is the central fact that clinches Paul's argument.
12. *Wounding their conscience* (*tuptontes autōn tēn suneidēsin*). Old verb *tuptō*, to smite with fist, staff, whip. The conscience is sensitive to a blow like that, a slap in the face. *Ye sin against Christ* (*eis Christon hamartanete*). That fact they were overlooking. Jesus had said to Saul that he was persecuting him when he persecuted his disciples (Acts 9:5). One may wonder if Paul knew the words of Jesus in Matt. 25:40, "ye did it unto me."
13. *Meat* (*brōma*). Food it should be, not flesh (*krea*). *Maketh my brother to stumble* (*skandalizei ton adelphon mou*). Late verb (LXX and N.T.) to set a trap-stick (Matt. 5:29) or stumbling-block like *proskomma* in verse 9 (cf. Rom. 14: 13, 21). Small boys sometimes set snares for other boys, not merely for animals to see them caught. *I will eat no flesh for evermore* (*ou mē phagō krea eis ton aiōna*). The strong double negative *ou mē* with the second aorist sub-junctive. Here Paul has *flesh* (*krea*) with direct reference to the flesh offered to idols. Old word, but in N.T. only here and Rom. 14:21. This is Paul's principle of love (verse 2) applied to the matter of eating meats offered to idols. Paul had rather be a vegetarian than to lead his weak brother to do what he considered sin. There are many questions of casuistry today that can only be handled wisely by Paul's ideal of love.

CHAPTER IX

1. *Am I not free?* (*Ouk eimi eleutheros;*). Free as a Christian from Mosaic ceremonialism (cf. 9:19) as much as any Christian and yet he adapts his moral independence to the principle of considerate love in 8:13. *Am I not an apostle?* (*ouk eimi apostolos;*). He has the exceptional privileges as an apostle to support from the churches and yet he foregoes these. *Have I not seen Jesus our Lord?* (*ouchi Iēsoun ton Kurion hēmōn heoraka;*). Proof (15:8; Acts 9:17, 27; 18:9; 22:14, 17f.; II Cor. 12:1ff.) that he has the qualification of an apostle (Acts 1:22) though not one of the twelve. Note strong form of the negative *ouchi* here. All these questions expect an affirmative answer. The perfect active *heoraka* from *horaō*, to see, does not here have double reduplication as in John 1:18. *Are not ye?* (*ou humeis este;*). They were themselves proof of his apostleship.

2. *Yet at least I am to you* (*alla ge humin eimi*). An argumentum ad hominem and a pointed appeal for their support. Note use of *alla ge* in the apodosis (cf. 8:6).

3. *My defence* (*hē emē apologia*). Original sense, not idea of apologizing as we say. See on Acts 22:1; 25:16. Refers to what precedes and to what follows as illustration of 8:13. *To them that examine me* (*tois eme anakrinousin*). See on I Cor. 2:15; 4:3. The critics in Corinth were "investigating" Paul with sharp eyes to find faults. How often the pastor is under the critic's spy-glass.

4. *Have we no right?* (*Mē ouk echomen exousian;*). Literary plural here though singular in 1–3. The *mē* in this double negative expects the answer "No" while *ouk* goes with the verb *echomen*. "Do we fail to have the right?" Cf. Rom. 10:18f. (Robertson, *Grammar*, p. 1173).

5. *Have we no right?* (*Mē ouk echomen exousian;*). Same idiom. *To lead about a wife that is a believer?* (*adelphēn gunaika periagein;*). Old verb *periagō*, intransitive in Acts 13:11. Two substantives in apposition, a sister a wife, a common Greek idiom. This is a plea for the support of the preacher's

wife and children. Plainly Paul has no wife at this time.
And Cephas (kai Kēphās). Why is he singled out by name?
Perhaps because of his prominence and because of the use
of his name in the divisions in Corinth (1:12). It was well
known that Peter was married (Matt. 8:14). Paul mentions
James by name in Gal. 1:19 as one of the Lord's brothers.
All the other apostles were either married or had the right
to be.

6. *Have we not a right to forbear working? (ouk echomen
exousian mē ergazesthai;)*. By *ē* (or) Paul puts the other side
about Barnabas (the only allusion since the dispute in Acts
15:39, but in good spirit) and himself. Perhaps (Hofmann)
Paul has in mind the fact that in the first great mission tour
(Acts 13 and 14), Barnabas and Paul received no help from
the church in Antioch, but were left to work their way along
at their own charges. It was not till the Philippian Church
took hold that Paul had financial aid (Phil. 4:15). Here
both negatives have their full force. Literally, Do we not
have (*ouk echomen*, expecting the affirmative reply) the
right not (*mē*, negative of the infinitive *ergazesthai*) to do
manual labour (usual meaning of *ergazomai* as in 4:12)?"
There was no more compulsion on Paul and Barnabas to
support themselves than upon the other workers for Christ.
They renounced no rights in being voluntarily independent.

7. *What soldier ever serveth? (tis strateuetai pote;)*. "Who
ever serves as a soldier?" serves in an army (*stratos*). Present
middle of old verb *strateuō*. *At his own charges (idiois op-
sōniois)*. This late word *opsōnion* (from *opson*, cooked meat
or relish with bread, and *ōneomai*, to buy) found in Menander,
Polybius, and very common in papyri and inscriptions in
the sense of rations or food, then for the soldiers' wages
(often provisions) or the pay of any workman. So of the
wages of sin (Rom. 6:23). Paul uses *labōn opsōnion* (receiving wages, the regular idiom) in II Cor. 11:8. See Moulton
and Milligan, *Vocabulary*; Deissmann, *Bible Studies*, pp. 148,
266; *Light from the Ancient East*, p. 168. To give proof of his
right to receive pay for preaching Paul uses the illustrations
of the soldier (verse 7), the husbandman (verse 7), the
shepherd (verse 7), the ox treading out the grain (8), the
ploughman (verse 10), the priests in the temple (13), proof
enough in all conscience, and yet not enough for some

churches who even today starve their pastors in the name of piety. *Who planteth a vineyard?* (*tis phuteuei ampelōna;*). *Ampelōn* no earlier than Diodorus, but in LXX and in papyri. Place of vines (*ampelos*), meaning of ending *-ōn*. *Who feedeth a flock?* (*tis poimainei poimnēn;*). Cognate accusative, both old words. Paul likens the pastor to a soldier, vinedresser, shepherd. He contends with the world, he plants churches, he exercises a shepherd's care over them (Vincent).

8. *Do I speak these things after the manner of men?* (*Mē kata anthrōpon tauta lalō;*). Negative answer expected. Paul uses *kata anthrōpon* six times (I Cor. 3:3; 9:8; 15:32; Gal. 1:11; 3:15; Rom. 3:5). The illustrations from human life are pertinent, but he has some of a higher order, from Scripture. *The law also* (*kai ho nomos*). Perhaps objection was made that the Scripture does not support the practice of paying preachers. That objection is still made by the stingy.

9. *Thou shalt not muzzle the ox when he treadeth out the corn* (*ou phimōseis boun aloōnta*). Quotation from Deut. 25:4. Prohibition by *ou* and the volitive future indicative. *Phimoō*, to muzzle (from *phimos*, a muzzle for dogs and oxen), appears first in Aristophanes (*Clouds*, 592) and not again till LXX and N.T., though in the papyri also. Evidently a vernacular word, perhaps a slang word. See metaphorical use in Matt. 22:12, 34. *Aloōnta* is present active participle of the old verb *aloaō*, occurs in the N.T. only here (and verse 10) and I Tim. 5:18 where it is also quoted. It is probably derived from *halos* or *halon*, a threshing-floor, or the disc of a shield or of the sun and moon. The Egyptians according to the monuments, used oxen to thresh out the grain, sometimes donkeys, by pulling a drag over the grain. The same process may be found today in Andalusia, Italy, Palestine. A hieroglyphic inscription at Eileithyas reads:

"Thresh ye yourselves, O oxen,
Measures of grain for yourselves,
Measures of grain for your masters."

Note *mē melei* expects the negative answer, impersonal verb with dative and genitive cases (*theōi*, God, *boōn*, oxen). *Altogether* (*pantōs*). But here probably with the notion of doubtless or assuredly. The editors differ in the verse divisions here. The Canterbury Version puts both these questions in verse 10, the American Standard the first in verse 9, the second in verse 10.

10. *He that plougheth (ho arotriōn).* Late verb *arotriaō*, to plough, for the old *aroō* from *arotron* (plough), in LXX and rare in papyri. *In hope of partaking (ep' elpidi tou metechein).* The infinitive *aloāin* is not repeated nor is *opheilei* though it is understood, "He that thresheth ought to thresh in hope of partaking." He that ploughs hardly refers to the ox at the plough as he that threshes does. The point is that all the workers (beast or man) share in the fruit of the toil.

11. *Is it a great matter? (mega;).* The copula *estin* has to be supplied. Note two conditions of first class with *ei*, both assumed to be true. On *pneumatika* and *sarkika* see on 2:14–3:3. This point comes out sharply also in Gal. 6:6.

12. *Over you (humōn).* Objective genitive after *exousian.* *Do not we yet more? (ou mallon hēmeis;).* Because of Paul's peculiar relation to that church as founder and apostle. *But we bear all things (alla panta stegomen).* Old verb to cover (*stegē*, roof) and so to cover up, to conceal, to endure (I Cor. 13:7 of love). Paul deliberately declined to use (usual instrumental case with *chraomai*) his right to pay in Corinth. *That we may cause no hindrance (hina mē tina enkopēn dōmen).* Late word *enkopē*, a cutting in (cf. *radio* or telephone) or hindrance from *enkoptō*, to cut in, rare word (like *ekkopē*) here only in N.T. and once in Vettius Valens. How considerate Paul is to avoid "a hindrance to the gospel of Christ" (*tōi euaggeliōi tou Christou*, dative case and genitive) rather than insist on his personal rights and liberties, an eloquent example for all modern men.

13. *Sacred things (ta hiera).* *Of the temple (tou hierou).* Play on the same word *hierou* (sacred). See Numb. 18:8–20 for the details. This is a very pertinent illustration. *They which wait upon the altar (hoi tōi thusiastēriōi paredreuontes).* Old word *paredreuō*, to sit beside, from *par—edros*, like Latin *assidere*, and so constant attendance. Only here in the N.T. Locative case *thusiastēriōi*, late word found so far only in LXX, Philo, Josephus, N.T., and ecclesiastical writers. See on Matt. 5:23.

14. *Even so did the Lord ordain (houtōs kai ho Kurios dietaxen).* Just as God gave orders about the priests in the temple, so did the Lord Jesus give orders for those who

preach the gospel to live out of the gospel (*ek tou euaggeliou zēin*). Evidently Paul was familiar with the words of Jesus in Matt. 10:10; Luke 10:7f. either in oral or written form. He has made his argument for the minister's salary complete for all time.

15. *For it were good for me to die, than that any man should make my glorying void* (*kalon gar moi mallon apothanein ē to kauchēma mou oudeis kenōsei*). The tangled syntax of this sentence reflects the intensity of Paul's feeling on the subject. He repeats his refusal to use his privileges and rights to a salary by use of the present perfect middle indicative (*kechrēmai*). By the epistolary aorist (*egrapsa*) he explains that he is not now hinting for a change on their part towards him in the matter, "in my case" (*en emoi*). Then he gives his reason in vigorous language without a copula (*ēn*, were): "For good for me to die rather than," but here he changes the construction by a violent anacoluthon. Instead of another infinitive (*kenōsai*) after *ē* (than) he changes to the future indicative without *hoti* or *hina*, "No one shall make my glorying void," viz., his independence of help from them. *Kenoō* is an old verb, from *kenos*, empty, only in Paul in N.T. See on I Cor. 1:17.

16. *For if I preach* (*ean gar euaggelizōmai*). Third class condition, supposable case. Same construction in verse 16 (*ean mē*). *For necessity is laid upon me* (*anagkē gar moi epikeitai*). Old verb, lies upon me (dative case *moi*). Jesus had called him (Acts 9:6, 15; Gal. 1:15f.; Rom. 1:14). He could do no other and deserves no credit for doing it. *Woe is me* (*ouai gar moi*). Explaining the *anagkē* (necessity). Paul had to heed the call of Christ that he had heard. He had a real call to the ministry. Would that this were the case with every modern preacher.

17. *Of mine own will* (*hekōn*)—*not of mine own will* (*akōn*). Both common adjectives, but only here in N.T. save *hekōn*, also in Rom. 8:20. The argument is not wholly clear. Paul's call was so clear that he certainly did his work *willingly* and so had a reward (see on Matt. 6:1 for *misthos*); but the only *reward* that he had for his willing work (Marcus Dods) was to make the gospel *free of expense* (*adapanon*, verse 18, rare word, here only in N.T., once in inscription at Priene). This was his *misthos*. It was glorying (*kauchēma*, to be able

THE EPISTLES OF PAUL 147

to say so as in Acts 20:33f.). *I have a stewardship intrusted to me (oikonomian pepisteumai)*. Perfect passive indicative with the accusative retained. I have been intrusted with a stewardship and so would go on with my task like any *oikonomos* (steward) even if *akōn* (unwilling).

18. *So as not to use to the full (eis to mē katachrēsasthai)*. *Eis to* for purpose with articular infinitive and perfective use of *kata* (as in 7:31) with *chrēsasthai* (first aorist middle infinitive).

19. *I brought myself under bondage (emauton edoulōsa)*. Voluntary bondage, I enslaved myself to all, though free. Causative verb in -oō (*douloō*, from *doulos*). *The more (tous pleionas)*. Than he could have done otherwise. Every preacher faces this problem of his personal attitude and conduct. Note *kerdēsō* (as in verses 20, 21, 22, but once *hina kerdanō* in 21, regular liquid future of *kerdainō*) with *hina* is probably future active indicative (James 4:13), though Ionic aorist active subjunctive from *kerdaō* is possible (Matt. 18:15). "He refuses payment in money that he may make the greater gain in souls" (Edwards).

20. *As a Jew (hōs Ioudaios)*. He was a Jew and was not ashamed of it (Acts 18:18; 21:26). *Not being myself under the law (mē ōn autos hupo nomon)*. He was emancipated from the law as a means of salvation, yet he knew how to speak to them because of his former beliefs and life with them (Gal. 4:21). He knew how to put the gospel to them without compromise and without offence.

21. *To them that are without law (tois anomois)*. The heathen, those outside the Mosaic law (Rom. 2:14), not lawless (Luke 22:37; Acts 2:23; I Tim. 1:9). See how Paul bore himself with the pagans (Acts 14:15; 17:23; 24:25), and how he quoted heathen poets. "Not being an outlaw of God, but an inlaw of Christ" (Evans, Estius has it *exlex*, *inlex*, *mē ōn anomos theou, all' ennomos Christou*). The genitive case of *theou* and *Christou* (specifying case) comes out better thus, for it seems unusual with *anomos* and *ennomos*, both old and regular adjectives.

22. *I became weak (egenomēn asthenēs)*. This is the chief point, the climax in his plea for the principle of love on the part of the enlightened for the benefit of the unenlightened (chapter 8). He thus brings home his conduct about renouncing pay for preaching as an illustration of love (8:13).

All things (*panta*) *to all men* (*tois pasin*, the whole number) *by all means* (*pantōs*). Pointed play on the word all, *that I may save some* (*hina tinas sōsō*). This his goal and worth all the cost of adaptation. In matters of principle Paul was adamant as about Titus the Greek (Gal. 2:5). In matters of expediency as about Timothy (Acts 16:3) he would go half way to win and to hold. This principle was called for in dealing with the problem of eating meat offered to idols (Rom. 14:1; 15:1; I Thess. 5:14).

23. *That I may be a joint partaker thereof* (*hina sunkoinōnos autou genōmai*). Literally, That I may become co-partner with others in the gospel. The point is that he may be able to share the gospel with others, his evangelistic passion. *Sunkoinōnos* is a compound word (*sun*, together with, *koinōnos*, partner or sharer). We have two genitives with it in Phil. 1:7, though *en* and the locative is used in Rev. 1:9. It is found only in the N.T. and a late papyrus. Paul does not wish to enjoy the gospel just by himself.

24 *In a race* (*en stadiōi*). Old word from *histēmi*, to place. A stated or fixed distance, 606¾ feet, both masculine *stadioi* (Matt. 14:24; Luke 24:13) and neuter as here. Most of the Greek cities had race-courses for runners like that at Olympia. *The prize* (*to brabeion*). Late word, in inscriptions and papyri. Latin *brabeum*. In N. T. only here and Phil. 3:14. The victor's prize which only one could receive. *That ye may attain* (*hina katalabēte*). Final use of *hina* and perfective use of *kata-* with *labēte* (effective aorist active subjunctive, grasp and hold). Old verb *katalambanō* and used in Phil. 3:12ff.

25. *That striveth in the games* (*ho agōnizomenos*). Common verb for contest in the athletic games (*agōn*), sometimes with the cognate accusative, *agōna agōnizomai* as in I Tim. 6:12; II Tim. 4:7. Probably Paul often saw these athletic games. *Is temperate in all things* (*panta egkrateuetai*). Rare verb, once in Aristotle and in a late Christian inscription, and I Cor. 7:9 and here, from *egkratēs*, common adjective for one who controls himself. The athlete then and now has to control himself (direct middle) in all things (accusative of general reference). This is stated by Paul as an athletic axiom. Training for ten months was required under the direction of trained judges. Abstinence from wine was required and a rigid diet and regimen of habits.

A corruptible crown (phtharton stephanon). *Stephanos* (crown) is from *stephō*, to put around the head, like the Latin *corona*, wreath or garland, badge of victory in the games. In the Isthmian games it was of pine leaves, earlier of parsley, in the Olympian games of the wild olive. "Yet these were the most coveted honours in the whole Greek world" (Findlay). For the crown of thorns on Christ's head see Matt. 27:29; Mark 15:17; John 19:2, 5. *Diadēma* (diadem) was for kings (Rev. 12:3). Favourite metaphor in N.T., the crown of righteousness (II Tim. 4:8), the crown of life (James 1:12), the crown of glory (I Peter 5:4), the crown of rejoicing (I Thess 2:9), description of the Philippians (4:1). Note contrast between *phtharton* (verbal adjective from *phtheirō*, to corrupt) like the garland of pine leaves, wild olive, or laurel, and *aphtharton* (same form with *a* privative) like the crown of victory offered the Christian, the amaranthine (unfading rose) crown of glory (I Peter 5:4).

26. *So (houtōs)*. Both with *trechō* (run) and *pukteuō* (fight). *As not uncertainly (hōs ouk adēlōs)*. Instead of exhorting them further Paul describes his own conduct as a runner in the race. He explains *houtōs*. *Adēlōs* old adverb, only here in N.T. His objective is clear, with Christ as the goal (Phil. 3:14). He kept his eye on Christ as Christ watched him. *Fight (pukteuō)*. Paul changes the metaphor from the runner to the boxer. Old verb (only here in N.T.) from *puktēs* (pugilist) and that from *pugmē* (fist). See on Mark 7:3). *As not beating the air (hōs ouk aera derōn)*. A boxer did this when practising without an adversary (cf. doing "the daily dozen") and this was called "shadow-fighting" (*skiamachia*). He smote something more solid than air. Probably *ou* negatives *aera*, though it still occurs with the participle as a strong and positive negative.

27. *But I buffet my body (alla hupōpiazō mou to sōma)*. In Aristophanes, Aristotle, Plutarch, from *hupōpion*, and that from *hupo* and *ops* (in papyri), the part of the face under the eyes, a blow in the face, to beat black and blue. In N.T. only here and Luke 18:5 which see. Paul does not, like the Gnostics, consider his *sarx* or his *sōma* sinful and evil. But "it is like the horses in a chariot race, which must be kept well in hand by whip and rein if the prize is to be secured" (Robertson and Plummer). The boxers often used boxing

gloves (*cestus*, of ox-hide bands) which gave telling blows. Paul was not willing for his body to be his master. He found good as the outcome of this self-discipline (II Cor. 12:7; Rom. 8:13; Col. 2:23; 3:5). *And bring it into bondage* (*kai doulagōgō*). Late compound verb from *doulagōgos*, in Diodorus Siculus, Epictetus and substantive in papyri. It is the metaphor of the victor leading the vanquished as captive and slave. *Lest by any means* (*mē pōs*). Common conjunction for negative purpose with subjunctive as here (*genōmai*, second aorist middle). *After that I have preached to others* (*allois kēruxas*). First aorist active participle of *kērussō* (see on 1:23), common verb to preach, from word *kērux* (herald) and that is probably the idea here. A *kērux* at the games announced the rules of the game and called out the competitors. So Paul is not merely a herald, but a competitor also. *I myself should be rejected* (*autos adokimos genōmai*). Literally, "I myself should become rejected." *Adokimos* is an old adjective used of metals, coin, soil (Heb. 6:8) and in a moral sense only by Paul in N.T. (I Cor. 9:27; II Cor. 13:5-7; Rom. 1:28; Titus 1:16; II Tim. 3:8). It means not standing the test (*dokimos* from *dokimazō*). Paul means rejected for the *prize*, not for the entrance to the race. He will fail to win if he breaks the rules of the game (Matt. 7:22f.). What is the prize before Paul? Is it that *reward* (*misthos*) of which he spoke in verse 18, his glorying of preaching a free gospel? So Edwards argues. Most writers take Paul to refer to the possibility of his rejection in his personal salvation at the end of the race. He does not claim absolute perfection (Phil. 3:12) and so he presses on. At the end he has serene confidence (II Tim. 4:7) with the race run and won. It is a humbling thought for us all to see this wholesome fear instead of smug complacency in this greatest of all heralds of Christ.

CHAPTER X

1. *For (gar)*. Correct text, not *de*. Paul appeals to the experience of the Israelites in the wilderness in confirmation of his statement concerning himself in 9:26f. and as a powerful warning to the Corinthians who may be tempted to flirt with the idolatrous practices of their neighbours. It is a real, not an imaginary peril. *All under the cloud (pantes hupo tēn nephelēn)*. They all marched under the pillar of cloud by day (Ex. 13:21; 14:19) which covered the host (Numb. 14:14; Psa. 95:39). This mystic cloud was the symbol of the presence of the Lord with the people.

2. *Were all baptized unto Moses in the cloud and in the sea (pantes eis ton Mōusēn ebaptisanto en tēi nephelēi kai en tēi thalassēi)*. The picture is plain enough. The mystic cloud covered the people while the sea rose in walls on each side of them as they marched across. B K L P read *ebaptisanto* (causative first aorist middle, got themselves baptized) while Aleph A C D have *ebaptisthēsan* (first aorist passive, were baptized). The immersion was complete for all of them in the sea around them and the cloud over them. Moses was their leader then as Christ is now and so Paul uses *eis* concerning the relation of the Israelites to Moses as he does of our baptism in relation to Christ (Gal. 3:27).

3. *The same spiritual meat (to auto pneumatikon brōma)*. Westcott and Hort needlessly bracket *to auto*. *Brōma* is food, not just flesh. The reference is to the manna (Ex. 16:13ff.) which is termed "spiritual" by reason of its supernatural character. Jesus called himself the true bread from heaven (John 6:35) which the manna typified.

4. *For they drank of a spiritual rock that followed them (epinon ek pneumatikēs akolouthousēs petras)*. Change to the imperfect *epinon* shows their continual access to the supernatural source of supply. The Israelites were blessed by the water from the rock that Moses smote at Rephidim (Ex. 17:6) and at Kadesh (Numb. 20:11) and by the well of Beer (Numb. 21:16). The rabbis had a legend that the water actually followed the Israelites for forty years, in one

form a fragment of rock fifteen feet high that followed the people and gushed out water. Baur and some other scholars think that Paul adopts this "Rabbinical legend that the water-bearing Rephidim rock journeyed onwards with the Israelites" (Findlay). That is hard to believe, though it is quite possible that Paul alludes to this fancy and gives it a spiritual turn as a type of Christ in allegorical fashion. Paul knew the views of the rabbis and made use of allegory on occasion (Gal. 4:24). *And the rock was Christ* (*hē petra de ēn ho Christos*). He definitely states here in symbolic form the preëxistence of Christ. But surely "we must not disgrace Paul by making him say that the pre-incarnate Christ followed the march of Israel in the shape of a lump of rock" (Hofmann). He does mean that Christ was the source of the water which saved the Israelites from perishing (Robertson and Plummer) as he is the source of supply for us today.

5. *With most of them* (*en tois pleiosin autōn*). "A mournful understatement," for only two (Caleb and Joshua) actually reached the Promised Land (Numb. 14:30–32). All the rest were rejected or *adokimoi* (9:27). *Were overthrown* (*katestrōthēsan*). First aorist passive indicative of *katastrōnnumi*, old compound verb, to stretch or spread down as of a couch, to lay low (Euripides), as if by a hurricane. Powerful picture of the desolation wrought by the years of disobedience and wanderings in the desert by this verb quoted from Numb. 14:16.

6. *Were our examples* (*tupoi hēmōn egenēthēsan*). More exactly, examples for us (objective genitive *hēmōn*, not subjective genitive, of us). The word *tupoi* (our types) comes from *tuptō*, to strike, and meant originally the mark of a blow as the print of the nails (John 20:25), then a figure formed by a blow like images of the gods (Acts 7:43), then an example to be imitated (I Peter 5:3; I Tim. 4:12; I Thess. 1:7; II Thess. 3:9), or to be avoided as here, and finally a type in a doctrinal sense (Rom. 5:14; Heb. 9:24). *To the intent we should not lust after* (*eis to mē einai hēmas epithumētas*). Purpose expressed by *eis* with the articular infinitive *to einai* and the accusative of general reference with *epithumētas* (lusters) in the predicate.

7. *Neither be ye idolaters* (*mēde eidōlolatrai ginesthe*). Literally, stop becoming idolaters, implying that some of them

had already begun to be. The word *eidōlolatrēs* seems to be a Christian formation to describe the Christian view. Eating *ta eidōlothuta* might become a stepping-stone to idolatry in some instances. *Drink (pein)*. Short form for *piein*, sometimes even *pin* occurs (Robertson, *Grammar*, p. 204). *To play (paizein)*. This old verb to play like a child occurs nowhere else in the N.T., but is common in the LXX and it is quoted here from Ex. 32:6. In idolatrous festivals like that witnessed by Moses when he saw the people singing and dancing around the golden calf (Ex. 32:18f.).

8. *Neither let us commit fornication (mēde porneuōmen)*. More exactly, And let us cease practicing fornication as some were already doing (I Cor. 6:11; 7:2). The connection between idolatry and fornication was very close (see Jowett, *Epistles of Paul*, II, p. 70) and see about Baal-Peor (Numb. 25:1–9). It was terribly true of Corinth where prostitution was part of the worship of Aphrodite. *In one day (miāi hēmerāi)*. An item that adds to horror of the plague in Numb. 25:9 where the total number is 24,000 instead of 23,000 as here for one day.

9. *Neither let us tempt the Lord (mēde ekpeirazōmen ton Kurion)*. So the best MSS. instead of Christ. This compound occurs in LXX and in N.T. always about Christ (here and Matt. 4:7; Luke 4:12; 10:25). Let us cease sorely (*ek-*) tempting the Lord by such conduct. *And perished by the serpents (kai hupo tōn opheōn apōllunto)*. Vivid imperfect middle (cf. aorist middle *apolonto* in verse 10), were perishing day by day. The story is told in Numb. 21:6. The use of *hupo* for agent with the intransitive middle of *apollumi* is regular. Note the Ionic uncontracted genitive plural *opheōn* rather than *ophōn*.

10. *Neither murmur ye (mēde gogguzete)*. Implying that some of them were murmuring. For this late picturesque onomatopoetic verb see on Matt. 20:11. The reference seems to be to Numb. 16:41f. after the punishment of Korah. *By the destroyer (hupo tou olothreutou)*. This word, from *olothreuō* (late verb from *olethros*, destruction) occurs only here, so far as known. The reference is to the destroying angel of Ex. 12:23 (*ho olothreuōn*).

11. *Now these things happened unto them (tauta de sunebainon ekeinois)*. Imperfect tense because they happened

from time to time. *By way of example (tupikōs)*. Adverb in
sense of *tupoi* in verse 6. Only instance of the adverb except
in ecclesiastical writers after this time, but adjective *tupikos*
occurs in a late papyrus. *For our admonition (pros nouthesian
hēmōn)*. Objective genitive (*hēmōn*) again. *Nouthesia* is late
word from *noutheteō* (see on Acts 20:31; I Thess. 5:12, 14)
for earlier *nouthetēsis* and *nouthetia*. *The ends of the ages have
come (ta telē tōn aiōnōn katentēken)*. Cf. Heb. 9:26 *hē sun-
teleia tōn aiōnōn*, the consummation of the ages (also Matt.
13:40). The plural seems to point out how one stage suc-
ceeds another in the drama of human history. *Katentēken*
is perfect active indicative of *katantaō*, late verb, to come
down to (see on Acts 16:1). Does Paul refer to the second
coming of Christ as in 7:26? In a sense the ends of the ages
like a curtain have come down to all of us.

12. *Lest he fall (mē pesēi)*. Negative purpose with *mē* and
second aorist active subjunctive of *piptō*.

13. *Hath taken (eilēphen)*. Perfect active indicative of
lambanō. *But such as man can bear (ei mē anthrōpinos)*. Except a human one. Old adjective meaning falling tò the lot
of man. *Above that ye are able (huper ho dunasthe)*. Ellipsis,
but plain. There is comfort in that God is faithful, trustworthy (*pistos*). *The way of escape (tēn ekbasin)*. "The way
out" is always there right along with (*sun*) the temptation.
This old word only here in N.T. and Heb. 13:7 about death.
It is cowardly to yield to temptation and distrustful of God.

14. *Wherefore (dioper)*. Powerfully Paul applies the example of the Israelites to the perilous state of the Corinthians about idolatry. See on verse 7 for word *eidōlolatreia*.

15. *As to wise men (hōs phronimois)*. No sarcasm as in II
Cor. 11:19, but plea that they make proper use of the mind
(*phrēn*) given them.

16. *The cup of blessing (to potērion tēs eulogias)*. The cup
over which we pronounce a blessing as by Christ at the institution of the ordinance. *A communion of the blood of
Christ (koinōnia tou haimatos tou Christou)*. Literally, a
participation in (objective genitive) the blood of Christ.
The word *koinōnia* is an old one from *koinōnos*, partner, and
so here and Phil. 2:1; 3:10. It can mean also fellowship
(Gal. 2:9) or contribution (II Cor. 8:4); Phil. 1:5). It is, of
course, a spiritual participation in the blood of Christ which

is symbolized by the cup. Same meaning for *koinōnia* in reference to "the body of Christ." *The bread which we break (ton arton hon klōmen).* The loaf. Inverse attraction of the antecedent *(arton)* to the case (accusative) of the relative *(hon)* according to classic idiom (Robertson, *Grammar*, p. 488). *Artos* probably from *arō*, to join or fit (flour mixed with water and baked). The mention of the cup here before the bread does not mean that this order was observed for see the regular order of bread and then cup in 11:24–27.

17. *One bread (heis artos).* One loaf. *Who are many (hoi polloi).* The many. *We all (hoi pantes).* We the all, the whole number, *hoi pantes* being in apposition with the subject *we (hēmeis* unexpressed). *Partake (metechomen).* Have a part with or in, share in. See on 9:12 and Heb. 2:14; 5:13 (partaking of milk). *Of the one bread (tou henos artou).* Of the one loaf, the article *tou* referring to one loaf already mentioned. *One body (hen sōma).* Here the mystical spiritual body of Christ as in 12:12f., the spiritual kingdom or church of which Christ is head (Col. 1:18; Eph. 5:23).

18. *After the flesh (kata sarka).* The literal Israel, the Jewish people, not the spiritual Israel *(Israēl kata pneuma)* composed of both Jews and Gentiles, the true children of faith (Rom. 2:28; 9:8; Gal. 3:7). *Communion with the altar (koinōnoi tou thusiastēriou).* Same idea in *koinōnoi* participators in, partners in, sharers in (with objective genitive). The word *thusiastērion* is from late verb *thusiazō*, to offer sacrifice, and that from *thusia*, sacrifice, and that from *thuō*, common verb to slay, to sacrifice (verse 20). The Israelites who offer sacrifices have a spiritual participation in the altar.

19. *A thing sacrificed to idols (eidōlothuton).* See on Acts 15:29; I Cor. 8:1, 4. *Idol (eidōlon).* Image of a god. See on Acts 7:41; 15:20; I Cor. 8:4, 7.

20. *But I say that (all' hoti).* The verb *phēmi* (I say) must be repeated from verse 19 before *hoti. To demons, and not to God (daimoniois kai ou theōi).* Referring to LXX text of Deut. 32:17. It is probable that by *ou theōi* Paul means "to a no-god" as also in Deut. 32:21 *ep' ouk ethnei (by a no-people).* This is Paul's reply to the heathen who claimed that they worshipped the gods represented by the images and not the mere wood or stone or metal idols. The word *daimonia* is an adjective *daimonios* from *daimōn*, an inferior

deity, and with same idea originally, once in this sense in
N.T. (Acts 17:18). Elsewhere in N.T. it has the notion of
evil spirits as here, those spiritual forces of wickedness (Eph.
6:12) that are under the control of Satan. The word *daimonia*, so common in the Gospels, occurs in Paul's writings
only here and I Tim. 4:1. Demonology is a deep and dark
subject here pictured by Paul as the explanation of heathenism which is a departure from God (Rom. 1:19-23) and a
substitute for the worship of God. It is a terrible indictment
which is justified by the licentious worship associated with
paganism then and now.

21. *Ye cannot (ou dunasthe)*. Morally impossible to drink
the Lord's cup and the cup of demons, to partake of the
Lord's table and the table of demons. *Of the table of the Lord*
(trapezēs Kuriou). No articles, but definite idea. *Trapeza*
is from *tetra* (four) and *peza* (a foot), four-footed. Here
table means, as often, what is on the table. See Luke 22:30
where Jesus says "at my table" *(epi tēs trapezēs mou)*, referring to the spiritual feast hereafter. Here the reference
is plainly to the Lord's Supper *(Kuriakon deipnon, I Cor.
11:20)*. See allusions in O.T. to use of the table in heathen
idol feasts (Isa. 65:11; Jer. 7:18; Ezek. 16:18f.; 23:41). The
altar of burnt-offering is called the table of the Lord in
Mal. 1:7 (Vincent).

22. *Provoke to jealousy (parazēloumen)*. The very word
used in Deut. 32:21 of the insolence of the old Israelites.
Quoted in Rom. 10:19. Such double-dealing now will do
this very thing. *Stronger than he (ischuroteroi autou)*. Comparative adjective followed by the ablative.

23. See on 6:12 for *lawful (exestin)* and *expedient (sumpherei)*. *Edify not (ouk oikodomei)*. Build up. Explanation
of *expedient (sumpherei)*.

24. *Let no man seek his own (mēdeis to heautou zēteitō)*.
This is Paul's rule for social relations (I Cor. 13:5; Gal. 6:2;
Rom. 14:7; 15:2; Phil. 2:1ff.) and is the way to do what is
expedient and what builds up. *His neighbour's good (to tou
heterou)*. Literally, "the affair of the other man." Cf. *ton
heteron* in Rom. 13:8 for this idea of *heteros* like *ho plēsion*
(the nigh man, the neighbour) in Rom 15:2. This is loving
your neighbour as yourself by preferring your neighbour's
welfare to your own (Phil. 2:4).

25. *In the shambles (en makellōi)*. Only here in N.T. A transliterated Latin word *macellum*, possibly akin to *maceria* and the Hebrew word for enclosure, though occurring in Ionic and Laconian and more frequent in the Latin. It occurs in Dio Cassius and Plutarch and in the papyri and inscriptions for "the provision market." Deissmann (*Light from the Ancient East*, p. 276) says: "In the Macellum at Pompeii we can imagine to ourselves the poor Christians buying their modest pound of meat in the Corinthian Macellum (I Cor. 10:25), with the same life-like reality with which the Diocletian maximum tariff called up the picture of the Galilean woman purchasing her five sparrows." *Asking no question for conscience sake (mēden anakrinontes dia tēn suneidēsin)*. As to whether a particular piece of meat had been offered to idols before put in the market. Only a part was consumed in the sacrifices to heathen gods. The rest was sold in the market. Do not be over-scrupulous. Paul here champions liberty in the matter as he had done in 8:4.

26. This verse gives the reason for Paul's advice. It is a quotation from Psa. 24:1 and was a common form of grace before meals. *Fulness (plērōma)*. Old word from *plēroō*, to fill, here that with which a thing is filled, whatever fills the earth.

27. *Biddeth you (kalei humas)*. To a general banquet, but not to a temple feast (8:10) which is prohibited. If a pagan invites Christians to their homes to a banquet, one is to act like a gentleman.

28. *But if any man say unto you (ean de tis humin eipēi)*. Condition of third class. Suppose at such a banquet a "weak" brother makes the point to you: "This hath been offered in sacrifice" *(touto hierothuton estin)*. *Hierothuton*, late word in Plutarch, rare in inscriptions and papyri, only here in N.T. *Eat not (mē esthiete)*. Present imperative with *mē* prohibiting the habit of eating then. Pertinent illustration to the point of doing what is expedient and edifying. *That shewed it (ton mēnusanta)*. First aorist active articular participle (accusative case because of *dia*) from *mēnuō*, old verb, to point out, to disclose. See Luke 20:37.

29. *For why is my liberty judged by another conscience? (hina ti gar hē eleutheria mou krinetai hupo allēs suneidēseōs;)*.

Supply *genētai* (deliberative subjunctive) after *ti*. Paul deftly puts himself in the place of the strong brother at such a banquet who is expected to conform his conscience to that of the weak brother who makes the point about a particular piece of meat. It is an abridgment of one's personal liberty in the interest of the weak brother. Two individualities clash. The only reason is love which builds up (8:2 and all of chapter 13). There is this eternal collision between the forces of progress and reaction. If they work together, they must consider the welfare of each other.

30. Paul carries on the supposed objective to his principle of love. Why incur the risk of being evil spoken of (*blasphēmoumai*) for the sake of maintaining one's liberty? Is it worth it? See Rom. 14:6 where Paul justifies the conscience of one who eats the meat and of one who does not. Saying grace over food that one should not eat seems inconsistent. We have this very word *blaspheme* in English.

31. *To the glory of God* (*eis doxan theou*). This is the ruling motive in the Christian's life, not just having his own way about whims and preferences.

32. *Give no occasion of stumbling* (*aproskopoi*). Late word and in papyri, only three times in N.T. (here; Phil. 1:10; Acts 24:16). See on Acts 24:16. Here in active sense, not tripping others by being a stumbling-block, as in Sirach 32:21, but passive in Acts 24:16.

33. *Mine own profit* (*to emoutou sumpheron*). Old word from *sumpherō*, to bear together, and explains use of verb in verse 23. *That they may be saved* (*hina sōthōsin*). First aorist passive subjunctive of *sōzō*, to save, with *hina* purpose clause with same high motive as in 9:22. This is the ruling passion of Paul in his dealings with men.

CHAPTER XI

1. *Imitators of me* (*mimētai mou*). In the principle of considerate love as so clearly shown in chapters 8 to 10 and in so far as (*kathōs*) Paul is himself an imitator of Christ. The preacher is a leader and is bound to set an example or pattern (*tupos*) for others (Titus 2:7). This verse clearly belongs to the preceding chapter and not to chapter 11.

2. *Hold fast the traditions* (*tas paradoseis katechete*). Hold down as in 15:2. *Paradosis* (tradition) from *paradidōmi* (*paredōka*, first aorist active indicative) is an old word and merely something handed on from one to another. The thing handed on may be bad as in Matt. 15:2f. (which see) and contrary to the will of God (Mark 7:8f.) or it may be wholly good as here. There is a constant conflict between the new and the old in science, medicine, law, theology. The obscurantist rejects all the new and holds to the old both true and untrue. New truth must rest upon old truth and is in harmony with it.

3. *But I would have you know* (*thelō de humas eidenai*). But I wish you to know, censure in contrast to the praise in verse 2. *The head of Christ is God* (*kephalē tou Christou ho theos*). Rather, God is the head of Christ, since *kephalē* is anarthrous and predicate.

4. *Having his head covered* (*kata kephalēs echōn*). Literally, having a veil (*kalumma* understood) down from the head (*kephalēs* ablative after *kata* as with *kata* in Mark 5:13; Acts 27:14). It is not certain whether the Jews at this time used the *tallith*, "a four-corned shawl having fringes consisting of eight threads, each knotted five times" (Vincent) as they did later. Virgil (*Aeneid* iii., 545) says: "And our heads are shrouded before the altar with a Phrygian vestment." The Greeks (both men and women) remained bareheaded in public prayer and this usage Paul commends for the men.

5. *With her head unveiled* (*akatakaluptōi tēi kephalēi*). Associative instrumental case of manner and the predicative adjective (compound adjective and feminine form same as masculine), "with the head unveiled." Probably some of

the women had violated this custom. "Amongst Greeks
only the *hetairai*, so numerous in Corinth, went about unveiled; slave-women wore the shaven head—also a punishment of the adulteress" (Findlay). Cf. Numb. 5:18. *One
and the same thing as if she were shaven (hen kai to auto tēi
exurēmenēi)*. Literally, "One and the same thing with the
one shaven" (associative instrumental case again, Robertson,
Grammar, p. 530). Perfect passive articular participle of the
verb *xuraō*, later form for the old *xureō*. It is public praying
and prophesying that the Apostle here has in mind. He does
not here condemn the act, but the breach of custom which
would bring reproach. A woman convicted of adultery had
her hair shorn (Isa. 7:20). The Justinian code prescribed
shaving the head for an adulteress whom the husband refused to receive after two years. Paul does not tell Corinthian Christian women to put themselves on a level with
courtesans.

6. *Let her also be shorn (kai keirasthō)*. Aorist middle imperative of *keirō*, to shear (as sheep). Let her cut her hair
close. A single act by the woman. *If it is a shame (ei de
aischron)*. Condition of first class assumed to be true.
Aischron is old adjective from *aischos*, bareness, disgrace.
Clearly Paul uses such strong language because of the effect
on a woman's reputation in Corinth by such conduct that
proclaimed her a lewd woman. Social custom varied in the
world then as now, but there was no alternative in Corinth.
To be shorn or shaven (to keirasthai kai xurasthai). Articular
infinitives subject of copula *estin* understood, *keirasthai* first
aorist middle, *xurasthai* present middle. Note change in
tense. *Let her be veiled (katakaluptesthō)*. Present middle
imperative of old compound *kata-kaluptō*, here alone in
N.T. Let her cover up herself with the veil (down, *kata*,
the Greek says, the veil hanging down from the head).

7. *The image and glory of God (eikōn kai doxa theou)*. Anarthrous substantives, but definite. Reference to Gen. 1:28
and 2:26 whereby man is made directly in the image (*eikōn*)
of God. It is the moral likeness of God, not any bodily re-
semblance. Ellicott notes that man is the glory (*doxa*) of
God as the crown of creation and as endowed with sovereignty like God himself. *The glory of the man (doxa andros)*.
Anarthrous also, man's glory. In Gen. 2:26 the LXX has

anthrōpos (Greek word for both male and female), not *anēr* (male) as here. But the woman (*gunē*) was formed from the man (*anēr*) and this priority of the male (verse 8) gives a certain superiority to the male. On the other hand, it is equally logical to argue that woman is the crown and climax of all creation, being the last.

9. *For the woman* (*dia tēn gunaika*). Because of (*dia* with accusative case) the woman. The record in Genesis gives the man (*anēr*) as the origin (*ek*) of the woman and the reason for (*dia*) the creation (*ektisthē*, first aorist passive of *ktizō*, old verb to found, to create, to form) of woman.

10. *Ought* (*opheilei*). Moral obligation therefore (*dia touto*, rests on woman in the matter of dress that does not (*ouk opheilei* in verse 7) rest on the man. *To have a sign of authority* (*exousian echein*). He means *sēmeion exousias* (symbol of authority) by *exousian*, but it is the sign of authority of the man over the woman. The veil on the woman's head is the symbol of the authority that the man with the uncovered head has over her. It is, as we see it, more a sign of subjection (*hypotagēs*, I Tim. 2:10) than of authority (*exousias*). *Because of the angels* (*dia tous aggelous*). This startling phrase has caused all kinds of conjecture which may be dismissed. It is not preachers that Paul has in mind, nor evil angels who could be tempted (Gen. 6:1f.), but angels present in worship (cf. I Cor. 4:9; Psa. 138:1) who would be shocked at the conduct of the women since the angels themselves veil their faces before Jehovah (Isa. 6:2).

11. *Howbeit* (*plēn*). This adversative clause limits the preceding statement. Each sex is incomplete without (*chōris*, apart from, with the ablative case) the other. *In the Lord* (*en Kuriōi*). In the sphere of the Lord, where Paul finds the solution of all problems.

12. *Of* (*ek*)—*by* (*dia*). Ever since the first creation man has come into existence by means of (*dia* with genitive) the woman. The glory and dignity of motherhood. Cf. *The Fine Art of Motherhood* by Ella Broadus Robertson.

13. *Is it seemly?* (*prepon estin;*). Periphrastic present indicative rather than *prepei*. See on Matt. 3:15. Paul appeals to the sense of propriety among the Corinthians.

14. *Nature itself* (*hē phusis autē*). He reënforces the appeal to custom by the appeal to nature in a question that

expects the affirmative answer (*oude*). *Phusis*, from old verb *phuō*, to produce, like our word nature (Latin *natura*), is difficult to define. Here it means native sense of propriety (cf. Rom. 2:14) in addition to mere custom, but one that rests on the objective difference in the constitution of things. 15. *Have long hair* (*komāi*). Present active subjunctive of *komaō* (from *komē*, hair), old verb, same contraction (-*aēi*= *āi*) as the indicative (*aei*=*āi*), but subjunctive here with *ean* in third class condition. Long hair is a glory to a woman and a disgrace to a man (as we still feel). The long-haired man! There is a papyrus example of a priest accused of letting his hair grow long and of wearing woollen garments. *For a covering* (*anti peribolaiou*). Old word from *periballō* to fling around, as a mantle (Heb. 1:12) or a covering or veil as here. It is not in the place of a veil, but answering to (*anti*, in the sense of *anti* in John 1:16), as a permanent endowment (*dedotai*, perfect passive indicative). 16. *Contentious* (*philoneikos*). Old adjective (*philos, neikos*), fond of strife. Only here in N.T. If he only existed in this instance, the disputatious brother. *Custom* (*sunētheian*). Old word from *sunēthēs* (*sun, ēthos*), like Latin *consuetudo*, intercourse, intimacy. In N.T. only here and 8:7 which see. "In the sculptures of the catacombs the women have a close-fitting head-dress, while the men have the hair short" (Vincent). 17. *This* (*touto*). Probably the preceding one about the head-dress of women, and transition to what follows. *I praise you not* (*ouk epainō*). In contrast to the praise in 11:2. *For the better* (*eis to kreisson*). Neuter articular comparative of *kratus*, but used as comparative of *kalos*, good. Attic form *kreitton*. *For the worse* (*eis to hēsson*). Old comparative from *hēka*, softly, used as comparative of *kakos*, bad. In N.T. only here and II Cor. 12:15. 18. *First of all* (*prōton men*). There is no antithesis (*deuteron de*, secondly, or *epeita de*, in the next place) expressed. This is the primary reason for Paul's condemnation and the only one given. *When ye come together in the church* (*sunerchomenōn hēmōn en ekklēsiāi*). Genitive absolute. Here *ekklēsia* has the literal meaning of assembly. *Divisions* (*schismata*). Accusative of general reference with the infinitive *huparchein* in indirect discourse. Old word for cleft, rent, from *schizō*. Example in papyri for splinter of wood. See on 1:10. Not yet formal cleavages into two or more organizations, but partisan divisions that showed in the love-feasts and at the Lord's Supper. *Partly (meros ti)*. Accusative of extent (to some part) like *panta* in 10:33. He could have said *ek merous* as in 13:9. The rumours of strife were so constant (I keep on hearing, *akouō*). 19. *Must be (dei einai)*. Since moral conditions are so bad among you (cf. chapters 1 to 6). Cf. Matt. 18:7. *Heresies (haireseis)*. The schisms naturally become *factions* or *parties*. Cf. strifes (*erides*) in 1:11. See on Acts 15:5 for *haireseis*, a choosing, taking sides, holding views of one party, heresy (our word). "Heresy is theoretical schism, schism practical heresy." Cf. Titus 3:10; II Peter 2:1. In Paul only here and Gal. 5:20. *That (hina)*. God's purpose in these factions makes *the proved ones (hoi dokimoi)* become *manifest (phaneroi)*. "These *haireseis* are a magnet attracting unsound and unsettled minds" (Findlay). It has always been so. Instance so-called Christian Science, Russellism, New Thought, etc., today.

20. *To eat the Lord's Supper (Kuriakon deipnon phagein)*. *Kuriakos*, adjective from *Kurios*, belonging to or pertaining to the Lord, is not just a biblical or ecclesiastical word, for it is found in the inscriptions and papyri in the sense of imperial (Deissmann, *Light from the Ancient East*, p. 358), as imperial finance, imperial treasury. It is possible that here the term applies both to the *Agapē* or Love-feast (a sort of church supper or club supper held in connection with, before or after, the Lord's Supper) and the Eucharist or Lord's Supper. *Deipnon*, so common in the Gospels, only here in Paul. The selfish conduct of the Corinthians made it impossible to eat a Lord's Supper at all.

21. *Taketh before (prolambanei)*. Before others. Old verb to take before others. It was conduct like this that led to the complete separation between the Love-feast and the Lord's Supper. It was not even a common meal together (*koinon deipnon*), not to say a Lord's *deipnon*. It was a mere grab-game. *This one is hungry (hos de peināi)*. Demonstrative *hos*. Nothing is left for him at the love-feast. *Another is drunken (hos de methuei)*. Such disgusting conduct was considered shameful in heathen club suppers. "Hungry

poor meeting intoxicated rich, at what was supposed to be a supper of the Lord" (Robertson and Plummer). On *methuō*, to be drunk, see on Matt. 24:49; Acts 2:15.

22. *What? Have ye not houses?* (*Mē gar oikias ouk echete;*) The double negative (*mē—ouk*) in the single question is like the idiom in 9:4f. which see. *Mē* expects a negative answer while *ouk* negatives the verb *echete*. "For do you fail to have houses?" Paul is not approving gluttony and drunkenness but only expressing horror at their sacrilege (despising, *kataphroneite*) of the church of God. *That have not* (*tous mē echontas*). Not those without houses, but those who have nothing, "the have-nots" (Findlay) like II Cor. 8:12, in contrast with *hoi echontes* "the haves" (the men of property). *What shall I say to you?* (*ti eipō humin;*) Deliberative subjunctive that well expresses Paul's bewilderment.

23. *For I received of the Lord* (*ego gar parelabon apo tou Kuriou*). Direct claim to revelation from the Lord Jesus on the origin of the Lord's Supper. Luke's account (Luke 22:17-20) is almost identical with this one. He could easily have read I Corinthians before he wrote his Gospel. See 15:3 for use of both *parelabon* and *paredōka*. Note *para* in both verbs. Paul received the account from (*para—apo*) the Lord and passed it on from himself to them, a true *paradosis* (tradition) as in 11:2. He was betrayed (*paredideto*). Imperfect passive indicative (irregular form for *paredidoto*, Robertson, *Grammar*, p. 340). Same verb as *paredōka* (first aorist active indicative just used for "I delivered").

24. *When he had given thanks* (*eucharistēsas*). First aorist active participle of *eucharisteō* from which word our word Eucharist comes, common late verb (see on 1:14). *Which is for you* (*to huper humōn*). *Klōmenon* (broken) of the Textus Receptus (King James Version) is clearly not genuine. Luke (22:19) has *didomenon* (given) which is the real idea here. As a matter of fact the body of Jesus was not broken (John 19:36). The bread was broken, but not the body of Jesus. *In remembrance of me* (*eis tēn emēn anamnēsin*). The objective use of the possessive pronoun *emēn*. Not my remembrance of you, but your remembrance of me. *Anamnēsis*, from *anamimnēskō*, to remind or to recall, is an old word, but only here in N.T. save Luke 22:19 which see.

25. *After supper (meta to deipnēsai)*. Meta and the articular aorist active infinitive, "after the dining" (or the supping) as in Luke 22:20. *The new covenant (hē kainē diathēkē)*. For *diathēkē* see on Matt. 26:28. For *kainos* see on Luke 5:38 and 22:20. The position of *estin* before *en tōi haimati* (in my blood) makes it a secondary or additional predicate and not to be taken just with *diathēkē* (covenant or will). *As oft as ye drink it (hosakis an pinēte)*. Usual construction for general temporal clause of repetition (*an* and the present subjunctive with *hosakis*). So in verse 26.

26. *Till he come (achri hou elthēi)*. Common idiom (with or without *an*) with the aorist subjunctive for future time (Robertson, *Grammar*, p. 975). In Luke 22:18 we have *heōs hou elthēi*. The Lord's Supper is the great preacher (*kataggellete*) of the death of Christ till his second coming (Matt. 26:29).

27. *Unworthily (anaxiōs)*. Old adverb, only here in N.T., not genuine in verse 29. Paul defines his meaning in verse 29f. He does not say or imply that we ourselves must be "worthy" (*axioi*) to partake of the Lord's Supper. No one would ever partake on those terms. Many pious souls have abstained from observing the ordinance through false exegesis here. *Shall be guilty (enochos estai)*. Shall be held guilty as in Matt. 5:21f. which see. Shall be guilty of a crime committed against the body and blood of the Lord by such sacrilege (cf. Heb. 6:6; 10:29).

28. *Let a man prove himself (dokimazetō anthrōpos heauton)*. Test himself as he would a piece of metal to see if genuine. Such examination of one's motives would have made impossible the disgraceful scenes in verses 20ff.

29. *If he discern not the body (mē diakrinōn to sōma)*. So-called conditional use of the participle, "not judging the body." Thus he eats and drinks judgment (*krima*) on himself. The verb *dia-krinō* is an old and common word, our *dis-cri-minate*, to distinguish. Eating the bread and drinking the wine as symbols of the Lord's body and blood in death probes one's heart to the very depths.

30. *And not a few sleep (kai koimōntai hikanoi)*. Sufficient number (*hikanoi*) are already asleep in death because of their desecration of the Lord's table. Paul evidently had knowledge of specific instances. A few would be too many.

31. *But if we discerned ourselves* (*ei de heautous diekri-nomen*). This condition of the second class, determined as unfulfilled, assumes that they had not been judging themselves discriminatingly, else they would not be judged (*ekrinometha*). Note distinction in the two verbs.

32. *We are chastened of the Lord* (*hupo tou Kuriou paideuo-metha*). On this sense of *paideuō*, from *pais*, child, to train a child (Acts 7:22), to discipline with words (II Tim. 2:25), to chastise with scourges see on Luke 23:16 (Heb. 12:7), and so by afflictions as here (Heb. 12:6). *Hupo tou Kuriou* can be construed with *krinomenoi* instead of with *paideuo-metha*. *With the world* (*sun tōi kosmōi*). Along with the world. Afflictions are meant to separate us from the doom of the wicked world. Final use of *hina mē* here with *kata-krithōmen* (first aorist passive subjunctive).

33. *Wait one for another* (*allēlous ekdechesthe*). As in John 5:3; Acts 17:16. That is common courtesy. Wait in turn. Vulgate has *invicem expectate*.

34. *At home* (*en oikōi*). If so hungry as all that (verse 22). *The rest* (*ta loipa*). He has found much fault with this church, but he has not told all. *I will set in order* (*diataxomai*). Not even Timothy and Titus can do it all. *Whensoever I come* (*hōs an elthō*). Common idiom for temporal clause of future time (conjunction like *hōs* with *an* and aorist subjunctive *elthō*).

CHAPTER XII

1. *Now concerning spiritual gifts (peri de tōn pneumatikōn).*
Clearly one of the items asked about in the letter to Paul
(7:1) and introduced precisely as the problem of meats
offered to idols (8:1). This question runs to the end of chapter 14. Plainly much trouble had arisen in Corinth in the
exercise of these gifts. 2. *Ye were led away (apagomenoi).*
The copula *ēte* is not
expressed (common ellipsis) with the participle (periphrastic
imperfect passive), but it has to be supplied to make sense.
Some scholars would change *hote* (when) to *pote* (once) and
so remove the difficulty. *Unto those dumb idols (pros ta
eidōla ta aphōna).* "Unto the idols the dumb." See Psa.
95:5–7 for the voicelessness (*a-phōna*, old adjective, without
voice, *phōnē*) of the idols. Pagans were led astray by demons
(I Cor. 10:19f.). *Howsoever ye might be led (hōs an ēgesthe).*
Rather, "as often as ye were led." For this use of *hōs an*
for the notion of repetition, regular *Koiné* idiom, see Robertson, *Grammar*, p. 974. Cf. *hopou an* in Mark 6:56.
3. *Wherefore I give you to understand (dio gnōrizō humin).*
Causative idea (only in Aeschylus in old Greek) in papyri
(also in sense of recognize) and N.T., from root *gnō* in
ginōskō, to know. *Speaking in the Spirit of God (en pneumati
theou lalōn).* Either sphere or instrumentality. No great
distinction here between *laleō* (utter sounds) and *legō* (to
say). *Jesus is anathema (anathema Iēsous).* On distinction
between *anathema* (curse) and *anathēma* (offering Luke 21:
5) see discussion there. In LXX *anathēma* means a thing
devoted to God without being redeemed, doomed to destruction (Lev. 27:28f.; Josh. 6:17; 7:12). See I Cor. 16:22;
Gal. 1:8f.; Rom. 9:3. This blasphemous language against
Jesus was mainly by the Jews (Acts 13:45; 18:6). It is even
possible that Paul had once tried to make Christians say
Anathema Iēsous (Acts 26:11). *Jesus is Lord (Kurios Iēsous).*
The term *Kurios*, as we have seen, is common in the LXX
for God. The Romans used it freely for the emperor in the

emperor worship. "Most important of all is the early establishment of a polemical parallelism between the cult of Christ and the cult of Caesar in the application of the term *Kurios*, 'lord.' The new texts have here furnished quite astonishing revelations" (Deissmann, *Light from the Ancient East*, p. 349). Inscriptions, ostraca, papyri apply the term to Roman emperors, particularly to Nero when Paul wrote this very letter (*ib.*, p. 353f.): "One with 'Nero Kurios' quite in the manner of a formula (without article, like the 'Kurios Jesus' in I Cor. 12:3." "The battle-cries of the spirits of error and of truth contending at Corinth" (Findlay). One is reminded of the demand made by Polycarp that he say *Kurios Caesar* and how each time he replied *Kurios Iēsous*. He paid the penalty for his loyalty with his life. Lighthearted men today can say "Lord Jesus" in a flippant or even in an irreverent way, but no Jew or Gentile then said it who did not mean it.

4. *Diversities (diaireseis)*. Old word for distinctions, differences, distributions, from *diaireō*, to distribute, as *diairoun* (dividing, distributing) in verse 11. Only here in the N.T. *Of gifts (charismatōn)*. Late word and chiefly in Paul (cf. Rom. 12:6) in N.T. (except I Peter 4:19), but some examples in papyri. It means a favour (from *charizomai*) bestowed or received without any merit as in Rom. 1:11.

5. *Of ministrations (diakoniōn)*. This old word is from *diakonos* and has a general meaning of service as here (Rom. 11:13) and a special ministration like that of Martha (Luke 10:40) and the collection (I Cor. 16:15; II Cor. 8:4).

6. *Of workings (energēmatōn)*. Late word, here only in N.T., the effect of a thing wrought (from *energeō*, to operate, perform, energize). Paul uses also the late kindred word *energeia* (Col. 1:29; 2:12) for efficiency. *Who worketh all things in all (ho energōn ta panta en pasin)*. Paul is not afraid to say that God is the Energy and the Energizer of the Universe. "I say that the magnet floats in space by the will of God" (Dr. W. R. Whitney, a world figure in science). This is his philosophic and scientific theory of the Cosmos. No one has shown Paul's philosophy and science to be wrong. Here he is speaking only of spiritual gifts and results as a whole, but he applies this principle to the universe (*ta panta*) in Col. 1:16 (of Christ) and in Rom. 11:36 (of God). Note

the Trinity in these verses: the same Spirit (verse 4), the same Lord (Jesus) in verse 5, the same God (the Father) in verse 6.

7. *Manifestation* (*phanerōsis*). Late word, in papyri, in N.T. only here and II Cor. 4:2, from *phaneroō*, to make manifest (*phaneros*). Each instance of the whole (verse 6) is repeatedly given (*didotai*, present passive indicative of *didōmi*). To profit withal (*pros to sumpheron*). See on 6:12; 10:23, 33 for Paul's guiding principle in such matters.

8. *To one* (*hōi men*). Demonstrative *hos* with *men* in dative case, to this one. The distribution or correlation is carried on by *allōi de* (verses 8, 9, 10), *heterōi de* (verses 9, 10) for variety, nine manifestations of the Spirit's work in verses 8 to 10. *The Word of wisdom* (*logos sophias*). Old words. *Logos* is reason, then speech. Wisdom is intelligence, then practical action in accord with it. Here it is speech full of God's wisdom (2:7) under the impulse of the Spirit of God. This gift is placed first (revelation by the Spirit). *The word of knowledge* (*logos gnōseōs*). This gift is insight (illumination) according to (*kata*) the same Spirit.

9. *Faith* (*pistis*). Not faith of surrender, saving faith, but wonder-working faith like that in 13:2 (Matt. 17:20; 21:21). Note here *en tōi autōi pneumati* (in the same Spirit) in contrast with *dia* and *kata* in verse 8. *Gifts of healings* (*charismata iamatōn*). *Iama*, old word from *iaomai*, common in LXX, in N.T. only in this chapter. It means acts of healing as in Acts 4:30 (cf. James 5:14) and Luke 7:21 (of Jesus). Note *en* here as just before.

10. *Workings of miracles* (*energēmata dunameōn*). Workings of powers. Cf. *energōn dunameis* in Gal. 3:5 and Heb. 2:4 where all three words are used (*sēmeia*, signs, *terata*, wonders, *dunameis*, powers). Some of the miracles were not healings as the blindness on Elymas the sorcerer. *Prophecy* (*prophēteia*). Late word from *prophētēs* and *prophēmi*, to speak forth. Common in papyri. This gift Paul will praise most (chapter 14). Not always prediction, but a speaking forth of God's message under the guidance of the Holy Spirit. *Discernings of spirits* (*diakriseis pneumatōn*). *Diakrisis* is old word from *diakrinō* (see 11:29) and in N.T. only here; Rom. 14:1; Heb. 5:14. A most needed gift to tell whether the gifts were really of the Holy Spirit and

supernatural (cf. so-called "gifts" today) or merely strange though natural or even diabolical (I Tim. 4:1; I John 4:1f.). *Divers kinds of tongues* (*genē glōssōn*). No word for "divers" in the Greek. There has arisen a great deal of confusion concerning the gift of tongues as found in Corinth. They prided themselves chiefly on this gift which had become a source of confusion and disorder. There were varieties (kinds, *genē*) in this gift, but the gift was essentially an ecstatic utterance of highly wrought emotion that edified the speaker (14:4) and was intelligible to God (14:2; 28). It was not always true that the speaker in tongues could make clear what he had said to those who did not know the tongue (14:13). It was not mere gibberish or jargon like the modern "tongues," but in a real language that could be understood by one familiar with that tongue as was seen on the great Day of Pentecost when people who spoke different languages were present. In Corinth, where no such variety of people existed, it required an interpreter to explain the tongue to those who knew it not. Hence Paul placed this gift lowest of all. It created wonder, but did little real good. This is the error of the Irvingites and others who have tried to reproduce this early gift of the Holy Spirit which was clearly for a special emergency and which was not designed to help spread the gospel among men. See on Acts 2:13–21; 10:44–46; 19:6. *The interpretation of tongues* (*hermēneia glōssōn*). Old word, here only and 14:26 in N.T., from *hermēneuō* from *Hermēs* (the god of speech). Cf. on *diermēneuō* in Luke 24:27; Acts 9:36. In case there was no one present who understood the particular tongue it required a special gift of the Spirit to some one to interpret it if any one was to receive benefit from it.

11. *Worketh* (*energei*). The same word that was used in verse 6 of God. *Severally* (*idiāi*). Separately. *Even as he will* (*kathōs bouletai*). Hence there is no occasion for conceit, pride, or faction (4:7).

12. *So also is Christ* (*houtōs kai ho Christos*). One would naturally expect Paul here to say *houtōs kai to sōma tou Christou* (so also is the body of Christ). He will later call Christ the Head of the Body the Church as in Col. 1:18, 24; Eph. 5:23, 30. Aristotle had used *sōma* of the state as the body politic. What Paul here means is Christ as the Head

of the Church has a body composed of the members who have varied gifts and functions like the different members of the human body. They are all vitally connected with the Head of the body and with each other. This idea he now elaborates in a remarkable manner.

13. *Were we all baptized into one body* (*hēmeis pantes eis hen sōma ebaptisthēmen*). First aorist passive indicative of *baptizō* and so a reference to a definite past event with each of them of different races, nations, classes, when each of them put on the outward badge of service to Christ, the symbol of the inward changes already wrought in them by the Holy Spirit (Gal. 3:27; Rom. 6:2ff.). *And were all made to drink of one Spirit* (*kai pantes hen pneuma epotisthēmen*). First aorist passive indicative of *potizō*, old verb, to give to drink. The accusative *hen pneuma* is retained in the passive as often with verbs that in the active take two accusatives. The reference is to a definite act in the past, probably to the inward experience of the Holy Spirit symbolized by the act of baptism.

14. *Is not one member* (*ouk estin hen melos*). The point sounds like a truism, but it is the key to the whole problem of church life both local and general. Vincent refers to the fable of the body and the members by Menenius Agrippa (Livy, II, 32), but it was an old parable. Socrates pointed out how absurd it would be if feet and hands should work against one another when God made them to coöperate (Xen., *Mem.* II. iii. 18). Seneca alludes to it as does Marcus Aurelius and Marcus Antoninus.

15. *If the foot shall say* (*ean eipēi ho pous*). Condition of third class (*ean* and second aorist subjunctive *eipēi*). In case the foot say. *I am not of the body* (*ouk eimi ek tou sōmatos*). I am independent of the body, not dependent on the body. *It is not therefore not of the body* (*ou para touto ouk estin ek tou sōmatos*). Thinking or saying so does not change the fact. *Para touto* here means "alongside of this" (cf. IV Macc. 10:19) and so "because of," a rare use (Robertson, *Grammar*, p. 616). The two negatives (*ou—ouk*) do not here destroy one another. Each retains its full force.

16. Points explained precisely as in verse 15.

17. *If the whole body were an eye* (*ei holon to sōma ophthalmos*). The eye is the most wonderful organ and supremely

useful (Numb. 10:31), the very light of the body (Luke 11: 34). And yet how grotesque it would be if there were nothing else but a great round rolling eye! A big "I" surely! *The smelling* (*hē osphrēsis*). Old word from *osphrainomai*, to smell. Here alone in N.T.

18. *But now* (*nun de*). But as things are, in contrast to that absurdity. *Hath God set* (*ho theos etheto*). Second aorist middle indicative. God did it and of himself. *Even as it pleased him* (*kathōs ēthelēsen*). Why challenge God's will? Cf. Rom. 9:20.

19. *One member* (*hen melos*). Paul applies the logic of verse 17 to any member of the body. The application to members of the church is obvious. It is particularly pertinent in the case of a "church boss."

20. *Many members, but one body* (*polla melē, hen de sōma*). The argument in a nutshell, in one epigram.

21. *Cannot say* (*ou dunatai eipein*). And be truthful. The superior organs need the inferior ones (the eye, the hand, the head, the feet).

22. *Nay, much rather* (*alla polloi mallon*). Adversative sense of *alla*, on the contrary. So far from the more dignified members like the eye and the head being independent of the subordinate ones like the hands and feet, they are "much more" (*argumentum a fortiori*, "by much more" *polloi mallon*, instrumental case) in need of them. *Those members of the body which seem to be more feeble are necessary* (*ta dokounta melē tou sōmatos asthenestera huparchein anagkaia estin*). Things are not always what they seem. The vital organs (heart, lungs, liver, kidneys) are not visible, but life cannot exist without them.

23. *We bestow* (*perititithemen*). Literally, We place around as if a garland (Mark 15:17) or a garment (Matt. 27:28). *More abundant comeliness* (*euschēmosunēn perissoteran*). One need only mention the mother's womb and the mother's breast to see the force of Paul's argument here. The word, common in old Greek, from *euschēmōn* (*eu*, well, *schēma*, figure), here only in N.T. One may think of the coal-miner who digs under the earth for the coal to keep us warm in winter. So *aschēmōn* (deformed, uncomely), old word, here only in N.T., but see 7:36 for *aschēmoneō*.

24. *Tempered the body together* (*sunekerasen to sōma*).

First aorist active indicative of *sunkerannumi*, to mix together, old word, but in N.T. only here and Heb. 4:2. Plato used this very word of the way God compounded (*sunekerasato*) the various elements of the body in creating soul and body. Paul rejects the idea of the later Gnostics that matter is evil and the physical organs degrading. He gives a noble picture of the body with its wonderful organs planned to be the temple of God's Spirit (6:19) in opposition to the Epicurean sensualists in Corinth. *To that part which lacked* (*tōi husteroumenōi*). It is a true instinct that gives superior honour to the unseen organs of life.

25. *That there should be no schism* (*hina mē ēi schisma*). Purpose of God in his plan for the body. Trouble in one organ affects the whole body. A headache may be due to trouble elsewhere and usually is. *Have the same care* (*to auto merimnōsin*). The very verb *merimnaō* used by Jesus of our anxiety (Matt. 6:27, 31). Paul here personifies the parts of the body as if each one is anxious for the others. The modern knowledge of the billions of cells in the body co-working for the whole confirms Paul's argument.

26. *Suffer with it* (*sunpaschei*). Medical term in this sense in Hippocrates and Galen. In N.T only here and Rom. 8:17 (of our suffering with Christ). One of Solon's Laws allowed retaliation by any one for another's injuries. Plato (*Republic*, V, 462) says the body politic "feels the hurt" as the whole body feels a hurt finger. *Rejoice with it* (*sunchairei*). This is fortunately true also. One may tingle with joy all over the body thanks to the wonderful nervous system and to the relation between mind and matter. See 13:6 for joy of love with truth.

27. *Severally* (*ek merous*). See Rom. 11:25 *apo merous* (in part). Each has his own place and function in the body of Christ.

28. *God hath set some* (*hous men etheto ho theos*). See verse 18 for *etheto ho theos*. Note middle voice (for his own use). Paul begins as if he means to say *hous men apostolous, hous de prophētas* (some apostles, some prophets), but he changes the construction and has no *hous de*, but instead *prōton, deuteron, epeita* (first, second, then, etc.). *In the church* (*en tēi ekklēsiāi*). The general sense of *ekklēsia* as in Matt. 16:18 and later in Col. 1:18, 24; Eph. 5:23, 32; Heb. 12:23.

See list also in Eph. 4:11. See on Matt. 10:2 for *apostolous*, the official title given the twelve by Jesus, and claimed by Paul though not one of the twelve. Prophets (*prophētas*). For-speakers for God and Christ. See the list of prophets and teachers in Acts 13:1 with Barnabas first and Saul last. Prophets are needed today if men will let God's Spirit use them, men moved to utter the deep things of God. *Teachers* (*didaskalous*). Old word from *didaskō*, to teach. Used to the Baptist (Luke 3:12), to Jesus (John 3:10; 13:13), and of Paul by himself along with *apostolos* (I Tim. 2:7). It is a calamity when the preacher is no longer a teacher, but only an exhorter. See Eph. 4:11. Then miracles (*epeita dunameis*). Here a change is made from the concrete to the abstract. See the reverse in Rom. 12:7. See these words (*dunameis, iamētōn, glōssōn*) in verses 9 and 10 with *glōssōn*, last again. But these two new terms (*helps, governments*). Helps (*antilēmpseis*). Old word, from *antilambanomai*, to lay hold of. In LXX, common in papyri, here only in N.T. Probably refers to the work of the deacons, help rendered to the poor and the sick. Governments (*kubernēseis*). Old word from *kubernaō* (cf. *Kubernētēs* in Acts 27:11) like Latin *gubernare*, our govern. So a governing. Probably Paul has in mind bishops (*episcopoi*) or elders (*presbuteroi*), the outstanding leaders (*hoi proistamenoi* in I Thess. 5:12; Rom. 12:8; *hoi hēgoumenoi* in Acts 15:22; Heb. 13:7, 17, 24). Curiously enough, these two offices (pastors and deacons) which are not named specifically are the two that survive today. See Phil. 1:1 for both officers.

29. *Are all* (*mē pantes*). The *mē* expects a negative answer with each group.

30. *Do all interpret?* (*mē pantes diermēneuousin?*). He adds this query to the list in 28, but it is in 10.

31. *The greater gifts* (*ta charismata ta meizona*). Paul unhesitatingly ranks some spiritual gifts above others. *Zēloō* here has good sense, not that of envy as in Acts 7:9 and I Cor. 13:4. *And a still more excellent way* (*kai eti kath' huperbolēn hodon*). In order to gain the greater gifts. "I show you a way *par excellence*," beyond all comparison (superlative idea in this adjunct, not comparative), like *kath' huperbolēn eis huperbolēn* (II Cor. 4:17). *Huperbolē* is old word from *huperballō*, to throw beyond, to surpass, to excel (II Cor.

3:10; Eph. 1:19). "I show you a supremely excellent way."
Chapter 13 is this way, the way of love already laid down
in 8:1 concerning the question of meats offered to idols
(cf. I John 4:7). Poor division of chapters here. This verse
belongs with chapter 13.

CHAPTER XIII

1. *With the tongues* (*tais glōssais*). Instrumental case. Mentioned first because really least and because the Corinthians put undue emphasis on this gift. Plato (*Symposium*, 197) and many others have written on love, but Paul has here surpassed them all in this marvellous prose-poem. It comes like a sweet bell right between the jangling noise of the gifts in chapters 12 and 14. It is a pity to dissect this gem or to pull to pieces this fragrant rose, petal by petal. Fortunately Paul's language here calls for little comment, for it is the language of the heart. "The greatest, strongest, deepest thing Paul ever wrote" (Harnack). The condition (*ean* and present subjunctive, *lalō kai mē echō*, though the form is identical with present indicative) is of the third class, a supposable case. *But have not love* (*agapēn de mē echō*). This is the *crux* of the chapter. Love is the way *par excellence* of 12:31. It is not yet clearly certain that *agapē* (a back-formation from *agapaō*) occurs before the LXX and the N.T. Plutarch used *agapēsis*. Deissmann (*Bible Studies*, p. 198) once suspected it on an inscription in Pisidia. It is still possible that it occurs in the papyri (Prayer to Isis). See *Light from the Ancient East*, p. 75 for details. The rarity of *agapē* made it easier for Christians to use this word for Christian love as opposed to *erōs* (sexual love). See also Moffatt's *Love in the N.T.* (1930) for further data. The word is rare in the Gospels, but common in Paul, John, Peter, Jude. Paul does not limit *agapē* at all (both toward God and man). Charity (Latin *caritas*) is wholly inadequate. "Intellect was worshipped in Greece, and power in Rome; but where did St. Paul learn the surpassing beauty of love?" (Robertson and Plummer). Whether Paul had ever seen Jesus in the flesh, he knows him in the spirit. One can substitute Jesus for love all through this panegyric. *I am become* (*gegona*). Second perfect indicative in the conclusion rather than the usual future indicative. It is put vividly, "I am already become." *Sounding brass* (*chalchos ēchōn*). Old words. Brass was the earliest metal that men learned to use.

Our word *echoing* is *ēchōn*, present active participle. Used in Luke 21:25 of the roaring of the sea. Only two examples in N.T. *Clanging cymbal* (*kumbalon alalazon*). Cymbal old word, a hollow basin of brass. *Alalazō*, old onomatopoetic word to ring loudly, in lament (Mark 5:38), for any cause as here. Only two N.T. examples.

2. The ecstatic gifts (verse 1) are worthless. Equally so are the teaching gifts (prophecy, knowledge of mysteries, all knowledge). Crasis here in *kán = kai ean*. Paul is not condemning these great gifts. He simply places love above them and essential to them. Equally futile is wonder-working faith "so as to remove mountains" (*hōste orē methistanein*) without love. This may have been a proverb or Paul may have known the words of Jesus (Matt. 17:20; 21:21). *I am nothing* (*outhen eimi*). Not *outheis*, nobody, but an absolute zero. This form in *th* rather than *d* (*ouden*) had a vogue for a while (Robertson, *Grammar*, p. 219).

3. *Bestow to feed* (*Psōmisō*). First aorist active subjunctive of *psōmizō*, to feed, to nourish, from *psōmos*, morsel or bit, and so to feed, by putting a morsel into the mouth like infant (or bird). Old word, but only here in N.T. *To be burned* (*hina kauthēsōmai*). First future passive subjunctive (Textus Receptus), but D *kauthēsomai* (future passive indicative of *kaiō*, old word to burn). There were even some who courted martyrdom in later years (time of Diocletian). This Byzantine future subjunctive does not occur in the old MSS. (Robertson, *Grammar*, p. 876). Aleph A B here read *kauchēsōmai*, first aorist middle subjunctive of *kauchaomai* (so Westcott and Hort), "that I may glory." This is correct. *It profiteth me nothing* (*ouden ōpheloumai*). Literally, I am helped nothing. *Ouden* in the accusative case retained with passive verb. See two accusatives with *ōpheleō* in 14:6. Verb is old and from *ophelos* (profit).

4. Verses 4 to 7 picture the character or conduct of love in marvellous rhapsody. *Suffereth long* (*makrothumei*). Late *Koiné* word (Plutarch) from *makros*, long, *thumos*, passion, ardour. Cf. James 5:7f. *Is kind* (*chrēsteuetai*). From *chrēstos* (useful, gracious, kind) and that from *chraomai*, to use. Not found elsewhere save in Clement of Rome and Eusebius. "Perhaps of Paul's coining" (Findlay). Perhaps a vernacular word ready for Paul. Gentle in behaviour. *Envieth not*

(*ou zēloi*). Present active indicative of *zēloō* (contraction *oei=oi*, same as subjunctive and optative forms). Bad sense of *zēlos* from *zeō*, to boil, good sense in 12:31. Love is neither jealous nor envious (both ideas). *Vaunteth not itself* (*ou perpereuetai*). From *perperos*, vainglorious, braggart (Polybius, Epictetus) like Latin *perperus*. Only here in N.T. and earliest known example. It means play the braggart. Marcus Anton. V. 5 uses it with *areskeuomai*, to play the toady. *Is not puffed up* (*ou phusioutai*). Present direct middle indicative of *phusioō* from *phusis* (late form for *phusaō*, *phusiaō* from *phusa*, bellows), to puff oneself out like a pair of bellows. This form in Herodas and Menander. Is not arrogant. See on 4:6.

5. *Doth not behave itself unseemly* (*ouk aschēmonei*). Old verb from *aschēmōn* (12:23). In N.T. only here and 7:36. Not indecent. *Seeketh not its own* (*ou zētei ta heautēs*). Its own interests (10:24, 33). *Is not provoked* (*ou paroxunetai*). Old word. In N.T. only here and Acts 17:16 which see. Irritation or sharpness of spirit. And yet Paul felt it in Athens (exasperation) and he and Barnabas had *paroxusmos* (paroxysm) in Antioch (15:39). See good sense of *paroxusmos* in Heb. 10:24. *Taketh not account of evil* (*ou logizetai to kakon*). Old verb from *logos*, to count up, to take account of as in a ledger or note-book, "the evil" (*to kakon*) done to love with a view to settling the account.

6. *Rejoiceth not in unrighteousness* (*ou chairei*). See Rom. 1:32 for this depth of degradation. There are people as low as that whose real joy is in the triumph of evil. *But rejoiceth with the truth* (*sunchairei de tēi alētheiāi*). Associative instrumental case after *sun-* in composition. Truth personified as opposed to unrighteousness (II Thess. 2:12; Rom. 2:8). Love is on the side of the angels. Paul returns here to the positive side of the picture (verse 4) after the remarkable negatives.

7. *Beareth all things* (*panta stegei*). *Stegō* is old verb from *stegē*, roof, already in I Cor. 9:12; I Thess. 3:1, 5 which see. Love covers, protects, forbears (*suffert*, Vulgate). See I Peter 4:8 "because love covers a multitude of sins" (*hoti agapē kaluptei phēthos hamartiōn*), throws a veil over. *Believeth all things* (*panta pisteuei*). Not gullible, but has faith in men. *Hopeth all things* (*panta elpizei*). Sees the bright

side of things. Does not despair. *Endureth all things (panta hupomenei)*. Perseveres. Carries on like a stout-hearted soldier. If one knows Sir Joshua Reynolds's beautiful painting of the Seven Virtues (the four cardinal virtues of the Stoics—temperance, prudence, fortitude, justice—and the three Christian graces—faith, hope, love), he will find them all exemplified here as marks of love (the queen of them all).

8. *Love never faileth (Hē agapē oudepote piptei)*. New turn for the perpetuity of love. *Piptei* correct text, not *ekpiptei*, as in Luke 16:17. Love survives everything. *They shall be done away (katargēthēsontai)*. First future passive of *katargeō*. Rare in old Greek, to make idle (*argos*), inoperative. All these special spiritual gifts will pass. It is amazing how little of human work lasts. *They shall cease (pausontai)*. Future middle indicative of *pauō*, to make cease. They shall make themselves cease or automatically cease of themselves.

9. *In part (ek merous)*. See on 12:27. As opposed to the whole.

10. *That which is perfect (to teleion)*. The perfect, the full-grown (*telos*, end), the mature. See on 2:6. *Hotan elthēi* is second aorist subjunctive with *hotan*, temporal clause for indefinite future time.

11. *A child (nēpios)*. See on 3:1 for *nēpios* in contrast with *teleios* (adult). *I spake (elaloun)*. Imperfect active, I used to talk. *I felt (ephronoun)*. Imperfect active, I used to think. Better, I used to understand. *I thought (elogizomēn)*. Imperfect middle, I used to reason or calculate. *Now that I am become (hote gegona)*. Perfect active indicative *gegona*, I have become a man (*anēr*) and remain so (Eph. 4:14). *I have put away (katērgēka)*. Perfect active indicative. I have made inoperative (verse 8) for good.

12. *In a mirror (di' esoptrou)*. By means of a mirror (*esoptron*, from *optō*, old word, in papyri). Ancient mirrors were of polished metal, not glass, those in Corinth being famous. *Darkly (en ainigmati)*. Literally, in an enigma. Old word from *ainissomai*, to express obscurely. This is true of all ancient mirrors. Here only in N.T., but often in LXX. "To see a friend's face in a cheap mirror would be very different from looking at the friend" (Robertson and Plummer). *Face to face (prosōpon pros prosōpon)*. Note triple use of

pros which means facing one as in John 1:1. *Prosōpon* is old word from *pros* and *ops*, eye, face. *Shall I know* (*epignō-somai*). I shall fully (*epi-*) know. Future middle indicative as *ginōskō* (I know) is present active and *epegnōsthēn* (I was fully known) is first aorist passive (all three voices).

31. *Abideth* (*menei*). Singular, agreeing in number with *pistis* (faith), first in list. *The greatest of these* (*meizōn toutōn*). Predicative adjective and so no article. The form of *meizōn* is comparative, but it is used as superlative, for the superlative form *megistos* had become rare in the *Koiné* (Robertson, *Grammar*, pp. 667ff.). See this idiom in Matt. 11:11; 18:1; 23:11. The other gifts pass away, but these abide forever. Love is necessary for both faith and hope. Does not love keep on growing? It is quite worth while to call attention to Henry Drummond's famous sermon *The Greatest Thing in the World* and to Dr. J. D. Jones's able book *The Greatest of These*. Greatest, Dr. Jones holds, because love is an attribute of God.

CHAPTER XIV

1. *Follow after love (diōkete tēn agapēn).* As if a veritable chase. Paul comes back to the idea in 12:31 (same use of *zēloute*) and proves the superiority of prophecy to the other spiritual gifts not counting faith, hope, love of 13:13. *But rather that ye may prophesy (mallon de hina prophēteuēte).* Distinct aim in view as in verse 5. Old verb from *prophētēs*, common in N.T. Present subjunctive, "that ye may keep on prophesying."

2. *For no man understandeth (oudeis gar akouei).* Literally, hears, gets the sense, understands. Verb *akouō* used either of hearing the sound only or getting the idea (cf. Acts 9:7; 22:9). *Mysteries (mustēria).* Unexplained mysteries (I Cor. 2:7).

3. *Edification (oikodomēn).* Building up. *Comfort (paraklēsin).* Encouragement, calling to one's side. *Consolation (paramuthian).* Old word (from *para, muthos, paramutheomai* I Thess. 2:12 which see, a stimulating word), nowhere else in N.T., but *paramuthion* in Phil. 2:1 with *paraklēsis* as here. Edification, cheer, incentive in these words.

4. *The church (ekklēsian).* No article, literally, "a church" (local use). Not *hē ekklēsia.*

5. *Except he interpret (ektos ei mē diermēneuēi).* Pleonastic combination of *ektos* (preposition except) and *ei mē* (if not, unless) as in 15:2; I Tim. 5:19. For use of *ei* with subjunctive rather than *ean* see Phil. 3:12 (common enough in the *Koiné*, Robertson, *Grammar*, pp. 1017f., condition of third class). On the verb see on 12:30; Luke 24:27; Acts 9:36. *Receive (labēi).* Second aorist (ingressive) active subjunctive of *lambanō*, may get edification.

6. *If I come (ean elthō).* Third class condition, supposable case (aorist subjunctive). *What shall I profit you (ti humas ōphelēsō).* Two accusatives with this verb (see 13:3). *Unless I speak (ean mē lalēsō).* Second condition (also third class) with the one conclusion (cf. I Tim. 2:5).

7. *Things without life (apsucha).* Without a soul (*a* privative, *psuchē*) or life. Old word only here in N.T. *Pipe*

(*aulos*). Old word (from *aō*, *auō*, to blow), only here in N.T. *Harp* (*kithara*). Old word. Stringed instrument as pipe, a wind instrument. *If they give not a distinction in the sounds* (*ean diastolēn tois phthoggois mē dōi*). Third class condition with second aorist active subjunctive *dōi* from *didōmi*. Common word in late Greek for difference (*diastellō*, to send apart). In N.T. only here and Rom. 3:22; 10:12. *Phthoggos* old word (from *phtheggomai*) for musical sounds vocal or instrumental. In N.T. only here and Rom. 10:18.

8. *An uncertain voice* (*adēlon phōnēn*). Old adjective (*a* privative, *dēlos*, manifest). In N.T. only here and Luke 11:44. Military trumpet (*salpigx*) is louder than pipe or harp. *Shall prepare himself* (*paraskeuasetai*). Direct middle future indicative of *paraskeuazō*, old verb, in N.T. only here, II Cor. 9:2ff.; Acts 10:10. From *para*, *skeuē* (*preparation*).

9. *Unless ye utter speech easy to be understood* (*ean mē eusēmon logon dōte*). Condition of third class again (*ean* and aorist subjunctive). *Eusēmon* (*eu*, well, *sēma*, sign) is old word, here only in N.T., well-marked, distinct, clear. Good enunciation, a hint for speakers. *Ye will be speaking into the air* (*esesthe eis aera laluntes*). Periphrastic future indicative (linear action). Cf. *aera derōn* (beating the air) in 9:26. Cf. our talking to the wind. This was before the days of radio.

10. *It may be* (*ei tuchoi*). Condition of fourth class (*ei* and aorist optative of *tugchanō*), if it should happen. Common enough idiom. Cf. *tuchon* in 16:6. *Without signification* (*aphōnon*). Old adjective (*a* privative and *phōnē*). Without the faculty of speech (12:2; Acts 8:32; II Peter 2:16).

11. *The meaning of the voice* (*tēn dunamin tēs phonēs*). The power (force) of the voice. *A barbarian* (*barbaros*). Jargon, bar-bar. The Egyptians called all *barbarous* who did not speak their tongue. The Greeks followed suit for all ignorant of Greek language and culture. They divided mankind into Hellenes and Barbarians. *Unto me* (*en emoi*). In my case, almost like a dative.

12. *Zealous of spiritual gifts* (*zēlōtai pneumatōn*). Zealots for spirits. So it looked. *That ye may abound* (*hina perisseuēte*). Purpose clause with the object by prolepsis stated beforehand "for the edification of the church."

13. *Let him pray that he may interpret* (*proseuchesthō hina diermēneuēi*). Else he had better cease talking in a tongue.

14. *But my understanding is unfruitful* (*ho de nous mou akarpos*). My intellect (*nous*) gets no benefit (*akarpos*, without fruit) from rhapsodical praying that may even move my spirit (*pneuma*).

15. *With the understanding also* (*kai tōi noï*). Instrumental case of *nous*. Paul is distinctly in favour of the use of the intellect in prayer. Prayer is an intelligent exercise of the mind. *And I will sing with the understanding also* (*psalō de kai tōi noï*). There was ecstatic singing like the rhapsody of some prayers without intelligent words. But Paul prefers singing that reaches the intellect as well as stirs the emotions. Solos that people do not understand lose more than half their value in church worship. *Psallō* originally meant to play on strings, then to sing with an accompaniment (Eph. 5:19), and here apparently to sing without regard to an instrument.

16. *Else if thou bless with the spirit* (*epei ean eulogēis en pneumati*). Third class condition. He means that, if one is praying and praising God (10:16) in an ecstatic prayer, the one who does not understand the ecstasy will be at a loss when to say "amen" at the close of the prayer. In the synagogues the Jews used responsive amens at the close of prayers (Neh. 5:13; 8:6; I Chron. 16:36; Psa. 106:48). *He that filleth the place of the unlearned* (*ho anaplērōn ton topon tou idiōtou*). Not a special part of the room, but the position of the *idiōtou* (from *idios*, one's own), common from Herodotus for private person (Acts 4:13), unskilled (II Cor. 11:6), uninitiated (unlearned) in the gift of tongues as here and verses 23f. *At thy giving of thanks* (*epi tēi sēi eucharistiāi*). Just the prayer, not the Eucharist or the Lord's Supper, as is plain from verse 17.

18. *More than you all* (*pantōn humōn mallon*). Ablative case after *mallon*. Astonishing claim by Paul that doubtless had a fine effect.

19. *Howbeit in church* (*alla en ekklēsiāi*). Private ecstasy is one thing (cf. II Cor. 12:1–9) but not in church worship. *That I may instruct* (*hina katēchēsō*). Final clause with *hina*. For the rare verb *katēcheō* see on Luke 1:4; Acts 18:25.

20. *Be not children in mind* (*mē paidia ginesthe tais phresin*). "Cease becoming children in your intellects," as some of them evidently were. Cf. Heb. 5:11–14 for a like complaint of intellectual dulness for being old babies. *In malice be ye*

babes (*tēi kakiāi nēpiazete*). *Be men* (*teleioi ginesthe*). Keep on becoming adults in your minds. A noble and a needed command, pertinent today.

21. *In the law it is written* (*en tōi nomōi gegraptai*). Isa. 28:11f. Freely quoted.

22. *For a sign* (*eis sēmeion*). Like the Hebrew and occasional *Koiné* idiom also.

23. *Will they not say that ye are mad?* (*ouk erousin hoti mainesthe?*). These unbelievers unacquainted (*idiōtai*) with Christianity will say that the Christians are raving mad (see on Acts 12:15; 26:24). They will seem like a congregation of lunatics.

24. *He is reproved by all* (*elegchetai hupo pantōn*). Old word for strong proof, is undergoing conviction. *Is judged* (*anakrinetai*). Is tested. Cf. I Cor. 2:15; 4:3f.

25. *That God is among you indeed* (*hoti ontōs en humin estin*). Recitative *hoti* and direct quotation from Isa. 45:15 (Hebrew rather than the LXX). "Really (*ontōs* Luke 24:34) God is in you."

26. *When ye come together* (*hotan sunerchēsthe*). Present middle subjunctive, repetition, whenever ye come together, in contrast with special case (*ean sunelthēi*, second aorist subjunctive) in verse 23.

27. *By two* (*kata duo*). According to two, ratio. *Or at most* (*ē to pleiston*). Adverbial accusative, "or at the most." *Three* (*treis*). *Kata* to be repeated. *And that in turn* (*kai ana meros*). One at a time and not over three in all.

28. *But if there be no interpreter* (*ean de mē ēi diermēneutēs*). Third class condition. Earliest known instance and possibly made by Paul from verb in verse 27. Reappears in Byzantine grammarians. *Keep silence in church* (*sigatō en ekklēsiāi*). Linear action (present active imperative). He is not even to speak in a tongue once. He can indulge his private ecstasy with God.

29. *By two or three* (*duo ē treis*). No *kata* here as in verse 27. Let two or three prophets speak. *Let the others discern* (*hoi alloi diakrinetōsan*). Whether what is said is really of the Spirit. Cf. 12:10 *diakriseis pneumatōn*.

30. *Let the first keep silence* (*ho prōtos sigatō*). To give the next one a chance.

31. *One by one* (*kath' ena*). Regular idiom.

32. *The spirits of the prophets are subject to the prophets* (*pneumata prophētōn prophētais hupotassetai*). A principle that some had forgotten.

33. *Not of confusion* (*ou—katastasias*). God is not a God of disorder, but of peace. We need this reminder today. *As in all the churches of the saints* (*hōs en pasais tais ekklēsiais tōn hagiōn*). Orderly reverence is a mark of the churches. This is a proper conclusion of his argument as in 11:16.

34. *Keep silence in the churches* (*en tais ekklēsiais sigatō-san*). The same verb used about the disorders caused by speakers in tongues (verse 28) and prophets (30). For some reason some of the women were creating disturbance in the public worship by their dress (11:2–16) and now by their speech. There is no doubt at all as to Paul's meaning here. In church the women are not allowed to speak (*lalein*) nor even to ask questions. They are to do that *at home* (*en oikōi*). He calls it a shame (*aischron*) as in 11:6 (cf. Eph. 5:12; Titus 1:11). Certainly women are still in subjection (*hupotas-sesthōsan*) to their husbands (or ought to be). But somehow modern Christians have concluded that Paul's commands on this subject, even I Tim. 2:12, were meant for specific conditions that do not apply wholly now. Women do most of the teaching in our Sunday schools today. It is not easy to draw the line. The daughters of Philip were prophetesses. It seems clear that we need to be patient with each other as we try to understand Paul's real meaning here.

37. *The commandment of the Lord* (*Kuriou entolē*). The prophet or the one with the gift of tongues or the disturbing woman would be quick to resent the sharp words of Paul. He claims inspiration for his position.

40. *Decently and in order* (*euschēmonōs kai kata taxin*). That is surely a good rule for all matters of church life and worship. It applies also to the function of women in church service.

CHAPTER XV

1. *I make known (gnōrizō)*. See on 12:3 for this common verb. *As if in reproach*. *The gospel which I preached unto you (to euaggelion ho euēggelisamēn humin)*. Cognate accusative, "the gospel which I gospelized unto you." Note augment *ē* after *eu-* like compound verb with preposition. Note repetition of relative (*ho, en hōi, di hou*, and *tini* like relative) without *kai* (and), asyndeton.

2. *In what words I preached it unto you (tini logoi euēggelisamēn humin)*. Almost certainly *tis (tini logoi*, locative or instrumental, in or with) here is used like the relative *hos* as is common in papyri (Moulton, *Prolegomena*, p. 93f.; Robertson, *Grammar*, p. 737f.). Even so it is not clear whether the clause depends on *gnōrizō* like the other relatives, but most likely so. *If we hold it fast (ei katechete)*. Condition of first class. Paul assumes that they are holding it fast. *Except ye believed in vain (ektos ei mē eikēi episteusate)*. For *ektos ei mē* see on 14:5. Condition of first class, unless in fact ye did believe to no purpose (*eikēi*, old adverb, only in Paul in N.T.). Paul holds this peril over them in their temptation to deny the resurrection.

3. *First of all (en prōtois)*. Among first things. *In primis*. Not to time, but to importance. *Which I also received (ho kai parelabon)*. Direct revelation claimed as about the institution of the Lord's Supper (11:23) and same verbs used (*paredōka, parelabon*). Four items given by Paul in explaining "the gospel" which Paul preached. Stanley calls it (verses 1–11) the creed of the early disciples, but "rather a sample of the exact form of the apostle's early teaching, than a profession of faith on the part of converts" (Vincent). The four items are presented by four verbs (*died, apethanen, was buried, etaphē, hath been raised, egēgertai, appeared, ōphthē*). *Christ died (Christos apethanen)*. Historical fact and crucial event. *For our sins (huper tōn hamartiōn hēmōn)*. *Huper* means literally over, in behalf, even instead of (Gal. 3:13), where used of persons. But here much in the sense of *peri* (Gal. 1:14) as is common in *Koiné*. In I Peter 3:18 we have

peri hamartiōn, huper adikōn. *According to the Scriptures* (*kata tas graphas*). As Jesus showed (Luke 22:37; 24:25) and as Peter pointed out (Acts 2:25–27; 3:35) and as Paul had done (Acts 13:24f.; 17:3). Cf. Rom. 1:2ff. 4. *And that he was buried* (*kai hoti etaphē*). Note *hoti* repeated before each of the four verbs as a separate item. Second aorist passive indicative of *thaptō*, old verb, to bury. This item is an important detail as the Gospels show. *And that he hath been raised* (*kai hoti egēgertai*). Perfect passive indicative, not *ēgerthē* like *rose* of the King James' Version. There is reason for this sudden change of tense. Paul wishes to emphasize the permanence of the resurrection of Jesus. He is still risen. *On the third day* (*tēi hēmerāi tēi tritēi*). Locative case of time. Whether Paul had seen either of the Gospels we do not know, but this item is closely identified with the fact of Christ's resurrection. We have it in Peter's speech (Acts 10:40) and Jesus points it out as part of prophecy (Luke 24:46). The other expression occasionally found "after three days" (Mark 10:34) is merely free vernacular for the same idea and not even Matt. 12:40 disturbs it. See on Luke 24:1 for record of the empty tomb on the first day of the week (the third day).

5. *And that he appeared to Cephas* (*kai hoti ōphthē Kēphāi*). First aorist passive indicative of the defective verb *horaō*, to see. Paul means not a mere "vision," but actual appearance. John uses *ephanerōthē* (John 21:14) from *phaneroō*, to make manifest, of Christ's appearance to the seven by the Sea of Galilee. Peter was listed first (*prōtos*) among the Apostles (Matt. 10:2). Jesus had sent a special message to him (Mark 16:7) after his resurrection. This special appearance to Peter is made the determining factor in the joyful faith of the disciples (Luke 24:34), though mentioned incidentally here. Paul had told all these four facts to the Corinthians in his preaching. He gives further proof of the fact of Christ's resurrection. There are ten appearances given besides the one to Paul. Nine are in the Gospels (Mary Magdalene in John and Mark, the other women in Matthew, the two going to Emmaus in Luke, Simon Peter in Luke and I Corinthians, the ten apostles and others in Luke and John and Mark, the eleven and others in John, the seven by the sea in John, to over five hundred in Galilee in Matthew and Paul and

Mark, to the apostles in Jerusalem in Luke and Mark and Acts and I Corinthians) and one in I Corinthians above (to James). It will be seen that Paul mentions only five of the ten, one, that to James, not given elsewhere. What he gives is conclusive evidence of the fact, particularly when reenforced by his own experience (the sixth appearance mentioned by Paul). The way to prove this great fact is to start with Paul's own witness given in this undoubted Epistle. The natural way to understand Paul's adverbs of time here is chronological: *then* (*eita*), *then* (*epeita*), *then* (*epeita*), *then* (*eita*), *last of all* (*eschaton pantōn*). *To the twelve* (*tois dōdeka*). The technical name. Only ten were present, for Judas was dead and Thomas was absent (John 20:24).

6. *To above five hundred brethren at once* (*epanō pentakosiois adelphois ephapax*). *Epanō* here is just an adverb with no effect on the case. As a preposition with the ablative see Matt. 5:14. This incident is the one described in Matt 28:16 the prearranged meeting on the mountain in Galilee. The strength of this witness lies in the fact that the majority (*hoi pleious*) of them were still living when Paul wrote this Epistle, say spring of A.D. 54 or 55, not over 25 years after Christ's resurrection.

7. *To James* (*Iakōbōi*). The brother of the Lord. This fact explains the presence of the brothers of Jesus in the upper room (Acts 1:14). *To all the apostles* (*tois apostolois pasin*). The Ascension of Christ from Olivet.

8. *As unto one born out of due time* (*hōsperei tōi ektrōmati*.) Literally, as to the miscarriage (or untimely birth). Word first occurs in Aristotle for abortion or miscarriage and occurs in LXX (Numb. 12:12; Job 3:16) and papyri (for miscarriage by accident). The verb *titrōskō* means to wound and *ek* is out. Paul means that the appearance to him came after Jesus had ascended to heaven.

9. *The least* (*ho elachistos*). True superlátive, not elative. Explanation of the strong word *ektrōma* just used. See Eph. 3:8 where he calls himself "less than the least of all saints" and I Tim. 1:15 the "chief" (*prōtos*) of sinners. Yet under attack from the Judaizers Paul stood up for his rank as equal to any apostle (II Cor. 11:5f., 23). *Because I persecuted the church of God* (*ediōxa tēn ekklēsian tou theou*). There were times when this terrible fact confronted Paul like a

nightmare. Who does not understand this mood of contrition?

10. *What I am* (*ho eimi*). Not, *who* (*hos*), but *what* (*ho*), neuter singular. His actual character and attainments. All "by the grace of God" (*chariti theou*). *I laboured more abundantly than they all* (*perissoteron autōn pantōn ekopiasa*). This is sober fact as shown by the Acts and Paul's Epistles. He had tremendous energy and used it. Genius is work, Carlyle said. Take Paul as a specimen.

11. *So we preach, and so ye believed* (*houtōs kērussomen, kai houtōs episteusate*). This is what matters both for preacher and hearers. This is Paul's gospel. Their conduct in response to his message was on record.

12. *Is preached* (*kērussetai*). Personal use of the verb, Christ is preached. *How say some among you?* (*pōs legousin en humin tines?*). The question springs naturally from the proof of the fact of the resurrection of Christ (verses 1–11) and the continual preaching which Paul here assumes by condition of the first class (*ei—kērussetai*). There were sceptics in Corinth, possibly in the church, who denied the resurrection of dead people just as some men today deny that miracles happen or ever did happen. Paul's answer is the resurrection of Christ as a fact. It all turns on this fact.

13. *Neither hath Christ been raised* (*oude Christos egēgertai*). He turns the argument round with tremendous force. But it is fair.

14. *Vain* (*kenon*). *Inanis*, Vulgate. Old word, empty. Both Paul's preaching and their faith are empty if Christ has not been raised. If the sceptics refuse to believe the fact of Christ's resurrection, they have nothing to stand on.

15. *False witnesses of God* (*pseudomartures tou theou*). Late word, but *pseudomartureō*, to bear false witness, old and common. The genitive (*tou theou*) can be either subjective (in God's service) or objective (concerning God). Either makes good sense. *Because we witnessed of God* (*hoti emarturēsamen kata tou theou*). Vulgate has *adversus Deum*. This is the more natural way to take *kata* and genitive, *against God* not as equal to *peri* (concerning). He would indeed make God play false in that case, *if so be that the dead are not raised* (*eiper ara nekroi ouk egeirontai*). Condition of

first class, assumed as true. Note both *per* intensive particle *indeed* and *ara* inferential particle *therefore*.

16. Repeats the position already taken in verse 13.
17. *Vain (mataia)*. Old word from adverb *matēn* (Matt. 15:9), devoid of truth, a lie. Stronger word than *kenon* in verse 14. *Ye are yet in your sins (eti este en tais hamartiais humōn)*. Because the death of Christ has no atoning value if he did not rise from the dead. In that case he was only a man like other men and did not die for our sins (verse 3).
18. *Then also (ara kai)*. Inevitable inference. *Have perished (apōlonto)*. Did perish. Second aorist middle indicative of *apollumi*, to destroy, middle, to perish (delivered up to eternal misery). Cf. 8:11.
19. *We have hoped (ēlpikotes esmen)*. Periphrastic perfect active indicative. Hope limited to this life even if "in Christ." *Only (monon)* qualifies the whole clause. *Most pitiable (eleeinoteroi)*. Comparative form, not superlative, of old adjective *eleeinos*, to be pitied, pitiable. If our hope is limited to this life, we have denied ourselves what people call pleasures and have no happiness beyond. The Epicureans have the argument on us. Paul makes morality turn on the hope of immortality. Is he not right? Witness the breaking of moral ties today when people take a merely animal view of life.
20. *But now (nuni de)*. Emphatic form of *nun* with -*i* added (cf. 12:18). It is the logical triumph of Paul after the *reductio ad impossibile* (Findlay) of the preceding argument. *The first-fruits (aparchē)*. Old word from *aparchomai*, to offer firstlings or first-fruits. In LXX for first-fruits. In papyri for legacy-duty, entrance-fee, and also first-fruits as here. See also verse 23; 16:15; Rom. 8:23, etc. Christ is "first-born from the dead" (Col. 1:18). Others raised from the dead died again, but not so Jesus. *That sleep (tōn kekoimēmenōn)*. Perfect middle participle as in Matt. 27:52 which see. Beautiful picture of death from which word (*koimaomai*) comes our *cemetery*.
21. *By man also (dai di' anthrōpou)*. That is Jesus, the God-man, the Second Adam (Rom. 5:12). The hope of the resurrection of the dead rests in Christ.
22. *Shall be made alive (zōopoiēthēsontai)*. First future

passive indicative of *zōopoieō*, late verb (Aristotle) to give
life, to restore to life as here. In verse 36 *zōopoieitai* is used
in the sense of natural life as in John 5:21; 6:63 of spiritual
life. It is not easy to catch Paul's thought here. He means
resurrection (restoration) by the verb here, but not necessarily eternal life or salvation. So also *pantes* may not coincide in both clauses. All who die die in Adam, all who will
be made alive will be made alive (restored to life) in Christ.
The same problem occurs in Rom. 5:18 about "all," and
in verse 19 about "the many."

23. *Order* (*tagmati*). Old military term from *tassō*, to
arrange, here only in N.T. Each in his own division, troop,
rank. *At his coming* (*en tēi parousiāi*). The word *parousia*
was the technical word "for the arrival or visit of the king
or emperor" and can be traced from the Ptolemaic period
into the second century A.D. (Deissmann, *Light from the
Ancient East*, p. 368). "Advent-coins were struck after a
parousia of the emperor." Paul is only discussing "those
that are Christ's" (3:23; Gal. 5:24) and so says nothing
about judgment (cf. I Thess. 2:19; 3:13; 4:15; 5:23).

24. *Then cometh the end* (*eita to telos*). No verb *ginetai* in
the Greek. Supply "at his coming," the end or consummation of the age or world (Matt. 13:39, 49; I Peter 4:7). *When
he shall deliver up* (*hotan paradidōi*). Present active subjunctive (not optative) of *paradidōmi* with *hotan*, whenever, and
so quite indefinite and uncertain as to time. Present subjunctive rather than aorist *paradōi* because it pictures a
future proceeding. *To God, even the Father* (*tōi theōi kai
patri*). Better, "to the God and Father" or to "His God
and Father." The Kingdom belongs to the Father. *When
he shall have abolished* (*hotan katargēsēi*). First aorist active
subjunctive with *hotan*, indefinite future time. Simply,
"whenever he shall abolish," no use in making it future
perfect, merely aorist subjunctive. On *katargeō* see I Cor.
6:13; 13:8, 10, 11. *Rule* (*archēn*), *authority* (*exousian*), *power*
(*dunamin*). All forms of power opposing the will of God.
Constative aorist tense covering the whole period of conflict with final victory as climax.

25. *Till he hath put* (*achri hou thēi*). Second aorist active
subjunctive of *tithēmi*, "till he put" (no sense in saying
"hath put," merely effective aorist tense for climax. *Achri*

(*hou*), *mechri* (*hou*), *heōs* (*hou*) all are used for the same idea of indefinite future time.

26. *The last enemy that shall be abolished is death* (*eschatos echthros katargeitai ho thanatos*). A rather free translation. Literally, "death (note article, and so subject) is done away (prophetic or futuristic use of present tense of same verb as in verse 24), the last enemy" (predicate and only one "last" and so no article as in I John 2:18).

27. *He put* (*hupetaxen*). First aorist active of *hupotassō*, to subject. Supply God (*theos*) as subject (Psa. 8:7). See Heb. 2:5–9 for similar use. Cf. Psa. 8. *But when he saith* (*hotan de eipēi*). Here Christ must be supplied as the subject if the reference is to his future and final triumph. The syntax more naturally calls for God as the subject as before. Either way makes sense. But there is no need to take *eipēi* (second aorist active subjunctive) as a *futurum exactum*, merely "whenever he shall say." *Are put in subjection* (*hupotetaktai*). Perfect passive indicative, state of completion, final triumph. *It is evident that* (*dēlon hoti*). Supply *estin* (is) before *hoti*. *He is excepted who did subject* (*ektos tou hupotaxantos*). "Except the one (God) who did subject (articular aorist active participle) the all things to him (Christ)."

28. *And when all things have been subjected* (*hotan de hupotagēi ta panta*). Second aorist passive subjunctive of *hupotassō*, not perfect. Merely, "when the all things are subjected unto him." The aorist subjunctive has given translators a deal of needless trouble in this passage. It is prophecy, of course. *That God may be all in all* (*hina ēi ho theos panta en pasin*). The final goal of all God's redemptive plans as Paul has so well said in Rom. 11:36. Precisely this language Paul will use of Christ (Col. 3:11).

29. *Else* (*epei*). Otherwise, if not true. On this use of *epei* with ellipsis see on 5:10; 7:14. *Which are baptized for the dead* (*hoi baptizomenoi huper tōn nekrōn*). This passage remains a puzzle. Stanley gives thirteen interpretations, no one of which may be correct. Over thirty have been suggested. The Greek expositors took it to be about the dead (*huper* in sense of *peri* as often as in II Cor. 1:6) since baptism is a burial and a resurrection (Rom. 6:2–6). Tertullian tells of some heretics who took it to mean baptized in the

place of dead people (unsaved) in order to save them. Some take it to be baptism over the dead. Others take it to mean that Paul and others were in peril of death as shown by baptism (see verse 30). *At all* (*holos*). See on 5:1.

30. *Why do we also stand in jeopardy every hour?* (*ti kai hēmeis kinduneuomen pasan hōran?*). We also as well as those who receive baptism which symbolizes death. Old verb from *kindunos* (peril, danger), in N.T. only here and Luke 8:23. Paul's Epistles and Acts (especially chapter 19) throw light on Paul's argument. He was never out of danger from Damascus to the last visit to Rome. There are perils in Ephesus of which we do not know (II Cor. 1:8f.) whatever may be true as to an Ephesian imprisonment. G. S. Duncan (*St. Paul's Ephesian Ministry*, 1930) even argues for several imprisonments in Ephesus. The accusative of time (*pasan hōran*) naturally means all through every hour (extension).

31. *I protest by that glorying in you* (*nē tēn humeteran kauchēsin*). No word for "I protest." Paul takes solemn oath by the use of *nē* (common in Attic) with the accusative. Only here in N.T., but in LXX (Gen. 42:15f.). For other solemn oaths by Paul see II Cor. 1:18, 23; 11:10f., 31; Rom. 9:1. For *kauchēsis* see on I Thess. 2:19. The possessive pronoun (*humeteran*) is objective as *emēn* in I Cor. 11:24. *I die daily* (*kath' hēmeran apothnēskō*). I am in daily peril of death (II Cor. 4:11; 11:23; Rom. 8:36).

32. *After the manner of men* (*kata anthrōpon*). Like men, for applause, money, etc. (4:9ff.; Phil. 3:7). *If I fought with wild beasts at Ephesus* (*ei ethēriomachēsa en Ephesōi*). Late verb from *thēriomachos*, a fighter with wild beasts. Found in inscriptions and in Ignatius. Those who argue for an Ephesian imprisonment for Paul and Ephesus as the place where he wrote the imprisonment epistles (see Duncan's book just mentioned) take the verb literally. There is in the ruins of Ephesus now a place called St. Paul's Prison. But Paul was a Roman citizen and it was unlawful to make such a one be a *thēriomachos*. If he were cast to the lions unlawfully, he could have prevented it by claiming his citizenship. Besides, shortly after this Paul wrote II Corinthians, but he does not mention so unusual a peril in the list in II Cor. 11:23f. The incident, whatever it was, whether literal or

figurative language, took place before Paul wrote I Corinthians. *What doth it profit me?* (*ti moi to ophelos?*). What the profit to me? *Let us eat and drink* (*phagōmen kai piōmen*). Volitive second aorist subjunctives of *esthiō* and *pinō*. Cited from Isa. 22:13. It is the outcry of the people of Jerusalem during the siege of Jerusalem by the Assyrians. At Anchiale near Tarsus is a statue of Sardanapalus with the inscription: "Eat, drink, enjoy thyself. The rest is nothing." This was the motto of the Epicureans. Paul is not giving his own view, but that of people who deny the resurrection.

33. *Be not deceived* (*mē planāsthe*). Do not be led astray (*planaō*) by such a false philosophy of life. *Evil company* (*homiliai kakai*). Evil companionships. Old word, *homilia*, from *homilos* (a crowd, gang, bunch). Only here in N.T. *Good manners* (*ēthē*). Old word (kin to *ethos*) custom, usage, morals. Good morals here. This line of poetry (iambic) occurs in Menander. It may be a current proverb. Paul could have gotten it from either source.

34. *Awake up righteously* (*eknēpsate dikaiōs*). Wake up as if from drunkenness. *Eknēphō*, only here in N.T. *Sin not* (*mē hamartanete*). Stop sinning. *No knowledge of God* (*agnōsian theou*). Old word for ignorance, in N.T. only here and I Peter 2:15. Ignorance of God, agnosticism. Some today (agnostics) even take pride in it instead of shame (*entropēn*, turning in on oneself). See on 6:5 for *entropē*.

35. *But some one will say* (*alla erei tis*). Paul knows what the sceptics were saying. He is a master at putting the standpoint of the imaginary adversary. *How* (*pōs*). This is still the great objection to the resurrection of our bodies. Granted that Jesus rose from the dead, for the sake of argument, these sceptics refuse to believe in the possibility of our resurrection. It is the attitude of Matthew Arnold who said, "Miracles do not happen." Scientifically we know the "how" of few things. Paul has an astounding answer to this objection. Death itself is the way of resurrection as in the death of the seed for the new plant (verses 36f.). *With what manner of body* (*poiōi sōmati*). This is the second question which makes plainer the difficulty of the first. The first body perishes. Will that body be raised? Paul treats this problem more at length (verses 38 to 54) and by analogy of nature (cf. Butler's famous *Analogy*). It is a spiritual, not a natural, body that is raised. *Sōma* here is an organism. Flesh (*sarx*) is the *sōma* for the natural man, but there is spiritual (*pneumatikon*) *sōma* for the resurrection.

36. *Thou foolish one* (*aphrōn*). Old word (*a* privative, *phrēn*), lack of sense. It is a severe term and justified by the implication "that the objector plumes himself on his acuteness" (Robertson and Plummer). Proleptic position of *su* (thou) sharpens the point. Sceptics (agnostics) pose as unusually intellectual (the intelligentsia), but the pose does not make one intelligent. *Except it die* (*ean mē apothanēi*). Condition of third class, possibility assumed. This is the answer to the "how" question. In plant life death precedes life, death of the seed and then the new plant.

37. *Not the body which shall be* (*ou to sōma to genēsomenon*). Articular future participle of *ginomai*, literally, "not the body that will become." The new *body* (*sōma*) is not yet in existence, but only the seed (*kokkos*, grain, old word, as in Matt. 13:31). *It may chance* (*ei tuchoi*). Fourth class condition as in 14:10 which see. Paul is rich in metaphors here, though usually not so (Howson, *Metaphors of St. Paul*). Paul was a city man. We sow seeds, not plants (bodies). The butterfly comes out of the dying worm.

38. *A body of its own* (*idion sōma*). Even under the microscope the life cells or germ plasm may seem almost identical, but the plant is quite distinct. On *sperma*, seed, old word from *speirō*, to sow, see on Matt. 13:24f.

39. *The same flesh* (*hē autē sarx*). Paul takes up animal life to show the great variety there is as in the plant kingdom. Even if evolution should prove to be true, Paul's argument remains valid. Variety exists along with kinship. Progress is shown in the different kingdoms, progress that even argues for a spiritual body after the body of flesh is lost. *Of beasts* (*ktēnōn*). Old word, from *ktaomai*, to possess, and so property. See Luke 10:34. *Of birds* (*ptēnōn*). Old word from *petomai*, to fly, winged, flying. Only here in N.T.

40. *Celestial* (*epourania*). Old word, from *epi*, upon, *ouranos*, heaven, existing in heaven. Paul now rises higher in the range of his argument, above the merely *terrestrial* (*epigeia*, upon earth, *epi*, *gē*) bodies. He has shown differences in the bodies here on earth in plants and in the animal

kingdom and now he indicates like differences to be seen in the heavens above us. *Is one (hetera men)—is another (hetera de)*. Antithesis that admits glory for bodies on earth and bodies in the heavens. Experience does not argue against a glory for the spiritual body (Phil. 3:21).

41. *For one star differeth from another star in glory (astēr gar asteros diapherei en doxēi)*. A beautiful illustration of Paul's point. *Asteros* is the ablative case after *diapherei* (old verb *diapherō*, Latin *differo*, our *differ*, bear apart). On *astēr* see Matt. 2:7 and *astron* Luke 21:25. Stars differ in magnitude and brilliancy. The telescope has added more force to Paul's argument. *In glory (en doxēi)*. Old word from *dokeō*, to think, to seem. So opinion, estimate, then the shekinah glory of God in the LXX, glory in general. It is one of the great words of the N.T. Jesus is termed the glory in James 2:1.

42. *So is the resurrection of the dead (houtōs kai hē anastasis tōn nekrōn)*. Paul now applies his illustrations to his argument to prove the kind of body we shall have after the resurrection. He does it by a series of marvellous contrasts that gather all his points. The earthly and the risen beings differ in duration, value, power (Wendt). *It is sown (speiretai)*. In death, like the seed (37). *In incorruption (en aphtharsiāi)*. Late word from *a* privative and *phtheirō*, to corrupt. In LXX, Plutarch, Philo, late papyrus of a Gnostic gospel, and quotation from Epicurus. Vulgate *incorruptio*. The resurrection body has undergone a complete change as compared with the body of flesh like the plant from the seed. It is related to it, but it is a different body of glory.

43. *In weakness (en astheneiāi)*. Lack of strength as shown in the victory of death. *In power (en dunamei)*. Death can never conquer this new body, "conformed to the body of His glory" (Phil. 3:21).

44. *A natural body (sōma psuchikon)*. See on 2:14 for this word, a difficult one to translate since *psuchē* has so many meanings. Natural is probably as good a rendering as can be made, but it is not adequate, for the body here is not all *psuchē* either as soul or life. The same difficulty exists as to a spiritual body (*sōma pneumatikon*). The resurrection body is not wholly *pneuma*. Caution is needed here in filling out details concerning the *psuchē* and the *pneuma*.

But certainly he means to say that the "spiritual body" has some kind of germinal connection with the "natural body," though the development is glorious beyond our comprehension though not beyond the power of Christ to perform (Phil. 3:21). The force of the argument remains unimpaired though we cannot follow fully into the thought beyond us. *If there is (ei estin).* "If there exists" (*estin* means this with accent on first syllable), a condition of first class assumed as true. *There is also (estin kai).* There exists also.

45. *Became a living soul (egeneto eis psuchēn zōsan).* Hebraistic use of *eis* in predicate from LXX. God breathed a soul (*psuchē*) into "the first man." *The last Adam became a life-giving spirit (ho eschatos Adam eis pneuma zōopoioun).* Supply *egeneto* (became). Christ is the crown of humanity and has power to give us the new body. In Rom. 5:12–19 Paul calls Christ the Second Adam.

46. *Howbeit that is not first which is spiritual, but that which is natural (all' ou prōton to pneumatikon, alla to psuchikon).* Literally, "But not first the spiritual, but the natural." This is the law of growth always.

47. *Earthly (choïkos).* Late rare word, from *chous,* dust. *The second man from heaven (ho deuteros anthrōpos ex ouranou).* Christ had a human (*psuchikon*) body, of course, but Paul makes the contrast between the first man in his natural body and the Second Man in his risen body. Paul saw Jesus after his resurrection and he appeared to him "from heaven." He will come again from heaven.

48. *As is the earthly (hoios ho choikos).* Masculine gender because of *anthrōpos* and correlative pronouns (*hoios, toioutoi*) of character or quality. All men of dust (*choïkoi*) correspond to "the man of dust" (*ho choïkos*), the first Adam. *As is the heavenly (hoios ho epouranios).* Christ in his ascended state (I Thess. 4:16; II Thess. 1:7; Eph. 2:6, 20; Phil. 3:20f.).

49. *We shall also bear (phoresomen kai).* Old MSS. (so Westcott and Hort) read *phoresōmen kai.* Volitive aorist active subjunctive, Let us also bear. Ellicott strongly opposes the subjunctive. It may be merely the failure of scribes to distinguish between long o and short o. Paul hardly means to say that our attaining the resurrection body depends on our own efforts! A late frequentative form of *pherō.*

50. *Cannot inherit* (*klēronomēsai ou dunantai*). Hence there must be a change by death from the natural body to the spiritual body. In the case of Christ this change was wrought in less than three days and even then the body of Jesus was in a transition state before the Ascension. He ate and could be handled and yet he passed through closed doors. Paul does not base his argument on the special circumstances connected with the risen body of Jesus.

51. *A mystery* (*mustērion*). He does not claim that he has explained everything. He has drawn a broad parallel which opens the door of hope and confidence. *We shall not all sleep* (*pantes ou koimēthēsometha*). Future passive indicative of *koimaomai*, to sleep. Not all of us shall die, Paul means. Some people will be alive when he comes. Paul does not affirm that he or any then living will be alive when Jesus comes again. He simply groups all under the phrase "we all." *But we shall all be changed* (*pantes de allagēsometha*). Second future passive indicative of *allassō*. Both living and dead shall be changed and so receive the resurrection body. See this same idea at more length in I Thess. 4:13-18.

52. *In a moment* (*en atomōi*). Old word, from *a* privative and *temnō*, to cut, indivisible: Scientific word for *atom* which was considered indivisible, but that was before the day of electrons and protons. Only here in N.T. *In the twinkling of an eye* (*en ripēi ophthalmou*). Old word *ripē* from *riptō*, to throw. Only here in N.T. Used by the Greeks for the flapping of a wing, the buzz of a gnat, the quivering of a harp, the twinkling of a star. *At the last trump* (*en tēi eschatēi salpiggi*). Symbolical, of course. See on I Thess. 4:16; Matt. 24:31.

53. *Must put on* (*dei endusasthai*). Aorist (ingressive) middle infinitive, put on as a garment. *Immortality* (*athanasian*). Old word from *athanatos*, undying, and that from *a* privative and *thnēskō*, to die. In N.T. only here and I Tim. 6:16 where God is described as having immortality.

54. *Shall have put on* (*endusētai*). First aorist middle subjunctive with *hotan* whenever, merely indefinite future, no *futurum exactum*, merely meaning, "whenever shall put on," not "shall have put on." *Is swallowed up* (*katepothē*). First aorist passive indicative of *katapinō*, old verb to drink down, swallow down. Perfective use of *kata-* where we say

"up," "swallow up." Timeless use of the aorist tense. Paul changes the active voice *katepien* in Isa. 25:8 to the passive. Death is no longer victory. Theodotion reads the Hebrew verb (*bulla*, for *billa*,) as passive like Paul. It is the "final overthrow of the king of Terrors" (Findlay) as shown in Heb. 2:15.

55. *Victory* (*nikos*). Late form of *nikē*. *O death* (*thanate*). Second instance. Here Paul changes Hades of the LXX for Hebrew Sheol (Hosea 13:14) to death. Paul never uses Hades. *Thy sting* (*sou to kentron*). Old word from *kentreō*, to prick, as in Acts 26:14. In Rev. 9:10 of the sting of locusts, scorpions. The serpent death has lost his poison fangs.

56. *The power of sin* (*hē dunamis tēs hamartias*). See Rom. 4:15; 5:20; 6:14; chapter 7; Gal. 2:16; 3:1–5:4 for Paul's ideas here briefly expressed. In man's unrenewed state he cannot obey God's holy law.

57. *But thanks be to God* (*tōi de theōi charis*). Exultant triumph through Christ over sin and death as in Rom. 7:25.

58. *Be ye steadfast, unmovable* (*hedraioi ginesthe, ametakinētoi*). "Keep on becoming steadfast, unshaken." Let the sceptics howl and rage. Paul has given rational grounds for faith and hope in Christ the Risen Lord and Saviour. Note practical turn to this great doctrinal argument. *Work* (*ergon*), *labour* (*kopos*, toil). The best answer to doubt is work.

CHAPTER XVI

1. *Now concerning the collection for the saints (peri de tēs logias tēs eis tous hagious).* Paul has discussed all the problems raised by the Corinthians. Now he has on his own heart the collection for the saints in Jerusalem (see chapters 8 and 9 in II Cor.). This word *logia* (or *-eia*) is now known to be derived from a late verb *logeuō*, to collect, recently found in papyri and inscriptions (Deissmann, *Bible Studies*, p. 143). The word *logia* is chiefly found in papyri, ostraca, and inscriptions that tell of religious collections for a god or a temple (Deissmann, *Light from the Ancient East*, p. 105). The introduction of this topic may seem sudden, but the Corinthians were behind with their part of it. They may even have asked further about it. Paul feels no conflict between discussion of the resurrection and the collection. *So also do ye (houtōs kai humas poiēsate).* Paul had given orders (*dietaxa*) to the churches of Galatia and now gives them like commands. As a matter of fact, they had *promised* a long time before this (II Cor. 8:10; 9:1-5). Now do what you pledged.

2. *Upon the first day of the week (kata mian sabbatou).* For the singular *sabbatou* (sabbath) for week see Luke 18:12; Mark 16:9. For the use of the cardinal *mian* in sense of ordinal *prōtēn* after Hebrew fashion in LXX (Robertson, *Grammar*, p. 672) as in Mark 16:2; Luke 24:1; Acts 20:7. Distributive use of *kata* also. *Lay by him in store (par' heautōi tithetō thēsaurizōn).* By himself, in his home. Treasuring it (cf. Matt. 6:19f. for *thēsaurizō*). Have the habit of doing it, *tithetō* (present imperative). *As he may prosper (hoti ean euodōtai).* Old verb from *eu*, well, and *hodos*, way or journey, to have a good journey, to prosper in general, common in LXX. In N.T. only here and Rom. 1:10; III John 2. It is uncertain what form *euodōtai* is, present passive subjunctive, perfect passive indicative, or even perfect passive subjunctive (Moulton, *Prolegomena*, p. 54). The old MSS. had no accents. Some MSS. even have *euodōthēi* (first aorist passive subjunctive). But the sense is not al-

tered. *Hoti* is accusative of general reference and *ean* can occur either with the subjunctive or indicative. This rule for giving occurs also in II Cor. 8:12. Paul wishes the collections to be made before he comes.

3. *When I arrive* (*hotan paragenōmai*). Whenever I arrive, indefinite temporal conjunction *hotan* and second aorist middle subjunctive. *Whomsoever ye shall approve by letters* (*hous ean dokimasēte di' epistolōn*). Indefinite relative with *ean* and aorist subjunctive of *dokimazō* (to test and so approve as in Phil. 1:10). "By letters" to make it formal and regular and Paul would approve their choice of messengers to go with him to Jerusalem (II Cor. 8:20ff.). Curiously enough no names from Corinth occur in the list in Acts 20:4. *To carry* (*apenegkein*). Second aorist active infinitive of *apopherō*, to bear away. *Bounty* (*charin*). Gift, grace, as in II Cor. 8:4-7. As a matter of fact, the messengers of the churches (*apostoloi ekklēsiōn* II Cor. 8:23) went along with Paul to Jerusalem (Acts 20:4f.).

4. *And if it be meet for me to go also* (*ean de axion ēi tou kāme poreuesthai*). "If the collection be worthy of the going as to me also." Condition of third class (*ean—ēi*) and the articular infinitive in the genitive (*tou*) after *axion*. The accusative of general reference (*kāme*, me also) with the infinitive. So the awkward phrase clears up.

5. *When I shall have passed through Macedonia* (*hotan Makedonian dielthō*). "Whenever I pass through (second aorist active subjunctive of *dierchomai*) Macedonia" (see construction in verse 3). *I do pass through* (*dierchomai*). I plan to pass through, futuristic use of present indicative.

6. *It may be* (*tuchon*). Neuter accusative of second aorist active participle of *tugchanō* used as an adverb (in Plato and Xenophon, but nowhere else in N.T.). *Or even winter* (*ē kai paracheimasō*). Future active of late verb *paracheimazō* (*cheimōn*, winter). See on Acts 27:12; 28:11; Titus 3:12. He did stay in Corinth for three months (Acts 20:3), probably the coming winter. *Whithersoever I go* (*hou ean poreuōmai*). Indefinite local clause with subjunctive. As a matter of fact, Paul had to flee from a conspiracy in Corinth (Acts 20:3).

7. *Now by the way* (*arti en parodōi*). Like our "by the way" (*parodos*), incidentally. *If the Lord permit* (*ean ho*

Kurios epitrepsēi). Condition of the third class. Paul did everything *en Kuriōi* (cf. Acts 18:21).

8. *Until Pentecost (heōs tēs pentēkostēs).* He writes them in the spring before pentecost. Apparently the uproar by Demetrius hurried Paul away from Ephesus (Acts 20:1).

9. *For a great and effectual door is opened unto me (thura gar moi aneōigen megalē kai energēs).* Second perfect active indicative of *anoigō,* to open. Intransitive, stands wide open at last after his years there (Acts 20:31). A wide open door. What does he mean by *energēs?* It is a late word in the *Koiné.* In the papyri a medical receipt has it for "tolerably strong." The form *energos* in the papyri is used of a mill "in working order," of "tilled land," and of "wrought iron." In the N.T. it occurs in Philemon 6 and Heb. 4:12 of "the word of God" as *"energēs"* (powerful). Paul means that he has at least a great opportunity for work in Ephesus. *And there are many adversaries (kai antikeimenoi polloi).* "And many are lying opposed to me," lined up against me. These Paul mentions as a reason for staying in, not for leaving, Ephesus. Read Acts 19 and see the opposition from Jews and Gentiles with the explosion under the lead of Demetrius. And yet Paul suddenly leaves. He hints of much of which we should like to know more. (I Cor. 15:32; II Cor. 1:8f.).

10. *That he be without fear (hina aphobōs genētai).* Evidently he had reason to fear the treatment that Timothy might receive in Corinth as shown in 4:17-21.

11. *For I expect him (ekdechomai gar auton).* Apparently later Timothy had to return to Ephesus without much success before Paul left and was sent on to Macedonia with Erastus (Acts 19:22) and Titus sent to Corinth whom Paul then arranged to meet in Troas (II Cor. 2:12).

12. *And it was not at all his will to come now (kai pantōs ouk ēn thelēma hina nun elthēi).* Adversative use of *kai=* "but." Apollos had left Corinth in disgust over the strife there which involved him and Paul (I Cor. 1 to 4). He had had enough of partisan strife over preachers.

13. *Watch ye (grēgoreite).* Stay awake. Late present from *egrēgora* second perfect of *egeirō,* to awake. *Quit you like men (andrizesthe).* Play the man. Middle voice, show yourselves men. From *anēr,* a man.

15. *Ye know (oidate).* *Koiné* form for second perfect in-

THE EPISTLES OF PAUL

dicative used as present of *horaō*. Parenthetic clause through rest of the verse. Stephanas is mentioned also in 1:16 and in 16:17. For *aparchē* see on 15:20, 23. *They have set themselves* (*etaxan heautous*). Remarkable statement worthy of attention today. This noble family appointed themselves to be ministers to the saints that needed it (the poor and needy). Personal work for Christ is still the only way to win the world for Christ, voluntary personal work. If all Christians did it!

16. *That ye also be in subjection unto such* (*hina kai humeis hupotassēsthe tois toioutois*). This is the exhortation begun in verse 15. The family of Stephanas took the lead in good works. Do ye also follow such leaders. This is our great problem today, to find great leaders and many loyal followers. This would solve all church problems, great leadership and great following. Lend a hand.

17. *At the coming* (*epi tēi parousiāi*). At the coming here of Stephanas, etc., the very word used of the *parousia* of Christ (15:23). *That which was lacking on your part they supplied* (*to humeteron husterēma houtoi aneplērōsan*). Either "these filled up my lack of you" or "these filled up your lack of me." Either makes perfectly good sense and both were true. Which Paul meant we cannot tell.

18. *For they refreshed my spirit and yours* (*anepausan gar to emon pneuma kai to humōn*). They did both. The very verb used by Jesus in Matt. 11:28 for the refreshment offered by him to those who come to him, fellowship with Jesus, and here fellowship with each other.

19. *The churches of Asia* (*hai ekklēsiai tēs Asias*). True of the Roman province (Acts 10:10, 26; Col. 1:6; 2:1; 4:13, 16). The gospel spread rapidly from Ephesus. *With the church that is in their house* (*sun tēi kat' oikon autōn ekklēsiāi*). Paul had long ago left the synagogue for the school house of Tyrannus (Acts 19:9). But Aquila and Prisca opened their house here for the services. The churches had to meet where they could. Paul had laboured and lived with this family in Corinth (Acts 18:2) and now again in Ephesus (Acts 18:19; 20:34). It was their habit wherever they lived (Rom. 16:5).

20. *With a holy kiss* (*en philēmati hagiōi*). In the synagogue men kissed men and women kissed women. This was

the Christian custom at a later date and apparently so here. See I Thess. 5:26; II Cor. 13:12; Rom. 3:8; I Peter 5:14. It seems never to have been promiscuous between the sexes.

21. *Of me Paul with mine own hand* (*tēi emēi cheiri Paulou*). Literally, "With the hand of me Paul." The genitive *Paulou* is in apposition with the possessive pronoun *emēi* which is in the instrumental case just as in II Thess. 3:17, the sign in every Epistle. He dictated, but signed at the end. If we only had that signature on that scrap of paper.

22. *Anathema.* The word seems a bit harsh to us, but the refusal to love Christ (*ou philei*) on the part of a nominal Christian deserves *anathema* (see on 12:3 for this word). *Maran atha.* This Aramaic phrase means "Our Lord (*maran*) cometh (*atha*)" or, used as a proleptic perfect, "has come." It seems to be a sort of watchword (cf. I Thess. 4:14ff.; James 5:7f.; Phil. 4:5; Rev. 1:7; 3:11; 22:20), expressing the lively hope that the Lord will come. It was a curious blunder in the King James Version that connected *Maran atha* with *Anathema.*

SECOND CORINTHIANS

FROM MACEDONIA A.D. 54 OR 55

BY WAY OF INTRODUCTION

The Pauline authorship is admitted by all real scholars, though there is doubt by some as to the unity of the Epistle. J. H. Kennedy (*The Second and Third Letters of St. Paul to the Corinthians*, 1900) has presented the arguments in a plausible, but not wholly convincing, manner for the plea that chapters 10 to 13 really represent a separate and earlier letter, the one referred to in II Cor. 2:3, which was later tacked on to chapters 1–9 as part of the same Epistle. This theory does explain the difference in tone between chapters 1 to 7 and 10 to 13, but that fact is sufficiently clear from the stubborn minority against Paul in Corinth reported by Titus after the majority had been won to Paul by First Corinthians and by Titus (II Cor. 2:1–11). There are in fact three obvious divisions in the Epistle. Chapters 1 to 7 deal with the report of Titus about the victory in Corinth and Paul's wonderful digression on the glory of the ministry in 2:12 to 6:10; chapters 8 and 9 discuss the collection for the poor saints in Jerusalem already mentioned in I Cor. 16:1f. and which Titus is to press to completion on his return to Corinth; chapters 10 to 13 deal sharply with the Judaizing minority who still oppose Paul's leadership. These three subjects are in no sense inconsistent with each other. The letter is a unity. Nowhere do we gain so clear an insight into Paul's own struggles and hopes as a preacher. It is a handbook for the modern minister of inestimable value. One can hear Paul's heart throb through these chapters. The syntax is often broken by anacolutha. The sentences are sometimes disconnected. Grammatical agreements are overlooked. But there is power here, the grip of a great soul holding on to the highest ideals in the midst of

205

manifold opposition and discouragements. Christ is Master of Paul at every turn.

The date of the Epistle is clearly after I Corinthians, for Paul has left Ephesus and is now in Macedonia (II Cor. 2:13), probably at Philippi, where he met Titus, though he had hoped to meet him at Troas on his return from Corinth. At a guess one may say that Paul wrote in the autumn of A.D. 54 or 55 of the same year in the spring of which he had written I Corinthians, and before he went on to Corinth himself where he wrote Romans (Acts 20:1–3; Rom. 16:1).

The occasion for writing is the return of Titus from Corinth with mixed news of the Pauline majority and the minority in opposition. So Titus is sent back with this Epistle to finish the task while Paul waits awhile for matters to clear up (13:1–10).

It is not certain whether the letter mentioned in II Cor. 2:3 is our I Corinthians or a lost letter like the one alluded to in I Cor. 5:9. If it is a lost one, we know of four Corinthian Epistles (the one in I Cor. 5:9, our I Corinthians, the one in II Cor. 2:3, our II Corinthians), assuming the unity of II Corinthians. Few things in Paul's ministry gave him more concern than the troubles in Corinth. The modern city pastor finds little in his work that Paul has not faced and mastered. There is consolation and courage for the preacher in the conduct and counsels of this greatest of all preachers.

The books on II Corinthians are mainly the same as those on I Corinthians. Some special discussions of II Corinthians deserve mention like Bachmann's *Der Zweite Brief des Paulus an die Korinther* in the Zahn *Kommentar* (1909), Barde's *Étude sur la épître aux Cor.* (1906), Belser's *Der Zweite Brief des Apostels Paulus an die Korinther* (1910), Bernard's *Second Corinthians* in the *Expositor's Greek Testament* (1903), Denney's *II Corinthians* in the *Expositor's Bible* (1911), Farrar's *II Corinthians* in the *Pulpit Commentary* (1883), Godet's *La seconde épître aux Corinthiens* (1914), Goudge's *The Mind of St. Paul in II Cor.* (1911), Heinrici's *II Kor.* in the Meyer *Komm.* (8th ed., 1900), Heinrici's *Das Zweite Sendschreiben des Apostels Paulus an die Kor.* (1887), J. H. Kennedy's *The Second and Third Letters of St. Paul to the Corinthians* (1900), Isaacs's *Second Epistle to the Corinthians*

(1921), Menzies's *The Second Epistle to the Corinthians* (1912), Parry's *II Cor.* in *Cambridge Greek Testament* (1916), Plummer's *II Corinthians* in *Int. Crit. Comm.* (1915), Rendall's *II Cor.*, A. T. Robertson's *The Glory of the Ministry* (II Cor. 2:12–6:10, 1911).

CHAPTER I

1. *And Timothy* (*kai Timotheos*). Timothy is with Paul, having been sent on to Macedonia from Ephesus (Acts 19:22). He is in no sense co-author any more than Sosthenes was in I Cor. 1:1. *In all Achaia* (*en holēi tēi Achaiāi*). The Romans divided Greece into two provinces (Achaia and Macedonia). Macedonia included also Illyricum, Epirus, and Thessaly. Achaia was all of Greece south of this (both Attica and the Peloponnesus). The restored Corinth was made the capital of Achaia where the pro-consul resided (Acts 18:12). He does not mention other churches in Achaia outside of the one in Corinth, but only "saints" (*hagiois*). Athens was in Achaia, but it is not clear that there was as yet a church there, though some converts had been won (Acts 17:34), and there was a church in Cenchreae, the eastern port of Corinth (Rom. 16:1). Paul in II Cor. 9:2 speaks of Achaia and Macedonia together. His language here would seem to cover the whole (*holēi*, all) of Achaia in his scope and not merely the environment around Corinth.

2. Identical with I Cor. 1:3 which see.

3. *Blessed* (*eulogētos*). From old verb *eulogeō*, to speak well of, but late verbal in LXX and Philo. Used of men in Gen. 24:31, but only of God in N.T. as in Luke 1:68 and chiefly in Paul (II Cor. 11:31; Rom. 1:25). Paul has no thanksgiving or prayer as in I Cor. 1:4-9, but he finds his basis for gratitude in God, not in them. *The God and Father* (*ho theos kai patēr*). So rightly, only one article with both substantives as in II Peter 1:1. Paul gives the deity of Jesus Christ as our Lord (*Kuriou*), but he does not hesitate to use the language here as it occurs. See I Peter 1:3; in Eph. 1:3 where the language is identical with that here. *The father of mercies* (*ho patēr tōn oiktirmōn*) *and God of all comfort* (*kai theos pasēs paraklēseōs*). Paul adds an item to each word. He is the compassionate Father characterized by mercies (*oiktirmōn*, old word from *oikteirō*, to pity, and here in plural, emotions and acts of pity). He is the God of all comfort (*paraklēseōs*, old word from *parakaleō*, to call to one's

side, common with Paul). Paul has already used it of God who gave eternal comfort (II Thess. 2:16). The English word comfort is from the Latin *confortis* (brave together). The word used by Jesus of the Holy Spirit as the Comforter or Paraklete is this very word (John 14:16; 16:7). Paul makes rich use of the verb *parakaleō* and the substantive *paraklēsis* in this passage (3–7). He urges all sorrowing and troubled hearts to find strength in God.

4. *In all our affliction (epi pasēi tēi thlipsei hēmōn)*. *Thlipsis* is from *thlibō*, to press, old and common word, as tribulation is from Latin *tribulum* (roller). See on Matt. 13:21 and I Thess. 1:6. The English affliction is Latin *afflictio* from *ad-fligere*, to strike on. *That we may be able to comfort (eis to dunasthai hēmas parakalein)*. Purpose clause with *eis* and the articular infinitive with the accusative of general reference, a common idiom. Paul here gives the purpose of affliction in the preacher's life, in any Christian's life, to qualify him for ministry to others. Otherwise it will be professional and perfunctory. *Wherewith (hēs)*. Genitive case of the relative attracted to that of the antecedent *paraklēseōs*. The case of the relative here could have been either the accusative *hēn* with the passive verb retained as in Mark 10:38 or the instrumental *hēi*. Either is perfectly good Greek (cf. Eph. 1:6; 4:1). Personal experience of God's comfort is necessary before we can pass it on to others.

5. *The sufferings of Christ (ta pathēmata tou Christou)*. Subjective genitive, Christ's own sufferings. *Abound unto us (perisseuei eis hēmas)*. Overflow unto us so that we suffer like sufferings and become fellow sufferers with Christ (4:10f.; Rom. 8:17; Phil. 3:10; Col. 1:24). *Through Christ (dia tou Christou)*. The overflow (*perisseuei*) of comfort comes also through Christ. Is Paul thinking of how some of the Jewish Christians in Corinth have become reconciled with him through Christ? Partnership with Christ in suffering brings partnership in glory also (Rom. 8:17; I Peter 4:13).

6. *Whether (eite)—or (eite)*. The alternatives in Paul's experience (afflicted *thlibometha*, comforted *parakaloumetha*) work out for their good when they are called on to endure like sufferings "which we also suffer" (*hōn kai hēmeis paschomen*). The relative *hōn* is attracted from neuter accusative

plural *ha* to genitive case of the antecedent *pathēmatōn* (sufferings).

7. *Our hope for you* (*hē elpis hēmōn huper humōn*). The old word *elpis*, from *elpizō*, to hope, has the idea of waiting with expectation and patience. So here it is "steadfast" (*bebaia*, stable, fast, from *bainō*, to plant the feet down). *Partakers* (*koinōnoi*). Partners as in Luke 5:10.

8. *Concerning our affliction* (*huper tēs thlipseōs hēmōn*)· Manuscripts read also *peri* for in the Koiné, *huper* (over) often has the idea of *peri* (around). Paul has laid down his philosophy of afflictions and now he cites a specific illustration in his own recent experience. *In Asia* (*en Asiāi*). Probably in Ephesus, but what it was we do not know whether sickness or peril. We do know that the disciples and the Asiarchs would not allow Paul to face the mob in the amphitheatre gathered by Demetrius (Acts 20:30f.). In Rom. 16:4 Paul says that Prisca and Aquila laid down their necks for him, risked their very lives for him. It may have been a later plot to kill Paul that hastened his departure from Ephesus (Acts 20:1). He had a trial so great that "we were weighed down exceedingly beyond our power" (*kath' huperbolēn huper dunamin ebarēthēmen*). Old verb from *baros*, weight, *barus*, weighty. First aorist passive indicative. See on I Cor. 12:31 for *kath' huperbolēn* (cf. our hyperbole). It was beyond Paul's power to endure if left to himself. *Insomuch that we despaired even of life* (*hōste exaporēthēnai hēmas kai tou zēin*). Usual clause of result with *hōste* and the infinitive. First aorist passive infinitive *exaporēthēnai*, late compound for utter despair (perfective use of *ex* and at a complete loss, *a* privative and *poros*, way). There seemed no way out. *Of life* (*tou zēin*). Ablative case of the articular infinitive, of living.

9. *Yea* (*alla*). Confirmatory use as in 7:11, rather than adversative. *The answer of death* (*to apokrima tou thanatou*). This late word from *apokrinomai*, to reply, occurs nowhere else in N.T., but is in Josephus, Polybius, inscriptions and papyri (Deissmann, *Bible Studies*, p. 257; Moulton and Milligan's *Vocabulary*), and always in the sense of decision or judgment rendered. But Vulgate renders it by *responsum* and that idea suits best here, unless Paul conceives God as rendering the decision of death. *We ourselves have had within*

ourselves (autoi en heautois eschēkamen). Regular perfect of *echō*, to have. And still have the vivid recollection of that experience. For this lively dramatic use of the present perfect indicative for a past experience see also *eschēka* in 2:13 (Moulton, *Prolegomena*, p. 143f.; Robertson, *Grammar*, p. 896f.). *That we should not trust in ourselves (hina mē pepoithotes ōmen eph' heautois).* A further purpose of God in affliction beyond that in verse 4. "This dreadful trial was sent to him in order to give him a precious spiritual lesson (12:7–10)" (Robertson and Plummer). Note periphrastic perfect active subjunctive of *peithō*, to persuade. *In (epi)*, upon, both ourselves and God.

10. *Out of so great a death (ek tēlikoutou thanatou).* He had considered himself as good as dead. *Delivered (erusato)—will deliver (rusetai).* Old verb *ruō*, middle, *ruomai*, draw oneself, as out of a pit, rescue. So Paul faces death without fear. *On whom we have set our hope (eis hon ēlpikamen).* Perfect active indicative of *elpizō*. We still have that hope, emphasized by *eti rusetai* (he will still deliver).

11. *Ye also helping together on our behalf (sunupourgountōn kai humōn huper hēmōn).* Genitive absolute with present active participle of late compound verb (*sun* and *hupourgeō* for *hupo* and *ergon*). Paul relied on God and felt the need of the prayer of God's people. *By means of many (ek pollōn prosōpōn).* *Prosōpon* means face (*pros, ops*). The word is common in all Greek. The papyri use it for face, appearance, person. It occurs twelve times in II Corinthians. It certainly means face in eight of them (3:7 twice, 13, 18; 8:24; 10:1, 7; 11:20). In 5:12 it means outward appearance. It may mean face or person here, 2:10; 4:6. It is more pictorial to take it here as face "that out of many upturned faces" thanks may be given (*hina—eucharistēthēi* first aorist passive subjunctive) for the gift to us by means of many (*dia pollōn*). It is indeed a difficult sentence to understand.

12. *Glorying (kauchēsis).* Act of glorying, while in verse 14 *kauchēma* is the thing boasted of. *The testimony of our conscience (to marturion tēs suneidēseōs hēmōn).* In apposition with *kauchēsis*. Sincerity of God (*eilikrineiāi tou theou*). Like *dikaiosunē theou* (Rom. 1:17; 3:21), the God-kind of righteousness. So the God-kind (genitive case) of sincerity. Late word from *eilikrinēs*. See on I Cor. 5:8. *Not in fleshly*

wisdom (ouk en sophiāi sarkikēi). See on I Cor. 1:17; 2:4,
13f. Paul uses *sarkikos* five times and it occurs only twice
elsewhere in N.T. See on I Cor. 3:3. *We behaved ourselves
(anestraphēmen).* Second aorist passive indicative of *anastrephō,* old verb, to turn back, to turn back and forth, to
walk. Here the passive is used as in late Greek as if middle.
More abundantly to you-ward (perissoterōs pros humas). They
had more abundant opportunity to observe how scrupulous
Paul was (Acts 18:11).
13. *Than what ye read (all' ē ha anaginōskete).* Note comparative conjunction *ē* (than) after *all'* and that after *alla*
(other things, same word in reality), "other than." Read
in Greek *(anaginōskō)* is knowing again, recognizing. See
on Acts 8:30. *Or even acknowledge (ē kai epiginōskete.* Paul
is fond of such a play on words *(anaginōskete, epiginōskete)*
or paronomasia. Does he mean "read between the lines,"
as we say, by the use of *epi* (additional knowledge)? *Unto
the end (heōs telous).* The report of Titus showed that the
majority now at last understood Paul. He hopes that it
will last (I Cor. 1:8).
14. *As also ye did acknowledge us in part (kathōs kai epegnōte hēmas apo merous).* Gracious acknowledgment (second
aorist active indicative of *epignōskō*) to the original Pauline
party (I Cor. 1:12; 3:4) that he had seemed to care so little
for them. And now in his hour of victory he shows that, if
he is their ground of glorying, they are his also (cf. I Thess.
2:19f.; Phil. 2:16).
15. *Confidence (pepoithēsei).* This late word (LXX,
Philo, Josephus) is condemned by the Atticists, but Paul
uses it a half dozen times (3:4 also). *I was minded to come
(eboulomēn elthein).* Imperfect, I was wishing to come,
picturing his former state of mind. *Before unto you (proteron pros humas).* This was his former plan *(proteron)* while
in Ephesus to go to Achaia directly from Ephesus. This he
confesses in verse 16 "and by you to pass into Macedonia."
*That ye might have a second benefit (hina deuteran charin
schēte).* Or second "joy" if we accept *charan* with Westcott
and Hort. This would be a real second blessing (or joy) if
they should have two visits from Paul.
16. *And again (kai palin).* This would have been the
second benefit or joy. But he changed his plans and did

not make that trip directly to Corinth, but came on to Macedonia first (Acts 19:21; 20:1f.; I Cor. 16:2; II Cor. 2:12). *To be set forward by you (huph' humōn propemphthēnai).* First aorist passive infinitive of *propempō.* Paul uses this same verb in Rom. 15:24 for the same service by the Roman Christians on his proposed trip to Spain. The Corinthians, especially the anti-Pauline party, took advantage of Paul's change of plans to criticize him sharply for vacillation and flippancy. How easy it is to find fault with the preacher! So Paul has to explain his conduct.

17. *Did I shew fickleness? (mēti ara tēi elaphriāi?).* An indignant negative answer is called for by *mēti.* The instrumental case of *elaphriāi* is regular after *echrēsamēn* from *chraomai,* to use. *Elaphria* is a late word for levity from the old adjective, *elaphros,* light, agile (II Cor. 10:17; Matt. 11:30). Here only in N.T. *Purpose (bouleuomai).* Paul raises the question of fickleness about any of his plans. *Yea yea (Nai nai)—nay nay (ou ou).* See a similar repetition in Matt. 5:37. It is plain in James 5:12 where "the yea" is "yea" and "the nay" is "nay." That seems to be Paul's meaning here, "that the Yea may be yea and the Nay may be nay."

18. *Is not yea and nay (ouk estin nai kai ou).* He is not a Yes and No man, saying Yes and meaning or acting No. Paul calls God to witness on this point.

19. *Was not Yea and Nay (ouk egeneto nai kai ou).* "Did not become Yes and No." *But in him is yea (alla Nai en autōi gegonen).* Rather, "But in him Yes has become yes," has proved true. So Paul appeals to the life of Christ to sustain his own veracity.

20. *In him is the yea (en autōi to Nai).* Supply *gegonen* from the preceding sentence, "In him was the Yea come true." This applies to all God's promises. *The Amen (to Amēn).* In public worship (I Cor. 14:16).

21. *Establishes (bebaiōn).* Present active participle from *bebaios,* firm. An apt metaphor in Corinth where confirmation of a bargain often took place (*bebaiōsis*) as Deissmann shows (*Bible Studies,* p. 109) and as verse 22 makes plain. *Anointed (chrisas).* From *chriō,* to anoint, old verb, to consecrate, with the Holy Spirit here as in I John 2:20.

22. *Sealed us (sphragisamenos hēmas).* From *sphragizō* old

verb, common in LXX and papyri for setting a seal to prevent opening (Dan. 6:17), in place of signature (I Kings 21:18). Papyri examples show a wide legal use to give validity to documents, to guarantee genuineness of articles as sealing sacks and chests, etc. (Deissmann, *Bible Studies*, p. 238; Moulton and Milligan's *Vocabulary*). *The earnest of the Spirit* (*ton arrabōna tou pneumatos*). A word of Semitic origin (possibly Phoenician) and spelled both *arabōn* and *arrabōn*. It is common in the papyri as earnest money in a purchase for a cow or for a wife (a dowry). In N.T. only here; 5:5; Eph. 1:14. It is part payment on the total obligation and we use the very expression today, "earnest money." It is God, says Paul, who has done all this for us and God is Paul's pledge that he is sincere. He will come to Corinth in due time. This earnest of the Spirit in our hearts is the witness of the Spirit that we are God's.

23. *But I call God for a witness upon my soul* (*Egō de martura ton theon epikaloumai epi tēn emēn psuchēn*). Solemn attestation, "calling heaven to witness is frequent in literature from Homer onwards" (Plummer). Thus God is described above (cf. I Thess. 2:5, 10; Rom. 1:9; Gal. 1:20; Phil. 1:8). *To spare you* (*pheidomenos humōn*). Present middle participle (causal rather than final) of *pheidomai*, old verb, to hold back, to spare. Ablative case *humōn*.

24. *We have lordship over* (*kurieuomen*). Old verb from *kurios*, to be lord of or over. See Luke 22:25. *Helpers of your joy* (*sunergoi tēs charas humōn*). Co-workers (I Cor. 3:8) in your joy. A delicate correction to present misapprehension (*epanorthōsis*).

CHAPTER II

1. *That I would not come again to you with sorrow* (*to mē palin en lupēi pros humas elthein*). Articular second aorist active infinitive with negative *mē* in apposition with *touto* (this) preceding. What does Paul mean by "again" (*palin*)? Had he paid another visit besides that described in Acts 18 which was in sorrow (*en lupēi*)? Or does he mean that having had one joyful visit (that in Acts 18) he does not wish the second one to be in sorrow? Either interpretation is possible as the Greek stands and scholars disagree. So in 12:14 "The third time I am ready to come" may refer to the proposed second visit (1:15f.) and the present plan (a third). And so as to 13:1. There is absolutely no way to tell clearly whether Paul had already made a second visit. If he had done so, it is a bit odd that he did not plainly say so in 1:15f. when he is apologizing for not having made the proposed visit ("a second benefit").

2. *Who then?* (*kai tis?*). For this use of *kai* see on Mark 10:26 and John 9:36. The *kai* accepts the condition (first class *ei—lupō*) and shows the paradox that follows. *Lupeō* is old word from *lupē* (sorrow) in causative sense, to make sorry. *Maketh glad* (*euphrainōn*). Present active participle of old word from *eu*, well, and *phrēn*, mind, to make joyful, causative idea like *lupeō*.

3. *I wrote this very thing* (*egrapsa touto auto*). Is this (and *egrapsa* in verses 4, 9, 12) the epistolary aorist referring to the present letter? In itself that is possible as the epistolary aorist does occur in the N.T. as in 8:18; 9:3 (Robertson, *Grammar*, p. 854f.). If not epistolary aorist as seems improbable from the context and from 7:8–12, to what Epistle does he refer? To I Cor. 5 or to a lost letter? It is possible, of course, that, when Paul decided not to come to Corinth, he sent a letter. The language that follows in verses 3 and 4 and 7:8–12 can hardly apply to I Corinthians. *Should have sorrow* (*lupēn schō*). Second aorist (ingressive) active subjunctive of *echō*, should get sorrow, after *hina mē* negative final particles. *From them of whom* (*aph' hōn*). Antecedent omitted, *apo toutōn aph' hōn* (from those from whom). *I ought* (*edei me*). Imperfect for unrealized present obligation

as often and like English. *Having confidence (pepoithōs).*
Second perfect active participle of *peithō* (1:9).

4. *Anguish (sunochēs).* Ablative case after *ek* (out of).
Old word from *sunechō*, to hold together. So contraction of
heart (Cicero, *contractio animi*), a spiritual *angina pectoris*.
In N.T. only here and Luke 21:25. *With many tears (dia
pollōn dakruōn).* He dictated that letter "through tears"
(accompanied by tears). Paul was a man of heart. He writes
to the Philippians with weeping *(klaiōn)* over the enemies
of the Cross of Christ (Phil. 3:18). He twice mentions his
tears in his speech at Miletus (Acts 20:19, 31). *But that ye
might know the love (alla tēn agapēn hina gnōte).* Proleptic
position of *agapēn* and ingressive second aorist active subjunctive *gnōte*, come to know.

5. *If any (ei tis).* Scholars disagree whether Paul refers
to I Cor. 5:1, where he also employs *tis, toioutos,* and *Satanās*
as here, or to the ringleader of the opposition to him. Either
view is possible. In both cases Paul shows delicacy of feeling
by not mentioning the name. *But in part (alla apo merous).*
"But to some extent to you all." The whole Corinthian
Church has been injured in part by this man's wrongdoing.
There is a parenthesis *(that I press not too heavily, hina mē
epibarō)* that interrupts the flow of ideas. *Epibareō,* to put
a burden on *(epi, baros),* is a late word, only in Paul in N.T.
(here and I Thess. 2:9; II Thess. 3:8). He does not wish to
give pain by too severe language.

6. *Punishment (epitimia).* Late word for old Greek *to
epitimion* (so papyri), from *epitimaō,* to show honour to, to
award, to adjudge penalty. Only here in N.T. *By the many
(hupo tōn pleionōn).* By the more, the majority. If Paul
refers to the case in I Cor. 5, they had taken his advice
and expelled the offender.

7. *So that on the contrary (hōste tounantion).* The natural
result expressed by *hōste* and the infinitive. *Tounantion* is
by crasis for *to enantion* and accusative of general reference.
Rather (mallon). Absent in some MSS. *Lest by any means
(mē pōs).* Negative purpose. *Swallowed up (katapothēi).*
First aorist passive subjunctive of *katapinō,* to drink down
(I Cor. 15:54). *With his overmuch sorrow (tēi perissoterāi
lupēi).* Instrumental case, "by the more abundant sorrow"
(comparative of adjective *perissos*).

8. *To confirm* (*kurōsai*). First aorist active infinitive of old verb *kuroō*, to make valid, to ratify, from *kuros* (head, authority). In N.T. only here and Gal. 3:15.

9. *That I might know the proof of you* (*hina gnō tēn dokimēn humōn*). Ingressive second aorist active subjunctive, come to know. *Dokimē* is proof by testing. Late word from *dokimos* and is in Dioscorides, medical writer in reign of Hadrian. Earliest use in Paul and only in him in N.T. (II Cor. 2:9; 8:2; 9:13; 13:3; Rom. 5:4; Phil. 2:22). *Obedient* (*hupēkooi*). Old word from *hupakouō*, to give ear. In N.T. only in Paul (II Cor. 2:9; Phil. 2:8 and Acts 7:39).

10. *In the person of Christ* (*en prosōpōi Christou*. More exactly, "in the presence of Christ," before Christ, in the face of Christ. Cf. *enōpion tou theou* (4:2) in the eye of God, *enōpion Kuriou* (8:21).

11. *That no advantage may be gained over us* (*hina mē pleonektēthōmen*). First aorist passive subjunctive after *hina mē* (negative purpose) of *pleonekteō*, old verb from *pleonektēs*, a covetous man (I Cor. 5:10f.), to take advantage of, to gain, to overreach. In N.T. only in I Thess. 4:6 and II Cor. 2:11; 7:2; 12:17f. "That we may not be overreached by Satan." *His devices* (*autou ta noēmata*). *Noēma* from *noeō* to use the *nous* is old word, especially for evil plans and purposes as here.

12. *To Troas* (*eis tēn Trōiada*). Luke does not mention this stop at Troas on the way from Ephesus to Macedonia (Acts 20:1f.), though he does mention two other visits there (Acts 16:8; 20:6). *When a door was opened unto me* (*thuras moi aneōigmenēs*). Genitive absolute with second perfect passive participle of *anoignumi*. Paul used this very metaphor in I Cor. 16:9. He will use it again in Col. 4:3. Here was an open door that he could not enter.

13. *I had no relief* (*ouk eschēka anesin*). Perfect active indicative like that in 1:9, vivid dramatic recital, not to be treated as "for" the aorist (Robertson, *Grammar*, p. 896, 898ff.). He still feels the shadow of that restlessness. *Anesis*, from *aniēmi*, to let up, to hold back, is old word for relaxing or release (Acts 24:34). *For my spirit* (*tōi pneumati mou*). Dative of interest. *Because I found not Titus* (*tōi mē heurein me Titon*). Instrumental case of the articular infinitive with negative *mē* and accusative of general reference *me*, "by the

not finding Titus as to me." *Taking my leave of them (apotaxamenos autois)*. First aorist middle participle of *apotassō*, old verb, to set apart, in middle in late Greek to separate oneself, to bid adieu to as in Mark 6:46.

14. *But thanks be unto God (tōi de theōi charis)*. Sudden outburst of gratitude in contrast to the previous dejection in Troas. Surely a new paragraph should begin here. In point of fact Paul makes a long digression from here to 6:10 on the subject of the Glory of the Christian Ministry as Bachmann points out in his *Kommentar* (p. 124), only he runs it from 2:12 to 7:1 (*Aus der Tiefe in die Hohe*, Out of the Depths to the Heights). We can be grateful for this emotional outburst, Paul's rebound of joy on meeting Titus in Macedonia, for it has given the world the finest exposition of all sides of the Christian ministry in existence, one that reveals the wealth of Paul's nature and his mature grasp of the great things in service for Christ. See my *The Glory of the Ministry (An Exposition of II Cor. 2:12–6:10)*. *Always (pantote)*. The sense of present triumph has blotted out the gloom at Troas. *Leadeth in triumph (thriambeuonti)*. Late common *Koiné* word from *thriambos* (Latin *triumphus*, a hymn sung in festal processions to Bacchus). Verbs in *-euō* (like *mathēteuō*, to make disciples) may be causative, but no example of *thriambeuō* has been found with this meaning. It is always to lead in triumph, in papyri sometimes to make a show of. Picture here is of Paul as captive in God's triumphal procession. *The savour (tēn osmēn)*. In a Roman triumph garlands of flowers scattered sweet odour and incense bearers dispensed perfumes. The knowledge of God is here the aroma which Paul had scattered like an incense bearer.

15. *A sweet savour of Christ (Christou euōdia)*. Old word from *eu*, well, and *ozō*, to smell. In N.T. only here and Phil. 4:18; Eph. 5:2. In spreading the fragrance of Christ the preacher himself becomes fragrant (Plummer). *In them that are perishing (en tois apollumenois)*. Even in these if the preacher does his duty.

16. *From death unto death (ek thanatou eis thanaton)*. From one evil condition to another. Some people are actually hardened by preaching. *And who is sufficient for these things?* (*kai pros tauta tis hikanos?*). Rhetorical question. In himself

no one is. But some one has to preach Christ and Paul proceeds to show that he is sufficient. *For we are not as the many (ou gar esmen hōs hoi polloi).* A bold thing to say, but necessary and only from God (3:6).

17. *Corrupting (kapēleuontes).* Old word from *kapēlos*, a huckster or peddlar, common in all stages of Greek for huckstering or trading. It is curious how hucksters were suspected of corrupting by putting the best fruit on top of the basket. Note Paul's solemn view of his relation to God as a preacher (*from God ek theou, in the sight of God katenanti theou, in Christ en Christōi*).

CHAPTER III

1. *To commend ourselves?* (*heautous sunistanein?*). Late (*Koiné* form of *sunistēmi*, to place one with another, to introduce, to commend. Paul is sensitive over praising himself, though his enemies compelled him to do it. *Epistles of commendation* (*sustatikōn epistolōn*). Late verbal adjective from *sunistēmi* and often 'in the papyri and in just this sense. In the genitive case here after *chrēizomen*. Such letters were common as seen in the papyri (Deissmann, *Light from the Ancient East*, p. 226). N.T. examples of commending individuals by letters occur in Acts 15:25f.; 18:27 (Apollos), I Cor. 16:10f. (Timothy); Rom. 16:1 (Phoebe with the verb *sunistēmi*); Col. 4:10 (Mark); II Cor. 8:22f. (Titus and his companion).

. 2. *Ye are our epistle* (*hē epistolē hēmōn humeis este*). Bold turn. Paul was writing in their hearts. *Known and read* (*ginōskomenē kai anaginōskomenē*). Play on the word. Literally true. Professing Christians are the Bible that men read and know.

3. *An epistle of Christ* (*epistolē Christou*). He turns the metaphor round and round. They are Christ's letter to men as well as Paul's. *Not with ink* (*ou melani*). Instrumental case of *melas*, black. Plato uses *to melan* for ink as here. See also II John 12; III John 13. *Of stone* (*lithinais*). Composed of stone (*lithos* and ending -*inos*). *Of flesh* (*sarkinais*). "Fleshen" as in I Cor. 3:1; Rom. 7:14.

4. *Through Christ* (*dia tou Christou*). It is not self-conceit on Paul's part, but through Christ.

5. *Of ourselves* (*aph' heautōn*). Starting from ourselves (reflexive pronoun). *As from ourselves* (*hōs ex hautōn*). He says it over again with preposition *ex* (out of). He has no originating power for such confidence. *Sufficiency* (*hikanotēs*). Old word, only here in N.T.

6. *Who also made us sufficient for such confidence* (*hos kai hikanōsen hēmas*). Late causative verb from *hikanos* (verse 5) first aorist active indicative, "who (God) rendered us fit." In N.T. only here and Col. 1:12. *As ministers of a new covenant* (*diakonous kainēs diathēkēs*). Predicate accusative

with *hikanōsen*. For *diathēkē* see on Matt. 26:28 and for *diakonos* on Matt. 20:26 and for *kainēs* (fresh and effective) on Luke 5:38. Only God can make us that.

7. *Of death* (*tou thanatou*). Subjective genitive, marked by death in its outcome (cf. I Cor. 15:56; Gal. 3:10). The letter kills. *Engraven on stones* (*entetupōmenē lithois*). Perfect passive participle of *entupoō*, late verb, to imprint a figure (*tupos*). Used by Aristias (67) of the "inlaid" work on the table sent by Ptolemy Philadelphus to Jerusalem. *Lithois* in locative case. *Came with glory* (*egenēthē en doxēi*). In glory. As it did, condition of first class, assumed as true. See Ex. 34:29, 35. *Look steadfastly* (*atenisai*). Late verb from *atenēs* (stretched, intent, *teinō* and *a* intensive) as in Luke 4:20; Acts 3:4. *Was passing away* (*katargoumenēn*). Late verb, to render of no effect, and present passive participle here as in I Cor. 2:6.

8. *How shall not rather?* (*pōs ouchi mallon?*). *Argumentum a minore ad majus* (from the less to the greater). *Of the spirit* (*tou pneumatos*). Marked by the spirit. Picture of the Christian ministry now.

9. *Of condemnation* (*tēs katakriseōs*). Genitive, that brings condemnation because unable to obey the law. *Is glory* (*doxa*). No copula, but makes the figure bolder. Paul freely admits the glory for the old dispensation. *Of righteousness* (*tēs dikaiosunēs*). Marked by and leading to righteousness. See 11:15. *Much more* (*pollōi mallon*). Instrumental case, by much more. *Exceed* (*perisseuei*). Overflow.

10. *In this respect* (*en toutōi tōi merei*). The glory on the face of Moses was temporary, though real, and passed away (verse 7), a type of the dimming of the glory of the old dispensation by the brightness of the new. The moon makes a dim light after the sun rises, "is not glorified" (*ou dedoxastai*, perfect passive indicative of *doxazō*). *By reason of the glory that surpasseth* (*heineken tēs huperballousēs doxēs*). The surpassing (*huper-ballō*, throwing beyond) glory. Christ as the Sun of Righteousness has thrown Moses in the shade. Cf. the claims of superiority by Christ in Matt. 5 to 7.

11. *Passeth away* (*katargoumenon*). In process of disappearing before the gospel of Christ. *Remaineth* (*menon*). The new ministry is permanent. This claim may be recommended to those who clamour for a new religion. Christianity

is still alive and is not dying. Note also *en doxēi*, in glory, in contrast with *dia doxēs*, with glory. *Boldness* (*parrēsiāi*). Instrumental case after *chrōmetha*. Old word, *panrēsis =* *parrēsis*, telling it all, absolute unreservedness. Surely Paul has kept nothing back here, no mental reservations, in this triumphant claim of superiority.

13. *Put a veil upon his face* (*etithei kalumma epi to prosō-pon autou*). Imperfect active of *tithēmi*, used to put (Ex. 34:33). *That the children of Israel should not look steadfastly* (*pros to mē atenisai tous huious*). Purpose expressed by *pros* and the articular infinitive with negative *mē* and the accusative of general reference. The Authorized Version had a wrong translation here as if to hide the glory on his face.

14. *But their minds were hardened* (*alla epōrōthē ta noēmata autōn*). Their thoughts (*noēmata*) literally. *Pōroō* (first aorist passive indicative here) is late verb from *pōros*, hard skin, to cover with thick skin (callus), to petrify. See on Mark 6:52; 8:17. *Of the old covenant* (*tēs palaias diathēkēs*). The Old Testament. *Palaios* (ancient) in contrast to *kainos* (fresh, verse 6). See Matt. 13:52. *The same veil* (*to auto kalumma*). Not that identical veil, but one that has the same effect, that blinds their eyes to the light in Christ. This is the tragedy of modern Judaism. *Unlifted* (*mē anaka-luptomenon*). Present passive participle of *anakaluptō*, old verb, to draw back the veil, to unveil. *Is done away* (*katar-geitai*). Same verb as in verses 7, 11.

15. *Whensoever Moses is read* (*hēnika an anaginōskētai Mōusēs*). Indefinite temporal clause with *hēnika an* and the present passive subjunctive. *A veil lieth upon their heart* (*epi tēn kardian autōn keitai*). Vivid and distressing picture, a fact that caused Paul agony of heart (Rom. 9:1-5). With wilful blindness the rabbis set aside the word of God by their tradition in the time of Jesus (Mark 7:8f.).

16. *It shall turn* (*epistrepsei*). The heart of Israel. *The veil is taken away* (*periaireitai to kalumma*). Present passive indicative of *periaireō*, old verb, to take from around, as of anchors (Acts 27:40), to cut loose (Acts 28:13), for hope to be taken away (Acts 27:20). Here Paul has in mind Ex. 34:34 where we find of Moses that *periēireito to kalumma* (the veil was taken from around his face) whenever he went

before the Lord. After the ceremony the veil is taken from around (*peri-*) the face of the bride.

17. *Now the Lord is the Spirit* (*ho de Kurios to pneuma estin*). Some, like E. F. Scott (*The Spirit in the N.T.*), take *Kurios* here to be Christ and interpret Paul as denying the personality of the Holy Spirit, identifying Christ and the Holy Spirit. But is not Bernard right here in taking *Kurios* (Lord) in the same sense here as in Ex. 34:34 (*enanti Kuriou*, before the Lord), the very passage that Paul is quoting? Certainly, the Holy Spirit is interchangeably called in the N.T. the Spirit of God and the Spirit of Christ (Rom. 8:9f.). Christ dwells in us by the Holy Spirit, but the language here in II Cor. 3:17 should not be pressed unduly (Plummer. See also P. Gardner, *The Religious Experience of St. Paul*, p. 176f.). Note "the Spirit of the Lord" here. *Liberty* (*eleutheria*). Freedom of access to God without fear in opposition to the fear in Ex. 34:30. We need no veil and we have free access to God.

18. *We all* (*hēmeis pantes*). All of us Christians, not merely ministers. *With unveiled face* (*anakekalummenōi prosōpōi*). Instrumental case of manner. Unlike and like Moses. *Reflecting as in a mirror* (*katoptrizomenoi*). Present middle participle of *katoptrizō*, late verb from *katoptron*, mirror (*kata*, *optron*, a thing to see with). In Philo (*Legis Alleg.* iii. 33) the word means beholding as in a mirror and that idea suits also the figure in I Cor. 13:12. There is an inscription of third century B.C. with *egkatoptrisasthai eis to hudōr*, to look at one's reflection in the water. Plutarch uses the active for mirroring or reflecting and Chrysostom takes it so here. Either makes good sense. The point that Paul is making is that we shall not lose the glory as Moses did. But that is true if we keep on beholding or keep on reflecting (present tense). Only here in N.T. *Are transformed* (*metamorphoumetha*). Present passive (are being transformed) of *metamorphoō*, late verb and in papyri. See on Matt. 17:2; Mark 9:2 where it is translated "transfigured." It is the word used for heathen mythological metamorphoses. *Into the same image* (*tēn autēn eikona*). Accusative retained with passive verb *metamorphoumetha*. Into the likeness of God in Christ (I Cor. 15:48-53; Rom. 8:17, 29; Col. 3:4; I John 3:2). *As from the Lord the Spirit* (*kathaper apo Kuriou pneumatos*). More likely, "as from the Spirit of the Lord."

CHAPTER IV

1. *We faint not (ouk egkakoumen)*. Present active indicative of *egkakeō*, late verb (*en, kakos*) to behave badly in, to give in to evil, to lose courage. In Symmachus (LXX), Polybius, and papyri. It is the faint-hearted coward. Paul speaks of himself (literary plural). Can he not speak for all of us?

2. *But we have renounced (alla apeipametha)*. Indirect middle second aorist (timeless aorist) indicative of *apeipon* (defective verb) with *a* of first aorist ending, to speak forth, to speak off or away from. Common verb in the active, but rare in middle and only here in N.T. *The hidden things of shame (ta krupta tēs aischunēs)*. They do attack the minister. His only safety is in instant and courageous defiance to all the powers of darkness. It is a terrible thing to see a preacher caught in the toils of the tempter. *In craftiness (en panourgiāi)*. Old word from *panourgos (pan, ergon)*, a doer of any deed (good or bad), clever, cunning, deceitful. See on Luke 20:23. *Handling deceitfully (dolountes)*. Present active participle of *doloō*, from *dolos*, deceit (from *delō*, to catch with bait), old and common verb, in papyri and inscriptions, to ensnare, to corrupt with error. Only here in N.T. Used of adulterating gold or wine. *To every conscience of men (pros pāsan suneidēsin anthrōpōn)*. Not to whim, foible, prejudice. See 3:1–6 for "commending" (*sunistanontes*).

3. *It is veiled in them that are perishing (en tois apollumenois estin kekalummenon)*. Periphrastic perfect passive of *kaluptō*, to veil in both condition (first class) and conclusion. See on 2:15f. for "the perishing."

4. *The god of this world (ho theos tou aiōnos toutou)*. "Age," more exactly, as in I Cor. 1:20. Satan is "the god of this age," a phrase nowhere else in the N.T., but Jesus uses the same idea in John 12:31; 14:30 and Paul in Eph. 2:2; 6:12 and John in I John 5:19. Satan claimed the rule over the world in the temptations with Jesus. *Blinded (etuphlōsen)*. First aorist active of *tuphloō*, old verb to blind (*tuphlos*,

blind). They refused to believe (*apistōn*) and so Satan got the power to blind their thoughts. That happens with wilful disbelievers. *The light (ton phōtismon)*. The illumination, the enlightening. Late word from *photizō*, to give light, in Plutarch and LXX. In N.T. only in II Cor. 4:4, 6. Accusative case of general reference here with the articular infinitive (*eis to mē augasai* (that should not dawn). That is, if *augasai* is intransitive as is likely, though it is transitive in the old poets (from *augē*, radiance. Cf. German *Auge*=eye). If it is transitive, the idea would be "that they should not see clearly the illumination, etc."

5. *For we preach not ourselves (ou gar heautous kērussomen)*. Surely as poor and disgusting a topic as a preacher can find. *But Christ Jesus as Lord (alla Christon Iēsoun Kurion)*. *Kurion* is predicate accusative in apposition. *As your servants for Jesus' sake (doulous humōn dia Iēsoun)*. Your bond-slave for the sake of Jesus. This is the sufficient reason for any preacher's sacrifice, "for Jesus' sake."

6. *God who said (ho theos ho eipōn)*. Paraphrase of Gen. 1:3. *Who shined (hos elampsen)*. Like a lamp in the heart (cf. Matt. 5:15). Miners carry a lamp on the forehead, Christians carry one in their hearts lit by the Spirit of God. *To give the light (pros phōtismon)*. For the illumination. *In the face of Jesus Christ (en prosōpōi Iēsou Christou)*. The Christian who looks on the face of Jesus Christ as Moses looked upon the glory of God will be able to give the illumination of the knowledge of the glory of God. See 2:10 for *prosōpon*.

7. *This treasure (ton thēsauron touton)*. On *thēsauron* see Matt. 6:19–21. It is the power of giving the illumination of the knowledge of the glory of God (verse 6). "The power is limitless, but it is stored in very unlikely receptacles" (Plummer). This warning Paul gives in contrast (*de*) with the exultation of verse 6 (Bernard). *In earthen vessels (en ostrakinois skeuesin)*. This adjective is common in the LXX with *skeuos, aggos* and *aggeion*. It occurs again in II Tim. 2:20 with *skeuē*. It is found also in the papyri with *skeuos* as here. It is from *ostrakon*, baked clay (same root as *osteon*, bone), so many fragments of which are found in Egypt with writing on them. We are but earthen jars used of God for his purposes (Rom. 9:20ff.) and so fragile. *The exceeding*

greatness (*hē huperbolē*). See on I Cor. 12:31 for this word, "the preëminence of the power." This is God's purpose (*hina—ēi*). God, not man, is the *dynamo* (*dunamis*). It comes from God (*tou theou*, ablative) and does not originate with us (*mē ex hēmōn*).

8. *Pressed* (*thlibomenoi*). From *thlibō*, to press as grapes, to contract, to squeeze. Series of present passive participles here through verse 9 that vividly picture Paul's ministerial career. *Yet not straitened* (*all' ou stenochōroumenoi*). Each time the exception is stated by *all' ou*. From *stenochōreō* (*stenochōros*, from *stenos*, narrow, *chōros*, space), to be in a narrow place, to keep in a tight place. Late verb, in LXX and papyri. In N.T. only here and II Cor. 6:12. *Yet not unto despair* (*all' ouk exaporoumenoi*). Late perfective compound with *ex-* of *exaporeō*. A very effective play on words here, lost, but not lost out.

9. *Forsaken* (*egkataleipomenoi*). Double compound of old verb *eg-kata-leipō*, to leave behind, to leave in the lurch. *Smitten down* (*kataballomenoi*). As if overtaken. *Destroyed* (*apollumenoi*). Perishing as in verse 3. Was Paul referring to Lystra when the Jews stoned him and thought him dead?

10. *Bearing about* (*peripherontes*). Ignatius was called *Theophoros*, God-bearer. See I Cor. 15:31 where Paul says "I die daily" and Phil. 3:10; Col. 1:24. *The dying of Jesus* (*tēn nekrōsin tou Iēsou*). Late word from *nekroō*, to put to death. In Galen. In N.T. only here and Rom. 4:19.

11. *Are alway delivered unto death* (*eis thanaton paradidometha*). This explains verse 10.

12. *Death worketh in us* (*ho thanatos en hēmin energeitai*). Middle voice present tense of the old verb to operate, be at work. Physical death works in him while spiritual life (paradox) works in them.

13. *According to that which is written* (*kata to gegrammenon*). This formula in legal documents in the papyri (*Bible Studies*, p. 250). Paul makes adaptation of the words in Psa. 95:1. *We also believe* (*kai hēmeis pisteuomen*). Like the Psalmist. And therefore can speak with effect. Otherwise useless. *Shall present us with you* (*kai parastēsei sun hēmin*). This shows that Paul was not certain that he would be alive when Jesus comes as has been wrongly inferred from I Cor. 7:29; 10:11; 15:51.

15. *Being multiplied through the many* (*pleonasasa dia tōn pleionōn*). Late word *pleonazō* from *pleon*, more, "making more through the more," with play on *pleon*. One can think of Bunyan's *Grace Abounding*.

16. *Wherefore we faint not* (*dio ouk egkakoumen*). Repeats from verse 1. *Our outward man* (*ho exō hēmōn anthrōpos*), *our inward man* (*ho esō hēmōn*). In Rom. 7:22; Col. 3:9; Eph. 4:22f., we have the inward man and the outward for the higher and the lower natures (the spirit and the flesh). "Here the decay (*diaphtheiretai*) of the bodily organism is set over against the growth in grace (*anakainoutai*, is refreshed) of the man himself" (Bernard). Plato (*Republ.* ix, p. 589) has *ho entos anthrōpos*. Cf. "the hidden man of the heart" (I Peter 3:4). *Day by day* (*hēmerāi kai hēmerāi*). This precise idiom is not in LXX nor rest of N.T. It may be colloquial use of locative in repetition.

17. *Our light affliction which is for the moment* (*to parautika elaphron tēs thlipeseōs hēmōn*). Literally, "the for the moment (old adverb *parautika*, here only in N.T.) lightness (old word, in N.T. only here and Matt. 11:30)." *More and more exceedingly* (*kath' huperbolēn eis huperbolēn*). Like piling Pelion on Ossa, "according to excess unto excess." See on I Cor. 12:31. *Eternal weight of glory* (*aiōnion baros doxēs*). Careful balancing of words in contrast (affliction vs. glory, lightness vs. weight, for the moment vs. eternal).

18. *While we look not* (*mē skopountōn hēmōn*). Genitive absolute with participle of *skopeō* from *skopos*, goal. *Temporal* (*proskaira*). Rather temporary, for a season (*pros kairon*). Late word. See on Matt. 13:21. See I Cor. 13:12; Heb. 11:1.

CHAPTER V

1. *If—be dissolved (ean—kataluthēi).* Third class condition, *ean* and first aorist passive subjunctive. The very word used (*kaluō*) for striking down a tent. *The earthly house of our tabernacle (hē epigeios hēmōn oikia tou skēnous).* Rather, "If our earthly (see on I Cor. 15:40 for *epigeios*) house of the tent (*skēnos*, another form of *skēnē*, tent, from root *ska*, to cover)." Appositive genitive, the house (*oikia*) is the tent. *We have (echomen).* Present indicative. We possess the title to it now by faith. "Faith is the title-deed (*hupostasis*) to things hoped for" (Heb. 11:7). *A building from God (oikodomēn ek theou).* This *oikodomē* (found in Aristotle, Plutarch, LXX, etc., and papyri, though condemned by Atticists) is more substantial than the *skēnos*. *Not made with hands (acheiropoiēton).* Found first in Mark 14:58 in charge against Jesus before the Sanhedrin (both the common verbal *cheiropoiēton* and the newly made vernacular *acheiropoiēton,* same verbal with *a* privative). Elsewhere only here and Col. 2:11. Spiritual, eternal home.

2. *To be clothed upon with our habitation which is from heaven (to oikētērion hēmōn to ex ouranou ependusasthai).* First aorist middle infinitive of late verb *ependuō*, double compound (*ep, en*) to put upon oneself. Cf. *ependutēs* for a fisherman's linen blouse or upper garment (John 21:7). *Oikētērion* is old word used here of the spiritual body as the abode of the spirit. It is a mixed metaphor (putting on as garment the dwelling-place).

3. *Being clothed (endusamenoi).* First aorist middle participle, having put on the garment. *Naked (gumnoi).* That is, disembodied spirits, "like the souls in Sheol, without form, and void of all power of activity" (Plummer).

4. *Not for that we would be unclothed (eph' hōi ou thelomen ekdusasthai).* Rather, "For that (*eph' hōi*) we do not wish to put off the clothing, but to put it on" (*all' ependusasthai*). The transposition of the negative *ou* weakens the sense. Paul does not wish to be a mere disembodied spirit without his spiritual garment. *That what is mortal may be swallowed*

up of life (hina katapothēi to thnēton hupo tēs zōēs). "Only what is mortal perishes; the personality, consisting of soul and body, survives," (Plummer). See on 1:22 for "the earnest of the spirit."

6. *At home in the body (endēmountes en tōi sōmati).* Rare verb *endēmeō* from *endēmos* (one among his own people as opposed to *ekdēmos*, one away from home). Both *ekdēmeō* (more common in the old Greek) and *endēmeō* occur in the papyri with the contrast made by Paul here.

7. *By sight (dia eidous).* Rather, by appearance.

8. *We are of good courage (tharroumen).* Good word for cheer and same root as *tharseō* (Matt. 9:2, 22). Cheer up. *Are willing rather (eudokoumen).* Rather, "We are well-pleased, we prefer" if left to ourselves. Cf. Phil. 1:21f. Same *eudokeō* used in Luke 3:22. *To be at home with the Lord (endēmēsai pros ton Kurion).* First aorist (ingressive) active infinitive, to attain that goal is bliss for Paul.

9. *We make it our aim (philotimoumetha).* Old and common verb, present middle, from *philotimos (philos, timē,* fond of honour), to act from love of honour, to be ambitious in the good sense (I Thess. 4:11; II Cor. 5:9; Rom. 15:20). The Latin *ambitio* has a bad sense from *ambire*, to go both ways to gain one's point. *To be well-pleasing to him (euarestoi autōi einai).* Late adjective that shows Paul's loyalty to Christ, his Captain. Found in several inscriptions in the *Koiné* period (Deissmann, *Bible Studies*, p. 214; Moulton and Milligan's *Vocabulary*).

10. *Before the judgment-seat of Christ (emprosthen tou bēmatos tou Christou).* Old word *bēma*, a step (from *bainō*), a platform, the seat of the judge (Matt. 27:19). Christ is Saviour, Lord, and Judge of us all *(tous pantas,* the all). *That each may receive (hina komisētai hekastos).* Receive as his due, *komizō* means, old verb. See on Matt. 25:27. *Bad (phaulon).* Old word, akin to German *faul*, worthless, of no account, base, wicked.

11. *The fear of the Lord (ton phobon tou Kuriou).* Many today regard this a played-out motive, but not so Paul. He has in mind verse 10 with the picture of the judgment seat of Christ. *We persuade (peithomen).* Conative present active, we try to persuade. It is always hard work. *Unto God (theōi).* Dative case. God understands whether men do or not. *That*

we are made manifest (*pephanerōsthai*). Perfect passive infinitive of *phaneroō* in indirect discourse after *elpizō*. Stand manifested, state of completion.

12. *As giving you occasion of glorying* (*aphormēn didontes humin kauchēmatos*). An old Greek word (*apo, hormē*, onset, rush), a base of operations, material with which to glory, as we say "a tip" only much more. *That ye may have wherewith to answer* (*hina echēte pros*). Literally, "That ye may have something against (for facing those, etc.)." Paul wishes his champions in Corinth to know the facts. *In appearance, and not in heart* (*en prosōpōi kai mē en kardiāi*). He means the Judaizers who were braggarts about their orthodox Judaism.

13. *Whether we are beside ourselves* (*eite exestēmen*). Second aorist active indicative of *existēmi*, old verb, here to stand out of oneself (intransitive) from *ekstasis*, ecstasy, comes as in Mark 5:42. It is literary plural, for Paul is referring only to himself. See on 1:6 for *eite—eite*. It is a condition of the first class and Paul assumes as true the charge that he was crazy (if I was crazy) for the sake of argument. Festus made it later (Acts 26:24). He spoke with tongues (I Cor. 14:18) and had visions (II Cor. 12:1–6) which probably the Judaizers used against him. A like charge was made against Jesus (Mark 3:21). People often accuse those whom they dislike with being a bit off.

14. *The love of Christ* (*hē agapē tou Christou*). Subjective genitive, Christ's love for Paul as shown by verse 15. *Constraineth us* (*sunechei hēmas*). Old and common verb, to hold together, to press the ears together (Acts 7:57), to press on every side (Luke 8:45), to hold fast (Luke 22:63), to hold oneself to (Acts 18:5), to be pressed (passive, Luke 12:50; Phil. 1:23). So here Paul's concepton of Christ's love for him holds him together to his task whatever men think or say. *Judging this* (*krinantas touto*). Having reached this conclusion, ever since his conversion (Gal. 1:17f.). *One died for all* (*heis huper pantōn apethanen*). This is the central tenet in Paul's theology and Christology. *Huper* (over) here is used in the sense of substitution as in John 11:50; Gal. 3:13, death in behalf so that the rest will not have to die. This use of *huper* is common in the papyri (Robertson, *Grammar*, p. 631). In fact, *huper* in this sense is more usual

in Greek than *anti, pro* or any other preposition. *Therefore all died (ara hoi pantes apethanon).* Logical conclusion (*ara,* corresponding), the one died for the all and so the all died when he did, all the spiritual death possible for those for whom Christ died. This is Paul's gospel, clear-cut, our hope today.

15. *Should no longer live unto themselves (hina mēketi heautois zōsin).* The high doctrine of Christ's atoning death carries a correspondingly high obligation on the part of those who live because of him. Selfishness is ruled out by our duty to live "unto him who for their sakes died and rose again."

16. *Henceforth (apo tou nun).* From the time that we gained this view of Christ's death for us. *After the flesh (kata sarka).* According to the flesh, the fleshy way of looking at men. He, of course, knows men "in the flesh (*en tēi sarki*), but Paul is not speaking of that. Worldly standards and distinctions of race, class, cut no figure now with Paul (Gal. 3:28) as he looks at men from the standpoint of the Cross of Christ. *Even though we have known Christ after the flesh (ei kai egnōkamen kata sarka Christon).* Concessive clause (*ei kai,* if even or also) with perfect active indicative. Paul admits that he had once looked at Christ *kata sarka,* but now no longer does it. Obviously he uses *kata sarka* in precisely the same sense that he did in verse 15 about men. He had before his conversion known Christ *kata sarka,* according to the standards of the men of his time, the Sanhedrin and other Jewish leaders. He had led the persecution against Jesus till Jesus challenged and stopped him (Acts 9:4). That event turned Paul clean round and he no longer knows Christ in the old way *kata sarka.* Paul may or may not have seen Jesus in the flesh before his death, but he says absolutely nothing on that point here.

17. *A new creature (kainē ktisis).* A fresh start is made (*kainē*). *Ktisis* is the old word for the act of creating (Rom. 1:20), but in N.T. by metonymy it usually bears the notion of *ktisma,* the thing created or creature as here. *The old things are passed away (ta archaia parēlthen).* Did pass by, he means. Second aorist active of *parerchomai,* to go by. The ancient (*archaia*) way of looking at Christ among other things. And yet today there are scholars who are trying to

revive the old prejudiced view of Jesus Christ as a mere man, a prophet, to give us "a reduced Christ." That was once Paul's view, but it passed by forever for him. It is a false view and leaves us no gospel and no Saviour. *Behold, they are become new* (*idou, gegone kaina*). Perfect active indicative of *ginomai*, have become new (fresh, *kaina*) to stay so.
18. *Who reconciled us to himself through Christ* (*tou katallaxantos hēmas heautōi dia Christou*). Here Paul uses one of his great doctrinal words, *katallassō*, old word for exchanging coins. *Diallassō*, to change one's mind, to reconcile, occurs in N.T. only in Matt. 5:24 though in papyri (Deissmann, *Light from the Ancient East*, p. 187), and common in Attic. *Katallassō* is old verb, but more frequent in later writers. We find *sunallassō* in Acts 7:26 and *apokatallassō* in Col. 1:20f.; Eph. 2:16 and the substantive *katallagē* in Rom. 5:11; 11:15 as well as here. It is hard to discuss this great theme without apparent contradiction. God's love (John 3:16) provided the means and basis for man's reconciliation to God against whom he had sinned. It is all God's plan because of his love, but God's own sense of justice had to be satisfied (Rom. 3:26) and so God gave his Son as a propitiation for our sins (Rom. 3:25; Col. 1:20; I John 2:2; 4:10). The point made by Paul here is that God needs no reconciliation, but is engaged in the great business of reconciling us to himself. This has to be done on God's terms and is made possible through (*dia*) Christ. *And gave unto us the ministry of reconciliation* (*kai dontos hēmin tēn diakonian tēs katallagēs*). It is a ministry marked by reconciliation, that consists in reconciliation. God has made possible through Christ our reconciliation to him, but in each case it has to be made effective by the attitude of each individual. The task of winning the unreconciled to God is committed to us. It is a high and holy one, but supremely difficult, because the offending party (the guilty) is the hardest to win over. We must be loyal to God and yet win sinful men to him.
19. *To wit, that* (*hōs hoti*). Latin puts it *quoniam quidem*. It is an unclassical idiom, but occurs in the papyri and inscriptions (Moulton, *Prol.*, p. 212; Robertson, *Grammar*, p. 1033). It is in Esther 4:14. See also II Cor. 11:21; II Thess. 2:2. It probably means "how that." *Not reckoning* (*mē logizomenos*). What Jesus did (his death for us) stands

to our credit (Rom. 8:32) if we make our peace with God. This is our task, "the word of reconciliation," that we may receive "the righteousness of God" and be adopted into the family of God.

20. *We are ambassadors therefore on behalf of Christ* (*huper Christou oun presbeuomen*). Old word from *presbus*, an old man, first to be an old man, then to be an ambassador (here and Eph. 6:20 with *en halusēi* in a chain added), common in both senses in the Greek. "The proper term in the Greek East for the Emperor's Legate" (Deissmann, *Light from the Ancient East*, p. 374), in inscriptions and papyri. So Paul has a natural pride in using this dignified term for himself and all ministers. The ambassador has to be *persona grata* with both countries (the one that he represents and the one to which he goes). Paul was Christ's *Legate* to act in his behalf and in his stead. *As though God were intreating by us* (*hōs tou theou parakalountos di' hēmōn*). Genitive absolute with *hōs* used with the participle as often to give the reason (apparent or real). Here God speaks through Christ's Legate. *Be ye reconciled to God* (*katallagēte tōi theōi*). Second aorist passive imperative of *katallassō* and used with the dative case. "Get reconciled to God," and do it now. This is the ambassador's message as he bears it to men from God.

21. *Him who knew no sin* (*ton mē gnonta hamartian*). Definite claim by Paul that Jesus did not commit sin, had no personal acquaintance (*mē gnonta*, second aorist active participle of *ginōskō*) with it. Jesus made this claim for himself (John 8:46). This statement occurs also in I Peter 2:22; Heb. 4:15; 7:26; I John 3:5. Christ was and is "a moral miracle" (Bernard) and so more than mere man. *He made to be sin* (*hamartian epoiēsen*). The words "to be" are not in the Greek. "Sin" here is the substantive, not the verb. God "treated as sin" the one "who knew no sin." But he knew the contradiction of sinners (Heb. 12:3). We may not dare to probe too far into the mystery of Christ's suffering on the Cross, but this fact throws some light on the tragic cry of Jesus just before he died: "My God, My God, why didst thou forsake me?" (Matt. 27:46). *That we might become* (*hina hēmeis genōmetha*). Note "become." This is God's purpose (*hina*) in what he did and in what Christ did. Thus alone can we obtain God's righteousness (Rom. 1:17).

CHAPTER VI

1. *Working together with him* (*sunergountes*). We are co-workers, partners with God (I Cor. 3:9), in this work of grace. *In vain* (*eis kenon*). Into emptiness. The plan of God, the work of Christ on the Cross, the pleas of the ambassador may all be nullified by the recipient of the message. 2. *Behold, now is the acceptable time* (*idou nun kairos euprosdektos*). Here is another "Pauline parenthesis" (Plummer) as in 5:7 by the quotation from Isa. 49:8. The LXX has *dektos* (*dektoi*) verbal of *dechomai*, but Paul employs the double compound (*eu, pros, dektos*), well-received. It occurs in Aristophanes, Plutarch, inscription, etc. 3. *Giving no occasion of stumbling in any thing* (*mēdemian en mēdeni didontes proskopēn*). *Proskopē*, late word (Polybius, LXX), from *proskoptō*, to strike against, to stumble. Only here in N.T. Note double negative in the Greek. *That the ministry be not blamed* (*hina mē mōmēthēi hē diakonia*). Negative purpose (*hina mē*). First aorist passive subjunctive of old verb *mōmaomai* from *mōmos*, blot, blemish. One can read with profit J. A. Hutton's Warrack Lectures, *That the Ministry Be Not Blamed*. 4. *But in everything commending ourselves* (*all' en panti sunistanontes heautous*). Paul gives a marvellous summary of his argument about the dignity and glory of ministers of Christ as *ministers of God* (*hōs theou diakonoi*) under three aspects, the first with *in* (*en*) verses 3 to 7a, the second with *by* (*dia*) verses 7b to 8, the third with *as* (*hōs*) verses 9 to 10. The negative view with *en* we have in verse 3, then the positive in verses 4 to 7a. Each word carries a story that can be filled in from Paul's own life as a preacher with an echo in that of us all. *In distresses* (*en stenochōriais*). In tight places (12:10). Late word from *stenochōreō* (see on 4:8). 5. *In stripes* (*en plēgais*). In blows, wounds (Luke 10:30; 12:48; Acts 16:23, 33). Our plague. *In tumults* (*en akatastasiais*). See on I Cor. 14:33). Instabilities, often from politics. *In watchings* (*en agrupniais*). In sleeplessnesses,

instances of insomnia. Old word, in N.T. only here and
11:27. Paul knew all about this.
6. *In love unfeigned* (*en agapēi anupokritōi*). Late and
rare word (*a* privative and *hupokritos*, from *hupokrinomai*).
This is the only love that is worth while (Rom. 12:9).
7. *On the right hand and on the left* (*tōn dexiōn kai aristerōn*).
Offensive weapons (*hoplōn*) on the right, defensive on the
left. See I Thess. 5:8; Eph. 6:11 for Paul's description of
the panoply of God and Rom. 6:13 for the phrase "weapons
of righteousness," the only kind that will stand the strain.
See also Book of Wisdom 5:18ff.
8. *By glory and dishonour* (*dia doxēs kai atimias*). Here
dia is no longer instrument, but state or condition. *Doxa*
here is glory. See Rom. 9:21 and II Tim. 2:20 for contrast
between honour and dishonour (*timē, atimia*). *By evil report
and good report* (*dia dusphēmias kai euphēmias*). Play on
the words with prefixes *dus-* and *eu-* and *phēmē*. *Dusphēmia*
is a late word, only here in N.T. *Euphēmia*, old and common
word, only here in N.T. *As deceivers and yet true* (*hōs planoi
kai alētheis*). Paul takes up *hōs* now in place of *dia* which
succeeded *en*. Note use of *kai* in sense of "and yet" (adversative). *Planos* is late word (Diodorus, Josephus) for
wandering, vagabond, impostor (cf. *planaō*, to lead astray,
used of Christ, John 7·12). In N.T. only here; Matt. 27:63
(of Christ by Pharisees); II John 7. "In the Clementines
St. Paul is expressly described by his adversaries as *planos*
and as disseminating deceit (*planēn*)" (Bernard). Such
slander from one's enemies is praise.
9. *As unknown and yet well known* (*hōs agnooumenoi kai
epiginoskomenoi*). "As ignored (as nonentities, obscure,
without proper credentials 3:2) and yet fully recognized (by
all who really matter as in 11:6)." *And behold, we live* (*kai
idou zōmen*). Cf. the hazards of his life (1:8; 4:10; 11:23).
His whole career is full of paradox).
10. *Always rejoicing* (*aei chairontes*). Even in sorrow
(11:9; I Thess. 5:16; Rom. 5:3-5; 9:2; Phil. 2:18, 27; 3:1;
4:4, 15). *Yet making many rich* (*pollous de ploutizontes*).
Old word from *ploutos* (wealth), to enrich. Spiritual riches
Paul has in mind as in I Cor. 1:5 (cf. Matt. 5:37). *As having
nothing and yet possessing all things* (*hōs mēden echontes kai
panta katechontes*). Contrast between *mēden* (nothing) and

panta (all things, cf. I Cor. 3:22) and *echō* (to have) and *katechō* (to hold down, to hold fast). Play on words (simple and compound) as in 3:2 and 4:8. Climax of Paul's panegyric on the Christian ministry. He now resumes the thread of the story broken off in 2:14.

11. *Our mouth is open unto you* (*to stoma hēmōn aneōigen pros humas*). Second perfect active indicative of *anoigō* and intransitive, stand open. He has kept back nothing in his portrayal of the glory of the ministry as the picture of the open mouth shows. *Our heart is enlarged* (*hē kardia hēmōn peplatuntai*). Perfect passive indicative of old verb *platunō*, to broaden, from *platus*, broad. In N.T. only here and Matt. 23:5 (cf. phylacteries). Hence his freedom of speech for "out of the abundance of the heart the mouth speaks" (Matt. 12:34).

12. *Ye are not straitened in us* (*ou stenochōreisthe en hēmin*). The same figure as in verse 11. See on 4:8 for *stenochōreō*. There is no restraint in me (my heart). My adversaries may have caused some of you to tighten up your affections (*splagchna* for affection as in James 5:11; I Peter 3:8).

13. *Now for a recompense in like kind* (*tēn de autēn antimisthian*). No example of this expressive word outside of this passage and Rom. 1:27 and later Christian writers. Paul may have found it in use in the *Koiné* vernacular or he may have coined it from *antimisthos*, remunerating (paying back). There is no verb here to explain the accusative which may be the accusative of general reference or the object of a verb not expressed. *Be ye also enlarged* (*platunthēte kai humeis*). As I have been (verse 11). First aorist passive imperative of *platunō*.

14. *Be not unequally yoked with unbelievers* (*mē ginesthe heterozugountes apistois*). No other example of this verb has yet been found, though the adjective from which it is apparently formed, *heterozugos* (yoked with a different yoke) occurs in Lev. 19:19 of the union of beasts of different kinds. In Deut. 22:10 we read: "Thou shalt not plough with an ox and an ass together." Literally, "Stop becoming (*mē ginesthe* present imperative, not *mē genēsthe* aorist subj.) unequally yoked with unconverted heathen (unbelievers)." Some were already guilty. Marriage is certainly included, but other unions may be in mind. Cf. Eph. 5:7. Paul gives

THE EPISTLES OF PAUL 237

as the reason (*gar*) for this prohibition five words in questions to distinguish the contrasts. *Fellowship* (*metochē*). Sharing with and followed by associative instrumental case of *dikaiosunēi* (righteousness) and iniquity (*anomiāi*). A pertinent challenge today when church members wink at violations of laws of the land and laws of God. *Communion* (*koinōnia*). Partnership to light (*phōti* dative case) with (*pros*), facing darkness.

15. *Concord* (*sumphōnēsis*). Symphony. Late word from *sumphōneō*, only here and ecclesiastical writers, though *sumphōnēma* in the papyri. *Belial* (*Belial*). Transliteration of Hebrew word for worthlessness and applied to Satan (*Book of Jubilees* 1.20) as here. Paul graphically sums up the contrast between Christ and Belial (Satan), the heads of the contending forces of good and evil. *Portion* (*meris*). The fourth of the words. Here by "unbeliever" (*apistou*) Paul means "disbeliever," not just an unconverted man who yet approves Christ.

16. *Agreement* (*sunkatathesis*). Fifth of these words. Late word, but common, though here only in N.T. Approved by putting together the votes. In the papyri *ek sunkatatheseōs* means "by agreement." On the temple of God and idols see I Cor. 10:14–22. See Luke 23:51 for the verb *sunkatatithēmi*. For we are the temple of the living God (*hēmeis gar naos theou esmen zōntos*). We, not temples (Acts 7:48; 17:24; I Cor. 3:16; 6:19). *As God said* (*kathōs eipen ho theos*). A paraphrase and catena of quotations, what J. Rendel Harris calls *Testimonia* (from Lev. 26:11f.; Isa. 52:11; Ezek. 20:34; 37:27; II Sam. 7:8, 14). Plummer notes that at the beginning "I will dwell in them" (*enoikēsō en autois*) is not in any of them. "As God said" points to Lev. 26:12 and Ezek. 37:27.

17. *Saith the Lord* (*legei Kurios*). Isa. 52:5 and Ezek. 20:33. Cf. Rev. 18:4. *Unclean thing* (*akathartou*). Or unclean person. Genitive case is the same for both.

18. *Saith the Lord Almighty* (*legei Kurios pantokratōr*). II Sam. 7:8. This use of *eis* is a Hebraism for Hebrew *le* instead of predicate nominative. *Pantokratōr* (*pās, krateō*, Ruler of all) is common in the LXX. Occurs also in the inscriptions and papyri. In the N.T. only here and in Revelation.

CHAPTER VII

1. *These promises* (*tautas tas epaggelias*). So many and so precious (II Peter 2:4 *epaggelmata;* Heb. 11:39f.). *Let us cleanse ourselves* (*katharisōmen heautous*). Old Greek used *kathairō* (in N.T. only in John 15:2, to prune). In *Koiné katharizō* occurs in inscriptions for ceremonial cleansing (Deissmann, *Bible Studies,* p. 216f.). Paul includes himself in this volitive aorist subjunctive. *From all defilement* (*apo pantos molusmou*). Ablative alone would have done, but with *apo* it is plainer as in Heb. 9:14. *Molusmos* is a late word from *molunō,* to stain (see on I Cor. 8:7), to pollute. In the LXX, Plutarch, Josephus. It includes all sorts of filthiness, physical, moral, mental, ceremonial, "of flesh and spirit." Missionaries in China and India can appreciate the atmosphere of pollution in Corinth, for instance. *Perfecting holiness* (*epitelountes hagiosunēn*). Not merely negative goodness (cleansing), but aggressive and progressive (present tense of *epiteleō*) holiness, not a sudden attainment of complete holiness, but a continuous process (I Thess. 3:13; Rom. 1:4; 1:6).

2. *Open your hearts to us* (*chōrēsate hēmas*). Old verb (from *chōros,* place), to leave a space, to make a space for, and transitive here as in Matt. 19:11. He wishes no further *stenochōria,* tightness of heart, in them (6:12). "Make room for us in your hearts." He makes this plea to all, even the stubborn minority. *We wronged no man* (*oudena ēdikēsamen*). A thing that every preacher ought to be able to say. Cf. 4:2; I Thess. 2:3; Acts 20:26f. *We corrupted no man* (*oudena ephtheiramen*). We ruined no one. "It may refer to money, or morals, or doctrine" (Plummer). He is answering the Judaizers. *We took advantage of no man* (*oudena epleonektēsamen*). That charge was made in Thessalonica (I Thess. 4:6) which see for this late verb and also on II Cor. 2:11. He got the best of (note *pleon* more in the root) no one in any evil way.

3. *Not to condemn you* (*pros katakrisin ou*). "Not for condemnation." Late word from *katakrinō,* found in Vettius

Valens, and here only in N.T. *To die together and live together* (*eis to sunapothanein kai sunzēin*). "For the dying together (second aorist ingressive active infinitive of *sunapothnēskō*) and living together (present active infinitive)." One article (*to*) with both infinitives. You are in our hearts to share death and life.

4. *I overflow with joy in all our affliction* (*huperperisseuomai tēi charāi epi pāsēi tēi thlipsei hēmōn*). A thoroughly Pauline sentiment. *Perisseuō* means to overflow, as we have seen. *Huper-perisseuō* (late word, so far only here and Byzantine writers) is to have a regular flood. Vulgate *superabundo*.

5. *When we had come* (*elthontōn hēmōn*). Genitive absolute with second aorist active participle of *erchomai*. Paul now returns to the incident mentioned in 2:12 before the long digression on the glory of the ministry. *Had no relief* (*oudemian escheken anesin*). Perfect active indicative precisely as in 2:13 which see, "has had no relief" (dramatic perfect). *Afflicted* (*thlibomenoi*). Present passive participle of *thlibō* as in 4:8, but with anacoluthon, for the nominative case agrees not with the genitive *hēmōn* nor with the accusative *hēmas* in verse 6. It is used as if a principal verb as in 9:11; 11:6; Rom. 12:16 (Moulton, *Prolegomena*, p. 182; Robertson, *Grammar*, pp. 1132–35). *Without were fightings* (*exōthen machai*). Asyndeton and no copula, a parenthesis also in structure. Perhaps pagan adversaries in Macedonia (cf. I Cor. 15:32). *Within were fears* (*esōthen phoboi*). Same construction. "Mental perturbations" (Augustine) as in 11:28.

6. *Comforteth* (*parakalōn*). See on 1:3–7 for this word. *The lowly* (*tous tapeinous*). See on Matt. 11:29. Literally, low on the ground in old sense (Ezek. 17:24). Low in condition as here; James 1:9. In II Cor. 10:1 regarded as abject. In this sense in papyri. "Humility as a sovereign grace is the creation of Christianity" (Gladstone, *Life*, iii, p. 466). *By the coming* (*en tēi parousiāi*). Same use of *parousia* as in I Cor. 16:7 which see. See also II Cor. 7:7; 10:10.

7. *Wherewith* (*hēi*). Either locative case with preceding *en* or instrumental of the relative with *pareklēthē* (first aorist passive indicative). "The manner in which Paul, so to speak, *fondles* this word [*parakaleō*] is most beautiful" (Vincent). *In you* (*eph' humin*). Over you, upon you. *Your longing* (*tēn humōn epipothēsin*). Late word from *epipotheō* (*epi,*

directive, longing towards, yearning). Only here in N.T. *Mourning* (*odurmon*). Old word from *oduromai*, to lament. Only here in N.T. *So that I rejoiced yet more* (*hōste me mallon charēnai*). Result expressed by *hōste* and the second aorist passive infinitive of *chairō* with accusative of general reference. 8. *Though* (*ei kai*). If also. Paul treats it as a fact. *With my epistle* (*en tēi epistolēi*). The one referred to in 2:3f. *I do not regret it* (*ou metamelomai*). This verb really means "repent" (be sorry again) which meaning we have transferred to *metanoeō*, to change one's mind (not to be sorry at all). See Matt. 21:30 and 27:3 for the verb *metamelomai*, to be sorry, to regret as here. Paul is now glad that he made them sorry. *Though I did regret* (*ei kai metemelomēn*). Imperfect indicative in the concessive clause. I was in a regretful mood at first. *For I see* (*blepō gar*). A parenthetical explanation of his present joy in their sorrow. B D do not have *gar*. The Latin Vulgate has *videns* (seeing) for *blepōn*. *For a season* (*pros hōran*). Cf. I Thess. 2:17. It was only "for an hour."

9. *Now I rejoice* (*nun chairō*). Now that Titus has come and told him the good news from Corinth (2:12f.). This was the occasion of the noble outburst in 2:12 to 6:10. *Unto repentance* (*eis metanoian*). Note the sharp difference here between "sorrow" (*lupē*) which is merely another form of *metamelomai* (regret, remorse) and "repentance" (*metanoia*) or change of mind and life. It is a linguistic and theological tragedy that we have to go on using "repentance" for *metanoia*. But observe that the "sorrow" has led to "repentance" and was not itself the repentance. *After a godly sort* (*kata theon*). In God's way. "God's way as opposed to man's way and the devil's way" (Plummer). It was not mere sorrow, but a change in their attitude that counted. *That ye might suffer loss by us in nothing* (*hina en mēdeni zēmiōthēte ex humōn*). Purpose clause with *hina* and first aorist passive subjunctive of *zēmioō*, old verb to suffer damage. See on Matt. 16:26. This was God's intention and so he overruled their sorrow to good.

10. *For godly sorrow* (*hē gar kata theon lupē*). "For the sorrow according to God" (God's ideal, verse 9). *Worketh repentance unto salvation a repentance without regret* (*meta-*

noian eis sōtērian ametamelēton ergazetai). This clause alone
should have prevented the confusion between mere "sorrow"
(*lupē*) as indicated in *metamelomai,* to regret (to be sorry
again) and "change of mind and life" as shown by *metanoian*
(*metanoeō*) and wrongly translated "repentance." The
sorrow according to God does work this "change of mind
and life" unto salvation, a change "not to be regretted"
(*ametamelēton,* an old verbal adjective of *metamelomai* and
a privative, but here alone in N.T.). It agrees with *metanoian,* not *sōtērian.* But *the sorrow of the world (hē de tou
kosmou lupē).* In contrast, the kind of sorrow that the world
has, grief "for failure, not for sin" (Bernard), for the results
as seen in Cain, Esau (his tears!), and Judas (remorse,
metemelēthē). Works out (perfective use of *kat-*) death in
the end.

11. *This selfsame thing (auto touto).* "This very thing,"
"the being made sorry according to God" (*to kata theon
lupēthēnai,* articular first aorist passive infinitive with which
auto touto agrees and the proleptic subject of the verb *kateirgasato.* Earnest care *(spouden).* Diligence, from *speudō,* to
hasten. Cf. Rom. 12:11. *Yea (alla).* Not adversative use
of *alla,* but copulative as is common (half dozen examples
here). *Clearing of yourselves (apologia).* In the old notion
of *apologia* (self-vindication, self-defence) as in I Peter 3:15.
Indignation (aganaktēsin). Old word, only here in N.T.
From *aganakteo* (Mark 10:14, etc.). *Avenging (ekdikēsin).*
Late word from *ekdikeō,* to avenge, to do justice (Luke 18:5;
21:22), vindication from wrong as in Luke 18:7, to secure
punishment (I Peter 2:14). *Pure (hagnous).* Kin to *hagios*
(*hazō,* to reverence), immaculate.

12. *But that your earnest care for us might be made manifest
(all' heineken tou phanerōthēnai tēn spouden humōn tēn huper
hēmōn).* So the correct text, not "our care for you." Easy
to interchange Greek *humōn* (your) and *hēmōn* (our). Usual
construction with preposition *heneken* and genitive of articular infinitive with accusative of general reference.

13. *We joyed the more exceedingly (perissoterōs mallon
echarēmen).* Double comparative (pleonastic use of *mallon,*
more, with *perissoterōs,* more abundantly) as is common in
the *Koinē* (Mark 7:36; Phil. 1:23). *For the joy of Titus (epi
tēi charāi Titou).* On the basis of (*epi*) the joy of Titus who

was proud of the outcome of his labours in Corinth. *Hath been refreshed* (*anapepautai*). Perfect passive indicative of *anapauō*. Cf. I Cor. 16:18 for this striking verb.

14. *If—I have gloried* (*ei—kekauchēmai*). Condition of first class. On this verb see I Cor. 3:21; II Cor. 5:12. *I was not put to shame* (*ou kateischunthēn*). First aorist passive indicative of *kataischunō*. Paul had assured Titus, who hesitated to go after the failure of Timothy, that the Corinthians were sound at bottom and would come round all right if handled properly. Paul's joy is equal to that of Titus. *In truth* (*en alētheiāi*). In the sharp letter as well as in I Corinthians. He had not hesitated to speak plainly of their sins. *Our glorying before Titus* (*hē kauchēsis epi Titou*). The two things were not inconsistent and were not contradictory as the outcome proved.

15. *Whilst he remembereth* (*anamimnēskomenou*). Present middle participle of *anamimnēskō*, to remind, in the genitive case agreeing with *autou* (his, of him). *The obedience of you all* (*tēn pantōn humōn hupakouēn*). A remarkable statement of the complete victory of Titus in spite of a stubborn minority still opposing Paul. *With fear and trembling* (*meta phobou kai tromou*). He had brought a stern message (I Cor. 5:5) and they had trembled at the words of Titus (cf. Eph. 6:5; Phil. 2:12). Paul had himself come to the Corinthians at first with a nervous dread (I Cor. 2:3).

16. *I am of good courage* (*tharrō*). The outcome has brought joy, courage, and hope to Paul.

CHAPTER VIII

1. *The grace (tēn charin).* As manifested in the collection in the churches, poor as they were. The Romans had lacerated Macedonia (Livy, XLV. 30). 2. *Proof (dokimēi).* Tests as of metals as in 2:9. *Abundance (perisseia).* Late word from *perisseuō,* to overflow. *Their deep poverty (hē kata bathous ptōcheia autōn). Ptōcheia* is old word from *ptōcheuō,* to be a beggar, as of Jesus in 8:9 (from *ptōchos,* cowering in fear and poverty, as in Luke 14:13, but ennobled by Christ as in Matt. 5:3; II Cor. 8:9). Poverty down deep. Strabo (LX 419) has *kata bathous,* down to the bottom. *Liberality (haplotētos).* From *haplous,* single, simple (Matt. 6:22). "The passage from single-mindedness or simplicity to liberality is not quite obvious" (Plummer). Perhaps "heartiness" supplies the connecting link. See also 9:11, 13.

3. *Beyond their power (para dunamin).* "Alongside" with accusative like *huper dunamin* in 1:8. Field (*Ot. Nov.*) quotes Josephus (*Ant.* iii. 6, 1) for *kata dunamin* and *para dunamin* as here. Few give *kata dunamin* (according to actual ability). Paul commends this high pressure collection because of the emergency. *Of their own accord (authairetoi).* Old verbal adjective (*autos, hairetos* from *haireomai,* to choose), of their own initiative, voluntary. Only here and verse 17 in N.T. Papyri often have *hekousiōs kai authairetōs* (willingly and voluntarily).

4. *Beseeching us with much intreaty in regard of this grace (meta pollēs paraklēseōs deomenoi hēmōn tēn charin).* Literally, "with much intreaty begging of us the favour and the partnership in the ministry to the saints." The accusative *(charin)* after *deomai* is unusual. By *charis* Paul means the privilege of giving (cf. Acts 24:27). Apparently Paul had been reluctant to press the Macedonians because of their manifest poverty. They demanded the right to have a share in it.

5. *We had hoped (ēlpisamen).* First aorist active indicative of *elpizō.* "Expected," he means. They went beyond his hopes about them. *First they gave their own selves (heautous*

243

edōkan prōton). First aorist active indicative of *didōmi* (k aorist). "Themselves they gave first." That is the explanation of the generous giving.

6. *Insomuch that we exhorted Titus (eis to parakalesai hēmas Titon).* Use of *eis to* and the infinitive for result with accusative of general reference (*hēmas*). See Robertson, *Grammar*, p. 1003. *He had made a beginning before (proenērxato).* First aorist active indicative of the double compound verb *pro-en-archomai*, still found only here and verse 10, to make a start before others. *Complete (epitelesei).* First aorist (effective) active subjunctive of *epiteleō*, to finish, with perfective use of *epi* in composition.

7. *In this grace also (kai en tautēi tēi chariti).* This gifted church (I Cor. 12–14) had fallen behind in the grace of giving. Kindly irony in this allusion.

8. *Proving (dokimazōn).* Testing and so proving. *The sincerity also of your love (kai to tēs humeteras agapēs gnēsion).* Old adjective, contraction of *genesios (ginomai),* legitimately born, not spurious. A collection is a test of one's love for Christ, not the only test, but a real one.

9. *Though he was rich (plousios ōn).* Concessive present participle *ōn* from *eimi,* to be. *He became poor (eptōcheusen).* Ingressive aorist active indicative of *ptōcheuō* (see verse 2 on *ptōcheia*). *Through his poverty (tēi ekeinou ptōcheiāi).* Instrumental case, by means of. *Might become rich (ploutēsēte).* Ingressive first aorist active subjunctive of *plouteō,* to be rich with *hina* (that). See on Luke 1:53 I Cor. 4:8.

10. *Judgment (gnōmēn).* Deliberate opinion, but not a "command" (*epitagē* verse 8). Cf. I Cor. 7:25. *A year ago (apo perusi).* From last year. *Not only to do, but also to will (ou monon to poiēsai, alla kai to thelein).* Articular infinitives the objects of *proenērxasthe* on which verb see verse 6). That is to say, the Corinthians promised before any others.

11. *The readiness to will (hē prothumia tou thelein).* Old word from *prothumos (pro, thumos),* forwardness, eagerness (Acts 17:11). They were quick to pledge. *The completion also (kai to epitelesai).* The finishing also (articular first aorist active infinitive). *Out of your ability (ek tou echein).* "Out of the having," literally, and so, "out of what you can give" (verse 12).

12. *Is there (prokeitai).* Lies before one. Old word. *Accept-*

able (euprosdektos). See on 6:2. *According as a man hath (katho ean echēi).* Indefinite comparative clause with *ean* and present subjunctive *echēi.* Clearly God does not expect us to give what we do not have. *Not according as he hath not (ou katho ouk echei).* Note present indicative rather than subjunctive because a specific case is presented. See 9:7; Mark 12:43.

13. *Others may be eased (allois anesis).* "Release to others." *Ye distressed (humin thlipsis).* "To you tribulation." The verb *ēi* (present subjunctive) with *hina* is not expressed.

14. *By equality (ex isotētos).* Old word from *isos,* fair, equal. In N.T. only here and Col. 4:1. *Abundancy (perisseuma).* Late word from *perisseuō* like *perisseia* (verse 2) Cf. Matt. 12:34. *Want (husterēma).* Late word from *hustereō,* to be in want. See also 9:12; Luke 21:4 (cf. *husterēsis* in Mark 12:44).

16. *Which putteth (tōi didonti).* Present active articular participle, "who is continually giving." Hence Titus is full of zealous care for you.

17. *Very earnest (spoudaioteros).* "More earnest than ordinarily," comparative adjective.

18. *We have sent with him (sunepempsamen met' autou).* Epistolary aorist. *The brother (ton adelphon).* This may be, probably is, Luke who may also be the brother of Titus (see also 12:18) according to a common Greek idiom where the article is used as "his." But this idiom is not necessary. As a matter of fact, we do not know who this brother is. *Is spread through all the churches (dia pasōn tōn ekklēsiōn).* No verb in the Greek (ellipsis).

19. *But who was also appointed (alla kai cheirotonētheis).* Anacoluthon. The first aorist passive participle *cheirotonētheis* is from *cheirotoneō,* old verb to stretch out the hands (*cheir teinō*) and so to vote in public. The idea is that this brother was chosen by the churches, not by Paul. Only here in N.T. save Acts 14:23 where it means to appoint without notion of raising the hands. In Acts 10:41 we have *procheirotoneō. To travel with us (sunekdēmos).* Late word for travelling companion. So in the inscriptions (*sun,* together with, *ekdēmos,* away from home).

20. *Avoiding this (stellomenoi touto).* Present middle participle of *stellō,* old verb, to set, to arrange. So "arranging

for ourselves this." *That any man should blame us* (*mē tis hēmas mōmēsētai*). Literally, "lest any one blame us" (negative purpose with *mē* and first aorist middle subjunctive of *mōmeomai*. See on 6:3, only other N.T. example). *Bounty* (*hadrotēti*). Old word from *hadros*, thick, stout, ripe, rich, great as in I Kings 1:9; II Kings 10:6. Only here in N.T.

21. *We take thought* (*pronoumen*). Old verb, to plan beforehand (*pro-*) as in Rom. 12:17; I Tim. 5:8. *But also in the sight of men* (*alla kai enōpion anthrōpōn*). It is not enough for one's financial accounts to be honourable (*kala*) as God sees them, but they should be so kept that men can understand them also. A timely warning. Paul took the utmost pains that no suspicion could be attached to him in this collection.

22. *Our brother* (*ton adelphon hēmōn*). Not Paul's personal brother, but a brother in Christ, one whom Paul had tested and was willing to trust. It may have been Tychicus or Apollos, but we do not know.

23. *About Titus* (*huper Titou*). There is no verb expressed. Supply "inquire." He endorses Titus up to the hilt. He is "my partner" (*koinōnos emos*) and "fellow-worker" (*sunergos*). *Messengers of the churches* (*apostoloi ekklēsiōn*). Apostles in the general sense of "sent ones" (from *apostellō*, to send) by the churches and responsible to the churches for the handling of the funds. *The glory of Christ* (*doxa Christou*). Financial agents, please observe.

24. *The proof of your love* (*tēn endeixin tēs agapēs humōn*). There is a word here for pastors and deacons who try to protect the churches from the denominational representatives of kingdom causes. *In the face of the churches* (*eis prosōpon tōn ekklēsiōn*). A great host is pictured as watching how the Corinthians will treat these duly accredited agents in the collection (Titus and the other two brethren). It requires courage to stand by such representatives of great causes before stingy saints.

CHAPTER IX

1. *Superfluous (perisson)*. All the same he does write. "The writing" (*to graphein*) ought to be superfluous. 2. *I glory (kauchōmai)*. Present middle indicative. I still am glorying, in spite of the poor performance of the Corinthians. *Hath been prepared (pareskeuastai)*. Perfect passive indicative of *paraskeuazō*, to make ready, "stands prepared." *Stirred up (ērethise)*. First aorist active indicative of *erethizō* (from *erethō*, to excite), to excite in a good sense here, in a bad sense in Col. 3:21, the only N.T. examples. *Very many of them (tous pleionas)*. The more, the majority. 3. *I sent (epempsa)*. Not literary plural with this epistolary aorist as in 18 and 22. *That ye may be prepared (hina pareskeuasmenoi ēte)*. Perfect passive subjunctive in the final clause, "that ye may really be prepared," "as I said" (*kathōs elegon*) and not just say that ye are prepared. Paul's very syntax tells against them. 4. *If there come with me any of Macedonia and find you unprepared (ean elthōsin sun emoi Makedones kai heurōsin humas aparaskeuastous)*. Condition of third class (undetermined, but stated as a lively possibility) with *ean* and the second aorist active subjunctive (*elthōsin, heurōsin*), a bold and daring challenge. *Aparaskeuastos* is a late and rare verbal adjective from *paraskeuazō* with *a* privative, only here in the N.T. *Lest by any means we should be put to shame (mē pōs kataischunthōmen hēmeis)*. Negative purpose with first aorist passive subjunctive of *kataischunō* (see on 7:14) in the literary plural. *That we say not, ye (hina mē legōmen humeis)*. A delicate syntactical turn for what he really has in mind. He does wish that they become ashamed of not paying their pledges. *Confidence (hupostasei)*. This word, common from Aristotle on, comes from *huphistēmi*, to place under. It always has the notion of substratum or foundation as here; 11:17; Heb. 1:3. The papyri give numerous examples (Moulton and Milligan's *Vocabulary*) of the word for "property" in various aspects. So in Heb. 11:1 "faith is

247

the title-deed of things hoped for." In the LXX it represents fifteen different Hebrew words.

5. *I thought* (*hegēsamēn*). Epistolary aorist again. See Phil. 2:25 for the expression here. *Go before* (*proelthōsin*). Second aorist active of *proerchomai*. Go to you before I come. *Make up beforehand* (*prokatartisōsi*). Late and rare double compound verb *prokatartizō* (in Hippocrates). Only here in N.T. See *katartizō* in I Cor. 1:10. *Your afore-promised bounty* (*tēn proepēggelmenēn eulogian humōn*). "Blessing" (*eulogia*) literally, but applied to good deeds also as well as good words (Gen. 33:11). Note third use of "*pro*" before. He literally rubs it in that the pledge was overdue. *That the same might be ready* (*tautēn hetoimēn einai*). Here the infinitive alone (*einai*) is used to express purpose without *hōste* or *eis to* or *pros to* with the accusative of general reference (*tautēn*). The feminine form *hetoimēn* is regular (I Peter 1:5) though *hetoimos* also occurs with the feminine like the masculine (Matt. 25:10). *And not of extortion* (*kai mē hōs pleonexian*). "And not as covetousness." Some offerings exhibit covetousness on the part of the giver by their very niggardliness.

6. *Sparingly* (*pheidomenōs*). Late and rare adverb made from the present middle participle *pheidomenos* from *pheidomai*, to spare. It occurs in Plutarch (Alex. 25).

7. *He hath purposed* (*proēirētai*). Perfect middle indicative of *proaireomai*, to choose beforehand, old verb, here only in N.T. Permanent purpose also. *Not grudgingly* (*mē ek lupēs*). The use of *mē* rather than *ou* shows that the imperative *poieitō* (do) or *didotō* (give) is to be supplied. Not give as out of sorrow. *Or of necessity* (*ē ex anagkēs*). As if it were like pulling eye-teeth. *For God loveth a cheerful giver* (*hilaron gar dotēn agapāi ho theos*). Our word "hilarious" comes from *hilaron* which is from *hilaos* (propitious), an old and common adjective, only here in N.T.

8. *Is able* (*dunatei*). Late verb, not found except here; 13:3; Rom. 14:4. So far a Pauline word made from *dunatos*, able. *All sufficiency* (*pāsan autarkeian*). Old word from *autarkēs* (Phil. 4:11), common word, in N.T. only here and I Tim. 6:6. The use of this word shows Paul's acquaintance with Stoicism. Paul takes this word of Greek philosophy and applies it to the Christian view of life as independent

of circumstances. But he does not accept the view of the Cynics in the avoidance of society. Note threefold use of "all" here (*en panti, pantote, pāsan*, in everything, always, all sufficiency).

9. *As it is written (kathōs gegraptai)*. Psa. 92:3, 9. Picture of the beneficent man. *He hath scattered abroad (eskorpisen)*. First aorist active indicative of *skorpizō*, to scatter, *Koiné* verb for *skedannumi* of the Attic. Probably akin to *skorpios* (scorpion) from root *skarp*, to cut asunder. See on Matt. 12:30. It is like sowing seed. *To the poor (tois penēsin)*. Old word from *penamai*, to work for one's living. Latin *penuria* and Greek *peinaō*, to be hungry, are kin to it. Only N.T. instance and to be distinguished from *ptōchos*, beggar, abjectly poor.

10. *Supplieth (epichorēgōn)*. Late *Koiné* compound verb from *epi* and *chorēgeō*, just below (I Peter 4:11). *Chorēgos* is old word for leader of a chorus *(choros, hēgeomai)* or chorus-leader. The verb means to furnish a chorus at one's own expense, then to supply in general. N.T. examples of *epichorēgeō* are II Cor. 9:10; Gal. 3:15; Col. 2:19; II Peter 1:5. *Shall multiply (plēthunei)*. Future active indicative of *plēthunō*, old verb from *plēthus*, fulness. Cf. Acts 6:1. *Fruits (genēmata)*. Correct reading (from *ginomai*, to become) and not *gennēmata* (from *gennaō*, to beget). This spelling is supported by LXX where Thackeray shows that *genēmata* in LXX refers to vegetables and *gennēmata* to animals. The papyri support this distinction (Moulton and Milligan's *Vocabulary*).

11. *Enriched (ploutizomenoi)*. Present passive participle of *ploutizō* for which see on I Cor. 1:5; II Cor. 6:10 only other N.T. examples. *Liberality (haplotēta)*. See on 8:2. Anacoluthon with nominative participle too far from *perisseuēte* for agreement. More like the independent use of the participle.

12. *Service (leitourgias)*. Old word from *leōs* (people, *laos*), *leitos* like *dēmosios*, public, and *ergon*, work. So public service either in worship to God (Luke 1:23) or benefaction to others (II Cor. 9:12; Phil. 2:30). Our word liturgy is this word. *Filleth up (estin prosanaplērousa)*. Present active periphrastic indicative of double compound verb *prosanaplēroō, Koiné* word, here and 11:9 only in N.T., to fill up

by adding to. The Corinthians simply added to the total from others. *Unto God (tōi theōi)*. Dative case and with a certain suddenness as at close of verse 11, really a parenthesis between in the somewhat tangled sentence. 13. *Seeing that they glorify God (doxazontes ton theon)*. Anacoluthon again. The nominative participle used independently like *ploutizomenoi* in verse 11. *Obedience (hupotagēi)*. Late and rare word from *hupotassō*, to subject, middle to obey. Only in Paul in N.T. *Of your confession (tēs homologias humōn)*. Old word from *homologeō (homologos, homou, legō)*, to say together. It is either to profess (Latin *profiteor*, to declare openly) or to confess (Latin *confiteor*, to declare fully, to say the same thing as another). Both confess and profess are used to translate the verb and each idea is present in the substantive. Only the context can decide. Actions speak louder than words. The brethren in Jerusalem will know by this collection that Gentiles make as good Christians as Jews. *For the liberality of your contribution (haplotēti tēs koinōnias)*. This is the point that matters just now. Paul drives it home. On this use of *koinōnia* see on 8:4. 14. *While they themselves long after you (autōn epipothountōn)*. Genitive absolute of present active participle of *epipotheō* (5:2). *In you (eph' humin)*. Upon you. 15. *Thanks be to God (charis tōi theōi)*. Third time (verses 11, 12, 15). *For his unspeakable gift (epi tēi anekdiēgētōi autou dōreāi)*. One of Paul's gems flashed out after the somewhat tangled sentence (verses 10–14) like a gleam of light that clears the air. Words fail Paul to describe the gift of Christ to and for us. He may have coined this word as it is not found elsewhere except in ecclesiastical writers save as a variant (B L) for *adiēgēton* in Aristeas 99 (*thaumasmon anekdiēgēton*, "wonder beyond description," Moulton and Milligan's *Vocabulary*). See similar word in Rom. 11:33 (*anexichniasta*, unsearchable) and Eph. 3:8.

CHAPTER X

1. *Now I Paul myself* (*Autos de egō Paulos*). Cf. Gal. 5:2. Paul now turns to the third part of the epistle in chapters 10 to 13 in which he vigorously defends himself against the accusations of the stubborn minority of Judaizers in Corinth. Great ministers of Christ through the ages have had to pass through fiery trials like these. Paul has shown the way for us all. He speaks of himself now plainly, but under compulsion, as is clear. It may be that at this point he took the pen from the amanuensis and wrote himself as in Gal 6:11. *By the meekness and gentleness of Christ* (*dia tes praütētos kai epieikias tou Christou*). This appeal shows (Plummer) that Paul had spoken to the Corinthians about the character of Christ. Jesus claimed meekness for himself (Matt. 11:29) and felicitated the meek (Matt. 5:5) and he exemplified it abundantly (Luke 23:34). See on Matt. 5:15 and I Cor. 4:21 for this great word that has worn thin with us. Plutarch combines *praütēs* with *epieikia* as Paul does here. Matthew Arnold suggested "sweet reasonableness" for *epieikeia* in Plato, Aristotle, Plutarch. It is in the N. T. only here and Acts 24:4 (*to epieikes* in Phil. 4:5). In Greek Ethics the equitable man was called *epieikēs*, a man who does not press for the last farthing of his rights (Bernard). *Lowly among you* (*tapeinos en humin*). The bad use of *tapeinos*, the old use, but here alone in N.T. in that meaning. Socrates and Aristotle used it for littleness of soul. Probably Paul here is quoting one of the sneers of his traducers in Corinth about his humble conduct while with them (I Cor. 2:23; II Cor. 7:6) and his boldness (*apōn tharrō*) when away (I Cor. 7:16). "It was easy to satirize and misrepresent a depression of spirits, a humility of demeanour, which were either the direct results of some bodily affliction, or which the consciousness of this affliction had rendered habitual" (Farrar). The words stung Paul to the quick.

2. *I beseech* (*deomai*). So here, but *parakalō* in verse 1. Perhaps, "I beg" suits the new turn here. *That I may not*

when present show courage (to mē parōn tharrēsai). Articular infinitive (aorist active of *tharreō*) in the accusative case with negative *mē* the direct object of *deomai.* Literally, "I beg the not when present (*parōn* nominative present participle agreeing with subject of *tharrō* in spite of being in the accusative infinitive clause, *to mē tharrēsai*) showing courage." The example of humility in Christ makes Paul drop "from magisterial exhortation to earnest entreaty" (Plummer). *As if we walked according to the flesh (hōs kata sarka peripatountas).* Another sneering charge as made plain by the use of *hōs* with the participle for the alleged reason.

3. *In the flesh (en sarki).* But that is a very different thing from walking *kata sarka* according to the standards of the flesh as his enemies charged. It is easy enough to make insinuations. *We war (strateuometha).* Literary plural again after *logizomai* in verse 2. Old word to lead an army (*stratos*). In N.T. only in the middle as here. Paul admits that he fights, but only the devil and his agents even if wearing the livery of heaven. Paul knew the Roman army well. He knows how to use the military metaphor.

4. *The weapons of our warfare (ta hopla tēs strateias).* *Strateia* (old word, in N.T. only here and I Tim. 1:18) is *campaign* and not army as some MSS. have (*stratia*). But both *strateia* and *stratia* occur in the papyri for the same word (Deissmann, *Bible Studies*, p. 181f.). For *hopla* (Latin *arma*) see on 6:7; Rom. 6:13; 13:12. *Of the flesh (sarkika).* See on I Cor. 3:3; II Cor. 1:12. They had accused him of artifices and craft. *Mighty before God (dunata tōi theōi).* This dative of personal interest (ethical dative) can be like *asteios tōi theōi* (Acts 7:20), in God's eyes, as it looks to God. *To the casting down of strongholds (pros kathairesin ochurōmatōn).* *Kathairesis* is old word from *kathaireō*, to take down, to tear down walls and buildings. Carries on the military metaphor. *Ochurōma* is old word, common in the Apocrypha, from *ochuroō*, to fortify, and that from *ochuros* (from *echō*, to hold fast). Nowhere else in N.T. In Cilicia the Romans had to tear down many rocky forts in their attacks on the pirates.

5. *Casting down imaginations (logismous kathairountes).* The same military figure (*kathairesis*) and the present active participle agreeing with *strateuometha* in verse 3 (verse 4 a parenthesis). The reasonings or imaginations (*logismous,* old

word from *logizomai*, to reckon, only here in N.T. and Rom. 2:15) are treated as forts or citadels to be conquered. *Every high thing that is exalted* (*pan hupsōma epairomenon*). Same metaphor. *Hupsōma* from *hupsoō* is late *Koiné* word (in LXX, Plutarch, Philo, papyri) for height and that figure carried on by *epairomenon*. Paul aims to pull down the topmost perch of audacity in their reasonings against the knowledge of God. We need Paul's skill and courage today. *Bringing every thought into captivity* (*aichmalōtizontes pān noēma*). Present active participle of *aichmalōtizō*, common *Koiné* verb from *aichmalōtos*, captive in war (*aichmē*, spear, *halōtos* verbal of *haliskomai*, to be taken). See on Luke 21:24. Paul is the most daring of thinkers, but he lays all his thoughts at the feet of Jesus. For *noēma* (device) see on 2:11. *To the obedience of Christ* (*eis tēn hupakoēn tou Christou*). Objective genitive, "to the obedience unto Christ." That is Paul's conception of intellectual liberty, freedom in Christ. Deissmann (*St. Paul*, p. 141) calls this "the mystic genitive."

6. *Being in readiness* (*en hetoimōi echontes*). This very idiom occurs in Polybius, Philo, etc. "Holding in readiness." In 12:14 we have *hetoimōs echō* for the same idea (adverb *hetoimōs*). *Disobedience* (*parakoēn*). Rare word (Plato, papyri) hearing amiss (aside), failing to hear, refusing to heed (cf. Matt. 18:17 for same idea in *parakouō*). In N.T. only here; Rom. 5:19; Heb. 2:2. In contrast with *hupakoē* (obedience) rather than the common *apeithia* (Rom. 11:30, 32). *When your obedience shall be fulfilled* (*hotan plērōthēi humōn hē hupakoē*). Indefinite temporal clause with *hotan* and first aorist passive subjunctive. Paul expects that the whole church will become obedient to Christ's will soon as came true.

7. *Ye look* (*Blepete*). Either indicative or imperative. Either makes sense but the indicative the best sense. *Before your face* (*kata prosōpon*). They ought to look below the surface. If it is imperative, they should see the facts. *That he is Christ's* (*Christou einai*). Predicate genitive in indirect discourse).

8. *Somewhat abundantly* (*perissoteron ti*). Comparative, "somewhat more abundantly" than I have, in order to show that he is as true a minister of Christ as his accusers are. Concessive (conditional) clause of third class. For *ean te*

see Rom. 14:8. *I shall not be put to shame* (*ouk aischunthē-somai*). As a convicted impostor or pretentious boaster (Plummer). First future passive, singular number (not literary plural as in verse 7).

9. *As if I would terrify you by my letters* (*hōs an ekphobein humas dia tōn epistolōn*). This use of *hōs an* with the infinitive is seen in the papyri (Moulton, *Prolegomena*, p. 167) and it is not *an* in the apodosis (Robertson, *Grammar*, pp. 974, 1040). The active of this old compound verb means to frighten, to terrify. Here only in N.T. It is common in the LXX (Job. 7:14; 33:16). Note plural (letters) here and cf. I Cor. 5:9 and II Cor. 2:3.

10. *They say* (*phasin*). Reading of B old Latin Vulgate, but Westcott and Hort prefer *phēsin* (says one, the leader). This charge Paul quotes directly. *Weighty and strong* (*bareiai kai ischurai*). These adjectives can be uncomplimentary and mean "severe and violent" instead of "impressive and vigorous." The adjectives bear either sense. *His bodily presence* (*hē parousia tou sōmatos*). This certainly is uncomplimentary. "The presence of his body." It seems clear that Paul did not have a commanding appearance like that of Barnabas (Acts 14:12). He had some physical defect of the eyes (Gal. 4:14) and a thorn in the flesh (II Cor. 12:7). In the second century *Acts of Paul and Thecla* he is pictured as small, short, bow-legged, with eye-brows knit together, and an aquiline nose. A forgery of the fourth century in the name of Lucian describes Paul as "the bald-headed, hook-nosed Galilean." However that may be, his accusers sneered at his personal appearance as "weak" (*asthenēs*). *His speech of no account* (*ho logos exouthenēmenos*). Perfect passive participle of *exoutheneō*, to treat as nothing (cf. I Cor. 1:28). The Corinthians (some of them) cared more for the brilliant eloquence of Apollos and did not find Paul a trained rhetorician (I Cor. 1:17; 2:1, 4; II Cor. 11:6). He made different impressions on different people. "Seldom has any one been at once so ardently hated and so passionately loved as St. Paul" (Deissmann, *St. Paul*, p. 70). "At one time he seemed like a man, and at another he seemed like an angel" (*Acts of Paul and Thecla*). He spoke like a god at Lystra (Acts 14:8-12), but Eutychus went to sleep on him (Acts 20:9). Evidently Paul winced under this biting criticism of his looks and speech.

11. *What we are* (*hoioi esmen*). Rather, "what sort" (*hoioi*), not *ho* (what) nor *hoi* (who). Literary plural. *Hoios* is qualitative just as *toioutoi* (such). Paul's quality in his letters when absent (*apontes*) and in his deeds when present (*parontes*) is precisely the same. 12. *To number or compare ourselves* (*enkrinai ē sunkrinai*). Paronomasia here, play on the two words. *Enkrinai* is first aorist active infinitive of old verb, but here only in N.T., to judge among, to judge one as worthy to be numbered among as here. The second verb *sunkrinai* (first aorist active infinitive of *sunkrinō*, old verb, in N.T. only here and I Cor. 2:13) originally meant to combine as in I Cor. 2:13 (which see), but here it has the sense of "compare" not found in the old Greek. The papyri use it to mean to decide. Plummer suggests "to pair and compare" for the play on the words here. *Measuring themselves by themselves* (*en heautois heautous metrountes*). Or "in themselves." Keenest sarcasm. Setting themselves up as the standards of orthodoxy these Judaizers always measure up to the standard while Paul falls short. *Comparing themselves with themselves* (*sunkrinontes heautous heautois*). Associate instrumental case *heautois* after *sunkrinontes* (verb just explained). Paul is not keen to fall into the trap set for him. *Are without understanding* (*ou suniāsin*). The regular form for present active indicative third plural of *suniēmi*, to comprehend, to grasp. Some MSS. have the late form *suniousin* (omega form *suniō*). It is a hard thing to see, but it is true. These men do not see their own picture so obvious to others (Eph. 5:17; I Tim. 1:7). Cf. Mark 8:17.

13. *Beyond our measure* (*eis ta ametra*). "Into the unmeasured things," "the illimitable." Old word, here only in N.T. *Of the province* (*tou kanonos*). Old word (*kanna* like Hebrew) a reed, a measuring rod. Numerous papyri examples for measuring rod and rules (our word canon). Only twice in N.T., here (also verse 15 and 16) and Gal. 6:16 (rule to walk by). *To reach even unto you* (*ephikesthai achri kai humōn*). Second aorist middle infinitive of *ephikneomai*, old verb, only here and verse 14 in N.T. Paul's measuring-rod extends to Corinth.

14. *We stretch not ourselves overmuch* (*ou huperekteinomen heautous*). Apparently Paul made this double compound

verb to express his full meaning (only in Gregory Nazianzen afterwards). "We do not stretch ourselves out beyond our rights." *We came even as far as unto you* (*achri kai humōn ephthasamen*). First aorist active indicative of *phthanō*, to come before, to precede, the original idea which is retained in Matt. 12:28 (Luke 11:20) and may be so here. If so, it means "We were the first to come to you" (which is true, Acts 18:1-18).

15. *In other men's labours* (*en allotriois kopois*). *Allotrios* means belonging to another as in Luke 16:12. Paul founded the church in Corinth. *As your faith groweth* (*auxanomenēs tēs pisteōs*). Genitive absolute of the present passive participle of *auxanō*, to grow. *We shall be magnified* (*megalunthēnai*). First aorist passive infinitive of *megalunō*, old verb (Luke 1:46) to make great (cf. Phil. 1:20 of Christ). Indirect discourse after *elpida* (hope) with the construction of *elpizō*, to hope.

16. *Even unto the parts beyond you* (*eis ta huperekeina humōn*). Compound adverb (*huper, ekeina*, beyond those places) used as preposition. Found only here and in ecclesiastical writers. *Things ready to our hand* (*ta hetoima*). He had a plenty besides that he could use.

17. Paul quotes Prov. 27:2.

18. *Is approved* (*dokimos*). Accepted (from *dechomai*) by the Lord. The Lord accepts his own recommendation (*sunistēsin*, see on II Cor. 3:1f.).

CHAPTER XI

1. *Would that ye could bear with me (ophelon aneichesthe mou).* *Koiné* way of expressing a wish about the present, *ophelon* (as a conjunction, really second aorist active indicative of *opheilō* without augment) and the imperfect indicative instead of *eithe* or *ei gar* (Robertson, *Grammar*, p. 1003). Cf. Rev. 3:15. See Gal. 5:12 for future indicative with *ophelon* and I Cor. 4:8 for aorist. *Mou* is ablative case after *aneichesthe* (direct middle, hold yourselves back from me). There is a touch of irony here. *Bear with me (anechesthe mou).* Either imperative middle or present middle indicative (ye do bear with me). Same form. *In a little foolishness (mikron ti aphrosunēs).* Accusative of general reference (*mikron ti*). "Some little foolishness" (from *aphrōn*, foolish). Old word only in this chapter in N.T.

2. *With a godly jealousy (theou zēloi).* Instrumental case of *zēlos.* With a jealousy of God. *I espoused (hērmosamēn).* First aorist middle indicative of *harmozō*, old verb to join, to fit together (from *harmos*, joint). Common for betrothed, though only here in N.T. The middle voice indicates Paul's interest in the matter. Paul treats the Corinthians as his bride.

3. *The serpent beguiled Eve (ho ophis exēpatēsen Heuan).* Paul's only mention of the serpent in Eden. The compound *exapataō* means to deceive completely. *Lest by any means (mē pōs).* Common conjunction after verbs of fearing. *Corrupted (phtharēi).* Second aorist passive subjunctive with *mē pōs* of *phtheirō*, to corrupt.

4. *Another Jesus (allon Iēsoun).* Not necessarily a different Jesus, but any other "Jesus" is a rival and so wrong. That would deny the identity. *A different spirit (pneuma heteron).* This is the obvious meaning of *heteron* in distinction from *allon* as seen in Acts 4:12; Gal. 1:6f. But this distinction in nature or kind is not always to be insisted on. *A different gospel (euaggelion heteron).* Similar use of *heteron.* *Ye do well to bear with him (kalōs anechesthe).* Ironical turn again.

258 WORD PICTURES IN NEW TESTAMENT

"Well do you hold yourselves back from him" (the coming one, whoever he is). Some MSS. have the imperfect *aneichesthe* (did bear with).

5. *That I am not a whit behind the very chiefest apostles* (*mēden husterēkenai tōn huperlian apostolōn*). Perfect active infinitive of *hustereō*, old verb to fall short with the ablative case. The rare compound adverb *huperlian* (possibly in use in the vernacular) is probably ironical also, "the super apostles" as these Judaizers set themselves up to be. "The extra-super apostles" (Farrar). Also in 12:11. He is not referring to the pillar-apostles of Gal. 2:9.

6. *Rude in speech* (*idiōtēs tōi logōi*). Locative case with *idiōtēs* for which word see on Acts 4:13; I Cor. 14:16, 23, 24. The Greeks regarded a man as *idiōtēs* who just attended to his own affairs (*ta idia*) and took no part in public life. Paul admits that he is not a professional orator (cf. 10:10), but denies that he is unskilled in knowledge (*all' ou tēi gnōsei*). *Among all men* (*en pāsin*). He has made his mastery of the things of Christ plain among all men. He knew his subject.

7. *In abasing myself* (*emauton tapeinōn*). Humbling myself by making tents for a living while preaching in Corinth. He is ironical still about "doing a sin" (*hamartian epoiēsa*). *For nought* (*dōrean*). Gratis. Accusative of general reference, common adverb. It amounts to sarcasm to ask if he did a sin in preaching the gospel free of expense to them "that ye may be exalted."

8. *I robbed* (*esulēsa*). Old verb to despoil, strip arms from a slain foe, only here in N.T. He allowed other churches to do more than their share. *Taking wages* (*labōn opsōnion*). For *opsōnion* see on I Cor. 9:7 and Rom. 6:17. He got his "rations" from other churches, not from Corinth while there.

9. *I was not a burden to any man* (*ou katenarkēsa outhenos*). First aorist active indicative of *katanarkaō*. Jerome calls this word one of Paul's *cilicisms* which he brought from Cilicia. But the word occurs in Hippocrates for growing quite stiff and may be a medical term in popular use. *Narkaō* means to become numb, torpid, and so a burden. It is only here and 12:13f. Paul "did not benumb the Corinthians by his demand for pecuniary aid" (Vincent). *From being burdensome* (*abarē*). Old adjective, free from weight or light

(*a* privative and *baros*, weight). See on I Thess. 2:9 for same idea. Paul kept himself independent.

10. *No man shall stop me of this glorying* (*hē kauchēsis hautē ou phragēsetai eis eme*). More exactly, "This glorying shall not be fenced in as regards me." Second future passive of *phrassō*, to fence in, to stop, to block in. Old verb, only here in N.T. *In the regions of Achaia* (*en tois klimasin tēs Achaias*). *Klima* from *klinō*, to incline, is *Koiné* word for declivity slope, region (our climate). See chapter 9 of I Corinthians for Paul's boast about preaching the gospel without cost to them.

11. *God knoweth* (*ho theos oiden*). Whether they do or not. He knows that God understands his motives.

12. *That I may cut off occasion* (*hina ekkopsō tēn aphormēn*). Purpose clause with *hina* and first aorist active subjunctive of *ekkoptō*, old verb to cut out or off (Matt. 3:10; 5:30). See II Cor. 5:12 for *aphormēn*. *From them which desire an occasion* (*tōn thelontōn aphormēn*). Ablative case after *ekkopsō*. There are always some hunting for occasions to start something against preachers. *They may be found* (*heurethōsin*). First aorist passive subjunctive of *heuriskō*, to find with final conjunction *hina*.

13. *False apostles* (*pseudapostoloi*). From *pseudēs*, false, and *apostolos*. Paul apparently made this word (cf. Rev. 2:2). In verse 26 we have *pseudadelphos*, a word of like formation (Gal. 2:4). See also *pseudochristoi* and *pseudoprophētai* in Mark 13:22. *Deceitful* (*dolioi*). Old word from *dolos* (lure, snare), only here in N.T. (cf. Rom. 16:18). *Fashioning themselves* (*metaschēmatizomenoi*). Present middle (direct) participle of the old verb *metaschēmatizō* for which see on I Cor. 4:6. Masquerading as apostles of Christ by putting on the outward habiliments, posing as ministers of Christ ("gentlemen of the cloth," nothing but cloth). Paul plays with this verb in verses 13, 14, 15.

14. *An angel of light* (*aggelon phōtos*). The prince of darkness puts on the garb of light and sets the fashion for his followers in the masquerade to deceive the saints. "Like master like man." Cf. 2:11 and Gal. 1:8. This terrible portrayal reveals the depth of Paul's feelings about the conduct of the Judaizing leaders in Corinth. In Gal. 2:4 he terms those in Jerusalem "false brethren."

15. *As ministers of righteousness* (*hōs diakonoi dikaiosunēs*). Jesus (John 10:1–21) terms these false shepherds thieves and robbers. It is a tragedy to see men in the livery of heaven serve the devil.

16. *Let no man think me foolish* (*mē tis me doxēi aphrona einai*). Usual construction in a negative prohibition with *mē* and the aorist subjunctive *doxēi* (Robertson, *Grammar*, p. 933). *But if ye do* (*ei de mē ge*). Literally, "But if not at least (or otherwise)," that is, If you do think me foolish. *Yet as foolish* (*kàn hōs aphrona*). "Even if as foolish." Paul feels compelled to boast of his career and work as an apostle of Christ after the terrible picture just drawn of the Judaizers. He feels greatly embarrassed in doing it. Some men can do it with complete composure (*sang froid*).

17. *Not after the Lord* (*ou kata Kurion*). Not after the example of the Lord. He had appealed to the example of Christ in 10:1 (the meekness and gentleness of Christ). Paul's conduct here, he admits, is not in keeping with that. But circumstances force him on.

18. *After the flesh* (*kata sarka*). It is *kata sarka* not *kata Kurion*. *I also* (*kágō*). But he knows that it is a bit of foolishness and not like Christ.

19. *Gladly* (*hēdeōs*). Irony again. Cf. *kalos* in 11:4 (Mark 7:9). So as to *phronimoi ontes* (being wise).

20. *For ye bear with a man* (*anechesthe gar*). "You tolerate tyranny, extortion, craftiness, arrogance, violence, and insult" (Plummer). Sarcasm that cut to the bone. Note the verb with each of the five conditional clauses (enslaves, devours, takes captive, exalteth himself, smites on the face). The climax of insult, smiting on the face.

21. *By way of disparagement* (*kata atimian*). Intense irony. Cf. 6:8. *As though* (*hōs hoti*). Presented as the charge of another. "They more than tolerate those who trample on them while they criticize as 'weak' one who shows them great consideration" (Plummer). After these prolonged explanations Paul "changes his tone from irony to direct and masterful assertion" (Bernard). *I am bold also* (*tolmō kágō*). Real courage. Cf. 10:2, 12.

22. *So am I* (*kágō*). This is his triumphant refrain with each challenge.

23. *As one beside himself* (*paraphronōn*). Present active

THE EPISTLES OF PAUL

participle of *paraphroneō*. Old verb from *paraphrōn* (*para, phrēn*), beside one's wits. Only here in N.T. Such open boasting is out of accord with Paul's spirit and habit. *I more* (*huper egō*). This adverbial use of *huper* appears in ancient Greek (Euripides). It has no effect on *egō*, not "more than I," but "I more than they." He claims superiority now to these "superextra apostles." *More abundant* (*perissoterōs*). See on 7:15. No verbs with these clauses, but they are clear. *In prisons* (*en phulakais*). Plural also in 6:5. Clement of Rome (*Cor.* V.) says that Paul was imprisoned seven times. We know of only five (Philippi, Jerusalem, Caesarea, twice in Rome), and only one before II Corinthians (Philippi). But Luke does not tell them all nor does Paul. Had he been in prison in Ephesus? So many think and it is possible as we have seen. *Above measure* (*huperballontōs*). Old adverb from the participle *huperballontōn* (*huperballō*, to hurl beyond). Here only in N.T. *In deaths oft* (*en thanatois pollakis*). He had nearly lost his life, as we know, many times (1:9f.; 4:11).

24. *Five times received I forty stripes save one* (*pentakis tesserakonta para mian elabon*). The Acts and the Epistles are silent about these Jewish floggings (Matt. 27:36). See on Luke 12:47 for omission of *plēgas* (stripes). Thirty-nine lashes was the rule for fear of a miscount (Deut. 25:1-3). Cf. Josephus (*Ant.* IV. 8, 1, 21).

25. *Thrice was I beaten with rods* (*tris errabdisthēn*). Roman (Gentile) punishment. It was forbidden to Roman citizens by the *Lex Porcia*, but Paul endured it in Philippi (Acts 16: 23, 37), the only one of the three named in Acts. First aorist passive of *rabdizō*, from *rabdos*, rod, Koiné word, in N.T. only here and Acts 16:22 which see. *Once was I stoned* (*hapax elithasthēn*). Once for all *hapax* means. At Lystra (Acts 14: 5-19). On *lithazō* Koiné verb from *lithos*, see on Acts 5:26. *Thrice I suffered shipwreck* (*tris enauagēsa*). First aorist active of *nauageō*, from *nauagos*, shipwrecked (*naus*, ship, *agnumi*, to break). Old and common verb, in N.T. only here and I Tim. 1:19. We know nothing of these. The one told in Acts 27 was much later. What a pity that we have no data for all these varied experiences of Paul. *Night and day* (*nuchthēmeron*). Rare word. Papyri give *nuktēmar* with the same idea (night-day). *Have I been in the deep* (*en*

tōi buthōi pepoiēka). Vivid dramatic perfect active indicative of *poieō*, "I have done a night and day in the deep." The memory of it survives like a nightmare. *Buthos* is old word (only here in N.T.) for bottom, depth of the sea, then the sea itself. Paul does not mean that he was a night and day under the water, not a Jonah experience, only that he was far out at sea and shipwrecked. This was one of the three shipwrecks already named.

26. *In journeyings* (*hodoiporiais*). Locative case of old word, only here in N.T. and John 4:6, from *hodoiporos*, wayfarer. *In perils* (*kindunois*). Locative case of *kindunos*, old word for danger or peril. In N.T. only this verse and Rom. 8:35. The repetition here is very effective without the preposition *en* (in) and without conjunctions (*asyndeton*). They are in contrasted pairs. The rivers of Asia Minor are still subject to sudden swellings from floods in the mountains. Cicero and Pompey won fame fighting the Cilician pirates and robbers (note *lēistōn*, not *kleptōn*, thieves, brigands or bandits on which see Matt. 26:55). The Jewish perils (*ek genous*, from my race) can be illustrated in Acts 9:23, 29; 13:50; 14:5; 17:5, 13; 18:12; 23:12; 24:27, and they were all perils in the city also. Perils from the Gentiles (*ex ethnōn*) we know in Philippi (Acts 16:20) and in Ephesus (Acts 19:23f.). Travel in the mountains and in the wilderness was perilous in spite of the great Roman highways. *Among false brethren* (*en pseudadelphois*). Chapters 10 and 11 throw a lurid light on this aspect of the subject.

27. *In labour and travail* (*kopōi kai mochthōi*). Both old words for severe work, combined here as in I Thess. 2:9; II Thess. 3:8, "by toil and moil" (Plummer). The rest of the list is like the items in II Cor. 6:4ff. *In cold* (*en psuchei*). Old word from *psuchō*, to cool by blowing. See Acts 28:2. See the picture of the aged Paul later in the Roman dungeon (II Tim. 4:9–18).

28. *Besides those things that are without* (*chōris tōn parektos*). Probably, "apart from those things beside these just mentioned." Surely no man ever found glory in such a peck of troubles as Paul has here recounted. His list should shame us all today who are disposed to find fault with our lot. *That which presseth upon me daily* (*hē epistasis moi hē kath' hēmeran*). For this vivid word *epistasis* see Acts 24:12, the

only other place in the N.T. where it occurs. It is like the
rush of a mob upon Paul. *Anxiety for all the churches* (*hē
merimna pasōn tōn ekklēsiōn*). Objective genitive after
merimna (distractions in different directions, from *merizō*)
for which word see on Matt. 13:22. Paul had the shepherd
heart. As apostle to the Gentiles he had founded most of
these churches.

29. *I burn* (*puroumai*). Present passive indicative of
puroō, old verb to inflame (from *pur*, fire). When a brother
stumbles, Paul is set on fire with grief.

30. *The things that concern my weakness* (*ta tēs astheneias
mou*). Like the list above.

31. *I am not lying* (*ou pseudomai*). The list seems so absurd and foolish that Paul takes solemn oath about it (cf.
1:23). For the doxology see Rom. 1:25; 9:5.

32. *The governor under Aretas* (*ho ethnarchēs Hareta*). How
it came to pass that Damascus, ruled by the Romans after
B.C. 65, came at this time to be under the rule of Aretas,
fourth of the name, King of the Nabatheans (II Macc. 5:8),
we do not know. There is an absence of Roman coins in
Damascus from A.D. 34 to 62. It is suggested (Plummer)
that Caligula, to mark his dislike for Antipas, gave Damascus to Aretas (enemy of Antipas). *Guarded* (*ephrourei*).
Imperfect active of *phroureō*, old verb (from *phrouros*, a
guard) to guard by posting sentries. In Acts 9:24 we read
that the Jews kept watch to seize Paul, but there is no conflict as they coöperated with the guard set by Aretas at
their request. *To seize* (*piasai*). Doric first aorist active infinitive of *piezō* (Luke 6:38) for which see on Acts 3:7.

33. *Through a window* (*dia thuridos*). For this late word
see on Acts 20:9, the only N.T. example. *Was I let down*
(*echalasthēn*). First aorist passive of *chalaō*, the very word
used by Luke in Acts 9:25. *In a basket* (*en sarganēi*). Old
word for rope basket whereas Luke (Acts 9:25) has *en
sphuridi* (the word for the feeding of the 4,000 while *kophinos*
is the one for the 5,000). This was a humiliating experience
for Paul in this oldest city of the world whither he had
started as a conqueror over the despised Christians.

CHAPTER XII

1. *I must needs glory (kauchasthai dei).* This is the reading of B L Latin Syriac, but Aleph D Bohairic have *de* while K M read *dē*. The first is probably correct. He must go on with the glorying already begun, foolish as it is, though it is not expedient (*ou sumpheron*). *Visions (optasias).* Late word from *optazō*. See on Luke 1:22; Acts 26:19. *Revelations of the Lord (apokalupseis Kuriou).* Unveilings (from *apokaluptō* as in Rev. 1:1). See on II Thess. 1:7; I Cor. 1:7; 14:26. Paul had both repeated visions of Christ (Acts 9:3; 16:9; 18:9; 22:17; 27:23f.) and revelations. He claimed to speak by direct revelation (I Cor. 11:23; 15:3; Gal. 1:12; Eph. 3:3, etc.).

2. *I know a man (oida anthrōpon).* Paul singles out one incident of ecstasy in his own experience that he declines to describe. He alludes to it in this indirect way as if it were some other personality. *Fourteen years ago (pro etōn dekatessarōn).* Idiomatic way of putting it, the preposition *pro* (before) before the date (Robertson, *Grammar*, p. 621f.) as in John 12:1. The date was probably while Paul was at Tarsus (Acts 9:30; 11:25). We have no details of that period. *Caught up (harpagenta).* Second aorist passive participle of *harpazō*, to seize (see on Matt. 11:12). *Even to the third heaven (heōs tritou ouranou).* It is unlikely that Paul alludes to the idea of seven heavens held by some Jews (*Test. of the Twelve Pat.*, Levi ii. iii.). He seems to mean the highest heaven where God is (Plummer).

3. *I do not know (ouk oida).* Paul declines to pass on his precise condition in this trance. We had best leave it as he has told it.

4. *Into Paradise (eis paradeison).* See on Luke 23:43 for this interesting word. Paul apparently uses Paradise as the equivalent of the third heaven in verse 2. Some Jews (*Book of the Secrets of Enoch*, chapter viii) make Paradise in the third heaven. The rabbis had various ideas (two heavens, three, seven). We need not commit Paul to any "celestial

gradation" (Vincent). *Unspeakable words (arrēta rēmata).*
Old verbal adjective (*a* privative, *rētos* from *reō*), only here
in N.T. *Not lawful (ouk exon).* Copula *estin* omitted.
Hence Paul does *not* give these words.
5. *But on mine own behalf (huper de emautou).* As if there
were two Pauls. In a sense there were. He will only glory
in the things mentioned above, the things of his weaknesses
(11:30).
6. *I shall not be foolish (ouk esomai aphrōn).* Apparent
contradiction to 11:1, 16. But he is here speaking of the
Paul "caught up" in case he should tell the things heard
(condition of the third class, *ean* and first aorist subjunctive
thelēsō). *Of me (eis eme).* To my credit, almost like dative
(cf. *en emoi* in I Cor. 14:11).
7. *By reason of the exceeding greatness (tēi huperbolēi).*
Instrumental case, "by the excess." *That I should not be
exalted overmuch (hina mē huperairōmai).* Present passive
subjunctive in final clause of *huperairō*, old verb to lift up
beyond, only here in N.T. This clause is repeated at the
end of the sentence. *A thorn in the flesh (skolops tēi sarki).*
This old word is used for splinter, stake, thorn. In the
papyri and inscriptions examples occur both for splinter and
thorn as the meaning. In the LXX it is usually thorn. The
case of *tēi sarki* can be either locative (in) or dative (for).
What was it? Certainly it was some physical malady that
persisted. All sorts of theories are held (malaria, eye-trouble,
epilepsy, insomnia, migraine or sick-headache, etc.). It is a
blessing to the rest of us that we do not know the particular
affliction that so beset Paul. Each of us has some such
splinter or thorn in the flesh, perhaps several at once. *Messenger of Satan (aggelos Satana).* Angel of Satan, the affliction personified. *Buffet (kolaphizēi).* See on Matt. 26:67
and I Cor. 4:11 for this late and rare word from *kolaphos,*
fist. The messenger of Satan kept slapping Paul in the face
and Paul now sees that it was God's will for it to be so.
8. *Concerning this thing (huper toutou).* More likely, "concerning this messenger of Satan." *That it might depart from
me (hina apostēi aph' emou).* Second aorist active (intransitive) subjunctive of *aphistēmi* in final clause, "that he stand
off from me for good."
9. *He hath said (eirēken).* Perfect active indicative, as if

a final word. Paul probably still has the thorn in his flesh and needs this word of Christ. *Is sufficient (arkei).* Old word of rich meaning, perhaps kin to Latin *arceo*, to ward off against danger. Christ's grace suffices and abides. *Is perfected (teleitai).* Present passive indicative of *teleō*, to finish. It is linear in idea. Power is continually increased as the weakness grows. See Phil. 4:13 for this same noble conception. The human weakness opens the way for more of Christ's power and grace. *Most gladly rather (hēdista mallon).* Two adverbs, one superlative *(hēdista)*, one comparative *(mallon).* "Rather" than ask any more (thrice already) for the removal of the thorn or splinter "most gladly will I glory in my weaknesses." Slowly Paul had learned this supreme lesson, but it will never leave him (Rom. 5:2; II Tim. 4:6–8). *May rest upon me (episkēnōsēi ep' eme).* Late and rare verb in first aorist active subjunctive with *hina* (final clause), to fix a tent upon, here upon Paul himself by a bold metaphor, as if the Shechinah of the Lord was overshadowing him (cf. Luke 9:34), the power *(dunamis)* of the Lord Jesus.

10. *Wherefore I take pleasure (dio eudokō).* For this noble word see on Matt. 3:17; II Cor. 5:8. The enemies of Paul will have a hard time now in making Paul unhappy by persecutions even unto death (Phil. 1:20–26). He is not courting martyrdom, but he does not fear it or anything that is "for Christ's sake" *(huper Christou).* *For when (hotan gar).* "For whenever," indefinite time. *Then I am strong (tote dunatos eimi).* At that very time, but not in myself, but in the fresh access of power from Christ for the emergency.

11. *I am become foolish (gegona aphrōn).* Perfect active indicative of *ginomai.* In spite of what he said in verse 6 that he would not be foolish if he gloried in the other Paul. But he feels that he has dropped back to the mood of 11:1, 16. He has been swept on by the memory of the ecstasy. *For I ought to have been commended by you (egō gar ōpheilon huph' humōn sunistasthai).* Explanation of "ye compelled me." Imperfect active *ōpheilon* of *opheilō*, to be under obligation, and the tense here expresses an unfulfilled obligation about the present. But *sunistasthai* is present passive infinitive, not aorist or perfect passive. He literally means, "I ought

now to be commended by you" instead of having to glorify myself. He repeats his boast already made (11:5f.), that he is no whit behind "the super-extra apostles" (the Judaizers), "though I am nothing" (*ei kai ouden eimi*). Even boasting himself against those false apostles causes a reaction of feeling that he has to express (cf. I Cor. 15:9; I Tim. 1:15f.).

12. *Of an apostle* (*tou apostolou*). "Of the apostle" (definite article). Note the three words here for miracles wrought by Paul (*sēmeia*, signs, *terata*, wonders, *dunameis*, powers or miracles) as in Heb. 2:4.

13. *Wherein ye were made inferior* (*ho hēssōthēte*). First aorist passive indicative of *hēssoomai*, the text of Aleph B D instead of the usual *hēttēthēte* from the common *hēttaomai* to be inferior or less from the comparative *hēttōn*. See *hēssōn* in verse 15. *Ho* is the neuter accusative with the passive verb (Robertson, *Grammar*, p. 479). *Forgive me this wrong* (*charisasthe moi tēn adikian tautēn*). Consummate irony to the stingy element in this church (cf. 11:9).

14. *Third time I am ready to come* (*triton touto hetoimōs echō*). Had he been already twice or only once? He had changed his plans once when he did not go (1:15f.). He will not change his plans now. This looks as if he had only been once (that in Acts 18). Note the third use of *katanarkaō* (11:9; 12:13, 14). They need not be apprehensive. He will be as financially independent of them as before. "I shall not sponge on you." *Not yours, but you* (*ou ta humōn, alla humas*). The motto of every real preacher. *To lay up* (*thēsaurizein*). For this use of the verb see I Cor. 16:2 (Matt. 6:19-21; James 5:3).

15. *I will most gladly spend and be spent* (*hēdista dapanēsō kai ekdapanēthēsomai*). Both future active of old verb *dapanaō* (Mark 5:26) to spend money, time, energy, strength and the future passive of *ekdapanaō*, late compound to spend utterly, to spend out, (*ek-*), to spend wholly. Only here in N.T.

16. *I did not myself burden you* (*egō ou katebarēsa humas*). First aorist active of late verb *katabareō*, to press a burden down on one. Only here in N.T. *Crafty* (*panourgos*). Old word from *pan*, all, and *ergo*, to do anything (good or bad). Good sense is skilful, bad sense cunning. Only here in N.T.

268 WORD PICTURES IN NEW TESTAMENT

and Paul is quoting the word from his enemies. *With guile* (*doloi*). Instrumental case of *dolos*, bait to catch fish with. The enemies of Paul said that he was raising this big collection for himself. Moffatt has done well to put these charges in quotation marks to make it plain to readers that Paul is ironical.

17. *Did I take advantage* (*epleonektēsa*). Paul goes right to the point without hedging. For this verb from *pleon* and *echō*, to have more, see on II Cor. 2:11 and 7:2. *By any one of them* (*tina—di' autou*). An anacoluthon for *tina* is left in the accusative without a verb and *di' autou* takes up the idea, "as to any one—by him." *Whom* (*hōn*). The genitive relative is attracted from the accusative *hous* into the case of the unexpressed antecedent *toutōn*). *Mē* expects the negative answer as does *mēti* in 18.

18. *The brother* (*ton adelphon*). Probably the brother of Titus (cf. 8:18). *Did Titus take advantage of you?* (*mēti epleonektēsen humas Titos?*). That puts the issue squarely. *By the same Spirit* (*tōi autōi pneumati*). That translation refers to the Holy Spirit and makes the case instrumental. The locative case, "in the same spirit," makes it mean that Paul's attitude is the same as that of Titus and most likely is correct, for "in the same steps" (*tois autois ichnesin*) is in locative case.

19. *Ye think all this time* (*palai dokeite*). Progressive present indicative, "for a long time ye have been thinking." *We are excusing ourselves* (*apologoumetha*). He is not just apologizing, but is in deadly earnest, as they will find out when he comes.

20. *Lest by any means, when I come, I should find you not such as I would* (*mē pōs elthōn ouch hoious thelō heurō humas*). An idiomatic construction after the verb of fearing (*phoboumai*) with *mē pōs* as the conjunction and with *ouch* as the negative of the verb *heurō* (second aorist active subjunctive of *heuriskō*), *mē* the conjunction, *ouch* the negative. See Robertson, *Grammar*, p. 995. *And I be found* (*kagō heurethō*). Same construction with first aorist passive subjunctive. *Such as ye would not* (*hoion ou thelete*). Neat change in voice just before and position of the negative here. *Lest by any means* (*mē pōs*). Still further negative purpose by repeating the conjunction. With graphic pen pictures Paul describes

what had been going on against him during his long absence. *Backbitings* (*katalaliai*). Late and rare word. In N.T. only here and I Peter 2:1. If it only existed nowhere else! *Whisperings* (*psithurismoi*). Late word from *psithurizō*, to whisper into one's ear. An onomatopoetic word for the sibilant murmur of a snake charmer (Eccl. 10:11). Only here in N.T. *Swellings* (*phusiōseis*). From *phusioō*, to swell up, late word only here and in ecclesiastical writers. Did Paul make up the word for the occasion? See on I Cor. 4:6 for verb. *Tumults* (*akatastasiai*). See on II Cor. 6:5.

21. *When I come again* (*palin elthontos mou*). Genitive absolute. Paul assumes it as true. *Lest my God humble me* (*mē tapeinōsei me ho theos mou*). Negative final clause (*mē* and first aorist active subjunctive), going back to *phoboumai* in 20. He means a public humiliation as his fear. The conduct of the church had been a real humiliation whether he refers to a previous visit or not. *That have sinned heretofore* (*tōn proēmartēkotōn*). Genitive plural of the articular perfect active participle of *proamartanō* to emphasize continuance of their sinful state as opposed to *mē metanoēsantōn* (did not repent) in the aorist tense.

CHAPTER XIII

1. *The third time I am coming (triton erchomai).* Either the third that he had planned to come or that he had been twice. The warning is made by quoting Deut. 19:15.

2. *As when I was present the second time (hōs parōn to deuteron).* This translation assumes the second visit as already made. It is a natural way to take the Greek *hōs parōn*. But *hōs* with *parōn* can also mean "as if present" the second time (Authorized Version). Probably "as when" is the more natural rendering, but the other cannot be ruled entirely out in view of 1:15-23. *If I come again (ean elthō eis to palin).* Condition of third class. The use of *palin* of itself suits the idea that Paul had not yet made the second visit as it means simply "again" or "back," but in Matt. 26:44 we find *palin ek tritou* (again a third time) and so it is not decisive.

3. *A proof of Christ (dokimēn tou Christou).* He will give it to them. "I will not spare." He will show that Christ speaks "in me" (*en emoi*).

4. *But we shall live with him through the power of God (alla zēsomen sun autōi ek dunameōs theou).* So real is Paul's sense of his union with Christ.

5. *Unless indeed ye be reprobate (ei mēti adokimoi este).* Paul challenged his opposers in Corinth to try (*peirazete*) themselves, to test (*dokimazete*) themselves, whether they were "in the faith" (*en tēi pistei*), a much more vital matter for them than trying to prove Paul a heretic. Such tests can be made, unless, alas, they are "reprobate" (*adokimoi*, the very adjective that Paul held up before himself as a dreadful outcome to be avoided, I Cor. 9:27).

6. *That ye shall know (hoti epignōsesthe).* Such a testing of themselves will give them full knowledge that Paul is not *reprobate (adokimos).* The best way for vacillating Christians to stop it is to draw close to Christ.

7. *Though we be as reprobate (hēmeis de hōs adokimoi ōmen).* Literally, "And that" (*hina de*). Paul wishes them to do

no wrong (*kakon mēden*). He has no desire to exercise his apostolic authority and "appear approved" (*dokimoi phanōmen*, second aorist passive subjunctive of *phainō*). He had far rather see them do "the noble thing" (*to kalon*) even if it should make him appear disapproved after all that he has said. 8. *Against the truth* (*kata tēs alētheias*). He means in the long run. We can hinder and hold down the truth by evil deeds (Rom. 1:18), but in the end the truth wins. 9. *For we rejoice* (*chairomen gar*). Paul had far rather be weak in the sense of failing to exercise his apostolic power because they did the noble thing. He is no Jonah who lamented when Ninevah repented. *Your perfecting* (*humōn katartisin*). Late word from *katartizō*, to fit, to equip (see verb in verse 11). In Plutarch, only here in N.T. 10. *That I may not when present deal sharply* (*hina parōn apotomōs chrēsōmai*). Late adverb from *apotomos*, curt, cut off. In N.T. only here and Titus 1:13. 12. *With a holy kiss* (*en hagiōi philēmati*). In the Jewish synagogues where the sexes were separated, men kissed men, the women, women. This apparently was the Christian custom also. It is still observed in the Coptic and the Russian churches. It was dropped because of charges made against the Christians by the pagans. In England in 1250 Archbishop Walter of York introduced a "pax-board" which was first kissed by the clergy and then passed around. Think of the germ theory of disease and that kissing tablet! 13. *The grace of the Lord Jesus Christ and the love of God, and the communion of the Holy Ghost, be with you all* (*hē charis tou Kuriou Iēsou Christou kai hē agapē tou theou kai hē koinōnia tou hagiou pneumatos meta pantōn humōn*). This benediction is the most complete of them all. It presents the persons of the Trinity in full form. From II Thess. 3:17 it appears that Paul wrote the greeting or benediction with his own hand. We know from Romans 15:19 that Paul went round about unto Illyricum before, apparently, he came on to Corinth. When he did arrive (Acts 20:1-3) the troubles from the Judaizers had disappeared. Probably the leaders left after the coming of Titus and the brethren with this Epistle. The reading of it in the church would make a stir of no small proportions. But it did the work.

THE EPISTLE TO THE GALATIANS
PROBABLE DATE A.D. 56 OR 57

BY WAY OF INTRODUCTION

It is a pity that we are not able to visualize more clearly the time and place of writing this powerful polemic against the Judaizers who were trying to draw away from the evangelical gospel the churches of Galatia. The data are not clear as in the Thessalonian and Corinthian Epistles. There are many things that can be said, but few are decisive. One is that the Epistle was written about seventeen years after Paul's conversion, adding the three years of Gal. 1:18 and the fourteen of 2:1, though not insisting on the full number in either case. Unfortunately we do not know the precise year of his conversion. It was somewhere between A.D. 31 and 36. Another thing that is clear is that the Epistle was written after the Conference in Jerusalem over the Judaizing controversy to which Paul refers in Gal. 2:1–10 and after the subsequent visit of Peter to Antioch (Gal. 2:11–14). The natural interpretation of Acts 15:1–33 is to understand it as the historical narrative of the public meetings of which Paul gives an inside view in Gal. 2:1–10. Not all scholars agree to this view, but the weight of the argument is for it. If so, that rules out the contention of Ramsay and others that Galatians is the earliest of Paul's Epistles. It was written then after that Conference which took place about A.D. 49. It seems clear also that it was written after the Epistles to the Thessalonians (A.D. 50–51) which were sent from Corinth.

Did Paul mean by Galatia the Roman province as he usually does or does he make an ethnographic use of the term and mean the real Celts of North Galatia? Luke uses geographical terms in either sense. Certainly Paul preached in South Galatia in his first mission tour. See Acts 16:6 for the discussion about the language there as bearing on his going into North Galatia. By "the churches of Galatia"

Paul can mean the whole of Galatia or either South or North Galatia. The various items mentioned, like the illness that led to his preaching (Gal. 4:13), "the first time" or "formerly" (4:13), "so quickly" (1:6), are not conclusive as to time or place. If Paul means only the South Galatian Churches (Pisidia, Lycaonia, Phrygia), then the Epistle, even if two visits had been made, could come some time after the second tour of Acts 16:1ff. The place could be Philippi, Corinth, Ephesus, Antioch. Even so room must be made for the seventeen years after his conversion plus the interval thereafter (some twenty years in all). If Paul includes North Galatia, the time would be more easily handled (the twenty years required from A.D. 31 to 36 to A.D. 51 to 57) and the place could be Ephesus, Philippi, or Corinth. Special treatises on the date of Galatians have been written by Askwith (1899), Round (1906), Steinmann (1908), Weber (1900).

Lightfoot held that the similarity of Galatians to Romans (written from Corinth spring of A.D. 56 or 57) naturally argues for the same general period and place. It is a possible hypothesis that, when Paul reached Corinth late autumn or early winter of A.D. 55 or 56 (Acts 20:1f.), he received alarming reports of the damage wrought by the Judaizers in Galatia. He had won his fight against them in Corinth (I and II Corinthians). So now he hurls this thunderbolt at them from Corinth and later, in a calmer mood, sends the fuller discussion to the church in Rome. This hypothesis is adopted here, but with full recognition of the fact that it is only hypothesis. The language and the topics and the treatment are the same that we find in Romans. Galatians thus fits in precisely between II Corinthians and Romans. It is a flaming torch in the Judaizing controversy. This Epistle was the battlecry of Martin Luther in the Reformation. Today it has served as a bulwark against the wild criticism that has sought to remove the Pauline Epistles from the realm of historical study. Paul is all ablaze in this Epistle with indignation as he faces the men who are undermining his work in Galatia.

SOME COMMENTARIES
(Only a few out of a vast number)

Adeney (1911), Bacon (1909), Beet (1885), Bousset (1907), Baljon (1889), Burton (1920), Ellicott (new ed. 1884), Emmet (1912), Findlay (1888), Girdlestone (1913), Hovey (1887), Lagrange (1918), Lietzmann (1910), Lightfoot (eleventh ed., 1905), Lipsius (1902), Martin Luther (1535; tr. 1575), MacGregor (1914), Mackenzie (1912), Ramsay (1900), Rendall (1903), Sieffert (Meyer Komm., 9 ed. 1899), Watkins (1914), Williams (1910), Windisch (2 aufl. 1926), Wood (1887), Zahn (2 aufl. 1907).

CHAPTER I

1. *Not from men, neither through men (ouk ap' anthrōpōn oude di' anthrōpou).* The bluntness of Paul's denial is due to the charge made by the Judaizers that Paul was not a genuine apostle because not one of the twelve. This charge had been made in Corinth and called forth the keenest irony of Paul (II Cor. 10 to 12). In Gal. 1 and 2 Paul proves his independence of the twelve and his equality with them as recognized by them. Paul denies that his apostleship had a human source (*ouk ap' anthrōpōn*) and that it had come to him through (*di' anthrōpou*) a human channel (Burton). *But through Jesus Christ and God the Father (alla dia Iēsou Christou kai theou patros).* The call to be an apostle came to Paul through Jesus Christ as he claimed in I Cor. 9:1 and as told in Acts 9:4-6; 22:7ff.; 26:16ff. He is apostle also by the will of God. *Who raised him from the dead (tou egeirantos auton ek nekrōn).* And therefore Paul was qualified to be an apostle since he had seen the Risen Christ (I Cor. 9:1; 15:8f.). This verb *egeirō* is often used in N.T. for raising from the sleep of death, to wake up the dead.

2. *All the brethren which are with me (hoi sun emoi pantes adelphoi).* The same phrase in Phil. 4:21 in distinction from the saints in verse 22. Probably the small company of travelling companions. *Unto the churches of Galatia (tais ekklēsiais tēs Galatias).* A circular letter therefore to all the churches in the province (both South Galatia and North Galatia if he really laboured there).

3. *Grace to you and peace (charis humin kai eirēnē).* As in I Thess., II Thess., I Cor., II Cor. (already written) and in all the later Epistles save that in I and II Timothy "mercy" is added. But this customary salutation (see on I Thess. 1:1) is not a perfunctory thing with Paul. He uses it here even when he has so much fault to find just as he did in I and II Corinthians.

4. *For our sins (huper tōn hamartiōn).* Some MSS. have *peri* (concerning). In the *Koiné* this use of *huper* as like

275

peri has come to be common. He refers to the death of Christ (cf. I Cor. 15:3; Gal. 2:20; Rom. 5:6f.). As a rule *peri* occurs of things, *huper* of persons. *Deliver (exelētai).* Second aorist middle subjunctive (final clause with *hopōs*) of *exaireō*, old verb to pluck out, to rescue (Acts 23:27). "Strikes the keynote of the epistle. The gospel is a rescue, an emancipation from a state of bondage" (Lightfoot). *Out of this present evil world (ek tou aiōnos tou enestōtos ponērou).* Literally, "out of the age the existing one being evil." The predicate position of *ponērou* calls emphatic attention to it. Each word here is of interest and has been already discussed. See on Matt. 13:22 for *aiōn*, Matt. 6:23 for *ponēros*. *Enestōtos* is genitive masculine singular of *enestōs* second perfect (intransitive) participle of *enistēmi* for which see on II Thess. 2:12; I Cor. 3:22; 7:26. It is present as related to future (Rom. 8:38; Heb. 9:9). *According to the will of God (kata to thelēma tou theou).* Not according to any merit in us.

5. *To whom be the glory (hōi hē doxa).* No verb in the Greek. For like doxologies see Rom. 9:5; 11:36; 16:27; Eph. 3:21; I Tim. 1:17.

6. *Ye are so quickly removing (houtōs tacheōs metatithesthe).* The present middle indicative of *metatithēmi*, to change places, to transfer. "You are transferring yourselves" and doing it "so quickly" either from the time of their conversion or most likely from the time when the Judaizers came and tempted them. So easily some of them are falling victims to these perverters of the gospel. That is a continuous amazement (*thaumazō*) to Paul and to men today that so many are so silly and so gullible to modern as to ancient charlatans. *Unto a different gospel (eis heteron euaggelion).* See on II Cor. 11:4 for distinction between *allo* and *heteron* as here. It is not here or there a mere difference in emphasis or spirit as in Phil. 1:18 so long as Christ is preached. These men as in II Cor. 11:4 preach "another Jesus" and a "different gospel" and so have fallen away from grace and have done away with Christ (Gal. 5:4). Hence the vehemence of Paul's words.

7. *Which is not another (ho ouk estin allo).* It is no "gospel" (good news) at all, but a yoke of bondage to the law and the abolition of grace. There is but one gospel and that is of grace, not works. The relative *ho* (which) refers to *heteron*

euaggelion (a different gospel) "taken as a single term and designating the erroneous teachings of the Judaizers" (Burton). *Only (ei mē)*. Literally, "except," that is, "Except in this sense," "in that it is an attempt to pervert the one true gospel" (Lightfoot). *Who disturb you (hoi tarassontes)*. The disturbers. This very verb *tarassō* is used in Acts 17:8 of the Jews in Thessalonica who "disturbed" the politarchs and the people about Paul. *Would pervert (thelontes metastrepsai)*. "Wish to turn about," change completely as in Acts 2:20; James 4:9. The very existence of the gospel of Christ was at stake.

8. *If we (ean hēmeis)*. Condition of third class (*ean* and aorist middle subjunctive *euaggelisētai*). Suppose I (literary plural) should turn renegade and preach "other than" (*par' ho*), "contrary to that which we preached." Preachers have turned away from Christ, alas, and preached "humanism" or some other new-fangled notion. The Jews termed Paul a renegade for leaving Judaism for Christianity. But it was before Paul had seen Christ that he clung to the law. Paul is dogmatic and positive here, for he knows that he is standing upon solid ground, the fact of Christ dying for us and rising again. He had seen the Risen Jesus Christ. No angel can change Paul now. *Let him be anathema (anathema estō)*. See on I Cor. 12:3 for this word.

9. *So say I now again (kai arti palin legō)*. Paul knows that he has just made what some will consider an extreme statement. But it is a deliberate one and not mere excitement. He will stand by it to the end. He calls down a curse on any one who proclaims a gospel to them contrary to that which they had received from him.

10. *Am I persuading? (peithō?)*. Conative present, trying to persuade like *zētō areskein* (seeking to please) where the effort is stated plainly. See II Cor. 5:11. *I should not be (ouk an ēmēn)*. Conclusion of second class condition, determined as unfulfilled. Regular construction here (*ei* and imperfect indicative in the condition *ēreskon, ouk an* and imperfect in the conclusion). About pleasing men see on I Thess. 2:4. In Col. 3:22 and Eph. 6:6 Paul uses the word "men-pleasers" (*anthrōpareskoi*).

11. *Which was preached (to euaggelisthen)*. Play on the word *euaggelion* by first aorist passive participle of *euaggelizō*,

"the gospel which was gospelized by me." *It is not after man*
(ouk estin kata anthrōpon). Not after a human standard and
so he does not try to conform to the human ideal. Paul alone
(I Cor. 3:3; 9:8; 15:32; Rom. 3:15) in the N.T. uses this old
and common idiom.

12. *Nor was I taught it (oute edidachthēn).* He did not
receive it "from man" *(para anthrōpōn,* which shuts out
both *apo* and *dia* of verse 1), whether Peter or any other
apostle, nor was he taught it in the school of Gamaliel in
Jerusalem or at the University of Tarsus. He "received"
his gospel in one way, "through revelation of Jesus Christ"
(di' apokalupseōs Iēsou Christou). He used *parelabon* in I
Cor. 15:3 about the reception of his message from Christ.
It is not necessary to say that he had only one (because of
the aorist active *parelabon,* from *paralambanō,* for it can
very well be constative aorist) revelation (unveiling) from
Christ. In fact, we know that he had numerous visions of
Christ and in I Cor. 11:23 he expressly says concerning the
origin of the Lord's Supper: "I received *(parelabon,* again)
from the Lord." The Lord Jesus revealed his will to Paul.

13. *My manner of life (tēn emēn anastrophēn).* Late word
in this sense from Polybius on from *anastrephomai.* In the
older writers it meant literally "return" or "turning back."
See I Peter 1:15. It is absent in this sense in the papyri
though the verb is common. *In the Jews' religion (en tōi
Ioudaismōi).* "In Judaism." The word in N.T. only here
and next verse, already in II Macc. 2:21; 8:1; 14:38; IV
Macc. 4:26. In these passages it means the Jewish religion
as opposed to the Hellenism that the Syrian Kings were
imposing upon the Jews. So later Justin Martyr (386 D)
will use *Christianismos* for Christianity. Both words are
made from verbs in -izō. *Beyond measure (kath' huperbolēn.*
"According to excess" (throwing beyond, *huperbolē). I persecuted (ediōkon).* Imperfect active, "I used to persecute"
(see Acts 7 to 9 for the facts). *Made havock of it (eporthoun
autēn).* Customary action again, imperfect of old verb
portheō, to lay waste, to sack. In N.T. only here, verse 23,
and Acts 9:31 (used by Christians in Damascus of Saul after
his conversion of his former conduct, the very word of Paul
here). Paul heard them use it of him and it stuck in his mind.

14. *I advanced (proekopton).* Imperfect active again of

prokoptō, old verb, to cut forward (as in a forest), to blaze a way, to go ahead. In N.T. only here, Rom. 13:12; II Tim. 2:16; 3:9, 13. Paul was a brilliant pupil under Gamaliel. See Phil. 3:4–6. He was in the lead of the persecution also. *Beyond many of mine own age* (*huper pollous sunēlikiōtas*). Later compound form for the Attic *hēlikiōtēs* which occurs in Dion Hal. and inscriptions (from *sun*, with, and *hēlikia*, age). Paul modestly claims that he went "beyond" (*huper*) his fellow-students in his progress in Judaism. *More exceedingly zealous* (*perissoterōs zēlotēs*). Literally, "more exceedingly a zealot." See on Acts 1:13; 21:20; I Cor. 14:12. Like Simon Zelotes. *For the traditions of my fathers* (*tōn patrikōn mou paradoseōn*). Objective genitive after *zēlotēs*. *Patrikōn* only here in N.T., though old word from *patēr* (father), paternal, descending from one's ·father. For *patrōios* see Acts 22:3, 14. Tradition (*paradosis*) played a large part in the teaching and life of the Pharisees (Mark 7:1–23). Paul now taught the Christian tradition (II Thess. 2:15).

15. *It was the good pleasure of God* (*eudokēsen ho theos*). Paul had no doubt about God's purpose in him (I Thess. 2:8). *Who separated me* (*ho aphorisas me*). *Aphorizō* is old word (from *apo* and *horos*) to mark off from a boundary or line. The Pharisees were the separatists who held themselves off from others. Paul conceives himself as a spiritual Pharisee "separated unto the gospel of God" (Rom. 1:1, the same word *aphōrismenos*). Before his birth God had his plans for him and called him.

16. *To reveal his Son in me* (*apokalupsai ton huion autou en emoi*). By "in me" (*en emoi*) Paul can mean to lay emphasis on his inward experience of grace or he may refer objectively to the vision of Christ on the way to Damascus, "in my case." Paul uses *en emoi* in this sense (in my case) several times (verse 24; II Cor. 13:3; Phil. 1:30; I Tim. 1:16). Once (I Cor. 14:11) *en emoi* is almost equivalent to the dative (to me). On the whole Lightfoot seems correct here in taking it to mean "in my case," though the following words suit either idea. Certainly Paul could not preach Christ among the Gentiles without the rich inward experience and in the objective vision he was called to that task. *I conferred not with flesh and blood* (*ou prosanethemēn sarki kai haimati*). Second aorist middle indicative of *prosanatithēmi*, old verb,

double compound (*pros, ana*), to lay upon oneself in addition, to betake oneself to another, to confer with, dative case as here. In N.T. only here and 2:6.

17. *Before me* (*pro emou*). The Jerusalem apostles were genuine apostles, but so is Paul. His call did not come from them nor did he receive confirmation by them. *Into Arabia* (*eis Arabian*). This visit to Arabia has to come between the two visits to Damascus which are not distinguished in Acts 9:22f. In verse 23 Luke does speak of "considerable days" and so we must place the visit to Arabia between verses 22 and 23.

18. *Then after three years* (*epeita meta tria etē*). A round number to cover the period from his departure from Jerusalem for Damascus to his return to Jerusalem. This stay in Damascus was an important episode in Paul's theological readjustment to his new experience. *To visit Cephas* (*historēsai Kēphān*). First aorist infinitive of *historeō*, old verb (from *histōr*, one who knows by inquiry), to gain knowledge by visiting. Only here in N.T. If we turn to Acts 9:26 to 30, we shall see that the visit of two weeks to Peter came after Barnabas endorsed Paul to the suspicious disciples in Jerusalem and probably while he was preaching in the city. It was a delightful experience, but Peter did not start Paul upon his apostleship. He visited him as an equal. Peter no doubt had much to say to Paul.

19. *Except James the brother of the Lord* (*ei mē Iakōbon ton adelphon tou Kuriou*). James the son of Zebedee was still living at that time. The rest of the twelve were probably away preaching and James, brother of the Lord, is here termed an apostle, though not one of the twelve as Barnabas is later so called. Paul is showing his independence of and equality with the twelve in answer to the attacks of the Judaizers.

20. *I lie not* (*ou pseudomai*). So important does he deem the point that he takes solemn oath about it.

21. *Into the region of Syria and Cilicia* (*eis ta klimata tēs Syrias kai tēs Kilikias*). This statement agrees with the record in Acts 9:30. On *klimata*, see II Cor. 11:10. Paul was not idle, but at work in Tarsus and the surrounding country.

22. *And I was still unknown* (*ēmēn de agnoumenos*). Peri-

phrastic imperfect passive of *agnoeō*, not to know. *By face* (*tōi prosōpōi*). Associative instrumental case. *Of Judea* (*tēs Ioudaias*). As distinct from Jerusalem, for he had once scattered the church there and had revisited them before coming to Tarsus (Acts 9:26–30). In Acts 9:31 the singular of *ekklēsia* is used, but in a geographic sense for Judea, Samaria, and Galilee.

23. *They only heard* (*monon akouontes ēsan*). Periphrastic imperfect, "They were only hearing from time to time." *That once persecuted us* (*ho diōkōn hēmas pote*). Present active articular participle, a sort of participle of antecedent time suggested by *pote*, "the one who used to persecute us once upon a time." *The faith* (*tēn pistin*). Here used in the sense of "the gospel" as in Acts 6:7.

24. *They glorified* (*edoxazon*). Imperfect, kept on doing it. *In me* (*en emoi*). In my case as in 1:16.

CHAPTER II

1. *Then after the space of fourteen years I went up again* (*epeita dia dekatessaron eton palin aneben*). This use of *dia* for interval between is common enough. Paul is not giving a recital of his visits to Jerusalem, but of his points of contact with the apostles in Jerusalem. As already observed, he here refers to the Jerusalem Conference given by Luke in Acts 15 when Paul and Barnabas were endorsed by the apostles and elders and the church over the protest of the Judaizers who had attacked them in Antioch (Acts 15:1f.). But Paul passes by another visit to Jerusalem, that in Acts 11:30 when Barnabas and Saul brought alms from Antioch to Jerusalem and delivered them to "the elders" with no mention of the apostles who were probably out of the city since the events in Acts 12 apparently preceded that visit and Peter had left for another place (Acts 12:17). Paul here gives the inside view of this private conference in Jerusalem that came in between the two public meetings (Acts 15:4f. and 6–29). *With Barnabas* (*meta Barnaba*). As in Acts 15:2. *Taking Titus also with me* (*sunparalabon kai Titon*). Second aorist active participle of *sunparalambano* the very verb used in Acts 15:37f. of the disagreement between Paul and Barnabas about Mark. Titus is not mentioned in Acts 15 nor anywhere else in Acts for some reason, possibly because he was Luke's own brother. But his very presence was a challenge to the Judaizers, since he was a Greek Christian.

2. *By revelation* (*kata apokalupsin*). In Acts 15:2 the church sent them. But surely there is no inconsistency here. *I laid before them* (*anethemen autois*). Second aorist middle indicative of old word *anatithemi*, to put up, to place before, with the dative case. But who were the "them" (*autois*)? Evidently not the private conference for he distinguishes this address from that, "but privately" (*kat' idian*). Just place Acts 15:4f. beside the first clause and it is clear: "I laid before them the gospel which I preach among the

282

Gentiles," precisely as Luke has recorded. Then came the private conference after the uproar caused by the Judaizers (Acts 15:5). *Before them who were of repute (tois dokousin).* He names three of them (Cephas, James, and John). James the Lord's brother, for the other James is now dead (Acts 12:1f.). But there were others also, a select group of real leaders. The decision reached by this group would shape the decision of the public conference in the adjourned meeting. So far as we know Paul had not met John before, though he had met Peter and James at the other visit. Lightfoot has much to say about the Big Four (St. Paul and the Three) who here discuss the problems of mission work among Jews and Gentiles. It was of the utmost importance that they should see eye to eye. The Judaizers were assuming that the twelve apostles and James the Lord's brother would side with them against Paul and Barnabas. Peter had already been before the Jerusalem Church for his work in Caesarea (Acts 11:1-18). James was considered a very loyal Jew. *Lest by any means I should be running or had run in vain (mē pōs eis kenon trechō ē edramon).* Negative purpose with the present subjunctive (*trechō*) and then by a sudden change the aorist indicative (*edramon*), as a sort of afterthought or retrospect (Moulton, *Prolegomena*, p. 201; Robertson, *Grammar*, p. 988). There are plenty of classical parallels. See also I Thess. 3:5 for both together again.

3. *Being a Greek (Hellēn ōn).* Concessive participle, though he was a Greek. *Was compelled to be circumcised (ēnagkasthē peritmēthēnai).* First aorist passive indicative of *anagkazō* and first aorist passive infinitive of *peritemnō.* Curiously enough some scholars interpret this language to mean that Paul voluntarily had Titus circumcised, instead of being compelled to do it, an impossible view in my opinion in the light of verse 5 and wholly inconsistent with the whole context. Paul means that he stood his ground against compulsion and all force.

4. *But because of the false brethren privately brought in (dia de tous pareisaktous pseudadelphous).* Late verbal adjective *pareisaktos* from the double compound verb *pareisagō,* found in papyri in the sense of brought in by the side or on the sly as here. Evidently some of the Judaizers or sympathizers whom Paul had not invited had come in as often happens.

Paul terms them "false brethren" like "the false apostles" in II Cor. 11:13 of the Judaizers in Corinth. *Who came in privily (hoitines pareisēlthon).* Repetition of the charge of their slipping in unwanted *(pareiserchomai,* late double compound, in Plutarch, in N.T. only here and Rom. 5:20). *To spy out (kataskopēsai).* First aorist active infinitive of *kataskopeō,* old Greek verb from *kataskopos,* a spy, to reconnoitre, to make a treacherous investigation. *That they might bring us into bondage (hina hēmas katadoulōsousin).* Future active indicative of this old compound, to enslave completely *(kata-)* as in II Cor. 11:20. Nowhere else in N.T. This was their purpose *(hina* and future active indicative of this causative verb). It was as serious a conflict as this. Spiritual liberty or spiritual bondage, which?

5. *No, not for an hour (oude pros hōran).* Pointed denial that he and Barnabas yielded at all "in the way of subjection" *(tēi hupotagēi,* in the subjection demanded of them). The compromisers pleaded for the circumcision of Titus "because of the false brethren" in order to have peace. The old verb *eikō,* to yield, occurs here alone in the N.T. See II Cor. 9:13 for *hupotagē. The truth of the gospel (hē alētheia tou euaggeliou).* It was a grave crisis to call for such language. The whole problem of Gentile Christianity was involved in the case of Titus, whether Christianity was to be merely a modified brand of legalistic Judaism or a spiritual religion, the true Judaism (the children of Abraham by faith). The case of Timothy later was utterly different, for he had a Jewish mother and a Greek father. Titus was pure Greek.

6. *Somewhat (ti).* Something, not somebody. Paul refers to the Big Three (Cephas, James, and John). He seems a bit embarrassed in the reference. He means no disrespect, but he asserts his independence sharply in a tangled sentence with two parentheses (dashes in Westcott and Hort). *Whatsoever they were (hopoioi pote ēsan).* Literally, "What sort they once were." *Hopoioi* is a qualitative word (I Thess. 1:9; I Cor. 3:13; James 1:24). Lightfoot thinks that these three leaders were the ones who suggested the compromise about Titus. That is a possible, but not the natural, interpretation of this involved sentence. The use of *de* (but) in verse 6 seems to make a contrast between the three

leaders and the pleaders for compromise in verses 4f. *They, I say, imparted nothing to me (emoi gar ouden prosanethento).* He starts over again after the two parentheses and drops the construction *apo tōn dokountōn* and changes the construction (anacoluthon) to *hoi dokountes* (nominative case), the men of reputation and influences whom he names in verses 8f. See the same verb in 1:16. They added nothing in the conference to me. The compromisers tried to win them, but they finally came over to my view. Paul won his point, when he persuaded Peter, James, and John to agree with him and Barnabas in their contention for freedom for the Gentile Christians from the bondage of the Mosaic ceremonial law.

7. *But contrariwise (alla tounantion).* But on the contrary (accusative of general reference, *to enantion*). So far from the three championing the cause of the Judaizers as some hoped or even the position of the compromisers in verses 4f., they came boldly to Paul's side after hearing the case argued in the private conference. This is the obvious interpretation rather than the view that Peter, James, and John first proposed the circumcision of Titus and afterwards surrendered to Paul's bold stand. *When they saw (idontes).* After seeing, after they heard our side of the matter. *That I had been intrusted with the gospel of the uncircumcision (hoti pepisteumai to euaggelion tēs akrobustias).* Perfect passive indicative of *pisteuō*, to intrust, which retains the accusative of the thing *(to euaggelion)* in the passive voice. This clear-cut agreement between the leaders "denotes a distinction of sphere, and not a difference of type" (Lightfoot). Both divisions in the work preach the same "gospel" (not like 1:6f., the Judaizers). It seems hardly fair to the Three to suggest that they at first championed the cause of the Judaizers in the face of Paul's strong language in verse 5.

8. *He that wrought for Peter unto the apostleship of the circumcision (ho gar energēsas Petrōi eis apostolēn tēs peritomēs).* Paul here definitely recognizes Peter's leadership (apostleship, *apostolēn*, late word, already in Acts 1:25; I Cor. 9:2) to the Jews and asserts that Peter acknowledges his apostleship to the Gentiles. This is a complete answer to the Judaizers who denied the genuineness of Paul's apostleship because he was not one of the twelve.

9. *They who were reputed to be pillars* (*hoi dokountes stuloi einai*). They had that reputation (*dokountes*) and Paul accepts them as such. *Stuloi*, old word for pillars, columns, as of fire (Rev. 10:1). So of the church (I Tim. 3:15). These were the Pillar Apostles. *Gave to me and Barnabas the right hands of fellowship* (*dexias edōkan emoi kai Barnabāi koinōnias*). Dramatic and concluding act of the pact for cooperation and coördinate, independent spheres of activity. The compromisers and the Judaizers were brushed to one side when these five men shook hands as equals in the work of Christ's Kingdom.

10. *Only* (*monon*). One item was emphasized. *We should remember* (*mnēmoneuōmen*). Present active subjunctive, "that we should keep on remembering." *Which very thing* (*ho—auto touto*). Repetition of relative and demonstrative, tautology, "which this very thing." In fact Barnabas and Saul had done it before (Acts 11:30). It was complete victory for Paul and Barnabas. Paul passes by the second public meeting and the letters to Antioch (Acts 15:6–29) and passes on to Peter's conduct in Antioch.

11. *I resisted him to the face* (*kata prosōpon autōi antestēn*). Second aorist active indicative (intransitive) of *anthistēmi*. "I stood against him face to face." In Jerusalem Paul faced Peter as his equal in rank and sphere of work. In Antioch he looked him in the eye as his superior in character and courage. *Because he stood condemned* (*hoti kategnōsmenos ēn*). Periphrastic past perfect passive of *kataginoskō*, old verb to know against, to find fault with. In N.T. only here and I John 3:20f.

12. *For before that certain came from James* (*pro tou gar elthein tinas apo Iakōbou*). The reason (*gar*) for Paul's condemnation of Peter. Articular infinitive in the genitive after *pro* with the accusative of general reference (*tinas*), "for before the coming as to some from James." Does Paul mean to say that these "certain" ones had been sent by James to Antioch to inspect the conduct of Peter and the other Jewish brethren? Some scholars think so. No doubt these brethren let the idea get out that they were emissaries "from James." But that idea is inconsistent with the position of James as president of the conference and the author of the resolution securing liberty to the Gentile Christians.

No doubt these brethren threatened Peter to tell James and the church about his conduct and they reminded Peter of his previous arraignment before the Jerusalem Church on this very charge (Acts 11:1–18). As a matter of fact the Jerusalem Conference did not discuss the matter of social relations between Jews and Gentiles though that was the charge made against Peter (Acts 11:1ff.). *He did eat with the Gentiles (meta tōn ethnōn sunēsthien).* It was his habit (imperfect tense). *He drew back (hupestellen).* Imperfect tense, inchoative action, "he began to draw himself *(heauton)* back." Old word *hupostellō.* See middle voice to dissemble (Acts 20:20, 27), to shrink (Heb. 10:38). *Separated himself (aphōrizen heauton).* Inchoative imperfect again, "began to separate himself" just like a Pharisee (see on 1:15) and as if afraid of the Judaizers in the Jerusalem Church, perhaps half afraid that James might not endorse what he had been doing. *Fearing them that were of the circumcision (phoboumenos tous ek peritomēs).* This was the real reason for Peter's cowardice. See Acts 11:2 for *"hoi ek peritomēs"* (they of the circumcision), the very phrase here. It was not that Peter had changed his views from the Jerusalem resolutions. It was pure fear of trouble to himself as in the denials at the trial of Christ.

13. *Dissembled likewise with him (sunupekrithēsan autōi kai).* First aorist passive indicative of the double compound verb *sunupokrinomai,* a late word often in Polybius, only here in N.T. One example in Polybius means to pretend to act a part with. That idea here would help the case of the rest of the Jews, but does not accord with Paul's presentation. *Insomuch that even Barnabas (hōste kai Barnabas).* Actual result expressed by *hōste* and the indicative and *kai* clearly means "even." *Was carried away with their dissimulation (sunapēchthē autōn tēi hupokrisei).* First aorist passive indicative of *sunapagō,* old verb, in N.T. only here and II Peter 3:17. *Hupokrisei* is in the instrumental case and can only mean hypocrisy in the bad sense (Matt. 23:28), not merely acting a part. It was a solemn moment when Paul saw the Jerusalem victory vanish and even Barnabas desert him as they followed the timid cowardice of Peter. It was *Paulus contra mundum* in the cause of spiritual freedom in Christ.

14. *But when I saw* (*All' hote eidon*). Paul did see and saw it in time to speak. *That they walked not uprightly* (*hoti orthopodousin*). Present active indicative retained in indirect discourse, "they are not walking straight." *Orthopodeō* (*orthos*, straight, *pous*, foot). Found only here and in later ecclesiastical writers, though *orthopodes bainontes* does occur. *According to the truth of the gospel* (*pros tēn alētheian tou euaggeliou*). Just as in 2:5. Paul brought them to face (*pros*) that. *I said unto Cephas before them all* (*eipon tōi Kēphāi emprosthen pantōn*). *Being a Jew* (*Ioudaios huparchōn*, though being a Jew). Condition of first class, assumed as true. It was not a private quarrel, but a matter of public policy. One is a bit curious to know what those who consider Peter the first pope will do with this open rebuke by Paul, who was in no sense afraid of Peter or of all the rest. *As do the Gentiles* (*ethnikōs*). Late adverb, here only in N.T. Like Gentiles. *As do the Jews* (*Ioudaikōs*). Only here in N.T., but in Josephus. *To live as do the Jews* (*Ioudaïzein*). Late verb, only here in the N.T. From *Ioudaios*, Jew. Really Paul charges Peter with trying to compel (conative present, *anagkazeis*) the Gentiles to live all like Jews, to Judaize the Gentile Christians, the very point at issue in the Jerusalem Conference when Peter so loyally supported Paul. It was a bold thrust that allowed no reply. But Paul won Peter back and Barnabas also. If II Peter is genuine, as is still possible, he shows it in II Peter 3:15. Paul and Barnabas remained friends (Acts 15:39f.; I Cor. 9:6), though they soon separated over John Mark.

15. *Not sinners of the Gentiles* (*ouk ex ethnōn hamartōloi*). The Jews regarded all Gentiles as "sinners" in contrast with themselves (cf. Matt. 26:45 "sinners" and Luke 18:32 "Gentiles"). It is not clear whether verses 15–21 were spoken by Paul to Peter or whether Paul is now simply addressing the Galatians in the light of the controversy with Peter. Burton thinks that he is "mentally addressing Peter, if not quoting from what he said to him."

16. *Is not justified* (*ou dikaioutai*). Present passive indicative of *dikaioō*, an old causative verb from *dikaios*, righteous (from *dikē*, right), to make righteous, to declare righteous. It is made like *axioō*, to deem worthy, and *koinoō*, to consider common. It is one of the great Pauline words

along with *dikaiosunē*, righteousness. The two ways of getting right with God are here set forth: by faith in Christ Jesus (objective genitive), by the works of the law (by keeping all the law in the most minute fashion, the way of the Pharisees). Paul knew them both (see Rom. 7). In his first recorded sermon the same contrast is made that we have here (Acts 13:39) with the same word *dikaioō*, employed. It is the heart of his message in all his Epistles. The terms faith (*pistis*), righteousness (*dikaiosunē*), law (*nomos*), works (*erga*) occur more frequently in Galatians and Romans because Paul is dealing directly with the problem in opposition to the Judaizers who contended that Gentiles had to become Jews to be saved. The whole issue is here in an acute form. *Save* (*ean mē*). Except. *Even we* (*kai hēmeis*). We Jews believed, had to believe, were not saved or justified till we did believe. This very point Peter had made at the Jerusalem Conference (Acts 15:10f.). He quotes Psa. 143:2. Paul uses *dikaiosunē* in two senses (1) Justification, on the basis of what Christ has done and obtained by faith. Thus we are set right with God. Rom. 1-5. (2) Sanctification. Actual goodness as the result of living with and for Christ. Rom. 6-8. The same plan exists for Jew and Gentile.

17. *We ourselves were found sinners* (*heurethēmen kai autoi hamartōloi*). Like the Gentiles, Jews who thought they were not sinners, when brought close to Christ, found that they were. Paul felt like the chief of sinners. *A minister of sin* (*hamartias diakonos*). Objective genitive, a minister to sin. An illogical inference. We were sinners already in spite of being Jews. Christ simply revealed to us our sin. *God forbid* (*mē genoito*). Literally, "May it not happen." Wish about the future (*mē* and the optative).

18. *A transgressor* (*parabatēn*). Peter, by his shifts had contradicted himself helplessly as Paul shows by this condition. When he lived like a Gentile, he tore down the ceremonial law. When he lived like a Jew, he tore down salvation by grace.

19. *I through the law died to the law* (*egō dia nomou nomōi apethanon*). Paradoxical, but true. See Rom. 7:4, 6 for picture of how the law waked Paul up to his real death to the law through Christ.

20. *I have been crucified with Christ* (*Christōi sunestaurō-mai*). One of Paul's greatest mystical sayings. Perfect passive indicative of *sustauroō* with the associative instrumental case (*Christōi*). Paul uses the same word in Rom. 6:6 for the same idea. In the Gospels it occurs of literal crucifixion about the robbers and Christ (Matt. 27:44; Mark 15:32; John 19:32). Paul died to the law and was crucified with Christ. He uses often the idea of dying with Christ (Gal. 5:24; 6:14; Rom. 6:8; Col. 2:20) and burial with Christ also (Rom. 6:4; Col. 2:12). *No longer I* (*ouketi egō*). So complete has become Paul's identification with Christ that his separate personality is merged into that of Christ. This language helps one to understand the victorious cry in Rom. 7:25. It is the union of the vine and the branch (John 15:1-6). *Which is in the Son of God* (*tēi tou huiou tou theou*). The objective genitive, not the faith of the Son of God. *For me* (*huper emou*). Paul has the closest personal feeling toward Christ. "He appropriates to himself, as Chrysostom observes, the love which belongs equally to the whole world. For Christ is indeed the personal friend of each man individually" (Lightfoot).

21. *I do not make void the grace of God* (*ouk athetō tēn charin tou theou*). Common word in LXX and Polybius and on, to make ineffective (*a* privative and *tithēmi*, to place or put). Some critic would charge him with that after his claim to such a close mystic union with Christ. *Then Christ died for nought* (*ara Christos dōrean apethanen*). Condition of first class, assumed as true. If one man apart from grace can win his own righteousness, any man can and should. Hence (*ara*, accordingly) Christ died gratuitously (*dōrean*), unnecessarily. Adverbial accusative of *dōrea*, a gift. This verse is a complete answer to those who say that the heathen (or any mere moralist) are saved by doing the best that they know and can. No one, apart from Jesus, ever did the best that he knew or could. To be saved by law (*dia nomou*) one has to keep all the law that he knows. That no one ever did.

CHAPTER III

1. *Who did bewitch you?* (*tis humas ebaskanen?*). Somebody "fascinated" you. Some aggressive Judaizer (5:7), some one man (or woman). First aorist active indicative of *baskainō*, old word kin to *phaskō* (*baskō*), to speak, then to bring evil on one by feigned praise or the evil eye (hoodoo), to lead astray by evil arts. Only here in the N.T. This popular belief in the evil eye is old (Deut. 28:54) and persistent. The papyri give several examples of the adjective *abaskanta*, the adverb *abaskantōs* (unharmed by the evil eye), the substantive *baskania* (witchcraft). *Before whose eyes Jesus Christ was openly set forth crucified* (*hois kat' ophthalmous Iēsous Christos proegraphē estaurōmenos*). Literally, "to whom before your very eyes Jesus Christ was portrayed as crucified." Second aorist passive indicative of *prographō*, old verb to write beforehand, to set forth by public proclamation, to placard, to post up. This last idea is found in several papyri (Moulton and Milligan's *Vocabulary*) as in the case of a father who posted a proclamation that he would no longer be responsible for his son's debts. *Graphō* was sometimes used in the sense of painting, but no example of *prographō* with this meaning has been found unless this is one. With that idea it would be to portray, to picture forth, a rendering not very different from placarding. The foolish Galatians were without excuse when they fell under the spell of the Judaizer. *Estaurōmenos* is perfect passive participle of *stauroō*, the common verb to crucify (from *stauros*, stake, cross), to put on the cross (Matt. 20:19), same form as in I Cor. 2:2.

2. *This only* (*touto monon*). Paul strikes at the heart of the problem. He will show their error by the point that the gifts of the Spirit came by the hearing of faith, not by works of the law.

3. *Are ye now perfected in the flesh?* (*nun sarki epiteleisthe?*). Rather middle voice as in I Peter 5:9, finishing of yourselves. There is a double contrast, between *enarxamenoi* (having

291

begun) and *epiteleisthe* (finishing) as in II Cor. 8:6 and Phil. 1:6, and also between "Spirit" (*pneumati*) and flesh (*sarki*). There is keen irony in this thrust.

4. *Did ye suffer?* (*epathete?*). Second aorist active indicative of *paschō*, to experience good or ill. But alone, as here, it often means to suffer ill (*tosauta*, so many things). In North Galatia we have no record of persecutions, but we do have records for South Galatia (Acts 14:2, 5, 19, 22). *If it be indeed in vain* (*ei ge kai eikēi*). On *eikēi* see I Cor. 15:2; Gal. 4:11. Paul clings to hope about them with alternative fears.

5. *Supplieth* (*epichorēgōn*). It is God. See on II Cor. 9:10 for this present active participle. Cf. Phil. 1:19; II Peter 1:5. *Worketh miracles* (*energōn dunameis*). On the word *energeō* see I Thess. 2:13; I Cor. 12:6. It is a great word for God's activities (Phil. 2:13). "In you" (Lightfoot) is preferable to "among you" for *en humin* (I Cor. 13:10; Matt. 14:2). The principal verb for "doeth he it" (*poiei*) is not expressed. Paul repeats the contrast in verse 2 about "works of the law" and "the hearing of faith."

6. *It was reckoned unto him for righteousness* (*elogisthē eis dikaiosunēn*). First aorist passive indicative of *logizomai*. See on I Cor. 13:5 for this old word. He quotes Gen. 15:6 and uses it at length in Rom. 4:3ff. to prove that the faith of Abraham was reckoned "for" (*eis*, good *Koiné* idiom though more common in LXX because of the Hebrew) righteousness before he was circumcised. James (2:23) quotes the same passage as proof of Abraham's obedience to God in offering up Isaac (beginning to offer him). Paul and James are discussing different episodes in the life of Abraham. Both are correct.

7. *The same are sons of Abraham* (*houtoi huioi eisin Abraham*). "These are." This is Paul's astounding doctrine to Jews that the real sons of Abraham are those who believe as he did, "they which be of faith" (*hoi ek pisteōs*), a common idiom with Paul for this idea (verse 9; Rom. 3:26; 4:16; 14:23), those whose spiritual sonship springs out of (*ek*) faith, not out of blood. John the Baptist denounced the Pharisees and Sadducees as vipers though descendants of Abraham (Matt. 3:7 = Luke 3:7) and Jesus termed the Pharisees children of the devil and not spiritual children of Abraham (not children of God) in John 8:37–44.

8. *Foreseeing* (*proidousa*). Second aorist active participle of *prooraō*. The Scripture is here personified. Alone in this sense of "sight," but common with *legei* or *eipen* (says, said) and really in verse 22 "hath shut up" (*sunekleisen*). *Would justify* (*dikaioi*). Present active indicative, "does justify." *Preached the gospel beforehand* (*proeuēggelisato*). First aorist middle indicative of *proeuaggelizomai* with augment on *a* though both *pro* and *eu* before it in composition. Only instance in N.T. It occurs in Philo. and Schol. Soph. This Scripture announced beforehand the gospel on this point of justification by faith. He quotes the promise to Abraham in Gen. 12:3; 18:18, putting *panta ta ethnē* (all the nations) in 18:18 for *pāsai hai phulai* (all the tribes) of the earth. It is a crucial passage for Paul's point, showing that the promise to Abraham included all the nations of the earth. The verb *eneulogeō* (future passive here) occurs in the LXX and here only in N.T. (not Acts 3:25 in correct text). *In thee* (*en soi*). "As their spiritual progenitor" (Lightfoot).

9. *With* (*sun*). Along with, in fellowship with. *The faithful* (*tōi pistōi*). Rather, "the believing" (cf. verse 6).

10. *Under a curse* (*hupo kataran*). Picture of the curse hanging over them like a Damocles' blade. Cf. Rom. 3:9 "under sin" (*huph' hamartian*). The word for "curse" (*katara*) is an old one (*kata*, down, *ara*, imprecation), often in LXX, in N.T. only here and 13 and James 3:10; II Peter 2:14. Paul quotes Deut. 27:26, the close of the curses on Mt. Ebal. He makes a slight explanatory modification of the LXX changing *logois* to *gegrammenois en tōi bibliōi*. The idea is made clearer by the participle (*gegrammenois*) and *bibliōi* (book). The curse becomes effective only when the law is violated. *Cursed* (*epikataratos*). Verbal adjective from *epikataraomai*, to imprecate curses, late word, common in LXX. In N.T. only here and verse 13, but in inscriptions also (Deissmann, *Light from the Ancient East*, p. 96). The emphasis is on "continueth" (*emmenei*) and "all" (*pāsin*).

11. *In the sight of God* (*para tōi theōi*). By the side of (*para*) God, as God looks at it, for the simple reason that no one except Jesus has ever kept *all* the law, God's perfect law.

12. *The law is not of faith* (*ho nomos ouk estin ek pisteōs*). Law demands complete obedience and rests not on mercy, faith, grace.

13. *Redeemed us* (*hēmas exēgorasen*). First aorist active of the compound verb *exagorazō* (Polybius, Plutarch, Diodorus), to buy from, to buy back, to ransom. The simple verb *agorazō* (I Cor. 6:20; 7:23) is used in an inscription for the purchase of slaves in a will (Deissmann, *Light from the Ancient East*, p. 324). See also Gal. 4:5; Col. 4:5; Eph. 5:16. Christ purchased us *from the curse of the law* (*ek tēs kataras tou nomou*). "Out from (*ek* repeated) under (*hupo* in verse 10) the curse of the law." *Having become a curse for us* (*genomenos huper hēmōn katara*). Here the graphic picture is completed. We were under (*hupo*) a curse, Christ became a curse *over* (*huper*) us and so between us and the overhanging curse which fell on him instead of on us. Thus he bought us out (*ek*) and we are free from the curse which he took on himself. This use of *huper* for substitution is common in the papyri and in ancient Greek as in the N.T. (John 11:50; II Cor. 5:14f.). *That hangeth on a tree* (*ho kremamenos epi xulou*). Quotation from Deut. 21:23 with the omission of *hupo theou* (by God). Since Christ was not cursed by God. The allusion was to exposure of dead bodies on stakes or crosses (Josh. 10:26). *Xulon* means wood, not usually tree, though so in Luke 23:31 and in later Greek. It was used of gallows, crosses, etc. See Acts 5:30; 10:39; I Peter 2:24. On the present middle participle from the old verb *kremannumi*, to hang, see on Matt. 18:6; Acts 5:30.

14. *That upon the Gentiles* (*hina eis ta ethnē*). Final clause (*hina* and *genētai*, aorist middle subjunctive). *That we might receive* (*hina labōmen*). Second final clause coördinate with the first as in II Cor. 9:3. So in Christ we all (Gentile and Jew) obtain the promise of blessing made to Abraham, through faith.

15. *After the manner of men* (*kata anthrōpon*). After the custom and practice of men, an illustration from life. *Though it be but a man's covenant, yet when it hath been confirmed* (*homōs anthrōpou kekurōmenēn diathēkēn*). Literally, "Yet a man's covenant ratified." On *Diathēkē* as both covenant and will see on Matt. 26:28; I Cor. 11:25; II Cor. 3:6; Heb. 9:16f. On *kuroō*, to ratify, to make valid, see on II Cor. 2:8. Perfect passive participle here, state of completion, authoritative confirmation. *Maketh it void* (*athetei*). See on 2:21 for this verb. Both parties can by agreement cancel a con-

tract, but not otherwise. *Addeth thereto* (*epidiatassetai*). Present middle indicative of the double compound verb *epidiatassomai*, a word found nowhere else as yet. But inscriptions use *diatassomai, diataxis, diatagē, diatagma* with the specialized meaning to "determine by testamentary disposition" (Deissmann, *Light from the Ancient East*, p. 90). It was unlawful to add (*epi*) fresh clauses or specifications (*diataxeis*).

16. *But as of one* (*all' hōs eph' henos*). But as in the case of one. *Which is Christ* (*hos estin Christos*). Masculine relative agreeing with *Christos* though *sperma* is neuter. But the promise to Abraham uses *sperma* as a collective substantive and applies to all believers (both Jews and Gentiles) as Paul has shown in verses 7 to 14, and as of course he knew full well. Here Paul uses a rabbinical refinement which is yet intelligible. The people of Israel were a type of the Messiah and he gathers up the promise in its special application to Christ. He does not say that Christ is specifically referred to in Gen. 13:15 or 17:7f.

17. *Now this I say* (*touto de legō*). Now I mean this. He comes back to his main point and is not carried afield by the special application of *sperma* to Christ. *Confirmed beforehand by God* (*prokekurōmenēn hupo tou theou*). Perfect passive participle of *prokuroō*, in Byzantine writers and earliest use here. Nowhere else in N.T. The point is in *pro* and *hupo tou theou* (by God) and in *meta* (after) as Burton shows. *Four hundred and thirty years after* (*meta tetrakosia kai triakonta etē*). Literally, "after four hundred and thirty years." This is the date in Ex. 12:40 for the sojourn in Egypt (cf. Gen. 15:13). But the LXX adds words to include the time of the patriarchs in Canaan in this number of years which would cut the time in Egypt in two. Cf. Acts 7:6. It is immaterial to Paul's argument which chronology is adopted except that "the longer the covenant had been in force the more impressive is his statement" (Burton). *Doth not disannul* (*ouk akuroi*). Late verb *akuroō*, in N.T. only here and Matt. 15:6; Mark 7:13 (from *a* privative and *kuros*, authority). On *katargēsai* see I Cor. 1:28; 2:6; 15:24, 26.

18. *The inheritance* (*hē klēronomia*). Old word from *klēronomos*, heir (*kleros*, lot, *nemomai*, to distribute). See on Matt. 21:38; Acts 7:5. This came to Israel by the promise

to Abraham, not by the Mosaic law. So with us, Paul argues. *Hath granted* (*kecharistai*). Perfect middle indicative of *charizomai*. It still holds good after the law came. 19. *What then is the law?* (*ti oun ho nomos?*). Or, why then the law? A pertinent question if the Abrahamic promise antedates it and holds on afterwards. *It was added because of transgressions* (*tōn parabaseōn charin prosetethē*). First aorist passive of *prostithēmi*, old verb to add to. It is only in apparent contradiction to verses 15ff., because in Paul's mind the law is no part of the covenant, but a thing apart "in no way modifying its provisions" (Burton). *Charin* is the adverbial accusative of *charis* which was used as a preposition with the genitive as early as Homer, in favour of, for the sake of. Except in I John 3:12 it is post-positive in the N.T. as in ancient Greek. It may be causal (Luke 7:47; I John 3:12) or telic (Titus 1:5, 11; Jude 16). It is probably also telic here, not in order to create transgressions, but rather "to make transgressions palpable" (Ellicott), "thereby pronouncing them to be from that time forward transgressions of the law" (Rendall). *Parabasis*, from *parabainō*, is in this sense a late word (Plutarch on), originally a slight deviation, then a wilful disregarding of known regulations or prohibitions as in Rom. 2:23. *Till the seed should come* (*achris an elthēi to sperma*). Future time with *achris an* and aorist subjunctive (usual construction). Christ he means by *to sperma* as in verse 16. *The promise hath been made* (*epēggeltai*). Probably impersonal perfect passive rather than middle of *epaggellomai* as in II Macc. 4:27. *Ordained through angels* (*diatageis di' aggelōn*). Second aorist passive participle of *diatassō* (see on Matt. 11:1). About angels and the giving of the law see on Deut. 33:2 (LXX); Acts 7:38, 52; Heb. 2:2; Josephus (*Ant.* XV. 5. 3). *By the hand of a mediator* (*en cheiri mesitou*). *En cheiri* is a manifest Aramaism or Hebraism and only here in the N.T. It is common in the LXX. *Mesitēs*, from *mesos* is middle or midst, is a late word (Polybius, Diodorus, Philo, Josephus) and common in the papyri in legal transactions for arbiter, surety, etc. Here of Moses, but also of Christ (I Tim. 2:5; Heb. 8:6; 9:15; 12:24).

20. *Is not a mediator of one* (*henos ouk estin*). That is, a middleman comes in between two. The law is in the nature

of a contract between God and the Jewish people with Moses as the mediator or middleman. *But God is one (ho de theos heis estin).* There was no middleman between God and Abraham. He made the promise directly to Abraham. Over 400 interpretations of this verse have been made! 21. *Against the promises (kata tōn epaggeliōn).* A pertinent question again. Far from it *(mē genoito).* *Which could make alive (ho dunamenos zōopoiēsai).* First aorist active infinitive of *zōopoieō,* late compound *(zōos,* alive, *poieō,* to make) verb for which see I Cor. 15:22. Spiritual life, he means, here and hereafter. *Verily (ontōs).* "Really" (cf. Mark 11:32; Luke 24:34). Condition and conclusion *(an ēn)* of second class, determined as unfulfilled. He had already said that Christ died to no purpose in that case (2:21).

22. *Hath shut up (sunekleisen).* Did shut together. First aorist active indicative of *sunkleiō,* old verb to shut together, on all sides, completely as a shoal of fish in a net (Luke 5:6). So verse 23; Rom. 11:32. *Under sin (hupo hamartian).* See *hupo kataran* in verse 10. As if the lid closed in on us over a massive chest that we could not open or as prisoners in a dungeon. He uses *ta panta* (the all things), the totality of everything. See Rom. 3:10-19; 11:32. *That (hina).* God's purpose, personifying scripture again. *Might be given (dothēi).* First aorist passive subjunctive of *didōmi* with *hina.*

23. *Before faith came (pro tou elthein tēn pistin).* "Before the coming (second aorist active infinitive of *erchomai,* definite event) as to the Faith" (note article, meaning the faith in verse 22 made possible by the historic coming of Christ the Redeemer), the faith in Christ as Saviour (verse 22). *We were kept in ward under the law (huper nomon ephrouroumetha).* Imperfect passive of *phroureō,* to guard (from *phrouros,* a guard). See on Acts 9:24; II Cor. 11:32. It was a long progressive imprisonment. *Unto the faith which should afterwards be revealed (eis tēn mellousan pistin apokaluphthēnai).* "Unto the faith (verse 22 again) about to be revealed." *Mellō* and the first aorist passive infinitive (regular idiom).

24. *Our tutor unto Christ (paidagōgos humōn eis Christon).* See I Cor. 4:15 for the only other N.T. example of this old and common word for the slave employed in Greek and

Roman families of the better class in charge of the boy from about six to sixteen. The paedagogue watched his behaviour at home and attended him when he went away from home as to school. Christ is our Schoolmaster and the law as paedagogue kept watch over us till we came to Christ. *That we might be justified by faith* (*hina ek pisteōs dikaiōthōmen*). This is the ultimate purpose of the law as paedagogue. *Now that faith is come* (*elthousēs tēs pisteōs*). Genitive absolute, "the faith (the time of the faith spoken of in verse 23) having come." *Under a tutor* (*hupo paidagōgon*). The pedagogue is dismissed. We are in the school of the Master.

26. *For ye are all sons of God* (*pantes gar huioi theou este*). Both Jews and Gentiles (3:14) and in the same way "through faith in Christ Jesus" (*dia tēs pisteōs en Christōi Iēsou*). There is no other way to become "sons of God" in the full ethical and spiritual sense that Paul means, not mere physical descendants of Abraham, but "sons of Abraham," "those by faith" (verse 7). The Jews are called by Jesus "the sons of the Kingdom" (Matt. 8:12) in privilege, but not in fact. God is the Father of all men as Creator, but the spiritual Father only of those who by faith in Christ Jesus receive "adoption" (*huiothesia*) into his family (verse 5; Rom. 8:15, 23). Those led by the Spirit are sons of God (Rom. 8:14).

27. *Were baptized into Christ* (*eis Christon ebaptisthēte*). First aorist passive indicative of *baptizō*. Better, "were baptized unto Christ" in reference to Christ. *Did put on Christ* (*Christon enedusasthe*). First aorist middle indicative of *enduō* (*-nō*). As a badge or uniform of service like that of the soldier. This verb is common in the sense of putting on garments (literally and metaphorically as here). See further in Paul (Rom. 13:14; Col. 3:9f.; Eph. 4:22–24; 6:11, 14). In I Thess. 5:8 Paul speaks of "putting on the breastplate of righteousness." He does not here mean that one enters into Christ and so is saved by means of baptism after the teaching of the mystery religions, but just the opposite. We are justified by faith in Christ, not by circumcision or by baptism. But baptism was the public profession and pledge, the soldier's *sacramentum*, oath of fealty to Christ, taking one's stand with Christ, the symbolic picture of the change wrought by faith already (Rom. 6:4–6).

28. *There can be neither* (*ouk eni*). Not a shortened form of *enesti*, but the old lengthened form of *en* with recessive accent. So *ouk eni* means "there is not" rather than "there cannot be," a statement of a fact rather than a possibility, as Burton rightly shows against Lightfoot. *One man* (*heis*). No word for "man" in the Greek, and yet *heis* is masculine, not neuter *hen*. "One moral personality" (Vincent). The point is that "in Christ Jesus" race or national distinctions ("neither Jew nor Greek") do not exist, class differences ("neither bond nor free," no proletarianism and no capitalism) vanish, sex rivalry ("no male and female") disappears. This radical statement marks out the path along which Christianity was to come in the sphere (*en*) and spirit and power of Christ. Candour compels one to confess that this goal has not yet been fully attained. But we are on the road and there is no hope on any way than on "the Jesus Road."

29. *If ye are Christ's* (*ei de humeis Christou*). This is the test, not the accident of blood, pride of race or nation, habiliments or environment of dress or family, whether man or woman. Thus one comes to belong to the seed of Abraham and to be an heir according to promise.

CHAPTER IV

1. *So long as (eph' hoson chronon).* "For how long a time," incorporation of the antecedent *(chronon)* into the relative clause. *The heir (ho klēronomos).* Old word *(klēros,* lot, *nemomai,* to possess). Illustration from the law of inheritance carrying on the last thought in 3:29. *A child (nēpios).* One that does not talk *(nē, epos,* word). That is a minor, an infant, immature intellectually and morally in contrast with *teleioi,* full grown (I Cor. 3:1; 14:20; Phil. 3:15; Eph. 4:13). *From a bondservant (doulou).* Slave. Ablative case of comparison after *diapherei* for which verb see on Matt. 6:26. *Though he is lord of all (Kurios pantōn ōn).* Concessive participle *ōn,* "being legally owner of all" (one who has the power, *ho echōn kuros).*

2. *Under guardians (hupo epitropous).* Old word from *epitrepō,* to commit, to intrust. So either an overseer (Matt. 20:8) or one in charge of children as here. It is common as the guardian of an orphan minor. Frequent in the papyri as guardian of minors. *Stewards (oikonomous).* Old word for manager of a household whether freeborn or slave. See Luke 12:42; I Cor. 4:2. Papyri show it as manager of an estate and also as treasurer like Rom. 16:23. No example is known where this word is used of one in charge of a minor and no other where both occur together. *Until the time appointed of the father (achri tēs prothesmias tou patros).* Supply *hēmeras* (day), for *prothesmios* is an old adjective "appointed beforehand" *(pro, thesmos,* from *tithēmi).* Under Roman law the *tutor* had charge of the child till he was fourteen when the curator took charge of him till he was twenty-five. Ramsay notes that in Graeco-Phrygia cities the same law existed except that the father in Syria appointed both tutor and curator whereas the Roman father appointed only the tutor. Burton argues plausibly that no such legal distinction is meant by Paul, but that the terms here designate two functions of one person. The point does not disturb Paul's illustration at all.

3. *When we were children (hote ēmen nēpioi).* Before the

epoch of faith came and we (Jews and Gentiles) were under the law as paedagogue, guardian, steward, to use all of Paul's metaphors. *We were held in bondage* (*hēmeis ēmetha dedoulō-menoi*). Periphrastic past perfect of *douloō*, to enslave, in a permanent state of bondage. *Under the rudiments of the world* (*hupo ta stoicheia tou kosmou*). Stoichos is row or rank, a series. So *stoicheion* is any first thing in a *stoichos* like the letters of the alphabet, the material elements in the universe (II Peter 3:10), the heavenly bodies (some argue for that here), the rudiments of any act· (Heb. 5:12; Acts 15:10; Gal. 5:1; 4:3, 9; Col. 2:8, 20). The papyri illustrate all the varieties in meaning of this word. Burton has a valuable excursus on the word in his commentary. Probably here (Lightfoot) Paul has in mind the rudimentary character of the law as it applies to both Jews and Gentiles, to all the knowledge of the world (*kosmos* as the orderly material universe as in Col. 2:8, 20). See on Matt. 13:38; Acts 17:24; I Cor. 3:22. All were in the elementary stage before Christ came.

4. *The fulness of the time* (*to plērōma tou chronou*). Old word from *plēroō*, to fill. Here the complement of the preceding time as in Eph. 1:10. Some examples in the papyri in the sense of complement, to accompany. God sent forth his preëxisting Son (Phil. 2:6) when the time for his purpose had come like the *prothesmia* of verse 2. *Born of a woman* (*genomenon ek gunaikos*). As all men are and so true humanity, "coming from a woman." There is, of course, no direct reference here to the Virgin Birth of Jesus, but his deity had just been affirmed by the words "his Son" (*ton huion autou*), so that both his deity and humanity are here stated as in Rom. 1:3. Whatever view one holds about Paul's knowledge of the Virgin Birth of Christ one must admit that Paul believed in his actual personal preëxistence with God (II Cor. 8:9; Phil. 2:5–11), not a mere existence in idea. The fact of the Virgin Birth agrees perfectly with the language here. *Born under the law* (*genomenon hupo nomon*). He not only became a man, but a Jew. The purpose (*hina*) of God thus was plainly to redeem (*exagorasēi*, as in 3:13) those under the law, and so under the curse. The further purpose (*hina*) was that we (Jew and Gentile) might receive (*apolabōmen*, second aorist active subjunctive of *apolambanō*), not get back (Luke 15:27), but get from (*apo*) God the adoption (*tēn huiothesian*). Late word common in

the inscriptions (Deissmann, *Bible Studies*, p. 239) and occurs in the papyri also and in Diogenes Laertes, though not in LXX. Paul adopts this current term to express his idea (he alone in the N.T.) as to how God takes into his spiritual family both Jews and Gentiles who believe. See also Rom. 8:15, 23; 9:4; Eph. 1:5. The Vulgate uses *adoptio filiorum*. It is a metaphor like the others above, but a very expressive one.

6. *Because ye are sons* (*hoti este huioi*). This is the reason for sending forth the Son (4:4 and here). We were "sons" in God's elective purpose and love. *Hoti* is causal (I Cor. 12:15; Rom. 9:7). *The Spirit of his Son* (*to pneuma tou huioi autou*). The Holy Spirit, called the Spirit of Christ (Rom. 8:9f.), the Spirit of Jesus Christ (Phil. 1:19). The Holy Spirit proceeds from the Father and from the Son (John 15:26). *Crying, Abba, Father* (*krazon Abba ho patēr*). The participle agrees with *pneuma* neuter (grammatical gender), not neuter in fact. An old, though rare in present as here, onomatopoetic word to croak as a raven (Theophrastus, like Poe's *The Raven*), any inarticulate cry like "the un-uttered groanings" of Rom. 8:26 which God understands. This cry comes from the Spirit of Christ in our hearts. *Abba* is the Aramaic word for father with the article and *ho patēr* translates it. The articular form occurs in the vocative as in John 20:28. It is possible that the repetition here and in Rom. 8:15 may be "a sort of affectionate fondness for the very term that Jesus himself used" (Burton) in the Garden of Gethsemane (Mark 14:36). The rabbis preserve similar parallels. Most of the Jews knew both Greek and Aramaic. But there remains the question why Jesus used both in his prayer. Was it not natural for both words to come to him in his hour of agony as in his childhood? The same thing may be true here in Paul's case.

7. *No longer a bondservant* (*ouketi doulos*). Slave. He changes to the singular to drive the point home to each one. The spiritual experience (3:2) has set each one free. Each is now a son and heir.

8. *To them which by nature are not gods* (*tois phusei mē ousi theois*). In I Cor. 10:20 he terms them "demons," the "so-called gods" (I Cor. 8:5), worshipping images made by hands (Acts 17:29).

9. *Now that ye have come to know God* (*nun de gnontes*).

Fine example of the ingressive second aorist active participle of *ginōskō*, come to know by experience through faith in Christ. *Rather to be known of God (mallon de gnōsthentes hupo theou)*. First aorist passive participle of the same verb. He quickly turns it round to the standpoint of God's elective grace reaching them (verse 6). *How (pōs)*. "A question full of wonder" (Bengel). See 1:6. *Turn ye back again? (epistrephete palin?)*. Present active indicative, "Are ye turning again?" See *metatithesthe* in 1:6. *The weak and beggarly rudiments (ta asthenē kai ptōcha stoicheia)*. The same *stoicheia* in verse 3 from which they had been delivered, "weak and beggarly," still in their utter impotence from the Pharisaic legalism and the philosophical and religious legalism and the philosophical and religious quests of the heathen as shown by Angus's *The Religious Quests of the Graeco-Roman World*. These were eagerly pursued by many, but they were shadows when caught. It is pitiful today to see some men and women leave Christ for will o' the wisps of false philosophy. *Over again (palin anōthen)*. Old word, from above (*anō*) as in Matt. 27:51, from the first (Luke 1:3), then "over again" as here, back to where they were before (in slavery to rites and rules).

10. *Ye observe (paratēreisthe)*. Present middle indicative of old verb to stand beside and watch carefully, sometimes with evil intent as in Luke 6:7, but often with scrupulous care as here (so in Dio Cassius and Josephus). The meticulous observance of the Pharisees Paul knew to a nicety. It hurt him to the quick after his own merciful deliverance to see these Gentile Christians drawn into this spider-web of Judaizing Christians, once set free, now enslaved again. Paul does not itemize the "days" (Sabbaths, fast-days, feast-days, new moons) nor the "months" (Isa. 66:23) which were particularly observed in the exile nor the "seasons" (passover, pentecost, tabernacles, etc.) nor the "years" (sabbatical years every seventh year and the Year of Jubilee). Paul does not object to these observances for he kept them himself as a Jew. He objected to Gentiles taking to them as a means of salvation.

11. *I am afraid of you (phoboumai humas)*. He shudders to think of it. *Lest by any means I have bestowed labour upon you in vain (mē pōs eikei kekopiaka eis humas)*. Usual construction after a verb of fearing about what has actually

happened (*mē pōs* and the perfect active indicative of *kopiaō*, to toil wearily). A fear about the future would be expressed by the subjunctive. Paul fears that the worst has happened.

12. *Be as I am* (*ginèsthe hōs egō*). Present middle imperative, "Keep on becoming as I am." He will not give them over, afraid though he is.

13. *Because of an infirmity of the flesh* (*di' astheneian tēs sarkos*). All that we can get from this statement is the fact that Paul's preaching to the Galatians "the first time" or "the former time" (*to proteron*, adverbial accusative) was due to sickness of some kind whether it was eye trouble (4:15) which was a trial to them or to the thorn in the flesh (II Cor. 12:7) we do not know. It can be interpreted as applying to North Galatia or to South Galatia if he had an attack of malaria on coming up from Perga. But the narrative in Acts 13 and 14 does not read as if Paul had planned to pass by Pisidia and by Lycaonia but for the attack of illness. The Galatians understood the allusion for Paul says "Ye know" (*oidate*).

14. *A temptation to you in my flesh* (*ton peirasmon humōn en tēi sarki mou*). "Your temptation (or trial) in my flesh." *Peirasmon* can be either as we see in James 1:2, 12ff. If trial here, it was a severe one. *Nor rejected* (*oude exeptusate*). First aorist active indicative of *ekptuō*, old word to spit out (Homer), to spurn, to loathe. Here only in N.T. Clemen (*Primitive Christianity*, p. 342) thinks it should be taken literally here since people spat out as a prophylactic custom at the sight of invalids especially epileptics. But Plutarch uses it of mere rejection. *As an angel of God* (*hōs aggelon theou*), *as Christ Jesus* (*hōs Christon Iēsoun*). In spite of his illness and repulsive appearance, whatever it was. Not a mere "messenger" of God, but a very angel, even as Christ Jesus. We know that at Lystra Paul was at first welcomed as Hermes the god of oratory (Acts 14:12f.). But that narrative hardly applies to these words, for they turned against Paul and Barnabas then and there at the instigation of Jews from Antioch in Pisidia and Iconium.

15. *That gratulation of yourselves* (*ho makarismos humōn*). "Your felicitation." Rare word from *makarizō*, to pronounce happy, in Plato, Aristotle, Plutarch. See also Rom. 4:6, 9. You no longer felicitate yourselves on my presence with

you. *Ye would have plucked out your eyes and given them to me (tous ophthalmous humōn exoruxantes edōkate moi)*. This is the conclusion of a condition of the second class without *an* expressed which would have made it clearer. But see John 16:22, 24; Rom. 7:7 for similar examples where the context makes it plain without *an*. It is strong language and is saved from hyperbole by "if possible" (*ei dunaton*). Did Paul not have at this time serious eye trouble?

16. *Your enemy (echthros humōn)*. Active sense of *echthros*, hater with objective genitive. They looked on Paul now as an enemy to them. So the Pharisees and Judaizers generally now regarded him. *Because I tell you the truth (alētheuōn humin)*. Present active participle of *alētheuō*, old verb from *alēthēs*, true. In N.T. only here and Eph. 4:15. "Speaking the truth." It is always a risky business to speak the truth, the whole truth. It may hit and hurt.

17. *They zealously seek you (zēlousin humas)*. *Zēloō* is an old and a good word from *zēlos* (zeal, jealousy), but one can pay court with good motives or evil. So here in contrast with Paul's plain speech the Judaizers bring their fawning flattery. *To shut you out (ekkleisai humas)*. From Christ as he will show (5:4). *That ye may seek them (hina autous zēloute)*. Probably present active indicative with *hina* as in *phusiousthe* (I Cor. 4:6) and *ginōskomen* (I John 5:20). The contraction *-oēte* would be *-ōte*, not *-oute* (Robertson, *Grammar*, p. 325).

18. *To be zealously sought in a good matter (zēlousthai en kalōi)*. Present passive infinitive. It is only in an evil matter that it is bad as here (*ou kalos*). *When I am present (en tōi pareinai me)*. "In the being present as to me."

19. *I am in travail (ōdinō)*. I am in birth pangs. Old word for this powerful picture of pain. In N.T. only here, verse 27; Rev. 12:2. *Until Christ be formed in you (mechris hou morphōthēi Christos en humin)*. Future temporal clause with *mechris hou* (until which time) and the first aorist passive subjunctive of *morphoō*, late and rare verb, in Plutarch, not in LXX, not in papyri, only here in N.T. This figure is the embryo developing into the child. Paul boldly represents himself as again the mother with birth pangs over them. This is better than to suppose that the Galatians are pregnant mothers (Burton) by a reversal of the picture as in I Thess. 2:7.

20. *I could wish* (*ēthelon*). Imperfect active, I was wishing like Agrippa's use of *eboulomēn* in Acts 25:22, "I was just wishing." "I was longing to be present with you just now (*arti*)." *To change my voice* (*allaxai tēn phōnēn mou*). Paul could put his heart into his voice. The pen stands between them. He knew the power of his voice on their hearts. He had tried it before. *I am perplexed* (*aporoumai*). I am at a loss and know not what to do. *Aporeō* is from *a* privative and *poros*, way. I am lost at this distance from you. *About you* (*en humin*). In your cases. For this use of *en* see II Cor. 7:16; Gal. 1:24.

21. *That desire to be under the law* (*hoi hupo nomon thelontes einai*). "Under law" (no article), as in 3:23; 4:4, legalistic system. Paul views them as on the point of surrender to legalism, as "wanting" (*thelontes*) to do it (1:6; 3:3; 4:11, 17). Paul makes direct reference to these so disposed to "hear the law." He makes a surprising turn, but a legitimate one for the legalists by an allegorical use of Scripture.

22. *By the handmaid* (*ek tēs paidiskēs*). From Gen. 16:1. Feminine diminutive of *pais*, boy or slave. Common word for damsel which came to be used for female slave or maidservant (Luke 12:45) or doorkeeper like Matt. 26:29. So in the papyri.

23. *Is born* (*gegennētai*). Perfect passive indicative of *gennaō*, stand on record so. *Through promise* (*di' epaggelias*). In addition to being "after the flesh" (*kata sarka*).

24. *Which things contain an allegory* (*hatina estin allēgoroumena*). Literally, "Which things are allegorized" (periphrastic present passive indicative of *allēgoreō*). Late word (Strabo, Plutarch, Philo, Josephus, ecclesiastical writers), only here in N.T. The ancient writers used *ainittomai* to speak in riddles. It is compounded of *allo*, another, and *agoreuō*, to speak, and so means speaking something else than what the language means, what Philo, the past-master in the use of allegory, calls the deeper spiritual sense. Paul does not deny the actual historical narrative, but he simply uses it in an allegorical sense to illustrate his point for the benefit of his readers who are tempted to go under the burden of the law. He puts a secondary meaning on the narrative just as he uses *tupikōs* in I Cor. 10:11 of the narrative. We need not press unduly the difference between allegory

and type, for each is used in a variety of ways. The allegory in one sense is a speaking parable like Bunyan's *Pilgrim's Progress*, the Prodigal Son in Luke 15, the Good Shepherd in John 10. But allegory was also used by Philo and by Paul here for a secret meaning not obvious at first, one not in the mind of the writer, like our illustration which throws light on the point. Paul was familiar with this rabbinical method of exegesis (Rabbi Akiba, for instance, who found a mystical sense in every hook and crook of the Hebrew letters) and makes skilful use of that knowledge here. Christian preachers in Alexandria early fell victims to Philo's allegorical method and carried it to excess without regard to the plain sense of the narrative. That startling style of preaching survives yet to the discredit of sound preaching. Please observe that Paul says here that he is using allegory, not ordinary interpretation. It is not necessary to say that Paul intended his readers to believe that this allegory was designed by the narrative. He illustrates his point by it. *For these are* (*hautai gar eisin*). Allegorically interpreted, he means. *From Mount Sinai* (*apo orous Sinā*). Spoken from Mount Sinai. *Bearing* (*gennōsa*). Present active participle of *gennaō*, to beget of the male (Matt. 1:1–16), more rarely as here to bear of the female (Luke 1:13, 57). *Which is Hagar* (*hētis estin Hagar*). Allegorically interpreted.

25. *This Hagar* (*to Hagar*). Neuter article and so referring to the word Hagar (not to the woman, *hē Hagar*) as applied to the mountain. There is great variety in the MSS. here. The Arabians are descendants of Abraham and Hagar (her name meaning wanderer or fugitive). *Answereth to* (*sunstoichei*). Late word in Polybius for keeping step in line (military term) and in papyri in figurative sense as here. Lightfoot refers to the Pythagorean parallels of opposing principles (*sunstoichiai*) as shown here by Paul (Hagar and Sarah, Ishmael and Isaac, the old covenant and the new covenant, the earthly Jerusalem and the heavenly Jerusalem). That is true, and there is a correlative correspondence as the line is carried on.

26. *The Jerusalem that is above* (*hē anō Ierousalēm*). Paul uses the rabbinical idea that the heavenly Jerusalem corresponds to the one here to illustrate his point without endorsing their ideas. See also Rev. 21:2. He uses the city of Jerusalem to represent the whole Jewish race (Vincent).

27. *Which is our mother* (*hētis estin mētēr hēmōn*). The mother of us Christians, apply the allegory of Hagar and Sarah to us. The Jerusalem above is the picture of the Kingdom of God. Paul illustrates the allegory by quoting Isa. 54:1, a song of triumph looking for deliverance from a foreign yoke. *Rejoice* (*euphranthēti*). First aorist passive imperative of *euphrainō*. *Break forth* (*rēxon*). First aorist active imperative of *rēgnumi*, to rend, to burst asunder. Supply *euphrosunēn* (joy) as in Isa. 49:13. *The desolate* (*tēs erēmou*). The prophet refers to Sarah's prolonged barrenness and Paul uses this fact as a figure for the progress and glory of Christianity (the new Jerusalem of freedom) in contrast with the old Jerusalem of bondage (the current Judaism). His thought has moved rapidly, but he does not lose his line.

28. *Now we* (*hēmeis de*). Some MSS. have *humeis de* (*now ye*). In either case Paul means that Christians (Jews and Gentiles) are children of the promise as Isaac was (*kata Isaak*, after the manner of Isaac).

29. *Persecuted* (*ediōken*). Imperfect active of *diōkō*, to pursue, to persecute. Gen. 21:9 has in Hebrew "laughing," but the LXX has "mocking." The Jewish tradition represents Ishmael as shooting arrows at Isaac. So now (*houtōs kai nun*) the Jews were persecuting Paul and all Christians (I Thess. 2:15f.).

30. *Cast out* (*ekbale*). Second aorist active imperative of *ekballō*. Quotation from Gen. 21:10 (Sarah to Abraham) and confirmed in 21:12 by God's command to Abraham. Paul gives allegorical warning thus to the persecuting Jews and Judaizers. *Shall not inherit* (*ou mē klēronomēsei*). Strong negative (*ou mē* and future indicative). "The law and the gospel cannot co-exist. The law must disappear before the gospel" (Lightfoot). See 3:18, 29 for the word "inherit."

31. *But of the freewoman* (*alla tēs eleutheras*). We are children of Abraham by faith (3:7).

CHAPTER V

1. *With freedom (tēi eleutheriāi)*. Rather dative case instead of instrumental, "for freedom," "for the (article) freedom that belongs to us children of the freewoman" (4:31). *Did Christ set us free (hēmas Christos eleutherōsen)*. Effective aorist active indicative of *eleutheroō* (from *erchomai*, to go, go free). *Stand fast therefore (stēkete oun)*. See on Mark 3:31; I Cor. 16:13 for this late word from perfect stem of *histēmi*, "keep on standing therefore," "stay free since Christ set you free." *Be not entangled again (mē palin enechesthe)*. "Stop being held in by a yoke of bondage." Common word for ensnare by trap. The Judaizers were trying to lasso the Galatians for the old yoke of Judaism.

2. *I Paul (egō Paulos)*. Asserts all his personal and apostolic authority. For both words see also I Thess. 2:16; II Cor. 10:1; Col. 1:23; Eph. 3:1. *If ye receive circumcision (ean peritemnēsthe)*. Condition of third class and present passive subjunctive, a supposable case, but with terrible consequences, for they will make circumcision a condition of salvation. In that case Christ will help them not at all.

3. *A debtor (opheiletēs)*. Common word from *opheilō*, to owe for one who has assumed an obligation. See on Matt. 6:12. See Gal. 3:10. He takes the curse on himself.

4. *Ye are severed from Christ (katērgēthēte apo Christou)*. First aorist passive of *katargeō*, to make null and void as in Rom. 7:2, 6. *Who would be justified by the law (hoitines en nomōi dikaiousthe)*. Present passive conative indicative, "ye who are trying to be justified in the law." *Ye are fallen away from grace (tēs charitos exepesate)*. Second aorist active indicative of *ekpiptō* (with *a* variable vowel of the first aorist) and followed by the ablative case. "Ye did fall out of grace," "ye left the sphere of grace in Christ and took your stand in the sphere of law" as your hope of salvation. Paul does not mince words and carries the logic to the end of the course. He is not, of course, speaking of occasional sins, but he has in mind a far more serious matter, that of substituting law for Christ as the agent in salvation.

5. *For we (hēmeis gar).* We Christians as opposed to the legalists. *Through the Spirit by faith (pneumati ek pisteōs).* By the Spirit (Holy Spirit) out of faith (not law). Clear-cut repetition to make it plain.

6. *Availeth anything (ischuei ti).* Old word to have strength (*ischūs*). See on Matt. 5:13. Neither Jew nor Greek has any recommendation in his state. See 3:28. All stand on a level in Christ. *Faith working through love (pistis di' agapēs energoumenē).* Middle voice of *energeō* and "through love," "the moral dynamic" (Burton) of Paul's conception of freedom from law.

7. *Who did hinder you? (tis humas enekopsen?).* First aorist active indicative of *enkoptō*, to cut in on one, for all the world like our use of one cutting in on us at the telephone. For this late verb see on Acts 24:4; I Thess. 2:18. Note the singular *tis*. There was some ringleader in the business. Some one "cut in" on the Galatians as they were running the Christian race and tried to trip them or to turn them.

8. *This persuasion (hē peismonē).* "The art of persuasion," the effort of the Judaizers to persuade you. Only here and in ecclesiastical writers.

9. This proverb Paul has in I Cor. 5:6. It is merely the pervasive power of leaven that is involved in the proverb as in Matt. 13:33, not the use of leaven as a symbol of evil.

10. *Whosoever he be (hostis ean ēi).* Indefinite relative clause with *ean* and subjunctive. It seems unlikely that Paul knew precisely who the leader was. In 1:6 he uses the plural of the same verb *tarassō* and see also *anastatountes* in verse 12.

11. *Why am I still persecuted? (ti eti diōkomai?).* Some of the Judaizers even circulated the slander that Paul preached circumcision in order to ruin his influence.

12. *I would (ophelon).* Would that, used as conjunction in wishes. See on I Cor. 4:2; II Cor. 11:1. Here a wish about the future with future indicative. *They which unsettle you (hoi anastatountes humas).* Late verb from *anastatos*, driven from one's abode, and in papyri in this sense as well as in sense of upsetting or disturbing one's mind (boy's letter) as here. In Acts 17:6; 21:38 we have it in sense of making a commotion. *Cut themselves off (apokopsontai).* Future middle of *apokoptō*, old word to cut off as in Acts 27:32, here to mutilate.

13. *Ye were called for freedom* (*ep' eleutheriāi eklēthēte*). The same point as in 5:1 made plainer by the use of *ep'* (on the basis of, for the purpose of). See I Thess. 4:7 for this use of *epi*. *Only use not* (*monon mē*). No word for "use" in the Greek. Probably supply *trepete* or *strephete*, "turn not your liberty into an occasion for the flesh" (*eis aphormēn tēi sarki*), as a spring board for license. On *aphormē*, see on II Cor. 5:12. Liberty so easily turns to license.

14. *Even in this* (*en tōi*). Just the article with *en*, "in the," but it points at the quotation from Lev. 19:18. Jews (Luke 10:29) confined "neighbour" (*plēsion*) to Jews. Paul uses here a striking paradox by urging obedience to the law against which he has been arguing, but this is the moral law as proof of the new love and life. See also Rom. 13:8, precisely as Jesus did (Matt. 22:40).

15. *If ye bite and devour one another* (*ei allēlous daknete kai katesthiete*). Condition of first class assumed as true. Two common and old verbs often used together of wild animals, or like cats and dogs. *That ye be not consumed one of another* (*mē hup' allēlōn analōthēte*). Negative final clause with first aorist passive subjunctive of *analiskō*, old word to consume or spend. In N.T. only here and Luke 9:54. There is a famous story of two snakes that grabbed each other by the tail and each swallowed the other.

16. *Ye shall not fulfil* (*ou mē telesēte*). Rather, "Ye will not fulfil." Strong double negative with aorist active subjunctive. *The lust of the flesh* (*epithumian sarkos*). Bad sense here as usual in Paul, but not so in I Thess. 2:17; Phil. 1:23. The word is just craving or longing (from *epi*, *thumos*, *yearning after*).

17. *Lusteth against* (*epithumei kata*). Like a tug of war. This use of *sarx* as opposed to the Spirit (Holy Spirit) personifies *sarx*. Lightfoot argues that *epithumei* cannot be used with the Spirit and so some other verb must be supplied for it. But that is wholly needless, for the verb, like *epithumia*, does not mean evil desire, but simply to long for. Christ and Satan long for the possession of the city of Man Soul as Bunyan shows. *Are contrary the one to the other* (*allēlois antikeitai*). Are lined up in conflict, face to face (*anti-*), a spiritual duel (cf. Christ's temptations), with dative case of personal interest (*allēlois*). *That ye may not do* (*hina mē poiēte*). "That ye may not keep on doing"

(present active subjunctive of *poieō*). *That ye would* (*ha ean thelēte*). "Whatever ye wish" (indefinite relative with *ean* and present subjunctive). 18. *Under the law* (*hupo nomon*). Instead of "under the flesh" as one might expect. See Gal. 3:2–6 for contrast between law and spirit. The flesh made the law weak (Rom. 8:3; Heb. 9:10, 13). They are one and the same in result. See same idea in Rom. 8:14. Note present tense of *agesthe* (if you are continually led by the Spirit). See verse 23. 19. *Manifest* (*phanera*). Opposed to "hidden" (*krupta*). Ancient writers were fond of lists of vices and virtues. Cf. Stalker's sermons on *The Seven Cardinal Virtues* and *The Seven Deadly Sins*. There are more than seven in this deadly list in verses 19 to 21. He makes the two lists in explanation of the conflict in verse 17 to emphasize the command in verses 13f. There are four groups in Paul's list of manifest vices: (1) Sensual sins like fornication (*porneia*, prostitution, harlotry), uncleanness (*akatharsia*, moral impurity), lasciviousness (*aselgeia*, wantonness), sexual vice of all kinds prevailed in heathenism. (2) Idolatry (*eidōlatreia*, worship of idols) and witchcraft (*pharmakeia* from *pharmakon*, a drug, the ministering of drugs, but the sorcerers monopolized the word for a while in their magical arts and used it in connection with idolatry. In N.T. only here and Rev. 18:23. See Acts 19:19 *perierga*, curious arts. (3) Personal relations expressed by eight words, all old words, sins of the spirit, like enmities (*exthrai*, personal animosities), strife (*eris*, rivalry, discord), jealousies (*zēlos* or *zēloi*, MSS. vary, our very word), wraths (*thumoi*, stirring emotions, then explosions), factions (*eritheiai*, from *erithos*, day labourer for hire, worker in wool, party spirit), divisions (*dichostasiai*, splits in two, *dicha* and *stasis*), heresies (*haireseis*, the very word, but really choosings from *haireomai*, preferences), envyings (*phthonoi*, feelings of ill-will). Surely a lively list. (4) *Drunkenness* (*methai*, old word and plural, drunken excesses, in N.T. only here and Luke 21:34; Rom. 13:13), revellings (*kōmoi*, old word also for drinking parties like those in honour of Bacchus, in N.T. only here and Rom. 13:13; I Peter 4:3). *And such like* (*kai ta·homoia toutois*). And the things like these (associative instrumental *toutois* after *homoia*, like). It is not meant to be exhaustive, but it is representative.

21. *Forewarn* (*prolegō*)—*did forewarn* (*proeipon*). Paul

repeats his warning given while with them. He did his duty
then. Gentile churches were peculiarly subject to these sins.
But who is not in danger from them? *Practise (prassontes).*
Prassō is the verb for habitual practice (our very word, in
fact), not *poieō* for occasional doing. The *habit* of these sins
is proof that one is not in the Kingdom of God and will
not inherit it.

22. *The fruit of the Spirit (ho karpos tou pneumatos).* Paul
changes the figure from *works (erga)* in verse 19 to fruit as
the normal out-cropping of the Holy Spirit in us. It is a
beautiful tree of fruit that Paul pictures here with nine
luscious fruits on it: *Love (agapē).* Late, almost Biblical
word. First as in I Cor. 13, which see for discussion as superior to *philia* and *erōs. Joy (chara).* Old word. See on I
Thess. 1:6. *Peace (eirēnē).* See on I Thess. 1:1. *Long-
suffering (makrothumia).* See on II Cor. 6:6. *Kindness
(chrēstotēs).* See on II Cor. 6:6. *Goodness (agathōsunē).* See
on II Thess. 1:11. *Faithfulness (pistis).* Same word as "faith."
See on Matt. 23:33; I Cor. 13:7, 13. *Meekness (praütēs).*
See on I Cor. 4:21; II Cor. 10:1. *Temperance (egkrateia).*
See on Acts 24:25. Old word from *egkratēs,* one holding
control or holding in. In N.T. only in these passages and
II Pet. 1:6. Paul has a better list than the four cardinal
virtues of the Stoics (temperance, prudence, fortitude,
justice), though they are included with better notes struck.
Temperance is alike, but kindness is better than justice,
long-suffering than fortitude, love than prudence.

24. *Crucified the flesh (tēn sarka estaurōsan).* Definite
event, first aorist active indicative of *stauroō* as in 2:19 (mystical union with Christ). Paul uses *sarx* here in the same
sense as in verses 16, 17, 19, "the force in men that makes
for evil" (Burton). *With (sun).* "Together with," emphasizing "the completeness of the extermination of this evil force"
and the guarantee of victory over one's passions and dis-
positions toward evil.

25. *By the Spirit let us also walk (pneumati kai stoichōmen).*
Present subjunctive (volitive) of *stoicheō,* "Let us also go on
walking by the Spirit." Let us make our steps by the help
and guidance of the Spirit.

26. *Let us not be (mē ginōmetha).* Present middle subjunctive (volitive), "Let us cease becoming vainglorious" (*keno-
doxoi*), late word only here in N.T. (*kenos, doxa*). Once in

Epictetus in same sense. *Provoking one another* (*allēlous prokaloumenoi*). Old word *prokaleō*, to call forth, to challenge to combat. Only here in N.T. and in bad sense. The word for "provoke" in Heb. 10:24 is *paroxusmon* (our "paroxysm"). *Envying* (*phthonountes*). Old verb from *phthonos*. Only here in N.T.

CHAPTER VI

1. *If a man be overtaken (ean kai prolēmphthēi anthrōpos).* Condition of third class, first aorist passive subjunctive of *prolambanō*, old verb to take beforehand, to surprise, to detect. *Trespass (paraptōmati).* Literally, a falling aside, a slip or lapse in the papyri rather than a wilful sin. In Polybius and Diodorus. *Koiné* word. *Ye which are spiritual (hoi pneumatikoi).* See on I Cor. 3:1. The spiritually led (5:18), the spiritual experts in mending souls. *Restore (katartizete).* Present active imperative of *katartizō*, the very word used in Matt. 4:21 of mending nets, old word to make *artios*, fit, to equip thoroughly. *Looking to thyself (skopōn seauton).* Keeping an eye on as in II Cor. 4:18 like a runner on the goal. *Lest thou also be tempted (mē kai su peirastheis).* Negative purpose with first aorist passive subjunctive. Spiritual experts (preachers in particular) need this caution. Satan loves a shining mark.

2. *Bear ye one another's burdens (allēlōn.ta barē bastazete).* Keep on bearing (present active imperative of *bastazō*, old word, used of Jesus bearing his Cross in John 19:17. *Baros* means weight as in Matt. 20:12 and II Cor. 4:17. It is when one's load (*phortion*, verse 5) is about to press one down. Then give help in carrying it. *Fulfil (anaplērōsate).* First aorist active imperative of *anaplēroō*, to fill up, old word, and see on Matt. 23:32; I Thess. 2:16; I Cor. 14:16. Some MSS. have future indicative (*anaplērōsete*).

3. *Something when he is nothing (ti mēden ōn).* Thinks he is a big number being nothing at all (neuter singular pronouns). He is really zero. *He deceiveth himself (phrenapatāi heauton).* Late compound word (*phrēn*, mind, *apataō*, lead astray), leads his own mind astray. Here for first time. Afterwards in Galen, ecclesiastical and Byzantine writers. He deceives no one else.

5. *Each shall bear his own burden (to idion phortion bastasei).* *Phortion* is old word for ship's cargo (Acts 27:10). Christ calls his *phortion* light, though he terms those of the Pharisees heavy (Matt. 23:4), meant for other people. The

terms are thus not always kept distinct, though Paul does make a distinction here from the *barē* in verse 2.

6. *That is taught* (*ho katēchoumenos*). For this late and rare verb *katēcheō*, see on Luke 1:4; Acts 18:25; I Cor. 14:19. It occurs in the papyri for legal instruction. Here the present passive participle retains the accusative of the thing. The active (*tōi katēchounti*) joined with the passive is interesting as showing how early we find paid teachers in the churches. Those who receive instruction are called on to "contribute" (better than "communicate" for *koinōneitō*) for the time of the teacher (Burton). There was a teaching class thus early (I Thess. 5:12; I Cor. 12:28; Eph. 4:11; I Thess. 5:17).

7. *Be not deceived* (*mē planāsthe*). Present passive imperative with *mē*, "stop being led astray" (*planaō*, common verb to wander, to lead astray as in Matt. 24:4f.). *God is not mocked* (*ou muktērizetai*). This rare verb (common in LXX) occurs in Lysias. It comes from *muktēr* (nose) and means to turn the nose up at one. That is done towards God, but never without punishment, Paul means to say. In particular, he means "an evasion of his laws which men think to accomplish, but, in fact, cannot" (Burton). *Whatsoever a man soweth* (*ho ean speirēi anthrōpos*). Indefinite relative clause with *ean* and the active subjunctive (either aorist or present, form same here). One of the most frequent of ancient proverbs (Job. 4:8; Arist., *Rhet.* iii. 3). Already in II Cor. 9:6. Same point in Matt. 7:16; Mark 4:26f. *That* (*touto*). That very thing, not something different. *Reap* (*therisei*). See on Matt. 6:26 for this old verb.

8. *Corruption* (*phthoran*). For this old word from *phtheirō*, see on I Cor. 15:42. The precise meaning turns on the context, here plainly the physical and moral decay or rottenness that follows sins of the flesh as all men know. Nature writes in one's body the penalty of sin as every doctor knows. *Eternal life* (*zōēn aiōnion*). See on Matt. 25:46 for this interesting phrase so common in the Johannine writings. Plato used *aiōnios* for perpetual. See also II Thess. 1:9. It comes as nearly meaning "eternal" as the Greek can express that idea.

9. *Let us not be weary in well-doing* (*to kalon poiountes mē enkakōmen*). Volitive present active subjunctive of *enkakeō* on which see Luke 18:1; II Thess. 3:13; II Cor. 4:1, 16 (*en,*

kakos, evil). Literally, "Let us not keep on giving in to evil while doing the good." It is curious how prone we are to give in and to give out in doing the good which somehow becomes prosy or insipid to us. *In due season (kairōi idiōi).* Locative case, "at its proper season" (harvest time). Cf. I Tim. 2:6; 6:15 (plural). *If we faint not (mē ekluomenoi).* Present passive participle (conditional) with *mē*. Cf. *ekluō*, old verb to loosen out. Literally, "not loosened out," relaxed, exhausted as a result of giving in to evil (*enkakōmen*). 10. *As we have opportunity (hōs kairon echōmen).* Indefinite comparative clause (present subjunctive without *an*). "As we have occasion at any time." *Let us work that which is good (ergazōmetha to agathon).* Volitive present middle subjunctive of *ergazomai*, "Let us keep on working the good deed." *Of the household of faith (tous oikeious tēs pisteōs).* For the obvious reason that they belong to the same family with necessary responsibility.

11. *With how large letters (pēlikois grammasin).* Paul now takes the pen from the amanuensis (cf. Rom. 16:22) and writes the rest of the Epistle (verses 11–18) himself instead of the mere farewell greeting (II Thess. 3:17; I Cor. 16:21; Col. 4:18). But what does he mean by "with how large letters"? Certainly not "how large a letter." It has been suggested that he employed large letters because of defective eyesight or because he could only write ill-formed letters because of his poor handwriting (like the print letters of children) or because he wished to call particular attention to this closing paragraph by placarding it in big letters (Ramsay). This latter is the most likely reason. Deissmann, (*St. Paul*, p. 51) argues that artisans write clumsy letters, yes, and scholars also. Milligan (*Documents*, p. 24; *Vocabulary*, etc.) suggests the contrast seen in papyri often between the neat hand of the scribe and the big sprawling hand of the signature. *I have written (egrapsa).* Epistolary aorist. *With mine own hand (tēi emēi cheiri).* Instrumental case as in I Cor. 16:21.

12. *To make a fair show (euprosōpēsai).* First aorist active infinitive of *euprosōpeō*, late verb from *euprosōpos*, fair of face (*eu, prosōpon*). Here only in N.T., but one example in papyri (Tebt. I. 19¹² B.C. 114) which shows what may happen to any of our N.T. words not yet found elsewhere. It is in

Chrysostom and later writers. *They compel (anagkazousin).*
Conative present active indicative, "they try to compel."
For the cross of Christ (tōi stauroi tou Christou). Instrumental
case (causal use, Robertson, *Grammar*, p. 532). Cf. II Cor.
2:13. "For professing the cross of Christ" (Lightfoot).

13. *They who receive circumcision (hoi peritemnomenoi).*
Present causative middle of *peritemnō*, those who are having
themselves circumcised. Some MSS. read *hoi peritetmē-
menoi*), "they who have been circumcised" (perfect passive
participle). Probably the present *(peritemnomenoi)* is correct as the harder reading.

14. *Far be it from me (emoi mē genoito).* Second aorist
middle optative of *ginomai* in a negative *(mē)* wish about
the future with dative case: "May it not happen to me."
See 2:17. The infinitive *kauchāsthai* (to glory) is the subject
of *genoito* as is common in the LXX, though not elsewhere
in the N.T. *Hath been crucified unto me (emoi estaurōtai).*
Perfect passive indicative of *stauroō*, stands crucified, with
the ethical dative again *(emoi).* This is one of the great
sayings of Paul concerning his relation to Christ and the
world in contrast with the Judaizers. Cf. 2:19f.; 3:13; 4:4f.;
I Cor. 1:23f.; Rom. 1:16; 3:21ff.; 4:25; 5:18. World *(kosmos)*
has no article, but is definite as in II Cor. 5:19. Paul's old
world of Jewish descent and environment is dead to him
(Phil. 3:3f.).

15. *A new creature (kainē ktisis).* For this phrase see on
II Cor. 5:17.

16. *By this rule (tōi kanoni toutōi).* For *kanōn*, see on II
Cor. 10:13, 15f.

17. *From henceforth (tou loipou).* Usually *to loipon*, the
accusative of general reference, "as for the rest" (Phil. 3:1;
4:8). The genitive case (as here and Eph. 6:10) means "in
respect of the remaining time." *The marks of Jesus (ta
stigmata tou Iēsou).* Old word from *stizō*, to prick, to stick,
to sting. Slaves had the names or stamp of their owners on
their bodies. It was sometimes done for soldiers also. There
were devotees also who stamped upon their bodies the names
of the gods whom they worshipped. Today in a round-up
cattle are given the owner's mark. Paul gloried in being
the slave of Jesus Christ. This is probably the image in
Paul's mind since he bore in his body brandmarks of suffer-

ing for Christ received in many places (II Cor. 6:4–6; 11:
23ff.), probably actual scars from the scourgings (thirty-
nine lashes at a time). If for no other reason, listen to me
by reason of these scars for Christ and "let no one keep on
furnishing trouble to me."

18. The farewell salutation is much briefer than that in
II Cor. 13:13, but identical with that in Philemon 25. He
calls them "brethren" (*adelphoi*) in spite of the sharp things
spoken to them.

THE EPISTLE TO THE ROMANS
Spring of a.d. 57

BY WAY OF INTRODUCTION

Integrity of the Epistle

The genuineness of the Epistle is so generally admitted by scholars that it is unnecessary to prove it here, for Loman, Steck, and the Dutch scholars (Van Manen, etc.) who deny it as Pauline are no longer taken seriously. He wrote it from Corinth because he sent it to Rome by Phoebe of Cenchreae (Rom. 16:2) if chapter 16 is acknowledged to be a part of the Epistle. Chapter 16 is held by some to be really a short epistle to Ephesus because of the long list of names in it, because of Paul's long stay in Ephesus, because he had not yet been to Rome, and because, in particular, Aquila and Priscilla are named (Rom. 16:3-5) who had been with Paul in Ephesus. But they had come from Rome before going to Corinth and there is no reason for thinking that they did not return to Rome. It was quite possible for Paul to have many friends in Rome whom he had met elsewhere. People naturally drifted to Rome from all over the empire. The old MSS. (Aleph A B C D) give chapter 16 as an integral part of the Epistle. Marcion rejected it and chapter 15 also for reasons of his own. Renan's theory that Romans was a circular letter like Ephesians sent in different forms to different churches (Rome, Ephesus, Thessalonica, etc.) has appealed to some scholars as explaining the several doxologies in the Epistle, but they cause no real difficulty since Paul interjected them in his other epistles according to his moods (II Cor. 1:20, for instance). That theory raises more problems than it solves as, for example, Paul's remarks about going to Rome (1:9-16) which apply to Rome. Lightfoot suggests the possibility that Paul added 16:25-27 some years after the original date so as to turn it into a circular letter. But the MSS. do not support that theory and that leaves 15:22-

33 in the Epistle quite unsuitable to a circular letter. Modern knowledge leaves the Epistle intact with occasional variations in the MSS. on particular points as is true of all the N.T.

THE TIME AND PLACE

The place is settled if we accept 16:1. The time of the year is in the spring if we combine statements in the Acts and the Epistle. He says: "I am now going to Jerusalem ministering to the saints" (Rom. 15:25). In Acts 20:3 we read that Paul spent three months in Corinth. In II Corinthians we have a full account of the collection for the poor saints in Jerusalem. The account of the journey from Corinth to Jerusalem is given in Acts 20:3-21:17. It was in the spring between passover at Philippi (Acts 20:6) and pentecost in Jerusalem (20:16; 21:17). The precise year is not quite so certain, but we may suggest A.D. 57 or 58 with reasonable confidence.

THE PURPOSE

Paul tells this himself. He had long cherished a desire to come to Rome (Acts 19:21) and had often made his plans to do so (Rom. 1:13) which were interrupted (15:22), but now he definitely plans to go from Jerusalem, after taking the contribution there (15:26), to Rome and then on to Spain (15:24, 28). Meanwhile he sends this Epistle that the Romans may know what Paul's gospel really is (1:15; 2:16). He is full of the issues raised by the Judaizing controversy as set forth in the Epistles to Corinth and to Galatia. So in a calmer mood and more at length he presents his conception of the Righteousness demanded by God (1:17) of both Gentile (1:18-32) and Jew (2:1-3:20) and only to be obtained by faith in Christ who by his atoning death (justification) has made it possible (3:21-5:21). This new life of faith in Christ should lead to holiness of life (sanctification, chapters 6-8). This is Paul's gospel and the remaining chapters deal with corollaries growing out of the doctrine of grace as applied to practical matters. It is a cause for gratitude that Paul did write out so full a statement of his message. He had a message for the whole world and was anxious to win the Roman Empire to Christ. It was important that he go to Rome for it was the centre of the world's life. No-where does Paul's Christian statesmanship show to better advantage than in this greatest of his Epistles. It is not a book of formal theology though Paul is the greatest of theologians. Here Paul is seen in the plenitude of his powers with all the wealth of his knowledge of Christ and his rich experience in mission work. The church in Rome is plainly composed of both Jews and Greeks, though who started the work there we have no way of knowing. Paul's ambition was to preach where no one else had been (Rom. 15:20), but he has no hesitation in going on to Rome.

COMMENTARIES

No one of Paul's Epistles has more helpful modern commentaries on it than this one, such as those by Barth (1919), Beet (9th ed., 1901), Cook (1930), Denney (1901), Feine (1903), Garvie (1901), Gifford (1881), Godet (Tr., 1883), Gore (Expos.), Grey (1910), Griffith-Thomas (1913), Hodge (1856), Hort (Intr., 1895), Jowett (3rd ed., 1894), Jülicher (2 Aufl., 1907), Kühl (1913), Lagrange (1916), Lard (1875), Liddon (Anal., 1893), Lietzmann (2 Aufl., 1919), Lightfoot (chapters 1–7, 1895), Luetgert (1913), Monk (1893), Plummer, Richter (1908), Sanday and Headlam (1895), Shedd (1893), Stifler (1897), Vaughan (1890), Weiss, B. (Meyer Komm., 9 Aufl., 1899), Westcott, F. B. (1913), Zahn (1910).

CHAPTER I

To the Romans (pros Rōmaious). This is the title in Aleph A B C, our oldest Greek MSS. for the Epistle. We do not know whether Paul gave any title at all. Later MSS. add other words up to the Textus Receptus: The Epistle of Paul to the Romans. The Epistle is put first in the MSS. because it is the most important of Paul's Epistles.

1. *Paul (Paulos).* Roman name *(Paulus).* See on Acts 13:9 for the origin of this name by the side of Saul. *Servant (doulos).* Bond-slave of Jesus Christ (or Christ Jesus as some MSS. give it and as is the rule in the later Epistles) for the first time in the Epistles in the opening sentence, though the phrase already in Gal. 1:10. Recurs in Phil. 1:1 and *desmios* (bondsman) in Philemon 1. *Called to be an apostle (klētos apostolos).* An apostle by vocation (Denney) as in I Cor. 1:1. In Gal. 1:1 *klētos* is not used, but the rest of the verse has the same idea. *Separated (aphōrismenos).* Perfect passive participle of *aphorizō* for which verb see on Gal. 1:15. Paul is a spiritual Pharisee (etymologically), separated not to the oral tradition, but to God's gospel, a chosen vessel (Acts 9:15). By man also (Acts 13:2). Many of Paul's characteristic words like *euaggelion* have been already discussed in the previous Epistles that will call for little comment from now on.

2. *He promised afore (proepēggeilato).* First aorist middle of *proepaggellō* for which verb see on II Cor. 9:5. *By (dia).* Through, by means of, intermediate agency like Matt. 1:22 which see. *In the holy scriptures (en graphais hagiais).* No article, yet definite. Perhaps the earliest use of the phrase (Sanday and Headlam). Paul definitely finds God's gospel in the Holy Scriptures.

3. *Concerning his Son (peri tou huiou autou).* Just as Jesus found himself in the O.T. (Luke 24:27, 46). The deity of Christ here stated. *According to the flesh (kata sarka).* His real humanity alongside of his real deity. For the descent from David see Matt. 1:1, 6, 20; Luke 1:27; John 7:42; Acts 13:23, etc.

4. *Who was declared* (*tou horisthentos*). Articular participle (first aorist passive) of *horizō* for which verb see on Luke 22:22; Acts 2:23. He was the Son of God in his preincarnate state (II Cor. 8:9; Phil. 2:6) and still so after his Incarnation (verse 3, "of the seed of David"), but it was the Resurrection of the dead (*ex anastaseōs nekrōn*, the general resurrection implied by that of Christ) that definitely marked Jesus off as God's Son because of his claims about himself as God's Son and his prophecy that he would rise on the third day. This event (cf. I Cor. 15) gave God's seal "with power" (*en dunamei*), "in power," declared so in power (II Cor. 13:4). The Resurrection of Christ is the miracle of miracles. "The resurrection only declared him to be what he truly was" (Denney). *According to the spirit of holiness* (*kata pneuma hagiōsunēs*). Not the Holy Spirit, but a description of Christ ethically as *kata sarka* describes him physically (Denney). *Hagiōsunē* is rare (I Thess. 3:13; II Cor. 7:1 in N.T.), three times in LXX, each time as the attribute of God. "The *pneuma hagiōsunēs*, though not the Divine nature, is that in which the Divinity or Divine Personality Resided" (Sanday and Headlam). *Jesus Christ our Lord* (*Iēsou Christou tou kuriou hēmōn*). These words gather up the total personality of Jesus (his deity and his humanity).

5. *Unto obedience of faith* (*eis hupakoēn pisteōs*). Subjective genitive as in 16:26, the obedience which springs from faith (the act of assent or surrender).

6. *Called to be Jesus Christ's* (*klētoi Iēsou Christou*). Predicate genitive after *klētoi* (verbal adjective from *kaleō*, to call), though it is possible to consider it the ablative case, "called of (or from) Jesus Christ."

7. *In Rome* (*en Rōmēi*). One late uncial (G of tenth century) and a cursive omit these words here and one or two other late MSS. omit *en Rōmēi* in verse 15. This possibly proves the Epistle was circulated as a circular to a limited extent, but the evidence is late and slight and by no means shows that this was the case in the first century. It is not comparable with the absence of *en Ephesōi* in Eph. 1:1 from Aleph and B (the two oldest and best MSS.). *Beloved of God* (*agapētois theou*). Ablative case of *theou* after the verbal adjective like *didaktoi theou* (taught of God) in John 6:45 (Robertson, *Grammar*, p. 516). *From God our Father and*

the Lord Jesus Christ (apo theou patros hēmōn kai kuriou Iēsou Christou). "St. Paul, if not formally enunciating a doctrine of the Divinity of Christ, held a view which cannot really be distinguished from it" (Sanday and Headlam). Paul's theology is clearly seen in the terms used in verses 1 to 7.

8. *First (prōton men).* Adverb in the accusative case, but no *epeita de* (in the next place) as in Heb. 7:2 or *epeita* as in James 3:17 follows. The rush of thoughts crowds out the balanced phraseology as in Rom. 3:2; I Cor. 11:18. *Through (dia).* As the mediator or medium of thanksgiving as in 7:25. *For (peri).* Concerning, about. *That (hoti).* Or because. Either declarative or causal *hoti* makes sense here. *Your faith (hē pistis humōn).* "Your Christianity" (Sanday and Headlam). *Is proclaimed (kataggelletai).* Present passive indicative of *kataggellō*, to announce *(aggellō)* up and down *(kata).* See also *anaggellō*, to bring back news (John 5:15), *apaggellō*, to announce from one as the source (Matt. 2:8), *prokataggellō*, to announce far and wide beforehand (Acts 3:18). *Throughout all the world (en holōi tōi kosmōi).* Natural hyperbole as in Col. 1:6; Acts 17:6. But widely known because the church was in the central city of the empire.

9. *I serve (latreuō).* Old verb from *latron*, hire, and *latris*, hireling, so to serve for hire, then to serve in general gods or men, whether sacred services (Heb. 9:9; 10:2) or spiritual service as here. Cf. Rom. 12:1; Phil. 3:3. *Unceasingly (adialeiptōs).* Late adverb for which see I Thess. 1:2f.; 2:13; 5:17, only other N.T. examples. *Always (pantote).* One might think that Paul prayed for no others, but he uses both adverbs in I Thess. 1:2. He seems to have had prayer lists. He never omitted the Romans.

10. *If by any means now at length (ei pōs ēdē pote).* A condition of the first class in the form of an indirect question (aim) or elliptical condition like Acts 27:12 (Robertson, *Grammar*, p. 1024). Note the four particles together to express Paul's feelings of emotion that now at length somehow it may really come true. *I may be prospered (euodōthēsomai).* First future passive indicative of *euodoō* for which verb see on I Cor. 16:2. *By the will of God (en tōi thelēmati tou theou).* Paul's way lay "in" God's will.

11. *Impart (metadō).* Second aorist active subjunctive of *metadidōmi*, to share with one. See on Luke 3:11; I Thess.

2:8. *To the end ye may be established* (*eis to stērichthēnai humas*). Final clause (common in Paul) with *eis to* and the first aorist passive infinitive of *stērizō* for which verb see on Luke 22:32; I Thess. 3:3, 13.

12. *That is* (*touto de estin*). "An explanatory correction" (Denney). The *de* should not be ignored. Instead of saying that he had a spiritual gift for them, he wishes to add that they also have one for him. *That I with you may be comforted* (*sunparaklēthēnai en humin*). "My being comforted in you (*en humin*) together. (*sun-*) with you," a mutual blessing to each party (you and me).

13. *Oftentimes I purposed* (*pollakis proethemēn*). Second aorist middle of *protithēmi*, old verb to place, to propose to oneself, in N.T. only here, 3:25; Eph. 1:9. See Acts 19:21 for this purpose. *And was hindered* (*kai ekōluthēn*). "But was hindered," adversative use of *kai*. *That I might have some fruit* (*hina tina karpon schō*). Second aorist (ingressive), active of *echō*, to have, and here means "might get (ingressive aorist) some fruit."

14. On *debtor* (*opheiletēs*) see Gal. 5:3. *Both to Greeks and to Barbarians* (*Hellēsin te kai barbarois*). The whole human race from the Greek point of view, Jews coming under *barbarois*. On this word see Acts 18:2, 4; I Cor. 4:11; Col. 3:11 (only N.T. instances). The Greeks called all others barbarians and the Jews termed all others Gentiles. Did Paul consider the Romans as Greeks? They had absorbed the Greek language and culture.

15. *So as much as in me is I am ready* (*houtō to kat' eme prothumon*). Literally, "Thus the according to me affair is ready" (*prothumos*, old adjective, *pro*, *thumos*). It is an awkward idiom like *to ex humōn* in 12:18. The plural *ta kat' eme* we find in Phil. 1:12; Col. 4:7; Eph. 6:21.

16. *It is the power of God* (*dunamis theou estin*). This Paul knew by much experience. He had seen the dynamite of God at work. *To the Jew first, and also to the Greek* (*Ioudaiōi te prōton kai Hellēni*). Jesus had taught this (John 4:22; 10:16; Luke 24:47; Acts 1:8). The Jew is first in privilege and in penalty (Rom. 2:9f.). It is not certain that *prōton* is genuine, but it is in 2:9f.

17. *For therein* (*gar en autōi*). In the gospel (verse 16) of which Paul is not ashamed. *A righteousness of God* (*dikaio-*

sunē theou). Subjective genitive, "a God kind of righteousness," one that each must have and can obtain in no other way save "from faith unto faith" (*ek pisteōs eis pistin*), faith the starting point and faith the goal (Lightfoot). *Is revealed* (*apokaluptetai*). It is a revelation from God, this God kind of righteousness, that man unaided could never have conceived or still less attained. In these words we have Paul's statement in his own way of the theme of the Epistle, the content of the gospel as Paul understands it. Every word is important: *sōtērian* (salvation), *euaggelion* (gospel), *apokaluptetai* (is revealed), *dikaiosunē theou* (righteousness of God), *pistis* (faith) and *pisteuonti* (believing). He grounds his position on Hab. 2:4 (quoted also in Gal. 3:11). By "righteousness" we shall see that Paul means both "justification" and "sanctification." It is important to get a clear idea of Paul's use of *dikaiosunē* here for it controls the thought throughout the Epistle. Jesus set up a higher standard of righteousness (*dikaiosunē*) in the Sermon on the Mount than the Scribes and Pharisees taught and practised (Matt. 5:20) and proves it in various items. Here Paul claims that in the gospel, taught by Jesus and by himself there is revealed a God kind of righteousness with two ideas in it (the righteousness that God has and that he bestows). It is an old word for quality from *dikaios*, a righteous man, and that from *dikē*, right or justice (called a goddess in Acts 28:4), and that allied with *deiknumi*, to show, to point out. Other allied words are *dikaioō*, to declare or make *dikaios* (Rom. 3:24, 26), *dikaiōma*, that which is deemed *dikaios* (sentence or ordinance as in 1:32; 2:26; 8:4), *dikaiōsis*, the act of declaring *dikaios* (only twice in N.T., 4:25; 5:18). *Dikaiosunē* and *dikaioō* are easy to render into English, though we use justice in distinction from righteousness and sanctification for the result that comes after justification (the setting one right with God). Paul is consistent and usually clear in his use of these great words.

18. *For the wrath of God is revealed* (*apokaluptetai gar orgē theou*). Note in Romans Paul's use of *gar*, now argumentative, now explanatory, now both as here. There is a parallel and antecedent revelation (see verse 17) of God's wrath corresponding to the revelation of God's righteousness, this an unwritten revelation, but plainly made known. *Orgē* is

from *orgaō*, to teem, to swell. It is the temper of God towards sin, not rage, but the wrath of reason and law (Shedd). The revelation of God's righteousness in the gospel was necessary because of the failure of men to attain it without it, for God's wrath justly rested upon all both Gentiles (1:18–32) and Jews (2:1–3:20). *Ungodliness* (*asebeian*). Irreligion, want of reverence toward God, old word (cf. II Tim. 2:16). *Unrighteousness* (*adikian*). Lack (*a* privative and *dikē*) of right conduct toward men, injustice (Rom. 9:14; Luke 18:6). This follows naturally from irreverence. The basis of ethical conduct rests on the nature of God and our attitude toward him, otherwise the law of the jungle (cf. Nietzsche, "might makes right"). *Hold down the truth* (*tēn alētheian katechontōn*). Truth (*alētheia, alēthēs,* from *a* privative and *lēthō* or *lanthanō,* to conceal) is out in the open, but wicked men, so to speak, put it in a box and sit on the lid and "hold it down in unrighteousness." Their evil deeds conceal the open truth of God from men. Cf. II Thess. 2:6f. for this use of *katechō,* to hinder.

19. *Because* (*dioti*). Gives the reason (*dia, hoti* like our "for that") for the revelation of God's wrath. *That which may be known of God* (*to gnōston tou theou*). Verbal adjective from *ginōskō,* either "the known" as elsewhere in N.T. (Acts 1:19; 15:18, etc.) or "the knowable" as usual in ancient Greek, that is "the knowledge" (*hē gnōsis*) of God. See Phil. 3:8. Cf. same use of the verbal *chrēston* in Rom. 2:4, *ametatheton* in Heb. 6:17. *Manifest in them* (*phaneron en autois*). In their hearts and consciences. *God manifested* (*ho theos ephanerōsen*). First aorist active indicative of *phaneroō.* Not mere tautology. See 2:14–16.

20. *The invisible things of him* (*ta aorata autou*). Another verbal adjective (*a* privative and *horaō,* to see), old word, either unseen or invisible as here and elsewhere in N.T. (Col. 1:15f., etc.). The attributes of God's nature defined here as "his everlasting power and divinity" (*hē te aidios autou dunamis kai theiotēs*). *Aidios* is for *aeidios* from *aei* (always), old word, in N.T. only here and Jude 6, common in Philo (*zōē aidios*), elsewhere *aiōnios. Theiotēs* is from *theios* (from *theos*) quality of *theos* and corresponds more to Latin *divinitas* from *divus,* divine. In Col. 2:9 Paul uses *theotēs* (Latin *deitas* from *deus*) *deity,* both old words and nowhere else

in the N.T. *Theotēs* is Divine Personality, *theiotēs*, Divine Nature and properties (Sanday and Headlam). *Since the creation of the world (apo ktiseōs kosmou).* He means by God and unto God as antecedent to and superior to the world (cf. Col. 1:15f. about Christ). *Are clearly seen (kathoratai).* Present passive indicative of *kathoraō* (perfective use of *kata-*), old word, only here in N.T., with direct reference to *aorata. Being perceived (nooumena).* Present passive participle of *noeō*, to use the *nous* (intellect). *That they may be without excuse (eis to einai autous anapologētous).* More likely, "so that they are without excuse." The use of *eis to* and the infinitive (with accusative of general reference) for result like *hōste* is reasonably clear in the N.T. (Moulton, *Prolegomena*, p. 219; Robertson, *Grammar*, p. 1003). *Anapologētous* is another verbal with *an* from *apologeomai.* Old word, in N.T. only here and Rom. 2:1 ("inexcusable" here).

21. *Because that (dioti).* As in verse 19. *Knowing God (gnontes ton theon).* Second aorist active participle of *ginōskō*, to know by personal experience. Definite statement that originally men had some knowledge of God. No people, however degraded, have yet been found without some yearning after a god, a seeking to find the true God and get back to him as Paul said in Athens (Acts 17:27). *Glorified not as God (ouch hōs theon edoxasan).* They knew more than they did. This is the reason for the condemnation of the heathen (2:12–16), the failure to do what they know. *Their senseless heart (hē asunetos autōn kardia). Kardia* is the most comprehensive term for all our faculties whether feeling (Rom. 9:2), will (I Cor. 4:5), intellect (Rom. 10:6). It may be the home of the Holy Spirit (Rom. 5:5) or of evil desires (1:24). See Mark 7:21f. for list of vices that come "out of the heart." *Asunetos* is a verbal adjective from *suniēmi*, to put together, and *a* privative, unintelligent, not able to put together the manifest evidence about God (verse 20). So darkness settled down on their hearts (*eskotisthē*, first aorist ingressive passive of *skotizō*, to darken).

22. *Professing themselves to be wise (phaskontes einai sophoi). Sophoi* is predicate nominative with *einai* in indirect discourse agreeing with *phaskontes* (old verb, from *phēmi*, to say, rare in N.T.) in case and number according to regular Greek idiom (Robertson, *Grammar*, p. 1038).

Became vain (*emataiōthēsan*). Ingressive first aorist passive indicative of *mataioō* from *mataios* (empty). Empty reasonings as often today. *Became fools* (*emōranthēsan*). Ingressive first aorist passive of *mōrainō*, to be a fool, old word from *mōros*, a fool. An oxymoron or sharp saying, true and one that cuts to the bone. *For the likeness of an image* (*en homoiōmati eikonos*). Both words, "a likeness which consists in an image or copy" (Lightfoot). See Phil. 2:7 for "likeness of men" and Col. 1:15 for "image of God." Paul shows indignant contempt for these grotesque efforts to present pictures of a deity that had been lost (Denney). Why is it that heathen images of gods in the form of men and beasts are so horrible to look upon?

24. *Wherefore* (*dio*). Paul's inexorable logic. See it also in verse 26 with the same verb and in verse 28 *kai* like "and so." *God gave them up* (*paredōken autous ho theos*). First aorist active indicative of *paradidōmi*, old and common verb to hand over (beside, *para*) to one's power as in Matt. 4:12. These people had already wilfully deserted God who merely left them to their own self-determination and self-destruction, part of the price of man's moral freedom. Paul refers to this stage and state of man in Acts 17:30 by "overlooked" (*huperidōn*). The withdrawal of God's restraint sent men deeper down. Three times Paul uses *paredōken* here (verses 24, 26, 28), not three stages in the giving over, but a repetition of the same withdrawal. The words sound to us like clods on the coffin as God leaves men to work their own wicked will. *That their bodies should be dishonoured* (*tou atimazesthai ta sōmata autōn*). Contemplated result expressed by *tou* (genitive article) and the passive infinitive *atimazesthai* (from *atimos*, *a* privative and *timos*, dishonoured) with the accusative of general reference. Christians had a new sense of dignity for the body (I Thess. 4:4; I Cor. 6:13). Heathenism left its stamp on the bodies of men and women.

25. *Exchanged* (*metēllaxan*). First aorist active indicative of *metallassō*, old word for exchanging trade, only here and verse 26 in N.T. What a bargain they made, "the truth of God for (*en*) the (*tōi*) lie." "The price of mythology" (Bengel). *Worshipped* (*esebasthēsan*). First aorist passive (used transitively) of *sebazomai*, old verb, used in late Greek

like *sebomai*, to worship. *Rather than the Creator (para ton ktisanta)*. Placed side by side (*para*, the Creator and the creature, *ktisis*) they preferred the creature. *Who is blessed forever. Amen (hos estin eulogētos. Amēn)*. One of Paul's doxologies which may come at any moment when he is greatly stirred, as in 9:5. *Eulogētos* is verbal of *eulogeō*.

26. *Unto vile passions (eis pathē atimias)*. Unto passions of dishonour. *Pathos*, old word from *paschō*, to experience, originally meant any feeling whether good or bad, but in N.T. always in bad sense as here, I Thess. 4:5; Col. 3:5 (only N.T. examples). *That which is against nature (tēn para phusin)*. The degradation of sex is what Paul here notes as one of the results of heathenism (the loss of God in the life of man). They passed by the Creator.

27. *Burned (exekauthēsan)*. First aorist passive indicative, causative aorist, of *ekkaiō*, old verb, to burn out, to set on fire, to inflame with anger or lust. Here only in N.T. *Lust (orexei)*. Only here in N.T. *Unseemliness (aschēmosunēn)*. Old word from *aschēmon* (deformed). In N.T. only here and Rev. 16:15. *Recompense (antimisthian)*. See on II Cor. 6:13 for only other N.T. instance of this late Pauline word, there in good sense, here in bad. *Which was due (hēn edei)*. Imperfect active for obligation still on them coming down from the past. This debt will be paid in full (*apolambanontes*, pay back as in Luke 6:34, and due as in Luke 23:41). Nature will attend to that in their own bodies and souls.

28. *And even as they refused (kai kathōs ouk edokimasan)*. "And even as they rejected" after trial just as *dokimazō* is used of testing coins. They tested God at first and turned aside from him. *Knowledge (epignōsei)*. Full knowledge (*epi* additional, *gnōsis*). They had a dim memory that was a caricature. *Unto a reprobate mind (eis adokimon noun)*. Play on *ouk edokimasan*. They rejected God and God rejected their mental attitude and gave them over (verses 24, 26, 28). See this adjective already in I Cor. 9:27; II Cor. 13:5–7. Like an old abandoned building, the home of bats and snakes, left "to do those things which are not fitting" (*poiein ta mē kathēkonta*), like the night clubs of modern cities, the dives and dens of the underworld, without God and in the darkness of unrestrained animal impulses. This was a technical term with Stoics (II Macc. 6:4).

29. *Being filled with (peplērōmenous).* Perfect passive participle of the common verb *plēroō*, state of completion, "filled to the brim with" four vices in the associative instrumental case *(adikiāi*, unrighteousness as in verse 18, *ponēriāi*, active wickedness as in Mark 7:22, *pleonexiāi*, covetousness as in I Thess. 2:5 and Luke 12:15, *kakiāi*, maliciousness or inward viciousness of disposition as in I Cor. 5:8). Note asyndeton, no connective in the lists in verses 29 to 31. Dramatic effect. The order of these words varies in the MSS. and *porneiāi*, fornication, is not genuine here (absent in Aleph A B C). *Full of (mestous).* Paul changes from participle to adjective. Old adjective, rare in the N.T., like *mestoō*, to fill full (only in Acts 2:13 in N.T.), stuffed full of (with genitive). Five substantives in the genitive *(phthonou*, envy, as in Gal. 5:21, *phonou*, murder, and so a paronomasia or combination with *phthonou*, of like sounding words, *eridos*, strife, as in II Cor. 12:16, *kakoēthias*, malignity, and here only in N.T. though old word from *kakoēthēs* and that from *kakos* and *ēthos*, a tendency to put a bad construction on things, depravity of heart and malicious disposition.

30. Paul changes the construction again to twelve substantives and adjectives that give vivid touches to this composite photograph of the God abandoned soul. *Whisperers (psithuristas).* Old word from *psithurizō*, to speak into the ear, to speak secretly, an onomatopoetic word like *psithurismos* (II Cor. 12:20) and only here in N.T. *Backbiters (katalalous).* Found nowhere else except in Hermas, compound like *katalaleō*, to talk back (James 4:11), and *katalalia*, talking back (II Cor. 12:20), talkers back whether secretly or openly. *Hateful to God (theostugeis).* Old word from *theos* and *stugeō*. All the ancient examples take it in the passive sense and so probably here. So *stugētos* (Titus 3:13). Vulgate has *deo odibiles. Insolent (hubristas).* Old word for agent from *hubrizō*, to give insult to, here alone in N.T. save I Tim. 1:13. *Haughty (huperēphanous).* From *huper* and *phainomai*, to appear above others, arrogant in thought and conduct, "stuck up." *Boastful (alazonas).* From *alē*, wandering. Empty pretenders, swaggerers, braggarts. *Inventors of evil things (epheuretas kakōn).* Inventors of new forms of vice as Nero was. Tacitus *(Ann.* IV. ii) describes Sejanus as

facinorum omnium repertor and Virgil (*Aen.* ii. 163) *scelerum inventor*. Disobedient to parents (*goneusin apeitheis*). Cf. I Tim. 1:9; II Tim. 3:2. An ancient and a modern trait. 31. *Without understanding* (*asunetous*). Same word in verse 21. *Covenant-breakers* (*asunthetos*). Another paronomasia or pun. *A* privative and verbal *sunthetos* from *suntithēmi*, to put together. Old word, common in LXX (Jer. 3:7), men "false to their engagements" (Sanday and Headlam), who treat covenants as "a scrap of paper." *Without natural affection* (*astorgous*). Late word, *a* privative and *storgē*, love of kindred. In N.T. only here and II Tim. 3:3. *Unmerciful* (*aneleēmonas*). From *a* privative and *eleēmōn*, merciful. Late word, only here in N.T. Some MSS. add *aspondous*, implacable, from II Tim. 3:3. It is a terrible picture of the effects of sin on the lives of men and women. The late Dr. R. H. Graves of Canton, China, said that a Chinaman who got hold of this chapter declared that Paul could not have written it, but only a modern missionary who had been to China. It is drawn to the life because Paul knew Pagan Graeco-Roman civilization. 32. *The ordinance of God* (*to dikaiōma tou theou*). The heathen knows that God condemns such evil practices. *But also consent with them* (*alla kai suneudokousin*). Late verb for hearty approval as in Luke 11:48; Acts 8:1; I Cor. 7:12. It is a tragedy of American city government that so many of the officials are proven to be hand in glove with the underworld of law-breakers.

CHAPTER II

1. *Wherefore* (*dio*). See 1:24, 26 for this relative conjunction, "because of which thing." *Without excuse* (*anapologētos*). See on 1:21. *Whosoever thou art that judgest* (*pas ho krinōn*). Literally, "every one that judgest," vocative case in apposition with *anthrōpe*. Paul begins his discussion of the failure of the Jew to attain to the God-kind of righteousness (2:1–3:20) with a general statement applicable to all as he did (1:18) in the discussion of the failure of the Gentiles (Lightfoot). The Gentile is readily condemned by the Jew when he sins and equally so is the Jew condemned by the Gentile in like case. *Krinō* does not of itself mean to condemn, but to pick out, separate, approve, determine, pronounce judgment, condemn (if proper). *Another* (*ton heteron*). Literally, "the other man." The notion of two in the word, one criticizing the other. *Thou condemnest thyself* (*seauton katakrineis*). Note *kata* here with *krinō*, to make plain the adverse judgment. *For* (*gar*). Explanatory reason for the preceding statement. The critic *practises* (*prasseis*, not single acts *poieō*, but the habit *prassō*) the same things that he condemns.

2. *Judgment* (*krima*). Decision rendered whether good or bad. *According to* (*kata* with accusative). As the rule of measure. Cf. John 7:24.

3. *And doest the same* (*kai poiōn auta*). "And doest them occasionally." *That thou shalt escape* (*su ekpheuxēi*). Emphasis on *su*, "thou conceited Jew expecting to escape God's *krima* because thou art a Jew." Cf. Matt. 3:8f. Paul justifies the bitter words of the Baptist to the Pharisees and Sadducees. The future middle of the old verb *ekpheugō* (cf. I Thess. 5:3). The Jew posed as immune to the ordinary laws of ethics because a Jew. Alas, some Christians affect the same immunity.

4. *Or despiseth thou?* (*ē kataphroneis?*). Another alternative, that of scorn of God's kindness (*chrēstotētos*, II Cor. 6:6) and forbearance (*anochēs*, old word, holding back from

334

anechō, only here in N.T.) and longsuffering (*makrothumias*, late word for which see II Cor. 6:4, 6). *Kataphroneō* is old verb to think down on (*kata, phroneō*) as in Matt. 6:24; I Cor. 11:22. This upstart Jew actually thinks down on God. And then "the riches" (*tou ploutou*) of all that comes from God. *Leadeth thee to repentance* (*eis metanoian se agei*). The very kindness (*to chrēston*, the kindly quality) of God is trying to lead (conative present *agei*) thee to a right-about face, a change of mind and attitude (*metanoian*) instead of a complacent self-satisfaction and pride of race and privilege.

5. *After thy hardness* (*kata tēn sklērotēta sou*). "According to thy hardness (old word from *sklēros*, hard, stiff, only here in N.T.) will God's judgment be." *And impenitent heart* (*kai ametanoēton kardian*). See *metanoian* just before. "Thy unreconstructed heart," "with no change in the attitude of thy heart." *Treasurest up for thyself* (*thēsaurizeis seautōi*). See for *thēsaurizō* on Matt. 6:19f.; Luke 12:21; II Cor. 12:14. Dative case *seautōi* (for thyself) with a touch of irony (Vincent). *Wrath* (*orgēn*). For such a Jew as already stated for the Gentile (1:18). There is a revelation (*apokalupseōs*) of God's wrath for both in the day of wrath and righteous judgment (*dikaiokrisias*, a late compound word, in LXX, two examples in the Oxyrhynchus papyri, only here in N.T.). See II Thess. 1:5 for *dikaias kriseōs*. Paul looks to the judgment day as certain (cf. II Cor. 5:10–12), the day of the Lord (II Cor. 1:14).

6. *Who will render* (*hos apodōsei*). Paul quotes Prov. 24:12 as in II Tim. 4:14. See also Matt. 16:27; Rev. 22:12. The rendering will be in accord with the facts.

7. *To them that seek* (*tois men—zētousin*). Dative plural of the articular present active participle of *zēteō* with *men* on the one hand. *Eternal life* (*zōēn aiōnion*). Accusative case object of *apodōsei* above.

8. *But unto them that are factious and obey not the truth but obey unrighteousness* (*tois de ex eritheias kai apeithousin tēi alētheiāi peithomenois de adikiāi*). The other side with *de* and the articular present participles in the dative again, only with *ex eritheias*, there is no participle *ousin*. But the construction changes and the substantives that follow are not the object of *apodōsei* like *zōēn ainōnion* above, but are in the nominative as if with *esontai* (shall be) understood

(anger and wrath, both *orgē* and *thumos*, tribulation and anguish, again a pair *thlipsis kai stenochōria* on which see II Cor. 5:4; 12:10).

9. *Every soul of man* (*pasan psuchēn anthrōpou*). See 13:1 for this use of *psuchē* for the individual. *Of the Jew first and also of the Greek* (*Ioudaiou te prōton kai Hellēnos*). See on 1:16. First not only in penalty as here, but in privilege also as in 2:11 and 1:16.

11. *Respect of persons* (*prosōpolēmpsia*). Milligan (*Vocabulary*) considers this word (in N.T. only here, Col. 3:25; Eph. 6:9) and *prosōpolēmptēs* (Acts 10:34) and *prosōpolēmpteō* (James 2:9) the earliest definitely known Christian words, not in LXX or non-Christian writings. See on Acts 10:34 for the formation in imitation of the Hebrew to take note of the face (*prosōpon, lambanō*), to judge by the face or appearance.

12. *Have sinned* (*hēmarton*). Constative aorist active indicative, "sinned," a timeless aorist. *Without law* (*anomōs*). Old adverb "contrary to law," "unjustly," but here in ignorance of the Mosaic law (or of any law). Nowhere else in N.T. *Shall also perish without law* (*anomōs kai apolountai*). Future middle indicative of *apollumi*, to destroy. This is a very important statement. The heathen who sin are lost, because they do not keep the law which they have, not because they do not have the Mosaic law or Christianity. *Under law* (*en nomōi*). In the sphere of the Mosaic law. *By the law* (*dia nomou*). The Jew has to stand or fall by the Mosaic law.

13. *Not the hearers—but the doers* (*ou gar hoi akroatai—all' hoi poiētai*). The law was read in the synagogue, but there was no actual virtue in listening. The virtue is in doing. See a like contrast by James between "hearers" and "doers" of the gospel (James 1:22–25). *Before God* (*para tōi theōi*). By God's side, as God looks at it. *Shall be justified* (*dikaiōthēsontai*). Future passive indicative of *dikaioō*, to declare righteous, to set right. "Shall be declared righteous." Like James 1:22–25.

14. *That have no law* (*ta mē nomon echonta*). Better, "that have not the law" (the Mosaic law). *By nature* (*phusei*). Instrumental case of *phusis*, old word from *phuō*, to beget. The Gentiles are without the Mosaic law, but not without

some knowledge of God in conscience and when they do right "they are a law to themselves" (*heautois eisin nomos*). This is an obvious reply to the Jewish critic. **15.** *In that they* (*hoitines*). "The very ones who," qualitative relative. *Written in their hearts* (*grapton en tais kardiais autōn*). Verbal adjective of *graphō*, to write. When their conduct corresponds on any point with the Mosaic law they practise the unwritten law in their hearts. *Their conscience bearing witness therewith* (*sunmarturousēs autōn tēs suneidēseōs*). On conscience (*suneidēsis*) see on I Cor. 8:7; 10:25f.; II Cor. 1:12. Genitive absolute here with present active participle *sunmarturousēs* as in 9:1. The word *suneidēsis* means co-knowledge by the side of the original consciousness of the act. This second knowledge is personified as confronting the first (Sanday and Headlam). The Stoics used the word a great deal and Paul has it twenty times. It is not in the O.T., but first in this sense in Wisdom 17:10. All men have this faculty of passing judgment on their actions. It can be over-scrupulous (I Cor. 10:25) or "seared" by abuse (I Tim. 4:12). It acts according to the light it has. *Their thoughts one with another accusing or also excusing them* (*metaxu allēlōn tōn logismōn katēgorountōn ē kai apologoumenōn*). Genitive absolute again showing the alternative action of the conscience, now accusing, now excusing. Paul does not say that a heathen's conscience always commends everything that he thinks, says, or does. In order for one to be set right with God by his own life he must always act in accord with his conscience and never have its disapproval. That, of course, is impossible else Christ died for naught (Gal. 2:21). Jesus alone lived a sinless life. For one to be saved without Christ he must also live a sinless life. **16.** *According to my gospel* (*kata to euaggelion mou*). What Paul preaches (I Cor. 15:1) and which is the true gospel (Gal. 1:6–9). **17.** *Bearest the name* (*eponomazēi*). Present passive indicative in condition of first class of *eponomazō*, old word, to put a name upon (*epi*), only here in N.T. "Thou art surnamed Jew" (Lightfoot). Jew as opposed to Greek denoted nationality while Hebrew accented the idea of language. *Restest upon the law* (*epanapauēi nomōi*). Late and rare double compound, in LXX and once in the Didache.

In N.T. only here and Luke 10:6 which see. It means to lean upon, to refresh oneself back upon anything, here with locative case (*nomōi*). It is the picture of blind and mechanical reliance on the Mosaic law. *Gloriest in God* (*kauchāsai en theōi*). Koiné vernacular form for *kauchāi* (*kauchaesai, kauchāsai*) of *kauchaomai* as in verse 23; I Cor. 4:7 and *katakauchāsai* in Rom. 11:18. The Jew gloried in God as a national asset and private prerogative (II Cor. 10:15; Gal. 6:13). *Approvest the things that are excellent* (*dokimazeis ta diapheronta*). Originally, "Thou testest the things that differ," and then as a result comes the approval for the excellent things. As in Phil. 1:10 it is difficult to tell which stage of the process Paul has in mind. *Instructed out of the law* (*katēchoumenos ek tou nomou*). Present passive participle of *katēcheō*, a rare verb to instruct, though occurring in the papyri for legal instruction. See on Luke 1:4; I Cor. 14:19. The Jew's "ethical discernment was the fruit of catechetical and synagogical instruction in the Old Testament" (Shedd).

19. *A guide of the blind* (*hodēgon tuphlōn*). Accusative *hodēgon* in predicate with *einai* to agree with *seauton*, accusative of general reference with infinitive *einai* in indirect discourse after *pepoithas*. Late word (Polybius, Plutarch) from *hodos*, way, and *hēgeomai*, to lead, one who leads the way. *Tuphlōn* is objective genitive plural. The Jews were meant by God to be guides for the Gentiles, for salvation is of the Jews (John 4:22). *A light* (*phōs*). "A light for those in darkness" (*tōn en skotei*, objective genitive again). But this intention of God about the Jews had resulted in conceited arrogance on their part.

20. *A corrector of the foolish* (*paideutēn aphronōn*). Old word (from *paideuō*) for instructor, in Plato, and probably so here, though corrector or chastiser in Heb. 12:9 (the only N.T. instances). See Luke 23:16. Late inscriptions give it as instructor (Preisigke). *Aphronōn* is a hard word for Gentiles, but it is the Jewish standpoint that Paul gives. Each termed the other "dogs." *Of babes* (*nēpiōn*). Novitiates or proselytes to Judaism just as in Gal. 4:1 Paul used it of those not of legal age. *The form* (*tēn morphōsin*). Rare word only in Theophrastus and Paul (here and II Tim. 3:5). Pallis regards it as a Stoical term for education. Lightfoot considers the *morphōsis* as "the rough-sketch, the pencilling of

THE EPISTLES OF PAUL 339

the *morphē*," the outline or framework, and in II Tim. 3:5
"the outline without the substance." This is Paul's picture
of the Jew as he sees himself drawn with consummate skill
and subtle irony.

21. *Thou therefore that teachest another* (*ho oun didaskōn
heteron*). Paul suddenly breaks off (anacoluthon) the long
sentence that began in verse 17 and starts over again with
a phrase that gathers it all up in small compass (*teachest*)
and drives it home (*therefore*) on the Jew (*thyself*). *Not to
steal* (*mē kleptein*). Infinitive with *mē* in indirect command
(indirect discourse) after *kerussōn*. *Dost thou steal?* (*klep-
teis?*). The preaching (*kerussōn*) was fine, but the practice?
A home-thrust. *Should not commit adultery* (*mē moicheuein*).
Infinitive in direct command again after *legōn*. "The Talmud
charges the crime of adultery upon the three most illustrious
Rabbins" (Vincent).

22. *That abhorrest* (*ho bdelussomenos*). Old word to make
foul, to stink, to have abhorrence for. In LXX, in N.T. only
here and Rev. 21:8. The very word used by Jesus to express
their horror of idols (*eidōla*, see on Acts 7:41; I Cor. 12:2).
See Matt. 24:15 for "abomination." *Dost thou rob temples?*
(*hierosuleis?*). Old verb from *hierosulos* (Acts 19:37) and
that from *hieron*, temple, and *sulaō*, to rob. The town clerk
(Acts 19:37) said that these Jews (Paul and his companions)
were "not robbers of temples," proof that the charge was
sometimes made against Jews, though expressly forbidden
the Jews (Josephus, *Ant.* IV. 8, 10). Paul refers to the crime
of robbing idol temples in spite of the defilement of contact
with idolatry.

23. *Through thy transgression of the law* (*dia tēs parabaseōs
tou nomou*). Old word for stepping across a line. Trench
calls attention to "the mournfully numerous group of words"
for the varieties of sin like *agnoēma*, ignorance, *anomia*,
violation of law, *hamartia*, missing the mark, *hettēma*, falling
short, *parabasis*, passing over the line, *parakoē*, disobedience
to a voice, *paranomia*, putting the law aside, *paraptōma*,
falling down, *plēmmeleia*, discord.

24. *Because of you* (*di' humas*). Free quotation from the
LXX of Isa. 52:5. The Jews were jealous for the Name of
God and would not pronounce the Tetragrammaton and yet
acted so that the Gentiles blasphemed that Name.

25. *If thou be a doer of the law* (*ean nomon prassēis*). Condition of third class and the present (continued action) subjunctive of *prassō*, a verb meaning to do as a habit. *Is become uncircumcision* (*akrobustia gegonen*). The Jew is then like the Gentile, with no privilege at all. Circumcision was simply the seal of the covenant relation of Israel with God.

26. *Keep* (*phulassēi*). Present subjunctive with *ean*, condition of third class, mere supposition like that in verse 25, "keep on keeping" perfectly, Paul means. *For* (*eis*). As often in N.T.

27. *If it fulfil the law* (*ton nomon telousa*). Present active participle (conditional use of the participle) of *teleō*, to finish, continually fulfilling to the end (as would be necessary). *Judge thee* (*krinei—se*). Unusual position of *se* (thee) so far from the verb *krinei*. *With the letter and circumcision* (*dia grammatos kai peritomēs*). *Dia* means here accompanied by, with the advantage of.

28. *Which is one outwardly* (*ho en tōi phanerōi*). *Ioudaios* (Jew) has to be repeated (ellipse) with the article, "the in the open Jew" (circumcision, phylacteries, tithes, etc.). Likewise repeat *peritomē* (circumcision).

29. *Who is one inwardly* (*ho en tōi kruptōi*). Repeat *Ioudaios* (Jew) here also, "the in the inward part Jew" (circumcision of the heart *peritomē kardias* and not a mere surgical operation as in Col. 2:11, in the spirit *en pneumati*, with which compare II Cor. 3:3, 6). This inward or inside Jew who lives up to his covenant relation with God is the high standard that Paul puts before the merely professional Jew described above. *Whose praise* (*hou ho epainos*). The antecedent of the relative *hou* is *Ioudaios* (Jew). Probably (Gifford) a reference to the etymology of Judah (praise) as seen in Gal. 49:8.

CHAPTER III

1. *What advantage then hath the Jew?* (*ti oun to perisson tou Ioudaiou?*). Literally, "What then is the overplus of the Jew?" What does the Jew have over and above the Gentile? It is a pertinent question after the stinging indictment of the Jew in chapter 2. *The profit* (*hē ōphelia*). The help. Old word, only here in N.T. See Mark 8:36 for *ōphelei*, the verb to profit.

2. *Much every way* (*polu kata panta*). *Polu* points back to *to perisson*. So it means the overplus of the Jew is much from every angle. *First of all* (*prōton men*). As in 1:8 and I Cor. 11:18 Paul does not add to his "first." He singles out one privilege of the many possessed by the Jew. *They were intrusted with* (*episteuthēsan*). First aorist passive indicative of *pisteuō*, to intrust, with accusative of the thing and dative of the person in the active. In the passive as here the accusative of the thing is retained as in I Thess. 2:4. *The oracles of God* (*ta logia tou theou*). In the accusative case, therefore, the object of *episteuthēsan*. *Logion* is probably a diminutive of *logos*, word, though the adjective *logios* also occurs (Acts 18:24). The word was early used for "oracles" from Delphi and is common in the LXX for the oracles of the Lord. But from Philo on it was used of any sacred writing including narrative. It occurs four times in the N.T. (Acts 7:38, which see; Rom. 3:2; Heb. 5:12; I Peter 4:11). It is possible that here and in Acts 7:38 the idea may include all the Old Testament, though the commands and promises of God may be all.

3. *For what if?* (*ti gar ei?*). But Westcott and Hort print it, *Ti gar? ei*. See Phil. 1:18 for this exclamatory use of *ti gar* (for how? How stands the case?). *Some were without faith* (*ēpistēsan*). First aorist active indicative of *apisteō*, old verb, to disbelieve. This is the common N.T. meaning (Luke 24:11, 41; Acts 28:24; Rom. 4:20). Some of them "disbelieved," these "depositaries and guardians of revelation" (Denney). But the word also means to be unfaithful to one's

341

trust and Lightfoot argues for that idea here and in II Tim. 2:13. The Revised Version renders it "faithless" there. Either makes sense here and both ideas are true of some of the Jews, especially concerning the Messianic promises and Jesus. *The faithfulness of God* (*tēn pistin tou theou*). Undoubtedly *pistis* has this sense here and not "faith." God has been faithful (II Tim. 2:13) whether the Jews (some of them) were simply disbelievers or untrue to their trust. Paul can use the words in two senses in verse 3, but there is no real objection to taking *epistēsan, apistian, pistin,* all to refer to faithfulness rather than just faith.

4. *Let God be found true* (*ginesthō ho theos alēthēs*). "Let God continue to be true" (present middle imperative). *But every man a liar* (*pās de anthrōpos pseustēs*). The contrast in *de* really means, "though every man be found a liar." Cf. Psa. 116:12. *As it is written* (*kathōs gegraptai*). Psa. 51:6. *That thou mightest be justified* (*hopōs an dikaiōtheis*). *Hopōs* rather than the common *hina* for purpose and *an* with the first aorist passive subjunctve of *dikaioō*. Used of God this verb here has to mean "declared righteous," not "made righteous." *Mightest prevail* (*nikēseis*). Future active indicative with *hopōs* of *nikaō,* to win a victory, though B L have *nikēsēis* (first aorist active subjunctive, the usual construction). *When thou comest into judgement* (*en tōi krinesthai se*). "In the being judged as to thee" (present passive infinitive or, if taken as middle, "in the entering upon trial as to thee"). Common construction in the LXX from the Hebrew infinitive construct.

5. *What shall we say?* (*ti eroumen?*). Rhetorical question, common with Paul as he surveys the argument. *Commendeth* (*sunistēsin*). This common verb *sunistēmi,* to send together, occurs in the N.T. in two senses, either to introduce, to commend (II Cor. 3:1; 4:2) or to prove, to establish (II Cor. 7:11; Gal. 2:18; Rom. 5:8). Either makes good sense here. *Who visiteth the wrath* (*ho epipherōn tēn orgēn*). "Who brings on the wrath," "the inflicter of the anger" (Vaughan). *I speak as a man* (*kata anthrōpon*). See Gal. 3:15 for same phrase. As if to say, "pardon me for this line of argument." Tholuck says that the rabbis often used *kata anthrōpon* and *ti eroumen.* Paul had not forgotten his rabbinical training.

6. *For then how* (*epei pōs*). There is a suppressed condition

between *epei* and *pōs*, an idiom occurring several times in the N.T. (I Cor. 15:29; Rom. 11:6, 22). "Since, if that were true, how."

7. *Through my lie* (*en tōi emōi pseusmati*). Old word from *pseudomai*, to lie, only here in N.T. Paul returns to the imaginary objection in verse 5. The MSS. differ sharply here between *ei de* (but if) and *ei gar* (for if). Paul "uses the first person from motives of delicacy" (Sanday and Headlam) in this supposable case for argument's sake as in I Cor. 4:6. So here he "transfers by a fiction" (Field) to himself the objection.

8. *And why not* (*kai mē*). We have a tangled sentence which can be cleared up in two ways. One is (Lightfoot) to supply *genētai* after *mē* and repeat *ti* (*kai ti mē genētai*, deliberative subjunctive in a question): And why should it not happen? The other way (Sanday and Headlam) is to take *mē* with *poiēsōmen* and make a long parenthesis of all in between. Even so it is confusing because *hoti* also (recitative *hoti*) comes just before *poiēsōmen*. The parenthesis is necessary anyhow, for there are two lines of thought, one the excuse brought forward by the unbeliever, the other the accusation that Paul affirms that very excuse that we may do evil that good may come. Note the double indirect assertion (the accusative and the infinitive *hēmās legein* after *phasin* and then the direct quotation with recitative *hoti* after *legein*, a direct quotation dependent on the infinitive in indirect quotation. *Let us do evil that good may come* (*poiēsōmen ta kaka hina elthēi ta agatha*). The volitive aorist subjunctive (*poiēsōmen*) and the clause of purpose (*hina* and the aorist subjunctive *elthēi*). It sounds almost uncanny to find this maxim of the Jesuits attributed to Paul in the first century by Jews. It was undoubtedly the accusation of Antinomianism because Paul preached justification by faith and not by works.

9. *What then?* (*ti oun?*). Paul's frequent query, to be taken with verses 1 and 2. *Are we in worse case than they?* (*proechometha?*). The American Revisers render it: "Are we in better case than they?" There is still no fresh light on this difficult and common word though it occurs alóne in the N.T. In the active it means to have before, to excel. But here it is either middle or passive. Thayer takes it to be

middle and to mean to excel to one's advantage and argues that the context demands this. But no example of the middle in this sense has been found. If it is taken as passive, Lightfoot takes it to mean, "Are we excelled" and finds that sense in Plutarch. Vaughan takes it as passive but meaning, "Are we preferred?" This suits the context, but no other example has been found. So the point remains unsettled. The papyri throw no light on it. *No, in no wise* (*ou pantōs*). "Not at all." See I Cor. 5:10. *We before laid to the charge* (*proeitiasametha*). First aorist middle indicative of *proaitiaomai*, to make a prior accusation, a word not yet found anywhere else. Paul refers to 1:18-32 for the Greeks and 2:1-29 for the Jews. The infinitive *einai* with the accusative *pantas* is in indirect discourse. *Under sin* (*hupo hamartian*). See Gal. 3:22 and Rom. 7:14.

10. *As it is written* (*kathōs gegraptai hoti*). Usual formula of quotation as in verse 4 with recitative *hoti* added as in verse 8. Paul here uses a catena or chain of quotations to prove his point in verse 9 that Jews are in no better fix than the Greeks for all are under sin. Dr. J. Rendel Harris has shown that the Jews and early Christians had *Testimonia* (quotations from the Old Testament) strung together for certain purposes as proof-texts. Paul may have used one of them or he may have put these passages together himself. Verses 10 to 12 come from Psa. 14:1-3; first half of 13 as far as *edoliousan* from Psa. 4:9, the second half from Psa. 140:3; verse 14 from Psa. 10:7; 15 to 17 from an abridgment of Isa. 59:7f.; verse 18 from Psa. 35:1. Paul has given compounded quotations elsewhere (II Cor. 6:16; Rom. 9:25f., 27f; 11:26f., 34f.; 12:19f.). Curiously enough this compounded quotation was imported bodily into the text (LXX) of Psa. 14 after verse 4 in Aleph B, etc. *There is none righteous, no, not one* (*ouk estin dikaios oude heis*). "There is not a righteous man, not even one." This sentence is like a motto for all the rest, a summary for what follows.

11. *That understandeth* (*suniōn*). Present active participle of *suniō*, late omega form of -mi verb *suniēmi*, to send together, to grasp, to comprehend. Some MSS. have the article *ho* before it as before *ekzētōn* (seeking out).

12. *They are together become unprofitable* (*hama ēchreōthēsan*). First aorist passive indicative of *achreoō*. Late word

in Polybius and Cilician inscription of first century A.D. Some MSS. read *ēchreiōthēsan* from *achreios*, useless (*a* privative and *chreios*, useful) as in Luke 17:10 and Matt. 25:30, but Westcott and Hort print as above from the rarer spelling *achreos*. Only here in N.T. The Hebrew word means to go bad, become sour like milk (Lightfoot). *No, not so much as one* (*ouk estin heōs henos*). "There is not up to one."

13. *Throat* (*larugx*). Old word, larynx. *Open sepulchre* (*taphos aneōigmenos*). Perfect passive participle of *anoigō*, "an opened grave." Their mouth (words) like the odour of a newly opened grave. "Some portions of Greek and Roman literature stink like a newly opened grave" (Shedd). *They have used deceit* (*edoliousan*). Imperfect (not perfect or aorist as the English implies) active of *dolioō*, only in LXX and here in the N.T. from the common adjective *dolios*, deceitful (II Cor. 11:13). The regular form would be *edolioun*. The *-osan* ending for third plural in imperfect and aorist was once thought to be purely Alexandrian because so common in the LXX, but it is common in the Boeotian and Aeolic dialects and occurs in *eichosan* in the N.T. (John 15:22, 24). "They smoothed their tongues" in the Hebrew. *Poison* (*ios*). Old word both for rust (James 5:3) and poison (James 3:8). *Of asps* (*aspidōn*). Common word for round bowl, shield, then the Egyptian cobra (a deadly serpent). Often in LXX. Only here in the N.T. The poison of the asp lies in a bag under the lips (*cheilē*), often in LXX, only here in N.T. Genitive case after *gemei* (is full).

15. *To shed* (*ekcheai*). First aorist active infinitive of *ekcheō*, to pour out, old verb with aorist active *exechea*.

16. *Destruction* (*suntrimma*). Rare word from *suntribō*, to rub together, to crush. In Lev. 21:19 for fracture and so in papyri. Only here in N.T. *Misery* (*talaipōria*). Common word from *talaipōros* (Rom. 7:24), only here in the N.T.

17. *The way of peace* (*hodon eirēnēs*). Wherever they go they leave a trail of woe and destruction (Denney).

18. *Before* (*apenanti*). Late double compound (*apo, en, anti*) adverbial preposition in LXX and Polybius, papyri and inscriptions. With genitive as here.

19. *That every mouth may be stopped* (*hina pān stoma phragēi*). Purpose clause with *hina* and second aorist passive subjunctive of *phrassō*, old verb to fence in, to block up.

See II Cor. 11:10. Stopping mouths is a difficult business.
See Titus 1:11 where Paul uses *epistomizein* (to stop up the
mouth) for the same idea. Paul seems here to be speaking
directly to Jews (*tois en tōi nomōi*), the hardest to convince.
With the previous proof on that point he covers the whole
ground for he made the case against the Gentiles in 1:18–32.
May be brought under the judgement of God (*hupodikos genētai
tōi theōi*). "That all the world (Jew as well as Gentile) may
become (*genētai*) answerable (*hupodikos*, old forensic word,
here only in N.T.) to God (dative case *tōi theōi*)." Every
one is "liable to God," in God's court.

20. *Because* (*dioti*, again, *dia*, *hoti*). *By the works of the
law* (*ex ergōn nomou*). "Out of works of law." Mosaic law
and any law as the source of being set right with God. Paul
quotes Psa. 43:2 as he did in Gal. 2:16 to prove his point.
The knowledge of sin (*epignōsis hamartias*). The effect of law
universally is rebellion to it (I Cor. 15:56). Paul has shown
this carefully in Gal. 3:19–22. Cf. Heb. 10:3. He has now
proven the guilt of both Gentile and Jew.

21. *But now apart from the law* (*nuni de chōris nomou*). He
now (*nuni* emphatic logical transition) proceeds carefully
in verses 21 to 31 the *nature* of the God-kind of righteousness which stands manifested (*dikaiosunē theou pephan-
erōtai*, perfect passive indicative of *phaneroō*, to make manifest), the *necessity* of which he has shown in 1:18 to 3:20.
This God kind of righteousness is "apart from law" of any
kind and all of grace (*chariti*) as he will show in verse 24.
But it is not a new discovery on the part of Paul, but "witnessed by the law and the prophets" (*marturoumenē*, present
passive participle, *hupo tou nomou kai tōn prophētōn*), made
plain continuously by God himself.

22. *Even* (*de*). Not adversative here. It defines here.
Through faith in Jesus Christ (*dia pisteōs* [*Iēsou*] *Christou*).
Intermediate agency (*dia*) is faith and objective genitive,
"in Jesus Christ," not subjective "of Jesus Christ," in spite
of Haussleiter's contention for that idea. The objective
nature of faith in Christ is shown in Gal. 2:16 by the addition
eis Christon Iēsoun episteusamen (we believed in Christ), by
tēs eis Christon pisteōs humōn (of your faith in Christ) in
Col. 2:5, by *en pistei tēi en Christōi Iēsou* (in faith that in
Christ Jesus) in I Tim. 3:13, as well as here by the added

THE EPISTLES OF PAUL

words "unto all them that believe" (*eis pantas tous pisteuontas*) in Jesus, Paul means. *Distinction* (*diastolē*). See on I Cor. 14:7 for the difference of sounds in musical instruments. Also in Rom. 10:12. The Jew was first in privilege as in penalty (2:9f.), but justification or setting right with God is offered to both on the same terms.

23. *Sinned* (*hērmarton*). Constative second aorist active indicative of *hamartanō* as in 5:12. This tense gathers up the whole race into one statement (a timeless aorist). *And fall short* (*kai husterountai*). Present middle indicative of *hustereō*, to be *husteros* (comparative) too late, continued action, still fall short. It is followed by the ablative case as here, the case of separation.

24. *Being justified* (*dikaioumenoi*). Present passive participle of *dikaioō*, to set right, repeated action in each case, each being set right. *Freely* (*dōrean*). As in Gal. 2:21. *By his grace* (*tēi autou chariti*). Instrumental case of this wonderful word *charis* which so richly expresses Paul's idea of salvation as God's free gift. *Through the redemption* (*dia tēs apolutrōseōs*). A releasing by ransom (*apo, lutrōsis* from *lutroō* and that from *lutron*, ransom). God did not set men right out of hand with nothing done about men's sins. We have the words of Jesus that he came to give his life a ransom (*lutron*) for many (Mark 10:45 = Matt. 20:28). *Lutron* is common in the papyri as the purchase-money in freeing slaves (Deissmann, *Light from the Ancient East*, pp. 327f.). *That is in Christ Jesus* (*tēi en Christōi Iēsou*). There can be no mistake about this redemption. It is like John 3:16.

25. *Set forth* (*proetheto*). Second aorist middle indicative. See on 1:13 for this word. Also in Eph. 1:9, but nowhere else in N.T. God set before himself (purposed) and did it publicly before (*pro*) the whole world. *A propitiation* (*hilastērion*). The only other N.T. example of this word is in Heb. 9:5 where we have the "cherubim overshadowing the mercy seat" (*to hilastērion*). In Hebrews the adjective is used as a substantive or as "the propitiatory place." But that idea does not suit here. Deissmann (*Bible Studies*, pp. 124-35) has produced examples from inscriptions where it is used as an adjective and as meaning "a votive offering" or "propitiatory gift." Hence he concludes about Rom. 3:25: "The crucified Christ is the votive gift of the Divine

Love for the salvation of men." God gave his Son as the means of propitiation (I John 2:2). *Hilastērion* is an adjective (*hilastērios*) from *hilaskomai*, to make propitiation (Heb. 2:17) and is kin in meaning to *hilasmos*, propitiation (I John 2:2; 4:10). There is no longer room for doubting its meaning in Rom. 3:25. *Through faith, by his blood* (*dia pisteōs en tōi autou haimati*). So probably, connecting *en toi haimati* (in his blood) with *proetheto*. *To show his righteousness* (*eis endeixin tēs dikaiosunēs autou*). See II Cor. 8:24. "For showing of his righteousness," the God-kind of righteousness. God could not let sin go as if a mere slip. God demanded the atonement and provided it. *Because of the passing over* (*dia tēn paresin*). Late word from *pariēmi*, to let go, to relax. In Dionysius Hal., Xenophon, papyri (Deissmann, *Bible Studies*, p. 266) for remission of punishment, especially for debt, as distinct from *aphesis* (remission). *Done aforetime* (*progegonotōn*). Second perfect active genitive participle of *proginomai*. The sins before the coming of Christ (Acts 14:16; 17:30; Heb. 9:15). *Forbearance* (*anochēi*). Holding back of God as in 2:4. In this sense Christ tasted death for every man (Heb. 2:9).

26. *For the shewing* (*pros tēn endeixin*). Repeats point of *eis endeixin* of 25 with *pros* instead of *eis*. *At this present season* (*en tōi nun kairōi*). "In the now crisis," in contrast with "done aforetime." *That he might himself be* (*eis to einai auton*). Purpose with *eis to* and the infinitive *einai* and the accusative of general reference. *Just and the justifier of* (*dikaion kai dikaiounta*). "This is the key phrase which establishes the connexion between the *dikaiosunē theou* and the *dikaiosunē ek pisteōs*" (Sanday and Headlam). Nowhere has Paul put the problem of God more acutely or profoundly. To pronounce the unrighteous righteous is unjust by itself (Rom. 4:5). God's mercy would not allow him to leave man to his fate. God's justice demanded some punishment for sin. The only possible way to save some was the propitiatory offering of Christ and the call for faith on man's part.

27. *It is excluded* (*exekleisthē*). First aorist (effective) passive indicative. "It is completely shut out." Glorying is on man's part. *Nay; but by a law of faith* (*ouchi, alla dia nomou pisteōs*). Strong negative, and note "law of faith," by the principle of faith in harmony with God's love and grace.

28. *We reckon therefore* (*logizometha oun*). Present middle indicative. Westcott and Hort read *gar* instead of *oun*. "My fixed opinion" is. The accusative and infinitive construction occurs after *logizometha* here. On this verb *logizomai*, see 2:3; 4:3f.; 8:18; 14:14. Paul restates verses 21f.

29. *Of Gentiles also* (*kai ethnōn*). Jews overlooked it then and some Christians do now.

30. *If so be that God is one* (*eiper heis ho theos*). Correct text rather than *epeiper*. It means "if on the whole." "By a species of rhetorical politeness it is used of that about which there is no doubt" (Thayer. Cf. I Cor. 8:5; 15:15; Rom. 8:9. *By faith* (*ek pisteōs*). "Out of faith," springing out of. *Through faith* (*dia tēs pisteōs*). "By means of the faith" (just mentioned). *Ek* denotes source, *dia* intermediate agency or attendant circumstance.

31. *Nay, we establish the law* (*alla nomon histanomen*). Present indicative active of late verb *histanō* from *histēmi*. This Paul hinted at in verse 21. Now he will show in chapter 4 how Abraham himself is an example of faith and in his life illustrates the very point just made. Besides, apart from Christ and the help of the Holy Spirit no one can keep God's law. The Mosaic law is only workable by faith in Christ.

CHAPTER IV

1. *What then shall we say?* (*ti oun eroumen?*). Paul is fond of this rhetorical question (4:1; 6:1; 7:7; 8:31; 9:14, 30). *Forefather* (*propatora*). Old word, only here in N.T. Accusative case in apposition with *Abraam* (accusative of general reference with the infinitive). *Hath found* (*heurēkenai*). Westcott and Hort put *heurēkenai* in the margin because B omits it, a needless precaution. It is the perfect active infinitive of *heuriskō* in indirect discourse after *eroumen*. The MSS. differ in the position of *kata sarka*.

2. *The Scripture* (*hē graphē*). Gen. 15:6. *Was justified by works* (*ex ergōn edikaiōthē*). Condition of first class, assumed as true for the sake of argument, though untrue in fact. The rabbis had a doctrine of the merits of Abraham who had a superfluity of credits to pass on to the Jews (Luke 3:8). *But not towards God* (*all' ou pros theon*). Abraham deserved all the respect from men that came to him, but his relation to God was a different matter. He had *there* no ground of boasting at all.

3. *It was reckoned unto him for righteousness* (*elogisthē eis dikaiosunēn*). First aorist passive indicative of *logizomai*, old and common verb to set down accounts (literally or metaphorically). It was set down on the credit side of the ledger "for" (*eis* as often) righteousness. What was set down? His believing God (*episteusen tōi theōi*).

4. *But as of debt* (*alla kata opheilēma*). An illustration of the workman (*ergazomenōi*) who gets his wages due him, "not as of grace" (*ou kata charin*).

5. *That justifieth the ungodly* (*ton dikaiounta ton asebē*). The impious, irreverent man. See 1:25. A forensic figure (Shedd). The man is taken as he is and pardoned. "The whole Pauline gospel could be summed up in this one word— God who justifies the ungodly" (Denney).

6. *Pronounceth blessing* (*legei ton makarismon*). Old word from *makarizō*, to pronounce blessed (Luke 1:48), felicitation, congratulation, in N.T. only here, verse 9; Acts 4:15.

7. *Blessed (makarioi).* See on Matt. 5:3. *Are forgiven (aphethēsan).* First aorist passive indicative of *aphiēmi*, without augment (*apheithēsan*, regular form). Paul quotes Psa. 32:1f. and as from David. Paul thus confirms his interpretation of Gen. 15:6. *Iniquities (anomiai).* Violations of law whereas *hamartiai* (sins) include all kinds. *Are covered (epekaluphthēsan).* First aorist passive of *epikaluptō*, old verb, to cover over (upon, *epi*) as a shroud. Only here in N.T. 8. *To whom (hōi).* But the best MSS. read *hou* like the LXX and so Westcott and Hort, "whose sin." *Will not reckon (ou mē logisētai).* Strong negation by double negative and aorist middle subjunctive. 9. *Is this blessing then pronounced? (ho makarismos oun houtos?).* "Is this felicitation then?" There is no verb in the Greek. Paul now proceeds to show that Abraham was said in Gen. 15:6 to be set right with God by faith *before* he was circumcised. 10. *When he was in circumcision (en peritomēi onti).* Dative masculine singular of the present active participle of *eimi;* "to him being in a state of circumcision or in a state of uncircumcision?" A pertinent point that the average Jew had not noticed. 11. *The sign of circumcision (sēmeion peritomēs).* It is the genitive of apposition, circumcision being the sign. *A seal of the righteousness of the faith (sphragida tēs dikaiosunēs tēs pisteōs).* *Sphragis* is old word for the seal placed on books (Rev. 5:1), for a signet-ring (Rev. 7:2), the stamp made by the seal (II Tim. 2:19), that by which anything is confirmed (I Cor. 9:2) as here. The circumcision did not convey the righteousness, but only gave outward confirmation. It came by faith and "the faith which he had while in uncircumcision" (*tēs en tēi akrobustiāi*), "the in the state of uncircumcision faith." Whatever parallel exists between baptism and circumcision as here stated by Paul argues for faith before baptism and for baptism as the sign and seal of the faith already had before baptism. *That he might be (eis to einai auton).* This idiom may be God's purpose (contemplated result) as in *eis to logisthēnai* below, or even actual result (so that he was) as in 1:20. *Though they be in uncircumcision (di' akrobustias).* Simply, "of those who believe while in the condition of uncircumcision."

12. *The father of circumcision (patera peritomēs).* The accusative with *eis to einai* to be repeated from verse 11. Lightfoot takes it to mean, not "a father of a circumcised progeny," but "a father belonging to circumcision," a less natural interpretation. *But who also walk (alla kai tois stoichousin).* The use of *tois* here is hard to explain, for *ou monon* and *alla kai* both come after the preceding *tois.* All the MSS. have it thus. A primitive error in a copyist is suggested by Hort who would omit the second *tois.* Lightfoot regards it less seriously and would repeat the second *tois* in the English: "To those who are, I do not say of circumcision only, but also to those who walk." *In the steps (tois ichnesin).* Locative case. See on II Cor. 12:18. *Stoicheō* is military term, to walk in file as in Gal. 5:25; Phil. 3:16.

13. *That he should be the heir of the world (to klēronomon auton einai kosmou).* The articular infinitive *(to einai)* with the accusative of general reference in loose apposition with *hē epaggelia* (the promise). But where is that promise? Not just Gen. 12:7, but the whole chain of promises about his son, his descendants like the stars in heaven, the Messiah and the blessing to the world through him. In these verses (13–17) Paul employs (Sanday and Headlam) the keywords of his gospel (faith, promise, grace) and arrays them against the current Jewish theology (law, works, merit).

14. *Be heirs (klēronomoi).* No predicate in the Greek *(eisin).* See on Gal. 4:1. If legalists are heirs of the Messianic promise to Abraham (condition of first class, assumed as true for argument's sake), the faith is emptied of all meaning *(kekenōtai,* perfect passive indicative of *kenoō)* and the promise to Abraham is made permanently idle *(katērgētai).*

15. *Worketh wrath (orgēn katergazetai).* Because of disobedience to it. *Neither is there transgression (oude parabasis).* There is no responsibility for the violation of a non-existent law.

16. *Of faith (ek pisteōs).* As the source. *According to grace (kata charin).* As the pattern. *To the end that (eis to einai).* Purpose again as in 11. *Sure (bebaian).* Stable, fast, firm. Old adjective from *bainō,* to walk. *Not to that only which is of the law (ou tōi ek tou nomou monon).* Another instance where *monon* (see verse 12) seems in the wrong place. Normally the order would be, *ou monon tōi ek tou nomou, alla kai ktl.*

17. *A father of many nations (patera pollōn ethnōn).* Quotation from Gen. 17:5. Only true in the sense of spiritual children as already explained, father of believers in God. *Before him whom he believed even God (katenanti hou episteusen theou).* Incorporation of antecedent into the relative clause and attraction of the relative *hōi* into *hou*. See Mark 11:2 for *katenanti,* "right in front of." *Calleth the things that are not as though they were (kalountos ta mē onta hōs onta).* "Summons the non-existing as existing." Abraham's body was old and decrepit. God rejuvenated him and Sarah (Heb. 11:19).

18. *In hope believed against hope (par' elpida ep' elpidi episteusen).* "Past hope in (upon) hope he trusted." Graphic picture. *To the end that he might become (eis to genesthai auton).* Purpose clause again with *eis to* and the infinitive as in verses 11 and 16.

19. *Without being weakened in faith (mē asthenēsas tēi pistei).* "Not becoming weak in faith." Ingressive first aorist active participle with negative *mē*. *Now as good as dead (ēdē nenekrōmenon).* Perfect passive participle of *nekroō,* "now already dead." B omits *ēdē.* He was, he knew, too old to become father of a child. *About (pou).* The addition of *pou* (somewhere, about) "qualifies the exactness of the preceding numeral" (Vaughan). The first promise of a son to Abraham and Sarah came (Gen. 15:3f.) before the birth of Ishmael (86 when Ishmael was born). The second promise came when Abraham was 99 years old (Gen. 17:1), calling himself 100 (Gen. 17:17).

20. *He wavered not through unbelief (ou diekrithē tēi apistiāi).* First aorist passive indicative of old and common verb *diakrinō,* to separate, to distinguish between, to decide between, to desert, to dispute, to be divided in one's own mind. This last sense occurs here as in Matt. 21:22; Mark 11:23; Rom. 14:23; James 1:6. "He was not divided in his mind by unbelief" (instrumental case). *Waxed strong through faith (enedunamōthē tēi pistei).* First aorist passive again of *endunamoō,* late word to empower, to put power in, in LXX and Paul and Acts 9:22.

21. *Being fully assured (plērophorētheis).* First aorist passive participle of *plērophoreō,* from *plērophoros* and this from *plērēs* and *pherō,* to bear or bring full (full measure), to

settle fully. Late word, first in LXX but frequent in papyri in sense of finishing off or paying off. See on Luke 1:1; Rom. 14:5. *What he had promised* (*ho epēggeltai*). Perfect middle indicative of *epaggellomai*, to promise, retained in indirect discourse according to usual Greek idiom. *He was able* (*dunatos estin*). Present active indicative retained in indirect discourse. The verbal adjective *dunatos* with *estin* is here used in sense of the verb *dunatai* (Luke 14:31; Acts 11:17).

23. *That* (*hoti*). Either recitative or declarative *hoti*. It makes sense either way.

24. *Him that raised up Jesus* (*ton egeiranta Iēsoun*). First aorist active articular participle of *egeirō*, to raise up. The fact of the Resurrection of Jesus is central in Paul's gospel (I Cor. 15:4ff.).

25. *For our justification* (*dia tēn dikaiōsin hēmōn*). The first clause (*paredothē dia ta paraptōmata*) is from Isa. 53:12. The first *dia* with *paraptōmata* is probably retrospective, though it will make sense as prospective (to make atonement for our transgressions). The second *dia* is quite clearly prospective with a view to our justification. Paul does not mean to separate the resurrection from the death of Christ in the work of atonement, but simply to show that the resurrection is at one with the death on the Cross in proof of Christ's claims.

CHAPTER V

1. *Being therefore justified by faith* (*dikaiōthentes oun ek pisteōs*). First aorist passive participle of *dikaioō*, to set right and expressing antecedent action to the verb *echōmen*. The *oun* refers to the preceding conclusive argument (chapters 1 to 4) that this is done by faith. *Let us have peace with God* (*eirēnēn echōmen pros ton theon*). This is the correct text beyond a doubt, the present active subjunctive, not *echomen* (present active indicative) of the Textus Receptus which even the American Standard Bible accepts. It is curious how perverse many real scholars have been on this word and phrase here. Godet, for instance. Vincent says that "it is difficult if not impossible to explain it." One has only to observe the force of the *tense* to see Paul's meaning clea ly. The mode is the volitive subjunctive and the present tense expresses linear action and so does not mean "make peace" as the ingressive aorist subjunctive *eirēnēn schōmen* would mean. A good example of *schōmen* occurs in Matt. 21:38 (*schōmen tēn klēronomian autou*) where it means: "Let us get hold of his inheritance." Here *eirēnēn echōmen* can only mean: "Let us enjoy peace with God" or "Let us retain peace with God." We have in Acts 9:31 *eichen eirēnēn* (imperfect and so linear), the church "enjoyed peace," not "made peace." The preceding justification (*dikaiōthentes*) "made peace with God." Observe *pros* (face to face) with *ton theon* and *dia* (intermediate agent) with *tou kuriou.*

2. *We have had* (*eschēkamen*). Perfect active indicative of *echō* (same verb as *echōmen*), still have it. *Our access* (*tēn prosagōgēn*). Old word from *prosagō*, to bring to, to introduce. Hence "introduction," "approach." Elsewhere in N.T. only Eph. 2:18; 3:12. *Wherein we stand* (*en hēi hestēkamen*). Perfect active (intransitive) indicative of *histēmi.* Grace is here present as a field into which we have been introduced and where we stand and we should enjoy all the privileges of this grace about us. *Let us rejoice* (*kauchōmetha*). "Let us exúlt." Present middle subjunctive (volitive) because *echōmen* is accepted as correct. The exhortation is

that we keep on enjoying peace with God and keep on exulting in hope of the glory of God.

3. *But let us also rejoice in our tribulations* (*alla kai kauchō-metha en tais thlipsesin*). Present middle subjunctive of same verb as in verse 2. *Kauchōmai* is more than "rejoice," rather "glory," "exult." These three volitive subjunctives (*echōmen*, *kauchōmetha*, twice) hold up the high ideal for the Christian after, and because of, his being set right with God. It is one thing to submit to or endure tribulations without complaint, but it is another to find ground of glorying in the midst of them as Paul exhorts here.

4. *Knowing* (*eidotes*). Second perfect participle of *eidon* (*oida*), giving the reason for the previous exhortation to glory in tribulations. He gives a linked chain, one linking to the other (tribulation *thlipsis*, patience *hupomonē*, experience *dokimē*, hope *elpis*) running into verse 5. On *dokimē*, see II Cor. 2:9.

5. *Hath been shed abroad* (*ekkechutai*). Perfect passive indicative of *ekcheō*, to pour out. "Has been poured out" in our hearts.

6. *For* (*eti gar*). So most documents, but B reads *ei ge* which Westcott and Hort use in place of *gar*. *While we were yet weak* (*ontōn hēmōn asthenōn eti*). Genitive absolute. The second *eti* (yet) here probably gave rise to the confusion of text over *eti gar* above. *In due season* (*kata kairon*). Christ came into the world at the proper time, the fulness of the time (Gal. 4:4; Eph. 1:10; Titus 1:3). *For the ungodly* (*huper asebōn*). In behalf, instead of. See about *huper* on Gal. 3:13 and also verse 7 here.

7. *Scarcely* (*molis*). Common adverb from *molos*, toil. See on Acts 14:18. As between *dikaios*, righteous, and *agathos*, good, Lightfoot notes "all the difference in the world" which he shows by quotations from Plato and Christian writers, a difference of sympathy mainly, the *dikaios* man being "absolutely without sympathy" while the *agathos* man "is beneficent and kind." *Would even dare* (*kai tolmāi*). Present active indicative of *tolmaō*, to have courage. "Even dares to." Even so in the case of the kindly sympathetic man courage is called for to make the supreme sacrifice. *Perhaps* (*tacha*). Common adverb (perhaps instrumental case) from *tachus* (swift). Only here in N.T.

8. *His own love (tēn heautou agapēn).* See John 3:16 as the best comment here. *While we were yet sinners (eti hamartōlōn ontōn).* Genitive absolute again. Not because we were Jews or Greeks, rich or poor, righteous or good, but plain sinners. Cf. Luke 18:13, the plea of the publican, *"moi tōi hamartōlōi."*

9. *Much more then (pollōi oun mallon).* Argument from the greater to the less. The great thing is the justification in Christ's blood. The final salvation (*sōthēsometha*, future passive indicative) is less of a mystery.

10. *We were reconciled to God (katēllagēmen tōi theōi).* Second aorist passive indicative of *katallassō* for which great Pauline word see on II Cor. 5:18f. The condition is the first class. Paul does not conceive it as his or our task to reconcile God to us. God has attended to that himself (Rom. 3:25f.). We become reconciled to God by means of the death of God's Son. "Much more" again we shall be saved "by his life" (*en tēi zōēi autou*). "In his life," for he does live, "ever living to intercede for them" (Heb. 7:25).

11. *But also glorying in God (alla kai kauchōmenoi en tōi theōi).* Basis of all the exultation above (verses 1 to 5). *Through whom we have now received the reconciliation (di hou nun tēn katallagēn elabomen).* Second aorist active indicative of *lambanō*, looked at as a past realization, "now" (*nun*) in contrast with the future consummation and a sure pledge and guarantee of it.

12. *Therefore (dia touto).* "For this reason." What reason? Probably the argument made in verses 1 to 11, assuming our justification and urging exultant joy in Christ because of the present reconciliation by Christ's death and the certainty of future final salvation by his life. *As through one man (hōsper di' henos anthrōpou).* Paul begins a comparison between the effects of Adam's sin and the effects of the redemptive work of Christ, but he does not give the second member of the comparison. Instead of that he discusses some problems about sin and death and starts over again in verse 15. The general point is plain that the effects of Adam's sin are transmitted to his descendants, though he does not say how it was done whether by the natural or the federal headship of Adam. It is important to note that Paul does not say that the whole race receives the full benefit of Christ's atoning

death, but only those who do. Christ is the head of all believers as Adam is the head of the race. In this sense Adam
"is a figure of him that was to come." *Sin entered into the
world* (*hē hamartia eis ton kosmon eisēlthen*). Personification
of sin and represented as coming from the outside into the
world of humanity. Paul does not discuss the origin of evil
beyond this fact. There are some today who deny the fact
of sin at all and who call it merely "an error of mortal mind"
(a notion) while others regard it as merely an animal inheritance devoid of ethical quality. *And so death passed unto
all men* (*kai houtōs eis pantas anthrōpous diēlthen*). Note use
of *dierchomai* rather than *eiserchomai*, just before, second
aorist active indicative in both instances. By "death" in
Gen. 2:17; 3:19 physical death is meant, but in verses 17 and
21 eternal death is Paul's idea and that lurks constantly behind physical death with Paul. *For that all sinned* (*eph' hōi
pantes hēmarton*). Constative (summary) aorist active indicative of *hamartanō*, gathering up in this one tense the
history of the race (committed sin). The transmission from
Adam became facts of experience. In the old Greek *eph' hōi*
usually meant "on condition that," but "because" in N.T.
(Robertson, *Grammar*, p. 963).

13. *Until the law* (*achri nomou*). Until the Mosaic law.
Sin was there before the Mosaic law, for the Jews were like
Gentiles who had the law of reason and conscience (2:12–16),
but the coming of the law increased their responsibility and
their guilt (2:9). *Sin is not imputed* (*hamartia de ouk ello-
geitai*). Present passive indicative of late verb *ellogaō* (*-eō*)
from *en* and *logos*, to put down in the ledger to one's account,
examples in inscription and papyri. *When there is no law*
(*mē ontos nomou*). Genitive absolute, no law of any kind,
he means. There was law *before* the Mosaic law. But what
about infants and idiots in case of death? Do they have
responsibility? Surely not. The sinful nature which they
inherit is met by Christ's atoning death and grace. No
longer do men speak of "elect infants."

14. *Even over them that had not sinned after the likeness of
Adam's transgression* (*kai epi tous mē hamartēsantas epi tōi
homoiōmati tēs parabaseōs Adam*). Adam violated an express command of God and Moses gave the law of God
clearly. And yet sin and death followed all from Adam on

till Moses, showing clearly that the sin of Adam brought terrible consequences upon the race. Death has come upon infants and idiots also as a result of sin, but one understands Paul to mean that they are not held responsible by the law of conscience. *A figure (tupos)*. See on Acts 7:43; I Thess. 1:7; II Thess. 3:9; I Cor. 10:6 for this word. Adam is a type of Christ in holding a relation to those affected by the headship in each case, but the parallel is not precise as Paul shows.

15. *But not as the trespass (all' ouch hōs)*. It is more contrast than parallel: "the trespass" *(to paraptōma*, the slip, fall to one side) over against the free gift *(to charisma*, of grace *charis)*. *Much more (polloi mallon)*. Another *a fortiori* argument. Why so? As a God of love he delights *much more* in showing mercy and pardon than in giving just punishment (Lightfoot). The gift surpasses the sin. It is not necessary to Paul's argument to make "the many" in each case correspond, one relates to Adam, the other to Christ.

16. *Through one that sinned (di' henos hamartēsantos)*. "Through one having sinned." That is Adam. Another contrast, difference in source *(ek)*. *Of one (ex henos)*. Supply *paraptōmatos*, Adam's one transgression. *Of many trespasses (ek pollōn paraptōmatōn)*. The gift by Christ grew out of manifold sins by Adam's progeny. *Justification (dikaiōma)*. Act of righteousness, result, ordinance (1:32; 2:26; 8:4), righteous deed (5:18), verdict as here (acquittal).

17. *Much more (polloi mallon)*. Argument *a fortiori* again. Condition of first class assumed to be true. Note balanced words in the contrast (transgression *paraptōmati*, grace *charitos;* death *thanatos*, life *zōēi;* the one or *Adam tou henos*, the one *Jesus Christ;* reign *basileuō* in both).

18. *So then (ara oun)*. Conclusion of the argument. Cf. 7:3, 25; 8:12, etc. Paul resumes the parallel between Adam and Christ begun in verse 12 and interrupted by explanation (13f.) and contrast (15–17). *Through one trespass (di' henos paraptōmatos)*. That of Adam. *Through one act of righteousness (di' henos dikaiōmatos)*. That of Christ. The first "unto all men" *(eis pantas anthrōpous)* as in verse 12, the second as in verse 17 "they that receive, etc."

19. Here again we have "the one" *(tou henos)* with both Adam and Christ, but "disobedience" *(parakoēs*, for which

see II Cor. 10:6) contrasted with "obedience" (*hupakoēs*), the same verb *kathistēmi*, old verb, to set down, to render, to constitute (*katestathēsan*, first aorist passive indicative, *katastathēsontai*, future passive), and "the many" (*hoi polloi*) in both cases (but with different meaning as with "all men" above).

20. *Came in beside* (*pareisēlthen*). Second aorist active indicative of double compound *pareiserchomai*, late verb, in N.T. only here and Gal. 2:4 which see. See also *eisēlthen* in verse 12. The Mosaic law came into this state of things, in between Adam and Christ. *That the trespass might abound* (*hina pleonasēi to paraptōma*). It is usual to explain *hina* here as final, as God's ultimate purpose. So Denney who refers to Gal. 3:19ff. and Rom. 7:7f. But Chrysostom explains *hina* here as *ekbasis* (result). This is a proper use of *hina* in the *Koinē* as we have seen. If we take it so here, the meaning is "so that the trespass abounded" (aorist active subjunctive of *pleonasō*, late verb, see on II Thess. 1:3; II Cor. 8:15). This was the actual effect of the Mosaic law for the Jews, the necessary result of all prohibitions. *Did abound more exceedingly* (*hupereperisseusen*). First aorist active indicative of *huperperisseuō*. Late verb, in N.T. only here and II Cor. 7:4 which see. A strong word. If *pleonazō* is comparative (*pleon*) *perisseuō* is superlative (Lightfoot) and then *huperperisseuō* goes the superlative one better. See *huperpleonazō* in 1 Tim. 1:14. The flood of grace surpassed the flood of sin, great as that was (and is).

21. *That—even so grace might reign* (*hina—houtōs kai hē charis basileusēi*). Final *hina* here, the purpose of God and the goal for us through Christ. Lightfoot notes the force of the aorist indicative (*ebasileusen*, established its throne) and the aorist subjunctive (*basileusēi*, might establish its throne), the ingressive aorist both times. "This full rhetorical close has almost the value of a doxology" (Denney).

CHAPTER VI

1. *What shall we say then?* (*ti oun eroumen?*). "A debater's phrase" (Morison). Yes, and an echo of the rabbinical method of question and answer, but also an expression of exultant victory of grace versus sin. But Paul sees the possible perversion of this glorious grace. *Shall we continue in sin?* (*epimenōmen tēi hamartiāi?*). Present active deliberative subjunctive of *epimenō*, old verb to tarry as in Ephesus (I Cor. 16:8) with locative case. The practice of sin as a habit (present tense) is here raised. *That grace may abound* (*hina hē charis pleonasēi*). Final clause with ingressive aorist subjunctive, to set free the superfluity of grace alluded to like putting money in circulation. Horrible thought (*mē genoito*) and yet Paul faced it. There are occasionally so-called pietists who actually think that God's pardon gives them liberty to sin without penalty (cf. the sale of indulgences that stirred Martin Luther).

2. *Died to sin* (*apethanomen tēi hamartiāi*). Second aorist active of *apothnēskō* and the dative case. When we surrendered to Christ and took him as Lord and Saviour. Qualitative relative (*hoitines*, we the very ones who). *How* (*pōs*). Rhetorical question.

3. *Were baptized into Christ* (*ebaptisthēmen eis Christon*). First aorist passive indicative of *baptizō*. Better, "were baptized unto Christ or in Christ." The translation "into" makes Paul say that the union with Christ was brought to pass by means of baptism, which is not his idea, for Paul was not a sacramentarian. *Eis* is at bottom the same word as *en*. Baptism is the public proclamation of one's inward spiritual relation to Christ attained before the baptism. See on Gal. 3:27 where it is like putting on an outward garment or uniform. *Into his death* (*eis ton thanaton autou*). So here "unto his death," "in relation to his death," which relation Paul proceeds to explain by the symbolism of the ordinance.

4. *We were buried therefore with him by means of baptism unto death* (*sunetaphēmen oun autōi dia tou baptismatos eis ton thanaton*). Second aorist passive indicative of *sunthaptō*,

361

old verb to bury together with, in N.T. only here and Col. 2:12. With associative instrumental case (*autōi*) and "by means of baptism unto death" as in verse 3. *In newness of life* (*en kainotēti zōēs*). The picture in baptism points two ways, backwards to Christ's death and burial and to our death to sin (verse 1), forwards to Christ's resurrection from the dead and to our new life pledged by the coming out of the watery grave to walk on the other side of the baptismal grave (F. B. Meyer). There is the further picture of our own resurrection from the grave. It is a tragedy that Paul's majestic picture here has been so blurred by controversy that some refuse to see it. It should be said also that a symbol is not the reality, but the picture of the reality.

5. *For if we have become united with him by the likeness of his death* (*ei gar sumphutoi gegonamen tōi homoiōmati tou thanatou autou*). Condition of the first class, assumed to be true. *Sumphutoi* is old verbal adjective from *sumphuō*, to grow together. Baptism as a picture of death and burial symbolizes our likeness to Christ in his death. *We shall be also united in the likeness of his resurrection* (*alla kai tēs anastaseōs esometha*). The conclusion to the previous condition introduced by *alla kai* as often and *tōi homoiōmati* (in the likeness) must be understood before *tēs anastaseōs* (of his resurrection). Baptism is a picture of the past and of the present and a prophecy of the future, the matchless preacher of the new life in Christ.

6. *Our old man* (*ho palaios hēmōn anthrōpos*). Only in Paul (here, Col. 3:9; Eph. 4:22). *Was crucified with him* (*sunestaurōthē*). See on Gal. 2:19 for this boldly picturesque word. This took place not at baptism, but only pictured there. It took place when "we died to sin" (verse 1). *The body of sin* (*to sōma tēs hamartias*). "The body of which sin has taken possession" (Sanday and Headlam), the body marked by sin. *That so we should no longer be in bondage to sin* (*tou mēketi douleuein hēmas tēi hamartiāi*). Purpose clause with *tou* and the present active infinitive of *douleuō*, continue serving sin (as slaves). Adds "slavery" to living in sin (verse 2).

7. *Is justified* (*dedikaiōtai*). Perfect passive indicative of *dikaioō*, stands justified, set free from, adding this great word to death and life of verses 1 and 2.

8. *With Christ (sun Christōi).* As pictured by baptism, the crucifixion with Christ of verse 6.

9. *Dieth no more (ouketi apothnēskei).* "Christ's particular death occurs but once" (Shedd). See Heb. 10:10. A complete refutation of the "sacrificial" character of the "mass."

10. *The death that he died (ho apethanen).* Neuter relative, cognative accusative with *apethanen.* *Once (ephapax).* Once and once only (Heb. 9:26f.), not *pote* (once upon a time). *The life that he liveth (ho zēi).* Cognate accusative of the relative.

11. *Reckon ye also yourselves (kai humeis logizesthe).* Direct middle imperative of *logizomai* and complete proof that Paul does not mean that baptism makes one dead to sin and alive to God. That is a spiritual operation "in Christ Jesus" and only pictured by baptism. This is a plea to live up to the ideal of the baptized life.

12. *Reign (basileuetō).* Present active imperative, "let not sin continue to reign" as it did once (5:12). *Mortal (thnētoi).* Verbal adjective from *thnēskō,* subject to death. The reign of sin is over with you. Self-indulgence is inconsistent with trust in the vicarious atonement. *That ye should obey (eis to hupakouein).* With a view to obeying.

13. *Neither present (mēde paristanete).* Present active imperative in prohibition of *paristanō,* late form of *paristēmi,* to place beside. Stop presenting your members or do not have the habit of doing so, "do not go on putting your members to sin as weapons of unrighteousness." *Instruments (hopla).* Old word for tools of any kind for shop or war (John 18:3; II Cor. 6:7; 10:4; Rom. 13:12). Possibly here figure of two armies arrayed against each other (Gal. 5:16–24), and see *hopla dikaiosunēs* below. The two sets of *hopla* clash. *But present yourselves unto God (alla parastēsate heautous tōi theōi).* First aorist active imperative of *paristēmi,* same verb, but different tense, do it now and completely. Our "members" (*melē*) should be at the call of God "as alive from the dead."

14. *Shall not have dominion (ou kurieusei).* Future active indicative of *kurieuō,* old verb from *kurios,* "shall not lord it over you," even if not yet wholly dead. Cf. II Cor. 1:24.

15. *What then? (ti oun?).* Another turn in the argument about the excess of grace. *Shall we sin? (hamartēsōmen?).*

First aorist active deliberative subjunctive of *hamartanō.*
"Shall we commit sin" (occasional acts of sin as opposed to
the life of sin as raised by *epimenōmen tēi hamartiāi* in
verse 1)? *Because* (*hoti*). The same reason as in verse 1 and
taken up from the very words in verse 14. Surely, the objector says, we may take a night off now and then and sin
a little bit "since we are under grace."

16. *His servants ye are whom ye obey* (*douloi este hōi hupakouete*). Bondservants, slaves of the one whom ye obey,
whatever one's profession may be, traitors, spies sometimes
they are called. As Paul used the figure to illustrate death
to sin and resurrection to new life in Christ and not in sin,
so now he uses slavery against the idea of occasional lapses
into sin. Loyalty to Christ will not permit occasional crossing
over to the other side to Satan's line.

17. *Whereas ye were* (*ēte*). Imperfect but no "whereas"
in the Greek. Paul is not grateful that they were once slaves
of sin, but only that, though they once were, they turned
from that state. *To that form of doctrine whereunto ye were
delivered* (*eis hon paredothēte tupon didachēs*). Incorporation
of the antecedent (*tupon didachēs*) into the relative clause:
"to which form of doctrine ye were delivered." See on 5:14
for *tupon*. It is hardly proper to take "form" here to refer
to Paul's gospel (2:16), possibly an allusion to the symbolism
of baptism which was the outward sign of the separation.

18. *Ye became servants of righteousness* (*edoulōthēte tēi dikaiosunēi*). First aorist passive indicative of *douloō*, to enslave. "Ye were made slaves to righteousness." You have
simply changed masters, no longer slaves of sin (set free
from that tyrant), but ye are slaves of righteousness. There
is no middle ground, no "no man's land" in this war.

19. *I speak after the manner of men* (*anthrōpinon legō*). "I
speak a human word." He begs pardon for using "slaving"
in connection with righteousness. But it is a good word,
especially for our times when self-assertiveness and personal
liberty bulk so large in modern speech. See 3:5 and Gal.
3:15 where he uses *kata anthrōpon*. *Because of the infirmity
of your flesh* (*dia tēn astheneian tēs sarkos humōn*). Because
of defective spiritual insight largely due to moral defects
also. *Servants to uncleanness* (*doula tēi akatharsiāi*). Neuter
plural form of *doulos* to agree with *melē* (members). Patently

true in sexual sins, in drunkenness, and all fleshly sins, absolutely slaves like narcotic fiends. *So now* (*houtōs nun*). Now that you are born again in Christ. Paul uses twice again the same verb *paristēmi*, to present (*parestēsate, parastēsate*). *Servants to righteousness* (*doula tēi dikaiosunēi*). Repeats the idea of verse 18. *Unto sanctification* (*eis hagiasmon*). This the goal, the blessed consummation that demands and deserves the new slavery without occasional lapses or sprees (verse 15). This late word appears only in LXX, N.T., and ecclesiastical writers so far. See on I Thess. 4:3; I Cor. 1:30. Paul includes sanctification in his conception of the God-kind (1:17) of righteousness (both justification, 1:18–5:21 and sanctification, chapters 6 to 8). It is a life process of consecration, not an instantaneous act. Paul shows that we ought to be sanctified (6:1–7:6) and illustrates the obligation by death (6:1–14), by slavery (6:15–23), and by marriage (7:1–6).

20. *Free in regard of righteousness* (*eleutheroi tēi dikaiosunēi*). Ye wore no collar of righteousness, but freely did as ye pleased. They were "free." Note dative case, personal relation, of *dikaiosunēi*.

21. *What fruit then had ye at that time?* (*tina oun karpon eichete tote?*). Imperfect active, used to have. A pertinent question. Ashes in their hands now. They are ashamed now of the memory of them. The end of them is death.

22. *Ye have your fruit unto sanctification* (*echete ton karpon humōn eis hagiasmon*). Freedom from sin and slavery to God bring permanent fruit that leads to sanctification. *And the end eternal life* (*to de telos zōēn aiōnion*). Note accusative case *zōēn aiōnion*, object of *echete* (ye have), though *thanatos* in contrast above is nominative.

23. *Wages* (*opsōnia*). Late Greek for wages of soldier, here of sin. See on Luke 3:14; I Cor. 9:7; II Cor. 11:8. Sin pays its wages in full with no cut. But eternal life is God's gift (*charisma*), not wages. Both *thanatos* and *zōēn* are eternal (*aiōnion*).

CHAPTER VII

1. *To men that know the law* (*ginōskousin nomon*). Dative plural of present active participle of *ginōskō*. The Romans, whether Jews or Gentiles, knew the principle of law. *A man* (*tou anthrōpou*). "The person," generic term *anthrōpos*, not *anēr*.

2. *The wife that hath a husband* (*hē hupandros gunē*). Late word, under (in subjection to) a husband. Here only in N.T. *Is bound* (*dedetai*). Perfect passive indicative, stands bound. *By law* (*nomōi*). Instrumental case. *To the husband while he liveth* (*tōi zōnti andri*). "To the living husband," literally. *But if the husband die* (*ean de apothanēi ho anēr*). Third class condition, a supposable case (*ean* and the second aorist active subjunctive). *She is discharged* (*katērgētai*). Perfect passive indicative of *katargeō*, to make void. She stands free from the law of the husband. Cf. 6:6.

3. *While the husband liveth* (*zōntos tou andros*). Genitive absolute of present active participle of *zaō*. *She shall be called* (*chrēmatisei*). Future active indicative of *chrēmatizō*, old verb, to receive a name as in Acts 11:26, from *chrēma*, business, from *chraomai*, to use, then to give an oracle, etc. *An adulteress* (*moichalis*). Late word, in Plutarch, LXX. See on Matt. 12:39. *If she be joined* (*ean genētai*). Third class condition, "if she come to." *So that she is no adulteress* (*tou mē einai autēn moichalida*). It is a fact that *tou* and the infinitive is used for result as we saw in 1:24. Conceived result may explain the idiom here.

4. *Ye also were made to the law* (*kai humeis ethanatōthēte*). First aorist indicative passive of *thanatoō*, old verb, to put to death (Matt. 10:21) or to make to die (extinct) as here and Rom. 8:13. The analogy calls for the death of the law, but Paul refuses to say that. He changes the structure and makes them dead to the law as the husband (6:3–6). The relation of marriage is killed "through the body of Christ" as the "propitiation" (3:25) for us. Cf. Col. 1:22. *That we should be joined to another* (*eis to genesthai heterōi*). Pur-

366

pose clause with *eis to* and the infinitive. First mention of the saints as wedded to Christ as their Husband occurs in I Cor. 6:13 and Gal. 4:26. See further Eph. 5:22–33. *That we might bring forth fruit unto God* (*hina karpophorēsōmen tōi theōi*). He changes the metaphor to that of the tree used in 6:22.

5. *In the flesh* (*en tēi sarki*). Same sense as in 6:19 and 7:18, 25. The "flesh" is not inherently sinful, but is subject to sin. It is what Paul means by being "under the law." He uses *sarx* in a good many senses. *Sinful passions* (*ta pathēmata tōn hamartiōn*). "Passions of sins" or marked by sins. *Wrought* (*energeito*). Imperfect middle of *energeō*, "were active." *To bring forth fruit unto death* (*eis to karpophorēsai tōi thanatōi*). Purpose clause again. Vivid picture of the seeds of sin working for death.

6. *But now* (*nuni de*). In the new condition. *Wherein we were holden* (*en hōi kateichometha*). Imperfect passive of *katechō*, picture of our former state (same verb in 1:18). *In newness of spirit* (*en kainotēti pneumatos*). The death to the letter of the law (the old husband) has set us free to the new life in Christ. So Paul has shown again the obligation on us to live for Christ.

7. *Is the law sin?* (*ho nomos hamartia?*). A pertinent query in view of what he had said. Some people today oppose all inhibitions and prohibitions because they stimulate violations. That is half-baked thinking. *I had not known sin* (*tēn hamartian ouk egnōn*). Second aorist indicative of *ginōskō*, to know. It is a conclusion of a second class condition, determined as unfulfilled. Usually *an* is used in the conclusion to make it plain that it is second class condition instead of first class, but occasionally it is not employed when it is plain enough without as here (John 16:22, 24). See on Gal. 4:15. So as to *I had not known coveting* (lust), *epithumian ouk ēidein*. But all the same the law is not itself sin nor the cause of sin. Men with their sinful natures turn law into an occasion for sinful acts.

8. *Finding occasion* (*aphormēn labousa*). See II Cor. 5:12; 11:12; Gal. 5:13 for *aphormēn*, a starting place from which to rush into acts of sin, excuses for doing what they want to do. Just so drinking men use the prohibition laws as "occasions" for violating them. *Wrought in me* (*kateirgasato en emoi*). First aorist active middle indicative of the intensive

verb *katergazomai*, to work out (to the finish), effective aorist. The command not to lust made me lust more. *Dead (nekra)*. Inactive, not non-existent. Sin in reality was there in a dormant state. 9. *I was alive (ezōn)*. Imperfect active. Apparently, "the lost paradise in the infancy of men" (Denney), before the conscience awoke and moral responsibility came, "a seeming life" (Shedd). *Sin revived (hē hamartia anezēsen)*. Sin came back to life, waked up, the blissful innocent stage was over, "the commandment having come" (*elthousēs tēs entolēs*, genitive absolute). *But I died (egō de apethanon)*. My seeming life was over for I was conscious of sin, of violation of law. I was dead before, but I did not know. Now I found out that I was spiritually dead.

10. *This I found unto death (heurethē moi—hautē eis thanaton)*. Literally, "the commandment the one for (meant for) life, this was found for me unto death." First aorist (effective) passive indicative of *heuriskō*, to find, not active as the English has it. It turned out so for me (ethical dative).

11. *Beguiled me (exēpatēsen me)*. First aorist active indicative of *exapataō*, old verb, completely (*ex*) made me lose my way (*a* privative, *pateō*, to walk). See on I Cor. 3:18; II Cor. 11:3. Only in Paul in N.T. *Slew me (apekteinen)*. First aorist active indicative of *apokteinō*, old verb. "Killed me off," made a clean job of it. Sin here is personified as the tempter (Gen. 3:13).

12. *Holy, and righteous, and good (hagia kai dikaia kai agathē)*. This is the conclusion (*wherefore, hōste*) to the query in verse 7. The commandment is God's and so holy like Him, just in its requirements and designed for our good. The modern revolt against law needs these words.

13. *Become death unto me? (emoi egeneto thanatos?)*. Ethical dative *emoi* again. New turn to the problem. Admitting the goodness of God's law, did it issue in death for me? Paul repels (*mē genoito*) this suggestion. It was sin that (*But sin, alla hē hamartia*) "became death for me." *That it might be shown (hina phanēi)*. Final clause, *hina* and second aorist passive subjunctive of *phainō*, to show. The sinfulness of sin is revealed in its violations of God's law. *By working death to me (moi katergazomenē thanaton)*. Present middle participle, as an incidental result. *Might become ex-*

ceedingly sinful (genētai kath' huperbolēn hamartōlos). Second aorist middle subjunctive of *ginomai* with *hina* in final clause. On *kath' huperbolēn*, see on I Cor. 12:31. Our *hyperbole* is the Greek *huperbolē*. The excesses of sin reveal its real nature. Only then do some people get their eyes opened.

14. *Spiritual (pneumatikos)*. Spirit-caused and spirit-given and like the Holy Spirit. See I Cor. 10:3f. *But I am carnal (egō de sarkinos eimi)*. "Fleshen" as in I Cor. 3:1 which see, more emphatic even than *sarkikos*, "a creature of flesh." *Sold under sin (pepramenos hupo tēn hamartian)*. Perfect passive participle of *pipraskō*, old verb, to sell. See on Matt. 13:46; Acts 2:45, state of completion. Sin has closed the mortgage and owns its slave.

15. *I know not (ou ginōskō)*. "I do not recognize" in its true nature. My spiritual perceptions are dulled, blinded by sin (II Cor. 4:4). The dual life pictured here by Paul finds an echo in us all, the struggle after the highest in us ("what I really wish," *ho thelō*, to practise it steadily, *prassō*) and the slipping into doing (*poiō*) "what I really hate" (*ho misō*) and yet sometimes do. There is a deal of controversy as to whether Paul is describing his struggle with sin before conversion or after it. The words "sold under sin" in verse 14 seem to turn the scale for the pre-conversion period. "It is the unregenerate man's experience, surviving at least in memory into regenerate days, and read with regenerate eyes" (Denney).

16. *I consent unto the law (sunphēmi tōi nomōi)*. Old verb, here only in N.T., with associative instrumental case. "I speak with." My wanting (*thelō*) to do the opposite of what I do proves my acceptance of God's law as good (*kalos*).

17. *So now (nuni de)*. A logical contrast, "as the case really stands." *But sin that dwelleth in me (all' hē enoikousa en emoi hamartia)*. "But the dwelling in me sin." Not my true self, my higher personality, but my lower self due to my slavery to indwelling sin. Paul does not mean to say that his whole self has no moral responsibility by using this paradox. "To be saved from sin, a man must at the same time own it and disown it" (Denney).

18. *In me (en emoi)*. Paul explains this by "in my flesh" (*en tēi sarki mou*), the unregenerate man "sold under sin" of verse 14. *No good thing (ouk—agathon)*. "Not absolutely

good." This is not a complete view of man even in his unregenerate state as Paul at once shows. *For to will is present with me (to gar thelein parakeitai moi)*. Present middle indicative of *parakeimai*, old verb, to lie beside, at hand, with dative *moi*. Only here in N.T. *The wishing* is the better self, *the doing* not the lower self.

19. *But the evil which I would not (alla ho ou thelō kakon)*. Incorporation of the antecedent into the relative clause, "what evil I do not wish." An extreme case of this practise of evil is seen in the drunkard or the dope-fiend.

20. *It is no more I that do it (ouketi egō katergazomai auto)*. Just as in verse 17, "no longer do I do it" (the real *Ego*, my better self), and yet there is responsibility and guilt for the struggle goes on.

21. *The law (ton nomon)*. The principle already set forth (*ara*, accordingly) in verses 18 and 19. This is the way it works, but there is no surcease for the stings of conscience.

22. *For I delight in (sunēdomai gar)*. Old verb, here alone in N.T., with associative instrumental case, "I rejoice with the law of God," my real self "after the inward man" (*kata ton esō anthrōpon*) of the conscience as opposed to "the outward man" (II Cor. 4:16; Eph. 3:16).

23. *A different law (heteron nomon)*. For the distinction between *heteros* and *allos*, see Gal. 1:6f. *Warring against (antistrateuomenon)*. Rare verb (*Xenophon*) to carry on a campaign against. Only here in N.T. *The law of my mind (tōi nomōi tou noos)*. The reflective intelligence Paul means by *noos*, "the inward man" of verse 22. It is this higher self that agrees that the law of God is good (12, 16, 22). *Bringing me into captivity (aichmalōtizonta)*. See on this late and vivid verb for capture and slavery Luke 21:24; II Cor. 10:5. Surely it is a tragic picture drawn by Paul with this outcome, "sold under sin" (14), "captivity to the law of sin" (23). The ancient writers (Plato, Ovid, Seneca, Epictetus) describe the same dual struggle in man between his conscience and his deeds.

24. *O wretched man that I am (talaipōros egō anthrōpos)*. "Wretched man I." Old adjective from *tlaō*, to bear, and *pōros*, a callus. In N.T. only here and Rev. 3:17. "A heart-rending cry from the depths of despair" (Sanday and Headlam). *Out of the body of this death (ek tou sōmatos tou thanatou*

toutou). So the order of words demands. See verse 13 for "death" which finds a lodgment in the body (Lightfoot). If one feels that Paul has exaggerated his own condition, he has only to recall I Tim. 1:15 when he describes himself a chief of sinners. He dealt too honestly with himself for Pharisaic complacency to live long.

25. *I thank God (charis tōi theōi).* "Thanks to God." Note of victory over death through Jesus Christ our Lord." *So then I myself (ara oun autos egō).* His whole self in his unregenerate state gives a divided service as he has already shown above. In 6:1-7:6 Paul proved the obligation to be sanctified. In 7:7 to 8:11 he discusses the possibility of sanctification, only for the renewed man by the help of the Holy Spirit.

CHAPTER VIII

1. *Therefore now* (*ara nun*). Two particles. Points back to the triumphant note in 7:25 after the preceding despair. *No condemnation* (*ouden katakrima*). As sinners we deserved condemnation in our unregenerate state in spite of the struggle. But God offers pardon "to those in Christ Jesus (*tois en Christōi Iēsou*). This is Paul's Gospel. The fire has burned on and around the Cross of Christ. There and there alone is safety. Those in Christ Jesus can lead the consecrated, the crucified, the baptized life.

2. *The law of the Spirit of life* (*ho nomos tou pneumatos tēs zōēs*). The principle or authority exercised by the Holy Spirit which bestows life and which rests "in Christ Jesus." *Made me free* (*eleutherōsen me*). First aorist active indicative of the old verb *eleutheroō* for which see Gal. 5:1. Aleph B have *se* (thee) instead of *me*. It matters little. We are pardoned, we are free from the old law of sin and death (7:7-24), we are able by the help of the Holy Spirit to live the new life in Christ.

3. *What the law could not do* (*to adunaton tou nomou*). Literally, "the impossibility of the law" as shown in 7:7-24, either nominative absolute or accusative of general reference. No syntactical connection with the rest of the sentence. *In that* (*en hōi*). "Wherein." *It was weak* (*esthenei*). Imperfect active, continued weak as already shown. *In the likeness of sinful flesh* (*en homoiōmati sarkos hamartias*). For "likeness" see Phil. 2:7, a real man, but more than man for God's "own Son." Two genitives "of flesh of sin" (marked by sin), that is the flesh of man is, but not the flesh of Jesus. *And for sin* (*kai peri hamartias*). Condensed phrase, God sent his Son also concerning sin (our sin). *Condemned sin in the flesh* (*katekrine tēn hamartian en tēi sarki*). First aorist active indicative of *katakrinō*. He condemned the sin of men and the condemnation took place in the flesh of Jesus. If the article *tēn* had been repeated before *en tēi sarki* Paul would have affirmed sin in the flesh of Jesus, but he carefully avoided that (Robertson, *Grammar*, p. 784).

4. *The ordinance of the law* (*to dikaiōma tou nomou*). "The requirement of the law." *Might be fulfilled* (*hina plērōthēi*). Purpose of the death of Christ by *hina* and first aorist passive subjunctive of *plēroō*. Christ met it all in our stead (3:21-26). *Not after the flesh, but after the Spirit* (*mē kata sarka alla kata pneuma*). The two laws of life (*kata sarka* in 7:7-24, *kata pneuma* 8:1-11). Most likely the Holy Spirit or else the renewed spirit of man.

5. *Do mind* (*phronousin*). Present active indicative of *phroneō*, to think, to put the mind (*phrēn*) on. See Matt. 16:23 and Rom. 12:16. For the contrast between *sarx* and *pneuma*, see Gal. 5:16-24.

6. *The mind* (*to phronēma*). The bent or will of the flesh is death as shown in 7:7-24. *Life* (*zōē*). In contrast with "death." *Peace* (*eirēnē*). As seen in 5:1-5.

7. *Is not subject* (*ouch hupotassetai*). Present passive indicative of *hupotassō*, late verb, military term for subjection to orders. Present tense here means continued insubordination. *Neither indeed can it be* (*oude gar dunatai*). "For it is not even able to do otherwise." This helpless state of the unregenerate man Paul has shown above apart from Christ. Hope lies in Christ (7:25) and the Spirit of life (8:2).

8. *Cannot please God* (*theōi aresai ou dunantai*). Because of the handicap of the lower self in bondage to sin. This does not mean that the sinner has no responsibility and cannot be saved. He is responsible and can be saved by the change of heart through the Holy Spirit.

9. *Not in the flesh* (*ouk en sarki*). Not sold under sin (7:14) any more. *But in the spirit* (*alla en pneumati*). Probably, "in the Holy Spirit." It is not Pantheism or Buddhism that Paul here teaches, but the mystical union of the believer with Christ in the Holy Spirit. *If so be that* (*eiper*). "If as is the fact" (cf. 3:30). *The Spirit of Christ* (*pneuma Christou*). The same as "the Spirit of God" just before. See also Phil. 1:19; I Peter 1:11. Incidental argument for the Deity of Christ and probably the meaning of II Cor. 3:18 "the Spirit of the Lord." Condition of first class, assumed as true.

10. *The body is dead* (*to men sōma nekron*). Has the seeds of death in it and will die "because of sin." *The spirit is life* (*to de pneuma zōē*). The redeemed human spirit. He uses

zōē (life) instead of *zōsa* (living), "God-begotten, God-sustained life" (Denney), if Christ is in you.

11. *Shall quicken* (*zōopoiēsei*). Future active indicative of *zōopoieō*, late verb from *zōopoios*, making alive. See on I Cor. 15:22. *Through his Spirit* (*dia tou pneumatos*). B D L have *dia to pneuma* (because of the Spirit). Both ideas are true, though the genitive is slightly more probably correct.

12. *We are debtors* (*opheiletai esmen*). See on Gal. 5:3; Rom. 1:14. *Not to the flesh* (*ou tēi sarki*). Negative *ou* goes with preceding verb and *tēi sarki*, not with the infinitive *tou zēin*.

13. *Ye must die* (*mellete apothnēskein*). Present indicative of *mellō*, to be about to do and present active infinitive of *apothnēskō*, to die. "Ye are on the point of dying." Eternal death. *By the spirit* (*pneumati*). Holy Spirit, instrumental case. *Ye shall live* (*zēsesthe*). Future active indicative of *zaō*. Eternal life.

14. *Sons of God* (*huioi theou*). In the full sense of this term. In verse 16 we have *tekna theou* (children of God). Hence no great distinction can be drawn between *huios* and *teknon*. The truth is that *huios* is used in various ways in the New Testament. In the highest sense, not true of any one else, Jesus Christ is God's Son (8:3). But in the widest sense all men are "the offspring" (*genos*) of God as shown in Acts 17:28 by Paul. But in the special sense here only those are "sons of God" who are led by the Spirit of God, those born again (the second birth) both Jews and Gentiles, "the sons of Abraham" (*huioi Abraam*, Gal. 3:7), the children of faith.

15. *The spirit of adoption* (*pneuma huiothesias*). See on this term *huiothesia*, Gal. 4:5. Both Jews and Gentiles receive this "adoption" into the family of God with all its privileges. "*Whereby we cry, Abba, Father*" (*en hēi krazomen Abbā ho patēr*). See Gal. 4:6 for discussion of this double use of Father as the child's privilege.

16. *The Spirit himself* (*auto to pneuma*). The grammatical gender of *pneuma* is neuter as here, but the Greek used also the natural gender as we do exclusively as in John 16:13 *ekeinos* (masculine *he*), *to pneuma* (neuter). See also John 16:26 (*ho—ekeinos*). It is a grave mistake to use the neuter "it" or "itself" when referring to the Holy Spirit. *Beareth witness with our spirit* (*summarturei tōi pneumati hēmōn*).

See on Rom. 2:15 for this verb with associative instrumental case. See I John 5:10f. for this double witness.

17. *Joint-heirs with Christ (sunklēronomoi Christou)*. A late rare double compound, in Philo, an Ephesian inscription of the imperial period (Deissmann, *Light from the Ancient East*, p. 92), papyri of the Byzantine period. See 8:29 for this idea expanded. Paul is fond of compounds of *sun*, three in this verse (*sunklēronomoi, sunpaschōmen, sundoxasthōmen*). The last (first aorist passive subjunctive of *sundoxazō* with *hina* (purpose), late and rare, here only in N.T.

18. *To us-ward (eis hēmās)*. We shall be included in the radiance of the coming glory which will put in the shadow the present sufferings. Precisely the same idiom here with *mellousan doxan* (aorist passive infinitive of *apokaluphthēnai*) occurs in Gal. 3:23 with *mellousan pistin*, which see.

19. *The earnest expectation of creation (hē apokaradokia tēs ktiseōs)*. This substantive has so far been found nowhere save here and Phil. 1:20, though the verb *apokaradokeō* is common in Polybius and Plutarch. Milligan (*Vocabulary*) thinks that Paul may have made the substantive from the verb. It is a double compound (*apo*, off from, *kara*, head, *dokeō*, Ionic verb, to watch), hence to watch eagerly with outstretched head. *Waiteth for (apekdechetai)*. See on I Cor. 1:7; Gal. 5:5 for this rare word (possibly formed by Paul, Milligan). "To wait it out" (Thayer). *The revealing of the sons of God (tēn apokalupsin tōn huiōn tou theou)*. Cf. I John 3:2; II Thess. 2:8; Col. 3:4. This mystical sympathy of physical nature with the work of grace is beyond the comprehension of most of us. But who can disprove it?

20. *Was subjected (hupetagē)*. Second aorist passive indicative of *hupatassō* (cf. verse 7). *To vanity (tēi mataiotēti)*. Dative case. Rare and late word, common in LXX. From *mataios*, empty, vain. Eph. 4:17; II Peter 2:18. *Not of its own will (ouch hekousa)*. Common adjective, in N.T. only here and I Cor. 9:27. It was due to the effect of man's sin. *But by reason of him (alla dia ton)*. Because of God. *In hope that (eph' helpidi hoti)*. Note the form *helpidi* rather than the usual *elpidi* and so *eph'*. *Hoti* can be causal "because" instead of declarative "that."

21. *The creation itself (autē hē ktisis)*. It is the hope of creation, not of the Creator. Nature "possesses in the feeling

of her unmerited suffering a sort of presentiment of her future deliverance" (Godet).

22. *Groaneth and travaileth in pain* (*sunstenazei kai sunōdinei*). Two more compounds with *sun*. Both rare and both here alone in N.T. Nature is pictured in the pangs of childbirth.

23. *The first fruits* (*tēn aparchēn*). Old and common metaphor. *Of the Spirit* (*tou pneumatos*). The genitive of apposition. The Holy Spirit came on the great Pentecost and his blessings continue as seen in the "gifts" in I Cor. 12–14, in the moral and spiritual gifts of Gal. 5:22f. And greater ones are to come (I Cor. 15:44ff.). *Even we ourselves* (*kai autoi*). He repeats for emphasis. We have our "groaning" (*stenazomen*) as well as nature. *Waiting for* (*apekdechomenoi*). The same verb used of nature in verse 19. *Our adoption* (*huiothesian*). Our full "adoption" (see verse 15), "the redemption of our body" (*tēn apolutrōsin tou sōmatos hēmōn*). That is to come also. Then we shall have complete redemption of both soul and body.

24. *For by hope were we saved* (*tēi gar elpidi esōthēmen*). First aorist passive indicative of *sōzō*. The case of *elpidi* is not certain, the form being the same for locative, instrumental and dative. Curiously enough either makes good sense in this context: "We were saved in hope, by hope, for hope" (of the redemption of the body).

25. *With patience* (*di' hupomonēs*). Paul repeats the verb *apekdechomai* of verse 23.

26. *Helpeth our infirmity* (*sunantilambanetai tēi astheneiāi hēmōn*). Present middle indicative of *sunantilambanomai*, late and striking double compound (Diodorus, LXX, Josephus, frequent in inscriptions, Deissmann, *Light, etc.*, p. 87), to lend a hand together with, at the same time with one. Only twice in N.T., here and Luke 10:40 in Martha's plea for Mary's help. Here beautifully Paul pictures the Holy Spirit taking hold at our side at the very time of our weakness (associative instrumental case) and before too late. *How to pray* (*to ti proseuxōmetha*). Articular clause object of *oidamen* (we know) and indirect question with the deliberative aorist middle subjunctive *proseuxōmetha*, retained in the indirect question. *As we ought* (*katho dei*). "As it is necessary." How true this is of all of us in our praying.

Maketh intercession (*huperentugchanei*). Present active indicative of late double compound, found only here and in later ecclesiastical writers, but *entugchanō* occurs in verse 27 (a common verb). It is a picturesque word of rescue by one who "happens on" (*entugchanei*) one who is in trouble and "in his behalf" (*huper*) pleads "with unuttered groanings" (instrumental case) or with "sighs that baffle words" (Denney). This is work of our Helper, the Spirit himself.

27. *He that searcheth* (*ho eraunōn*). God (I Sam. 16:7). *According to the will of God* (*kata theon*). See II Cor. 7:9–11 for this phrase *kata theon* (according to God). The Holy Spirit is the "other Paraclete" (John 14:16) who pleads God's cause with us as Christ is our Paraclete with the Father (I John 2:1). But more is true as here, for the Holy Spirit interprets our prayers to God and "makes intercession for us in accord with God's will."

28. *All things work together* (*panta sunergei*). A B have *ho theos* as the subject of *sunergei* (old verb, see on I Cor. 16:16; II Cor. 6:1). That is the idea anyhow. It is God who makes "all things work together" in our lives "for good" (*eis agathon*), ultimate good. *According to his purpose* (*kata prothesin*). Old word, seen already in Acts 27:13 and for "shewbread" in Matt. 12:4. The verb *protithēmi* Paul uses in 3:24 for God's purpose. Paul accepts fully human free agency but behind it all and through it all runs God's sovereignty as here and on its gracious side (9:11; 3:11; II Tim. 1:9).

29. *Foreknew* (*proegnō*). Second aorist active indicative of *proginōskō*, old verb as in Acts 26:5. See Psa. 1:6 (LXX) and Matt. 7:23. This fore-knowledge and choice is placed in eternity in Eph. 1:4. *He foreordained* (*proōrisen*). First aorist active indicative of *proorizō*, late verb to appoint beforehand as in Acts 4:28; I Cor. 2:7. Another compound with *pro-* (for eternity). *Conformed to the image* (*summorphous tēs eikonos*). Late adjective from *sun* and *morphē* and so an inward and not merely superficial conformity. *Eikōn* is used of Christ as the very image of the Father (II Cor. 4:4; Col. 1:15). See Phil. 2:6f. for *morphē*. Here we have both *morphē* and *eikōn* to express the gradual change in us till we acquire the likeness of Christ the Son of God so that we ourselves shall ultimately have the family likeness of sons of God. Glorious destiny. *That he might be* (*eis*

to einai auton). Common idiom for purpose. *First born among many brethren* (*prōtotokon en pollois adelphois*). Christ is "first born" of all creation (Col. 1:15), but here he is "first born from the dead" (Col. 1:18), the Eldest Brother in this family of God's sons, though "Son" in a sense not true of us.

30. *Called* (*ekalesen*)—*Justified* (*edikaiōsen*)—*Glorified* (*edoxasen*). All first aorist active indicatives of common verbs (*kaleō, dikaioō, doxazō*). But the glorification is stated as already consummated (constative aorists, all of them), though still in the future in the fullest sense. "The step implied in *edoxasen* is both complete and certain in the Divine counsels" (Sanday and Headlam).

31. *To these things* (*pros tauta*). From 8:12 on Paul has made a triumphant presentation of the reasons for the certainty of final sanctification of the sons of God. He has reached the climax with glorification (*edoxasen* in verse 30). But Paul lets the objector have his say as he usually does so that in verses 31 to 39 he considers the objections. *If God is for us, who is against us?* (*ei ho theos huper hēmōn, tis kath' hēmōn?*). This condition of the first class carries Paul's challenge to all doubters. There is no one on a par with God. Note the two prepositions in contrast (*huper*, over, *kata*, down or against).

32. *He that* (*hos ge*). "Who as much as this" (*ge* here magnifying the deed, intensive particle). *Spared not* (*ouk epheisato*). First aorist middle of *pheidomai*, old verb used about the offering of Isaac in Gen. 22:16. See Acts 20:29. *Also with him* (*kai sun autōi*). The gift of "his own son" is the promise and the pledge of the all things for good of verse 28. Christ is all and carries all with him.

33. *Who shall lay anything to the charge of God's elect?* (*tis egkalesei kata eklektōn theou?*). Future active indicative of *egkaleō*, old verb, to come forward as accuser (forensic term) in case in court, to impeach, as in Acts 19:40; 23:29; 26:2, the only N.T. examples. Satan is the great Accuser of the brethren. *It is God that justifieth* (*theos ho dikaiōn*). God is the Judge who sets us right according to his plan for justification (3:21-31). The Accuser must face the Judge with his charges.

34. *Shall condemn* (*katakrinōn*). Can be either present

active participle (condemns) or the future (shall condemn).
It is a bold accuser who can face God with false charges or
with true ones for that matter for we have an "Advocate"
at God's Court (I John 2:1), "who is at the right hand of
God" (*hos estin en dexiāi tou theou*) "who also maketh intercession for us" (*hos kai entugchanei huper hēmōn*). Our
Advocate paid the debt for our sins with his blood. The
score is settled. We are free (8:1).

35. *Shall separate* (*chōrisei*). Future active of old verb
chorizō from adverb *chōris* and that from *chōra*, space. Can
any one put a distance between Christ's love and us (objective genitive)? Can any one lead Christ to cease loving
us? Such things do happen between husband and wife, alas.
Paul changes the figure from "who" (*tis*) to "what" (*ti*).
The items mentioned will not make Christ love us less.
Paul here glories in tribulations as in 5:3ff.

36. *Even as it is written* (*kathōs gegraptai*). He quotes Psa.
44:23. *We are killed* (*thanatoumetha*). Present passive indicative of *thanatoō* for which see on 7:4. Same idea of
continuous martyrdom in I Cor. 15:31. *As sheep for the
slaughter* (*hōs probata sphagēs*). Objective genitive (*sphagēs*).

37. *Nay* (*alla*). On the contrary, we shall not be separated.
We are more than conquerors (*hupernikōmen*). Late and rare
compound. Here only in N.T. "We gain a surpassing victory through the one who loved us."

38. *For I am persuaded* (*pepeismai gar*). Perfect passive
participle of *peithō*, "I stand convinced." The items mentioned are those that people dread (life, death, supernatural
powers, above, below, any creature to cover any omissions).

39. *To separate us* (*hēmās chōrisai*). Aorist active infinitive of *chorizō* (same verb as in 35). God's love is victor
over all possible foes, "God's love that is in Christ Jesus."
Paul has reached the mountain top. He has really completed his great argument concerning the God-kind of
righteousness save for its bearing on some special problems.
The first of these concerns the fact that the Jews (God's
chosen people) have so largely rejected the gospel (chapters
9 to 11).

CHAPTER IX

1. *In Christ (en Christōi).* Paul really takes a triple oath here so strongly is he stirred. He makes a positive affirmation in Christ, a negative one (not lying), the appeal to his conscience as "co-witness" (*sunmarturousēs*, genitive absolute as in 2:15 which see) "in the Holy Spirit."

2. *Sorrow (lupē).* Because the Jews were rejecting Christ the Messiah. "We may compare the grief of a Jew writing after the fall of Jerusalem" (Sanday and Headlam). *Unceasing pain in my heart (adialeiptos odunē tēi kardiāi).* Like *angina pectoris. Odunē* is old word for consuming grief, in N.T. only here and and I Tim. 6:10. *Unceasing (adialeiptos).* Late and rare adjective (in an inscription 1 cent. B.C.), in N.T. only here and II Tim. 1:3. Two rare words together and both here only in N.T. and I and II Timothy (some small argument for the Pauline authorship of the Pastoral Epistles).

3. *I could wish (ēuchomēn).* Idiomatic imperfect, "I was on the point of wishing." We can see that *euchomai* (I do wish) would be wrong to say. *An ēuchomēn* would mean that he does not wish (conclusion of second class condition). *An euchoimēn* would be conclusion of fourth class condition and too remote. He is shut up to the imperfect indicative (Robertson, *Grammar*, p. 886). *Anathema (anathema).* See for this word as distinct from *anathēma* (offering) I Cor. 12:3 and Gal. 1:8f. *I myself (autos egō).* Nominative with the infinitive *einai* and agreeing with subject of *ēuchomēn. According to the flesh (kata sarka).* As distinguished from Paul's Christian brethren.

4. *Who (hoitines).* The very ones who, inasmuch as they. *Israelites (Israēleitai).* Covenant name of the chosen people. *Whose (hōn).* Predicate genitive of the relative, used also again with *hoi pateres.* For "the adoption" (*hē huiothesia*) see 8:15. *The glory (hē doxa).* The Shekinah Glory of God (3:23) and used of Jesus in James 2:1. *The covenants (hai diathēkai).* Plural because renewed often (Gen. 6:18; 9:9;

15:18; 17:2, 7, 9; Ex. 2:24). *The giving of the law* (*hē nomo-
thesia*). Old word, here only in N.T., from *nomos* and *tithēmi*.
The service (*hē latreia*). The temple service (Heb. 9:1, 6). *The
fathers* (*hoi pateres*). The patriarchs (Acts 3:13; 7:32).
5. *Of whom* (*ex hōn*). Fourth relative clause and here
with *ex* and the ablative. *Christ* (*ho Christos*). The Messiah.
As concerning the flesh (*to kata sarka*). Accusative of general
reference, "as to the according to the flesh." Paul limits the
descent of Jesus from the Jews to his human side as he did
in 1:3f. *Who is over all, God blessed for ever* (*ho on epi pantōn
theos eulogētos*). A clear statement of the deity of Christ
following the remark about his humanity. This is the natural
and the obvious way of punctuating the sentence. To make
a full stop after *sarka* (or colon) and start a new sentence
for the doxology is very abrupt and awkward. See Acts
20:28 and Titus 2:13 for Paul's use of *theos* applied to Jesus
Christ.
6. *But it is not as though* (*ouch hoion de hoti*). Supply *estin*
after *ouch:* "But it is not such as that," an old idiom, here
alone in N.T. *Hath come to nought* (*ekpeptōken*). Perfect
active indicative of *ekpiptō*, old verb, to fall out. *For they
are not all Israel, which are of Israel* (*ou gar pantes hoi ex
Israēl houtoi Israēl*). "For not all those out of Israel (the
literal Jewish nation), these are Israel (the spiritual Israel)."
This startling paradox is not a new idea with Paul. He had
already shown (Gal. 3:7–9) that those of faith are the true
sons of Abraham. He has amplified that idea also in Rom. 4.
So he is not making a clever dodge here to escape a difficulty.
He now shows how this was the original purpose of God to
include only those who believed. *Seed of Abraham* (*sperma
Abraam*). Physical descent here, but spiritual seed by
promise in verse 8. He quotes Gen. 21:12f.
8. *The children of the promise* (*ta tekna tēs epaggelias*). Not
through Ishmael, but through Isaac. Only the children of
the promise are "children of God" (*tekna tou theou*) in the
full sense. He is not speaking of Christians here, but simply
showing that the privileges of the Jews were not due to
their physical descent from Abraham. Cf. Luke 3:8.
9. *A word of promise* (*epaggelias ho logos houtos*). Literally,
"this word is one of promise." Paul combines Gen. 18:10
and 14 from the LXX.

382 WORD PICTURES IN NEW TESTAMENT

10. *Having conceived of one* (*ex henos koitēn echousa*). By metonomy with cause for the effect we have this peculiar idiom (*koitē* being bed, marriage bed), "having a marriage bed from one" husband. One father and twins.

11. *The children being not yet born* (*mēpō gennēthentōn*). Genitive absolute with first aorist passive participle of *gennaō*, to beget, to be born, though no word for children nor even the pronoun *autōn* (they). *Neither having done anything good or bad* (*mēde praxantōn ti agathon ē phaulon*). Genitive absolute again with first active participle of *prassō*. On *phaulon*, see II Cor. 5:10. *The purpose of God* (*hē prothesis tou theou*). See 8:28 for *prothesis*. *According to election* (*kat' eklogēn*). Old word from *eklegō*, to select, to choose out. See I Thess. 1:4. Here it is the purpose (*prothesis*) of God which has worked according to the principles of election. *Not of works* (*ouk ex ergōn*). Not of merit.

12. *But of him that calleth* (*all' ek tou kalountos*). Present active articular participle of *kaleō* in the ablative case after *ek*. The source of the selection is God himself. Paul quotes Gen. 25:33 (LXX).

13. Paul quotes Mal. 1:2f. *But Esau I hated* (*ton de Ēsau emisēsa*). This language sounds a bit harsh to us. It is possible that the word *miseō* did not always carry the full force of what we mean by "hate." See Matt. 6:24 where these very verbs (*miseō* and *agapaō*) are contrasted. So also in Luke 14:26 about "hating" (*miseō*) one's father and mother if coming between one and Christ. So in John 12:25 about "hating" one's life. There is no doubt about God's preference for Jacob and rejection of Esau, but in spite of Sanday and Headlam one hesitates to read into these words here the intense hatred that has always existed between the descendants of Jacob and of Esau.

14. *Is there unrighteousness with God?* (*mē adikia para tōi theōi?*). Paul goes right to the heart of the problem. *Mē* expects a negative answer. "Beside" (*para*) God there can be no injustice to Esau or to any one because of election.

15. *For he says to Moses* (*tōi Mōüsei gar legei*). He has an Old Testament illustration of God's election in the case of Pharaoh (Ex. 33:19). *On whom I have mercy* (*hon an eleō*). Indefinite relative with *an* and the present active subjunctive of *eleaō*, late verb only here and Jude 23 in N.T. "On

THE EPISTLES OF PAUL

whomsoever I have mercy." The same construction in *hon an oikteirō*, "on whomsoever I have compassion."
16. *So then (ara oun)*. In view of this quotation. *It is not of (ou)*. We must supply *estin eleos* with *ou*. "Mercy is not of." The articular participles (*tou thelontos, tou trechontos, tou eleōntos*) can be understood as in the genitive with *eleos* understood (mercy is not a quality of) or as the predicate ablative of source like *epiluseōs* in II Peter 1:20. Paul is fond of the metaphor of running.
17. *To Pharaoh (tōi Pharaō)*. There is a national election as seen in verses 7–13, but here Paul deals with the election of individuals. He "lays down the principle that God's grace does not necessarily depend upon anything but God's will" (Sanday and Headlam). He quotes Ex. 9:16. *Might be published (diaggelēi)*. Second aorist passive subjunctive of *diaggellō*.
18. *He hardeneth (sklērunei)*. Pharaoh hardened his own heart also (Ex. 8:15, 32; 9:34), but God gives men up also (1:24, 26, 28). This late word is used by the Greek physicians Galen and Hippocrates. See on Acts 19:9. Only here in Paul.
19. *Why doth he still find fault? (ti eti memphetai?)*. Old verb, to blame. In N.T. only here and Heb. 8:8. Paul's imaginary objector picks up the admission that God hardened Pharaoh's heart. "Still" (*eti*) argues for a change of condition since that is true. *Withstandeth his will (tōi boulēmati autou anthestēken)*. Perfect active indicative of *anthistēmi*, old verb, maintains a stand (the perfect tense). Many have attempted to resist God's will (*boulēma*, deliberate purpose, in N.T. only here and Acts 27:43; I Peter 4:3). Elsewhere *thelēma* (Matt. 6:10).
20. *Nay, but, O man, who art thou? (O anthrōpe, men oun ge su tis ei?)*. "O man, but surely thou who art thou?" Unusual and emphatic order of the words, prolepsis of *su* (thou) before *tis* (who) and *men oun ge* (triple particle, *men*, indeed, *oun*, therefore, *ge*, at least) at the beginning of clause as in Rom. 10:18; Phil. 3:8 contrary to ancient idiom, but so in papyri. *That repliest (ho antapokrinomenos)*. Present middle articular participle of double compound verb *antapokrinomai*, to answer to one's face (*anti-*) late and vivid combination, also in Luke 14:6, nowhere else in N.T., but in LXX. *The thing formed (to plasma)*. Old word (Plato,

Aristophanes) from *plassō*, to mould, as with clay or wax, from which the aorist active participle used here (*tōi plasanti*) comes. Paul quotes these words from Isa. 29:16 verbatim. It is a familiar idea in the Old Testament, the absolute power of God as Creator like the potter's use of clay (Isa. 44:8; 45:8–10; Jer. 18:6). *Mē* expects a negative answer. *Why didst thou make me thus?* (*ti me epoiēsas houtōs?*). The original words in Isaiah dealt with the nation, but Paul applies them to individuals. This question does not raise the problem of the origin of sin for the objector does not blame God for that but why God has used us as he has, made some vessels out of the clay for this purpose, some for that. Observe "thus" (*houtōs*). The potter takes the clay as he finds it, but uses it as he wishes.

21. *Or hath not the potter a right over the clay?* (*ē ouk echei exousian ho kerameus tou pēlou?*). This question, expecting an affirmative answer, is Paul's reply to the previous one, "Why didst thou make me thus?" *Pēlos*, old word for clay, is mud or wet clay in John 9:6, 11, 14f. The old word for potter (*kerameus*) in N.T. only here and Matt. 27:7, 10. *Lump* (*phuramatos*). Late word from *phuraō*, to mix (clay, dough, etc.). *One part* (*ho men*)—*another* (*ho de*). Regular idiom for contrast (*men—de*) with the old demonstrative *ho* (this), "this vessel (*skeuos*, old word as in Mark 11:16) for honour, that for dishonour." Paul thus claims clearly God's sovereign right (*exousian*, power, right, authority, from *exesti*) to use men (already sinners) for his own purpose.

22. *Willing* (*thelōn*). Concessive use of the participle, "although willing," not causal, "because willing" as is shown by "with much long-suffering" (*en pollēi makrothumiāi*, in much long-suffering). *His power* (*to dunaton autou*). Neuter singular of the verbal adjective rather than the substantive *dunamin*. *Endured* (*ēnegken*). Constative second aorist active indicative of the old defective verb *pherō*, to bear. *Vessels of wrath* (*skeuē orgēs*). The words occur in Jer. 50 (LXX 27): 25, but not in the sense here (objective genitive like *tekna orgēs*, Eph. 2:3, the objects of God's wrath). *Fitted* (*katērtismena*). Perfect passive participle of *katartizō*, old verb to equip (see Matt. 4:21; II Cor. 13:11), state of readiness. Paul does not say here that God did it or that they did it. That they are responsible may be seen from I Thess.

2:15f. *Unto destruction* (*eis apōleian*). Endless perdition (Matt. 7:13; II Thess. 2:3; Phil. 3:19), not annihilation.

23. *Vessels of mercy* (*skeuē eleous*). Objective genitive like *skeuē orgēs*. *Afore prepared* (*proētoimasen*). First aorist active indicative of *proetoimazō*, old verb to make ready (from *hetoimos*, ready) and *pro*, before, in N.T. only here and Eph. 2:10. But same idea in Rom. 8:28-30.

24. *But also from the Gentiles* (*alla kai ex ethnōn*). Paul had already alluded to this fact in 9:6f. (cf. Gal. 3:7-9). Now he proceeds to prove it from the Old Testament.

25. *In Hosea* (*en tōi Hōsēe*). He quotes 2:23 with some freedom. Hosea refers to the ten tribes and Paul applies the principle stated there to the Gentiles. Hosea had a son named *Lo-ammi*=*ou laos*. So here *ho ou laos mou* "the not people of mine." *Ou* with substantives obliterates the meaning of the substantive, an idiom seen in Thucydides and other Greek writers. See also Rom. 10:19; I Peter 2:10. *Which was not beloved* (*tēn ouk ēgapēmenēn*). The LXX rendering of *Lo-ruhamah* (not mercy, without mercy or love), name of Hosea's daughter. The use of *ouk* with the perfect passive participle is emphatic, since *mē* is the usual negative of the participle in the *Koiné*.

26. *Ye are not my people* (*ou laos mou humeis*). Quotation from Hosea 1:10 (LXX 2:1). *There* (*ekei*). Palestine in the original, but Paul applies it to scattered Jews and Gentiles everywhere.

27. *Isaiah* (*Ēsaias*). Shortened quotation from Isa. 10:22 (LXX). *It is the remnant that shall be saved* (*to hupoleimma sōthēsetai*). First future passive of *sōzō*. Literally, "the remnant will be saved." Late word from *hupoleipō*, to leave behind (11:3), here only in N.T. Textus Receptus has *kataleimma*, but Aleph A B have *hupoleimma*. Isaiah cries in anguish over the outlook for Israel, but sees hope for the remnant.

28. *Finishing it and cutting it short* (*suntelōn kai suntemnōn*). Present active participles and note *sun*- with each (perfective use of the preposition, finishing completely as in Luke 4:13, cutting off completely or abridging and here only in N.T.) The quotation is from Isa. 28:22.

29. *Hath said before* (*proeirēken*). Perfect active indicative of *proeipon* (defective verb). Stands on record in Isa. 1:9.

Had left (egkatelipen). Second aorist active indicative of old verb *egkataleipō*, to leave behind. Condition of second class, determined as unfulfilled, with *an egenēthēmen* and *an hōmoiōthēmen* as the conclusions (both first aorist passives of *ginomai* and *homoioō*, common verbs). *A seed (sperma).* The remnant of verse 27.

30. *Attained (katelaben).* Second aorist active indicative of *katalambanō*, old verb, to grasp, to seize, to overtake (carrying out the figure in *diōkō* (to pursue). It was a curious paradox. *Which is of faith (tēn ek pisteōs).* As Paul has repeatedly shown, the only way to get the God-kind of righteousness.

31. *Did not arrive at that law (eis nomon ouk ephthasen).* First aorist active indicative of *phthanō*, old verb to anticipate (I Thess. 4:15), now just to arrive as here and II Cor. 10:14. The word "that" is not in the Greek. Legal righteousness Israel failed to reach, because to do that one had to keep perfectly all the law.

32. We must supply the omitted verb *ediōxa* (pursued) from verse 31. That explains the rest. *They stumbled at the stone of stumbling (prosekopsan tōi lithōi tou proskommatos).* The quotation is from Isa. 8:14. *Proskoptō* means to cut (*koptō*) against (*pros*) as in Matt. 4:6; John 11:9f. The Jews found Christ a *skandalon* (I Cor. 1:23).

33. Paul repeats the phrase just used in the whole quotation from Isa. 8:14 with the same idea in "a rock of offence" (*petran skandalou*, "a rock of snare," a rock which the Jews made a cause of stumbling). The rest of the verse is quoted from Isa. 28:16. However, the Hebrew means "shall not make haste" rather than "shall not be put to shame." In I Peter 2:8 we have the same use of these Scriptures about Christ. Either Peter had read Romans or both Paul and Peter had a copy of Christian *Testimonia* like Cyprian's later.

CHAPTER X

1. *Desire (eudokia)*. No papyri examples of this word, though *eudokēsis* occurs, only in LXX and N.T., but no example for "desire" unless this is one, though the verb *eudokeō* is common in Polybius, Diodorus, Dion, Hal. It means will, pleasure, satisfaction (Matt. 11:26; II Thess. 1:11; Phil. 1:15; 2:13; Eph. 1:5, 9). *Supplication (deēsis)*. Late word from *deomai*, to want, to beg, to pray. In the papyri. See Luke 1:13. It is noteworthy that, immediately after the discussion of the rejection of Christ by the Jews, Paul prays so earnestly for the Jews "that they may be saved" (*eis sōtērian*), literally "unto salvation." Clearly Paul did not feel that the case was hopeless for them in spite of their conduct. Bengel says: *Non orasset Paul si absolute reprobati essent* (Paul would not have prayed if they had been absolutely reprobate). Paul leaves God's problem to him and pours out his prayer for the Jews in accordance with his strong words in 9:1–5.

2. *A zeal for God (zēlon theou)*. Objective genitive like Phil. 3:9, "through faith in Christ" (*dia pisteōs Christou*). *But not according to knowledge (all' ou kat' epignōsin)*. They had knowledge of God and so were superior to the Gentiles in privilege (2:9–11), but they sought God in an external way by rules and rites and missed him (9:30–33). They became zealous for the letter and the form instead of for God himself.

3. *Being ignorant of God's righteousness (agnoountes tēn tou theou dikaiosunēn)*. A blunt thing to say, but true as Paul has shown in 2:1–3:20. They did not understand the God-kind of righteousness by faith (1:17). They misconceived it (2:4). *They did not subject themselves (ouch hupetagēsan)*. Second aorist passive indicative of *hupotassō*, common *Koinē* verb, to put oneself under orders, to obey, here the passive in sense of the middle (James 4:7) like *apekrithēn*, I answered.

4. *The end of the law (telos nomou)*. Christ put a stop to

the law as a means of salvation (6:14; 9:31; Eph. 2:15; Col.
2:14) as in Luke 16:16. Christ is the goal or aim of the law
(Gal. 3:24). Christ is the fulfilment of the law (Matt. 5:17;
Rom. 13:10; I Tim. 1:5). But here (Denney) Paul's main
idea is that Christ ended the law as a method of salvation
for "every one that believeth" whether Jew or Gentile.
Christ wrote *finis* on law as a means of grace.

5. *Thereby* (*en autēi*). That is by or in "the righteousness
that is from law." He stands or falls with it. The quotation
is from Lev. 18:5.

6. *Saith thus* (*houtōs legei*). Paul personifies "the from
faith righteousness" (*hē ek pisteōs dikaiosunē*). A free re-
production from Deut. 30:11-14. Paul takes various phrases
from the LXX and uses them for "his inspired conviction
and experiences of the gospel" (Denney). He does not quote
Moses as saying this or meaning this. *Say not in thy heart*
(*mē eipēis en tēi kardiāi sou*). Second aorist active subjunctive with *mē* like Deut. 8:17. To say in the heart is to think
(Matt. 3:9). *That is, to bring Christ down* (*tout' estin Christon
katagagein*). Second aorist active infinitive of the common
verb *katagō*, to bring or lead down. It is dependent on the
preceding verb *anabēsetai* (shall ascend). *Tout' estin* (that
is) is what is called *Midrash* or interpretation as in 9:8. It
occurs three times here (verses 6 to 8). Paul applies the
words of Moses to Christ. There is no need for one to go to
heaven to bring Christ down to earth. The Incarnation is
already a glorious fact. Today some men scout the idea of
the Deity and Incarnation of Christ.

7. *Into the abyss* (*eis tēn abusson*). See Luke 8:31 for this
old Greek word (*a* privative and *bussos*) bottomless like
sea (Psa. 106:26), our abyss. In Rev. 9:1 it is the place of
torment. Paul seems to refer to Hades or Sheol (Acts 2:27,
31), the other world to which Christ went after death. *To
bring Christ up* (*Christon anagagein*). Second aorist active
infinitive of *anagō* and dependent on *katabēsetai* (shall de-
scend). Christ has already risen from the dead. The deity
and resurrection of Christ are precisely the two chief points
of attack today on the part of sceptics.

8. *But what saith it?* (*alla ti legei?*). That is "the from
faith righteousness." *The word of faith* (*to rēma tēs pisteōs*).
The gospel message concerning faith (objective genitive).

Only here. In contrast to the law. *Which we preach (ho kērussomen)*. The living voice brings home to every one the faith kind of righteousness. Paul seizes upon the words of Moses with the orator's instinct and with rhetorical skill (Sanday and Headlam) applies them to the facts about the gospel message about the Incarnation and Resurrection of Christ.

9. *If thou shalt confess (ean homologēsēis)*. Third class condition (*ean* and first aorist active subjunctive of *homologeō*). *With thy mouth Jesus as Lord (en tōi stomati sou Kurion Iēsoun)*. This is the reading of nearly all the MSS. But B 71 Clem of Alex. read *to rēma en tōi stomati sou hoti Kurios Iēsous* (the word in thy mouth that Jesus is Lord). The idea is the same, the confession of Jesus as Lord as in I Cor. 12:3; Phil. 2:11. No Jew would do this who had not really trusted Christ, for *Kurios* in the LXX is used of God. No Gentile would do it who had not ceased worshipping the emperor as *Kurios*. The word *Kurios* was and is the touchstone of faith. *And shalt believe (kai pisteusēis)*. Same construction. Faith precedes confession, of course.

10. *Man believeth (pisteuetai)*. Impersonal construction, "it is believed" (present passive indicative of *pisteuō*). The order is reversed in this verse and the true order (faith, then confession). *Confession is made (homologeitai)*. Impersonal construction again, "it is confessed," "man confesses." Both *kardiāi* (heart) and *stomati* (mouth) are in the instrumental case.

11. *Every one (pās)*. Paul adds this word to the quotation from Isa. 28:16 already made in 9:33.

12. *Distinction (diastolē)*. See on this word 3:22. Here it is followed by the ablative case *Ioudaiou te kai Hellēnos* (between Jew and Greek). *Lord of all (Kurios pantōn)*. See Gal. 3:28. *Rich (ploutōn)*. Present active participle of *plouteō*. See Eph. 3:8 "the unsearchable riches of Christ."

13. Paul here quotes Joel 3:5 (2:32 LXX).

14. *How then shall they call? (pōs oun epikalesōntai?)*. Deliberative subjunctive (first aorist middle) of *epikaleomai* (see verses 12 and 13). The antecedent of *eis hon* (in whom) is not expressed. *How shall they believe? (pos pisteusōsin?)*. Deliberative subjunctive again (first aorist active of *pisteuō* just used). Each time Paul picks up the preceding verb and

challenges that. Here again the antecedent *eis touton* before *hon* is not expressed. *How shall they hear?* (*pos akousōsin?*). Deliberative subjunctive (first aorist active of *akouō*). *Without a preacher?* (*chōris kērussontos?*). Preposition *chōris* with ablative singular masculine present active participle of *kērussō*, "without one preaching." *How shall they preach?* (*pōs kēruxōsin?*). Deliberative subjunctive again (first aorist active *kērussō*, to preach). *Except they be sent?* (*ean mē apostalōsin?*). Second aorist passive deliberative subjunctive of *apostellō*, to send, from which verb *apostolos* apostle comes. Negative condition of third class. In graphic style Paul has made a powerful plea for missions. It is just as true today as then.

15. *How beautiful* (*Hōs hōraioi*). A quotation from Isa. 52:7 more like the Hebrew than the LXX, picturing the messengers of the restoration from the Jewish captivity. Paul assumes that the missionaries (*apostoloi*) have been sent as implied in verse 14.

16. *But they did not all hearken* (*ou pantes hupēkousan*). They heard, but did not heed. Some disbelieve now (3:3) as they did then. On obedience and disobedience see 5:19; I Thess. 2:13; Gal. 3:2. He quotes Isa. 53:1 to show how Isaiah felt. *Report* (*akoēi*). Literally, "hearing" (Matt. 14:1; Mark 13:7).

17. *By the word of Christ* (*dia rēmatos Christou*). "By the word about Christ" (objective genitive).

18. *Did they not hear?* (*mē ouk ēkousan?*). Rather, "Did they fail to hear?" (expecting the negative answer *mē*, while *ouk* blends with the verb). See on I Cor. 9:5 for this construction. *Yea, verily* (*menounge*). Triple particle (*men, oun, ge*) as in 9:20. *Sound* (*phthoggos*). Vibration of a musical string. See on I Cor. 14:7. Only two N.T. examples. *The world* (*tēs oikoumenēs*). The inhabited earth as in Luke 2:1.

19. *Did Israel not know?* (*mē Israel ouk egnō?*). "Did Israel fail to know?" See above. *First* (*prōtos*). Moses first before any one else. LXX quotation Deut. 32:21. See on I Cor. 10:22 for *parazēlōsō* (I will provoke you to jealousy). *With that which is no nation* (*ep' ouk ethnei*). The Jews had worshipped "no-gods" and now God shows favours to a "no-nation" (people). *Will I anger you* (*parorgiō humas*). Future

active (Attic future) of *parorgizō*, rare word, to rouse to wrath.

20. *Is very bold* (*apotolmāi*). Present active indicative of *apotolmaō*, old word, to assume boldness (*apo*, off) and only here in N.T. Isaiah "breaks out boldly" (Gifford). Paul cites Isa. 65:1 in support of his own courage against the prejudice of the Jews. See 9:30–33 for illustration of this point. *I was found* (*heurethēn*). First aorist passive indicative of *heuriskō*.

21. *All the day long* (*holēn tēn hēmeran*). Accusative of extent of time. He quotes Isa. 65:2. *Did I spread out* (*exepetasa*). First aorist active indicative of *ekpetannumi*, old verb, to stretch out, bold metaphor, only here in N.T. *Unto a disobedient and a gainsaying people* (*pros laon apeithounta kai antilegonta*). "Unto a people disobeying and talking back." The two things usually go together. Contrary and contradictory (Luke 13:34f.).

CHAPTER XI

1. *I say then (legō oun).* As in verse 11. *Oun* looks back to 9:16–33 and 10:19–21. *Did God cast off? (mē apōsato ho theos?).* An indignant negative answer is called for by *mē* and emphasized by *mē genoito* (God forbid). Paul refers to the promise in the O.T. made three times: I Sam. 12:22; Psa. 94 (93 LXX):14; 94 (94 LXX):4. First aorist middle indicative (without augment) of *apōtheō*, to push away, to repel, middle, to push away from one as in Acts 7:27. *For I also (kai gar egō).* Proof that not all the Jews have rejected Christ. See Phil. 3:5 for more of Paul's pedigree.

2. *Whom he foreknew (hon proegnō).* The same form and sense as in 8:29, which see. Probably the Hebrew sense of choice beforehand. The nation of Israel was God's chosen people and so all the individuals in it could not be cast off. *Wot ye not? (ouk oidate?).* "Know ye not?" Why keep the old English "wot"? *Of Elijah (en Ēleiāi).* "In the case of Elijah." Cf. "in the bush" (Mark 12:26). *He pleadeth (entugchanei).* See on 8:27. *Entugchanō* means to happen on one and so to converse with (Acts 25:24), to plead for (Rom. 8:27, 34), to plead against as here with *kata*, but the "against" is in *kata*.

3. *They have digged down (kateskapsan).* First aorist active indicative of *kataskaptō*, to dig under or down. Old verb, here only in N.T. (critical text). LXX has *katheilan* "pulled down." Paul has reversed the order of the LXX of I Kings 19:10, 14, 18. *Altars (thusiastēria).* Late word (LXX, Philo, Josephus, N.T. eccl. writers) from *thusiazō*, to sacrifice. See Acts 17:23. *And I am left alone (kágō hupeleiphthēn monos).* First aorist passive indicative of *hupoleipō*, old word, to leave under or behind, here only in N.T. Elijah's mood was that of utter dejection in his flight from Jezebel. *Life (psuchēn).* It is not possible to draw a clear distinction between *psuchē* (soul) and *pneuma* (spirit). *Psuchē* is from *psuchō*, to breathe or blow, *pneuma* from *pneō*, to blow. Both are used for the personality and for the immortal part of

392

man. Paul is usually dichotomous in his language, but sometimes trichotomous in a popular sense. We cannot hold Paul's terms to our modern psychological distinctions.

4. *The answer of God* (*ho chrēmatismos*). An old word in various senses like *chrēmatizō*, only here in N.T. See this use of the verb in Matt. 2:12, 22; Luke 2:26; Acts 10:22. *To Baal* (*tēi Baal*). Feminine article. In the LXX the name *Baal* is either masculine or feminine. The explanation is that the Jews put *Bosheth* (*aischunē*, shame) for Baal and in the LXX the feminine article occurs because *aischunē* is so, though here the LXX has the masculine *tōi*.

5. *Remnant* (*limma*). Old word, but only here in N.T., but in papyri also and with this spelling rather than *leimma*. From *leipō*, to leave. *According to the election of grace* (*kat' eklogēn charitos*). As in 9:6-13. The election is all of God. Verse 6 explains it further.

6. *Otherwise* (*epei*). Ellipse after *epei* (since), "since, in that case." *Is no more* (*ouketi ginetai*). "No longer becomes" grace, loses its character as grace. Augustine: *Gratia nisi gratis sit gratia non est.*

7. *What then?* (*ti oun?*). Since God did not push Israel away (verse 1), what is true? *The election* (*hē eklogē*). Abstract for concrete (the elect). *Obtained* (*epetuchen*). Second aorist active indicative of *epitugchanō*, old verb, to hit upon, only here in Paul. See 9:30-33 for the failure of the Jews. *Were hardened* (*epōrōthēsan*). First aorist passive indicative of *pōroō*, late verb, to cover with thick skin (*pōros*). See on II Cor. 3:14; Mark. 3:5.

8. *A spirit of stupor* (*pneuma katanuxeōs*). The quotation is a combination of Deut. 19:4; Isa. 29:10; 6:9f. This phrase is from Isa. 29:10. *Katanuxis* is a late and rare word from *katanussō*, to prick or stick (Acts 2:37), in LXX, here only in N.T., one example in *Pelagia-Legende*. The torpor seems the result of too much sensation, dulled by incitement into apathy. *That they should not see* (*tou mē blepein*). Genitive articular infinitive of negative purpose. *That they should not hear* (*tou mē akouein*). So here also. See Stephen's speech (Acts 7:51f.).

9. *David says* (*Daueid legei*). From Psa. 69 (68 LXX): 23f.; 34:8; 28:4 (combined quotation). *Table* (*trapeza*). For what is on the table, "a feast." *A snare* (*eis pagida*). From

pēgnumi, to make fast, old word for snares for birds and beasts. See on Luke 21:35. *Eis* in predicate with *ginomai* is a translation-Hebraism. *A trap (eis thēran)*. Old word for hunting of wild beasts, then a trap. Only here in N.T. *A stumbling-block (eis skandalon)*. A third word for trap, snare, trap-stick or trigger over which they fall. See on I Cor. 1:23; Rom. 9:33. *A recompense (eis antapodoma)*. Late word from double compound verb *antapodidōmi*, to repay (both *anti* and *apo*). Ancient Greeks used *antapodosis*. In LXX and Didache. In N.T. only here (bad sense) and Luke 14:12 (good sense).

10. *Let their eyes be darkened (skotisthētōsan hoi ophthalmoi autōn)*. First aorist passive imperative of *skotizō*, to darken. A terrible imprecation. *That they may not see (tou mē blepein)*. Repeated from verse 8. *Bow down (sunkampson)*. First aorist active imperative of *sunkamptō*, old verb, to bend together as of captives whose backs (*nōton*, another old word, only here in N.T.) were bent under burdens. Only here in N.T.

11. *Did they stumble that they might fall? (mē eptaisan hina pesōsin?)*. Negative answer expected by *mē* as in verse 1. First aorist active indicative of *ptaiō*, old verb, to stumble, only here in Paul (see James 3:2), suggested perhaps by *skandalon* in verse 9. If *hina* is final, then we must add "merely" to the idea, "merely that they might fall" or make a sharp distinction between *ptaiō*, to stumble, and *piptō*, to fall, and take *pesōsin* as effective aorist active subjunctive to fall completely and for good. *Hina*, as we know, can be either final, sub-final, or even result. See I Thess. 5:4; I Cor. 7:29; Gal. 5:17. Paul rejects this query in verse 11 as vehemently as he did that in verse 1. *By their fall (tōi autōn paraptōmati)*. Instrumental case. For the word, a falling aside or a false step from *parapiptō*, see 5:15–20. *Is come*. No verb in the Greek, but *ginetai* or *gegonen* is understood. *For to provoke them to jealousy (eis to parazēlōsai)*. Purpose expressed by *eis* and the articular infinitive, first aorist active, of *parazēloō*, for which verb see I Cor. 10:22. As an historical fact Paul turned to the Gentiles when the Jews rejected his message (Acts 13:45ff.; 28:28, etc.). *The riches of the world (ploutos kosmou)*. See 10:12. *Their loss (to hēttēma autōn)*. So perhaps in I Cor. 6:7, but in Isa. 31:8

defeat is the idea. Perhaps so here. *Fulness (plērōma)*. Perhaps "completion," though the word from *plēroō*, to fill, has a variety of senses, that with which anything is filled (I Cor. 10:26, 28), that which is filled (Eph. 1:23). *How much more? (posōi mallon)*. Argument *a fortiori* as in verse 24. Verse 25 illustrates the point.

13. *To you that are Gentiles (humin tois ethnesin)*. "To you the Gentiles." He has a serious word to say to them. *Inasmuch then (eph' hoson men oun)*. Not temporal, *quamdiu*, "so long as" (Matt. 9:15), but qualitative *quatenus* "in so far then as" (Matt. 25:40). *I glorify my ministry (tēn diakonian mou doxazō)*. As apostle to the Gentiles (*ethnōn apostolos*, objective genitive). Would that every minister of Christ glorified his ministry. *If by any means (ei pōs)*. This use of *ei* with purpose or aim is a kind of indirect discourse. *I may provoke (parazēlōsō)*. Either future active indicative or first aorist active subjunctive, see same uncertainty in Phil. 3:10 *katantēsō*, but in 3:11 *katalabō* after *ei* is subjunctive. The future indicative is clear in Rom. 1:10 and the optative in Acts 27:12. Doubtful whether future indicative or aorist subjunctive also in *sōsō* (save).

15. *The casting away of them (hē apobolē autōn)*. Objective genitive (*autōn*) with *apobolē*, old word from *apoballō*, to throw off (Mark 10:50), in N.T. only here and Acts 27:22. *The reconciling of the world (katallagē kosmou)*. See 5:10f. for *katallagē* (reconciling). It explains verse 12. *The receiving (hē proslēmpsis)*. Old word from *proslambanō*, to take to oneself, only here in N.T. *Life from the dead (zōē ek nekrōn)*. Already the conversion of Jews had become so difficult. It is like a miracle of grace today, though it does happen. Many think that Paul means that the general resurrection and the end will come when the Jews are converted. Possibly so, but it is by no means certain. His language may be merely figurative.

16. *First fruit (aparchē)*. See on I Cor. 15:20, 23. The metaphor is from Numb. 15:19f. The LXX has *aparchēn phuramatos*, first of the dough as a heave offering. *The lump (to phurama)*. From which the first fruit came. See on 9:21. Apparently the patriarchs are the first fruit. *The root (hē riza)*. Perhaps Abraham singly here. The metaphor is changed, but the idea is the same. Israel is looked on as

a tree. But one must recall and keep in mind the double sense of Israel in 9:6f. (the natural and the spiritual).

17. *Branches* (*kladōn*). From *klaō*, to break. *Were broken off* (*exeklasthēsan*). First aorist passive indicative of *ekklaō*. Play oň the word *klados* (branch) and *ekklaō*, to break off. Condition of first class, assumed as true. Some of the individual Jews (natural Israel) were broken off the stock of the tree (spiritual Israel). *And thou* (*kai su*). An individual Gentile. *Being a wild olive* (*agrielaios ōn*). This word, used by Aristotle, occurs in an inscription. Ramsay (*Pauline Studies*, pp. 219ff.) shows that the ancients used the wild-olive graft upon an old olive tree to reinvigorate the tree precisely as Paul uses the figure here and that both the olive tree and the graft were influenced by each other, though the wild olive graft did not produce as good olives as the original stock. But it should be noted that in verse 24 Paul expressly states that the grafting of Gentiles on to the stock of the spiritual Israel was "contrary to nature" (*para phusin*). *Wast grafted in* (*enekentristhēs*). First aorist passive indicative of *enkentrizō*, to cut in, to graft, used by Aristotle. Belongs "to the higher *Koinē*" (literary *Koinē*) according to Milligan. *Partaker* (*sunkoinōnos*). Co-partner. *Fatness* (*piotētos*). Old word from *piōn* (fat), only here in N.T. Note three genitives here "of the root of the fatness of the olive."

18. *Glory not over the branches* (*mē katakauchō tōn kladōn*). Genitive case after *kata*. Present middle imperative second person singular of *katakauchaomai* with negative *mē*, "stop glorying" or "do not have the habit of glorying over the branches." The conclusion of the preceding condition. *Gloriest* (*katakauchāsai*). Late form -*aesai* retaining *s*. *Not thou* (*ou su*). Very emphatic position. The graft was upon the stock and root, though each affected the other.

19. *Thou wilt say then* (*ereis oun*). A presumptuous Gentile speaks. *That I might be grafted in* (*hina egō enkentristhō*). Purpose clause with *hina* and first aorist passive subjunctive. He shows contempt for the cast-off Jews.

20. *Well* (*kalōs*). Perhaps ironical, though Paul may simply admit the statement (cf. Mark 12:32) and show the Gentile his real situation. *By unbelief* (*tēi apistiāi*)—*by faith* (*pistei*). Instrumental case with both contrasted words (by unbelief, by belief).

21. *Be not highminded* (*mē hupsēla phronei*). "Stop thinking high (proud) thoughts." *If God spared not* (*ei gar ho theos ouk epheisato*). It is not *ei mē* (unless), but the *ouk* negatives the verb *epheisato* (first aorist middle indicative of *pheidomai*, to spare. Condition of first class.

22. *The goodness and the severity of God* (*chrēstotēta kai apotomian theou*). See on Rom. 2:2 for *chrēstotēs*, kindness of God. *Apotomia* (here alone in the N.T.) is from *apotomos*, cut off, abrupt, and this adjective from *apotemnō*, to cut off. This late word occurs several times in the papyri. *If thou continue* (*ean epimenēis*). Third class condition, *ean* and present active subjunctive. *Otherwise* (*epei*). Ellipse after *epei*, "since if thou dost not continue." *Thou also* (*kai su*). Precisely as the Jewish branches of verse 17 were. *Shalt be cut off* (*ekkopēsei*). Second future passive of *ekkoptō*, to cut out.

23. *If they continue not in their unbelief* (*ean mē epimenōsi tēi apistiāi*). Third class condition with the same verb used in verse 22 of the Gentile. Locative case of *apistiāi* here (same form as the instrumental in verse 20). *For God is able* (*dunatos gar estin ho theos*). See this use of *dunatos estin* in 4:21 rather than *dunatai*. This is the *crux* of the whole matter. God is able.

24. *Contrary to nature* (*para phusin*). This is the gist of the argument, the power of God to do what is contrary to natural processes. He put the wild olive (Gentile) into the good olive tree (the spiritual Israel) and made the wild olive (contrary to nature) become the good olive (*kallielaios*, the garden olive, *kallos* and *elaia* in Aristotle and a papyrus). *Into their own olive tree* (*tēi idiāi elaiāi*). Dative case. Another argument *a fortiori*, "how much more" (*pollōi mallon*). God can graft the natural Israel back upon the spiritual Israel, if they become willing.

25. *This mystery* (*to mustērion touto*). Not in the pagan sense of an esoteric doctrine for the initiated (from *mueō*, to blink, to wink), unknown secrets (II Thess. 2:7), or like the mystery religions of the time, but the revealed will of God now made known to all (I Cor. 2:1, 7; 4:1) which includes Gentiles also (Rom. 16:25; Col. 1:26f.; Eph. 3:3f.) and so far superior to man's wisdom (Col. 2:2; 4:13; Eph. 3:9; 5:32; 6:19; Matt. 13:11 = Mark 4:11). Paul has covered every point of difficulty concerning the failure of the Jews to accept Jesus as the Messiah and has shown how God has overruled it for the blessing of the Gentiles with a ray of hope still held out for the Jews. "In early ecclesiastical Latin *mustērion* was rendered by *sacramentum*, which in classical Latin means *the military oath*. The explanation of the word *sacrament*, which is so often founded on this etymology, is therefore mistaken, since the meaning of sacrament belongs to *mustērion* and not to *sacramentum* in the classical sense" (Vincent). *Wise in your own conceits* (*en heautois phronimoi*). "Wise in yourselves." Some MSS. read *par' heautois* (by yourselves). Negative purpose here (*hina mē ēte*), to prevent self-conceit on the part of the Gentiles who have believed. They had no merit in themselves. *A hardening* (*pōrōsis*). Late word from *pōroō* (11:7). Occurs in Hippocrates as a medical term, only here in N.T. save Mark 3:5; Eph. 4:18. It means obtuseness of intellectual discernment, mental dulness. *In part* (*apo merous*). Goes with the verb *gegonen* (has happened in part). For *apo merous*, see II Cor. 1:14; 2:5; Rom. 15:24; for *ana meros*, see I Cor. 14:27; for *ek merous*, see I Cor. 12:27; 13:9; for *kata meros*, see Heb. 9:5; for *meros ti* (adverbial accusative) partly see I Cor. 11:18. Paul refuses to believe that no more Jews will be saved. *Until the fulness of the Gentiles be come in* (*achri hou to plērōma tōn ethnōn eiselthēi*). Temporal clause with *achri hou* (until which time) and the second aorist active subjunctive of *eiserchomai*, to come in (Matt. 7:13, 21). For *fulness of the Gentiles* (*to plērōma tōn ethnōn*) see on verse 12, the complement of the Gentiles.

26. *And so* (*kai houtōs*). By the complement of the Gentiles stirring up the complement of the Jews (verses 11f.). *All Israel* (*pās Israēl*). What does Paul mean? The immediate context (use of *pās* in contrast with *apo merous*, *plērōma* here in contrast with *plērōma* in verse 12) argues for the Jewish people "as a whole." But the spiritual Israel (both Jews and Gentiles) may be his idea in accord with 9:6 (Gal. 6:16) as the climax of the argument. At any rate we should strive for and pray for the conversion of Jews as a whole. Paul here quotes from Isa. 59:20f.; 27:9. *The Deliverer* (*ho ruomenos*). Present middle articular participle of *ruomai*, to rescue, to deliver. See on I Thess. 1:10;

II Cor. 1:10. The Hebrew *Goel*, the Avenger, the Messiah, the Redeemer (Deut. 25:5–10; Job 19:25; Ruth 3:12f.). Paul interprets it of Jesus as Messiah.

27. *My covenant (hē par' emou diathēkē)*. "The from me covenant," "my side of the covenant I have made with them" (Sanday and Headlam). Cf. Jer. 31:31ff. Not a political deliverance, but a religious and ethical one. *When I shall take away (hotan aphelōmai)*. Second aorist middle subjunctive of *aphaireō*, old and common verb, to take away.

28. *As touching the gospel (kata to euaggelion)*. "According to (*kata* with the accusative) the gospel" as Paul has shown in verses 11–24, the gospel order as it has developed. *Enemies (echthroi)*. Treated as enemies (of God), in passive sense, because of their rejection of Christ (verse 10), just as *agapētoi* (beloved) is passive. *As touching the election (kata tēn eklogēn)*. "According to the election" (the principle of election, not as in verses 5f. the elect or abstract for concrete). *For the fathers' sake (dia tous pateras)*. As in 9:4; 11:16f.

29. *Without repentance (ametamelēta)*. See on II Cor. 7:10 for this word (*a* privative and *metamelomai*, to be sorry afterwards). It is not *ametanoēton* (Rom. 2:5) from *a* privative and *metanoeō*, to change one's mind. God is not sorry for his gifts to and calling of the Jews (9:4f.).

30. *Ye in time past (humeis pote)*. Ye Gentiles (1:18–32). *Were disobedient (epeithēsate)*. First aorist active indicative of *apeitheō*, to disbelieve and then to disobey. "Ye once upon a time disobeyed God." *By their disobedience (tēi toutōn apeithiāi)*. Instrumental case, "by the disobedience of these" (Jews). Note "now" (*nun*) three times in this sentence.

31. *By the mercy shown to you (tōi humeterōi eleei)*. Objective sense of *humeteros* (possessive pronoun, your). Proleptic position also for the words go with *eleēthōsin* (first aorist passive subjunctive of *eleeō*, from *eleos* with *hina*, purpose clause). God's purpose is for the Jews to receive a blessing yet.

32. *Hath shut up (sunekleisen)*. First aorist active indicative of *sunkleiō*, to shut together like a net (Luke 5:6). See Gal. 3:22 for this word with *hupo hamartian* (under sin). This is a resultant (effective) aorist because of the disbelief

and disobedience of both Gentile (1:17–32) and Jew (2:1–3:20). *All (tous pantas)*. "The all" (both Gentiles and Jews). *That he might have mercy (hina—eleēsēi)*. Purpose with *hina* and aorist active subjunctive. No merit in anyone, but all of grace. "The all" again, who receive God's mercy, not that "all" men are saved.

33. *O the depth (O bathos)*. Exclamation with omega and the nominative case of *bathos* (see on II Cor. 8:2; Rom. 8:39). Paul's argument concerning God's elective grace and goodness has carried him to the heights and now he pauses on the edge of the precipice as he contemplates God's wisdom and knowledge, fully conscious of his inability to sound the bottom with the plummet of human reason and words. *Unsearchable (anexerauntēta)*. Double compound (*a* privative and *ex*) verbal adjective of *ereunaō* (old spelling -*eu*-), late and rare word (LXX, Dio Cassius, Heraclitus), only here in N.T. Some of God's wisdom can be known (1:20f.), but not all. *Past tracing out (anexichniastoi)*. Another verbal adjective from *a* privative and *exichniazō*, to trace out by tracks (*ichnos* Rom. 4:12). Late word in Job (5:9; 9:10; 34:24) from which use Paul obtained it here and Eph. 3:8 (only N.T. examples). Also in ecclesiastical writers. Some of God's tracks he has left plain to us, but others are beyond us.

34. *Who hath known? (tis egnō?)*. Second aorist active indicative of *ginōskō*, a timeless aorist, did know, does know, will know. Quotation from Isa. 40:13. Quoted already in I Cor. 2:16. *Counsellor (sumboulos)*. Old word from *sun* and *boulē*. Only here in N.T. *His (autou)*. Objective genitive, counsellor to him (God). Some men seem to feel competent for the job.

35. *First driven to him (proedōken autōi)*. First aorist active indicative of *prodidōmi*, to give beforehand or first. Old verb, here alone in N.T. From Job 41:11, but not like the LXX, Paul's own translation. *Shall be recompensed (antapodothēsetai)*. First future passive of double compound *antapodidōmi*, to pay back (both *anti* and *apo*), old word in good sense, as here and Luke 14:14; I Thess. 3:9 and in bad sense as II Thess. 1:6; Rom. 12:19.

36. *Of him (ex autou), through him (di' autou), unto him (eis auton)*. By these three prepositions Paul ascribes the

universe (*ta panta*) with all the phenomena concerning creation, redemption, providence to God as the *Source* (*ex*), the *Agent* (*di*), the *Goal* (*eis*). For ever (*eis tous aiōnas*). "For the ages." Alford terms this doxology in verses 33 to 36 "the sublimest apostrophe existing even in the pages of inspiration itself."

CHAPTER XII

1. *Therefore (oun)*. This inferential participle gathers up all the great argument of chapters 1 to 11. Now Paul turns to exhortation *(parakalō)*, "I beseech you." *By the mercies (dia tōn oiktirmōn)*. "By means of the mercies of God" as shown in his argument and in our lives. See II Cor. 1:3 for "the Father of mercies." *To present (parastēsai)*. First aorist active infinitive of *paristēmi*, for which verb see 6:13, a technical term for offering a sacrifice (Josephus, *Ant*. IV. 6. 4), though not in the O.T. Used of presenting the child Jesus in the temple (Luke 2:22), of the Christian presenting himself (Rom. 6:13), of God presenting the saved (Eph. 5:27), of Christ presenting the church (Col. 1:28). *Bodies (sōmata)*. So literally as in 6:13, 19; II Cor. 5:10 and in contrast with *nous* (mind) in verse 2. *A living sacrifice (thusian zōsan)*. In contrast with the Levitical sacrifices of slain animals. Cf. 6:8, 11, 13. Not a propitiatory sacrifice, but one of praise. *Acceptable (euareston)*. "Well-pleasing." See on II Cor. 5:9. *Which is your reasonable service (tēn logikēn humōn latreian)*. "Your rational (spiritual) service (worship)." For *latreia*, see on 9:4. *Logikos* is from *logos*, reason. The phrase means here "worship rendered by the reason (or soul)." Old word, in N.T. only here and I Peter 2:2 *to logikon gala* (not logical milk, but the milk nourishing the soul).

2. *Be not fashioned (mē sunschēmatizesthe)*. Present passive imperative with *mē*, stop being fashioned or do not have the habit of being fashioned. Late Greek verb *suschēmatizō*, to conform to another's pattern (I Cor. 7:31; Phil. 2:7f.). In N.T. only here and I Peter 1:14. *According to this world (tōi aiōni toutōi)*. Associative instrumental case. Do not take this age as your fashion plate. *Be ye transformed (metamorphousthe)*. Present passive imperative of *metamorphoō*, another late verb, to transfigure as in Matt. 17:2 (=Mark 9:2); II Cor. 3:18, which see. On the distinction between *schēma* and *morphē*, see Phil. 2:7. There must be a radical change in the inner man for one to live rightly in

this evil age, "by the renewing of your mind" (*tēi anakai-nōsei tou noos*). Instrumental case. The new birth, the new mind, the new (*kainos*) man. *That ye may prove (eis to dokimazein)*. Infinitive of purpose with *eis to*, "to test" what is God's will, "the good and acceptable and perfect" (*to agathon kai euareston kai teleion*).

3. *Not to think of himself more highly than he ought to think* (*mē huperphronein par' ho dei phronein*). Indirect negative command after *legō* (I say). Play on the two infinitives *phronein*, to think, and *huperphronein* (old verb from *huper-phrōn*, over-proud, here only in N.T.) to "over-think" with *par' ho* (beyond what) added. Then another play on *phronein* and *sōphronein* (old verb from *sōphrōn*, sober-minded), to be in one's right mind (Mark 5:15; II Cor. 5:13). Self-conceit is here treated as a species of insanity. *A measure of faith (metron pisteōs)*. Accusative case, the object of the verb *emerisen*. Each has his gift from God (I Cor. 3:5; 4:7). There is no occasion for undue pride. *To each man (hekas-tōi)*. Emphatic position before *hōs* (as) and emphasizes the diversity.

4. *The same office (tēn autēn praxin)*. Mode of acting or function. Cf. Acts 19:18; Tim. 8:13.

5. *And severally (to de kath' heis)*. A difficult late idiom where the preposition *kath'* (*kata*) is treated adverbially with no effect on the nominative case *heis* like *huper egō* (II Cor. 11:23). So *heis kath' heis* (Mark 14:19) and in Modern Greek *katheis* as a distributive pronoun. But we have *kath' hena* in I Cor. 14:31. The use of the neuter article here *to* with *kath' heis* is probably the accusative of general reference, "as to each one."

6. *Differing (diaphora)*. Old adjective from *diapherō*, to differ, to vary. So Heb. 9:10. *According to the proportion of our faith (kata tēn analogian tēs pisteōs)*. The same use of *pistis* (faith) as in verse 3 "the measure of faith." Old word. *analogia* (our word "analogy") from *analogos* (analogous, conformable, proportional). Here alone in N.T. The verb *prophēteuōmen* (present active volitive subjunctive, let us prophesy) must be supplied with which *echontes* agrees. The context calls for the subjective meaning of "faith" rather than the objective and outward standard though *pistis* does occur in that sense (Gal. 1:23; 3:23).

7. *Let us give ourselves.* There is no verb in the Greek. We must supply *dōmen heautous* or some such phrase. *Or he that teacheth (eite ho didaskōn).* Here the construction changes and no longer do we have the accusative case like *diakonian* (general word for Christian service of all kinds including ministers and deacons) as the object of *echontes*, but the nominative articular participle. A new verb must be supplied of which *ho didaskōn* is the subject as with the succeeding participles through verse 8. Perhaps in each instance the verb is to be repeated from the participle like *didasketō* here (let him teach) or a general term *poieitō* (let him do it) can be used for all of them as seems necessary before "with liberality" in verse 8 (*en haplotēti*, in simplicity, for which word, see Matt. 6:22; II Cor. 8:2; 9:11, 13). *He that ruleth (ho proistamenos).* "The one standing in front" for which see I Thess. 5:12. *With diligence (en spoudēi).* "In haste" as if in earnest (Mark 6:25; II Cor. 7:11f., 8:8, 16), from *speudō*, to hasten. Again verse 11. *With cheerfulness (en hilarotēti).* Late word, only here in N.T., from *hilaros* (II Cor. 9:7) cheerful, hilarious.

9. *Without hypocrisy (anupokritos).* Late double compound adjective for which see II Cor. 6:6. Hypocritical or pretended love is no love at all as Paul describes *agapē* in I Cor. 13. *Abhor (apostugountes).* Old verb with intensive (*apo*) dislike, only here in N.T. The present active participle is here employed in the sense of the present active indicative as sometimes happens with the independent participle (Robertson, *Grammar*, pp. 1132ff.). This same idiom appears with *kollōmenoi* (cleaving) for which verb see on I Cor. 6:17, with *proēgoumenoi* (preferring) in verse 10 (old verb here only in N.T.), and with the participles in verses 11 to 13 and again in verses 16 to 18. One can supply *este* if he prefers.

10. *In love of the brethren (tēi philadelphiāi).* Late word for brotherly love for which see I Thess. 4:9. *Tenderly affectioned (philostorgoi).* Old compound adjective from *philos* and *storgē* (mutual love of parents and children), here alone in N.T.

11. *Slothful (oknēroi).* Old adjective from *okneō*, to hesitate, to be slow. Slow and "poky" as in Matt. 25:26.

12. *Patient in tribulation (tēi thlipsei hupomenontes).* So soon this virtue became a mark of the Christians.

13. *Communicating (koinōnountes)*. "Contributing." From *koinōneō* for which see II Cor. 9:13. Paul had raised a great collection for the poor saints in Jerusalem. *Given to hospitality (tēn philoxenian diōkontes)*. "Pursuing (as if in a chase or hunt) hospitality" (*philoxenia*, old word from *philoxenos*, fond of strangers, *philos* and *xenos* as in I Tim. 3:2). In N.T. only here and Heb. 13:2. See II Cor. 3:1. They were to pursue (*diōkō*) hospitality as their enemies pursued (*diōkontas*) them.

14. *And curse not (kai mē katarāsthe)*. Present middle imperative with *mē*. Like Matt. 5:44 in spirit, not a quotation, but a reminiscence of the words of Jesus. The negative addition gives emphasis. See Luke 6:28 for the old verb *kataraomai* from *katara* (curse).

15. *Rejoice (chairein)*. Present active infinitive of *chairō*, absolute or independent use of the infinitive as if a finite verb as occurs sometimes (Robertson, *Grammar*, pp. 1092ff.). Literally here, "Rejoicing with rejoicing people, weeping with weeping people."

16. *Be of the same mind (to auto phronountes)*. Absolute or independent use of the participle again as with all the participles through verse 18, "thinking the same thing." *Set not your mind on high things (mē ta hupsēla phronountes)*. "Not thinking the high things" (*hupsēlos* from *hupsos*, height). Cf. I Cor. 13:5. *Condescend to things that are lowly (tois tapeinois sunapagomenoi)*. "Be carried away with (borne along with) the lowly things" (in contrast with *ta hupsēla*, though the associative instrumental case may be masculine, "with lowly men." See Gal. 2:13 and II Peter 3:17 for the only other N.T. examples of this old verb. *Be not wise (mē ginesthe phronimoi)*. "Do not have the habit of becoming (*ginesthe*) wise in your own conceits" (*par' heautois*, beside yourselves). Note the imperative in the midst of infinitives and participles.

17. *Render to no man (mēdeni apodidontes)*. "Giving back to no man." Independent participle again. *Evil for evil (kakon anti kakou)*. Directly opposite to the law of retaliation of the Pharisees as in Matt. 5:39; I Thess. 5:15; I Cor. 13:5f. *Take thought of (pronooumenoi)*. "Taking thought beforehand." Old word. See II Cor. 8:21.

18. *As much as in you lieth (to ex humōn)*. Accusative of

general reference, "so far as what proceeds from you" ("the from you part"). See *to kat' eme* in 1:15. This phrase explains "if it be possible" (*ei dunaton*). "All *your* part is to be peace" (Alford). For "be at peace" (*eirēneuontes*) see II Cor. 13:11.

19. *Avenge not* (*mē ekdikountes*). Independent participle again of late verb *ekdikeō* from *ekdikos*, exacting justice (13:4). See already Luke 18:5; II Cor. 10:6. *But give place unto wrath* (*alla dote topon tēi orgēi*). Second aorist active imperative of *didōmi*, to give. "Give room for the (note article as in 5:9; I Thess. 2:16) wrath" of God instead of taking vengeance in your own hands. See Eph. 4:27 for *didote topon*. Paul quotes Deut. 32:35 (the Hebrew rather than the LXX). So have Heb. 10:30 and the Targum of Onkelos, but the relation between them and Paul we cannot tell. Socrates and Epictetus condemned personal vindictiveness as Paul does here. *I will recompense* (*antapodōsō*). Future active of the double compound verb quoted also in 11:35.

20. *Feed him* (*psōmize auton*). Quotation from LXX text of Prov. 25:21f. Present active imperative of verb from *psōmos*, a morsel, and so to feed crumbs to babies, then to feed in general. In N.T. only here and I Cor. 13:3. *Thou shalt heap* (*sōreuseis*). Future active of old verb *sōreuō* from *sōros*, a heap. In N.T. only here and II Tim. 3:6. *Coals of fire* (*anthrakas puros*). That is, burning or live coals. *Anthrax* (our "anthracite") is an old word, only here in N.T. It is a metaphor for keen anguish. The Arabs have a proverb "coals in the heart," "fire in the liver." Such kindness may lead to repentance also.

21. *Be not overcome of evil* (*mē nikō hupo tou kakou*). Present passive imperative of *nikaō*, to conquer. "Stop being conquered by the evil (thing or man)," *But overcome evil with good* (*alla nika en tōi agathōi to kakon*). "But keep on conquering the evil in the good." Drown the evil in the good. Seneca: *Vincit malos pertinax bonitas.*

CHAPTER XIII

1. *Every soul* (*pāsa psuchē*). As in 2:9; Acts 2:43. A Hebraism for *pās anthrōpos* (every man). *To the higher powers* (*exousiais huperechousais*). Abstract for concrete. See Mark 2:10 for *exousia*. *Huperechō* is an old verb to have or hold over, to be above or supreme, as in I Peter 2:13. *Except by God* (*ei mē hupo theou*). So the best MSS. rather than *apo theou* (from God). God is the author of order, not anarchy. *The powers that be* (*hai ousai*). "The existing authorities" (supply *exousiai*). *Are ordained* (*tetagmenai eisin*). Periphrastic perfect passive indicative of *tassō*, "stand ordained by God." Paul is not arguing for the divine right of kings or for any special form of government, but for government and order. Nor does he oppose here revolution for a change of government, but he does oppose all lawlessness and disorder.

2. *He that resisteth* (*ho antitassomenos*). Present middle articular participle of *antitassō*, old verb to range in battle against as in Acts 18:6, "he that lines himself up against." *Withstandeth* (*anthestēken*). Perfect active indicative of *anthistēmi* and intransitive, "has taken his stand against." *The ordinance of God* (*tēi tou theou diatagēi*). Late word, but common in papyri (Deissmann, *Light, etc.*, p. 89), in N.T. only here and Acts 7:53. Note repetition of root of *tassō*. *To themselves* (*heautois*). Dative of disadvantage. See Mark 12:40 for "shall receive a judgment" (*krina lēmpsontai*). Future middle of *lambanō*.

3. *A terror* (*phobos*). This meaning in Isa. 8:13. Paul does not approve all that rulers do, but he is speaking generally of the ideal before rulers. Nero was Emperor at this time. *From the same* (*ex autēs*). "From it" (*exousia*, personified in verse 4).

4. *A minister of God* (*theou diakonos*). General sense of *diakonos*. Of course even Nero was God's minister "to thee (*soi* ethical dative) for good (*eis to agathon*, for the good)." That is the ideal, the goal. *Beareth* (*phorei*). Present active

indicative of *phoreō*, old frequentative form of *pherō*, to bear, to wear. *But if thou do (ean de poiēis).* Condition of third class, *ean* and present active subjunctive of *poieō*, "if thou continue to do." *Sword (machairan).* Symbol of authority as to-day policemen carry clubs or pistols. "The Emperor Trajan presented to a provincial governor on starting for his province, a dagger, with the words, '*For me.* If I deserve it, *in* me'" (Vincent). *An avenger (ekdikos).* Old adjective from *ek* and *dikē* (right), "outside of penalty," unjust, then in later Greek "exacting penalty from one," in N.T. only here and I Thess. 4:6.

5. *Ye must needs (anagkē).* "There is necessity," both because of the law and because of conscience, because it is right (2:15; 9:1).

6. *Ye pay (teleite).* Present active indicative (not imperative) of *teleō*, to fulfil. *Tribute (phorous).* Old word from *pherō*, to bring, especially the annual tax on lands, etc. (Luke 20:22; 23:1). Paying taxes recognizes authority over us. *Ministers of God's service (leitourgoi theou).* Late word for public servant (unused *leitos* from Attic *leōs*, people, and *ergō*, to work). Often used of military servants, servants of the king, and temple servants (Heb. 8:2). Paul uses it also of himself as Christ's *leitourgos* (Rom. 15:16) and of Epaphroditus as a minister to him (Phil. 2:25). See *theou diakonos* in verse 4. *Attending continually (proskarterountes).* Present active participle of the late verb *proskartereō* (*pros* and *kartereō* from *kartos* or *kratos*, strength) to persevere. See on Acts 2:42; 8:13.

7. *Dues (opheilas).* Debts, from *opheilō*, to owe. Often so in the papyri, though not in Greek authors. In N.T. only here, Matt. 18:32; I Cor. 7:3. Paying debts needs emphasis today, even for ministers. *To whom tribute is due (tōi ton phoron).* We must supply a participle with the article *tōi* like *apaitounti* ("to the one asking tribute"). So with the other words (*to whom custom, tōi to telos apaitounti; to whom fear, tōi ton phobon apaitounti; to whom honour, tōi tēn timēn apaitounti*). *Phoros* is the tribute paid to a subject nation (Luke 20:22), while *telos* is tax for support of civil government (Matt. 17:25).

8. *Save to love one another (ei mē to allēlous agapāin).* "Except the loving one another." This articular infinitive

is in the accusative case the object of *opheilete* and partitive
apposition with *mēden* (nothing). This debt can never be
paid off, but we should keep the interest paid up. *His
neighbour* (*ton heteron*). "The other man," "the second
man." "Just as in the relations of man and God *pistis* has
been substituted for *nomos*, so between man and man *agapē*
takes the place of definite legal relations" (Sanday and
Headlam). See Matt. 22:37-40 for the words of Jesus on
this subject. Love is the only solution of our social relations
and national problems.

9. *For this* (*to gar*). For the article (*to*) pointing to a sentence see 8:26, here to the quotation. The order of the commandments here is like that in Luke 18:20 and James 2:11
and in B for Deut. 5, but different from that of the Hebrew
in Ex. 20 and Deut. 5. The use of *ou* with the volitive future
in prohibitions in place of *mē* and the imperative or subjunctive is a regular Greek idiom. *And if there be any other*
(*kai ei tis hetera*). Paul does not attempt to give them all.
It is summed up (*anakephalaioutai*). Present passive indicative of *anakephalaioō*, late literary word or "rhetorical term"
(*ana, kephalaion*, head or chief as in Heb. 8:1). Not in the
papyri, but *kephalaion*, quite common for sum or summary.
In N.T. only here and Eph. 1:10. *Namely* (*en tōi*). See *to
gar* at the beginning of the verse, though omitted by B F.
The quotation is from Lev. 19:18. Quoted in Matt. 5:43;
22:39; Mark 12:31; Luke 10:27; Gal. 5:14 and in James 2:8
it is called *basilikos nomos* (royal law). *Thy neighbour* (*ton
plēsion sou*). *Plēsion* is an adverb and with the article it
means "the one near thee." See on Matt. 5:43.

10. *The fulfilment of the law* (*plērōma nomou*). "The filling
up or complement of the law" like *peplērōken* (perfect active
indicative of *plēroō*, stands filled up) in verse 8. See I Cor.
13 for the fuller exposition of this verse.

11. *And this* (*kai touto*). Either nominative absolute or
accusative of general reference, a common idiom for "and
that too" (I Cor. 6:6, 8, etc.). *Knowing* (*eidotes*). Second
perfect active participle, nominative plural without a principal verb. Either we must supply a verb like *poiēsōmen*
(let us do it) or *poiēsate* (do ye do it) or treat it as an independent participle as in 12:10f. *The season* (*ton kairon*).
The critical period, not *chronos* (time in general). *High*

time (*hōra*). Like our the "hour" has come, etc. MSS. vary between *hēmās* (us) and *humās* (you), accusative of general reference with *egerthēnai* (first aorist passive infinitive of *egeirō*, to awake, to wake up), "to be waked up out of sleep" (*ex hupnou*). *Nearer to us* (*egguteron hēmōn*). Probably so, though *hēmōn* can be taken equally well with *hē sōtēria* (our salvation is nearer). Final salvation, Paul means, whether it comes by the second coming of Christ as they all hoped or by death. It is true of us all.

12. *Is far spent* (*proekopsen*). First aorist active indicative of *prokoptō*, to cut forward, to advance, old word for making progress. See Luke 2:52; Gal. 1:14; II Tim. 2:16; 3:9. *Is at hand* (*ēggiken*). Perfect active indicative, "has drawn nigh." Vivid picture for day-break. *Let us therefore cast off* (*apothōmetha oun*). Aorist middle subjunctive (volitive) of *apotithēmi*, to put off from oneself "the works of darkness" (*ta erga tou skotous*) as we do our night-clothes. *Let us put on* (*endusōmetha*). Aorist middle subjunctive (volitive) of *enduō*, to put on. For this same contrast between putting off (*apotithēmi* and *apekduō*) and putting on (*enduō*) see Col. 3:8–12. *The armour of light* (*ta hopla tou photos*). The weapons of light, that belong to the light (to the day time). For the metaphor of the Christian armour see I Thess. 5:8; II Cor. 6:7; Rom. 6:13; Eph. 6:13ff.

13. *Honestly* (*euschēmonōs*). Paul is fond of the metaphor "walk" (*peripateō*), 33 times though not in the Pastoral Epistles. This old adverb (from *euschēmōn*, graceful) occurs also in I Thess. 4:12; I Cor. 14:40. The English word "honest" means honourable (Latin *honor*) and so decent. Wycliff translates I Cor. 12:32 by "unhonest," "honesty," "honest" for "less honourable, honour, honourable." *Not in revelling* (*mē kōmois*). Plural "revellings." See on Gal. 5:21. *Drunkenness* (*methais*). Plural again, "drunkennesses." See on Gal. 5:21. *In chambering* (*koitais*). Plural also. See on Rom. 9:10. *Wantonness* (*aselgeiais*). Plural likewise. See on II Cor. 12:21; Gal. 5:19. *Not in strife and jealousy* (*mē eridi kai zēlōi*). Singular here, but some MSS. have the plural like the previous words. Quarrelling and jealousy go with the other vices (Shedd).

14. *Put ye on* (*endusasthe*). The same metaphor as in verse 12. The Lord Jesus Christ is the garment that we all

need. See Gal. 3:27 with baptism as the symbol. *Provision* (*pronoian*). Old word for forethought (from *pronoos*). In N.T. only here and Acts 24:2(3). *For the flesh* (*tēs sarkos*). Objective genitive. *To fulfil the lusts thereof* (*eis epithumias*). "For lusts." No verb.

CHAPTER XIV

1. *Him that is weak (ton asthenounta)*. See on I Cor. 8:7–12; 9:22; Rom. 4:19. *Receive ye (proslambanesthe)*. Present middle imperative (indirect), "take to yourselves." *Yet not to doubtful disputations (mē eis diakriseis dialogismōn)*. "Not for decisions of opinions." Note *dia* (between, two or *duo*) in both words. Discriminations between doubts or hesitations. For *diakrisis*, see I Cor. 12:10 and Heb. 5:14 (only N.T. examples). For *dialogismos* see Luke 2:35; 24:38; Phil. 2:14. The "strong" brother is not called upon to settle all the scruples of the "weak" brother. But each takes it on himself to do it.

2. *One man (hos men)*. "This one," demonstrative pronoun *hos* with *men*. *Hath faith (pisteuei)*. Like *echei pistin* (Acts 14:9). *But he that is weak (ho de asthenōn)*. One would expect *hos de* (but that one) in contrast with *hos men*. *Ho* is demonstrative with *de* sometimes, but here is probably just the article with *asthenōn*. *Herbs (lachana)*. From *lachanō*, to dig. Hence garden herbs or vegetables. Denney feels certain that Paul has in mind a party of vegetarians in Rome.

3. *Set at nought (exoutheneitō)*. Present active imperative of *exoutheneō*, to treat as nothing and so with contempt (Luke 23:11; I Thess. 5:20). *Judge (krinetō)*. Present active imperative of *krinō*, criticize. One side (the meat-eaters) despises the vegetarians, while the vegetarians criticize the meat-eaters. *Received him (auton proselabeto)*. Aorist middle (indirect) of *proslambanō*, same verb used in verse 1. God took both sides into his fellowship without requiring that they be vegetarians or meat-eaters.

4. *Who art thou? (su tis ei?)*. Proleptic position of *su*, "thou who art thou?" *The servant of another (allotrion oiketēn)*. Not another (*allon*) servant (household servant, *oiketēn*), but "another's servant." For the adjective *allotrios*, see Luke 16:12; II Cor. 10:15f. *Shall be made to stand (stathēsetai)*. Future passive of *histēmi*. In spite of your sharp

criticisms of one another. *Hath power (dunatei)*. Verb found only in Paul (II Cor. 9:8; 13:3; Rom. 14:4), from verbal adjective *dunatos*.

5. *One man (hos men), another (hos de)*. Regular idiom of contrasted demonstratives (this one, that one). *One day above another (hēmeran par' hēmeran)*. "Day beyond day." For this use of *para* (beside) in comparison see 1:25; Luke 13:2. *Be fully assured (plērophoreisthō)*. Present passive imperative of *plērophoreō*, late compound verb for which see on Luke 1:1 and Rom. 4:21. *In his own mind (en tōi idiōi noi)*. Intelligent and honest decision according to the light possessed by each.

6. *Regardeth (phronei)*. "Thinks of," "esteems," "observes," "puts his mind on" (from *phrēn*, mind). The Textus Receptus has also "he that regardeth not," but it is not genuine. *Unto the Lord (kuriōi)*. Dative case. So as to *tōi theōi* (unto God). He eats unto the Lord, he eats not unto the Lord. Paul's principle of freedom in non-essentials is most important. The Jewish Christians still observed the Seventh day (the Sabbath). The Gentile Christians were observing the first day of the week in honour of Christ's Resurrection on that day. Paul pleads for liberty.

7. *To himself (heautōi)*. Dative of advantage again. But to the Lord as he shows in verse 8. Life and death focus in the Lord.

8. *Whether—or (ean te—ean te)*. "Both if—and if" (condition of third class with present subjunctive (*zōmen—apothnēskōmen*). Both living and dying are "to the Lord." Paul repeats the idiom (*ean te—ean te*) with the conclusion "we are the Lord's (*tou kuriou esmen*). Predicate genitive, "we belong to the Lord."

9. *And lived again (kai ezēsen)*. First ingressive aorist active indicative of *zaō*, "he came to life." *Might be lord of (kurieusei)*. Ingressive aorist active subjunctive of *kurieuō*, "become Lord of." Purpose clause with *hina* (that). Old verb from *kurios*, lord. See Luke 22:25; Rom. 6:9.

10. *But thou, why dost thou judge? (su de ti su krineis?)*. Referring to the conduct of the "weak" brother in verse 3. *Or thou again (ē kai su)*. Referring to the "strong" brother. *Shall stand before (parastēsometha)*. Future middle of *paristēmi* and intransitive, to stand beside (*para*) with the locative

case (*tōi bemati*, the judgment seat) as in Acts 27:24. See the same figure of God in II Cor. 5:10.

11. *As I live* (*zō egō*). "I live." The LXX here (Isa. 45:23) has *kat' emautou omnnuō*, "I swear by myself." *Shall confess to God* (*exomologēsetai tōi theōi*). Future middle of *exomologeō*, to confess openly (*ex*) with the accusative as in Matt. 3:6. With the dative as here the idea is to give praise to, to give gratitude to (Matt. 11:25).

12. *Shall give account* (*logon dōsei*). So Aleph A C rather than *apodōsei* of Textus Receptus, Common use of *logos* for account (bookkeeping, ledger) as in Luke 16:2.

13. *Let us not therefore judge one another any more* (*mēketi oun allēlous krinōmen*). Present active subjunctive (volitive). "Let us no longer have the habit of criticizing one another." A wonderfully fine text for modern Christians and in harmony with what the Master said (Matt. 7:1). *That no man put a stumbling block in his brother's way or an occasion of falling* (*to mē tithenai proskomma tōi adelphōi ē skandalon*). Articular present active infinitive of *tithēmi* in apposition with *touto*, accusative case after *krinate:* "Judge this rather, the not putting a stumbling block (see 9:32 for *proskomma*) or a trap (*skandalon*, 9:33) for his brother" (*adelphōi*, dative of disadvantage).

14. *I know and am persuaded in the Lord Jesus* (*oida kai pepeismai en kuriōi Iēsou*). He knows it and stands persuaded (perfect passive indicative of *peithō*, to persuade), but in the sphere of the Lord Jesus (cf. 9:1), not by mere rational processes. *Unclean of itself* (*kainon di' heautou*). So Paul takes his stand with the "strong" as in I Cor. 8:4f., but he is not a libertine. Paul's liberty as to food is regulated by his life in the Lord. For this use of *koinos*, not as common to all (Acts 2:44; 4:32), but unhallowed, impure, see on Mark 7:2, 5; Acts 10:14, 28. God made all things for their own uses. *Save that* (*ei mē*). The exception lies not in the nature of the food (*di' heautou*), but in the man's view of it (*to him*, *ekeinōi*, dative case).

15. *Because of meat* (*dia brōma*). "Because of food." *In love* (*kata agapēn*). "According to love" as the regulating principle of life. See I Cor. 8 where Paul pleads for love in place of knowledge on this point. *Destroy not* (*mē apollue*). Present active imperative of *apolluō*, the very argument

made in I Cor. 8:1of. *With thy meat (tōi brōmati sou).* Instrumental case, "with thy food." It is too great a price to pay for personal liberty as to food.

16. *Your good (humōn to agathon).* "The good thing of you"=the liberty or Christian freedom which you claim. *Be evil spoken of (blasphēmeisthō).* Present passive imperative of *blasphēmeō* for which see Matt. 9:3; Rom. 3:8.

17. *The kingdom of God (hē basileia tou theou).* Not the future kingdom of eschatology, but the present spiritual kingdom, the reign of God in the heart, of which Jesus spoke so often. See I Cor. 4:21. Paul scores heavily here, for it is not found in externals like food and drink, but in spiritual qualities and graces.

18. *Herein (en toutōi).* "On the principle implied by these virtues" (Sanday and Headlam). *Approved of men (dokimos tois anthrōpois).* "Acceptable to men." Stands the test for men. See I Cor. 11:19; II Cor. 10:18; II Tim. 2:15.

19. *So then (ara oun).* Two inferential particles, "accordingly therefore." *Let us follow after (diōkōmen).* Present active subjunctive (volitive). "Let us pursue." Some MSS. have present indicative, "we pursue." *The things which make for peace (ta tēs eirēnēs).* "The things of peace," literally, genitive case. So "the things of edification for one another" (ta tēs oikodomēs tēs eis allēlous).

20. *Overthrow not (mē katalue).* "Destroy not," "do not loosen down" (carrying on the metaphor in *oikodomē*, building). *The work of God (to ergon tou theou).* The brother for whom Christ died, verse 15. Perhaps with a side-glance at Esau and his mess of pottage. *But it is evil (alla kakon).* Paul changes from the plural *koina* to the singular *kakon*. *With offence (dia proskommatos).* "With a stumbling-block" as in verse 13. This use of *dia* (accompaniment) is common. So then it is addressed to the "strong" brother not to cause a stumbling-block by the way he eats and exercises his freedom.

21. *Not to eat (to mē phagein).* "The not eating." Articular infinitive (second aorist active of *esthiō*) and subject of *kalon estin* (copula, understood). *Flesh (kreas).* Old word, in N.T. only here and I Cor. 8:13. *To drink (pein).* Shortened form for *piein* (second aorist activei nfinitive of *pinō*). *Whereby (en hōi).* "On which thy brother stumbleth" (*proskoptei*).

22. *Have thou to thyself before God* (*su—kata seauton eche enōpion tou theou*). Very emphatic position of *su* at the beginning of the sentence, "Thou there." The old MSS. put *hēn* (relative "which") after *pistin* and before *echeis*. This principle applies to both the "strong" and the "weak." He is within his rights to act "according to thyself," but it must be "before God" and with due regard to the rights of the other brethren. *In that which he approveth* (*en hōi dokimazei*). This beatitude cuts both ways. After testing and then approving (1:28; 2:18) one takes his stand which very act may condemn himself by what he says or does. "It is a rare felicity to have a conscience untroubled by scruples" (Denney).

23. *He that doubteth* (*ho diakrinomenos*). Present middle participle of *diakrinō*, to judge between (*dia*), to hesitate. See James 1:6f. for this same picture of the double-minded man. Cf. Rom. 4:20 and Mark 11:23. *Is condemned* (*katakekritai*). Perfect passive indicative of *katakrinō* (note *kata-*), "stands condemned." *If he eat* (*ean phagēi*). Third class condition, *ean* and second aorist active subjunctive. If in spite of his doubt, he eat. *Whatsoever is not of faith is sin* (*pan ho ouk ek pisteōs hamartia estin*). Faith (*pistis*) here is subjective, one's strong conviction in the light of his relation to Christ and his enlightened conscience. To go against this combination is sin beyond a doubt. Some MSS. (A L etc.) put the doxology here which most place in 16:25-27. But they all give chapters XV and XVI. Some have supposed that the Epistle originally ended here, but that is pure speculation. Some even suggest two editions of the Epistle. But chapter XV goes right on with the topic discussed in chapter XIV.

CHAPTER XV

1. *We the strong* (*hēmeis hoi dunatoi*). Paul identifies himself with this wing in the controversy. He means the morally strong as in II Cor. 12:10; 13:9, not the mighty as in I Cor. 1:26. *The infirmities* (*ta asthenēmata*). "The weaknesses" (cf. *asthenōn* in 14:1 and 2), the scruples "of the not strong" (*tōn adunatōn*). See Acts 14:8 where it is used of the man weak in his feet (impotent). *To bear* (*bastazein*). As in Gal. 6:2, common in the figurative sense. *Not to please ourselves* (*mē heautois areskein*). Precisely Paul's picture of his own conduct in I Cor. 10:33.

2. *For that which is good* (*eis to agathon*). "For the good." As in 14:16, 19. Not to please men just for popular favours, but for their benefit.

3. *Pleased not himself* (*ouch heautōi ēresen*). Aorist active indicative of *areskō* with the usual dative. The supreme example for Christians. See 14:15. He quotes Psa. 69:9 (Messianic Psalm) and represents the Messiah as bearing the reproaches of others.

4. *Were written aforetime* (*proegraphē*). Second aorist passive indicative of *prographō*, old verb, in N.T. only here, Gal. 3:1 (which see); Eph. 3:3; Jude 4. *For our learning* (*eis tēn hēmeteran didaskalian*). "For the instruction of us." Objective sense of possessive pronoun *hēmeteros*. See Matt. 15:9; II Tim. 3:16 for *didaskalian* (from *didaskō*, to teach). *We might have hope* (*tēn elpida echōmen*). Present active subjunctive of *echō* with *hina* in final clause, "that we might keep on having hope." One of the blessed uses of the Scriptures.

5. *The God of patience and comfort* (*ho theos tēs hupomonēs kai tēs paraklēseōs*). Genitive case of the two words in verse 4 used to describe God who uses the Scriptures to reveal himself to us. See II Cor 1:3 for this idea; Rom. 15:13 for "the God of hope"; 15:33 for "the God of peace." *Grant you* (*dōiē humin*). Second aorist active optative (*Koiné* form for older *doiē*) as in II Thess. 3:16; Eph. 1:17; II Tim. 1:16,

417

18; 2:25, though MSS. vary in Eph. 1:17 and II Tim. 2:25 for *dōei* (subjunctive). The optative here is for a wish for the future (regular idiom). *According to Christ Jesus (kata Christon Iēsoun)*. "According to the character or example of Christ Jesus" (II Cor. 11:17; Col. 2:8; Eph. 5:24).

6. *With one accord (homothumadon)*. Here alone in Paul, but eleven times in Acts (1:14, etc.). *With one mouth (en heni stomati)*. Vivid outward expression of the unity of feeling. *May glorify (doxazēte)*. Present active subjunctive of *doxazō*, final clause with *hina* "that ye may keep on glorifying." For "the God and Father of our Lord Jesus Christ" see II Cor. 1:3; 9:31 for discussion. It occurs also in Eph. 1:3; I Peter 1:3.

7. *Receive ye (proslambanesthe* as in 14:1), *received (proselabeto*, here of Christ as in 14:3 of God). The repetition here is addressed to both the strong and the weak and the "us" (*hēmas*) includes all.

8. *A minister of the circumcision (diakonon peritomēs)*. Objective genitive, "a minister to the circumcision." *Diakonon* is predicate accusative with *gegenēsthai* (perfect passive infinitive of *ginomai* in indirect assertion after *legō*, I say) and in apposition with *Christon*, accusative of general reference with the infinitive. See Gal. 4:4f. *That he might confirm (eis to bebaiōsai)*. Purpose clause with *eis to* and the infinitive *bebaiōsai* (first aorist active of *bebaioō*, to make stand). *The promises given unto the fathers (tas epaggelias tōn paterōn)*. No "given" in the Greek, just the objective genitive, "the promises to the fathers." See 9:4, 5.

9. *And that the Gentiles might praise (ta de ethnē doxasai)*. Coördinate with *bebaiōsai* and *eis to*, to be repeated with *ta ethnē*, the accusative of general reference and *ton theon* the object of *doxasai*. Thus the Gentiles were called through the promise to the Jews in the covenant with Abraham (4:11f., 16f.). Salvation is of the Jews. Paul proves his position by a chain of quotations from the O.T., the one in verse 9 from Psa. 18:50. For *exomologeō*, see 14:10. *I will sing (psalō)*. Future active of *psallō*, for which verb see on I Cor. 14:15.

10. *Rejoice, ye Gentiles (euphranthēte)*. First aorist passive imperative of *euphrainō*, old word from *eu*, well and *phrēn*, mind. See Luke 15:32. Quotation from Deut. 32:43 (LXX).

11. *All the Gentiles (panta ta ethnē)*. From Psa. 117:1 with slight variations from the LXX text. 12. *The root (hē riza)*. Rather here, as in Rev. 5:5; 23:16, the sprout from the root. From Isa. 11:10. *On him shall the Gentiles hope (ep' autōi ethnē elpiousin)*. Attic future of *elpizō* for the usual *elpisousin*. 13. *The God of hope (ho theos tēs elpidos)*. Taking up the idea in verse 12 as in verse 5 from 4. *Fill you (plērōsai humas)*. Optative (first aorist active of *pleroō*) of wish for the future. Cf. *dōiē* in verse 5. *In believing (en tōi pisteuein)*. "In the believing" (*en* with locative of the articular infinitive, the idiom so common in Luke's Gospel). *That ye may abound (eis to perisseuein humas)*. Purpose clause with *eis to*, as in verse 8, with *perisseuein* (present active infinitive of *perisseuō*, with accusative of general reference, *humas*). This verse gathers up the points in the preceding quotations. 14. *I myself also (kai autos egō)*. See 7:25 for a like emphasis on himself, here in contrast with "ye yourselves" (*kai autoi*). The argument of the Epistle has been completed both in the main line (chapters 1 to 8) and the further applications (9:1–15:13). Here begins the Epilogue, the personal matters of importance. *Full of goodness (mestoi agathosunēs)*. See II Thess. 1:11 and Gal. 5:22 for this LXX and Pauline word (in ecclesiastical writers also) made from the adjective *agathos*, good, by adding *-sunē* (common ending for words like *dikaiosunē*. See 1:29 for *mestos* with genitive and *peplērōmenoi* (perfect passive participle of *pleroō* as here), but there with instrumental case after it instead of the genitive. Paul gives the Roman Christians (chiefly Gentiles) high praise. The "all knowledge" is not to be pressed too literally, "our Christian knowledge in its entirety" (Sanday and Headlam). *To admonish (nouthetein)*. To put in mind (from *nouthetēs* and this from *nous* and *tithēmi*). See on I Thess 5:12, 14. "Is it laying too much stress on the language of compliment to suggest that these words give a hint of St. Paul's aim in this Epistle?" (Sanday and Headlam). The strategic position of the church in Rome made it a great centre for radiating and echoing the gospel over the world as Thessalonica did for Macedonia (I Thess. 1:8). 15. *I write (egrapsa)*. Epistolary aorist. *The more boldly (tolmēroteros)*. Old comparative adverb from *tolmēros*. Most

MSS. read *tolmēroteron*. Only here in N.T. *In some measure* (*apo merous*). Perhaps referring to some portions of the Epistle where he has spoken plainly (6:12, 19; 8:9; 11:17; 14:3, 4, 10, etc.). *As putting you again in remembrance* (*hōs epanamimnēskōn humas*). Delicately put with *hōs* and *epi* in the verb, "as if calling back to mind again" (*epi*). This rare verb is here alone in the N.T.

16. *That I should be* (*eis to einai me*). The *eis to* idiom with the infinitive again (verses 8, 13). *Minister* (*leitourgon*). Predicate accusative in apposition with *me* and see 13:6 for the word. "The word here derives from the context the priestly associations which often attach to it in the LXX" (Denney). But this purely metaphorical use does not show that Paul attached a "sacerdotal" character to the ministry. *Ministering* (*hierourgounta*). Present active participle of *hierourgeō*, late verb from *hierourgos* (*hieros, ergō*), in LXX, Philo, and Josephus, only here in N.T. It means to work in sacred things, to minister as a priest. Paul had as high a conception of his work as a preacher of the gospel as any priest did. *The offering up of the Gentiles* (*hē prosphora tōn ethnōn*). Genitive of apposition, the Gentiles being the offering. They are Paul's offering. See Acts 21:26. *Acceptable* (*euprosdektos*). See II Cor. 6:2; 8:12. Because "sanctified in the Holy Spirit" (*hēgiasmenē en pneumati hagiōi*, perfect passive participle of *hagiazō*).

17. *In things pertaining to God* (*ta pros ton theon*). Accusative of general reference of the article used with the prepositional phrase, "as to the things relating to (*pros*, facing) God."

18. *Any things save those which Christ wrought through me* (*ti hōn ou kateirgasato Christos di' emou*). Rather, "any one of those things which Christ did not work through me." The antecedent of *hōn* is the unexpressed *toutōn* and the accusative relative *ha* (object of *kateirgasato*) is attracted into the genitive case of *toutōn* after a common idiom. *By word and deed* (*logōi kai ergōi*). Instrumental case with both words. By preaching and life (Luke 24:19; Acts 1:1; 7:22; II Cor. 10:11).

19. *In power of signs and wonders* (*en dunamei sēmeiōn kai teratōn*). Note all three words as in Heb. 2:4, only here *dunamis* is connected with *sēmeia* and *terata*. See all three

words used of Paul's own work in II Cor. 12:12 and in II
Thess 2:9 of the Man of Sin. See I Thess. 1:5; I Cor. 2:4
for the "power" of the Holy Spirit in Paul's preaching. Note
repetition of *en dunamei* here with *pneumatos hagiou*. *So
that* (*hōste*). Result expressed by the perfect active infinitive
peplērōkenai (from *plēroō*) with the accusative *me* (general
reference). *Round about even unto Illyricum* (*kuklōi mechri
tou Illurikou*). "In a ring" (*kuklōi*, locative case of *kuklos*).
Probably a journey during the time when Paul left Macedonia and waited for II Corinthians to have its effect before
coming to Corinth. If so, see II Cor. 13 and Acts 20:1–3.
When he did come, the trouble with the Judaizers was over.
Illyricum seems to be the name for the region west of Macedonia (Dalmatia). Strabo says that the Egnatian Way
passed through it. Arabia and Illyricum would thus be the
extreme limits of Paul's mission journeys so far.

20. *Yea* (*houtōs de*). "And so," introducing a limitation
to the preceding statement. *Making it my aim* (*philotimou-
menon*). Present middle participle (accusative case agreeing
with *me*) of *philotimeomai*, old verb, to be fond of honour
(*philos*, *timē*). In N.T. only here and I Thess. 4:11; II Cor.
5:9. A noble word in itself, quite different in aim from the
Latin word for *ambition* (*ambio*, to go on both sides to carry
one's point). *Not where* (*ouch hopou*). Paul was a pioneer
preacher pushing on to new fields after the manner of Daniel
Boone in Kentucky. *That I might not build upon another
man's foundation* (*hina mē ep' allotrion themelion oikodomō*).
For *allotrios* (not *allos*) see 14:4. For *themelion*, see Luke
6:48f.; 1 Cor. 3:11. This noble ambition of Paul's is not
within the range of some ministers who can only build on
another's foundation as Apollos did in Corinth. But the
pioneer preacher and missionary has a dignity and glory all
his own.

21. *As it is written* (*kathōs gegraptai*). From Isa. 52:15.
Paul finds an illustration of his word about his own ambition
in the words of Isaiah. Fritzsche actually argues that Paul
understood Isaiah to be predicting his (Paul's) ministry!
Some scholars have argued against the genuineness of verses
19 to 21 on wholly subjective and insufficient grounds.

22. *I was hindered* (*enekoptomēn*). Imperfect passive
(repetition) of *enkoptō*, late verb, to cut in, to cut off, to

interrupt. Seen already in Acts 24:4; I Thess. 2:18; Gal. 5:7. Cf. modern telephone and radio and automobile. *These many times* (*ta polla*). "As to the many things." In 1:13 Paul used *pollakis* (many times) and B D read it here. But Paul's work (*ta polla*) had kept him away. *From coming to you* (*tou elthein pros humas*). Ablative case (after the verb of hindering) of the articular infinitive, "from the coming."

23. *Having no more any place in these regions* (*mēketi topon echōn en tois klimasin*). Surprising frankness that the average preacher would hardly use on such a matter. Paul is now free to come to Rome because there is no demand for him where he is. For *klima* (from *klinō*, to incline), slope, then tract of land, region, see already II Cor. 11:10; Gal. 1:21 (the only N.T. examples). *A longing* (*epipotheian*). A *hapax legomenon*, elsewhere *epipothēsis* (II Cor. 7:7, 11), from *epipotheō* as in Rom. 1:11. *These many years* (*apo hikanōn etōn*). "From considerable years." So B C, but Aleph A D have *pollōn*, "from many years."

24. *Whensoever I go* (*hōs an poreuōmai*). Indefinite temporal clause with *hōs an* and the present middle subjunctive (cf. I Cor. 11:34; Phil. 2:23 with aorist subjunctive). *Into Spain* (*eis tēn Spanian*). It was a, Roman province with many Jews in it. The Greek name was *Iberia*, the Latin *Hispania*. The Textus Receptus adds here *eleusomai pros humas* (I shall come to you), but it is not in Aleph A B C D and is not genuine. Without it we have a parenthesis (or anacoluthon) through the rest of verse 24. *In my journey* (*diaporeuomenos*). Present middle participle, "passing through." Paul planned only a brief stay in Rome since a strong church already existed there. *To be brought on my way thitherward* (*propemphthēnai ekei*). "To be sent forward there." First aorist passive infinitive of *propempō*, common word for escorting one on a journey (I Cor. 16:6, 11; II Cor. 1:16; Titus 3:13; II John 6). *If first in some measure I shall have been satisfied with your company* (*ean humōn prōton apo merous emplēsthō*). Condition of third class with *ean* and first aorist passive subjunctive of *empimplēmi*, old verb, to fill up, to satisfy, to take one's fill. See Luke 6:25. Literally, "if I first in part be filled with you" (get my fill of you). A delicate compliment for the Roman church.

25. *But now* (*nuni de*). Repeats the very words used in

23. *I go (poreuomai).* Futuristic present as in John 14:2. *Ministering unto the saints (diakonon tois hagiois).* Present active participle of purpose like *eulogounta* in Acts 3:26. This collection had been one of Paul's chief cares for over a year now (see II Cor. 8 and 9). See II Cor. 8:4.

26. *For it hath been the good pleasure of Macedonia and Achaia (eudokēsan gar Makedonia kai Achaia).* "For Macedonia and Achaia took pleasure." The use of *eudokēsan* (first aorist active indicative of *eudokeō*) shows that it was voluntary (II Cor. 8:4). Paul does not here mention Asia and Galatia. *A certain contribution (koinōnian tina).* Put thus because it was unknown to the Romans. For this sense of *koinōnian*, see II Cor. 8:4; 9:13. *For the poor among the saints (eis tous ptōchous tōn hagiōn).* Partitive genitive. Not all there were poor, but Acts 4:32–5:11; 6:1–6; 11:29f. and Gal. 2:10 prove that many were.

27. *Their debtors (opheiletai autōn).* Objective genitive: the Gentiles are debtors to the Jews. See the word *opheiletēs* in 1:14; 8:12. *For if (ei gar).* Condition of the first class, assumed as true, first aorist active indicative (*ekoinōnēsan*, from *koinōneō*, to share) with associative instrumental case (*pneumatikois*, spiritual things). *To minister unto (leitourgēsai*, first aorist active infinitive of *leitourgeō* with dative case *autois*, to them), but here certainly with no "sacerdotal" functions (cf. verse 16). *In carnal things (en tois sarkikois).* Things which belong to the natural life of the flesh (*sarx*), not the sinful aspects of the flesh at all.

28. *Have sealed (sphragisamenos).* First aorist middle participle (antecedent action, having sealed) of *sphragizō*, old verb from *sphragis*, a seal (Rom. 4:11), to stamp with a seal for security (Matt. 27:66) or for confirmation (II Cor. 1:22) and here in a metaphorical sense. Paul was keenly sensitive that this collection should be actually conveyed to Jerusalem free from all suspicion (II Cor. 8:18–23). *I will go on by you (apeleusomai di' humōn).* Future middle of *aperchomai*, to go off or on. Note three prepositions here (*ap'* from Rome, *di'* by means of you or through you, *eis* unto Spain). He repeats the point of verse 24, his temporary stay in Rome with Spain as the objective. How little we know what is ahead of us and how grateful we should be for our ignorance on this point.

29. *When I come* (*erchomenos*). Present middle participle of *erchomai* with the time of the future middle indicative *eleusomai* (coming I shall come). *In the fulness of the blessing of Christ* (*en plērōmati eulogias Christou*). On *plērōmati*, see 11:12. Paul had already (1:11f.) said that he had a *charisma pneumatikon* (spiritual blessing) for Rome. He did bring that to them.

30. *By* (*dia*). The intermediate agents of the exhortation (the Lord Jesus and the love of the Spirit) as *dia* is used after *parakalō* in 12:1. *That ye strive together with me* (*sunagōnisasthai moi*). First aorist middle infinitive of *sunagōni zomai*, old compound verb, only here in N.T., direct object of *parakalō*, and with associative instrumental case *moi*, the simplex *agōnizomenos*, occurring in Col. 4:12 of the prayers of Epaphras. For Christ's agony in prayer see Matt. 26:42; Luke 22:44.

31. *That I may be delivered* (*hina rusthō*). First aorist passive subjunctive of *ruomai*, old verb to rescue. This use of *hina* is the sub-final one after words of beseeching or praying. Paul foresaw trouble all the way to Jerusalem (Acts 20:23; 21:4, 13). *May be acceptable to the saints* (*euprosdektos tois hagiois genētai*). "May become (second aorist middle subjunctive of *ginomai*) acceptable to the saints." The Judaizers would give him trouble. There was peril of a schism in Christianity.

32. *That* (*hina*). Second use of *hina* in this sentence, the first one sub-final (*hina rusthō*), this one final with *sunanapausōmai*, first aorist middle subjunctive of the double compound verb *sunanapauomai*, late verb to rest together with, to refresh (*anapauō* as in Matt. 11:28) one's spirit with (*sun*), with the associative instrumental case *humin* (with you), only here in the N.T.

33. *The God of peace* (*ho theos tēs eirēnēs*). One of the characteristics of God that Paul often mentions in benedictions (1 Thess. 5:23; II Thess. 3:16; II Cor. 13:11; Phil. 4:9; Rom. 16:20). Because of the "amen" here some scholars would make this the close of the Epistle and make chapter 16 a separate Epistle to the Ephesians. But the MSS. are against it. There is nothing strange at all in Paul's having so many friends in Rome though he had not yet been there himself. Rome was the centre of the world's life as Paul realized (1:15). All men sooner or later hoped to see Rome.

CHAPTER XVI

1. *I commend* (*sunistēmi*). The regular word for letters of commendation as in II Cor. 3:1 (*sustatikōn epistolōn*). See also Rom. 3:5. So here verses 1 and 2 constitute Paul's recommendation of Phoebe, the bearer of the Epistle. Nothing else is known of her, though her name (*Phoibē*) means bright or radiant. *Sister* (*adelphēn*). In Christ, not in the flesh. *Who is a servant of the church* (*ousan diakonon tēs ekklēsias*). The etymology of *diakonos* we have had repeatedly. The only question here is whether it is used in a general sense or in a technical sense as in Phil. 1:1 and I Tim. 3:8–13. In favour of the technical sense of "deacon" or "deaconess" is the addition of "*tēs ekklēsias*" (of the church). In some sense Phoebe was a servant or minister of the church in Cenchreae. Besides, right in the midst of the discussion in I Tim. 3:8–13 Paul has a discussion of *gunaikas* (verse 11) either as women as deaconesses or as the wives of deacons (less likely though possible). The *Apostolic Constitutions* has numerous allusions to deaconesses. The strict separation of the sexes made something like deaconesses necessary for baptism, visiting the women, etc. Cenchreae, as the eastern port of Corinth, called for much service of this kind. Whether the deaconesses were a separate organization on a par with the deacons we do not know nor whether they were the widows alluded to in I Tim. 5:9f.

2. *Worthily of the saints* (*axiōs tōn hagiōn*). Adverb with the genitive as in Phil. 1:27 because the adjective *axios* is used with the genitive (Luke 3:8). "Receive her in a way worthy of the saints." This word *hagios* had come to be the accepted term for followers of Christ. *Assist her* (*paristēte*). Second aorist (intransitive) active subjunctive of *paristēmi*, to stand by, with the dative case ("beside her"), the very word used by Paul of the help of Jesus in his trial (*parestē*, II Tim. 4:17). Used with *hina* as *prosdexēsthe*. *In whatsoever matter* (*en hōi pragmati*). Incorporation of the antecedent (*pragmati*) into the relative clause (*hōi*). *She may have need of you* (*an humōn chrēizēi*). Indefinite relative

425

clause with *an* and the present subjunctive of *chrēizō* with genitive. *A succourer* (*prostatis*). Old and rare feminine form for the masculine *prostatēs*, from *proistēmi* (*prostateō*, common, but not in the N.T.), here only in the N.T. and not in the papyri. The word illustrates her work as *diakonon* and is perhaps suggested here by *parastēte*, just before. *Of mine own self* (*emou autou*). "Of me myself."

3. In verses 3 to 16 Paul sends his greetings to various brethren and sisters in Rome. *Prisca and Aquila* (*Priskan kai Akulan*). This order always (Acts 18:18, 26; II Tim. 4:19, and here) save in Acts 18:2 and I Cor. 16:19, showing that Prisca was the more prominent. Priscilla is a diminutive of Prisca, a name for women in the Acilian gens. She may have been a noble Roman lady, but her husband was a Jew of Pontus and a tent-maker by trade. They were driven from Rome by Claudius, came to Corinth, then to Ephesus, then back to Rome, and again to Ephesus. They were good travelling Christians. *My fellow-workers* (*tous sunergous mou*). Both in tent-making and in Christian service in Corinth and Ephesus.

4. *Laid down their own necks* (*ton heautōn trachelon hupethēkan*). First aorist active of *hupotithēmi*, old verb to place under (the axe of the executioner), only here in N.T. in this sense, though in I Tim. 4:16 to suggest. If literal or figurative, the incident may be connected with the uproar created by Demetrius in Ephesus. Certainly Paul felt deep obligation toward them (see Acts 20:34). *Not only I* (*ouk egō monos*). Rather, "not I alone" (adjective *monos*). The Gentile churches also (great mission workers).

5. *The church that is in their house* (*tēn kat' oikon autōn ekklēsian*). The early Christians had no church buildings. See also Acts 12:2; I Cor. 16:19; Philemon 2; Col. 4:15. The Roman Christians had probably several such homes where they would meet. *Epainetus* (*Epaineton*). Nothing is known of him except this item, "the first-fruits of Asia" (*aparchē tēs Asias*). An early convert from the province of Asia. Cf. Acts 2:9 and I Cor. 16:15 (about Stephanus and Achaia).

6. *Mary* (*Marian*). Some MSS. have *Mariam*, the Hebrew form. The name indicates a Jewish Christian in Rome. Paul praises her toil. See Luke 5:5.

7. *Andronicus and Junias* (*Andronicou kai Iounian*). The

first is a Greek name found even in the imperial household. The second name can be either masculine or feminine. *Kinsmen (suggeneis)*. Probably only fellow-countrymen as in 9:13. *Fellow-prisoners (sunaichmalōtus)*. Late word and rare (in Lucian). One of Paul's frequent compounds with *sun*. Literally, fellow captives in war. Perhaps they had shared one of Paul's numerous imprisonments (II Cor. 11:23). In N.T. only here, Philemon 23; Col. 4:10. *Of note (episēmoi)*. Stamped, marked (*epi sēma*). Old word, only here and Matt. 27:16 (bad sense) in N.T. *Among the apostles (en tois apostolois)*. Naturally this means that they are counted among the apostles in the general sense true of Barnabas, James, the brother of Christ, Silas, and others. But it can mean simply that they were famous in the circle of the apostles in the technical sense. *Who have been in Christ before me (hoi kai pro emou gegonan en Christōi)*. Andronicus and Junias were converted before Paul was. Note *gegonan* (*Koiné* form by analogy) instead of the usual second perfect active indicative form *gegonasin*, which some MSS. have. The perfect tense notes that they are still in Christ.

8. *Ampliatus (Ampliaton)*. Some MSS. have a contracted form Amplias.

9. *Urbanus (Ourbanon)*. "A common Roman slave name found among members of the household" (Sanday and Headlam). A Latin adjective from *urbs*, city (city-bred). *Stachys (Stachun)*. A Greek name, rare, but among members of the imperial household. It means a head or ear of grain (Matt. 12:1).

10. *Apelles (Apellēn)*. A name among Jews and a famous tragic actor also. *The approved (ton dokimon)*. The tried and true (I Cor. 11:19; II Cor. 10:18; 13:7). *Them which are of the household of Aristobulus (tous ek tōn Aristoboulou)*. The younger Aristobulus was a grandson of Herod the Great. Lightfoot suggests that some of the servants in this household had become Christians, Aristobulus being dead.

11. *Herodion (Herōidiōna)*. Probably one belonging to the Herod family like that above. *Kinsman (suggenē)*. Merely fellow-countryman. *Them of the household of Narcissus (tous ek tōn Narkissou)*. "Narcissiani." There was a famous freedman of this name who was put to death by Agrippa. Perhaps members of his household.

12. *Tryphaena and Tryphosa* (*Truphainan kai Truphōsan*). Probably sisters and possibly twins. Both names come from the same root, the verb *truphaō*, to live luxuriously (James, 5:5). Denney suggests "Dainty and Disdain." *Persis* (*Persida*). A freedwoman was so named. She is not Paul's "beloved," but the "beloved" of the whole church.

13. *Rufus* (*Rouphon*). A very common slave name, possibly the Rufus of Mark 15:21. The word means "red." *The chosen* (*ton eklekton*). Not "the elect," but "the select." *And mine* (*kai emou*). Paul's appreciation of her maternal care once, not his real mother.

14. *Asyncritus* (*Asunkriton*). There is an inscription of a freedman of Augustus with this name. *Phlegon* (*Phlegonta*). No light on this name till the historian of the second century A.D. *Hermes* (*Hermēn*). A very common slave name. *Patrobas* (*Patroban*). Name of a freedman of Nero, abbreviated form of Patrobius. *Hermas* (*Hermān*). Not the author of the Shepherd of Hermas. Common as a slave name, shortened form of Hermagoras, Hermogenes, etc. *The brethren that are with them* (*tous sun autois adelphous*). Perhaps a little church in the house of some one.

15. *Philologus* (*Philologon*). Another common slave name. *Julia* (*Ioulian*). The commonest name for female slaves in the imperial household because of Julius Caesar. Possibly these two were husband and wife. *Nereus* (*Nērea*). Found in inscriptions of the imperial household. But the sister's name is not given. One wonders why. *Olympas* (*Olumpān*). Possibly an abbreviation for Olympiodorus. *All the saints that are with them* (*tous sun autois pantas hagious*). Possibly another church in the house. These unnamed, the "and others," constitute the great majority in all our churches.

16. *With a holy kiss* (*en philēmati hagiōi*). The near-east mode of salutation as hand-shaking in the Western. In China one shakes hands with himself. Men kissed men and women kissed women. See I Thess. 5:26; I Cor. 16:20 II; Cor. 13:12.

17. *Mark* (*skopeite*). Keep an eye on so as to avoid. *Skopos* is the goal, *skopeō* means keeping your eye on the goal. *Divisions* (*dichostasias*). Old word for "standings apart," cleavages. In N.T. only here and Gal. 5:20. *Those which are causing* (*tous—poiountas*). This articular participle

clause has within it not only the objects of the participle but the relative clause *hēn humeis emathete* (which you learned), a thoroughly Greek idiom.

18. *But their own belly* (*alla tēi heautōn koiliāi*). Dative case after *douleuousin*. A blunt phrase like the same picture in Phil. 3:19 "whose god is the belly," more truth than caricature in some cases. *By their smooth and fair speech* (*dia tēs chrēstologias kai eulogias*). Two compounds of *logos* (speech), the first (from *chrēstos* and *logos*) is very rare (here only in N.T.), the second is very common (*eu* and *logos*). *Beguile* (*exapatōsin*). Present active indicative of the double compound verb *exapataō* (see II Thess. 2:3; I Cor. 3:18). *Of the innocent* (*tōn akakōn*). Old adjective (*a* privative and *kakos*), without evil or guile, in N.T. only here and Heb. 7:26 (of Christ).

19. *Is come abroad* (*aphiketo*). Second aorist middle indicative of *aphikneomai*, old verb, to come from, then to arrive at, only here in N.T. *Over you* (*eph' humin*). "Upon you." *Simple unto that which is evil* (*akeraious eis to kakon*). Old adjective from *a* privative and *kerannumi*, to mix. Unmixed with evil, unadulterated.

20. *Shall bruise* (*suntripsei*). Future active of *suntribō*, old verb, to rub together, to crush, to trample underfoot. Blessed promise of final victory over Satan by "the God of peace." "Shortly" (*en tachei*). As God counts time. Meanwhile patient loyalty from us.

21. Verses 21 to 23 form a sort of postscript with greetings from Paul's companions in Corinth. Timothy was with Paul in Macedonia (II Cor. 1:1) before he came to Corinth. Lucius may be the one mentioned in Acts 13:1. Jason was once Paul's host (Acts 17:5-9) in Thessalonica, Sosipater may be the longer form of Sopater of Acts 20:4. They are all Paul's fellow-countrymen (*suggeneis*).

22. *I Tertius* (*egō Tertios*). The amanuensis to whom Paul dictated the letter. See II Thess. 3:17; I Cor. 16:21; Col. 4:18.

23. *Gaius my host* (*Gaios ho xenos mou*). Perhaps the same Gaius of I Cor. 1:14 (Acts 19:29; 20:4), but whether the one of III John 1 we do not know. *Xenos* was a guest friend, and then either a stranger (Matt. 25:35) or a host of strangers as here. This Gaius was plainly a man of some

means as he was the host of all the church. Erastus (II Tim. 4:20) was "the treasurer of the city" (*ho oikonomos tēs poleōs*), one of the outstanding men of Corinth, the "steward" (house-manager) or city manager. See Luke 12:42 and 16:1. He is probably the administrator of the city's property. *Quartus (Kouartos)*. Latin name for fourth. Verse 24 is not genuine, not in Aleph A B C Coptic.

25. Verses 25 to 27 conclude the noble Epistle with the finest of Paul's doxologies. *To him that is able (tōi dunamenōi)*. Dative of the articular participle of *dunamai*. See similar idiom in Eph. 3:20. *To stablish (stērixai)*. First aorist active infinitive of *stērizō*, to make stable. *According to my gospel (kata to euaggelion mou)*. Same phrase in 2:16; II Tim. 2:8. Not a book, but Paul's message as here set forth. *The preaching (to kērugma)*. The proclamation, the heralding. *Of Jesus Christ (Iēsou Christou)*. Objective genitive, "about Jesus Christ." *Revelation (apokalupsin)*. "Unveiling." *Of the mystery (mustēriou)*. Once unknown, but now revealed. *Kept in silence (sesigēmenou)*. Perfect passive participle of *sigaō*, to be silent, state of silence. *Through times eternal (chronois aiōniois)*. Associative instrumental case, "along with times eternal" (Robertson, *Grammar*, p. 527). See I Cor. 2:6, 7, 10.

26. *But now is manifested (phanerōthentos de nun)*. First aorist passive participle of *phaneroō*, to make plain, genitive case in agreement with *mustēriou*. *By the scriptures of the prophets (dia graphōn prophētikōn)*. "By prophetic scriptures." Witnessed by the law and the prophets (3:21). This thread runs all through Romans. *According to the command of the eternal God (kat' epitagēn tou aiōniou theou)*. Paul conceives that God is in charge of the redemptive work and gives his orders (1:1–5; 10:15f.). The same adjective *aiōnios* is here applied to God that is used of eternal life and eternal punishment in Matt. 25:46. *Unto obedience of faith (eis hupakoēn tēs pisteōs)*. See 1:5. *Made known unto all the nations (eis panta ta ethnē gnōristhentos)*. First aorist passive participle of *gnōrizō*, still the genitive case agreeing with *mustēriou* in verse 25.

27. *To the only wise God (monōi sophōi theōi)*. Better, "to God alone wise." See I Tim. 1:17 without *sophōi*. *To whom (hōi)*. Some MSS. omit.

THE THIRD GROUP OF PAUL'S EPISTLES
Philippians
Philemon
Colossians
Ephesians

Written from Rome, Probably a.d. 61 to 63

CHIEF TOPIC CHRISTOLOGY
Against Incipient Gnosticism

EPISTLE TO THE PHILIPPIANS
From Rome about a.d. 61

BY WAY OF INTRODUCTION

There is something to be said for the idea that Paul wrote the Epistle to the Philippians while a prisoner in Ephesus if he ever was a prisoner there. All that can be said for that view has been presented by Professor George S. Duncan in *St. Paul's Ephesian Ministry* (1930). But, when all is considered carefully in the light of the facts in the Acts and the Epistles, the best that one can say is that a possible case is made out with many difficulties remaining unexplained. The argument is more ingenious than convincing. It is not possible here to review the arguments *pro* and *con* that convince me that Paul was in Rome when he wrote this letter to Philippi. It is not clear whether it was written before the three that went together (Philemon, Colossians, Ephesians) or afterwards. Probably there was no great difference in time, but there was time for Epaphroditus to come to Rome, to fall sick, for the news to reach Philippi and for Epaphroditus to hear of their concern about him. The church in Philippi was Paul's joy and pride and they had helped him before as they did this time.

The Epistle is a beautiful expression of gratitude for the love and gifts of the Philippian saints. He is a prisoner of hope in Rome with possible death before him, but with the note of joy running through all that Paul says. He hopes to be set free and to see them again.

Meanwhile he tells the Philippians about the difficulties and triumphs in Rome. The Judaizers have followed Paul here and there is an echo in chapters 1 and 3 of their opposition. But Paul rises to full stature in the great Christological passages in chapters 2 and 3 which prepare the way for the controversy with the Gnostics over the Person of Christ in Colossians and Ephesians.

Some special books on Philippians are those by Beet (1891),

Burns (1917), Dibelius (1911), Ellicott (new ed. 1890), Wohlenberg in Zahn Komm. (3rd ed. 1917), Haupt in Meyer Komm. (8 ed. 1902), Jones in Westm. Comm. (1920), Johnstone (1904), Jowett (1909), Kennedy in Exp. Gk. Test. (1903), Klöpper (1893), Knabenbauer (1913), Lightfoot (9 ed. 1891), Lipsius (1893), Lohmeyer in Meyer Komm. (8 ed. 1930), Lueken (1906), Martin (New Cent. Bible), Michael (1928), Moule (Phil. Studies), Plummer (1919), Rainy (Exp. Bible 1893), Robertson (1917), Vincent (Int. Crit., 2 ed. 1910).

CHAPTER I

1. *Paul* (*Paulos*). He does not mention his apostleship as he usually does. Omitted also in I and II Thess. and Philemon. *Timothy* (*Timotheos*). In no sense the author, but associated with Paul because with him here in Rome as in Corinth when I and II Thessalonians written and in Ephesus when I Corinthians sent and in Macedonia when II Corinthians written. Timothy was with Paul when the Philippian church was founded (Acts 16:1, 13; 17:14). He had been there twice since (Acts 19:22; 20:3f.). *To all the saints* (*pāsi tois hagiois*). The word saint (*hagios*) here is used for the professing Christians as in I Cor. 1:2 which see as well as Rom. 1:7 for the origin of the word. The word "all" (*pāsi*) means that all individual believers are included. Paul employs this word frequently in Philippians. *In Christ Jesus* (*en Christōi Iēsou*). The centre for all Christian relations and activities for Paul and for us. *In Philippi* (*en Philippois*). See on Acts 16:12 for discussion of this name. *With the bishops* (*sun episkopois*). "Together with bishops," thus singled out from "all the saints." See Acts 20:17 and 28 for the use of this most interesting word as equivalent to *presbuteros* (elder). It is an old word from *episkeptomai*, to look upon or after, to inspect, so the overseer or superintendent. In the second century *episcopos* (Ignatius) came to mean one superior to elders, but not so in the N.T. The two New Testament church officers are here mentioned (bishops or elders and deacons). The plural is here employed because there was usually one church in a city with several pastors (bishops, elders). *And deacons* (*kai diakonois*). Technical sense here of the other church officers as in I Tim. 3:8–13, not the general use as in Matt. 22:13. The origin of the office is probably seen in Acts 6:1–6. The term is often applied to preachers (I Cor. 3:5; II Cor. 3:6). The etymology (*dia, konis*) suggests raising a dust by hastening.

3. *Upon* (*epi*). Basis of the thanksgiving. *All* (*pāsēi*). Note frequent use of "all" here (*pāsēi, pantote*, always,

435

pāsēi, again, *pantōn humōn*, you all). The use of "you all" recurs several times (4, 7 *bis*, 8).

4. *With joy* (*meta charas*). Keynote of the Epistle. Paul is a happy prisoner as in Philippi when he and Silas sang praises at midnight though in prison (Acts 16:25).

5. *For your fellowship* (*epi tēi koinōniāi humōn*). "On the basis of your contribution" as in II Cor. 8:4; 9:13 and Acts 2:42. The particular kind of "partnership" or "fellowship" involved is the contribution made by the Philippians for the spread of the gospel (1:7 *sugkoinōnous* and 4:14 where *sugkoinōnēsantes* occurs). *In furtherance of the gospel* (*eis to euaggelion*). "For the gospel." *From the first day until now* (*apo tēs prōtēs hēmeras achri tou nun*). As when in Thessalonica (Phil. 4:15f.), in Corinth (Acts 18:5; II Cor. 11:7–10), and now in Rome.

6. *Being confident* (*pepoithōs*). Second perfect active of *peithō*, to persuade. *This very thing* (*auto touto*). Accusative of the inner object with *pepoithōs*, "this thing itself." *Will perfect it* (*epitelesei*). Future active indicative of *epiteleō*, will fully (*epi-*) finish. God began and God will consummate it (see II Cor. 8:6; Gal. 3:3 where both words occur together as here), but not without their coöperation and partnership. *Until the day of Jesus Christ* (*achri hēmeras Christou Iēsou*). The second coming as in verse 10. See I Thess. 5:2, 4; II Thess. 1:10; 2:2; I Cor. 1:18; 3:13; II Cor. 1:14; Rom. 13:12. Paul never sets the time for the Lord's return, but he is cheered by that blessed hope.

7. *Because I have you in my heart* (*dia to echein me en tēi kardiāi humas*). Or "because you hold me in your heart." Literally, "because of the holding me (or you) in the heart as to you (or me)." One accusative is the object of the infinitive *echein*, the other is the accusative of general reference. There is no way to decide which is the idea meant except to say that love begets love. The pastor who, like Paul, holds his people in his heart will find them holding him in their hearts. *In the defence* (*en tēi apologiāi*). Old word (our word apology, but not our idea of apologizing), in the original sense in Acts 22:1; 25:16. So also in verse 16 below. *Confirmation* (*bebaiōsei*). Old word from *bebaioō* (*bebaios, bainō*), to make stable. In N.T. only here and Heb. 6:16 about oath. *Partakers with me of grace* (*sugkoinōnous mou tēs*

charitos). Literally, "my co-sharers in grace" (objective genitive). "Grace prompted them to alleviate his imprisonment, to coöperate with him in defending and propagating the gospel, and to suffer for its sake" (Vincent, *Int. Crit. Comm.*).

8. *My witness* (*martus mou*). Same solemn oath in Rom. 1:9. *I long after* (*epipothō*). Longing (*pothos*) directed toward (*epi*) the Philippians. Old word, chiefly in Paul in N.T. *In the tender mercies* (*en splagchnois*). Literally "in the bowels" as the seat of the affections.

9. *May abound* (*perisseuēi*). Present active subjunctive of *perisseuō*, may keep on overflowing, a perpetual flood of love, "yet more and more" (*eti mallon kai mallon*), but with necessary limitations (river banks), "in knowledge" (*en epignōsei*, in full knowledge) "and all discernment" (*pāsēi aisthēsei*). The delicate spiritual perception (*aisthēsis*, old word from *aisthanomai*, only here in N.T. as the verb only in Luke 9:45 in N.T.) can be cultivated as in *aisthētērion* (Heb. 5:14).

10. *So that ye may* (*eis to humas*). Either purpose or result (*eis to* plus infinitive as in Rom. 1:11, 20; 3:26, etc.). *Approve the things that are excellent* (*dokimazein ta diapheronta*). Originally, "test the things that differ." Cf. same idiom in Rom. 2:28. The verb was used for assaying metals. Either sense suits this context, but the first step is to distinguish between good and evil and that is not always easy in our complex civilization. *Sincere* (*eilikrineis*). Old word of uncertain origin from *krinō*, to judge, by *heilē* (sunlight) or to sift by rapid rolling (*eilos*). At any rate it means pure, unsullied. *Void of offence* (*aproskopoi*). Alpha privative *pros* and *koptō*, to cut, "not stumbled against" (not causing others to stumble) or if active "not stumbling against." Passive sense probably, not active as in I Cor. 10:32. Common in the papyri, though not in ancient Greek writers.

11. *Fruits of righteousness* (*karpon dikaiosunēs*). Singular, collective idea, fruit of righteousness. Accusative case retained with perfect passive participle.

12. *The things which happened unto me* (*ta kat' eme*). "The things concerning me" = "my affairs" as common in Josephus. *Have fallen out rather* (*mallon elēluthen*). "Have come rather." Second perfect active indicative of *erchomai*.

Unto the progress (eis prokopēn). Late word from *prokoptō*, common verb, to cut or strike forward, but this late substantive does not occur in classical Greek. It is a technical term in Stoic philosophy for "progress toward wisdom" and it appears also in the papyri and the LXX. In N.T. only here, verse 25, and I Tim. 4:15.

13. *Throughout the whole praetorian guard (en holōi tōi praitōriōi).* There were originally ten thousand of these picked soldiers, concentrated in Rome by Tiberius. They had double pay and special privileges and became so powerful that emperors had to court their favour. Paul had contact with one after another of these soldiers. It is a Latin word, but the meaning is not certain, for in the other New Testament examples (Matt. 27:27; Mark 15:16; John 18:28, 33; 19:9; Acts 23:35) it means the palace of the provincial governor either in Jerusalem or Caesarea. In Rome "palace" would have to be the emperor's palace, a possible meaning for Paul a provincial writing to provincials (Kennedy). Some take it to mean the camp or barracks of the praetorian guard. The Greek, "in the whole praetorium," allows this meaning, though there is no clear example of it. Mommsen and Ramsay argue for the judicial authorities (*praefecti praetorio*) with the assessors of the imperial court. At any rate Paul, chained to a soldier, had access to the soldiers and the officials.

14. *The most of the brethren (tous pleionas tōn adelphōn).* "The more part of the brethren." The comparative with the article with the sense of the superlative as often in the *Koiné*. *In the Lord (en Kuriōi).* It is not clear whether this phrase is to be connected with "brethren" or with "being confident" (*pepoithotas*), probably with *pepoithotas*. If so, then "through my bonds" (*tois desmois mou*) would be the instrumental case and mean that by means of Paul's bonds the brethren "are more abundantly bold" (*perissoterōs tolmāin*).

15. *Even of envy and strife (kai dia phthonon kai erin).* "Even because of" (accusative after *dia*). Surely the lowest of motives for preaching Christ. Envy is an old word and an old sin and strife (*eris*) is more rivalry than schism. It is petty and personal jealousy of Paul's power and prowess by the Judaizers in Rome whom Paul has routed in the east,

but who now exult at the opportunity of annoying their great antagonist by their interpretation of Christ. Jealousy is always against those of one's own class or profession as preachers with preachers, doctors with doctors. *Of goodwill* (*di' eudokian*). Because of goodwill toward Paul.

16. *Of love* (*ex agapēs*). Out of love to Paul as well as to Christ. Put I Cor. 13 here as a flash-light.

17. *Of faction* (*ex eritheias*). Out of partisanship. From *eritheuō*, to spin wool, and that from *erithos*, a hireling. The papyri examples suit the idea of selfish ambition (Moulton and Milligan's *Vocabulary*). See II Cor. 12:20; Gal. 5:20. *Not sincerely* (*ouch hagnōs*). "Not purely," that is with mixed and impure motives. *To raise up affliction for my bonds* (*thlipsin egeirein tois desmois mou*). Now that Paul is down they jump on him in mean and nagging ways. Dative case in *desmois*. "To make my chains gall me" (Lightfoot).

18. *What then?* (*ti gar?*). Sharp problem put up to Paul by the conduct of the Judaizers. *Only that* (*plēn hoti*). Same idiom in Acts 20:23. *Plēn* is adverb *pleon* (more besides). As a preposition *plēn* means "except." This essential thing Paul sees in spite of all their envy and selfishness that Christ is preached. *Whether in pretence* (*eite prophasei*). Either from *prophainō*, to shew forth, or *prophēmi*, to speak forth, the ostensible presentation often untrue. See Acts 27:30. Paul sees clearly through the pious pretence of these Judaizers and rejoices that people get some knowledge of Christ. Some Christ is better than no Christ. *Yea, and will rejoice* (*alla kai charēsomai*). Note affirmative, not adversative, use of *alla*. Volitive use of the future (second future passive) indicative (*charēsomai*) of *chairō*. Paul is determined to rejoice in spite of the efforts of the Judaizers to prod him to anger.

19. *Will turn* (*apobēsetai*). Future middle indicative of *apobainō*, old verb, to come from, to come back, to turn out. *To my salvation* (*eis sōtērian*). For his release from prison as he strongly hopes to see them again (1:26). Lightfoot takes the word to be Paul's eternal salvation and it must be confessed that verse 20 (the close of this sentence) does suit that idea best. Can it be that Paul carried both conceptions in the word here? *Supply* (*epichorēgias*). Late and

rare word (one example in inscription of first century A.D.). In N.T. only here and Eph. 4:16. From the late verb *epichorēgeō* (double compound, *epi, choros, hēgeomai*, to furnish supply for the chorus) which see in II Cor. 9:10; Gal. 3:5.

20. *Earnest expectation (apokaradokian)*. In Paul alone from *apokaradokeō* (in papyri). See on Rom. 8:19 for only other example. *Shall be magnified (megalunthēsetai)*. Future passive indicative of *megalunō*, old verb, to make great, from *megas* (great). See Acts 19:17. *In my body (en tōi sōmati mou)*. See Rom. 12:1f. It is harder often to make Christ great in the body than in the spirit.

21. *For to me (emoi gar)*. Fine example of the ethical dative. Paul gives his own view of living. *To live is Christ (to zēin Christos)*. No copula (*estin*), but *to zēin* (the act of living present active infinitive) is the subject as is shown by the article *to*. Living is coextensive with Christ. *Gain (kerdos)*. Old word for any gain or profit, interest on money (so in papyri). In N.T. only here, Phil. 3:7; Titus 1:11. *To die (to apothanein*, second aorist active infinitive, single act) is to cash in both principal and interest and so to have more of Christ than when living. So Paul faces death with independence and calm courage.

22. *If this is the fruit of my work (touto moi karpos ergou)*. There is no *ei* (if) here in the Greek, but *touto* (this) seems to be resumptive and to repeat the conditional clause just before. If so, *kai* just after means *then* and introduces the conclusion of the condition. Otherwise *touto* introduces the conclusion and *kai* means *and*. *I wot not (ou gnōrizō)*. "I know not." It seems odd to preserve the old English word "wot" here. But it is not clear that *gnōrizō* (old causative verb from *ginōskō*) means just to know. Elsewhere in the N.T., as in Luke 2:15 and Rom. 9:22, it means to make known, to declare. The papyri examples mean to make known. It makes perfectly good sense to take its usual meaning here, "I do not declare what I shall choose."

23. *I am in a strait (sunechomai)*. "I am held together." Present passive indicative of the common compound verb *sunechō*, to hold together, to hem together as in Luke 8:45. "I am hemmed in on both sides" (Lightfoot). *Betwixt the two (ek tōn duo)*. "From the two (sides)." Pressure to live

on, pressure to die and be with Christ. *To depart (eis to analusai).* Purpose clause, *eis to* and the aorist active infinitive *analusai*, old compound verb, to unloose (as threads), to break up, to return (Luke 12:36, only other N.T. example), to break up camp (Polybius), to weigh anchor and put out to sea, to depart (often in old Greek and papyri). Cf. *kataluō* in II Cor 5:1 for tearing down the tent. *Very far better (polloi mallon kreisson).* Double comparative (triple Lightfoot calls it because of *polloi*) like Isocrates and the *Koine* often. See II Cor. 7:13 for *perissoterōs mallon*. *Polloi* is the instrumental case of measure (by much).

24. *In the flesh (en tēi sarki).* So B D G, but Aleph A C do not have *en*. Unnecessary with *epimenō*, to abide by (common verb).

25. *And abide with you all (kai paramenō pāsin humin).* Common Pauline idiom to repeat the simple verb *(menō)* as a compound *(paramenō,* future active indicative), old verb, to remain beside followed by locative case. See same idiom in *chairō, sunchairō* (Phil. 2:17).

26. *In Christ Jesus in me (en Christōi Iēsou en emoi).* "In Christ Jesus" as the basis for the glorying *(kauchēma),* "in me" as the instance in point. *Through my presence (dia tēs emēs parousias).* The word so often used of the second coming of Christ, but here in its ordinary sense as in 2:12 and I Cor. 16:17.

27. *Let your manner of life (politeuesthe).* Old verb from *politēs,* citizen, and that from *polis,* city, to be a citizen, to manage a state's affairs, to live as a citizen. Only twice in N.T.,here and Acts 23:1. Philippi as a colony possessed Roman citizenship and Paul was proud of his own possession of this right. The Authorized Version missed the figure completely by the word "conversation" which did refer to conduct and not mere talk as now, but did not preserve the figure of citizenship. Better render, "Only do ye live as citizens." *Striving (sunathlountes).* Rather, "striving together" as in an athletic contest. Late and rare word (Diodorus). "The very energy of the Christian faith to produce energetic individualities" (Rainy). "Striving in concert" (Lightfoot). *For the faith (tēi pistei).* For the teaching of the gospel, objective sense of *pistis* (faith).

28. *Affrighted (pturomenoi).* Present passive participle of

pturō, old verb, to frighten. The metaphor is of a timid or scared horse and from *ptoeō* (*ptoa*, terror). "Not startled in anything." *By the adversaries* (*hupo tōn antikeimenōn*). These men who were lined up against (present middle participle of *antikeimai*) may have been Jews or Gentiles or both. See II Thess. 2:4 for this late verb. Any preacher who attacks evil will have opposition. *Evident token* (*endeixis*). Old word for proof. See II Cor. 8:24; Rom. 3:25f. "An Attic law term" (Kennedy) and only in Paul in N.T. *Perdition* (*apōleias*). "Loss" in contrast with "salvation" (*sōtērias*). *And that* (*kai touto*). Idiomatic adverbial accusative. "It is a direct indication from God. The Christian gladiator does not anxiously await the signal of life or death from the fickle crowd" (Lightfoot).

29. *In the behalf of Christ* (*to huper Christou*). Literally, "the in behalf of Christ." But Paul divides the idea and uses the article *to* again both with *pisteuein* and with *paschein*. Suffering in behalf of Christ is one of God's gifts to us.

30. *Conflict* (*agōna*). Athletic or gladiatorial contest as in I Tim. 6:12; II Tim. 4:7. The Philippians saw Paul suffer (Acts 16:19-40; I Thess. 2:2) as now they have heard about it in Rome.

CHAPTER II

1. *If (ei).* Paul uses four conditions in this verse, all of the first class, assuming the condition to be true. *Comfort (paraklēsis).* Rather, "ground of appeal to you in Christ." See I Cor. 1:10; Eph. 4:1. *Consolation (paramuthion).* Old word from *paramutheomai,* persuasive address, incentive. *Of love (agapēs).* Objective genitive, "in love" (undefined as in I Cor. 13). *Fellowship (koinōnia).* Partnership in the Holy Spirit "whose first fruit is love" (Gal. 5:22). *Any tender mercies (tis splagchna).* Common use of this word for the nobler *viscera* and so for the higher emotions. But *tis* is masculine singular and *splagchna* is neuter plural. Lightfoot suggests an error of an early transcriber or even of the amanuensis in writing *ei tis* instead of *ei tina.*

2. *Fulfil (plērōsate).* Better here, "fill full." Paul's cup of joy will be full if the Philippians will only keep on having unity of thought and feeling (*to auto phronēte,* present active subjunctive, keep on thinking the same thing). *Being of one accord (sunpsuchoi).* Late word here for the first time, from *sun* and *psuchē,* harmonious in soul, souls that beat together, in tune with Christ and with each other. *Of one mind (to hen phronountes).* "Thinking the one thing." Like clocks that strike at the same moment. Perfect intellectual telepathy. Identity of ideas and harmony of feelings.

3. *Through vainglory (kata kenodoxian).* Late word, only here in N.T., from *kenodoxos (kenos, doxa,* Gal. 5:26, only here in N.T.), empty pride. *In lowliness of mind (tēi tapeinophrosunēi).* Late and rare word. Not in O.T. or early Greek writers. In Josephus and Epictetus in bad sense (pusillanimity). For ostentatious humility in Col. 2:18, 23. One of the words, like *tapeinos* (Matt. 11:29) and *tapeinophrōn* (I Peter 3:8, here alone in N.T.) that Christianity has ennobled and dignified (Acts 20:19). *Better than himself (huperechontas heautōn).* Present active participle of *huperechō* in intransitive sense to excel or surpass with the ablative, "excelling themselves." See Rom. 12:10.

443

4. *Looking* (*skopountes*). Present active participle of *skopeō* from *skopos* (aim, goal). Not keeping an eye on the main chance for number one, but for the good of others.

5. *Have this mind in you* (*touto phroneite en humin*). "Keep on thinking this in you which was also in Christ Jesus" (*ho kai en Christōi Iēsou*). What is that? Humility. Paul presents Jesus as the supreme example of humility. He urges humility on the Philippians as the only way to secure unity.

6. *Being* (*huparchōn*). Rather, "existing," present active participle of *huparchō*. *In the form of God* (*en morphēi theou*). *Morphē* means the essential attributes as shown in the form. In his preincarnate state Christ possessed the attributes of God and so appeared to those in heaven who saw him. Here is a clear statement by Paul of the deity of Christ. *A prize* (*harpagmon*). Predicate accusative with *hēgēsato*. Originally words in -*mos* signified the act, not the result (-*ma*). The few examples of *harpagmos* (Plutarch, etc.) allow it to be understood as equivalent to *harpagma*, like *baptismos* and *baptisma*. That is to say Paul means a prize to be held on to rather than something to be won ("robbery"). *To be on an equality with God* (*to einai isa theoi*). Accusative articular infinitive object of *hēgēsato*, "the being equal with God" (associative instrumental case *theoi* after *isa*). *Isa* is adverbial use of neuter plural with *einai* as in Rev. 21:16. *Emptied himself* (*heauton ekenōse*). First aorist active indicative of *kenoō*, old verb from *kenos*, empty. Of what did Christ empty himself? Not of his divine nature. That was impossible. He continued to be the Son of God. There has arisen a great controversy on this word, a *Kenosis* doctrine. Undoubtedly Christ gave up his environment of glory. He took upon himself limitations of place (space) and of knowledge and of power, though still on earth retaining more of these than any mere man. It is here that men should show restraint and modesty, though it is hard to believe that Jesus limited himself by error of knowledge and certainly not by error of conduct. He was without sin, though tempted as we are. "He stripped himself of the insignia of majesty" (Lightfoot).

7. *The form of a servant* (*morphēn doulou*). He took the characteristic attributes (*morphēn* as in verse 6) of a slave.

His humanity was as real as his deity. *In the likeness of men (en homoiōmati anthrōpōn).* It was a likeness, but a real likeness (Kennedy), no mere phantom humanity as the Docetic Gnostics held. Note the difference in tense between *huparchōn* (eternal existence in the *morphē* of God) and *genomenos* (second aorist middle participle of *ginomai*, becoming, definite entrance in time upon his humanity).

8. *In fashion (schēmati).* Locative case of *schēma*, from *echō*, to have, to hold. Bengel explains *morphē* by *forma*, *homoiōma* by *similitudo*, *schēma* by *habitus*. Here with *schēma* the contrast "is between what He is in Himself, and what He *appeared* in the eyes of men" (Lightfoot). *He humbled himself (etapeinōsen heauton).* First aorist active of *tapeinoō*, old verb from *tapeinos*. It is a voluntary humiliation on the part of Christ and for this reason Paul is pressing the example of Christ upon the Philippians, this supreme example of renunciation. See Bruce's masterpiece, *The Humiliation of Christ.* *Obedient (hupēkoos).* Old adjective, giving ear to. See Acts 7:39; II Cor. 2:9. *Unto death (mechri thanatou).* "Until death." See "until blood" (*mechris haimatos*, Heb. 12:4). *Yea, the death of the cross (thanatou de staurou).* The bottom rung in the ladder from the Throne of God. Jesus came all the way down to the most despised death of all, a condemned criminal on the accursed cross.

9. *Wherefore (dio).* Because of which act of voluntary and supreme humility. *Highly exalted (huperupsōse).* First aorist indicative of *huperupsoō (huper* and *hupsos*) late and rare word (LXX and Byzantine). Here only in N.T. Because of Christ's voluntary humiliation God lifted him above or beyond (*huper*) the state of glory which he enjoyed before the Incarnation. What glory did Christ have after the Ascension that he did not have before in heaven? What did he take back to heaven that he did not bring? Clearly his humanity. He returned to heaven the Son of Man as well as the Son of God. *The name which is above every name (to onoma to huper pan onoma).* What name is that? Apparently and naturally the name *Jesus,* which is given in verse 10. Some think it is "Jesus Christ," some "Lord," some the ineffable name Jehovah, some merely dignity and honour.

10. *That in the name of Jesus every knee should bow (hina en tōi onomati Iēsou pan gonu kampsēi).* First aorist active

subjunctive of *kamptō*, old verb, to bend, to bow, in purpose clause with *hina*. Not perfunctory genuflections whenever the name of Jesus is mentioned, but universal acknowledgment of the majesty and power of Jesus who carries his human name and nature to heaven. This universal homage to Jesus is seen in Rom. 8:22; Eph. 1:20–22 and in particular Rev. 5:13. *Under the earth* (*katachthoniōn*). Homeric adjective for departed souls, subterranean, simply the dead. Here only in the N.T.

11. *Should confess* (*exomologēsētai*). First aorist middle subjunctive of *exomologeomai* with *hina* for purpose. *Lord* (*Kurios*). Peter (Acts 2:36) claimed that God made Christ "Lord." See also I Cor. 8:6; 12:3; Rom. 10:9. Kennedy laments that the term Lord has become one of the most lifeless in the Christian vocabulary, whereas it really declares the true character and dignity of Jesus Christ and "is the basis and the object of worship."

12. *Not as in my presence only* (*mē hōs en tēi parousiāi monon*). B and a few other MSS. omit *hōs*. The negative *mē* goes with the imperative *katergazesthe* (work out), not with *hupēkousate* (obeyed) which would call for *ouch*. *Much more* (*polloi mallon*). They are not to render eye-service only when Paul is there, but much more when he is away. *Work out* (*katergazesthe*). Perfective use of *kata* (down) in composition, work on to the finish. This exhortation assumes human free agency in the carrying on the work of one's salvation. *With fear and trembling* (*meta phobou kai tromou*). "Not slavish terror, but wholesome, serious caution" (Vincent). "A nervous and trembling anxiety to do right" (Lightfoot). Paul has no sympathy with a cold and dead orthodoxy or formalism that knows nothing of struggle and growth. He exhorts as if he were an Arminian in addressing men. He prays as if he were a Calvinist in addressing God and feels no inconsistency in the two attitudes. Paul makes no attempt to reconcile divine sovereignty and human free agency, but boldly proclaims both.

13. *Which worketh in you* (*ho energōn en humin*). Articular present active participle of *energeō* from *energos* (*en*, *ergon*) one at work, common verb from Aristotle on, to be at work, to energize. God is the Energy and the Energizer of the universe. Modern scientists, like Eddington, Jeans, and

Whitney, are not afraid to agree with Paul and to put God back of all activity in nature. *Both to will and to work (kai to thelein kai to energein).* "Both the willing and the working (the energizing)." God does it all, then. Yes, but he puts us to work also and our part is essential, as he has shown in verse 12, though secondary to that of God. *For his good-pleasure (huper tēs eudokias).* So Whitney puts "the will of God" behind gravitation and all the laws of nature.

14. *Without murmurings (chōris goggusmōn).* See on Acts 6:1 for this late onomatopoetic word from *gogguzō,* to mutter, to grumble. *Disputings (dialogismōn).* Or questionings as in Luke 24:38. The grumblings led to disputes.

15. *That ye may be (hina genēsthe).* Rather, "that ye may become" (second aorist middle subjunctive of *ginomai,* to become). *Blameless (amemptoi).* Free from censure (*memphomai,* to blame). *Harmless (akeraioi).* Unmixed, unadulterated as in Rom. 16:19. *Without blemish (amōma).* Without spot, "unblemished in reputation and in reality" (Vincent). *In the midst of (meson).* Preposition with genitive. *Crooked (skolias).* Old word, curved as opposed to *orthos,* straight. See on Acts 2:40. *Perverse (diestrammenēs).* Perfect passive participle of *diastrephō,* to distort, to twist, to turn to one side (*dia,* in two). Old word. See Matt. 17:17; Acts 13:10.

16. *As lights in the world (hōs phōstēres en kosmōi).* As luminaries like the heavenly bodies. Christians are the light of the world (Matt. 5:14) as they reflect the light from Christ (John 1:4; 8:12), but here the word is not *phōs* (light), but *phōstēres* (luminaries, stars). The place for light is the darkness where it is needed. *Holding forth (epechontes).* Present active participle of *epechō.* Probably not connected with the preceding metaphor in *phōstēres.* The old meaning of the verb *epechō* is to hold forth or to hold out (the word of life as here). The context seems to call for "holding fast." It occurs also with the sense of attending to (Acts 3:5). *That I may have (emoi).* Ethical dative, "to me as a ground of boasting."

17. *And if I am offered (ei kai spendomai).* Though I am poured out as a libation. Old word. In N.T. only here and II Tim. 4:6. Paul pictures his life-blood as being poured

upon (uncertain whether heathen or Jewish offerings meant and not important) the sacrifice and service of the faith of the Philippians in mutual service and joy (both *chairō* and *sunchairō* twice in the sentence). Joy is mutual when the service is mutual. Young missionaries offer their lives as a challenge to other Christians to match their money with their blood.

19. *That I also may be of good comfort* (*hina kágō eupsuchō*). Present subjunctive with *hina* in purpose clause of the late and rare verb *eupsucheō*, from *eupsuchos* (cheerful, of good spirit). In papyri and *eupsuchei* (be of good cheer) common in sepulchral inscriptions. *When I know* (*gnous*). Second aorist active participle of *ginōskō*.

20. *Likeminded* (*isopsuchon*). Old, but very rare adjective (*isos, psuchē*), like *isotimos* in II Peter 1:1. Only here in N.T. Likeminded with Timothy, not with Paul. *Truly* (*gnēsiōs*). "Genuinely." Old adverb, only here in N.T., from *gnēsios* (Phil. 4:3), legitimate birth, not spurious.

21. *They all* (*hoi pantes*). "The whole of them." Surely Luke was away from Rome at this juncture.

22. *The proof* (*tēn dokimēn*). "The test" as of metals (II Cor. 2:9; 9:13). Three times they had seen Timothy (Acts 16:13; 19:22; 20:3f.). *With me* (*sun emoi*). Paul's delicacy of feeling made him use *sun* rather than *emoi* alone. Timothy did not serve Paul. *In furtherance of* (*eis*). See Phil. 1:5 for this use of *eis*.

23. *So soon as I shall see* (*hōs an aphidō*). Indefinite temporal clause with *hōs an* and the second aorist active subjunctive of *aphoraō*. The oldest MSS. (Aleph A B D) have *aphidō* (old aspirated form) rather than *apidō*. *How it will go with me* (*ta peri eme*). On the force of *apo* with *horaō* (look away) see Heb. 12:2. "The things concerning me," the outcome of the trial. Cf. I Cor. 4:17, 19.

24. *In the Lord* (*en Kuriōi*). Not a perfunctory use of this phrase. Paul's whole life is centred in Christ (Gal. 2:20).

25. *I counted it* (*hēgēsamēn*). Epistolary aorist from the point of view of the readers. *Epaphroditus* (*Epaphroditon*). Common name, though only in Philippians in N.T., contracted into Epaphras, though not the same man as Epaphras in Col. 1:7. Note one article *ton* (the) with the three epithets given in an ascending scale (Lightfoot), brother (*adelphon*,

common sympathy), fellow-worker (*sunergon*, common work), fellow-soldier (*sunstratiōtēn*, common danger as in Philemon 2). *Mou* (my) and *humōn* (your) come together in sharp contrast. *Messenger* (*apostolon*). See II Cor. 8:23 for this use of *apostolos* as messenger (missionary). *Minister* (*leitourgon*). See on Rom. 13:6 and 15:16 for this ritualistic term.

26. *He longed after* (*epipothōn ēn*). Periphrastic imperfect of *epipotheō* (Phil. 1:8), "he was yearning after." *You all* (*pantas humas*). So again (1:5, 7, 8). *Was sore troubled* (*adēmonōn*). Periphrastic imperfect again (repeat *ēn*) of the old word *adēmoneō* either from an unused *adēmōn* (a privative and *dēmos*, away from home, homesick) or from *adēmōn*, *adēsai* (discontent, bewilderment). The *Vocabulary* of Moulton and Milligan gives one papyrus example in line with the latter etymology. See already Matt. 26:37; Mark 14:33. In any case the distress of Epaphroditus was greatly increased when he knew that the Philippians (the home-folks) had learned of his illness, "because ye had heard that he was sick" (*dioti ēkousate hoti ēsthenēse*), "because ye heard that he fell sick" (ingressive aorist). *He was sick* (*ēsthenēse*). Ingressive aorist, "he did become sick." *Nigh unto death* (*paraplēsion thanatōi*). Only example in N.T. of this compound adverbial preposition (from the adjective *paraplēsios*) with the dative case.

28. *Ye may rejoice* (*charēte*). Second aorist passive subjunctive with *hina* in final clause of *chairō*, to rejoice. *That I may be the less sorrowful* (*kágō alupoteros ō*). Present subjunctive with *hina* and comparative of old compound adjective *alupos* (a privative and *lupē*, more free from grief). Beautiful expression of Paul's feelings for the Philippians and for Epaphroditus.

29. *In honour* (*entimous*). Old compound adjective (*en*, *timē*), prized, precious (Luke 7:2; 14:8; I Peter 2:4, 6). Predicate accusative. Noble plea in behalf of Christ's minister.

30. *Hazarding his life* (*paraboleusamenos tēi psuchēi*). First aorist middle participle of *paraboleuō* (from the adjective *parabolos*), to place beside. The old Greek writers used *paraballomai*, to expose oneself to danger. But Deissmann (*Light from the Ancient East*, p. 88) cites an example

of *paraboleusamenos* from an inscription at Olbia or the Black Sea of the second century A.D. where it plainly means "exposing himself to danger" as here. Lightfoot renders it here "having gambled with his life." The word *parabolani* (riskers) was applied to the Christians who risked their lives for the dying and the dead.

CHAPTER III

1. *Finally* (*to loipon*). Accusative of general reference, literally, "as for the rest." So again in 4:8. It (or just *loipon*) is a common phrase towards the close of Paul's Epistles (II Thess. 3:1; II Cor. 13:11). In Eph. 6:10 we have *tou loipou* (genitive case). But Paul uses the idiom elsewhere also as in I Cor. 7:29; I Thess. 4:1 before the close of the letter is in sight. It is wholly needless to understand Paul as about to finish and then suddenly changing his mind like some preachers who announce the end a half dozen times. *To write the same things* (*ta auta graphein*). Present active articular infinitive, "the going on writing the same things." What things? He has just used *chairete* (go on rejoicing) again and he will repeat it in 4:4. But in verse 2 he uses *blepete* three times. At any rate Paul, as a true teacher, is not afraid of repetition. *Irksome* (*oknēron*). Old adjective from *okneo*, to delay, to hesitate. It is not tiresome to me to repeat what is "safe" (*asphales*) for you. Old adjective from *a* privative and *sphallō*, to totter, to reel. See Acts 21:34.

2. *Beware* (*blepete*). Three times for urgency and with different epithet for the Judaizers each time. *The dogs* (*tous kunas*). The Jews so termed the Gentiles which Jesus uses in a playful mood (*kunariois*, little dogs) to the Syro-Phoenician woman (Matt. 15:26). Paul here turns the phrase on the Judaizers themselves. *The evil workers* (*tous kakous ergatas*). He had already called the Judaizers "deceitful workers" (*ergatai dolioi*) in II Cor. 11:13. *The concision* (*tēn katatomēn*). Late word for incision, mutilation (in contrast with *peritomē*, circumcision). In Symmachus and an inscription. The verb *katatemnō* is used in the LXX only of mutilations (Lev. 21:5; I Kings 18:28).

3. *For we* (*hēmeis gar*). We believers in Christ, the children of Abraham by faith, whether Jew or Gentile, the spiritual circumcision in contrast to the merely physical (Rom. 2:25–29; Col. 2:11; Eph. 2:11). See Gal. 5:12 for *apotemnein* (to

cut off) in sense of mutilation also. *By the Spirit of God*
(*pneumati theou*). Instrumental case, though the dative case
as the object of *latreuō* makes good sense also (worshipping
the Spirit of God) or even the locative (worshipping in the
Spirit of God). *No* (*ouk*). Actual condition rather than *mē*
with the participle. *In the flesh* (*en sarki*). Technical term
in Paul's controversy with the Judaizers (II Cor. 11:18;
Gal. 6:13f.). External privileges beyond mere flesh.

4. *Might have* (*echōn*). Rather, "even though myself
having." *Confidence* (*pepoithēsin*). Late word, condemned
by the Atticists, from *pepoitha* (just used). See II Cor. 1:15;
3:4.

5. *Thinketh to have confidence* (*dokei pepoithenai*). Second
perfect active infinitive. Old idiom, "seems to himself to
have confidence." Later idiom like Matt. 3:9 "think not
to say" and I Cor. 11:16, "thinks that he has ground of
confidence in himself." *I yet more* (*egō mallon*). "I have
more ground for boasting than he" and Paul proceeds to
prove it in the rest of verses 5 and 6. *Circumcised the eighth
day* (*peritomēi oktaēmeros*). "In circumcision (locative case)
an eighth day man." Use of the ordinal with persons like
tetartaios (John 11:39). Ishmaelites were circumcised in the
thirteenth year, proselytes from Gentiles in mature age,
Jews on the eighth day (Luke 2:21). *Of the stock of Israel*
(*ek genous Israēl*). Of the original stock, not a proselyte.
Benjamin (*Beniamin*). Son of the right hand (that is, left-
handed), son of Rachel. The first King, Saul (Paul's own
Hebrew name) was from this little tribe. The battle cry of
Israel was "After thee, O Benjamin" (Judg. 5:14). *A
Hebrew of the Hebrews* (*Ebraios ex Ebraiōn*). Of Hebrew
parents who retained the characteristic qualities in language
and custom as distinct from the Hellenistic Jews (Acts 6:1).
Paul was from Tarsus and knew Greek as well as Aramaic
(Acts 21:40; 22:2) and Hebrew, but he had not become
Hellenized. *A Pharisee* (*Pharisaios*). In distinction from
the Sadducees (Gal. 1:14) and he continued a Pharisee in
many essential matters like the doctrine of the resurrection
(Acts 23:6). Cf. II Cor. 11:22.

6. *As touching zeal* (*kata zēlos*). So the old MSS. treating
zēlos as neuter, not masculine. He was a zealot against Christianity, "persecuting the church" (*diōkōn tēn ekklēsian*). He

was the ringleader in the persecution from the death of Stephen till his own conversion (Acts 8:1–9:9). *Found blameless (genomenos amemptos).* "Having become blameless" (Gal. 1:14). He knew and practised all the rules of the rabbis. A marvellous record, scoring a hundred in Judaism.

7. *Were gain to me (en moi kerdē).* "Were gains (plural, see on 1:21) to me (ethical dative)." Paul had natural pride in his Jewish attainments. He was the star of hope for Gamaliel and the Sanhedrin. *Have I counted (hēgēmai).* Perfect middle indicative, state of completion and still true. *Loss (zēmian).* Old word for damage, loss. In N.T. only in Phil. and Acts 27:10, 21. Debit side of the ledger, not credit.

8. *Yea, verily, and (alla men oun ge kai).* Five particles before Paul proceeds (yea, indeed, therefore, at least, even), showing the force and passion of his conviction. He repeats his affirmation with the present middle indicative (*hēgoumai*), "I still count all things loss for the excellency of the knowledge (*to huperechon*, the surpassingness, neuter articular participle of *huperechō*, Phil. 2:3) of Christ Jesus my Lord." *Dung (skubala).* Late word of uncertain etymology, either connected with *skōr* (dung) or from *es kunas ballō*, to fling to the dogs and so refuse of any kind. It occurs in the papyri. Here only in the N.T. *That I may gain Christ (hina Christon kerdēsō).* First aorist active subjunctive of *kerdaō*, Ionic form for *kerdainō* with *hina* in purpose clause. Paul was never satisfied with his knowledge of Christ and always craved more fellowship with him.

9. *Be found in him (heurethō en autōi).* First aorist (effective) passive subjunctive with *hina* of *heuriskō*. At death (II Cor. 5:3) or when Christ comes. Cf. 2:8; Gal. 2:17. *Through faith in Christ (dia pisteōs Christou).* The objective genitive *Christou*, not subjective, as in Gal. 2:16, 20; Rom. 3:22. Explained further by *epi tēi pistei* (on the basis of faith) as in Acts 3:16.

10. *That I may know him (tou gnōnai auton).* Genitive of the articular second aorist (ingressive) active infinitive (purpose) of *ginōskō*, to have personal acquaintance or experience with. This is Paul's major passion, to get more knowledge of Christ by experience. *The power of his resurrection (tēn dunamin tēs anastaseōs autou).* Power (Lightfoot)

in the sense of assurance to believers in immortality (I Cor. 15:14f.; Rom. 8:11), in the triumph over sin (Rom. 4:24f.), in the dignity of the body (I Cor. 6:13ff.; Phil. 3:21), in stimulating the moral and spiritual life ˋ(Gal. 2:20; Rom. 6:4f.; Col. 2:12; Eph. 2:5). See Westcott's *The Gospel of the Resurrection*, ii #31. *The fellowship of his sufferings* (*tēn koinōnian tōn pathēmatōn autou*). Partnership in (objective genitive) his sufferings, an honour prized by Paul (Col. 1:24). *Becoming conformed to his death* (*summorphizomenos tōi thanatōi autou*). Present passive participle of *summorphizō*, late verb from *summorphos*, found only here and ecclesiastical writers quoting it. The Latin Vulgate uses *configuro*. See Rom. 6:4 for *sumphutoi* in like sense and II Cor. 4:10. "The agony of Gethsemane, not less than the agony of Calvary, will be reproduced however faintly in the faithful servant of Christ" (Lightfoot). "In this passage we have the deepest secrets of the Apostle's Christian experience unveiled" (Kennedy).

11. *If by any means I may attain* (*ei pōs katantēsō*). Not an expression of doubt, but of humility (Vincent), a modest hope (Lightfoot). For *ei pōs*, see Rom. 1:10; 11:14 where *parazēlōsō* can be either future indicative or aorist subjunctive like *katantēsō* here (see subjunctive *katalabō* in verse 12), late compound verb *katantaō*. *Resurrection* (*exanastasin*). Late word, not in LXX, but in Polybius and one papyrus example. Apparently Paul is thinking here only of the resurrection of believers out from the dead and so double *ex* (*tēn exanastasin tēn ek nekrōn*). Paul is not denying a general resurrection by this language, but emphasizing that of believers.

12. *Not that* (*ouch hoti*). To guard against a misunderstanding as in John 6:26; 12:6; II Cor. 1:24; Phil. 4:11, 17. *I have already obtained* (*ēdē elabon*). Rather, "I did already obtain," constative second aorist active indicative of *lambanō*, summing up all his previous experiences as a single event. *Or am already made perfect* (*ē ēdē teteleiōmai*). Perfect passive indicative (state of completion) of *teleioō*, old verb from *teleios* and that from *telos* (end). Paul pointedly denies that he has reached a spiritual impasse of nondevelopment. Certainly he knew nothing of so-called sudden absolute perfection by any single experience. Paul has

made great progress in Christlikeness, but the goal is still before him, not behind him. *But I press on (diōkō de)*. He is not discouraged, but encouraged. He keeps up the chase (real idea in *diōkō*, as in I Cor. 14:1; Rom. 9:30; I Tim. 6:11). *If so be that (ei kai)*. "I follow after." The condition (third class, *ei—katalabō*, second aorist active subjunctive of *katalambanō*) is really a sort of purpose clause or aim. There are plenty of examples in the *Koiné* of the use of *ei* and the subjunctive as here (Robertson, *Grammar*, p. 1017), "if I also may lay hold of that for which (*eph' hōi*, purpose expressed by *epi*) I was laid hold of (*katelēmphthēn*, first aorist passive of the same verb *katalambanō*) by Christ Jesus." His conversion was the beginning, not the end of the chase.

13. *Not yet (oupō)*. But some MSS. read *ou* (not). *To have apprehended (kateilēphenai)*. Perfect active infinitive of same verb *katalambanō* (perfective use of *kata*, to grasp completely). Surely denial enough. *But one thing (hen de)*. No verb in the Greek. We can supply *poiō* (I do) or *diōkō* (I keep on in the chase), but no verb is really needed. "When all is said, the greatest art is to limit and isolate oneself" (Goethe), concentration. *Forgetting the things which are behind (ta men opisō epilanthanomenos)*. Common verb, usually with the genitive, but the accusative in the *Koiné* is greatly revived with verbs. Paul can mean either his old pre-Christian life, his previous progress as a Christian, or both (all of it). *Stretching forward (epekteinomenos)*. Present direct middle participle of the old double compound *epekteinō* (stretching myself out towards). Metaphor of a runner leaning forward as he runs.

14. *Toward the goal (kata skopon)*. "Down upon the goal," who is Jesus himself to whom we must continually look as we run (Heb. 12:2). The word means a watchman, then the goal or mark. Only here in N.T. *Unto the prize (eis to brabeion)*. Late word (Menander and inscriptions) from *brabeus* (umpire who awards the prize). In N.T. only here and I Cor. 9:24. *Of the high calling (tēs anō klēseōs)*. Literally, "of the upward calling." The goal continually moves forward as we press on, but yet never out of sight.

15. *As many as be perfect (hosoi teleioi)*. Here the term *teleioi* means relative perfection, not the absolute perfection so pointedly denied in verse 12. Paul here includes himself

in the group of spiritual adults (see Heb. 5:13). *Let us be thus minded* (*touto phronōmen*). Present active volitive subjunctive of *phroneō*. "Let us keep on thinking this," viz. that we have not yet attained absolute perfection. *If ye are otherwise minded* (*ei ti heterōs phroneite*). Condition of first class, assumed as true. That is, if ye think that ye are absolutely perfect. *Shall God reveal unto you* (*ho theos humin apokalupsei*). He turns such cases over to God. What else can he do with them? *Whereunto we have already come* (*eis ho ephthasamen*). First aorist active indicative of *phthanō*, originally to come before as in I Thess. 4:15, but usually in the *Koiné* simply to arrive, attain to, as here.

16. *By that same rule let us walk* (*tōi autōi stoichein*). Aleph A B do not have *kanoni* (rule). Besides *stoichein* is the absolute present active infinitive which sometimes occurs instead of the principal verb as in Rom. 12:15. Paul means simply this that, having come thus far, the thing to do is to go "in the same path" (*tōi autōi*) in which we have been travelling so far. A needed lesson for Christians weary with the monotony of routine in religious life and work.

17. *Imitators together of me* (*sunmimētai mou*). Found only here so far, though Plato uses *summimeisthai*. "Vie with each other in imitating me" (Lightfoot). *Mark* (*skopeite*). Old verb from *skopos* (verse 14). "Keep your eyes on me as goal." Mark and follow, not avoid as in Rom. 16:17. *An ensample* (*tupon*). Originally the impression left by a stroke (John 20:25), then a pattern (mould) as here (cf. I Thess. 1:7; I Cor. 10:6, 11; Rom. 5:14; 6:17).

18. *I told you often* (*pollakis elegon*). Imperfect active, repetition in Paul's warnings to them. *Even weeping* (*kai klaiōn*). Deep emotion as he dictated the letter and recalled these recreant followers of Christ (cf. II Cor. 2:4). *The enemies of the cross of Christ* (*tous echthrous tou staurou tou Christou*). Either the Judaizers who denied the value of the cross of Christ (Gal. 5:11; 6:12, 14) or Epicurean antinomians whose loose living gave the lie to the cross of Christ (I John 2:4).

19. *Whose god is the belly* (*hou to theos hē koilia*). The comic poet Eupolis uses the rare word *Koiliodaimōn* for one who makes a god of his belly and Seneca speaks of one who *abdomini servit*. Sensuality in food, drink, sex then as now

mastered some men. These men posed as Christians and gloried in their shame. *Who mind earthly things* (*hoi ta epigeia phronountes*). Anacoluthon. The nominative does not refer to *polloi* at the beginning, but with the accusative *tous echthrous* in between. See Mark 12:40.

20. *Our citizenship* (*hēmōn to politeuma*). Old word from *piliteuō* (Phil. 1:27), but only here in N.T. The inscriptions use it either for citizenship or for commonwealth. Paul was proud of his Roman citizenship and found it a protection. The Philippians were also proud of their Roman citizenship. But Christians are citizens of a kingdom not of this world (John 18:36). Milligan (*Vocabulary*) doubts if commentators are entitled to translate it here: "We are a colony of heaven," because such a translation reverses the relation between the colony and the mother city. But certainly here Paul's heart is in heaven. *We wait for* (*apekdechometha*). Rare and late double compound (perfective use of prepositions like wait out) which vividly pictures Paul's eagerness for the second coming of Christ as the normal attitude of the Christian colonist whose home is heaven.

21. *Shall fashion anew* (*metaschēmatisei*). Future active indicative of *metaschēmatizō* for which see I Cor. 4:6; II Cor. 11:13ff. *Conformed to* (*summorphon*). For which (*sun, morphē*) see Rom. 8:29, only N.T. examples. With associative instrumental case. The body of our state of humiliation will be made suitable to associate with the body of Christ's glory (I Cor. 15:54f.). *According to the working* (*kata tēn energeian*). "According to the energy." If any one doubts the power of Christ to do this transformation, Paul replies that he has power "even to subject all things unto himself."

CHAPTER IV

1. *Longed for* (*epipothētoi*). Late and rare verbal adjective (here alone in N.T.) from *epipotheō*. *So stand fast* (*houto stēkete*). Present active imperative of *stēkō* (late present from perfect *hestēka* from *histēmi*). See 1:27. They were tempted to defection. Standing firm is difficult when a panic starts.

2. *Euodia* (*Euodian*). This name means literally "prosperous journey" (*eu, hodos*). It occurs in the inscriptions. *Syntyche* (*Suntuchēn*). From *suntugchanō*, to meet with and so "pleasant acquaintance" or "good-luck." Occurs in the inscriptions and identified with Lydia by some. Klöpper suggests that each of these rival women had church assemblies in their homes, one a Jewish-Christian church, the other a Gentile-Christian church. Vincent doubts the great influence of women in Macedonia held by Lightfoot who also suggests that these two were ladies of rank or perhaps deaconesses of the church in Philippi. Schinz suggests that in such a pure church even slight bickerings would make a real disturbance. "It may have been accidental friction between two energetic Christian women" (Kennedy).

3. *True yokefellow* (*gnēsie sunzuge*). All sorts of suggestions have been made here, one that it was Lydia who is termed Paul's wife by the word *sunzuge*. Unfortunately for that view *gnēsie* is masculine vocative singular. Some have suggested it as a proper name though it is not found in the inscriptions, but the word does occur as an appellative in one. Lightfoot even proposes Epaphroditus, the bearer of the Epistle, certainly a curious turn to take to address him. After all it matters little that we do not know who the peacemaker was. *Help these women* (*sunlambanou autais*). Present middle imperative of *sunlambanō*, to seize (Matt. 26:55), to conceive (Luke 1:24), then to take hold together with one (associative instrumental case), to help as here (Luke 5:7). "Take hold with them." *They laboured with me* (*sunēthlēsan moi*). First aorist active indicative of *sunath-*

458

leō (for which see 1:27) with associative instrumental case (*moi*). *With Clement also* (*meta kai Klēmentos*). There is no evidence that he was Clement of Rome as the name is common. *In the book of life* (*en biblōi zōēs*). The only instance of this expression in the N.T. outside of the Apocalypse (3:5; 13:8; 17:8, etc.). Hence real Christians in spite of their bickerings.

4. *Again I will say* (*palin erō*). Future active indicative of defective verb *eipon*. *Rejoice* (*chairete*). Present active imperative as in 3:1, repeated for emphasis in spite of discouragements. Not in the sense of "Farewell" here.

5. *Your forbearance* (*to epieikes humōn*). "Your gentleness," "your sweet reasonableness" (Matthew Arnold), "your moderation." Old adjective (*epi*, *eikos*) as in James 3:17; I Tim. 3:3. Article and neuter singular here=*hē epieikeia* (Acts 24:4; II Cor. 10:1) like *to chrēston* in Rom. 2:4. *The Lord is at hand* (*ho kurios eggus*). "The Apostle's watchword" (Lightfoot), as in I Cor. 16:22 (*Maran atha*, Aramaic equivalent, Our Lord cometh). Unless, indeed, *eggus* here means *near* in space instead of *nigh* in time.

6. *In nothing be anxious* (*mēden merimnāte*). Present imperative in prohibition, "stop being anxious." See *mē merimnāte* in Matt. 6:31. *With thanksgiving* (*meta eucharistias*). In all the forms of prayer here named thanksgiving should appear.

7. *The peace of God* (*hē eirēnē tou theou*). See in II Thess. 3:16 "the Lord of peace" (*ho Kurios tēs eirēnēs*) and verse 9 for "the God of peace" (*ho theos tēs eirēnēs*). *Shall guard* (*phrourēsei*). "Shall garrison," future active indicative of *phroureō*, old verb from *phrouros* (*pro-horos*, *prooraō*, to see before, to look out). See Acts 9:24; II Cor. 11:32. God's peace as a sentinel mounts guard over our lives as Tennyson so beautifully pictures Love as doing.

8. *Finally* (*to loipon*). See on 3:1. *Whatsoever* (*hosa*). Thus he introduces six adjectives picturing Christian ideals, old-fashioned and familiar words not necessarily from any philosophic list of moral excellencies Stoic or otherwise. Without these no ideals can exist. They are pertinent now when so much filth is flaunted before the world in books, magazines and moving-pictures under the name of realism (the slime of the gutter and the cess-pool). *Honourable* (*semna*).

Old word from *sebō*, to worship, revere. So revered, venerated (I Tim. 3:8). *Pure (hagna)*. Old word for all sorts of purity. There are clean things, thoughts, words, deeds. *Lovely (prosphilē)*. Old word, here only in N.T., from *pros* and *phileō*, pleasing, winsome. *Of good report (euphēma*. Old word, only here in N.T., from *eu* and *phēmē*, fair-speaking, attractive. *If there be any (ei tis)*. Paul changes the construction from *hosa* (whatsoever) to a condition of the first class, as in 2:1, with two substantives. *Virtue (aretē)*. Old word, possibly from *areskō*, to please, used very often in a variety of senses by the ancients for any mental excellence or moral quality or physical power. Its very vagueness perhaps explains its rarity in the N.T., only four times (Phil. 4:8; I Peter 2:9; II Peter 1:3, 5). It is common in the papyri, but probably Paul is using it in the sense found in the LXX (Isa. 42:12; 43:21) of God's splendour and might (Deissmann, *Bible Studies*, p. 95) in connection with "praise" *(epainos)* as here or even meaning praise. *Think on these things (tauta logizesthe)*. Present middle imperative for habit of thought. We are responsible for our thoughts and can hold them to high and holy ideals.

9. *In me (en emoi)*. Paul dares to point to his life in Philippi as an illustration of this high thinking. The preacher is the interpreter of the spiritual life and should be an example of it. *These things do (tauta prassete)*. Practise as a habit *(prassō*, not *poieō)*.

10. *I rejoice (echarēn)*. Second aorist passive indicative of *chairō*, a timeless aorist. I did rejoice, I do rejoice. *Greatly (megalōs)*. Old adverb, only here in N.T., from *megas* (great). *Now at length (ēdē pote)*. In N.T. only here and Rom. 1:10. *Pote* is indefinite past (interval), *ēdē* immediate present. *Ye have revived (anethalete)*. Second aorist active indicative of old poetic word (Homer), *anathallō*, to sprout again, to shoot up, to blossom again. So in the LXX five times, though rare and literary word. *Your thought for me (to huper emou phronein)*. Accusative case of the articular present active infinitive the object of *anethalete* used transitively. "You caused your thinking of me to bloom afresh." *Wherein (eph' hōi)*. "In which," "upon which" (locative case). A loose reference to Paul's interests as involved in their thinking of him. *Ye did indeed take thought (kai ephroneite)*. In-

perfect active, "ye were also (or had been also) thinking."
Ye lacked opportunity (ēkaireisthe). Imperfect middle of
akaireomai, late and rare word, here only in N.T., from
akairos (*a* privative, *kairos*), not to have a chance, the
opposite of *eukaireō* (Mark 6:31).
11. *In respect of want (kath' husterēsin)*. Late and rare
word from *hustereō*, to be behind or too late, only here and
Mark 12:44 in N.T. *I have learned (emathon)*. Simply, "I
did learn" (constative second aorist active indicative of
manthanō, to learn, looking at his long experience as a unit.
In whatsoever state I am (en hois eimi). "In what things
(circumstances) I am." *To be content (autarkēs einai)*.
Predicate nominative with the infinitive of the old adjective
autarkēs (from *autos* and *arkeō*, to be self-sufficient), self-
sufficing. Favourite word with the Stoics, only here in N.T.,
though *autarkeia* occurs in II Cor. 9:8 and I Tim. 6:6. Paul
is contented with his lot and he learned that lesson long ago.
Socrates said as to who is wealthiest: "He that is content
with least, for *autarkeia* is nature's wealth."
12. *I know how (oida)*. Followed by the infinitive *oida*
has this sense. So here twice, with *tapeinousthai*, to be
humbled, from *tapeinos*, and with *perisseuein*, to overflow.
Have I learned the secret (memuēmai). Perfect passive indicative of *mueō*, old and common word from *muō*, to close
(Latin *mutus*), and so to initiate with secret rites, here only
in N.T. The common word *mustērion* (mystery) is from
mustēs (one initiated) and this from *mueō*, to initiate, to
instruct in secrets. Paul draws this metaphor from the
initiatory rites of the pagan mystery-religions. *To be filled*
(*chortazesthai*). Old verb from *chortos* (grass, hay) and so to
fatten like an animal. *To be hungry (peināin)*. Old verb
from *peina* (hunger) and kin to *penēs*, poor man who has to
work for his living (*penomai*).
13. *I can do all things (panta ischuō)*. Old verb to have
strength (*ischus*). *In him that strengtheneth me (en tōi en-
dunamounti me)*. Late and rare verb (in LXX) from adjective *endunamos (en, dunamis)*. Causative verb to empower,
to pour power into one. See same phrase in I Tim. 1:12 *tōi
endunamōsanti me* (aorist tense here). Paul has such strength
so long as Jesus keeps on putting power (*dunamis*) into him.
14. *That ye had fellowship (sunkoinōnēsantes)*. First aorist

active participle (simultaneous action with the principal verb *kalōs epoiēsate*). "Ye did well contributing for my affliction."
15. *In the beginning of the gospel* (*en archēi tou euaggeliou*). After he had wrought in Philippi (II Thess. 2:13). *Had fellowship* (*ekoinōnēsen*). "Had partnership" (first aorist active indicative). *In the matter* (*eis logon*). "As to an account." No other church opened an account with Paul. *Of giving and receiving* (*doseōs kai lēmpseōs*). Credit and debit. A mercantile metaphor repeated in verse 17 by *eis logon humōn* (to your account). Paul had to keep books then with no other church, though later Thessalonica and Beroea joined Philippi in support of Paul's work in Corinth (II Cor. 11:8f.). *But ye only* (*ei mē humeis monoi*). Not even Antioch contributed anything but good wishes and prayers for Paul's work (Acts 13:1–3).
16. *Once and again* (*kai hapax kai dis*). "Both once and twice" they did it "even in Thessalonica" and so before Paul went to Corinth." See the same Greek idiom in I Thess. 2:18.
17. *I seek for* (*epizētō*). Old verb, in N.T. only here and Rom. 11:7 (linear present, I am seeking for). Lightfoot calls it "the Apostle's nervous anxiety to clear himself" of wanting more gifts. Why not say his delicate courtesy?
18. *I have all things* (*apechō panta*). As a receipt in full in appreciation of their kindness. *Apechō* is common in the papyri and the ostraca for "receipt in full" (Deissmann, *Bible Studies*, p. 110). See Matt. 6:2, 5, 16. *I am filled* (*peplērōmai*). Perfect passive indicative of *plēroō*. "Classical Greek would hardly use the word in this personal sense" (Kennedy). *An odour of a sweet smell* (*osmēn euōdias*). *Osmē*, old word from *ozō*, to smell. *Euōdia*, old word from *eu* and *ozō*. In Eph. 5:2 both words come together as here and in II Cor. 2:15 we have *euōdia* (only other N.T. example) and in verse 16 *osmē* twice. *Euōdias* here is genitive of quality. *Sacrifice* (*thusian*). Not the act, but the offering as in Rom. 12:1. *Well-pleasing* (*euareston*). As in Rom. 12:1.
19. *According to his riches in glory* (*kata to ploutos autou en doxēi*). God has an abundant treasure in glory and will repay the Philippians for what they have done for Paul. The spiritual reward is what spurs men into the ministry and holds them to it.

20. *The glory (hē doxa).* "The doxology flows out of the joy of the whole epistle" (Bengel).

21. *They that are of Caesar's household (hoi ek tēs Kaisaros oikias).* Not members of the imperial family, but some connected with the imperial establishment. The term can apply to slaves and freedmen and even to the highest functionaries. Christianity has begun to undermine the throne of the Caesars. Some day a Christian will sit on this throne. The gospel works upward from the lower classes. It was so at Corinth and in Rome. It is true today. It is doubtful if Nero had yet heard of Paul for his case may have been dismissed by lapse of time. But this obscure prisoner who has planted the gospel in Caesar's household has won more eternal fame and power than all the Caesars combined. Nero will commit suicide shortly after Paul has been executed. Nero's star went down and Paul's rose and rises still.

THE EPISTLE TO PHILEMON

FROM ROME A.D. 63

BY WAY OF INTRODUCTION

This little letter was sent to Philemon by Onesimus, a converted runaway slave of Philemon, along with Tychicus who is going to Colossae with Onesimus (Col. 4:7–9) as the bearer also of the so-called Epistle to the Ephesians (Eph. 6:21f.). Hence it is clear that these three Epistles were carried to the Province of Asia at the same time. Colossians was probably written before Ephesians which appears to be a general treatment of the same theme. Whether Philemon was actually penned before the other two there is no way of knowing. But it is put first here as standing apart. Probably Paul wrote it himself without dictation because in verse 19 it constitutes a note in his own hand to Philemon for what Onesimus may owe him. Paul applies the spirit of Christianity to the problem of slavery in words that have ultimately set the slaves free from bondage to men.

1. *A prisoner of Christ Jesus* (*desmios Christou Iēsou*). As verse 9 and in Eph. 3:1 and 4:1. Old adjective from *desmos* (bond, *deō*, to bind). Apparently used here on purpose rather than *apostolos* as more effective with Philemon and a more touching occasion of pride as Paul writes with his manacled right hand. *Timothy* (*Timotheos*). With Paul in Ephesus (Acts 19:22) and probably known to Philemon. Associated with Paul also in I and II Thess., II Cor., Philipp., Col. *To Philemon* (*Philēmoni*). A resident of Colossae and a convert of Paul's (verse 19), perhaps coming to Ephesus while Paul was there when his ministry had so much influence over the province of Asia (Acts 19:9f., 26; I Cor. 16:19). The name Philemon occurs in the legend of Baucis and Philemon (Ovid's *Metamorphoses*), but with no connection with the brother here. He was active in the church in Colossae ("our co-worker," *sunergōi hēmōn*) and was beloved (*agapētōi*) by Paul.

2. *To Apphia our sister* (*Apphiāi tēi adelphēi*). Dative
case in address. A common name in Phrygian inscriptions
and apparently the wife of Philemon. "Sister" is in the
Christian sense. *To Archippus* (*Archippōi*). Dative case
in address. It is uncertain whether he is the son of Philemon
or not. Apparently he is prominent in the church in Colossae,
possibly even pastor, probably not in Laodicea as some
understand Col. 4:17 to imply. *Fellow-soldier* (*sunstratiōtēi*).
Old word, only here and Phil. 2:25 in N.T. In metaphorical
sense. Perhaps while Paul was in Ephesus. *To the church
in thy house* (*tēi kat' oikon sou ekklēsiāi*). The church that
met in the house of Philemon. In large cities there would be
several meeting-places. Before the third century there is
no certain evidence of special church buildings for worship
(White, *Exp. Grk. T.*). See Acts 12:12 for Mary's house in
Jerusalem, I Cor. 16:19 for the house of Aquila and Prisca
in Ephesus, Rom. 16:5 for the house of Prisca and Aquila in
Rome, Col. 4:15 for the house of Nympha in Laodicea.

4. *Always* (*pantote*). Goes with *eucharistō* though so far
away in the Greek sentence. *Making mention of thee* (*mneian
sou poioumenos*). See I Thess. 1:2 for this phrase. *In* (*epi*).
Upon the occasion of.

5. *Hearing* (*akouōn*). Through Epaphras (Col. 1:7, 8;
4:12), possibly from Onesimus also. *And towards all the
saints* (*kai eis pantas tous hagious*). He spoke of "thy love
and faith" (*sou tēn agapēn kai tēn pistin*) "towards the Lord
Jesus" (*pros ton Kurion Iēsoun*) and by a sort of momentum
(Vincent) he carries both words over to the saints, though
it can be explained as chiasm (Gal. 4:4) also.

6. *That* (*hopōs*). Rather than the more common final
particle *hina*. Connected with *mneian poioumenos*. *The
fellowship of thy faith* (*hē koinōnia tēs pisteōs sou*). Partnership like Phil. 1:5 in (objective genitive, *pisteōs*). *Effectual*
(*energēs*). Common adjective, like *energos* (at work), in
N.T. only here, I Cor. 16:9; Heb. 4:12. Papyri use *energos*
of a mill in working order, of ploughed land, etc. *In you* (*en
humin*). Some MSS. have *en hēmin* (in us), itacism and
common.

7. *I had* (*eschon*). Ingressive second aorist active indicative of *echō*, not *eichomēn* as the Textus Receptus has it.
Paul refers to his joy when he first heard the good news

about Philemon's activity (verse 5). *The hearts* (*ta splagchna*). See Phil. 1:8 for this use of this word for the nobler viscera (heart, lungs, liver) and here for the emotional nature. *Have been refreshed* (*anapepautai*). Perfect passive indicative of old compound verb *anapauō* as in Matt. 11:28, a relief and refreshment whether temporary (Mark 6:31) or eternal (Rev. 14:13). 8. *Though I have* (*echōn*). Concessive participle (present active). *That which is befitting* (*to anēkon*). Neuter singular accusative of the articular participle (present active) of *anēkō*, to come up to requirements and so to be befitting. For idea in *anēkō*, see Col. 3:18; Eph. 5:4. This idiom is in later writers. *I rather beseech* (*mallon parakalō*). Rather than command (*epitassō*) which he has a perfect right to do. 9. *Paul the aged* (*Paulos presbutēs*). Paul is called *neanias* (a young man) at the stoning of Stephen (Acts 7:58). He was perhaps a bit under sixty now. Hippocrates calls a man *presbutēs* from 49 to 56 and *gerōn* after that. The papyri use *presbutēs* for old man as in Luke 1:18 of Zacharias and in Titus 2:2. But in Eph. 6:20 Paul says *presbeuō en halusei* (I am an ambassador in a chain). Hence Lightfoot holds that here *presbutēs=presbeutēs* because of common confusion by the scribes between *u* and *eu*. In the LXX four times the two words are used interchangeably. There is some confusion also in the papyri and the inscriptions. Undoubtedly ambassador (*presbeutēs*) is possible here as in Eph. 6:20 (*presbeuō*) though there is no real reason why Paul should not term himself properly "Paul the aged." 10. *For my child* (*peri tou emou teknou*). Tender and affectionate reference to Onesimus as his spiritual child. *Whom I have begotten in my bonds* (*hon egennēsa en tois desmois*). First aorist active indicative of *gennaō*, to beget. See I Cor. 4:15 for this figurative sense. Paul is evidently proud of winning Onesimus to Christ though a prisoner himself. 11. *Onesimus* (*Onēsimon*). A common name among slaves and made like Chresimus, Chrestus. The word is from *onēsis* (profit) and that from *oninēmi*, to profit, to help. *Who was aforetime unprofitable to thee* (*ton pote soi achrēston*). "The once to thee useless one." Play (pun) on the meaning of the name Onesimus (*onēsimos*, useful) as once "useless" (*achrēstos*, verbal adjective, *a* privative and *chraomai*, to use). *But now is profitable to thee and to me (nuni de soi kai emoi euchrēston).* "But now to thee and to me useful." Still further play on the name Onesimus by *euchrēston* (verbal adjective from *eu* and *chraomai*, to use). Ethical dative here (*soi, emoi*).

12. *I have sent back (anepempsa).* Epistolary aorist. As it will look when Onesimus arrives. *In his own person (auton).* "Himself," intensive pronoun with *hon* (whom). *My very heart (ta ema splagchna).* As in verse 7. He almost loves Onesimus as his own son.

13. *I would fain have kept (eboulomēn katechein).* Imperfect middle and present infinitive, "I was wishing to hold back." Again from the standpoint of the arrival of Onesimus. *In thy behalf (huper sou).* So "in thy stead," "in place of thee." *He might minister (diakonēi).* Present active subjunctive (retained after *eboulomēn*) with *hina*, purpose continued, "that he might keep on ministering."

14. *Without thy mind (chōris tēs sēs gnōmēs).* Judgment, purpose (I Cor. 1:10; 7:25). Ablative case with *chōris* (apart from). *I would do nothing (ouden ēthelēsa poiēsai).* First aorist active indicative of *thelō*, I decided, I wished, decision reached (cf. *eboulomēn* in verse 13. *Thy goodness (to agathon sou).* Neuter articular adjective (thy good deed). *As of necessity (hōs kata anagkēn).* "As if according to compulsion." See II Cor. 9:7. *But of free will (alla kata hekousion).* According to what is voluntary (Numb. 15:3). Perhaps *tropon* (way, manner) is to be understood with the adjective *hekousios* (old word, here alone in N.T.), from *hekōn* (I Cor. 9:17; Rom. 8:20).

15. *Perhaps (tacha).* Old adverb, in N.T. only here and Rom. 5:7. *That thou shouldst have him (hina auton apecheis).* Final clause with *hina* and present active subjunctive of *apechō*, to have back, "that thou might keep on having him back." *For ever (aiōnion).* "Eternal," here and hereafter. Surely a noble thing for Paul to say and a word that would touch the best in Philemon.

16. *No longer as a servant (ouketi hōs doulon).* "No longer as a slave." So it has to be here. So it should be always. Paul sends Onesimus, the converted runaway slave, back to his legal master, but shows that he expects Philemon the Christian to treat Onesimus as a brother in Christ, not as a

slave. *But more than a servant (all' huper doulon).* "But beyond a slave." *A brother beloved (adelphon agapēton).* A brother in Christ. *How much rather to thee (posōi de mallon soi).* "By how much more to thee," because of Philemon's legal ownership of this now Christian slave. "In the flesh Philemon had the brother for a slave; in the Lord he had the slave for a brother" (Meyer).

17. *If then thou countest me a partner (ei oun me echeis koinōnon).* As I assume that you do, condition of the first class. *Receive him as myself (proslabou auton hōs eme).* "Take him to thyself (indirect second aorist middle of *proslambanō* as in Acts 18:26) as myself." Surpassing delicacy and consummate tact. These words sound the death-knell of human slavery wherever the spirit of Christ is allowed to have its way. It has been a long and hard fight to break the shackles of human bondage even in Christian countries and there are still millions of slaves in pagan and Mohammedan lands. Paul wrote these words with wisdom and courage and sincerity.

18. *But if he hath wronged thee at all (ei de ti ēdikēse se).* Condition of the first class, assumed to be true. Onesimus did wrong (*ēdikēse*, first aorist active indicative of *adikeō*, to wrong, without justice). He had probably robbed Philemon before he ran away. *Or oweth (ē opheilei).* Delicate way of putting the stealing. *Put that to mine account (touto emoi ellogā).* Present active imperative of *ellogaō*. In the Koiné verbs in -eō often appear in -aō like *eleeō, eleaō.* So with *ellogeō* as *ellogaō*, late verb in inscriptions and papyri (Deissmann, *Light,* etc., p. 84), though in N.T. only here and Rom. 5:13. It means to set to one's account.

19. *Write (egrapsa).* Epistolary aorist. *With mine hand (tēi emēi cheiri).* Instrumental case and a note of hand that can be collected. See II Thess. 3:17; I Cor. 16:21; Col. 4:18. *I will repay it (egō apotisō).* Future active indicative of *apotinō (apotiō)* to pay back, to pay off. The more usual word was *apodōsō.* This is Paul's promissory note. Deissmann (*Light,* etc., p. 331) notes how many of the papyri are concerning debts. *That I say not (hina mē legō).* Neat idiom as in II Cor. 9:4, delicately reminding Philemon that Paul had led him also to Christ. *Thou owest to me even thine own self besides (kai seauton moi prosopheileis).* Old verb, only here in N.T., Paul using the verb *opheilō* of verse 18

with *pros* added. He used every available argument to bring Philemon to see the higher ground of brotherhood in Christ about Onesimus.

20. *Let me have joy of thee* (*ego sou onaimēn*). Second aorist middle optative of *oninēmi*, old verb, only here in N.T. Optative the regular construction for a wish about the future. "May I get profit from thee in the Lord." *Refresh my heart in Christ* (*anapauson mou ta splagchna en Christōi*). See verse 7 for *anapauson* (first aorist active imperative of *anapauō*) and *splagchna* (3 times in this letter, 7, 12, 20).

21. *Obedience* (*hupakoēi*). "Compliance" seems less harsh to us in the light of 9. *I write* (*egrapsa*). Epistolary aorist again. *Even beyond what I say* (*kai huper ha legō*). That can only mean that Paul "knows" (*eidōs*, second perfect active participle of *oida*) that Philemon will set Onesimus free. He prefers that it come as Philemon's idea and wish rather than as a command from Paul. Paul has been criticized for not denouncing slavery in plain terms. But, when one considers the actual conditions in the Roman empire, he is a wise man who can suggest a better plan than the one pursued here for the ultimate overthrow of slavery.

22. *But withal* (*hama de*). Along with your kindly reception of Onesimus. On *hama*, see Acts 24:26; 27:40. *A lodging* (*xenian*). Old word from *xenos*, stranger. In N.T. only here and Acts 28:23. *I shall be granted unto you* (*charisthēsomai humin*). First future passive of *charizomai*. Used either as a favour as here and Acts 3:14 or for destruction (Acts 25:11).

23. *Epaphras* (*Epaphrās*). The Colossian preacher who apparently started the work in Colossae, Hierapolis, and Laodicea, and who had come to Rome to enlist Paul's help in the fight against incipient Gnosticism in the Lycus Valley. *My fellow-prisoner* (*ho sunaichmalōtos mou*). See on Rom. 16:7 for this word, also in Col. 4:10. Used metaphorically like the verb *aichmalōtizō* in II Cor. 10:5, though some hold that Epaphras became a prisoner with Paul in Rome.

24. The other "co-workers" (*sunergoi*) here (Mark, Aristarchus, Demas, Luke) are all named in detail in Col. 4:10-14 with kindly words.

25. *Grace* (*hē charis*). This great word occurred in the greeting (verse 3) as it does in the farewell.

THE EPISTLE TO THE COLOSSIANS
FROM ROME A.D. 63

BY WAY OF INTRODUCTION

GENUINENESS

The author claims to be Paul (1:1) and there is no real doubt about it in spite of Baur's denial of the Pauline authorship which did not suit his *Tendenz* theory of the New Testament books. There is every mark of Paul's style and power in the little Epistle and there is no evidence that any one else took Paul's name to palm off this striking and vigorous polemic.

THE DATE

Clearly it was sent at the same time with the Epistle to Philemon and the one to the Ephesians since Tychicus the bearer of the letter to Ephesus (Eph. 6:21f.) and the one to Colossae (Col. 4:7f.) was a companion of Onesimus (Col. 4:9) the bearer of that to Philemon (10–12). If Paul is a prisoner (Col. 4:3; Eph. 6:20; Philemon 9) in Rome, as most scholars hold, and not in Ephesus as Deissmann and Duncan argue, the probable date would be A.D. 63. I still believe that Paul is in Rome when he sends out these epistles. If so, the time would be after the arrival in Rome from Jerusalem as told in Acts 28 and before the burning of Rome by Nero in A.D. 64. If Philippians was already sent, A.D. 63 marks the last probable year for the writing of this group of letters.

THE OCCASION

The Epistle itself gives it as being due to the arrival of Epaphras from Colossae (1:7–9; 4:12f.). He is probably one of Paul's converts while in Ephesus who in behalf of Paul (1:7) evangelized the Lycus Valley (Colossae, Hierapolis, Laodicea) where Paul had never been himself (2:1; 4:13–16). Since Paul's departure for Rome, the "grievous wolves" whom he foresaw in Miletus (Acts 20:29f.) had

470

descended upon these churches and were playing havoc with many and leading them astray much as new cults today mislead the unwary. These men were later called Gnostics (see Ignatius) and had a subtle appeal that was not easy to withstand. The air was full of the mystery cults like the Eleusinian mysteries, Mithraism, the vogue of Isis, what not. These new teachers professed new thought with a world-view that sought to explain everything on the assumption that matter was essentially evil and that the good God could only touch evil matter by means of a series of aeons or emanations so far removed from him as to prevent contamination by God and yet with enough power to create evil matter. This jejune theory satisfied many just as today some are content to deny the existence of sin, disease, death in spite of the evidence of the senses to the contrary. In his perplexity Epaphras journeyed all the way to Rome to obtain Paul's help.

PURPOSE OF THE EPISTLE

Epaphras did not come in vain, for Paul was tremendously stirred by the peril to Christianity from the Gnostics (*hoi gnōstikoi*, the knowing ones). He had won his fight for freedom in Christ against the Judaizers who tried to fasten Jewish sacramentarianism upon spiritual Christianity. Now there is an equal danger of the dissipation of vital Christianity in philosophic speculation. In particular, the peril was keen concerning the Person of Christ when the Gnostics embraced Christianity and applied their theory of the universe to him. They split into factions on the subject of Christ. The Docetic (from *dokeō*, to seem) Gnostics held that Jesus did not have a real human body, but only a phantom body. He was, in fact, an aeon and had no real humanity. The Cerinthian (followers of Cerinthus) Gnostics admitted the humanity of the man Jesus, but claimed that the Christ was an aeon that came on Jesus at his baptism in the form of a dove and left him on the Cross so that only the man Jesus died. At once this heresy sharpened the issue concerning the Person of Christ already set forth in Phil. 2:5-11. Paul met the issue squarely and powerfully portrayed his full-length portrait of Jesus Christ as the Son of God and the Son of Man (both deity and humanity) in opposition to both types of Gnostics. So then Colossians seems written expressly for our own day when so many are trying to rob Jesus Christ of his deity. The Gnostics took varying views of moral issues also as men do now. There were the ascetics with rigorous rules and the licentious element that let down all the bars for the flesh while the spirit communed with God. One cannot understand Colossians without some knowledge of Gnosticism such as may be obtained in such books as Angus's *The Mystery-Religions and Christianity*, Glover's *The Conflict of Religion in the Early Roman Empire*, Kennedy's *St. Paul and the Mystery-Religions*, Lightfoot's *Commentary on Colossians*.

SOME BOOKS ABOUT COLOSSIANS

One may note commentaries by T. K. Abbott (*Int. Crit.* 1897), Gross Alexander (1910), Dargan (1887), Dibelius (1912), Ellicott (1890), Ewald (1905), Griffith-Thomas (1923), Findlay (1895), Haupt (1903), M. Jones (1923), Lightfoot (1904), Maclaren (1888), Meinertz (1917), Moule (1900), Mullins (1913), Oltramare (1891), Peake (1903), Radford (1931), A. T. Robertson (1926), Rutherford (1908), E. F. Scott (1930), Von Soden (1893), F. B. Westcott (1914), Williams (1907).

CHAPTER I

1. *Of Christ Jesus (Christou Iēsou).* This order in the later epistles shows that *Christos* is now regarded as a proper name and not just a verbal adjective (Anointed One, Messiah). Paul describes himself because he is unknown to the Colossians, not because of attack as in Gal. 1:1. *Timothy* (*Timotheos*). Mentioned as in I and II Thess. when in Corinth, II Cor. when in Macedonia, Phil. and Philemon when in Rome as here.

2. *At Colossae (en Kolossais).* The spelling is uncertain, the MSS. differing in the title (*Kolassaeis*) and here (*Kolossais*). Colossae was a city of Phrygia on the Lycus, the tributaries of which brought a calcareous deposit of a peculiar kind that choked up the streams and made arches and fantastic grottoes. In spite of this there was much fertility in the valley with two other prosperous cities some ten or twelve miles away (Hierapolis and Laodicea). "The church at Colossae was the least important of any to which Paul's epistles were addressed" (Vincent). But he had no greater message for any church than he here gives concerning the Person of Christ. There is no more important message today for modern men.

3. *God the Father of our Lord Jesus Christ (tōi theōi patri tou kuriou hēmōn Iēsou Christou).* Correct text without *kai* (and) as in 3:17, though usually "the God and Father of our Lord Jesus Christ" (II Cor. 1:3; 11:31; Rom. 15:6; I Peter 1:3; Rev. 1:6). In verse 2 we have the only instance in the opening benediction of an epistle when the name of "Jesus Christ" is not joined with "God our Father." *Always* (*pantote*). Amphibolous position between *eucharistoumen* (we give thanks) and *proseuchomenoi* (praying). Can go with either.

4. *Having heard of (akousantes).* Literary plural unless Timothy is included. Aorist active participle of *akouō* of antecedent action to *eucharistoumen.* Epaphras (verse 8o had told Paul. *Your faith in Jesus Christ (tēn pistin humōn*

en Iēsou Christōi). See Eph. 1:15 for similar phrase. No
article is needed before *en* as it is a closely knit phrase and
bears the same sense as the objective genitive in Gal. 2:16
(*dia pisteōs Christou Iēsou*, by faith in Christ Jesus). *Which
ye have (hēn echete).* Probably genuine (Aleph A C D),
though B omits it and others have the article (*tēn*). There
is a real distinction here between *en* (sphere or basis) and *eis*
(direction towards), though they are often identical in idea.
5. *Because of the hope (dia tēn elpida).* See Rom. 8:24.
It is not clear whether this phrase is to be linked with
eucha istoumen at the beginning of verse 3 or (more likely)
with *tēn agapēn* just before. Note also here *pistis* (faith),
agapē (love), *elpis* (hope), though not grouped together so
sharply as in I Cor. 13:13. Here hope is objective, the goal
ahead. *Laid up (apokeimeinēn).* Literally, "laid away or
by." Old word used in Luke 19:20 of the pound laid away
in a napkin. See also *apothēsaurizō*, to store away for future
use (I Tim. 6:19). The same idea occurs in Matt. 6:20
(treasure in heaven) and I' Pet. 1:4 and it is involved in
Phil. 3:20. *Ye heard before (proēkousate).* First aorist indicative active of this old compound *proakouō*, though only
here in the N.T. Before what? Before Paul wrote? Before
the realization? Before the error of the Gnostics crept in?
Each view is possible and has advocates. Lightfoot argues
for the last and it is probably correct as is indicated by the
next clause. *In the word of the truth of the gospel (en tōi logōi
tēs alētheias tou euaggeliou).* "In the preaching of the truth
of the gospel" (Gal. 2:5, 14) which is come (*parontos*, present
active participle agreeing with *euaggeliou*, being present, a
classical use of *pareimi* as in Acts 12:20). They heard the
pure gospel from Epaphras before the Gnostics came.
6. *In all the world (en panti tōi kosmōi).* A legitimate
hyperbole, for the gospel was spreading all over the Roman
Empire. *Is bearing fruit (estin karpophoroumenon).* Periphrastic present middle indicative of the old compound
karpophoreō, from *karpophoros* (Acts 14:17) and that from
karpos and *pherō*. The periphrastic present emphasizes the
continuity of the process. See the active participle *karpophorountes* in verse 10. *Increasing (auxanomenon).* Periphrastic present middle of *auxanō*. Repeated in verse 10.
The growing and the fruit-bearing go on simultaneously- as

always with Christians (inward growth and outward expression). *Ye heard and knew (ēkousate kai epegnōte).* Definite aorist indicative. They heard the gospel from Epaphras and at once recognized and accepted (ingressive second aorist active of *epiginōskō,* to know fully or in addition). They fully apprehended the grace of God and should be immune to the shallow vagaries of the Gnostics.

7. *Of Epaphras (apo Epaphrā).* "From Epaphras" who is the source of their knowledge of Christ. *On our behalf (huper hēmōn).* Clearly correct (Aleph A B D) and not *huper humōn* (on your behalf). In a true sense Epaphras was Paul's messenger to Colossae.

8. *Who also declared (ho kai dēlōsas).* Articular first aorist active participle of *dēloō,* old verb, to make manifest. Epaphras told Paul about their "love in the Spirit," grounded in the Holy Spirit.

9. *That ye may be filled with (hina plērōthēte).* First aorist (effective) passive subjunctive of *plēroō,* to fill full. *The knowledge of his will (tēn epignōsin tou thelēmatos autou).* The accusative case is retained with this passive verb. *Epignōsis* is a *Koiné* word (Polybius, Plutarch, etc.) for additional *(epi)* or full knowledge. The word is the keynote of Paul's reply to the conceit of Gnosticism. The cure for these intellectual upstarts is not ignorance, not obscurantism, but more knowledge of the will of God. *In all spiritual wisdom and understanding (en pasēi sophiāi kai sunesei pneumatikēi).* Both *pasēi* (all) and *pneumatikēi* (spiritual) are to be taken with both *sophiāi* and *sunesei.* In Eph. 1:8 Paul uses *phronēsei* (from *phrēn,* intellect) rather than *sunesei* (grasp, from *suniēmi,* to send together). *Sunesis* is the faculty of deciding in particular cases while *sophia* gives the general principles (Abbott). Paul faces Gnosticism with full front and wishes the freest use of all one's intellectual powers in interpreting Christianity. The preacher ought to be the greatest man in the world for he has to deal with the greatest problems of life and death.

10. *To walk worthily of the Lord (peripatēsai axiōs tou Kuriou).* This aorist active infinitive may express purpose or result. Certainly this result is the aim of the right knowledge of God. "The end of all knowledge is conduct" (Lightfoot). See I Thess. 2:12; Phil. 1:27; Eph. 4:1 for a like use

of *axiōs* (adverb) with the genitive. *In the knowledge of God* (*tēi epignōsei tou theou*). Instrumental case, "by means of the full knowledge of God." This is the way for fruit-bearing and growth to come. Note both participles (*karpophorountes kai auxanomenoi*) together as in verse 6. *Unto all pleasing* (*eis pāsan areskian*). In order to please God in all things (I Thess. 4:1). *Areskia* is late word from *areskeuō*, to be complaisant (Polybius, Plutarch) and usually in bad sense (obsequiousness). Only here in N.T., but in good sense. It occurs in the good sense in the papyri and inscriptions.

11. *Strengthened* (*dunamoumenoi*). Present passive participle of late verb *dunamoō* (from *dunamis*), to empower, "empowered with all power." In LXX and papyri and modern Greek. In N.T. only here and Heb. 11:34 and MSS. in Eph. 6:10 (W H in margin). *According to the might of his glory* (*kata to kratos tēs doxēs autou*). *Kratos* is old word for perfect strength (cf. *krateō, kratilos*). In N.T. it is applied only to God. Here his might is accompanied by glory (*Shekinah*). *Unto all patience and longsuffering* (*eis pāsan hupomonēn kai makrothumian*). See both together also in James 5:10f.; II Cor. 6:4, 6; II Tim. 3:10. *Hupomonē* is remaining under (*hupomenō*) difficulties without succumbing, while *makrothumia* is the long endurance that does not retaliate (Trench).

12. *Who made us meet* (*tōi hikanōsanti hēmās*). Or "you" (*humās*). Dative case of the articular participle of *hikanoō*, late verb from *hikanos* and in N.T. only here and II Cor. 3:6 (which see), "who made us fit or adequate for." *To be partakers* (*eis merida*). "For a share in." Old word for share or portion (from *meros*) as in Acts 8:21; 16:12; II Cor. 6:15 (the only other N.T. examples). *Of the inheritance* (*tou klērou*). "Of the lot," "for a share of the lot." Old word. First a pebble or piece of wood used in casting lots (Acts 1:26), then the allotted portion or inheritance as here (Acts 8:21). Cf. Heb. 3:7-4:11. *In light* (*en tōi phōti*). Taken with *merida* (portion) "situated in the kingdom of light" (Lightfoot).

13. *Delivered* (*erusato*). First aorist middle indicative of *ruomai*, old verb, to rescue. This appositional relative clause further describes God the Father's redemptive work and

marks the transition to the wonderful picture of the person and work of Christ in nature and grace in verses 14 to 20, a full and final answer to the Gnostic depreciation of Jesus Christ by speculative philosophy and to all modern efforts after a "reduced" picture of Christ. *God rescued us out from* (*ek*) *the power* (*exousias*) *of the kingdom of darkness* (*skotous*) *in which we were held as slaves. Translated metes-tēsen).* First aorist active indicative of *methistēmi*) and transitive (not intransitive like second aorist *metestē*). Old word. See I Cor. 13:2. Changed us from the kingdom of darkness to the kingdom of light. *Of the Son of his love* (*tou huiou tēs agapēs autou*). Probably objective genitive (*agapēs*), the Son who is the object of the Father's love like *agapētos* (beloved) in Matt. 3:17. Others would take it as describing love as the origin of the Son which is true, but hardly pertinent here. But Paul here rules out the whole system of aeons and angels that the Gnostics placed above Christ. It is Christ's Kingdom in which he is King. He has moral and spiritual sovereignty.

14. *In whom* (*en hōi*). In Christ as in Eph. 1:7. This great sentence about Christ carries on by means of three relatives (*en hōi* 14, *hos* 15, *hos* 18) and repeated personal pronoun (*autos*), twice with *hoti* (16, 19), thrice with *kai* (17, 18, 20), twice alone (16, 20). *Our redemption* (*tēn apolutrōsin*). See on Rom. 3:24 for this great word (*Koinē*), a release on payment of a ransom for slave or debtor (Heb. 9:15) as the inscriptions show (Deissmann, *Light, etc.*, p. 327). *The forgiveness of our sins* (*tēn aphesin tōn hamartiōn*). Accusative case in apposition with *apolutrōsin* as in Eph. 1:7 (*remission*, sending away, *aphesis*, after the *redemption apolutrōsis*, buying back). Only here we have *hamartiōn* (sins, from *hamartanō*, to miss) while in Eph. 1:7 we find *paraptōmatōn* (slips, fallings aside, from *parapiptō*).

15. *The image* (*eikōn*). In predicate and no article. On *eikōn*, see II Cor. 4:4; 3:18; Rom. 8:29; Col 3:10. Jesus is the very stamp of God the Father as he was before the Incarnation (John 17:5) and is now (Phil. 2:5–11; Heb. 1:3). *Of the invisible God* (*tou theou tou aoratou*). But the one who sees Jesus has seen God (John 14:9). See this verbal adjective (*a* privative and *horaō*) in Rom. 1:20. *The first born* (*prōtotokos*). Predicate adjective again and anarthrous.

This passage is parallel to the *Logos* passage in John 1:1–18 and to Heb. 1:1–4 as well as Phil. 2:5–11 in which these three writers (John, author of Hebrews, Paul) give the high conception of the Person of Christ (both Son of God and Son of Man) found also in the Synoptic Gospels and even in Q (the Father, the Son). This word (LXX and N.T.) can no longer be considered purely "Biblical" (Thayer), since it is found in inscriptions (Deissmann, *Light, etc.*, p. 91) and in the papyri (Moulton and Milligan, *Vocabulary, etc.*). See it already in Luke 2:7 and Aleph for Matt. 1:25; Rom. 8:29. The use of this word does not show what Arius argued that Paul regarded Christ as a creature like "all creation" (*pāsēs ktiseōs*, by metonymy the *act* regarded as *result*). It is rather the comparative (superlative) force of *prōtos* that is used (first-born of all creation) as in Col. 1:18; Rom. 8:29; Heb. 1:6; 12:23; Rev. 1:5. Paul is here refuting the Gnostics who pictured Christ as one of the aeons by placing him before "all creation" (angels and men). Like *eikōn* we find *prōtotokos* in the Alexandrian vocabulary of the *Logos* teaching (Philo) as well as in the LXX. Paul takes both words to help express the deity of Jesus Christ in his relation to the Father as *eikōn* (Image) and to the universe as *prōtotokos* (First-born).

16. *All things* (*ta panta*). The universe as in Rom. 11:35, a well-known philosophical phrase. It is repeated at the end of the verse. *In him were created* (*en autōi ektisthē*). Paul now gives the reason (*hoti*, for) for the primacy of Christ in the work of creation (16f.). It is the constative aorist passive indicative *ektisthē* (from *ktizō*, old verb, to found, to create (Rom. 1:25). This central activity of Christ in the work of creation is presented also in John 1:3 and Heb. 1:2 and is a complete denial of the Gnostic philosophy. The whole of creative activity is summed up in Christ including the angels in heaven and everything on earth. God wrought through "the Son of his love." All earthly dignities are included. *Have been created* (*ektistai*). Perfect passive indicative of *ktizō*, "stand created," "remain created." The permanence of the universe rests, then, on Christ far more than on gravity. It is a Christo-centric universe. *Through him* (*di' autou*). As the intermediate and sustaining agent. He had already used *en autōi* (in him) as the sphere of

activity. *And unto him* (*kai eis auton*). This is the only remaining step to take and Paul takes it (I Cor. 15:28). See Eph. 1:10 for similar use of *en autōi* of Christ and in Col. 1:19–20 again we have *en autōi, di' autou, eis auton* used of Christ. See Heb. 2:10 for *di' hon* (because of whom) and *di' hou* (by means of whom) applied to God concerning the universe (*ta panta*). In Rom. 11:35 we find *ex autou kai di' autou kai eis auton ta panta* referring to God. But Paul does not use *ex* in this connection of Christ, but only *en*, *dia*, and *eis*. See the same distinction preserved in I Cor. 8:6 (*ex* of God, *dia*, of Christ).

17. *Before all things* (*pro pantōn*). *Pro* with the ablative case. This phrase makes Paul's meaning plain. The precedence of Christ in time and the preëminence as Creator are both stated sharply. See the claim of Jesus to eternal timeless existence in John 8:58; 17:5. See also Rev. 23:13 where Christ calls himself the Alpha and the Omega, the Beginning (*archē*) and the End (*telos*). Paul states it also in II Cor. 8:9; Phil. 2:6f. *Consist* (*sunestēken*). Perfect active indicative (intransitive) of *sunistēmi*, old verb, to place together and here to cohere, to hold together. The word repeats the statements in verse 16, especially that in the form *ektistai*. Christ is the controlling and unifying force in nature. The Gnostic philosophy that matter is evil and was created by a remote aeon is thus swept away. The Son of God's love is the Creator and the Sustainer of the universe which is not evil.

18. *The head of the body* (*hē kephalē tou sōmatos*). Jesus is first also in the spiritual realm as he is in nature (verses 18–20). Paul is fond of the metaphor of the body (*sōma*) for believers of which body Christ is the head (*kephalē*) as seen already in I Cor. 11:3; 12:12, 27; Rom. 12:5. See further Col. 1:24; 2:19; Eph. 1:22f.; 4:2, 15; 5:30. *The church* (*tēs ekklēsias*). Genitive case in explanatory apposition with *tou sōmatos*. This is the general sense of *ekklēsia*, not of a local body, assembly, or organization. Here the contrast is between the realm of nature (*ta panta*) in verses 15 to 17 and the realm of·spirit or grace in verses 18 to 20. A like general sense of *ekklēsia* occurs in Eph. 1:22f.; 5:24–32; Heb. 12:23. In Eph. 2:11–22 Paul uses various figures for the kingdom of Christ (commonwealth *politeia*, verse 12, one new man

eis hena kainon anthrōpon, verse 15, one body *en heni sōmati*, verse 16, family of God *oikeioi tou theou*, verse 19, building or temple *oikodomē* and *naos*, verses 20 to 22). *Who* (*hos*). Causal use of the relative, "in that he is." *The beginning* (*hē archē*). It is uncertain if the article (*hē*) is genuine. It is absolute without it. Christ has priority in time and in power. See Rev. 3:14 for his relation as *archē* to creation and I Cor. 15:20, 23 for *aparchē* used of Christ and the resurrection and Acts 3:14 for *archēgos* used of him as the author of life and Heb. 2:10 of Jesus and salvation and Heb. 12:2 of Jesus as the pioneer of faith. *That in all things he might have the preëminence* (*hina genētai en pāsin autos prōteuōn*). Purpose clause with *hina* and the second aorist middle subjunctive of *ginomai*, "that he himself in all things (material and spiritual) may come to (*genētai*, not *ēi*, be) hold the first place" (*prōteuōn*, present active participle of *prōteuō*, old verb, to hold the first place, here only in the N.T.). Christ is first with Paul in time and in rank. See Rev. 1:5 for this same use of *prōtotokos* with *tōn nekrōn* (the dead).

19. *For it was the good pleasure of the Father* (*hoti eudokēsen*). No word in the Greek for "the Father," though the verb calls for either *ho theos* or *ho patēr* as the subject. This verb *eudokeō* is common in the N.T. for God's will and pleasure (Matt. 3:17; I Cor. 10:5). *All the fulness* (*pān to plērōma*). The same idea as in 2:9 *pān to plērōma tēs theotētos* (all the fulness of the Godhead). "A recognized technical term in theology, denoting the totality of the Divine powers and attributes" (Lightfoot). It is an old word from *plēroō*, to fill full, used in various senses as in Mark 8:20 of the baskets, Gal. 4:10 of time, etc. The Gnostics distributed the divine powers among various aeons. Paul gathers them all up in Christ, a full and flat statement of the deity of Christ. *Should dwell* (*katoikēsai*). First aorist active infinitive of *katoikeō*, to make abode or home. All the divine attributes are at home in Christ (*en autōi*).

20. *Through him* (*di' autou*). As the sufficient and chosen agent in the work of reconciliation (*apokatallaxai*, first aorist active infinitive of *apokatallassō*, further addition to *eudokēsen*, was pleased). This double compound (*apo, kata* with *allassō*) occurs only here, verse 22, and Eph. 2:16, and no-

where else so far as known. Paul's usual word for "reconcile" is *katallassō* (II Cor. 5:18-20; Rom. 5:10), though *diallassō* (Matt. 5:24) is more common in Attic. The addition of *apo* here is clearly for the idea of complete reconciliation. See on II Cor. 5:18-20 for discussion of *katallassō*, Paul's great word. The use of *ta panta* (the all things, the universe) as if the universe were somehow out of harmony reminds us of the mystical passage in Rom. 8:19-23 which see for discussion. Sin somehow has put the universe out of joint. Christ will set it right. *Unto himself* (*eis auton*). Unto God, though *auton* is not reflexive unless written *hauton*. *Having made peace* (*eirēnopoiēsas*). Late and rare compound (Prov. 10:10 and here only in N.T.) from *eirēnopoios*, peacemaker (Matt. 5:9; here only in N.T.). In Eph. 2:15 we have *poiōn eirēnēn* (separate words) *making peace*. Not the masculine gender, though agreeing with the idea of Christ involved even if *plērōma* be taken as the subject of *eudokēsen*, a participial anacoluthon (construction according to sense as in 2:19). If *theos* be taken as the subject of *eudokēsen* the participle *eirēnopoiēsas* refers to Christ, not to *theos* (God). *Through the blood of his cross* (*dia tou haimatos tou staurou autou*). This for the benefit of the Docetic Gnostics who denied the real humanity of Jesus and as clearly stating the *causa medians* (Ellicott) of the work of reconciliation to be the Cross of Christ, a doctrine needed today. *Or things in the heavens* (*eite ta en tois ouranois*). Much needless trouble has been made over this phrase as if things in heaven were not exactly right. It is rather a hypothetical statement like verse 16 not put in categorical form (Abbott), *universitas rerum* (Ellicott).

21. *And you* (*kai humās*). Accusative case in a rather loose sentence, to be explained as the object of the infinitive *parastēsai* in verse 22 (note repeated *humās* there) or as the anticipated object of *apokatēllaxen* if that be the genuine form in verse 22. It can be the accusative of general reference followed by anacoluthon. See similar idiom in Eph. 2:1, 12. *Being in time past alienated* (*pote ontas apēllotriōmenous*). Periphrastic perfect passive participle (continuing state of alienation) of *apallotrioō*, old word from Plato on, to estrange, to render *allotrios* (belonging to another), alienated from God, a vivid picture of heathenism as in Rom.

1:20-23. Only other N.T. examples in Eph. 2:12; 4:18. *Enemies* (*exthrous*). Old word from *echthos* (hatred). Active sense here, *hostile* as in Matt. 13:28; Rom. 8:7, not passive *hateful* (Rom. 11:28). *In your mind* (*tēi dianoiāi*). Locative case. *Dianoia* (*dia, nous*), mind, intent, purpose. Old word. It is always a tragedy to see men use their minds actively against God. *In your evil works* (*en tois ergois tois ponērois*). Hostile purpose finds natural expression in evil deeds.

22. *Yet now* (*nuni de*). Sharpened contrast with emphatic form of *nun*, "now" being not at the present moment, but in the present order of things in the new dispensation of grace in Christ. *Hath he reconciled* (*apokatēllaxen*). First aorist (effective, timeless) active indicative (a sort of parenthetical anacoluthon). Here B reads *apokatallagēte*, be ye reconciled like *katallagēte* in II Cor. 5:20 while D has *apokatallagentes*. Lightfoot prefers to follow B here (the hard reading), though Westcott and Hort only put it in the margin. On the word see verse 20. *In the body of his flesh* (*en tōi sōmati tēs sarkos autou*). See the same combination in 2:11 though in Eph. 2:14 only *sarki* (flesh). Apparently Paul combines both *sōma* and *sarx* to make plain the actual humanity of Jesus against incipient Docetic Gnostics who denied it. *Through death* (*dia tou thanatou*). The reconciliation was accomplished by means of Christ's death on the cross (verse 20) and not just by the Incarnation (the body of his flesh) in which the death took place. *To present* (*parastēsai*). First aorist active (transitive) infinitive (of purpose) of *paristēmi*, old verb, to place beside in many connections. See it used of presenting Paul and the letter from Lysias to Felix (Acts 23:33). Repeated in Col. 2:28. See also II Cor. 11:2 and II Cor. 4:14. Paul has the same idea of his responsibility in rendering an account for those under his influence seen in Heb. 13:17. See Rom. 12:1 for use of living sacrifice. *Holy* (*hagious*). Positively consecrated, separated unto God. Common in N.T. for believers. Haupt holds that all these terms have a religious and forensic sense here. *Without blemish* (*amōmous*). Without spot (Phil. 2:15). Old word *a* privative and *mōmos* (blemish). Common in the LXX for ceremonial purifications. *Unreproveable* (*anegklētous*). Old verbal adjective from *a* privative and *egkaleō*, to call to account, to pick flaws in. These three adjectives give

a marvellous picture of complete purity (positive and negative, internal and external). This is Paul's ideal when he presents the Colossians "before him" (*katenōpion autou*), right down in the eye of Christ the Judge of all.

23. *If so be that ye continue in the faith* (*ei ge epimenete tēi pistei*). Condition of the first class (determined as fulfilled), with a touch of eagerness in the use of *ge* (at least). *Epi* adds to the force of the linear action of the present tense (continue and then some). *Pistei* is in the locative case (in faith). *Grounded* (*tethemeliōmenoi*). Perfect passive participle of *themelioō*, old verb from *themelios* (adjective, from *thema* from *tithēmi*, laid down as a foundation, substantive, I Cor. 3:11f.). Picture of the saint as a building like Eph. 2:20. *Steadfast* (*hedraioi*). Old adjective from *hedra* (seat). In N.T. only here, I Cor. 7:37; 15:58. Metaphor of seated in a chair. *Not moved away* (*mē metakinoumenoi*). Present passive participle (with negative *mē*) of *metakineō*, old verb, to move away, to change location, only here in N.T. Negative statement covering the same ground. *From the hope of the gospel* (*apo tēs elpidos tou euaggeliou*). Ablative case with *apo*. The hope given by or in the gospel and there alone. *Which ye heard* (*hou ēkousate*). Genitive case of relative either by attraction or after *ēkousate*. The Colossians had in reality heard the gospel from Epaphras. *Preached* (*kēruchthentos*). First aorist passive participle of *kērussō*, to herald, to proclaim. *In all creation* (*en pasēi ktisei*). *Ktisis* is the act of founding (Rom. 1:20) from *ktizō* (verse 16), then a created thing (Rom. 1:25), then the sum of created things as here and Rev. 3:14. It is hyperbole, to be sure, but Paul does not say that all men are converted, but only that the message has been heralded abroad over the Roman Empire in a wider fashion than most people imagine. *A minister* (*diakonos*). General term for service (*dia, konis*, raising a dust by speed) and used often as here of preachers like our "minister" today, one who serves. Jesus used the verb *diakonēsai* of himself (Mark 10:45). Our "deacon" is this word transliterated and given a technical meaning as in Phil. 1:1.

24. *Now I rejoice* (*nun chairomen*). This is not a new note for Paul. See him in jail in Philippi (Acts 16:25) and in II Cor. 11:16–33; Rom. 5:3; Phil. 2:18. *Fill up on my part*

(*antanaplērō*). Very rare double compound verb (here only in N.T.) to fill (*pleroō*) up (*ana*), in turn (*anti*). It is now Paul's "turn" at the bat, to use a baseball figure. Christ had his "turn," the grandest of all and suffered for us all in a sense not true of any one else. It is the idea of balance or correspondence in *anti* as seen in Demosthenes's use of this verb (*De Symm.*, p. 282), "the poor balancing the rich." And yet Christ did not cause suffering to cease. There is plenty left for Paul and for each of us in his time. *That which is lacking (ta husterēmata)*. "The left-overs," so to speak. Late word from *hustereō*, to come behind, to be left, to fail. See Luke 21:4; I Thess. 3:10; II Cor. 8:14; 9:12. *For his body's sake (huper tou sōmatos autou)*. As Paul showed in his exultation in suffering in II Cor. 11:16–33, though not in the same sense in which Christ suffered and died for us as Redeemer. Paul attaches no atoning value whatever to his own sufferings for the church (see also verse 18).

25. *According to the dispensation of God (kata tēn oikonomian tou theou)*. "According to the economy of God." An old word from *oikonomeō*, to be a house steward (*oikos, nemō*) as in Luke 16:2–4; I Cor. 9:17; Eph. 1:9; 3:9. It was by God's stewardship that Paul was made a minister of Christ. *To fulfil the word of God (plērōsai ton logon tou theou)*. First aorist active infinitive of purpose (*pleroō*), a fine phrase for a God-called preacher, to fill full or to give full scope to the Word of God. The preacher is an expert on the word of God by profession. See Paul's ideal about preaching in II Thess. 3:1.

26. *The mystery (to mustērion)*. See on I Cor. 2:7 for this interesting word from *mustēs* (initiate), from *mueō*, to wink, to blink. The Gnostics talked much of "mysteries." Paul takes their very word (already in common use, Matt. 13:11) and uses it for the gospel. *Which hath been hid (to apokekrummenon)*. Perfect passive articular participle from *apokruptō*, old verb, to hide, to conceal from (I Cor. 2:7; Eph. 3:9). *But now it hath been manifested (nun de ephanerōthē)*. First aorist passive indicative of *phaneroō*, to make manifest (*phaneros*). The construction is suddenly changed (anacoluthon) from the participle to the finite verb.

27. *God was pleased (ethelēsen ho theos)*. First aorist active indicative of *thelō*, to will, to wish. "God willed" this change

from hidden mystery to manifestation. *To make known* (*gnōrisai*). First aorist active infinitive of *gnōrizō* (from *ginōskō*). *Among the Gentiles* (*en tois ethnesin*). This is the crowning wonder to Paul that God had included the Gentiles in his redemptive grace, "the riches of the glory of this mystery" (*to ploutos tēs doxēs tou mustēriou toutou*) and that Paul himself has been made the minister of this grace among the Gentiles (Eph. 3:1-12). He feels the high honour keenly and meets the responsibility humbly. *Which* (*ho*). Grammatical gender (neuter) agreeing with *mustēriou* (mystery), supported by A B P Vulg., though *hos* (who) agreeing with *Christos* in the predicate is read by Aleph C D L. At any rate the idea is simply that the personal aspect of "this mystery" is "Christ in you the hope of glory" (*Christos en humin hē elpis tēs doxēs*). He is addressing Gentiles, but the idea of *en* here is *in*, not *among*. It is the personal experience and presence of Christ in the individual life of all believers that Paul has in mind, the indwelling Christ in the heart as in Eph. 3:17. He constitutes also the hope of glory for he is the *Shekinah* of God. Christ is our hope now (I Tim. 1:1) and the consummation will come (Rom. 8:18).

28. *Whom* (*hon*). That is, "Christ in you, the hope of glory." *We proclaim* (*kataggellomen*). Paul, Timothy and all like-minded preachers against the Gnostic depreciation of Christ. This verb originally (Xenophon) meant to denounce, but in N.T. it means to announce (*aggellō*) throughout (*kata*), to proclaim far and wide (Acts 13:5). *Admonishing* (*nouthetountes*). Old verb from *nouthetēs*, admonisher (from *nous, tithēmi*). See already Acts 20:31; I Thess. 5:12, 14; II Thess. 3:15, etc. Warning about practice and teaching (*didaskontes*) about doctrine. Such teaching calls for "all wisdom." *Every man* (*panta anthrōpon*). Repeated three times. "In opposition to the doctrine of an intellectual exclusiveness taught by the false teachers" (Abbott). *That we may present* (*hina parastēsōmen*). Final use of *hina* and first aorist active subjunctive of *paristēmi*, for which see 1:22, the final presentation to Christ. *Perfect* (*teleion*). Spiritual adults in Christ, no longer babes in Christ (Heb. 5:14), mature and ripened Christians (4:22), the full-grown man in Christ (Eph. 4:13). The relatively perfect (Phil. 3:15) will on that day of the presentation be fully developed

as here (Col. 4:12; Eph. 4:13). The Gnostics used *teleios* of the one fully initiated into their mysteries and it is quite possible that Paul here has also a sidewise reference to their use of the term. 29. *Whereunto* (*eis ho*). That is "to present every man perfect in Christ." *I labour also* (*kai kopiō*). Late verb *kopiaō*, from *kopos* (toil), to grow weary from toil (Matt. 11:28), to toil on (Phil. 2:16), sometimes for athletic training. In papyri. *Striving* (*agōnizomenos*). Present middle participle of common verb *agōnizomai* (from *agōn*, contest, as in 2:1), to contend in athletic games, to agonize, a favourite metaphor with Paul who is now a prisoner. *Working* (*energeian*). Our word "energy." Late word from *energēs* (*en*, *ergon*), efficiency (at work). Play on the word here with the present passive participle of *energeō*, *energoumenēn* (energy energized) as in Eph. 1:19f. Paul was conscious of God's "energy" at work in him "mightily" (*en dunamei*), "in power" like dynamite.

CHAPTER II

1. *How greatly I strive* (*hēlikon agōna echō*). Literally, "how great a contest I am having." The old adjectival relative *hēlikos* (like Latin *quantus*) is used for age or size, in N.T. only here and James 3:5 (twice, how great, how small). It is an inward contest of anxiety like the *merimna* for all the churches (II Cor. 11:28). *Agōna* carries on the metaphor of *agōnizomenos* in 1:29. *For them at Laodicea* (*tōn en Laodikiāi*). Supply *huper* as with *huper humōn*. Paul's concern extended beyond Colossae to Laodicea (4:16) and to Hierapolis (4:13), the three great cities in the Lycus Valley where Gnosticism was beginning to do harm. Laodicea is the church described as lukewarm in Rev. 3:14. *For as many as have not seen my face* (*hosoi ouch heorakan to prosōpon mou*). The phrase undoubtedly includes Hierapolis (4:13), and a few late MSS. actually insert it here. Lightfoot suggests that Hierapolis had not yet been harmed by the Gnostics as much as Colossae and Laodicea. Perhaps so, but the language includes all in that whole region who have not seen Paul's face in the flesh (that is, in person, and not in picture). How precious a real picture of Paul would be to us today. The antecedent to *hosoi* is not expressed and it would be *toutōn* after *huper*. The form *heorakan* (perfect active indicative of *horaō* instead of the usual *heōrakasin* has two peculiarities *o* in Paul's Epistles (I Cor. 9:1) instead of *ō* (see John 1:18 for *heōraken*) and *-an* by analogy in place of *-asin*, which short form is common in the papyri. See Luke 9:36 *heōrakan*.

2. *May be comforted* (*paraklēthōsin*). First aorist passive subjunctive of *parakaleō* (for which see II Cor. 1:3-7) in final clause with *hina*. *Being knit together* (*sunbibasthentes*). First aorist passive participle of *sunbibazō*, old verb, causal of *bainō*, to make go together, to coalesce in argument (Acts 16:10), in spiritual growth (Col. 2:19), in love as here. Love is the *sundesmos* (3:14) that binds all together. *Unto all riches* (*eis pan ploutos*). Probably some distinction intended

487

between *en* (in love as the sphere) and *eis* (unto as the goal). *Of the full assurance of understanding* (*tēs plērophorias tēs suneseōs*). On *plērophoria*, see I Thess. 1:5. From *plērophoreō* (see Luke 1:1) and only in N.T. (I Thess. 1:5; Col. 2:2; Heb. 6:11; 10:22), Clement of Rome (*Cor.* 42) and one papyrus example. Paul desires the full use of the intellect in grasping the great mystery of Christ and it calls for the full and balanced exercise of all one's mental powers. *That they may know* (*eis epignōsin*). "Unto full knowledge." This use of *epignōsis* (full, additional knowledge) is Paul's reply to the Gnostics with the limited and perverted *gnōsis* (knowledge). *The mystery of God, even Christ* (*tou mustēriou tou theou, Christou*). The MSS. differ widely here, but this is Westcott and Hort's reading. Genitive (objective) with *epignōsin* and *Christou* in apposition. Christ is "the mystery of God," but no longer hidden, but manifested (1:26) and meant for us to know to the fulness of our capacity.

3. *In whom* (*en hōi*). This locative form can refer to *mustēriou* or to *Christou*. It really makes no difference in sense since Christ is the mystery of God. *All the treasures of wisdom and knowledge* (*pantes hoi thēsauroi tēs sophias kai gnōseōs*). See on Matt. 2:11; 6:19–21 for this old word, our thesaurus, for coffer, storehouse, treasure. Paul confronts these pretentious intellectuals (Gnostics) with the bold claim that Christ sums up all wisdom and knowledge. These treasures are hidden (*apokruphoi*, old adjective from *apokruptō*, to hide away, Mark 4:22) whether the Gnostics have discovered them or not. They are there (in Christ) as every believer knows by fresh and repeated discovery.

4. *This I say* (*touto legō*). Paul explains why he has made this great claim for Christ at this point in his discussion. *May delude* (*paralogizētai*). Present middle subjunctive of *paralogizomai*, old verb, only here in N.T., from *para* and *logizomai*, to count aside and so wrong, to cheat by false reckoning, to deceive by false reasoning (Epictetus). *With persuasiveness of speech* (*en pithanologiāi*). Rare word (Plato) from *pithanos* and *logos*, speech, adapted to persuade, then speciously leading astray. Only here in N.T. One papyrus example. The art of persuasion is the height of oratory, but it easily degenerates into trickery and momentary and flashy deceit such as Paul disclaimed in I Cor. 2:4 (*ouk en pithois*

sophias logois) where he uses the very adjective *pithos* (persuasive) of which *pithanos* (both from *peithō*) is another form. It is curious how winning champions of error, like the Gnostics and modern faddists, can be with plausibility that catches the gullible.

5. *Though (ei kai)*. Not *kai ei* (even if). *Yet (alla)*. Common use of *alla* in the apodosis (conclusion) of a conditional or concessive sentence. *Your order (tēn taxin)*. The military line (from *tassō*), unbroken, intact. A few stragglers had gone over to the Gnostics, but there had been no panic, no breach in the line. *Steadfastness (stereōma)*. From *stereoō* (from *stereos*) to make steady, and probably the same military metaphor as in *taxin* just before. The solid part of the line which can and does stand the attack of the Gnostics. See Acts 16:5 where the verb *stereoō* is used with *pistis* and I Peter 5:9 where the adjective *stereos* is so used. In II Thess. 3:6, 8, 11 Paul speaks of his own *taxis* (orderly conduct).

6. *As therefore ye received (hōs oun parelabete)*. Second aorist active indicative of *paralambanō* in same sense as in I Thess. 4:1; Phil. 4:9 (both *manthanō* and *paralambanō*) that is like *manthanō*, to learn (1:7), from Epaphras and others. *Christ Jesus the Lord (ton Christon Iēsoun ton Kurion)*. This peculiar phrase occurs nowhere else by Paul. We have often *ho Christos* (the Christ or Messiah) as in Phil. 1:15, *Iēsous Christos* (Jesus Christ), *Christos Iēsous* (Christ Jesus), *ho Kurios Iēsous* (the Lord Jesus, very often), but nowhere else *ho Christos Iēsous* and *Iēsous ho Kurios*. Hence it is plain that Paul here meets the two forms of Gnostic heresy about the Person of Christ (the recognition of the historical Jesus in his actual humanity against the Docetic Gnostics, the identity of the Christ or Messiah with this historical Jesus against the Cerinthian Gnostics, and the acknowledgment of him as Lord). "As therefore ye received the Christ (the Messiah), Jesus the Lord." Ye were taught right. *Walk in him (en autōi peripateite)*. "Go on walking in him" (present active indicative of *peripateō*). Stick to your first lessons in Christ.

7. *Rooted (errizōmenoi)*. Perfect passive participle of old verb *rizoō* from *riza*, root. In N.T. only here and Eph. 3:17 (18). Paul changes the figure from walk to growing tree.

Builded up in him (*epoikodomoumenoi en autōi*). Present passive participle (rooted to stay so) of *epoikodomeō*, old verb, to build upon as in I Cor. 3:10, 12. The metaphor is changed again to a building as continually going up (present tense). *Stablished* (*bebaioumenoi*). Present passive participle of *bebaioō*, old verb from *bebaios* (from *bainō, baiō*), to make firm or stable. *In your faith* (*tēi pistei*). Locative case, though the instrumental case, *by your faith*, makes good sense also. *Even as ye were taught* (*kathōs edidachthēte*). First aorist passive indicative of *didaskō*, an allusion to *parelabete* in verse 6 and to *emathete* in 1:7. *In thanksgiving* (*en eucharistiāi*). Hence they had no occasion to yield to the blandishments of the Gnostic teachers.

8. *Take heed* (*blepete*). Present active imperative second person plural of *blepō*, common verb for warning like our "look out," "beware," "see to it." *Lest there shall be any one* (*mē tis estai*). Negative purpose with the future indicative, though the aorist subjunctive also occurs as in II Cor. 12:6. *That maketh spoil of you* (*ho sulagōgōn*). Articular present active participle of *sulagōgeō*, late and rare (found here first) verb (from *sulē*, booty, and *agō*, to lead, to carry), to carry off as booty a captive, slave, maiden. Only here in N.T. Note the singular here. There was some one outstanding leader who was doing most of the damage in leading the people astray. *Through his philosophy* (*dia tēs philosophias*). The only use of the word in the N.T. and employed by Paul because the Gnostics were fond of it. Old word from *philosophos* (*philos, sophos*, one devoted to the pursuit of wisdom) and in N.T. only in Acts 17:18. Paul does not condemn knowledge and wisdom (see verse 2), but only this false philosophy, "knowledge falsely named" (*pseudō-numos gnōsis*, I Tim. 6:20), and explained here by the next words. *And vain deceit* (*kai kenēs apatēs*). Old word for trick, guile, like riches (Matt. 13:22). Descriptive of the philosophy of the Gnostics. *Tradition* (*paradosin*). Old word from *paradidōmi*, a giving over, a passing on. The word is colourless in itself. The tradition may be good (II Thess. 2:15; 3:6) or bad (Mark 7:3). Here it is worthless and harmful, merely the foolish theories of the Gnostics. *Rudiments* (*stoicheia*). Old word for anything in a *stoichos* (row, series) like the letters of the alphabet, the materials

of the universe (II Peter 3:10, 12), elementary teaching (Heb. 5:12), elements of Jewish ceremonial training (Acts 15:10; Gal. 4:3, 9), the specious arguments of the Gnostic philosophers as here with all their aeons and rules of life. *And not after Christ (kai ou kata Christon)*. Christ is the yardstick by which to measure philosophy and all phases of human knowledge. The Gnostics were measuring Christ by their philosophy as many men are doing today. They have it backwards. Christ is the measure for all human knowledge since he is the Creator and the Sustainer of the universe.

9. *For in him dwelleth all the fulness of the Godhead bodily (hoti en autōi katoikei pān to plērōma tēs theotētos sōmatikōs)*. In this sentence, given as the reason (*hoti*, because) for the preceding claim for Christ as the measure of human knowledge Paul states the heart of his message about the Person of Christ. There dwells (at home) in Christ not one or more aspects of the Godhead (the very *essence* of God, from *theos*, *deitas*) and not to be confused with *theiotes* in Rom. 1:20 (from *theios*, the *quality* of God, *divinitas*), here only in N.T. as *theiotēs* only in Rom. 1:20. The distinction is observed in Lucian and Plutarch. *Theiotēs* occurs in the papyri and inscriptions. Paul here asserts that "all the *plērōma* of the Godhead," not just certain aspects, dwells in Christ and in bodily form (*sōmatikōs*, late and rare adverb, in Plutarch, inscription, here only in N.T.), dwells now in Christ in his glorified humanity (Phil. 2:9–11), "the body of his glory" (*tōi sōmati tēs doxēs*). The fulness of the Godhead was in Christ before the Incarnation (John 1:1, 18; Phil. 2:6), during the Incarnation (John 1:14, 18; I John 1:1–3). It was the Son of God who came in the likeness of men (Phil. 2:7). Paul here disposes of the Docetic theory that Jesus had no human body as well as the Cerinthian separation between the man Jesus and the aeon Christ. He asserts plainly the deity and the humanity of Jesus Christ in corporeal form.

10. *Ye are made full (este peplērōmenoi)*. Periphrastic perfect passive indicative of *plēroō*, but only one predicate, not two. Christ is our fulness of which we all partake (John 1:16; Eph. 1:23) and our goal is to be made full of God in Christ (Eph. 3:19). "In Christ they find the satisfaction

of every spiritual want" (Peake). *The head* (*hē kaphalē*).
There is no other place for Christ. He is first (1:18) in time
and in rank. All rule and authority comes after Christ
whether angels, aeons, kings, what not. 11. *Ye were also circumcised* (*kai perietmēthēte*). First
aorist passive indicative of *peritemnō*, to circumcise. But
used here as a metaphor in a spiritual sense as in Rom. 2:29
"the circumcision of the heart." *Not made with hands*
(*acheiropoiētoi*). This late and rare negative compound verbal
occurs only in the N.T. (Mark 14:58; II Cor. 5:1; Col. 2:11)
by merely adding *a* privative to the old verbal *cheiropoiētos*
(Acts 7:48; Eph. 2:11), possibly first in Mark 14:58 where
both words occur concerning the temple. In II Cor. 5:1
the reference is to the resurrection body. The feminine form
of this compound adjective is the same as the masculine.
In the putting off (*en tēi apekdusei*). As if an old garment
(the fleshly body). From *apekduomai* (Col. 2:15, possibly
also coined by Paul) and occurring nowhere else so far as
known. The word is made in a perfectly normal way by
the perfective use of the two Greek prepositions (*apo, ek*),
"a resource available for and generally used by any real
thinker writing Greek" (Moulton and Milligan, *Vocabulary*).
Paul had as much right to mint a Greek compound as any
one and surely no one ever had more ideas to express and
more power in doing it. *Of Christ* (*tou Christou*). Specifying
genitive, the kind of circumcision that belongs to Christ,
that of the heart. 12. *Having been buried with him in baptism* (*suntaphentes
autōi en tōi baptismati*). Second aorist passive participle of
sunthaptō, old word, in N.T. only here and Rom. 6:4, followed by associative instrumental case (*autōi*). Thayer's
Lexicon says: "For all who in the rite of baptism are plunged
under the water, thereby declare that they put faith in the
expiatory death of Christ for the pardon of their past sins."
Yes, and for all future sins also. This word gives Paul's
vivid picture of baptism as a symbolic burial with Christ
and resurrection also to newness of life in him as Paul shows
by the addition "wherein ye were also raised with him"
(*en hōi kai sunēgerthēte*). "In which baptism" (*baptismati*,
he means). First aorist passive indicative of *sunegeirō*, late
and rare verb (Plutarch for waking up together), in LXX,

in N.T. only in Col. 2:12; 3:1; Eph. 2:6. In the symbol of baptism the resurrection to new life in Christ is pictured with an allusion to Christ's own resurrection and to our final resurrection. Paul does not mean to say that the new life in Christ is caused or created by the act of baptism. That is grossly to misunderstand him. The Gnostics and the Judaizers were sacramentalists, but not so Paul the champion of spiritual Christianity. He has just given the spiritual interpretation to circumcision which itself followed Abraham's faith (Rom. 4:10-12). Cf. Gal. 3:27. Baptism gives a picture of the change already wrought in the heart "through faith" (*dia tēs pisteōs*). *In the working of God* (*tēs energeias tou theou*). Objective genitive after *pisteōs*. See 1:29 for *energeia*. God had power to raise Christ from the dead (*tou egeirantos*, first aorist active participle of *egeirō*, the fact here stated) and he has power (energy) to give us new life in Christ by faith.

13. *And you* (*kai humas*). Emphatic position, object of the verb *sunezōopoiēsen* (did he quicken) and repeated (second *humās*). You Gentiles as he explains. *Being dead through your trespasses* (*nekrous ontas tois paraptōmasin*). Moral death, of course, as in Rom. 6:11; Eph. 2:1, 5. Correct text does not have *en*, but even so *paraptōmasin* (from *parapiptō*, to fall beside or to lapse, Heb. 6:6), a lapse or misstep as in Matt. 6:14; Rom. 5:15-18; Gal. 6:1, can be still in the locative, though the instrumental makes good sense also. *And the uncircumcision of your flesh* (*kai tēi akroboustiāi tēs sarkos humōn*). "Dead in your trespasses and your alienation from God, of which the uncircumcision of your flesh was a symbol" (Abbott). Clearly so, "the uncircumcision" used merely in a metaphorical sense. *Did he quicken together with him* (*sunezōopoiēsen sun autōi*). First aorist active indicative of the double compound verb *sunzōopoieō*, to make alive (*zōos, poieō*) with (*sun*, repeated also with *autōi*, associative instrumental), found only here and in Eph. 2:5, apparently coined by Paul for this passage. Probably *theos* (God) is the subject because expressly so stated in Eph. 2:4f. and because demanded by *sun autōi* here referring to Christ. This can be true even if Christ be the subject of *ērken* in verse 14. *Having forgiven us* (*charisamenos hēmin*). First aorist middle participle of *charizomai*,

common verb from *charis* (favour, grace). Dative of the person common as in 3:13. The act of forgiving is simultaneous with the quickening, though logically antecedent. 14. *Having blotted out* (*exaleipsas*). And so "cancelled." First aorist active participle of old verb *exaleiphō*, to rub out, wipe off, erase. In N.T. only in Acts 3:19 (LXX); Rev. 3:5; Col. 2:14. Here the word explains *charisamenos* and is simultaneous with it. Plato used it of blotting out a writing. Often MSS. were rubbed or scraped and written over again (palimpsests, like Codex C). *The bond written in ordinances that was against us* (*to kath' hēmōn cheirographon tois dogmasin*). The late compound *cheirographon* (*cheir*, hand, *graphō*) is very common in the papyri for a certificate of debt or bond, many of the original *cheirographa* (handwriting, "chirography"). See Deissmann, *Bible Studies*, p. 247. The signature made a legal debt or bond as Paul says in Philemon 18f.: "I Paul have written it with mine own hand, I will repay it." Many of the papyri examples have been "crossed out" thus X as we do today and so cancelled. One decree is described as "neither washed out nor written over" (Milligan, *N.T. Documents*, p. 16). Undoubtedly "the handwriting in decrees" (*dogmasin*, the Mosaic law, Eph. 2:15) was against the Jews (Ex. 24:3; Deut. 27:14–26) for they accepted it, but the Gentiles also gave moral assent to God's law written in their hearts (Rom. 2:14f.). So Paul says "against us" (*kath' hēmōn*) and adds "which was contrary to us" (*ho ēn hupenantion hēmin*) because we (neither Jew nor Gentile) could not keep it. *Hupenantios* is an old double compound adjective (*hupo, en, antios*) set over against, only here in N.T. except Heb. 10:27 when it is used as a substantive. It is striking that Paul has connected the common word *cheirographon* for bond or debt with the Cross of Christ (Deissmann, *Light*, etc., p. 332). *And he hath taken it out of the way* (*kai ērken ek tou mesou*). Perfect active indicative of *airō*, old and common verb, to lift up, to bear, to take away. The word used by the Baptist of Jesus as "the Lamb of God that bears away (*airōn*) the sin of the world" (John 1:29). The perfect tense emphasizes the permanence of the removal of the bond which has been paid and cancelled and cannot be presented again. Lightfoot argues for Christ as the subject of *ērken*, but that is not necessary, though Paul does use sudden anacolutha. God has taken the bond against us "out of the midst" (*ek tou mesou*). *Nailing it to the cross* (*proselōsas auto tōi staurōi*). First aorist active participle of old and common verb *proseloō*, to fasten with nails to a thing (with dative *staurōi*). Here alone in N.T., but in III Macc. 4:9 with the very word *staurōi*. The victim was nailed to the cross as was Christ. "When Christ was crucified, God nailed the Law to His cross" (Peake). Hence the "bond" is cancelled for us. Business men today sometimes file cancelled accounts. No evidence exists that Paul alluded to such a custom here.

15. *Having put off from himself* (*apekdusamenos*). Only here and 3:9 and one MS. of Josephus (*apekdus*). Both *apoduō* and *ekduō* occur in ancient writers. Paul simply combines the two for expression of complete removal. But two serious problems arise here. Is God or Christ referred to by *apekdusamenos*? What is meant by "the principalities and the powers" (*tas archas kai tas exousias*)? Modern scholars differ radically and no full discussion can be attempted here as one finds in Lightfoot, Haupt, Abbott, Peake. On the whole I am inclined to look on God as still the subject and the powers to be angels such as the Gnostics worshipped and the verb to mean "despoil" (American Standard Version) rather than "having put off from himself." In the Cross of Christ God showed his power openly without aid or help of angels. *He made a show of them* (*edeigmatisen*). First aorist active indicative of *deigmatizō*, late and rare verb from *deigma* (Jude 7), an example, and so to make an example of. Frequent in the papyri though later than *paradeigmatizō* and in N.T. only here and Matt. 1:19 of Joseph's conduct toward Mary. No idea of disgrace is necessarily involved in the word. The publicity is made plain by "openly" (*en parrēsiāi*). *Triumphing over them on it* (*thriambeusas autous en autōi*). On the Cross the triumph was won. This late, though common verb in *Koiné* writers (*ekthriambeuō* in the papyri) occurs only twice in the N.T., once "to lead in triumph" (II Cor. 2:14), here to celebrate a triumph (the usual sense). It is derived from *thriambos*, a hymn sung in festal procession and is kin to the Latin *triumphus* (our triumph), a triumphal procession of victorious Roman generals. God won a complete triumph over

all the angelic agencies (*autous*, masculine regarded as personal agencies). Lightfoot adds, applying *thriambeusas* to Christ: "The convict's gibbet is the victor's car." It is possible, of course, to take *autōi* as referring to *cheirographon* (bond) or even to Christ.

16. *Let no one judge you* (*mē tis humas krinetō*). Prohibition present active imperative third singular, forbidding the habit of passing judgment in such matters. For *krinō* see on Matt. 7:1. Paul has here in mind the ascetic regulations and practices of one wing of the Gnostics (possibly Essenic or even Pharisaic influence). He makes a plea for freedom in such matters on a par with that in I Cor. 8 to 9 and Rom. 14 and 15. The Essenes went far beyond the Mosaic regulations. For the Jewish feasts see on Gal. 4:10. Josephus (*Ant.* III. 10, 1) expressly explains the "seventh day" as called "*sabbata*" (plural form as here, an effort to transliterate the Aramaic *sabbathah*).

17. *A shadow* (*skia*). Old word, opposed to substance (*sōma*, body). In Heb. 10:1 *skia* is distinguished from *eikōn* (picture), but here from *sōma* (body, substance). The *sōma* (body) casts the *skia* (shadow) and so belongs to Christ (*Christou*, genitive case).

18. *Rob you of your prize* (*katabrabeuetō*). Late and rare compound (*kata, brabeuō*, Col. 3:15) to act as umpire against one, perhaps because of bribery in Demosthenes and Eustathius (two other examples in Preisigke's *Wörterbuch*), here only in the N.T. So here it means to decide or give judgment against. The judge at the games is called *brabeus* and the prize *brabeion* (I Cor. 9:24; Phil. 3:14). It is thus parallel to, but stronger than, *krinetō* in verse 16. *By a voluntary humility* (*thelōn en tapeinophrosunēi*). Present active participle of *thelō*, to wish, to will, but a difficult idiom. Some take it as like an adverb for "wilfully" somewhat like *thelontas* in II Peter 3:5. Others make it a Hebraism from the LXX usage, "finding pleasure in humility." The Revised Version margin has "of his own mere will, by humility." Hort suggested *en ethelotapeinophrosunēi* (in gratuitous humility), a word that occurs in Basil and made like *ethelothrēskia* in verse 23. *And worshipping of the angels* (*kai thrēskeiāi tōn aggelōn*). In 3:12 humility (*tapeinophrosunēn*) is a virtue, but it is linked with worship of the angels which is

idolatry and so is probably false humility as in verse 23. They may have argued for angel worship on the plea that God is high and far removed and so took angels as mediators as some men do today with angels and saints in place of Christ. *Dwelling in the things which he hath seen (ha heoraken embateuōn)*. Some MSS. have "not," but not genuine. This verb *embateuō* (from *embatēs*, stepping in, going in) has given much trouble. Lightfoot has actually proposed *kenembateuōn* (a verb that does not exist, though *kenembateō* does occur) with *aiōra*, to tread on empty air, an ingenious suggestion, but now unnecessary. It is an old word for going in to take possession (papyri examples also). W. M. Ramsay (*Teaching of Paul*, pp. 287ff.) shows from inscriptions in Klaros that the word is used of an initiate in the mysteries who "set foot in" (*enebateusen*) and performed the rest of the rites. Paul is here quoting the very work used of these initiates who "take their stand on" these imagined revelations in the mysteries. *Vainly puffed up (eikēi phusioumenos)*. Present passive participle of *phusioō*, late and vivid verb from *phusa*, pair of bellows, in N.T. only here and I Cor. 4:6, 18f.; 8:1. Powerful picture of the self-conceit of these bombastic Gnostics.

19. *Not holding fast the Head (ou kratōn tēn kephalēn)*. Note negative *ou*, not *mē*, actual case of deserting Christ as the Head. The Gnostics dethroned Christ from his primacy (1:18) and placed him below a long line of aeons or angels. They did it with words of praise for Christ as those do now who teach Christ as only the noblest of men. The headship of Christ is the keynote of this Epistle to the Colossians and the heart of Paul's Christology. *From whom (ex hou)*. Masculine ablative rather than *ex hēs (kephalēs)* because Christ is the Head. He develops the figure of the body of which Christ is Head (1:18, 24). *Being supplied (epichorēgoumenon)*. Present passive participle (continuous action) of *epichorēgeō*, for which interesting verb see already II Cor. 9:10; Gal. 3:5 and further II Peter 1:5. *Knit together (sunbibazomenon)*. Present passive participle also (continuous action) of *sunbibazō*, for which see Col. 2:2. *Through the joints (dia tōn haphōn)*. Late word *haphē* (from *haptō*, to fasten together), connections (*junctura* and *nexus* in the Vulgate). *And bonds (kai sundesmōn)*. Old word from

sundeō, to bind together. Aristotle and Galen use it of the human body. Both words picture well the wonderful unity in the body by cells, muscles, arteries, veins, nerves, skin, glands, etc. It is a marvellous machine working together under the direction of the head. *Increaseth with the increase of God* (*auxei tēn auxēsin tou theou*). Cognate accusative (*auxēsin*) with the old verb *auxei*.

20. *If ye died* (*ei apethanete*). Condition of the first class, assumed as true, *ei* and second aorist active indicative of *apothnēskō*, to die. He is alluding to the picture of burial in baptism (2:12). *From the rudiments of the world* (*apo tōn stoicheiōn tou kosmou*). See 2:8. *As though living in the world* (*hōs-zōntes en kosmōi*). Concessive use of the participle with *hōs*. The picture is that of baptism, having come out (F. B. Meyer) on the other side of the grave, we are not to act as though we had not done so. We are in the Land of Beulah. *Why do ye subject yourselves to ordinances?* (*ti dogmatizesthe?*). Late and rare verb (three examples in inscriptions and often in LXX) made from *dogma*, decree or ordinance. Here it makes good sense either as middle or passive. In either case they are to blame since the bond of decrees (2:14) was removed on the Cross of Christ. Paul still has in mind the rules of the ascetic wing of the Gnostics (2:16ff.).

21. *Handle not, nor taste, nor touch* (*mē hapsēi mēde geusēi mēde thigēis*). Specimens of Gnostic rules. The Essenes took the Mosaic regulations and carried them much further and the Pharisees demanded ceremonially clean hands for all food. Later ascetics (the Latin commentators Ambrose, Hilary, Pelagius) regard these prohibitions as Paul's own instead of those of the Gnostics condemned by him. Even today men are finding that the noble prohibition law needs enlightened instruction to make it effective. That is true of all law. The Pharisees, Essenes, Gnostics made piety hinge on outward observances and rules instead of inward conviction and principle. These three verbs are all in the aorist subjunctive second person singular with *mē*, a prohibition against handling or touching these forbidden things. Two of them do not differ greatly in meaning. *Hapsēi* is aorist middle subjunctive of *haptō*, to fasten to, middle, to cling to, to handle. *Thigēis* is second aorist active subjunc-

tive of *thigganō*, old verb, to touch, to handle. In N.T. only here and Heb. 11:28; 12:20. *Geusei* is second aorist middle subjunctive of *geuō*, to give taste of, only middle in N.T. to taste as here.

22. *Are to perish with the using* (*estin eis phthoran tēi apochrēsei*). Literally, "are for perishing in the using." *Phthora* (from *phtheirō*) is old word for decay, decomposition. *Apochrēsis* (from *apochraomai*, to use to the full, to use up), late and rare word (in Plutarch), here only in N.T. Either locative case here or instrumental. These material things all perish in the use of them.

23. *Which things* (*hatina*). "Which very things," these ascetic regulations. *Have indeed a show of wisdom* (*estin logon men echonta sophias*). Periphrastic present indicative with *estin* in the singular, but present indicative *echonta* in the plural (*hatina*). *Logon sophias* is probably "the repute of wisdom" (Abbott) like Plato and Herodotus. *Men* (in deed) has no corresponding *de*. *In will-worship* (*en ethelothrēskiāi*). This word occurs nowhere else and was probably coined by Paul after the pattern of *ethelodouleia*, to describe the voluntary worship of angels (see 2:18). *And humility* (*kai tapeinophrosunēi*). Clearly here the bad sense, "in mock humility." *And severity to the body* (*kai apheidiāi sōmatos*). Old word (Plato) from *apheidēs*, unsparing (*a* privative, *pheidomai*, to spare). Here alone in N.T. Ascetics often practice flagellations and other hardnesses to the body. *Not of any value* (*ouk en timēi tini*). *Timē* usually means honour or price. *Against the indulgence of the flesh* (*pros plēsmonēn tēs sarkos*). These words are sharply debated along with *time* just before. It is not unusual for *pros* to be found in the sense of "against" rather than "with" or "for." See *pros* in sense of *against* in 3:13; Eph. 6:11f.; II Cor. 5:12; I Cor. 6:1. *Plēsmonē* is an old word from *pimplēmi*, to fill and means satiety. It occurs here only in the N.T. Peake is inclined to agree with Hort and Haupt that there is a primitive corruption here. But the translation in the Revised Version is possible and it is true that mere rules do not carry us very far in human conduct as every father or mother knows, though we must have some regulations in family and state and church. But they are not enough of themselves.

CHAPTER III

1. *If then ye were raised together with Christ (ei oun sun-ēgerthēte tōi Christōi).* Condition of the first class, assumed as true, like that in 2:20 and the other half of the picture of baptism in 2:12 and using the same form *sunēgerthēte* as then which see for the verb *sunegeirō.* Associative instrumental case of *Christōi. The things that are above (ta anō).* "The upward things" (cf. Phil. 3:14), the treasure in heaven (Matt. 6:20). Paul gives this ideal and goal in place of merely ascetic rules. *Seated on the right hand of God (en dexiāi tou theou kathēmenos).* Not periphrastic verb, but additional statement. Christ is up there and at God's right hand. Cf. 2:3.

2. *Set your mind on (phroneite).* "Keep on thinking about." It does matter what we think and we are responsible for our thoughts. *Not on the things that are upon the earth (mē ta epi tēs gēs).* Paul does not mean that we should never think the things upon the earth, but that these should not be our aim, our goal, our master. The Christian has to keep his feet upon the earth, but his head in the heavens. He must be heavenly-minded here on earth and so help to make earth like heaven.

3. *For ye died (apethanete gar).* Definite event, aorist active indicative, died to sin (Rom. 6:2). *Is hid (kekruptai).* Perfect passive indicative of *kruptō,* old verb, to hide, remains concealed, locked "together with" (*sun*) Christ, "in" (*en*) God. No hellish burglar can break that combination.

4. *When Christ shall be manifested (hotan ho Christos phanerōthēi).* Indefinite temporal clause with *hotan* and the first aorist passive subjunctive of *phaneroō,* "whenever Christ is manifested," a reference to the second coming of Christ as looked for and longed for, but wholly uncertain as to time. See this same verb used of the second coming in I John 3:2. *Ye also together with him (kai humeis sun autōi).* That is the joy of this blessed hope. He repeats the verb about us *phanerōthēsesthe* (future passive indicative) and

500

adds *en doxēi* (in glory). Not to respond to this high appeal is to be like Bunyan's man with the muck-rake.

5. *Mortify* (*nekrōsate*). First aorist active imperative of *nekroō*, late verb, to put to death, to treat as dead. Latin Vulgate *mortifico*, but "mortify" is coming with us to mean putrify. Paul boldly applies the metaphor of death (2:20; 3:3) pictured in baptism (2:12) to the actual life of the Christian. He is not to go to the other Gnostic extreme of license on the plea that the soul is not affected by the deeds of the body. Paul's idea is that the body is the temple of the Holy Spirit (I Cor. 6:19). He mentions some of these "members upon the earth" like fornication (*porneian*), uncleanness (*akatharsian*), passion (*pathos*), evil desire (*epithumian kakēn*), covetousness (*pleonexian*) "the which is idolatry" (*hētis estin eidōlolatria*). See the longer list of the works of the flesh in Gal. 5:19-21, though covetousness is not there named, but it is in Eph. 4:19; 5:5.

6. *Cometh the wrath of God* (*erchetai hē orgē tou theou*). Paul does not regard these sins of the flesh as matters of indifference, far otherwise. Many old MSS. do not have "upon the sons of disobedience," genuine words in Eph. 5:6.

7. *Walked aforetime* (*periepatēsate pote*). First aorist (constative) indicative referring to their previous pagan state. *When ye lived* (*hote ezēte*). Imperfect active indicative of *zaō*, to live, "ye used to live" (customary action). Sharp distinction in the tenses.

8. *But now* (*nuni de*). Emphatic form of *nun* in decided contrast (to *pote* in verse 7) in the resurrection life of 2:12; 3:1. *Put ye also away* (*apothesthe kai humeis*). Second aorist middle imperative of old verb *apotithēmi*, to put away, lay aside like old clothes. This metaphor of clothing Paul now uses with several verbs (*apothesthe* here, *apekdusamenoi* in verse 9, *endusamenoi* in verse 10, *endusasthe* in verse 12). *All these* (*ta panta*). The whole bunch of filthy rags (anger *orgēn*, wrath *thumon*, malice *kakian*, railing *blasphēmian*, shameful speaking *aischrologian*). See somewhat similar lists of vices in Col. 3:5; Gal. 5:20; Eph. 4:29-31. These words have all been discussed except *aischrologian*, an old word for low and obscene speech which occurs here only in the N.T. It is made from *aischrologos* (*aischros* as in I Cor. 11:6 and that from *aischos*, disgrace). Note also the

addition of "out of your mouth" (*ek tou stomatos humōn*). The word was used for both abusive and filthy talk and Lightfoot combines both ideas as often happens. Such language should never come out of the mouth of a Christian living the new life in Christ.

9. *Lie not to another* (*mē pseudesthe eis allēlous*). Lying (*pseudos*) could have been included in the preceding list where it belongs in reality. But it is put more pointedly thus in the prohibition (*mē* and the present middle imperative). It means either "stop lying" or "do not have the habit of lying." *Seeing that ye have put off* (*apekdusamenoi*). First aorist middle participle (causal sense of the circumstantial participle) of the double compound verb *apekduomai*, for which see 2:15. The *apo* has the perfective sense (wholly), "having stripped clean off." The same metaphor as *apothesthe* in verse 8. *The old man* (*ton palaion anthrōpon*). Here Paul brings in another metaphor (mixes his metaphors as he often does), that of the old life of sin regarded as "the ancient man" of sin already crucified (Rom. 6:6) and dropped now once and for all as a mode of life (aorist tense). See same figure in Eph. 4:22. *Palaios* is ancient in contrast with *neos* (young, new) as in Matt. 9:17 or *kainos* (fresh, unused) as in Matt. 13:52. *With his doings* (*sun tais praxesin autou*). Practice must square with profession.

10. *And have put on* (*kai endusamenoi*). First aorist middle participle (in causal sense as before) of *endunō*, old and common verb (Latin *induo*, English endue) for putting on a garment. Used of putting on Christ (Gal. 3:27; Rom. 13:14). *The new man* (*ton neon*). "The new (young as opposed to old *palaion*) man" (though *anthrōpon* is not here expressed, but understood from the preceding phrase). In Eph. 4:24 Paul has *endusasthai ton kainon* (fresh as opposed to worn out) *anthrōpon*. *Which is being renewed* (*ton anakainoumenon*). Present passive articular participle of *anakainoō*. Paul apparently coined this word on the analogy of *ananeomai*. *Anakainizō* already existed (Heb. 6:6). Paul also uses *anakainōsis* (Rom. 12:2; Titus 3:5) found nowhere before him. By this word Paul adds the meaning of *kainos* to that of *neos* just before. It is a continual refreshment (*kainos*) of the new (*neos*, young) man in Christ Jesus. *Unto knowledge* (*eis epignōsin*). "Unto full (additional) knowl-

edge," one of the keywords in this Epistle. *After the image (kat' eikona)*. An allusion to Gen. 1:26, 28. The restoration of the image of God in us is gradual and progressive (II Cor. 3:18), but will be complete in the final result (Rom. 8:29; I John 3:2). 11. *Where (hopou)*. In this "new man" in Christ. Cf. Gal. 3:28. *There cannot be (ouk eni)*. *Eni* is the long (original) form of *en* and *estin* is to be understood. "There does not exist." This is the ideal which is still a long way ahead of modern Christians as the Great War proved. Race distinctions (Greek *Hellēn* and Jew *Ioudaios*) disappear in Christ and in the new man in Christ. The Jews looked on all others as Greeks (Gentiles). Circumcision *(peritomē)* and uncircumcision *(akrobustia)* put the Jewish picture with the cleavage made plainer (cf. Eph. 2). The Greeks and Romans regarded all others as barbarians *(barbaroi*, Rom. 1:14), users of outlandish jargon or gibberish, onomatopoetic repetition *(barbar)*. A Scythian *(Skuthēs)* was simply the climax of barbarity, *bar-baris barbariores* (Bengel), used for any rough person like our "Goths and Vandals." *Bondman (doulos*, from *deō*, to bind), *freeman (eleutheros*, from *erchomai*, to go). Class distinctions vanish in Christ. In the Christian churches were found slaves, freedmen, freemen, masters. Perhaps Paul has Philemon and Onesimus in mind. But labour and capital still furnish a problem for modern Christianity. *But Christ is all (alla panta Christos)*. Demosthenes and Lucian use the neuter plural to describe persons as Paul does here of Christ. The plural *panta* is more inclusive than the singular *pān* would be. *And in all (kai en pāsin)*. Locative plural and neuter also. "Christ occupies the whole sphere of human life and permeates all its developments" (Lightfoot). Christ has obliterated the words barbarian, master, slave, all of them and has substituted the word *adelphos* (brother).

12. *Put on therefore (endusasthe oun)*. First aorist middle imperative of *endunō* (verse 10). He explains and applies *(oun* therefore) the figure of "the new man" as "the new garment." *As God's elect (hōs eklektoi tou theou)*. Same phrase in Rom. 8:33; Titus 1:1. In the Gospels a distinction exists between *klētos* and *eklektos* (Matt. 24:22, 24, 31), but no distinction appears in Paul's writings. Here further described as "holy and beloved" *(hagioi kai ēgapēmenoi)*. The

items in the new clothing for the new man in Christ Paul now gives in contrast with what was put off (3:8). The garments include a heart of compassion (*splagchna oiktirmou*, the nobler *viscera* as the seat of emotion as in Luke 1:78; Phil. 1:8), kindness (*chrēstotēta*, as in Gal. 5:22), humility (*tapeinophrosunēn*, in the good sense as in Phil. 2:3), meekness (*praütēta*, in Gal. 5:23 and in Eph. 4:2 also with *tapeinophrosunē*), long-suffering (*makrothumian*, in Gal. 5:22; Col. 1:11; James 5:10).

13. *Forbearing one another* (*anechomenoi allēlōn*). Present middle (direct) participle of *anechō* with the ablative case (*allēlōn*), "holding yourselves back from one another." *Forgiving each other* (*charizomenoi heautois*). Present middle participle also of *charizomai* with the dative case of the reflexive pronoun (*heautois*) instead of the reciprocal just before (*allēlōn*). *If any man have* (*ean tis echēi*). Third class condition (*ean* and present active subjunctive of *echō*). *Complaint* (*momphēn*). Old word from *memphomai*, to blame. Only here in N.T. Note *pros* here with *tina* in the sense of against for comparison with *pros* in 2:31. *Even as the Lord* (*kathōs kai ho Kurios*). Some MSS. read *Christos* for *Kurios*. But Christ's forgiveness of us is here made the reason for our forgiveness of others. See Matt. 6:12, 14f. where our forgiveness of others is made by Jesus a prerequisite to our obtaining forgiveness from God.

14. *And above all these things* (*epi pāsin de toutois*). "And upon all these things." *Put on love* (*tēn agapēn*). See Luke 3:20. The verb has to be supplied (*endusasthe*) from verse 12 as the accusative case *agapēn* shows. *Which is* (*ho estin*). Neuter singular of the relative and not feminine like *agapē* (the antecedent) nor masculine like *sundesmos* in the predicate. However, there are similar examples of *ho estin* in the sense of *quod est* (*id est*), "that is," in Mark 14:42; 15:42, without agreement in gender and number. So also Eph. 5:5 where *ho estin*="which thing." *The bond of perfectness* (*sundesmos tēs teleiotētos*). See 2:19 for *sundesmos*. Here it is apparently the girdle that holds the various garments together. The genitive (*teleiotētos*) is probably that of apposition with the girdle of love. In a succinct way Paul has here put the idea about love set forth so wonderfully in I Cor. 13.

15. *The peace of Christ (hē eirēnē tou Christou).* The peace that Christ gives (John 14:27). *Rule (brabeuetō).* Imperative active third singular of *brabeuō*, to act as umpire (*brabeus*), old verb, here alone in N.T. See I Cor. 7:15 for called in peace. *In one body (en heni sōmati).* With one Head (Christ) as in 1:18, 24. *Be ye thankful (eucharistoi ginesthe).* "Keep on becoming thankful." Continuous obligation. 16. *The word of Christ (ho logos tou Christou).* This precise phrase only here, though "the word of the Lord" in I Thess. 1:8; 4:15; II Thess. 3:1. Elsewhere "the word of God." Paul is exalting Christ in this Epistle. *Christou* can be either the subjective genitive (the word delivered by Christ) or the objective genitive (the word about Christ). See I John. 2:14. *Dwell (enoikeitō).* Present active imperative of *enoikeō*, to make one's home, to be at home. *In you (en humin).* Not "among you." *Richly (plousiōs).* Old adverb from *plousios* (rich). See I Tim. 6:17. The following words explain *plousiōs*. *In all wisdom (en pasēi sophiāi).* It is not clear whether this phrase goes with *plousiōs* (richly) or with the participles following (*didaskontes kai nouthetountes*, see 1:28). Either punctuation makes good sense. The older Greek MSS. had no punctuation. There is an anacoluthon here. The participles may be used as imperatives as in Rom. 12:11f., 16. *With psalms (psalmois*, the Psalms in the Old Testament originally with musical accompaniment), *hymns (humnois*, praises to God composed by the Christians like I Tim. 3:16), spiritual songs (*ōidais pneumatikais*, general description of all whether with or without instrumental accompaniment). The same song can have all three words applied to it. *Singing with grace (en chariti āidontes).* In God's grace (II Cor. 1:12). The phrase can be taken with the preceding words. The verb *āidō* is an old one (Eph. 5:19) for lyrical emotion in a devout soul. *In your hearts (en tais kardiais humōn).* Without this there is no real worship "to God" (*tōi theōi*). How can a Jew or Unitarian in the choir lead in the worship of Christ as Saviour? Whether with instrument or with voice or with both it is all for naught if the adoration is not in the heart. 17. *Whatsoever ye do (pān hoti ean poiēte).* Indefinite relative (everything whatever) with *ean* and the present active subjunctive, a common idiom in such clauses. *Do all (panta).*

The imperative *poieite* has to be supplied from *poiēte* in the relative clause. *Panta* is repeated from *pān* (singular), but in the plural (all things). *Pān* is left as a nominative absolute as in Matt. 10:32; Luke 12:10. This is a sort of Golden Rule for Christians "in the name of the Lord Jesus" (*en onomati Kuriou Iēsou*), in the spirit of the Lord Jesus (Eph. 5:20). What follows (directions to the various groups) is in this same vein. Sociological problems have always existed. Paul puts his finger on the sore spot in each group with unerring skill like a true diagnostician.

18. *Wives* (*kai gunaikes*). The article here distinguishes class from class and with the vocative case can be best rendered "Ye wives." So with each group. *Be in subjection to your husbands* (*hupotassesthe tois andrasin*). "Own" (*idiois*) is genuine in Eph. 5:22, but not here. The verb *hupotassomai* has a military air, common in the Koiné for such obedience. Obedience in government is essential as the same word shows in Rom. 13:1, 5. *As is fitting in the Lord* (*hōs anēken en Kuriōi*). This is an idiomatic use of the imperfect indicative with verbs of propriety in present time (Robertson, *Grammar*, p. 919). Wives have rights and privileges, but recognition of the husband's leadership is essential to a well-ordered home, only the assumption is that the husband has a head and a wise one.

19. *Love your wives* (*agapāte tas gunaikas*). Present active imperative, "keep on loving." That is precisely the point. *Be not bitter* (*mē pikrainesthe*). Present middle imperative in prohibition: "Stop being bitter" or "do not have the habit of being bitter." This is the sin of husbands. *Pikrainō* is an old verb from *pikros* (bitter). In N.T. only here and Rev. 8:11; 10:9f. The bitter word rankles in the soul.

20. *Obey your parents* (*hupakouete tois goneusin*). Old verb to listen under (as looking up), to hearken, to heed, to obey. *In all things* (*kata panta*). This is the hard part for the child, not occasional obedience, but continual. Surely a Christian father or mother will not make unreasonable or unjust demands of the child. Nowhere does modern civilization show more weakness than just here. Waves of lawlessness sweep over the world because the child was not taught to obey. Again Paul argues that this is "in the Lord" (*en Kuriōi*).

21. *Provoke not* (*mē erethizete*). Present imperative of old

verb from *erethō*, to excite. Only twice in N.T., here in bad sense, in good sense in II Cor. 9:2 (to stimulate). Here it means to nag and as a habit (present tense). *That they be not discouraged* (*hina mē athumōsin*). Negative purpose (*hina mē*) with the present subjunctive (continued discouragement) of *athumeō*, old verb, but only here in N.T., from *athumos* (dispirited, *a* privative, *thumos*, spirit or courage). One does not have to read *Jane Eyre* or *Oliver Twist* to know something of the sorrows of childhood as is witnessed by runaway children and even child suicides.

22. *Your masters according to the flesh* (*tois kata sarka kuriois*). "Lords" really, but these Christian slaves (*douloi*) had Christ as Lord, but even so they were to obey their lords in the flesh. *Not with eye-service* (*mē en ophthalmodouliais*). Another Pauline word (here only and Eph. 6:6), elsewhere only in Christian writers after Paul, an easy and expressive compound, service while the master's eye was on the slave and no longer. *Men-pleasers* (*anthrōpareskoi*). Late compound only in LXX and Paul (here and Eph. 6:6). *In singleness of heart* (*en haplotēti kardias*). So in Eph. 6:5. Old and expressive word from *haplous* (simple, without folds). See II Cor. 11:3. *Fearing the Lord* (*phoboumenoi ton Kurion*). Rather than the lords according to the flesh.

23. *Whatsoever ye do* (*ho ean poiēte*). See same idiom in 3:17 except *ho* instead of *pān hoti*. *Heartily* (*ek psuchēs*). From the soul and not with mere eye service. In Eph. 6:7 Paul adds *met' eunoias* (with good will) in explanation of *ek psuchēs*. *As unto the Lord* (*hōs tōi Kuriōi*). Even when unto men. This is the highest test of worthwhile service. If it were only always true!

24. *Ye shall receive* (*apolēmpsesthe*). Future middle indicative of *apolambanō*, old verb, to get back (*apo*), to recover. *The recompense* (*antapodosin*). "The full recompense," old word, in LXX, but only here in N.T., but *antapodoma* twice (Luke 14:12; Rom. 11:9). Given back (*apo*) in return (*anti*). *Ye serve the Lord Christ* (*to Kuriōi Christōi douleuete*). As his slaves and gladly so. Perhaps better as imperatives, keep on serving.

25. *Shall receive again for the wrong that he hath done* (*komisetai ho ēdikēsen*). It is not clear whether *ho adikōn* (he that doeth wrong) is the master or the slave. It is true

of either and Lightfoot interprets it of both, "shall receive back the wrong which he did." This is a general law of life and of God and it is fair and square. *There is no respect of persons (ouk estin prosōpolēmpsia).* There is with men, but not with God. For this word patterned after the Hebrew see Rom. 2:11; Eph. 6:9; James 2:1 The next verse should be in this chapter also.

CHAPTER IV

1. *That which is just and equal (to dikaion kai tēn isotēta).* Paul changes from *to ison* (like *to dikaion*, neuter singular adjective with article for abstract idea) to the abstract substantive *isotēs*, old word, in N.T. only here and II Cor. 8:13f. If employers always did this, there would be no labour problem. *A Master in heaven (Kurion en ouranōi).* A wholesome reminder to the effect that he keeps his eye on the conduct of masters of men here towards their employes.

2. *Continue steadfastly (proskartereite).* See Mark 3:9; Acts 2:42, 46 for this interesting word from *pros* and *karteros* (strong), common in the Koiné. *Watching (grēgorountes).* Present active participle of *grēgoreō*, late present made on perfect active stem *egrēgora* with loss of *e-*, found first in Aristotle.

3. *Withal (hama).* At the same time. *That God may open (hina ho theos anoixēi).* Common use of *hina* and the subjunctive (aorist), the sub-final use so common in the N.T. as in the Koiné. *A door for the word (thuran tou logou).* Objective genitive, a door for preaching. It is comforting to other preachers to see the greatest of all preachers here asking prayer that he may be set free again to preach. He uses this figure elsewhere, once of a great and open door with many adversaries in Ephesus (I Cor. 16:9), once of an open door that he could not enter in Troas (II Cor. 2:12). *The mystery of Christ (to mustērion tou Christou).* The genitive of apposition, the mystery which is Christ (2:2), one that puts out of comparison the foolish "mysteries" of the Gnostics. *For which I am also in bonds (di' ho kai dedemai).* Perfect passive indicative of *deō*. Paul is always conscious of this limitation, this chain. At bottom he is a prisoner because of his preaching to the Gentiles.

4. *As I ought to speak (hōs dei me lalēsai).* Wonderful as Paul's preaching was to his hearers and seems to us, he was never satisfied with it. What preacher can be?

5. *Toward them that are without (pros tous exō).* A Pauline

509

phrase for those outside the churches (I Thess. 5:12; I Cor. 5:12f.). It takes wise walking to win them to Christ. *Redeeming the time* (*ton kairon exagorazomenoi*). We all have the same time. Paul goes into the open market and buys it up by using it rightly. See the same metaphor in Eph. 5:16.

6. *Seasoned with salt* (*halati ērtumenos*). The same verb *artuō* (old verb from *airō*, to fit, to arrange) about salt in Mark 9:50; Luke 14:34. Nowhere else in the N.T. Not too much salt, not too little. Plutarch uses salt of speech, the wit which flavours speech (cf. Attic salt). Our word salacious is this same word degenerated into vulgarity. Grace and salt (wit,·sense) make an ideal combination. Every teacher will sympathize with Paul's desire "that ye know how ye must answer each one" (*eidenai pōs dei humas heni ekastōi apokrinesthai*). Who does know?

7. *All my affairs* (*ta kat' eme panta*). "All the things relating to me." The accusative case the object of *gnōrisei*. The same idiom in Acts 25:14; Phil. 1:2. *Tychicus* (*Tuchikos*). Mentioned also in Eph. 6:21 as the bearer of that Epistle and with the same verb *gnōrisei* (future active of *gnōrizō*) and with the same descriptive epithet as here (*ho agapētos adelphos kai pistos diakonos en Kuriōi*, the beloved brother and faithful minister in the Lord) except that here we have also *kai sundoulos* (and fellow-servant). Abbott suggests that Paul adds *sundoulos* because he had used it of Epaphras in 1:7. Perhaps *pistos* goes with both substantives and means faithful to Paul as well as to Christ.

8. *I have sent* (*epempsa*). Epistolary aorist active indicative of *pempō* as in Eph. 6:22. *That ye may know* (*hina gnōte*). Second aorist (ingressive) active subjunctive of *ginōskō*, "that ye may come to know." This the correct text, not *gnoi* (third singular). *Our estate* (*ta peri hēmōn*). "The things concerning us." *May comfort* (*parakalesēi*). First aorist active subjunctive. Proper rendering here and not "may exhort."

9. *Together with Onesimus* (*sun Onēsimōi*). Co-bearer of the letter with Tychicus and praised on a par with him, runaway slave though he is. *Who is one of you* (*hos estin ex humōn*). Said not as a reproach to Colossae for having such a man, but as a privilege to the church in Colossae to give

a proper welcome to this returning converted slave and to treat him as a brother as Paul argues to Philemon.

10. *Aristarchus* (*Aristarchos*). He was from Thessalonica and accompanied Paul to Jerusalem with the collection (Acts 19:29; 20:4) and started with Paul to Rome (Acts 27:2; Philemon 24). Whether he has been with Paul all the time in Rome we do not know, but he is here now. *My fellow-prisoner* (*ho sunaichmalōtos mou*). One of Paul's compounds, found elsewhere only in Lucian. Paul uses it of Epaphras in Philemon 23, but whether of actual voluntary imprisonment or of spiritual imprisonment like *sunstratiōtes* (fellow-soldier) in Phil. 2:25; Philemon 2 we do not know. Abbott argues for a literal imprisonment and it is possible that some of Paul's co-workers (*sun-ergoi*) voluntarily shared imprisonment with him by turns. *Mark* (*Markos*). Once rejected by Paul for his defection in the work (Acts 15:36–39), but now cordially commended because he had made good again. *The cousin of Barnabas* (*ho anepsios Barnabā*). It was used for "nephew" very late, clearly "cousin" here and common so in the papyri. This kinship explains the interest of Barnabas in Mark (Acts 12:25; 13:5; 15:36–39). *If he come unto you, receive him* (*ean elthēi pros humas dexasthe auton*). This third class conditional sentence (*ean* and second aorist active subjunctive of *erchomai*) gives the substance of the commands (*entolas*) about Mark already sent, how we do not know. But Paul's commendation of Mark is hearty and unreserved as he does later in II Tim. 4:11. The verb *dechomai* is the usual one for hospitable reception (Matt. 10:14; John 4:45) like *prosdechomai* (Phil. 2:29) and *hupodechomai* (Luke 10:38).

11. *Jesus which is called Justus* (*Iēsous ho legomenos Ioustos*). Another illustration of the frequency of the name Jesus (Joshua). The surname Justus is the Latin *Justus* for the Greek *Dikaios* and the Hebrew *Zadok* and very common as a surname among the Jews. The name appears for two others in the N.T. (Acts 1:23; 18:7). *Who are of the circumcision* (*hoi ontes ek peritomēs*). Jewish Christians certainly, but not necessarily Judaizers like those so termed in Acts 11:3 (*hoi ek peritomēs*. Cf. Acts 35:1, 5). *These only* (*houtoi monoi*). "Of the circumcision" (Jews) he means. *A comfort unto me* (*moi parēgoria*). Ethical dative of personal

interest. *Parēgoria* is an old word (here only in N.T.) from
parēgoreō, to make an address) and means solace, relief. A
medical term. Curiously enough our word paregoric comes
from it (*parēgorikos*).

12. *Epaphras who is one of you* (*Epaphrās ho ex humōn*).
See 1:7 for previous mention of this brother who had brought
Paul news from Colossae. *Always striving for you* (*pantote
agōnizomenos huper hēmōn*). See 1:29 of Paul. *That ye may
stand* (*hina stathēte*). Final clause, first aorist passive subjunctive (according to Aleph B) rather than the usual second
aorist active subjunctives (*stēte*) of *histēmi* (according to
A C D). *Fully assured* (*peplērophorēmenoi*). Perfect passive
participle of *plērophoreō*, late compound, for which see Luke
1:1; Rom. 14:5.

13. *And for them in Hierapolis* (*kai tōn en Hierāi Polei*).
The third of the three cities in the Lycus Valley which had
not seen Paul's face (2:1). It was across the valley from
Laodicea. Probably Epaphras had evangelized all three
cities and all were in peril from the Gnostics.

14. *Luke, the beloved physician* (*Loukas ho iatros ho aga-
pētos*). Mentioned also in Philemon 24 and II Tim. 4:11.
The author of the Gospel and the Acts. Both Mark and
Luke are with Paul at this time, possibly also with copies of
their Gospels with them. The article here (repeated) may
mean "my beloved physician." It would seem certain that
Luke looked after Paul's health and that Paul loved him.
Paul was Luke's hero, but it was not a one-sided affection.
It is beautiful to see preacher and physician warm friends
in the community. *Demas* (*Dēmas*). Just his name here (a
contraction of Demetrius), but in II Tim. 4:10 he is mentioned as one who deserted Paul.

15. *Nymphas* (*Numphan*). That is masculine, if *autou*
(his) is genuine (D E K L) after *kat' oikon*, but *Numpha*
(feminine) if *autēs* (her) is read (B 67). Aleph A C P read
autōn (their), perhaps including *adelphous* (brethren) and
so locating this church (*ekklēsia*) in Laodicea. It was not
till the third century that separate buildings were used for
church worship. See Rom. 16:5 for Prisca and Aquila. It
is not possible to tell whether it is "her" or "his" house
here.

16. *When this epistle hath been read among you* (*hotan*

anagnōsthēi par' humin hē epistolē). Indefinite temporal clause with *hotan (hote an)* and the first aorist passive subjunctive of *anaginōskō.* The epistle was read in public to the church (Rev. 1:3). *Cause that (poiēsate hina).* Same idiom in John 11:37; Rev. 13:15. Old Greek preferred *hopōs* for this idiom. See I Thess. 5:27 for injunction for public reading of the Epistle. *That ye also read (kai humeis anagnōte).* Second aorist active subjunctive of *anaginōskō,* to read. *And the epistle from Laodicea (kai tēn ek Laodikias).* The most likely meaning is that the so-called Epistle to the Ephesians was a circular letter to various churches in the province of Asia, one copy going to Laodicea and to be passed on to Colossae as the Colossian letter was to be sent on to Laodicea. This was done usually by copying and keeping the original. See Eph. 1:1 for further discussion of this matter.

17. *Take heed (blepe).* Keep an eye on. *Thou hast received in the Lord (parelabes en Kuriōi).* Second aorist active indicative of *paralambanō,* the verb used by Paul of getting his message from the Lord (I Cor. 15:3). Clearly Archippus had a call "in the Lord" as every preacher should have. *That thou fulfil it (hina autēn plērois).* Present active subjunctive of *pleroō,* "that thou keep on filling it full." It is a life-time job.

18. *Of me Paul with mine own hand (tēi emēi cheiri Paulou).* More precisely, "with the hand of me Paul." The genitive *Paulou* is in apposition with the idea in the possessive pronoun *emēi,* which is itself in the instrumental case agreeing with *cheiri.* So also II Thess. 3:17 and I Cor. 16:21. *My bonds (mou tōn desmōn).* Genitive case with *mnemoneuete* (remember). The chain (*en halusei* Eph. 6:20) clanked afresh as Paul took the pen to sign the salutation. He was not likely to forget it himself.

THE EPISTLE TO THE EPHESIANS
From Rome a.d. 63

BY WAY OF INTRODUCTION

There are some problems of a special nature that confront us about the so-called Epistle to the Ephesians.

THE AUTHORSHIP

It is not admitted by all that Paul wrote it, though no other adequate explanation of its origin has ever been given. So far as subject matter and vocabulary and style are concerned, if Colossians is Pauline, there is little or nothing to be said against the Pauline authorship of this Epistle.

RELATION TO COLOSSIANS

As we have seen, the two Epistles were sent at the same time, but clearly Colossians was composed first. Ephesians bears much the same relation to Colossians that Romans does to Galatians, a fuller treatment of the same general theme in a more detached and impersonal manner.

THE DESTINATION

The oldest documents (Aleph and B) do not have the words *en Ephesōi* (in Ephesus) in 1:1 (inserted by a later hand). Origen did not have them in his copy. Marcion calls it the Epistle to the Laodiceans. We have only to put here Col. 4:16 "the letter from Laodicea" to find the probable explanation. After writing the stirring Epistle to the Colossians Paul dictated this so-called Epistle to the Ephesians as a general or circular letter for the churches in Asia (Roman province). Perhaps the original copy had no name in 1:1 as seen in Aleph and B and Origen, but only a blank space. Marcion was familiar with the copy in Laodicea. Basil in the fourth century mentions some MSS. with no name in the address. Most MSS. were copies from the one in Ephesus and so it came to be called the Epistle to the

Ephesians. The general nature of the letter explains also the absence of names in it, though Paul lived three years in Ephesus.

THE DATE

The same date must be assigned as for Philemon and Colossians, probably A.D. 63.

THE PLACE OF WRITING

This would also be the same, that is Rome, though Deissmann and Duncan argue for Ephesus itself as the place of writing. Some scholars even suggest Caesarea.

THE CHARACTER OF THE EPISTLE

The same Gnostic heresy is met as in Colossians, but with this difference. In Colossians the emphasis is on the Dignity of Christ as the Head of the Church, while in Ephesians chief stress is placed upon the Dignity of the Church as the Body of Christ the Head. Paul has written nothing more profound than chapters 1 to 3 of Ephesians. Stalker termed them the profoundest thing ever written. He sounds the depths of truth and reaches the heights. Since Ephesians covers the same ground so largely as Colossians, only the words in Ephesians that differ or are additional will call for discussion.

SPECIAL BOOKS ON EPHESIANS

One may note Abbott (*Int. Crit. Comm.* 1897), Gross Alexander (1910), Beet (1891), Belser (1908), Candlish (1895), Dale (*Lectures on Ephesians*), Dibelius (*Handbuch*, 1912), Eadie (1883), Ellicott (1884), Ewald (*Zahn Komm.*, 2 Auf. 1910), Findlay (1892), Gore (*Practical Exposition*, 1898), Haupt (*Meyer Komm.*, 8 Auf. 1902), Hitchcock (1913), Hort (*Intr.* 1895), Knabenbauer (1913), Krukenberg (1903), Lidgett (1915), Lock (1929), Lueken (1906), Martin (*New Century Bible*), McPhail (1893), McPherson (1892), Meinertz (1917), Moule (1900), Mullins (1913), Murray (1915), Oltramare (1891), Robinson (1903), Salmond (1903), E. F. Scott (*Moffatt Comm.*, 1930), Stroeter (*The Glory of the Body of Christ*, 1909), Von Soden (2 Aufl. 1893), F. B. Westcott (1906), Wohlenberg (1895).

CHAPTER I

1. *Of Christ Jesus (Christou Iēsou).* So B D, though Aleph A L have *Iēsou Christou.* Paul is named as the author and so he is. Otherwise the Epistle is pseudepigraphic. *By the will of God (dia thelēmatos theou).* As in 1 Cor. 1:1; II Cor. 1:1; Rom. 1:1. *At Ephesus (en Ephesōi).* In Aleph and B these words are inserted by later hands, though both MSS. give the title *Pros Ephesious.* Origen explains the words *tois hagiois tois ousin* as meaning "the saints that are" (genuine saints), showing that his MSS. did not have the words *en Ephesōi.* The explanation of the insertion of these words has already been given in the remarks on "The Destination" as one copy of the general letter that was preserved in Ephesus. It is perfectly proper to call it the Epistle to the Ephesians if we understand the facts.

3. *Blessed (eulogētos).* Verbal of *eulogeō,* common in the LXX for Hebrew *baruk* (Vulgate *benedictus*) and applied usually to God, sometimes to men (Gen. 24:31), but in N.T. always to God (Luke 1:68), while *eulogēmenos* (perfect passive participle) is applied to men (Luke 1:42). "While *eulogēmenos* points to an isolated act or acts, *eulogētos* describes the intrinsic character" (Lightfoot). Instead of the usual *eucharistoumen* (Col. 1:3) Paul here uses *eulogētos,* elsewhere only in II Cor. 1:3 in opening, though in a doxology in Rom. 1:25; 9:5; II Cor. 11:31. The copula here is probably *estin* (is), though either *estō* (imperative) or *eiē* (optative as wish) will make sense. *The God and Father of our Lord Jesus Christ (ho theos kai patēr tou Kuriou hēmōn Iēsou Christou).* *Kai* is genuine here, though not in Col. 1:3. The one article (*ho*) with *theos kai patēr* links them together as in I Thess. 1:3; 3:11, 13; Gal. 1:4. See also the one article in II Peter 1:1, 11. In Eph. 1:17 we have *ho theos tou Kuriou hēmōn Iēsou Christou,* and the words of Jesus in John 20:17. *Who hath blessed us (ho eulogēsas humās).* First aorist active participle of *eulogeō,* the same word, antecedent action to the doxology (*eulogētos*). *With (en).* So-called instrumental

use of *en* though *in* is clear. *Every spiritual blessing (pasēi eulogiāi pneumatikēi)*. Third use of the root *eulog* (verbal, verb, substantive). Paul lovingly plays with the idea. The believer is a citizen of heaven and the spiritual blessings count for most to him. *In the heavenly places in Christ (en tois epouraniois en Christōi)*. In four other places in Eph. (1:20; 2:6; 3:10; 6:12). This precise phrase (with *en*) occurs nowhere else in the N.T. and has a clearly local meaning in 1:20; 2:6; 3:10, doubtful in 6:12, but probably so here. In 2:6 the believer is conceived as already seated with Christ. Heaven is the real abode of the citizen of Christ's kingdom (Phil. 3:20) who is a stranger on earth (Phil. 1:27; Eph. 2:19). The word *epouranios* (heavenly) occurs in various passages in the N.T. in contrast with *ta epigeia* (the earthly) as in John 3:12; I Cor. 15:40, 48, 49; Phil. 2:10, with *patris* (country) in Heb. 11:16, with *klēsis* (calling) in Heb. 3:1, with *dōrea* (gift) in Heb. 6:4, with *basileia* (kingdom) in II Titus 4:18.

4. *Even as he chose us in him (kathōs exelexato hēmās en autōi)*. First aorist middle indicative of *eklegō*, to pick out, to choose. Definitive statement of God's elective grace concerning believers in Christ. *Before the foundation of the world (pro katabolēs kosmou)*. Old word from *kataballō*, to fling down, used of the deposit of seed, the laying of a foundation. This very phrase with *pro* in the Prayer of Jesus (John 17:24) of love of the Father toward the Son. It occurs also in I Peter 1:20. Elsewhere we have *apo* (from) used with it (Matt. 25:34; Luke 11:50; Heb. 4:3; 9:26; Rev. 13:8; 17:8). But Paul uses neither phrase elsewhere, though he has *apo tōn aiōnōn* (from the ages) in Eph. 3:9. Here in Eph. 1:3–14. Paul in summary fashion gives an outline of his view of God's redemptive plans for the race. *That we should be (einai hēmās)*. Infinitive of purpose with the accusative of general reference (*hēmās*). See Col. 1:22 for the same two adjectives and also *katenōpion autou*.

5. *Having foreordained us (Proorisas hēmās)*. First aorist active participle of *proorizō*, late and rare compound to define or decide beforehand. Already in Acts 4:28; I Cor. 2:7; Rom. 8:29. See also verse 11. Only other N.T. example in verse 11. To be taken with *exelexato* either simultaneous or antecedent (causal). *Unto adoption as sons (eis huiothesian)*.

For this interesting word see Gal. 4:5; Rom. 8:15; 9:4. *Unto himself* (*eis auton*). Unto God. *According to the good pleasure of his will* (*kata tēn eudokian tou thelēmatos autou*). Here *eudokian* means *purpose* like *boulēn* in verse 11 rather than *benevolence* (good pleasure). Note the preposition *kata* here for standard.

6. *To the praise* (*eis epainon*). Note the prepositions in this sentence. *Which* (*hēs*). Genitive case of the relative *hēn* (cognate accusative with *echaritōsen* (he freely bestowed), late verb *charitoō* (from *charis*, grace), in N.T. attracted to case of antecedent *charitos* only here and Luke 1:28. *In the Beloved* (*en tōi ēgapēmenōi*). Perfect passive participle of *agapaō*. This phrase nowhere else in the N.T. though in the Apostolic Fathers.

7. *In whom* (*en hōi*). Just like Col. 1:14 with *paraptōmatōn* (trespasses) in place of *hamartiōn* (sins) and with the addition of *dia tou haimatos autou* (through his blood) as in Col. 1:20. Clearly Paul makes the blood of Christ the cost of redemption, the ransom money (*lutron*, Matt. 20:28=Mark 10:45; *antilutron*, I Tim. 2:6). See Col. 1:9.

8. *According to the riches of his grace* (*kata to ploutos tēs charitos autou*). A thoroughly Pauline phrase, riches of kindness (Rom. 2:4), riches of glory (Col. 1:27; Eph. 3:16; Phil. 4:19), riches of fulness of understanding (Col. 2:7), riches of Christ (Eph. 3:8), and in Eph. 2:7 "the surpassing riches of grace." *Which* (*hēs*). Genitive attracted again to case of antecedent *charitos*.

9. *The mystery of his will* (*to mustērion tou thelēmatos autou*). Once hidden, now revealed as in Col. 1:26 which see. See also Col. 2:3. *Which he purposed* (*hēn proetheto*). Second aorist middle of *protithēmi*, old verb, for which see Rom. 1:13; 3:25.

10. *Unto a dispensation of the fulness of the times* (*eis oikonomian tou plērōmatos tōn kairōn*). See Col. 1:25 for *oikonomian*. In Gal. 4:4 "the fulness of the time" (*to plērōma tou chronou*) the time before Christ is treated as a unit, here as a series of epochs (*kairōn*). Cf. Mark 1:15; Heb. 1:1. On *plērōma* see also Rom. 11:26; Eph. 3:19; 4:13. *To sum up* (*anakephalaiōsasthai*). Purpose clause (amounting to result) with first aorist middle infinitive of *anakephalaioō*, late compound verb *ana* and *kephalaioō* (from *kephalaion*, Heb. 8:1,

and that from *kephalē*, head), to head up all things in Christ, a literary word. In N.T. only here and Rom. 13:9. For the headship of Christ in nature and grace see Col. 1:15-20.

11. *In him* (*en autōi*). Repeats the idea of *en tōi Christōi* of verse 10. *We were made a heritage* (*eklērōthēmen*). First aorist passive of *klēroō*, an old word, to assign by lot (*klēros*), to make a *klēros* or heritage. So in LXX and papyri. Only time in N.T., though *prosklēroō* once also (Acts 17:4). *Purpose* (*prothesin*). Common substantive from *protithēmi*, a setting before as in Acts 11:23; 27:13.

12. *To the end that we should be* (*eis to einai hēmās*). Final clause with *eis to* and the infinitive *einai* (see the mere infinitive *einai* in verse 4) and the accusative of general reference. *Who had before hoped in Christ* (*tous proēlpikotas en tōi Christōi*). Articular perfect active participle of *proelpizō*, late and rare compound (here only in N.T.) and the reference of *pro* not clear. Probably the reference is to those who like Paul had once been Jews and had now found the Messiah in Jesus, some of whom like Simeon and Anna had even looked for the spiritual Messiah before his coming.

13. *Ye also* (*kai humeis*). Ye Gentiles (now Christians), in contrast to *hēmās* (we) in 12. *In whom* (*en hōi*). Repeated third time (once in verse 11, twice in 13), and note *ho* or *hos* in 14. *Ye were sealed* (*esphragisthēte*). First aorist passive indicative of *sphragizō*, old verb, to set a seal on one as a mark or stamp, sometimes the marks of ownership or of worship of deities like *stigmata* (Gal. 6:17). Marked and authenticated as God's heritage as in 4:30. See II Cor. 1:22 for the very use of the metaphor here applied to the Holy Spirit even with the word *arrabōn* (earnest). *Spirit* (*pneumati*). In the instrumental case.

14. *An earnest* (*arrabōn*). See II Cor. 1:22 for discussion of *arrabōn*. Here "of promise" (*tēs epaggelias*) is added to the Holy Spirit to show that Gentiles are also included in God's promise of salvation. *Of our inheritance* (*tēs klēronomias hēmōn*). God's gift of the Holy Spirit is the pledge and first payment for the final inheritance in Christ. *Of God's own possession* (*tēs peripoiēseōs*). The word *God's* is not in the Greek, but is implied. Late and rare word (from *peripoieō*, to make a survival) with the notion of obtaining (I Thess. 5:9; II Thess. 3:14) and then of preserving (so in the papyri).

So in I Peter 2:9; Heb. 10:39, and here. God has purchased us back to himself. The sealing extends (*eis*) to the redemption and to the glory of God.

15. *And which yé shew toward all the saints* (*kai tēn eis pantas tous hagious*). The words "ye show" do not occur in the Greek. The Textus Receptus has *tēn agapēn* (the love) before *tēn* supported by D G K L Syr., Lat., Copt., but Aleph A B P Origen do not have the word *agapēn*. It could have been omitted, but is probably not genuine. The use of the article referring to *pistin* and the change from *en* to *eis* probably justifies the translation "which ye shew toward."

16. *I do not cease* (*ou pauomai*). Singular present middle, while in Col. 1:9 Paul uses the plural (literary, or including Timothy), *ou pauometha*.

17. *The Father of glory* (*ho patēr tēs doxēs*). The God characterized by glory (the Shekinah, Heb. 9:5) as in Acts 7:2; I Cor. 2:8; II Cor. 1:3; James 2:1. *That—may give* (*hina—dōiē*). In Col. 1:9 *hina* is preceded by *aitoumenoi*, but here the sub-final use depends on the general idea asking in the sentence. The form *dōiē* is a late *Koiné* optative (second aorist active) for the usual *doiē*. It occurs also in II Thess. 3:16; Rom. 15:5; II Tim. 1:16, 18 in the text of Westcott and Hort. Here B 63 read *dōi* (like John 15:16) second aorist active subjunctive, the form naturally looked for after a primary tense (*pauomai*). This use of the volitive optative with *hina* after a primary tense is rare, but not unknown in ancient Greek. *A spirit of wisdom and revelation* (*pneuma sophias kai apokalupseōs*). The Revised Version does not refer this use of *pneuma* to the Holy Spirit (cf. Gal. 6:1; Rom. 8:15), but it is open to question if it is possible to obtain this wisdom and revelation apart from the Holy Spirit. *In the knowledge of him* (*en epignōsei autou*). In the full knowledge of Christ as in Colossians.

18. *Having the eyes of your heart enlightened* (*pephōtismenous tous ophthalmous tēs kardias humōn*). A beautiful figure, the heart regarded as having eyes looking out toward Christ. But the grammar is difficult. There are three possible interpretations. One is an anacoluthon, the case of *pephōtismenous* being changed from the dative *humin* (to you) to the accusative because of the following infinitive like

eklexamenous (Acts 15:22) after *apostolois.* Another way of explaining it is to regard it as a tertiary predicate of *doië,* a loose expansion of *pneuma.* The third way is to regard the construction as the accusative absolute, a rare idiom possible in Acts 26:3; I Cor. 16:3; I Tim. 2:6. In this case, the participle merely agrees with *tous ophthalmous,* not with *humin,* "the eyes of your heart having been enlightened." Otherwise *tous ophthalmous* is the accusative retained after the passive participle. *That ye may know* (*eis to eidenai*). Final use of *eis to* and the infinitive (second perfect of *oida*) as in verse 12. Note three indirect questions after *eidenai* (what the hope *tis hē elpis,* what the riches *tis ho ploutos,* and what the surpassing greatness *kai ti to huperballon megethos*). When the Holy Spirit opens the eyes of the heart, one will be able to see all these great truths. *In the saints* (*en tois hagiois*). Our riches is in God, God's is in his saints.

19. *The exceeding greatness of his power* (*to huperballon megethos tēs dunameōs autou*). *Megethos* is an old word (from *megas*), but here only in N.T. *Huperballon,* present active participle of *huperballō,* reappears in 2:7 and 3:19 and seen already in II Cor. 3:10; 9:14. To enlightened eyes the greatness of God's power is even more "surpassing."

20. *Which he wrought* (*enērgēken*). Reading of A B rather than aorist *enērgēsen.* Perfect active indicative, "which he has wrought." *Hēn* is cognate accusative of the relative referring to *energeian* (energy) with *enērgēken* and note also *kratous* (strength) and *ischuos* (might), three words trying to express what surpasses (*huperballon*) expression or comprehension. *Made him to sit* (*kathisas*). First aorist active participle of *kathizō* in causative sense as in I Cor. 6:4. Metaphorical local expression like *dexiāi* and *en tois epour aniois.*

21. *Far above all rule* (*huperanō pasēs archēs*). Late compound adverbial preposition (*huper, anō*) with the ablative case. In N.T. only here and Heb. 9:5. As in Colossians 1:16, so here Paul claims primacy for Jesus Christ above all angels, aeons, what not. These titles all were used in the Gnostic speculations with a graduated angelic hierarchy. *World* (*aiōni*). "Age." See this identical expression in Matt. 12:32 for the present time (Gal. 1:4; I Tim. 6:17) and the future life (Eph. 2:7; Luke 20:35). Both combined in Mark 10:30; Luke 18:30.

22. *He put all things in subjection* (*panta hupetaxen*). First aorist active indicative of *hupotassō*, quoted from Psa. 8:7 as in I Cor. 15:27. *Gave him to be head* (*auton edōken kephalēn*). Gave (*edōken*, first aorist active indicative of *didōmi*) to the church (the universal spiritual church or kingdom as in Col. 1:18, 24) Christ as Head (*kephalēn*, predicate accusative). This conception of *ekklēsia* runs all through Ephesians (3:10, 21; 5:23, 24, 25, 27, 29, 32).

23. *Which* (*hētis*). "Which in fact is," explanatory use of *hētis* rather than *hē*. *The fulness of him that filleth all in all* (*to plērōma tou ta panta en pāsin plēroumenou*). This is probably the correct translation of a much disputed phrase. This view takes *plērōma* in the passive sense (that which is filled, as is usual, Col. 1:19) and *plēroumenou* as present middle participle, not passive. All things are summed up in Christ (1:10), who is the *plērōma* of God (Col. 1:19), and in particular does Christ fill the church universal as his body. Hence we see in Ephesians the Dignity of the Body of Christ which is ultimately to be filled with the fulness (*plērōma*) of God (3:19) when it grows up into the fulness (*plērōma*) of Christ (4:13, 16).

CHAPTER II

1. *And you did he quicken* (*kai humās*). The verb for *did he quicken* does not occur till verse 5 and then with *hēmās* (us) instead of *humās* (you). There is a like ellipsis or anacoluthon in Col. 1:21 and 22, only there is no change from *humās* to *hēmās*. *When ye were dead* (*ontas nekrous*). Present active participle referring to their former state. Spiritually dead. *Trespasses and sins* (*paraptōmasin kai hamartiais*). Both words (locative case) though only one in verse 5.

2. *According to the course of this world* (*kata ton aiōna tou kosmou toutou*). Curious combinations of *aiōn* (a period of time), *kosmos* (the world in that period). See I Cor. 1:20 for "this age" and I Cor. 3:9 for "this world." *The prince of the power of the air* (*ton archonta tēs exousias tou aeros*). *Aēr* was used by the ancients for the lower and denser atmosphere and *aithēr* for the higher and rarer. Satan is here pictured as ruler of the demons and other agencies of evil. Jesus called him "the prince of this world" (*ho archōn tou kosmou toutou*, John 16:11). *That now worketh* (*tou nun energountos*). Those who deny the existence of a personal devil cannot successfully deny the vicious tendencies, the crime waves, in modern men. The power of the devil in the lives of men does explain the evil at work "in the sons of disobedience" (*en tois huiois tēs apethias*). In 5:6 also. A Hebrew idiom found in the papyri like "sons of light" (I Thess. 5:5).

3. *We also all* (*kai hēmeis pantes*). We Jews. *Once lived* (*anestraphēmen pote*). Second aorist passive indicative of *anastrephō*, old verb, to turn back and forth, to live (II Cor. 1:12). Cf. *pote periepatēsate*, of the Gentiles in verse 2. *The desires* (*ta thelēmata*). Late and rare word except in LXX and N.T., from *thelō*, to will, to wish. Plural here "the wishes," "the wills" of the flesh like *tais epithumiais tēs sarkos* just before. Gentiles had no monopoly of such sinful impulses. *Of the mind* (*tōn dianoiōn*). Plural again, "of the thoughts or purposes." *Were by nature children of wrath* (*ēmetha tekna phusei orgēs*). This is the proper order of these

words which have been the occasion of much controversy. There is no article with *tekna*. Paul is insisting that Jews as well as Gentiles ("even as the rest") are the objects of God's wrath (*orgēs*) because of their lives of sin. See Rom. 2:1–3:20 for the full discussion of this to Jews unpalatable truth. The use of *phusei* (associative instrumental case of manner) is but the application of Paul's use of "all" (*pantes*) as shown also in Rom. 3:20 and 5:12. See *phusei* of Gentiles in Rom. 2:14. The implication of original sin is here, but not in the form that God's wrath rests upon little children before they have committed acts of sin. The salvation of children dying before the age of responsibility is clearly involved in Rom. 5:13f.

4. **But God** (*ho de theos*). Change in the structure of the sentence here, resuming verse 1 after the break. **Being rich in mercy** (*plousios ōn en eleei*). More than *eleēmōn* (being merciful). **Wherewith** (*hēn*). Cognate accusative with *ēgapēsen* (loved).

5. **Even when we were dead** (*kai ontas hēmās nekrous*). Repeats the beginning of verse 1, but he changes *humās* (you Gentiles) to *hēmās* (us Jews). **Quickened us together with Christ** (*sunezōopoiēsen tōi Christōi*). First aorist active indicative of the double compound verb *sunzōopoieō* as in Col. 2:13 which see. Associative instrumental case in *Christōi*. Literal resurrection in the case of Jesus, spiritual in our case as pictured in baptism. **By grace have ye been saved** (*chariti este sesōsmenoi*). Instrumental case of *chariti* and perfect passive periphrastic indicative of *sōzō*. Parenthetical clause interjected in the sentence. All of grace because we were dead.

6. **In Christ Jesus** (*en Christōi Iēsou*). All the preceding turns on this phrase. See Col. 3:1 for the word *sunēgeiren*. **Made to sit with him** (*sunekathisen*). First aorist active indicative of *sunkathizō*, old causative verb, but in N.T. only here and Luke 22:55.

7. **That he might shew** (*hina endeixētai*). Final clause with *hina* and first aorist middle subjunctive of *endeiknumi*. See 1:7 for "riches of grace" and 1:19 for "exceeding" (*huperballon*). **In kindness toward us** (*en chrēstotēti eph' hēmās*). See Rom. 2:7 for this word from *chrēstos* and that from *chraomai*, here God's benignity toward us.

8. *For by grace (tēi gar chariti)*. Explanatory reason. "By the grace" already mentioned in verse 5 and so with the article. *Through faith (dia pisteōs)*. This phrase he adds in repeating what he said in verse 5 to make it plainer. "Grace" is God's part, "faith" ours. *And that (kai touto)*. Neuter, not feminine *tautē*, and so refers not to *pistis* (feminine) or to *charis* (feminine also), but to the act of being saved by grace conditioned on faith on our part. Paul shows that salvation does not have its source (*ex humōn*, out of you) in men, but from God. Besides, it is God's gift (*dōron*) and not the result of our work.

9. *That no man should glory (hina mē tis kauchēsētai)*. Negative final clause (*hina mē*) with first aorist middle subjunctive of *kauchaomai*. It is all of God's grace.

10. *Workmanship (poiēma)*. Old word from *poieō* with the ending -*mat* meaning result. In N.T. only here and Rev. 1:20. *Created (ktisthentes)*. First aorist passive participle of *ktizō*, not the original creation as in Col. 1:16; Eph. 3:9, but the moral and spiritual renewal in Christ, the new birth, as in Eph. 2:15; 4:24. *For good works (epi ergois agathois)*. Probably the true dative of purpose here with *epi* (Robertson, *Grammar*, p. 605). Purpose of the new creation in Christ. *Which (hois)*. Attraction of the relative *ha* (accusative after *proētoimasen*) to case of the antecedent *ergois*. *Afore prepared (proētoimasen)*. First aorist active indicative of *proetoimazō*, old verb to make ready beforehand. In N.T. only here and Rom. 9:23. Good works by us were included in the eternal foreordination by God. *That we should walk in them (hina en autois peripatēsōmen)*. Expexegetic final clause explanatory of the election to good works.

11. *Wherefore (dio)*. This conjunction applies to the Gentile Christians the arguments in 2:1-10. *That aforetime ye (hoti pote humeis)*. No verb is expressed, but in verse 12 Paul repeats *hoti en tōi kairōi ekeinōi* (for *pote*) "that at that time" and inserts *ēte* (ye were). *Uncircumcision (akrobustia)*, *circumcision (peritomēs)*. The abstract words are used to describe Gentiles and Jews as in Gal. 5:6; Rom. 2:27. *Made by hands (cheiropoiētou)*. Agreeing with *peritomēs*. Verbal (Mark 14:58) from *cheiropoieō* like *acheiropoiētos* in Col. 2:11.

12. *Separate from Christ (chōris Christou)*. Ablative case with adverbial preposition *chōris*, describing their former condition as heathen. *Alienated from the commonwealth of Israel (apēllotriōmenoi tēs politeias tou Israēl)*. Perfect passive participle of *apallotrioō*, for which see Col. 1:21. Here followed by ablative case *politeias*, old word from *politeuō*, to be a citizen (Phil. 1:27) from *politēs* and that from *polis* (city). Only twice in N.T., here as commonwealth (the spiritual Israel or Kingdom of God) and Acts 22:28 as citizenship. *Strangers from the covenants of the promise (xenoi tōn diathēkōn tēs epaggelias)*. For *xenos* (Latin *hospes*, as stranger see Matt. 25:35, 38, 43f.), as guest-friend see Rom. 16:23. Here it is followed by the ablative case *diathēkōn*. *Having no hope (elpida mē echontes)*. No hope of any kind. In Gal. 4:8 *ouk* (strong negative) occurs with *eidotes theon*, but here *mē* gives a more subjective picture (I Thess. 4:5). *Without God (atheoi)*. Old Greek word, not in LXX, only here in N.T. Atheists in the original sense of being without God and also in the sense of hostility to God from failure to worship him. See Paul's words in Rom. 1:18–32. "In the world" (*en tōi kosmōi*) goes with both phrases. It is a terrible picture that Paul gives, but a true one.

13. *But now (nuni de)*. Strong contrast, as opposed to "at that time." *Afar off (makran)*. Adverb (accusative feminine adjective with *hodon* understood). From the *politeia* and its hope in God. *Are made nigh (egenēthēte eggus)*. First aorist passive indicative of *ginomai*, a sort of timeless aorist. Nigh to the commonwealth of Israel in Christ. *In the blood of Christ (en tōi haimati tou Christou)*. Not a perfunctory addition, but essential (1:7), particularly in view of the Gnostic denial of Christ's real humanity.

14. *For he is our peace (autos gar estin hē eirēnē hēmōn)*. He himself, not just what he did (necessary as that was and is). He is our peace with God and so with each other (Jews and Gentiles). *Both one (ta amphotera hen)*. "The both" (Jew and Gentile). Jesus had said "other sheep I have which are not of this fold" (John 10:16). *One (hen)* is neuter singular (oneness, unity, identity) as in Gal. 3:28. Race and national distinctions vanish in Christ. If all men were really in Christ, war would disappear. *Brake down the middle wall of partition (to mesotoichon tou phragmou lusas)*. "Having

loosened (first aorist active participle of *luō*, see John 2:19)
the middle-wall (late word, only here in N.T., and very rare
anywhere, one in papyri, and one inscription) of partition
(*phragmou*, old word, fence, from *phrassō*, to fence or hedge,
as in Matt. 21:33)." In the temple courts a partition wall
divided the court of the Gentiles from the court of Israel
with an inscription forbidding a Gentile from going further
(Josephus, *Ant.* VIII. 3, 2). See the uproar when Paul was
accused of taking Trophimus beyond this wall (Acts 21:28).
15. *Having abolished* (*katargēsas*). First aorist active participle of *katargeō*, to make null and void. *The enmity* (*tēn
echthran*). But it is very doubtful if *tēn echthran* (old word
from *echthros*, hostile, Luke 23:12) is the object of *katargēsas*. It looks as if it is in apposition with *to mesotoichon*
and so the further object of *lusas*. The enmity between Jew
and Gentile was the middle wall of partition. And then it
must be decided whether "in his flesh" (*en tēi sarki autou*)
should be taken with *lusas* and refer especially to the Cross
(Col. 1:22) or be taken with *katargēsas*. Either makes sense,
but better sense with *lusas*. Certainly "the law of commandments in ordinances (*ton nomon tōn entolōn en dogmasin*) is
governed by *katargēsas*. *That he might create* (*hina ktisēi*).
Final clause with first aorist active subjunctive of *ktizō*.
The twain (*tous duo*). The two men (masculine here, neuter
in verse 14), Jew and Gentile. *One new man* (*eis hena kainon
anthrōpon*). Into one fresh man (Col. 3:9–11) "in himself"
(*en hautōi*). Thus alone is it possible. *Making peace* (*poiōn
eirēnēn*). Thus alone can it be done. Christ is the peacemaker between men, nations, races, classes.
16. *And might reconcile* (*kai apokatallaxēi*). Final clause
with *hina* understood of first aorist active subjunctive of
apokatallassō for which see Col. 1:20, 22. *Them both* (*tous
amphoterous*). "The both," "the two" (*tous duo*), Jew and
Gentile. *In one body* (*en heni sōmati*). The "one new man"
of verse 15 of which Christ is Head (1:23), the spiritual
church. Paul piles up metaphors to express his idea of the
Kingdom of God with Christ as King (the church, the body,
the commonwealth of Israel, oneness, one new man in
Christ, fellow-citizens, the family of God, the temple of God).
Thereby (*en autōi*). On the Cross where he slew the enmity
(repeated here) between Jew and Gentile.

17. *Preached peace* (*euēggelisato eirēnēn*). First aorist middle of *euaggelizō*. "He gospelized peace" to both Jew and Gentile, "to the far off ones" (*tois makran*) and "to the nigh ones" (*tois eggus*). By the Cross and after the Cross Christ could preach that message. 18. *Through him* (*di' autou*). Christ. *We both* (*hoi amphoteroi*). "We the both" (Jew and Gentile). *Our access* (*tēn prosagōgēn*). The approach, the introduction as in Rom. 5:2. *In one Spirit* (*en heni pneumati*). The Holy Spirit. *Unto the Father* (*pros ton patera*). So the Trinity as in 1:13f. The Three Persons all share in the work of redemption. 19. *So then* (*ara oun*). Two inferential particles (accordingly therefore). *No more* (*ouketi*). No longer. *Sojourners* (*paroikoi*). Old word for dweller by (near by, but not in). So Acts 7:6, 29; I Peter 2:11 (only other N.T. examples). Dwellers just outside the house or family of God. *Fellowcitizens* (*sunpolitai*, old, but rare word, here only in N.T.), members now of the *politeia* of Israel (verse 12), the opposite of *xenoi kai paroikoi*. *Of the household of God* (*oikeioi tou theou*). Old word from *oikos* (house, household), but in N.T. only here, Gal. 6:10; I Tim. 5:8. Gentiles now in the family of God (Rom. 8:29). 20. *Being built upon* (*epoikodomēthentes*). First aorist passive participle of *epoikodomeō*, for which double compound verb see I Cor. 3:10; Col. 2:17. *The foundation* (*epi tōi themeliōi*). Repetition of *epi* with the locative case. See I Cor. 3:11 for this word. *Of the apostles and prophets* (*tōn apostolōn kai prophētōn*). Genitive of apposition with *themeliōi*, consisting in. If one is surprised that Paul should refer so to the apostles, he being one himself, Peter does the same thing (II Peter 3:2). Paul repeats this language in 3:5. *Christ Jesus himself being the chief corner stone* (*ontōs akrogōnianiou autou Christou Iēsou*). Genitive absolute. The compound *akrogōniaios* occurs only in the LXX (first in Isa. 28:16) and in the N.T. (here, I Peter 2:6). *Lithos* (*stone*) is understood. Jesus had spoken of himself as the stone, rejected by the Jewish builders (experts), but chosen of God as the head of the corner (Matt. 21:42), *eis kephalēn gōnias*. "The *akrogōniaios* here is the primary foundation-stone at the angle of the structure by which the architect

fixes a standard for the bearings of the walls and cross-walls throughout" (W. W. Lloyd).

21. *Each several building* (*pāsa oikodomē*). So without article Aleph B D G K L. *Oikodomē* is a late word from *oikos* and *demō*, to build for building up (edification) as in Eph. 4:29, then for the building itself as here (Mark 13:1f.). Ordinary Greek idiom here calls for "every building," not for "all the building" (Robertson, *Grammar*, p. 772), though it is not perfectly clear what that means. Each believer is called a *naos theou* (I Cor. 3:16). One may note the plural in Mark 13:1 (*oikodomai*) of the various parts of the temple. Perhaps that is the idea here without precise definition of each *oikodomē*. But there are examples of *pās* without the article where "all" is the idea as in *pāsēs ktiseōs* (all creation) in Col. 1:15. *Fitly framed together* (*sunarmologoumenē*). Double compound from *sun* and *harmologos* (binding, *harmos*, joint and *legō*), apparently made by Paul and in N.T. only here and Eph. 4:16. Architectural metaphor. *Into a holy temple* (*eis naon hagion*). The whole structure with all the *oikodomai*. Another metaphor for the Kingdom of God with which compare Peter's "spiritual house" (*oikos pneumatikos*) in which each is a living stone being built in (I Peter 2:5).

22. *Ye also are builded together* (*kai humeis sunoikodomeisthe*). Ye Gentiles also. Present passive indicative (continuous process) of common old verb *sunoikodomeō*, to build together with others or out of varied materials as here. Only here in N.T. In I Peter 2:5 Peter uses *oikodomeisthe* for the same process. *For a habitation* (*eis katoikētērion*). Late word (LXX), in N.T. only here and Rev. 18:2. From *katoikeō*, to dwell, as Eph. 3:17. Possibly each of us is meant here to be the "habitation of God in the Spirit" and all together growing (*auxei*) "into a holy temple in the Lord," a noble conception of the brotherhood in Christ.

CHAPTER III

1. *For this cause* (*toutou charin*). Use of *charin* (accusative of *charis*) as a preposition with the genitive and referring to the preceding argument about God's elective grace. It is possible that Paul started to make the prayer that comes in verses 14–21 when he repeats *toutou charin*. If so, he is diverted by his own words "the prisoner of Christ Jesus in behalf of you Gentiles" (*ho desmios tou Christou Iēsou huper humōn tōn ethnōn*) to set forth in a rich paragraph (1–13) God's use of him for the Gentiles.

2. *If so be that ye have heard* (*ei ge ēkousate*). Condition of first class with *ei* and first aorist active indicative and with the intensive particle *ge* that gives a delicate touch to it all. On *oikonomian* (stewardship, dispensation) see 1:9; 3:9 and Col. 1:25.

3. *By revelation* (*kata apokalupsin*). Not essentially different from *di' apokalupseōs* (Gal. 1:12). This was Paul's qualification for preaching "the mystery" (*to mustērion*. See 1:9). *As I wrote afore* (*kathōs proegrapsa*). First aorist active indicative of *prographō* as in Rom. 15:4, not picture forth as Gal. 3:1. But when and where? Epistolary aorist for this Epistle? That is possible. A previous and lost Epistle as in I Cor. 5:9? That also is abstractly possible. To the preceding discussion of the Gentiles? Possible and also probable. *In few words* (*en oligōi*). Not = *pro oligou*, shortly before, but as in Acts 26:28 "in brief space or time" = *suntonōs* (Acts 24:4), "briefly."

4. *Whereby* (*pros ho*). "Looking to which," "according to which." *When ye read* (*anaginōskontes*). This Epistle will be read in public. *My understanding in the mystery of Christ* (*tēn sunesin mou en tōi mustēriōi tou Christou*). My "comprehension" (*sunesin*, Col. 1:9; 2:2). Every sermon reveals the preacher's grasp of "the mystery of Christ." If he has no insight into Christ, he has no call to preach.

5. *In other generations* (*heterais geneais*). Locative case of time. He had already claimed this revelation for himself (verse 3). Now he claims it for all the other apostles and prophets of God.

530

6. *To wit.* Not in the Greek. But the infinitive (*einai*) clause is epexegetical and gives the content of the revelation, a common idiom in the N.T. *Ta ethnē* is in the accusative of general reference. Paul is fond of compounds with *sun* and here uses three of them. *Fellow-heirs (sunklēronoma).* Late and rare (Philo, inscriptions and papyri). See also Rom. 8:17. *Fellow-members of the body (sunsōma).* First found here and only here save in later ecclesiastical writers. Preuschen argues that it is equivalent to *sundoulos* in Col. 1:7 (*sōma* in sense of *doulos*). *Fellow-partakers (sunmetocha).* Another late and rare word (Josephus). Only here in N.T. In one papyrus in sense of joint possessor of a house.

7. For this verse see Col. 1:25; Eph. 1:19f.; 3:2.

8. *Unto me who am less than the least of all saints (emoi tōi elachistoterōi pantōn hagiōn).* Dative case *emoi* with *elothē.* The peculiar form *elachistoterōi* (in apposition with *emoi*) is a comparative (*-teros*) formed on the superlative *elachistos.* This sort of thing was already done in the older Greek like *eschatoteros* in Xenophon. It became more common in the *Koiné.* So the double comparative *meizoteran* in III John 4. The case of *hagiōn* is ablative. This was not mock humility (15:19), for on occasion Paul stood up for his rights as an apostle (II Cor. 11:5). *The unsearchable riches of Christ (to anexichniaston ploutos tou Christou).* *Anexichniastos* (*a* privative and verbal of *exichniazō,* to track out, *ex* and *ichnos,* track) appears first in Job 5:9; 9:10. Paul apparently got it from Job. Nowhere else in N.T. except Rom. 11:33. In later Christian writers. Paul undertook to track out the untrackable in Christ.

9. *To make see (phōtisai).* First aorist active infinitive of *photizō,* late verb, to turn the light on. With the eyes of the heart enlightened (Eph. 1:18) one can then turn the light for others to see. See Col. 1:26.

10. *To the intent that (hina).* Final clause. *Might be made known (gnōristhēi).* First aorist passive subjunctive of *gnōrizō* with *hina.* The mystery was made known to Paul (3:3) and now he wants it blazoned forth to all powers (Gnostic aeons or what not). *Through the church (dia tēs ekklēsias).* The wonderful body of Christ described in chapter 2. *The manifold wisdom of God (hē polupoikilos sophia tou theou).* Old and rare word, much-variegated,

with many colours. Only here in N.T. *Poikilos* (variegated) is more common (Matt. 4:24).

11. *According to the eternal purpose (kata prothesin tōn aiōnōn).* "According to the purpose (1:11) of the ages." God's purpose runs on through the ages. "Through the ages one eternal purpose runs."

12. *In confidence (en pepoithēsei).* Late and rare word from *pepoitha.* See II Cor. 1:15. *Through our faith in him (dia tēs pisteōs autou).* Clearly objective genitive *autou* (in him).

13. *That ye faint not (mē enkakein).* Object infinitive with *mē* after *aitoumai.* The infinitive (present active) *enkakein* is a late and rare word (see already Luke 18:1; II Thess. 3:13; II Cor. 4:1, 16; Gal. 6:9) and means to behave badly in, to give in to evil (*en, kakos*). Paul urges all his apostolic authority to keep the readers from giving in to evil because of his tribulations for them. *Your glory (doxa humōn).* As they could see.

14. *I bow my knees (kamptō ta gonata mou).* He now prays whether he had at first intended to do so at 3:1 or not. Calvin supposes that Paul knelt as he dictated this prayer, but this is not necessary. This was a common attitude in prayer (Luke 22:41; Acts 7:40; 20:36; 21:5), though standing is also frequent (Mark 11:25; Luke 18:11, 13).

15. *Every family (pāsa patria).* Old word (*patra* is the usual form) from *patēr,* descent from a common ancestor as a tribe or race. Some take it here as = *patrotēs,* fatherhood, but that is most unlikely. Paul seems to mean that all the various classes of men on earth and of angels in heaven get the name of family from God the Father of all.

16. *That he would grant you (hina dōi humin).* Sub-final clause with *hina* and the second aorist active subjunctive of *didōmi,* to give. There are really five petitions in this greatest of all Paul's prayers (one already in 1:16–23), two by the infinitives after *hina dōi (krataiōthēnai, katoikēsai),* two infinitives after *hina exischusēte (katalabesthai, gnōnai),* and the last clause *hina plērōthēte.* Nowhere does Paul sound such depths of spiritual emotion or rise to such heights of spiritual passion as here. The whole seems to be coloured with "the riches of His glory." *That ye may be strengthened (krataiōthēnai).* First aorist passive infinitive of *krataioō,*

late and rare (LXX, N.T.) from *krataios*, late form from *kratos* (strength). See Luke 1:80. Paul adds *dunamei* (with the Spirit). Instrumental case. *In the inward man (eis ton esō anthrōpon)*. Same expression in II Cor. 4:16 (in contrast with the outward *exō*, man) and in Rom. 7:22.

17. *That Christ may dwell (katoikēsai ton Christon)*. Another infinitive (first aorist active) after *hina dōi*. *Katoikeō* is an old verb to make one's home, to be at home. Christ (*Christon* accusative of general reference) is asked to make his home in our hearts. This is the ideal, but a deal of fixing would have to be done in our hearts for Christ. *Being rooted and grounded in love (en agapēi errizōmenoi kai tethemeliō-menoi)*. But it is not certain whether *en agapēi* should go with these participles or with the preceding infinitive *katoikēsai* (dwell). Besides, these two perfect passive participles (from *rizoō*, old verb, in N.T. only here and Col. 2:7, and from *themelioō*, see also Col. 1:23) are in the nominative case and are to be taken with *hina exischusēte* and are pro-leptically placed before *hina*. Verse 18 should really begin with these participles. Paul piles up metaphors (dwelling, rooted, grounded).

18. *That ye may be strong (hina exischusēte)*. Sub-final clause again with *hina* and the first aorist active subjunctive of *exischuō*, a late and rare compound (from *ex, ischuō*) to have full strength. Here only in N.T. *To apprehend (katala-besthai)*. Second aorist middle infinitive of *katalambanō*, old and common verb, to lay hold of effectively (*kata-*), here with the mind, to grasp (Acts 25:25). *With all the saints (sun pasin tois hagiois)*. No isolated privilege. Fellowship open to all. Paul gives a rectangular (four dimension) measure of love (breadth *platos*, length *mēkos*, height *hupsos*, depth *bathos*, all common enough words).

19. *And to know (gnōnai te)*. Second aorist active infin-itive with *exischusēte*. *Which passeth knowledge (tēn huper-ballousan tēs gnōseōs)*. Ablative case *gnōseōs* after *huper-ballousan* (from *huperballō*). All the same Paul dares to scale this peak. *That ye may be filled with all the fulness of God (hina plērōthēte eis pān to plērōma tou theou)*. Final clause again (third use of *hina* in the sentence) with first aorist passive subjunctive of *plēroō* and the use of *eis* after it. One hesitates to comment on this sublime climax in

Paul's prayer, the ultimate goal for followers of Christ in harmony with the injunction in Matt. 5:48 to be perfect (*teleioi*) as our heavenly Father is perfect. There is nothing that any one can add to these words. One can turn to Rom. 8:29 again for our final likeness to God in Christ.

20. *That is able to do* (*tōi dunamenōi poiēsai*). Dative case of the articular participle (present middle of *dunamai*). Paul is fully aware of the greatness of the blessings asked for, but the Doxology ascribes to God the power to do them for us. *Above all* (*huper panta*). Not simply *panta*, but *huper* beyond and above all. *Exceedingly abundantly* (*huperekperissou*). Late and rare double compound (*huper, ek, perissou*) adverb (LXX, I Thess. 3:10; 5:13; Eph. 3:20). It suits well Paul's effort to pile Pelion on Ossa. *That we ask* (*hōn aitoumetha*). Ablative of the relative pronoun attracted from the accusative *ha* to the case of the unexpressed antecedent *toutōn*. Middle voice (*aitoumetha*) "we ask for ourselves." *Or think* (*ē nooumen*). The highest aspiration is not beyond God's "power" (*dunamin*) to bestow.

21. *In the church* (*en tēi ekklēsiāi*). The general church, the body of Christ. *And in Christ Jesus* (*kai en Christōi Iēsou*). The Head of the glorious church.

CHAPTER IV

1. *Wherewith ye were called (hēs eklēthēte).* Attraction of the relative *hēs* to the genitive of the antecedent *klēseōs* (calling) from the cognate accusative *hēn* with *eklēthēte* (first aorist passive indicative of *kaleō*, to call. For the list of virtues here see Col. 3:12. To *anechomenoi allēlōn* (Col. 3:13) Paul here adds "in love" (*en agapēi*), singled out in Col. 3:14.

3. *The unity (tēn henotēta).* Late and rare word (from *heis*, one), in Aristotle and Plutarch, though in N.T. only here and verse 13. *In the bond of peace (en tōi sundesmōi tēs eirēnēs).* In Col. 3:14 *agapē* (love) is the *sundesmos* (bond). But there is no peace without love (verse 2).

4. *One body (hen sōma).* One mystical body of Christ (the spiritual church or kingdom, cf. 1:23; 2:16). *One Spirit (hen pneuma).* One Holy Spirit, grammatical neuter gender (not to be referred to by "it," but by "he"). *In one hope (en miāi elpidi).* The same hope as a result of their calling for both Jew and Greek as shown in chapter 2.

5. *One Lord (heis Kurios).* The Lord Jesus Christ and he alone (no series of aeons). *One faith (mia pistis).* One act of trust in Christ, the same for all (Jew or Gentile), one way of being saved. *One baptism (hen baptisma).* The result of baptizing (*baptisma*), while *baptismos* is the act. Only in the N.T. (*baptismos* in Josephus) and ecclesiastical writers naturally. See Mark 10:38. There is only one act of baptism for all (Jews and Gentiles) who confess Christ by means of this symbol, not that they are made disciples by this one act, but merely so profess him, put Christ on publicly by this ordinance.

6. *One God and Father of all (heis theos kai patēr pantōn).* Not a separate God for each nation or religion. One God for all men. See here the Trinity again (Father, Jesus, Holy Spirit). *Who is over all (ho epi pantōn), and through all (kai dia pantōn), and in all (kai en pāsin).* Thus by three prepositions (*epi, dia, en*) Paul has endeavoured to express the

universal sweep and power of God in men's lives. The pronouns (*pantōn, pantōn, pāsin*) can be all masculine, all neuter, or part one or the other. The last "in all" is certainly masculine and probably all are.

7. *According to the measure of the gifts of Christ* (*kata to metron tēs dōreas tou Christou*). Each gets the gift that Christ has to bestow for his special case. See I Cor. 12:4ff.; Rom. 12:4-6.

8. *Wherefore he saith* (*dio legei*). As a confirmation of what Paul has said. No subject is expressed in the Greek and commentators argue whether it should be *ho theos* (God) or *hē graphē* (Scripture). But it comes to God after all. See Acts 2:17. The quotation is from Psa. 68:18, a Messianic Psalm of victory which Paul adapts and interprets for Christ's triumph over death. *He led captivity captive* (*ēichmalōteusen aichmalōsian*). Cognate accusative of *aichmalōsian*, late word, in N.T. only here and Rev. 13:10. The verb also (*aichmalōteuō*) is from the old word *aichmalōtos*, captive in war (in N.T. only in Luke 4:18), in LXX and only here in N.T.

9. *Now this* (*to de*). Paul picks out the verb *anabas* (second aorist active participle of *anabainō*, to go up), changes its form to *anebē* (second aorist indicative), and points the article (*to*) at it. Then he concludes that it implied a previous *katabas* (coming down). *Into the lower parts of the earth* (*eis ta katōtera tēs gēs*). If the *anabas* is the Ascension of Christ, then the *katabas* would be the Descent (Incarnation) to earth and *tēs gēs* would be the genitive of apposition. What follows in verse 10 argues for this view. Otherwise one must think of the death of Christ (the descent into Hades of Acts 2:31).

10. *Is the same also* (*autos estin*). Rather, "the one who came down (*ho katabas*, the Incarnation) is himself also the one who ascended (*ho anabas*, the Ascension)." *Far above* (*huperanō*). See 1:21. *All the heavens* (*pantōn tōn ouranōn*). Ablative case after *huperanō*. For the plural used of Christ's ascent see Heb. 4:14; 7:27. Whether Paul has in mind the Jewish notion of a graded heaven like the third heaven in II Cor. 12:2 or the seven heavens idea one does not know. *That he might fill all things* (*hina plērōsēi ta panta*). This purpose we can understand, the supremacy of Christ (Col. 2:9f.).

11. *And he gave* (*kai autos edōken*). First aorist active indicative of *didōmi*. In I Cor. 12:28 Paul uses *etheto* (more common verb, appointed), but here repeats *edōken* from the quotation in verse 8. There are four groups (*tous men, tous de* three times, as the direct object of *edōken*). The titles are in the predicate accusative (*apostolous, prophētas, poimenas kai didaskalous*). Each of these 'words occurs in I Cor. 12:28 (which see for discussion) except *poimenas* (shepherds). This word *poimēn* is from a root meaning to protect. Jesus said the good shepherd lays down his life for the sheep (John 10:11) and called himself the Good Shepherd. In Heb. 13:20 Christ is the Great Shepherd (cf. I Peter 2:25). Only here are preachers termed shepherds (Latin *pastores*) in the N.T. But the verb *poimainō*, to shepherd, is employed by Jesus to Peter (John 21:16), by Peter to other ministers (I Peter 5:2), by Paul to the elders (bishops) of Ephesus (Acts 20:28). Here Paul groups "shepherds and teachers" together. All these gifts can be found in one man, though not always. Some have only one.

12. *For the perfecting* (*pros ton katartismon*). Late and rare word (in Galen in medical sense, in papyri for house-furnishing), only here in N.T., though *katartisis* in II Cor. 13:9, both from *katartizō*, to mend (Matt. 4:21; Gal. 6:1). "For the mending (repair) of the saints." *Unto the building up* (*eis oikodomēn*). See 2:21. This is the ultimate goal in all these varied gifts, "building up."

13. *Till we all attain* (*mechri katantēsōmen hoi pantes*). Temporal clause with purpose idea with *mechri* and the first aorist active subjunctive of *katantaō*, late verb, to come down to the goal (Phil. 3:11). "The whole" including every individual. Hence the need of so many gifts. *Unto the unity of the faith* (*eis tēn henotēta tēs pisteōs*). "Unto oneness of faith" (of trust) in Christ (verse 3) which the Gnostics were disturbing. *And of the knowledge of the Son of God* (*kai tēs epignōseōs tou huiou tou theou*). Three genitives in a chain dependent also on *tēn henotēta*, "the oneness of full (*epi-*) knowledge of the Son of God," in opposition to the Gnostic vagaries. *Unto a full-grown man* (*eis andra teleion*). Same figure as in 2:15 and *teleios* in sense of adult as opposed to *nēpioi* (infants) in 14. *Unto the measure of the stature* (*eis metron hēlikias*). So apparently *hēlikia* here as in Luke 2:52,

not age (John 9:21). Boys rejoice in gaining the height of a man. But Paul adds to this idea "the fulness of Christ" (*tou plērōmatos tou Christou*), like "the fulness of God" in 3:19. And yet some actually profess to be "perfect" with a standard like this to measure by! No pastor has finished his work when the sheep fall so far short of the goal.

14. *That we may be no longer children* (*hina mēketi ōmen nēpioi*). Negative final clause with present subjunctive. Some Christians are quite content to remain "babes" in Christ and never cut their eye-teeth (Heb. 5:11-14), the victims of every charlatan who comes along. *Tossed to and fro* (*kludōnizomenoi*). Present passive participle of *kludōnizomai*, late verb from *kludōn* (wave, James 1:6), to be agitated by the waves, in LXX, only here in N.T. One example in Vettius Valens. *Carried about* (*peripheromenoi*). Present passive participle of *peripherō*, old verb, to carry round, whirled round "by every wind (*anemōi*, instrumental case) of teaching." In some it is all wind, even like a hurricane or a tornado. If not anchored by full knowledge of Christ, folks are at the mercy of these squalls. *By the sleight* (*en tēi kubiāi*). "In the deceit," "in the throw of the dice" (*kubia*, from *kubos*, cube), sometimes cheating. *In craftiness* (*en panourgiāi*). Old word from *panourgos* (*pan, ergon*, any deed, every deed), cleverness, trickiness. *After the wiles of error* (*pros tēn methodian tēs planēs*). *Methodia* is from *methodeuō* (*meta, hodos*) to follow after or up, to practise deceit, and occurs nowhere else (Eph. 4:13; 6:11) save in late papyri in the sense of method. The word *planēs* (wandering like our "planet") adds to the evil idea in the word. Paul has covered the whole ground in this picture of Gnostic error.

15. *In love* (*en agapēi*). If truth were always spoken only in love! *May grow into him* (*auxēsōmen eis auton*). Supply *hina* and then note the final use of the first aorist active subjunctive. It is the metaphor of verse 13 (the full-grown man). We are the body and Christ is the Head. We are to grow up to his stature.

16. *From which* (*ex hou*). Out of which as the source of energy and direction. *Fitly framed* (*sunarmologoumenon*). See 2:21 for this verb. *Through that which every joint supplieth* (*dia pasēs haphēs tēs epichorēgias*). Literally, "through every joint of the supply." See Col. 2:19 for *haphē* and Phil.

1:19 for the late word *epichorēgia* (only two examples in N.T.) from *epichorēgeō*, to supply (Col. 2:19). *In due measure (en metrōi)*. Just "in measure" in the Greek, but the assumption is that each part of the body functions properly in its own sphere. *Unto the building up of itself (eis oikodomēn heautou)*. Modern knowledge of cell life in the human body greatly strengthens the force of Paul's metaphor. This is the way the body grows by coöperation under the control of the head and all "in love" *(en agapēi)*.

17. *That ye no longer walk (mēketi humas peripatein)*. Infinitive (present active) in indirect command (not indirect assertion) with accusative *humas* of general reference. *In vanity of their mind (en mataiotēti tou noos autōn)*. "In emptiness (from *mataios*, late and rare word. See Rom. 8:20) of their intellect (*noos*, late form for earlier genitive *nou*, from *nous*)."

18. *Being darkened (eskotōmenoi ontes)*. Periphrastic perfect passive participle of *skotoō*, old verb from *skotos* (darkness), in N.T. only here and Rev. 9:2; 16:10. *In their understanding (tēi dianoiāi)*. Locative case. Probably *dianoia (dia, nous)* includes the emotions as well as the intellect *(nous)*. It is possible to take *ontes* with *apēllotriōmenoi* (see 2:12) which would then be periphrastic (instead of *eskotōmenoi*) perfect passive participle. *From the life of God (tēs zōēs tou theou)*. Ablative case *zōēs* after *apēllotriōmenoi* (2:12). *Because of the ignorance (dia tēn agnoian)*. Old word from *agnoeō*, not to know. Rare in N.T. See Acts 3:17. *Hardening (pōrōsin)*. Late medical term (Hippocrates) for callous hardening. Only other N.T. examples are Mark 3:5; Rom. 11:25.

19. *Being past feeling (apēlgēkotes)*. Perfect active participle of *apalgeō*, old word to cease to feel pain, only here in N.T. *To lasciviousness (tēi aselgeiāi)*. Unbridled lust as in II Cor. 12:21; Gal. 5:19. *To work all uncleanness (eis ergasïan akatharsias pasēs)*. Perhaps prostitution, "for a trading (or work) in all uncleanness." Certainly Corinth and Ephesus could qualify for this charge. *With greediness (en pleonexiāi)*. From *pleonektēs*, one who always wants more whether money or sexual indulgence as here. The two vices are often connected in the N.T.

20. *But ye did not so learn Christ (Humeis de ouch houtōs*

emathete ton Christon). In sharp contrast to pagan life
(houtōs). Second aorist active indicative of *manthanō.*
21. *If so be that (ei ge).* "If indeed." Condition of first
class with aorist indicatives here, assumed to be true *(ēkousate kai edidachthēte).* *Even as truth is in Jesus (kathōs estin
alētheia en tōi Iēsou).* It is not clear what Paul's precise
idea is here. The Cerinthian Gnostics did distinguish between the man Jesus and the aeon Christ. Paul here identifies
Christ (verse 20) and Jesus (verse 21). At any rate he flatly
affirms that there is "truth in Jesus" which is in direct opposition to the heathen manner of life and which is further
explained by the epexegetical infinitives that follow *(apothesthai, ananeousthai de, kai endusasthai).*
22. *That ye put away (apothesthai).* Second aorist middle
infinitive of *apotithēmi* with the metaphor of putting off
clothing or habits as *apothesthe* in Col. 3:8 (which see) with
the same addition of "the old man" *(ton palaion anthrōpon)*
as in Col. 3:9. For *anastrophēn* (manner of life) see Gal. 1:13.
Which waxeth corrupt (ton phtheiromenon). Either present
middle or passive participle of *phtheirō,* but it is a process
of corruption (worse and worse).
23. *That ye be renewed (ananeousthai).* Present passive
infinitive (epexegetical, like *apothesthai,* of *alētheia en tōi
Iēsou)* and to be compared with *anakainoumenon* in Col.
3:10. It is an old verb, *ananeoō,* to make new (young) again,
though only here in N.T. *The spirit (tōi pneumati).* Not
the Holy Spirit, but the human spirit.
24. *Put on (endusasthai).* First aorist middle infinitive of
enduō (-nō), for which see Col. 3:10. *The new man (ton
kainon anthrōpon).* "The brand-new (see 2:15) man,"
though *ton neon* in Col. 3:10. *After God (kata theon).* After
the pattern God, the new birth, the new life in Christ, destined to be like God in the end (Rom. 8:29).
25. *Wherefore (dio).* Because of putting off the old man,
and putting on the new man. *Putting away (apothemenoi).*
Second aorist middle participle of *apotithēmi* (verse 22).
Lying (pseudos), truth (alētheian) in direct contrast. *Each
one (hekastos).* Partitive apposition with *laleite.* See Col.
3:8 *mē pseudesthe.*
26. *Be ye angry and sin not (orgizesthe kai mē hamartanete).*
Permissive imperative, not a command to be angry. Pro-

hibition against sinning as the peril in anger. Quotation
from Psa. 4:4. *Let not the sun go down upon your wrath (ho
hēlios mē epiduetō epi parorgismōi).* Danger in settled mood
of anger. *Parorgismos* (provocation), from *parorgizō*, to
exasperate to anger, occurs only in LXX and here in N.T.
27. *Neither give place to the devil (mēde didote topon tōi
diabolōi).* Present active imperative in prohibition, either
stop doing it or do not have the habit. See Rom. 12:19 for
this idiom. 28. *Steal no more (mēketi kleptetō).* Clearly here, cease
stealing (present active imperative with *mēketi*). *The thing
that is good (to agathon).* "The good thing" opposed to his
stealing and "with his hands" (*tais chersin*, instrumental
case) that did the stealing. See II Thess. 3:10. Even un-
employment is no excuse for stealing. *To give (metadidonai).*
Present active infinitive of *metadidōmi*, to share with one.
29. *Corrupt (sapros).* Rotten, putrid, like fruit (Matt.
7:17f.), fish (Matt. 13:48), here the opposite of *agathos*
(good). *For edifying as the need may be (pros oikodomēn tēs
chreias).* "For the build-up of the need," "for supplying
help when there is need." Let no other words come out.
That it may give (hina dōi). For this elliptical use of *hina*
see on 5:33.
30. *Grieve not the Holy Spirit of God (mē lupeite to pneuma
to hagion tou theou).* "Cease grieving" or "do not have the
habit of grieving." Who of us has not sometimes grieved
the Holy Spirit? *In whom (en hōi).* Not "in which." *Ye
were sealed (esphragisthēte).* See 1:13 for this verb, and 1:14
for *apolutrōseōs*, the day when final redemption is realized.
31. *Bitterness (pikria).* Old word from *pikros* (bitter), in
N.T. only here and Acts 8:23; Rom. 3:14; Heb. 12:15.
Clamour (kraugē). Old word for outcry (Matt. 25:6; Luke
1:42). See Col. 3:8 for the other words. *Be put away (ar-
thetō).* First aorist passive imperative of *airō*, old verb, to
pick up and carry away, to make a clean sweep.
32. *Be ye kind to one another (ginesthe eis allēlous chrēstoi).*
Present middle imperative of *ginomai*, "keep on becoming
kind (*chrēstos*, used of God in Rom. 2:4) toward one another." See Col. 3:12f. *Tenderhearted (eusplagchnoi).* Late
word (*eu, splagchna*) once in Hippocrates, in LXX, here and
I Peter 3:8 in N.T.

CHAPTER V

1. *Imitators of God (mimētai tou theou).* This old word from *mimeomai* Paul boldly uses. If we are to be like God, we must imitate him.

2. *An offering and a sacrifice to God (prosphoran kai thusian tōi theōi).* Accusative in apposition with *heauton* (himself). Christ's death was an offering to God "in our behalf" (*huper hēmōn*) not an offering to the devil (Anselm), a ransom (*lutron*) as Christ himself said (Matt. 20:28), Christ's own view of his atoning death. *For an odour of a sweet smell (eis osmēn euōdias).* Same words in Phil. 4:18 from Lev. 4:31 (of the expiatory offering). Paul often presents Christ's death as a propitiation (Rom. 3:25) as in 1 John 2:2.

3. *Or covetousness (ē pleonexia).* In bad company surely. Debasing like sensuality. *As becometh saints (kathōs prepei hagiois).* It is "unbecoming" for a saint to be sensual or covetous.

4. *Filthiness (aischrotēs).* Old word from *aischros* (base), here alone in N.T. *Foolish talking (mōrologia).* Late word from *mōrologos (mōros, logos),* only here in N.T. *Jesting (eutrapelia).* Old word from *eutrapelos (eu, trepō,* to turn) nimbleness of wit, quickness in making repartee (so in Plato and Plutarch), but in low sense as here ribaldry, scurrility, only here in N.T. All of these disapproved vices are *hapax legomena* in the N.T. *Which are not befitting (ha ouk anēken).* Same idiom (imperfect with word of propriety about the present) in Col. 3:18. Late MSS. read *ta ouk anēkonta* like *ta mē kathēkonta* in Rom. 1:28.

5. *Ye know of a surety (iste ginōskontes).* The correct text has *iste,* not *este.* It is the same form for present indicative (second person plural) and imperative, probably indicative here, "ye know." But why *ginōskontes* added? Probably, "ye know recognizing by your own experience." *No (pās— ou).* Common idiom in the N.T. like the Hebrew=*oudeis* (Robertson, *Grammar,* p. 732). *Covetous man (pleonektēs, pleon echō).* Old word, in N.T. only here and I Cor. 5:10f.;

542

6:10. *Which is (ho estin).* So Aleph B. A D K L have *hos* (who), but *ho* is right. See Col. 3:14 for this use of *ho* (which thing is). On *eidōlolatrēs* (idolater) see I Cor. 5:10f. *In the Kingdom of Christ and God (en tēi basileiāi tou Christou kai theou).* Certainly the same kingdom and Paul may here mean to affirm the deity of Christ by the use of the one article with *Christou kai theou.* But Sharp's rule cannot be insisted on here because *theos* is often definite without the article like a proper name. Paul did teach the deity of Christ and may do it here.

6. *With empty words (kenois lŏgois).* Instrumental case. Probably Paul has in mind the same Gnostic praters as in Col. 2:4f. See 2:2.

7. *Partakers with them (sunmetochoi autōn).* Late double compound, only here in N.T., joint (*sun*) shares with (*metochoi*) them (*autōn*). These Gnostics.

8. *But now light (nŭn de phōs).* Jesus called his disciples the light of the world (Matt. 5:14).

9. *The fruit of light (ho karpos tou phōtos).* Two metaphors (fruit, light) combined. See Gal. 5:22 for "the fruit of the Spirit." The late MSS. have "spirit" here in place of "light." *Goodness (agathosunēi).* Late and rare word from *agathos.* See II Thess. 1:11; Gal. 5:22.

10. *Proving (dokimazontes).* Testing and so proving.

11. *Have no fellowship with (mē sunkoinōneite).* No partnership with, present imperative with *mē.* Followed by associative instrumental case *ergois* (works). *Unfruitful (akarpois).* Same metaphor of verse 9 applied to darkness (*skotos*). *Reprove (elegchete).* Convict by turning the light on the darkness.

12. *In secret (kruphēi).* Old adverb, only here in N.T. Sin loves the dark. *Even to speak of (kai legein).* And yet one must sometimes speak out, turn on the light, even if to do so is disgraceful (*aischron,* like I Cor. 11:6).

13. *Are made manifest by the light (hupo tou phōtos phaneroutai).* Turn on the light. Often the preacher is the only man brave enough to turn the light on the private sins of men and women or even those of a community.

14. *Wherefore he saith (dio legei).* Apparently a free adaptation of Isa. 26:19 and 60:1. The form *anasta* for *anastēthi* (second person singular imperative second aorist active of *anistēmi*) occurs in Acts 12:7. *Shall shine (epi-phausei).* Future active of *epiphauskō*, a form occurring in Job (25:5; 31:26), a variation of *epiphōskō.* The last line suggests the possibility that we have here the fragment of an early Christian hymn like I Tim. 3:16.

15. *Carefully (akribōs).* Aleph B 17 put *akribōs* before *pōs* (how) instead of *pōs akribōs* (how exactly ye walk) as the Textus Receptus has it. On *akribōs* (from *akribēs*) see Matt. 2:8; Luke 1:3. *Unwise (asophoi).* Old adjective, only here in N.T.

16. *Redeeming the time (exagorazomenoi ton kairon).* As in Col. 4:5 which see.

17. *Be ye not foolish (mē ginesthe aphrones).* "Stop. becoming foolish."

18. *Be not drunken with wine (mē methuskesthe oinōi).* Present passive imperative of *methuskō*, old verb to intoxicate. Forbidden as a habit and to stop it also if guilty. Instrumental case *oinōi. Riot (asōtia).* Old word from *asōtos* (adverb *asōtōs* in Luke 15:13), in N.T. only here, Titus 1:6; I Peter 4:4. *But be filled with the Spirit (alla plērousthe en pneumati).* In contrast to a state of intoxication with wine.

19. *To the Lord (tōi Kuriōi).* The Lord Jesus. In Col. 3:16 we have *tōi theōi* (to God) with all these varieties of praise, another proof of the deity of Christ. See Col. 3:16 for discussion.

20. *In the name of our Lord Jesus Christ (en onomati tou Kuriou hēmōn Iēsou Christou).* Jesus had told the disciples to use his name in prayer (John 16:23f.). *To God, even the Father (tōi theōi kai patri).* Rather, "the God and Father."

21. *Subjecting yourselves to one another (hupotassomenoi allēlois).* Present middle participle of *hupotassō*, old military figure to line up under (Col. 3:18). The construction here is rather loose, coördinate with the preceding participles of praise and prayer. It is possible to start a new paragraph here and regard *hupotassomenoi* as an independent participle like an imperative.

22. *Be in subjection.* Not in the Greek text of B and Jerome knew of no MS. with it. K L and most MSS. have *hupotassesthe* like Col. 3:18, while Aleph A P have *hupotassesthōsan* (let them be subject to). But the case of *andrasin* (dative) shows that the verb is understood from verse 21

if not written originally. *Idiois* (*own*) is genuine here, though not in Col. 3:18. *As unto the Lord* (*hōs tōi Kuriōi*). So here instead of *hōs anēken en Kuriōi* of Col. 3:18.

23. *For the husband is the head of the wife* (*hoti anēr estin kephalē tēs gunaikos*). "For a husband is head of the (his) wife." No article with *anēr* or *kephalē*. *As Christ also is the head of the church* (*hōs kai ho Christos kephalē tēs ekklēsias*). No article with *kephalē*, "as also Christ is head of the church." This is the comparison, but with a tremendous difference which Paul hastens to add either in an appositional clause or as a separate sentence. *Himself the saviour of the body* (*autos sōtēr tou sōmatos*). He means the church as the body of which Christ is head and Saviour.

24. *But* (*alla*). Perhaps, "nevertheless," in spite of the difference just noted. Once again the verb *hupotassō* has to be supplied in the principal clause before *tois andrasin* either as indicative (*hupotassontai*) or as imperative (*hupotassesthōsan*).

25. *Even as Christ also loved the church* (*kathōs kai ho Christos ēgapēsen tēn ekklēsian*). This is the wonderful new point not in Col. 3:19 that lifts this discussion of the husband's love for his wife to the highest plane.

26. *That he might sanctify it* (*hina autēn hagiasēi*). Purpose clause with *hina* and the first aorist active subjunctive of *hagiazō*. Jesus stated this as his longing and his prayer (John 17:17–19). This was the purpose of Christ's death (verse 25). *Having cleansed it* (*katharisas*). First aorist active participle of *katharizō*, to cleanse, either simultaneous action or antecedent. *By the washing of water* (*tōi loutrōi tou hudatos*). If *loutron* only means bath or bathing-place (=*loutron*), then *loutrōi* is in the locative. If it can mean bathing or washing, it is in the instrumental case. The usual meaning from Homer to the papyri is the bath or bathing-place, though some examples seem to mean bathing or washing. Salmond doubts if there are any clear instances. The only other N.T. example of *loutron* is in Titus 3:5. The reference here seems to be to the baptismal bath (immersion) of water, "in the bath of water." See I Cor. 6:11 for the bringing together of *apelousasthe* and *hēgiasthēte*. Neither there nor here does Paul mean that the cleansing or sanctification took place in the bath save in a symbolic fashion as in Rom.

6:4–6. Some think that Paul has also a reference to the bath of the bride before marriage. Still more difficult is the phrase "with the word" (*en rēmati*). In John 17:17 Jesus connected "truth" with "sanctify." That is possible here, though it may also be connected with *katharisas* (having cleansed). Some take it to mean the baptismal formula.

27. *That he might present* (*hina parastēsēi*). Final clause with *hina* and first aorist active subjunctive of *paristēmi* (see Col. 1:22 for parallel) as in II Cor. 11:2 of presenting the bride to the bridegroom. Note both *autos* (himself) and *heautōi* (to himself). *Glorious* (*endoxon*). Used of splendid clothing in Luke 7:25. *Spot* (*spilos*). Late word, in N.T. only here and II Peter 2:13, but *spiloō*, to defile in James 3:6; Jude 23. *Wrinkle* (*rutida*). Old word from *ruō*, to contract, only here in N.T. *But that it should be holy and without blemish* (*all' hina ēi hagia kai amōmos*). Christ's goal fcʳ the church, his bride and his body, both negative purity and positive.

28. *Even so ought* (*houtōs opheilousin*). As Christ loves the church (his body). And yet some people actually say that Paul in I Cor. 7 gives a degrading view of marriage. How can one say that after reading Eph. 5:22–33 where the noblest picture of marriage ever drawn is given?

29. *Nourisheth* (*ektrephei*). Old compound with perfective sense of *ek* (to nourish up to maturity and on). In N.T. only here and 6:4. *Cherisheth* (*thalpei*). Late and rare word, once in a marriage contract in a papyrus. In N.T. only here and I Thess. 2:7. Primarily it means to warm (Latin *foveo*), then to foster with tender care as here. *Even as Christ also* (*kathōs kai ho Christos*). Relative (correlative) adverb pointing back to *houtōs* at the beginning of the sentence (verse 28) and repeating the statement in verse 25.

30. *Of his flesh and of his bones* (*ek tēs sarkos autou kai ek tōn osteōn autou*). These words are in the Textus Receptus (Authorized Version) supported by D G L P cursives Syriac, etc., though wanting in Aleph A B 17 Bohairic. Certainly not genuine.

31. *For this cause* (*anti toutou*). "Answering to this" = *heneken toutou* of Gen. 2:24, in the sense of *anti* seen in *anth' hōn* (Luke 12:3). This whole verse is a practical quotation and application of the language to Paul's argument here.

In Matt. 19:5 Jesus quotes Gen. 2:24. It seems absurd to make Paul mean Christ here by *anthrōpos* (man) as some commentators do.

32. *This mystery is great (to mustērion touto mega estin)*. For the word "mystery" see 1:9. Clearly Paul means to say that the comparison of marriage to the union of Christ and the church is the mystery. He makes that plain by the next words. *But I speak (egō de legō)*. "Now I mean." Cf. I Cor. 7:29; 15:50. *In regard of Christ and of the church (eis Christon kai [eis] tēn ekklēsian)*. "With reference to Christ and the church." That is all that *eis* here means.

33. *Nevertheless (plēn)*. "Howbeit," not to dwell unduly (Abbott) on the matter of Christ and the church. *Do ye also severally love (kai humeis hoi kath' hena hekastos agapātō)*. An unusual idiom. The verb *agapātō* (present active imperative) agrees with *hekastos* and so is third singular instead of *agapāte* (second plural) like *humeis*. The use of *hoi kath' hena* after *humeis* = "ye one by one" and then *hekastos* takes up (individualizes) the "one" in partitive apposition and in the third person. *Let the wife see that she fear (hē gunē hina phobētai)*. There is no verb in the Greek for "let see" (*blepetō*). For this use of *hina* with the subjunctive as a practical imperative without a principal verb (an elliptical imperative) see Mark 5:23; Matt. 20:32; I Cor. 7:29; II Cor. 8:7; Eph. 4:29; 5:33 (Robertson, *Grammar*, p. 994). "Fear" (*phobētai*, present middle subjunctive) here is "reverence."

CHAPTER VI

1. *Right* (*dikaion*). In Col. 3:20 it is *euareston* (well-pleasing).

2. *Which* (*hētis*). "Which very" = "for such is." *The first commandment with promise* (*entolē prōtē en epaggeliāi*). *En* here means "accompanied by" (Alford). But why "with a promise"? The second has a general promise, but the fifth alone (Ex. 20:12) has a specific promise. Perhaps that is the idea. Some take it to be first because in the order of time it was taught first to children, but the addition of *en epaggeliāi* here to *prōtē* points to the other view.

3. *That it may be well with thee* (*hina eu soi genētai*). From Ex. 20:12, "that it may happen to thee well." *And thou mayest live long on the earth* (*kai esēi makrochronios epi tēs gēs*). Here *esēi* (second person singular future middle) takes the place of *genēi* in the LXX (second person singular second aorist middle subjunctive). *Makrochronios* is a late and rare compound adjective, here only in N.T. (from LXX, Ex. 20:12).

4. *Provoke not to anger* (*mē parorgizete*). Rare compound, both N.T. examples (here and Rom. 10:19) are quotations from the LXX. The active, as here, has a causative sense. Parallel in sense with *mē erethizete* in Col. 3:21. Paul here touches the common sin of fathers. *In the chastening and admonition of the Lord* (*en paideiāi kai nouthesiāi tou kuriou*). *En* is the sphere in which it all takes place. There are only three examples in the N.T. of *paideia*, old Greek for training a *pais* (boy or girl) and so for the general education and culture of the child. Both papyri and inscriptions give examples of this original and wider sense (Moulton and Milligan, *Vocabulary*). It is possible, as Thayer gives it, that this is the meaning here in Eph. 6:4. In II Tim. 3:16 adults are included also in the use. In Heb. 12:5, 7, 11 the narrower sense of "chastening" appears which some argue for here. At any rate *nouthesia* (from *nous*, *tithēmi*), common from Aristophanes on, does have the idea of correction. In N.T. only here and I Cor. 10:11; Titus 3:10.

5. *With fear and trembling* (*meta phobou kai tromou*). This addition to Col. 3:22.

6. *But as servants of Christ* (*all' hōs douloi Christou*). Better "slaves of Christ" as Paul rejoiced to call himself (Phil. 1:1). *Doing the will of God* (*poiountes to thelēma tou theou*). Even while slaves of men.

7. *With good will* (*met' eunoias*). Not in Col. Old word from *eunoos*, only here in N.T. as *eunoeō* is in N.T. only in Matt. 5:25.

8. *Whatsoever good thing each one doeth* (*hekastos ean ti poiēsēi agathon*). Literally, "each one if he do anything good." Condition of third class, undetermined, but with prospect. Note use here of *agathon* rather than *adikon* (one doing wrong) in Col. 3:25. So it is a reward (*komisetai*) for good, not a penalty for wrong, though both are true, "whether he be bond or free" (*eite doulos eite eleutheros*).

9. *And forbear threatening* (*anientes tēn apeilēn*). Present active participle of *aniēmi*, old verb, to loosen up, to relax. "Letting up on threatening." *Apeilē* is old word for threat, in N.T. only here and Acts 4:29; 9:1. *Both their Master and yours* (*kai autōn kai humōn ho kurios*). He says to "the lords" (*hoi kurioi*) of the slaves. Paul is not afraid of capital nor of labour. *With him* (*par' autōi*). "By the side of him (God)."

10. *Finally* (*tou loipou*). Genitive case, "in respect of the rest," like Gal. 6:17. D G K L P have the accusative *to loipon* (as for the rest) like II Thess. 3:1; Phil. 3:1; 4:8. *Be strong in the Lord* (*endunamousthe en kuriōi*). A late word in LXX and N.T. (Acts 9:22; Rom. 4:20; Phil. 4:13), present passive imperative of *endunamoō*, from *en* and *dunamis*, to empower. See 1:10 for "in the strength of his might." Not a hendiadys.

11. *Put on* (*endusasthe*). Like 3:12. See also 4:24. *The whole armour* (*tēn panoplian*). Old word from *panoplos* (wholly armed, from *pan, hoplon*). In N.T. only Luke 11:22; Eph. 6:11, 13. Complete armour in this period included "shield, sword, lance, helmet, greaves, and breastplate" (Thayer). Our "panoply." Polybius gives this list of Thayer. Paul omits the lance (spear). Our museums preserve specimens of this armour as well as the medieval coat-of-mail. Paul adds girdle and shoes to the list of Polybius, not

armour but necessary for the soldier. Certainly Paul could claim knowledge of the Roman soldier's armour, being chained to one for some three years. *That ye may be able to stand* (*pros to dunasthai humās stēnai*). Purpose clause with *pros to* and the infinitive (*dunasthai*) with the accusative of general reference (*humās*) and the second aorist active infinitive *stēnai* (from *histēmi*) dependent on *dunasthai*. *Against* (*pros*). Facing. Another instance of *pros* meaning "against" (Col. 2:23). *The wiles of the devil* (*tas methodias tou diabolou*). See already 4:14 for this word. He is a crafty foe and knows the weak spots in the Christian's armour.

12. *Our wrestling is not* (*ouk estin hēmin hē palē*). "To us the wrestling is not." *Palē* is an old word from *pallō*, to throw, to swing (from Homer to the papyri, though here only in N.T.), a contest between two till one hurls the other down and holds him down (*katechō*). Note *pros* again (five times) in sense of "against," face to face conflict to the finish. *The world-rulers of this darkness* (*tous kosmokratoras tou skotous toutou*). This phrase occurs here alone. In John 14:30 Satan is called "the ruler of this world" (*ho archōn tou kosmou toutou*). In II Cor. 4:4 he is termed "the god of this age" (*ho theos tou aiōnos toutou*). The word *kosmokratōr* is found in the Orphic Hymns of Satan, in Gnostic writings of the devil, in rabbinical writings (transliterated) of the angel of death, in inscriptions of the Emperor Caracalla. These "world-rulers" are limited to "this darkness" here on earth. *The spiritual hosts of wickedness* (*ta pneumatika tēs ponērias*). No word for "hosts" in the Greek. Probably simply, "the spiritual things (or elements) of wickedness." *Ponēria* (from *ponēros*) is depravity (Matt. 22:18; I Cor. 5:8). *In the heavenly places* (*en tois epouraniois*). Clearly so here. Our "wrestling" is with foes of evil natural and supernatural. We sorely need "the panoply of God" (furnished by God).

13. *Take up* (*analabete*). Second aorist active imperative of *analambanō*, old word and used (*analabōn*) of "picking up" Mark in II Tim. 4:11. *That ye may be able to withstand* (*hina dunēthēte antistēnai*). Final clause with *hina* and first aorist passive subjunctive of *dunamai* with *antistēnai* (second aorist active infinitive of *anthistēmi*, to stand face to face, against). *And having done all to stand* (*kai hapanta katergasa*

menoi stēnai). After the fight (wrestle) is over to stand (*stēnai*) as victor in the contest. Effective aorist here.

14. *Stand therefore* (*stēte oun*). Second aorist active imperative of *histēmi* (intransitive like the others). Ingressive aorist here, "Take your stand therefore" (in view of the arguments made). *Having girded your loins with truth* (*perizōsamenoi tēn osphun humōn en alētheiāi*). First aorist middle participle (antecedent action) of *perizōnnuō*, old verb, to gird around, direct middle (gird yourselves) in Luke 12:37; but indirect here with accusative of the thing, "having girded your own loins." So *endusamenoi* (having put on) is indirect middle participle. *The breast-plate of righteousness* (*ton thōraka tēs dikaiosunēs*). Old word for breast and then for breastplate. Same metaphor of righteousness as breastplate in I Thess. 5:8.

15. *Having shod* (*hupodēsamenoi*). "Having bound under" (sandals). First aorist middle participle of *hupodeō*, old word, to bind under (Mark 6:9; Acts 12:8, only other N.T. example). *With the preparation* (*en hetoimasiāi*). Late word from *hetoimazō*, to make ready, only here in N.T. Readiness of mind that comes from the gospel whose message is peace.

16. *Taking up* (*analabontes*). See verse 13. *The shield of faith* (*ton thureon tēs pisteōs*). Late word in this sense a large stone against the door in Homer, from *thura*, door, large and oblong (Latin *scutum*), *aspis* being smaller and circular, only here in N.T. *To quench* (*sbesai*). First aorist active infinitive of *sbennumi*, old word, to extinguish (Matt. 12:20). *All the fiery darts* (*panta ta belē ta pepurōmena*). *Belos* is an old word for missile, dart (from *ballō*, to throw), only here in N.T. *Pepurōmena* is perfect passive participle of *puroō*, old verb, to set on fire, from *pur* (fire). These darts were sometimes ablaze in order to set fire to the enemies' clothing or camp or homes just as the American Indians used to shoot poisoned arrows.

17. *The helmet of salvation* (*tēn perikephalaian tou sōtēriou*). Late word (*peri, kephalē*, head, around the head), in Polybius, LXX, I Thess. 5:8 and Eph. 6:17 alone in N.T. *Which is the word of God* (*ho estin to rēma tou theou*). Explanatory relative (*ho*) referring to the sword (*machairan*) The sword given by the Spirit to be wielded as offensive weapon (the others defensive) by the Christian is the word of God. See

Heb. 4:12 where the word of God is called "sharper than any two-edged sword."

18. *At all seasons (en panti kairōi).* "On every occasion." Prayer is needed in this fight. The panoply of God is necessary, but so is prayer.

"Satan trembles when he sees
The weakest saint upon his knees."

19. *That utterance may be given unto me (hina moi dothēi logos).* Final clause with *hina* and first aorist passive subjunctive of *didōmi*, to give. See a like request in Col. 4:3. Paul wishes their prayer for courage for himself.

20. *For which I am an ambassador in chains (huper hou presbeuō en halusei).* "For which mystery" of the gospel (verse 19). *Presbeuō* is an old word for ambassador (from *presbus*, an old man) in N.T. only here and II Cor. 5:20. Paul is now an old man (*presbutēs*, Philemon 9) and feels the dignity of his position as Christ's ambassador though "in a chain" (*en halusei*, old word *halusis*, from *a* privative and *luō*, to loosen). Paul will wear a chain at the close of his life in Rome (II Tim. 1:16). *In it (en autōi).* In the mystery of the gospel. This is probably a second purpose (*hina*), the first for utterance (*hina dothēi*), this for boldness (*hina parrēsiasōmai*, first aorist middle subjunctive, old word to speak out boldly). See I Thess. 2:2. See Col. 4:4 for "as I ought."

21. *That ye also may know (hina eidēte kai humeis).* Final clause with *hina* and second perfect subjunctive active of *oida*. For Tychicus, see Col. 4:7f.

22. *That ye may know (hina gnōte).* Second aorist active subjunctive of *ginōskō*. Just as in Col. 4:8 he had not written *hina eidēte* in verse 21. *Our state (ta peri hēmōn).* "The things concerning us," practically the same as *ta kat' eme* of verse 21. See both phrases in Col. 4:7 and 8.

23. *Love and faith (agapē meta pisteōs).* Love of the brotherhood accompanied by faith in Christ and as an expression of it.

24. *In uncorruptness (en aphtharsiāi).* A never diminishing love. See I Cor. 15:42 for *aphtharsia*.

THE FOURTH GROUP

THE PASTORAL EPISTLES

First Timothy
Titus
Second Timothy
A.D. 65 to 68

BY WAY OF INTRODUCTION

It is necessary to discuss introductory matters concerning the three because they are common to them all. It is true that some modern scholars admit as Pauline the personal passages in II Tim. 1:15-18; 4:9-22 while they deny the genuineness of the rest. But that criticism falls by its own weight since precisely the same stylistic characteristics appear in these admitted passages as in the rest and no earthly reason can be advanced for Paul's writing mere scraps or for the omission of the other portions and the preservation of these by a second century forger.

The external evidence for the Pauline authorship is strong and conclusive (Clement, Polycarp, Irenaeus, Tertullian, Theophilus, the Muratorian Canon). "Traces of their circulation in the church before Marcion's time are clearer than those which can be found for Romans and II Corinthians" (Zahn, *Introduction to the N.T.*, tr. II, p. 85). Marcion and Tatian rejected them because of the condemnation of asceticism by Paul.

Objections on internal grounds are made on the lines laid down by Baur and followed by Renan. They are chiefly four. The "most decisive" as argued by McGiffert (*History of Christianity in the Apostolic Age*, p. 402) is that "the Christianity of the Pastoral Epistles is not the Christianity of Paul." He means as we know Paul in the other Epistles. But this charge is untrue. It is true that Paul here lists faith with the virtues, but he does that in Gal. 5:22. Nowhere does Paul give a loftier word about faith than in I Tim. 1:12-17. Another objection urged is that the ecclesiastical organization seen in the Pastoral Epistles belongs to the second century, not to the time of Paul's life. Now we have the Epistles of Ignatius in the early part of the second century in which "bishop" is placed over "elders" of which there is no trace in the New Testament (Lightfoot). A forger in the second century would certainly have reproduced the ecclesiastical organization of that century instead of the first as we have it in the Pastoral Epistles. There is only here the normal development of bishop (=elder) and deacon. A third objection is made on the ground that there is no room in Paul's life as we know it in the Acts and the other Pauline Epistles for the events alluded to in the Pastoral Epistles and it is also argued on late and inconclusive testimony that Paul was put to death A.D. 64 and had only one Roman imprisonment. If Paul was executed A.D. 64, this objection has force in it, though Bartlet (*The Apostolic Age*) tries to make room for them in the period covered by the Acts. Duncan makes the same attempt for the Pauline scraps admitted by him as belonging to the hypothecated imprisonment in Ephesus. But, if we admit the release of Paul from the first Roman imprisonment, there is ample room before his execution in A.D. 68 for the events referred to in the Pastoral Epistles and the writing of the letters (his going east to Ephesus, Macedonia, to Crete, to Troas, to Corinth, to Miletus, to Nicopolis, to Rome), including the visit to Spain before Crete once planned for (Rom. 15: 24, 28) and mentioned by Clement of Rome as a fact ("the limit of the west"). The fourth objection is that of the language in the Pastoral Epistles. Probably more men are influenced by this argument than by any other. The ablest presentation of this difficulty is made by P. N. Harrison in *The Problem of the Pastoral Epistles* (1921). Besides the arguments Dr. Harrison has printed the Greek text in a fashion to help the eye see the facts. Words not in the other Pauline Epistles are in red, Pauline phrases (from the other ten) are underlined, *hapax legomena* are marked by an asterisk. At a superficial glance one can see that the words here not in the other Pauline Epistles and the common Pauline phrases are about equal. The data as to mere words are broadly as follows according to Harrison: Words in the Pastorals, not elsewhere in the N.T. (Pastoral *hapax legomena*) 175 (168 according to Rutherford); words in the other ten Pauline Epistles not elsewhere in the N.T. 470 (627 according to Rutherford). Variations in MSS. will account for some of the difficulty of counting. Clearly there is a larger proportion of new words in the Pastorals (about twice as many) than in the other Pauline Epistles. But Harrison's tables show remarkable differences in the

other Epistles also. The average of such words per page in
Romans is 4, but 5.6 in II Corinthians, 6.2 in Philippians,
and only 4 in Philemon. Parry (*Comm.*, p. CXVIII) notes
that of the 845 words in the Pastorals as compared with
each other 278 occur only in I Tim., 96 only in Titus,
185 only in II Tim. "If vocabulary alone is taken, this
would point to separate authorship of each epistle." And
yet the same style clearly runs through all three. After all
vocabulary is not wholly a personal problem. It varies
with age in the same person and with the subject matter
also. Precisely such differences exist in the writings of
Shakespeare and Milton as critics have long ago observed.
The only problem that remains is whether the differences
are so great in the Pastoral Epistles as to prohibit the
Pauline authorship when "Paul the aged" writes on the
problem of pastoral leadership to two of the young ministers
trained by him who have to meet the same incipient Gnostic
heresy already faced in Colossians and Ephesians. My
judgment is that, all things considered, the contents and
style of the Pastoral Epistles are genuinely Pauline, mellowed
by age and wisdom and perhaps written in his own hand or
at least by the same amanuensis in all three instances. Lock
suggests Luke as the amanuensis for the Pastorals.

The conclusion of Lock is that "either they are genuine
'letters' or artificial 'Epistles'" (*Int. Crit. Comm.*, p. XXV).
If not genuine, they are forgeries in Paul's name (pseudepigraphic). "The argument from style is in favour of the
Pauline authorship, that from vocabulary strongly, though
not quite conclusively, against it" (Lock, *op. cit.*, p. XXIX).
I should put the case for the Pauline authorship more
strongly than that and shall treat them as Paul's own.
Parry (*Comm.*, p. CXIII) well says: "It is not reasonable
to expect that a private letter, addressed to a personal
friend, for his own instruction and consideration, should
exhibit the same features as a letter addressed to a community for public, oral communication."

Special Books on the Pastoral Epistles (besides Introduc-
tions to the N.T., Apostolic History, Lives of Paul, the
Epistles of Paul as a whole): Belser (1907), Bernard (*Cambridge Gr. T.*, 1899), E. F. Brown (*Westminster*, 1917),

Bowen (*Dates of P. Letters*, 1900), Dibelius (*Handbuch*, 1913), Ellicott (1883), P. Fairbairn, P. N. Harrison (*Problem of the Past. Eps.*, 1921), Harvey (1890), Hesse (*Die Entst.*, 1889), Humphreys (*Camb. B.*, 1897), Huther (1890), H. J. Holtzmann (1880), James (*Genuineness and Authorship of P. Eps.*, 1906), Köhler (*Schriften N.T.*, 2 Aufl. 1907), Knabenbauer (1913), Kraukenberg (1901), Laughlin (*Past. Eps. in Light of One Rom. Imp.*, 1905), Lilley (1901), W. Lock (*Int. & Crit. Comm.*, 1924), Lütgert (*Die Irrlehre d. P.*, 1909), Maier (*Die Hauptprobleme d. P.*, 1910), Mayer (1913), Meinertz (1913), Michaelis, W (Pastoralbriefe etc. zur Echtheitsfrage der Pastoralbriefe, 1930), Niebergall (*Handbuch*, 1909), Parry (1920), Plummer (*Exp. B.*, 1896), Pope (1901), Riggenbach (1898), Stock (*Plain Talks on*, 1914), Strachan (*Westm. N.T.*, 1910), von Soden (*Hand-Comm.*, 1891), Wace (*Sp. Comm.*, 1885), B. Weiss (*Meyer Komm.*, ed. 5, 1886), White (*Exp. Grk. T.*, 1910), Wohlenberg (*Zahn's Komm.*, 1906).

FIRST TIMOTHY

Probably a.d. 65

From Macedonia

BY WAY OF INTRODUCTION

Assuming the Pauline authorship the facts shape up after this fashion. Paul had been in Ephesus (1 Tim. 1:3) after his arrival from Rome, which was certainly before the burning of Rome in a.d. 64. He had left Timothy in charge of the work in Ephesus and has gone on into Macedonia (I Tim. 1:3), possibly to Philippi as he had hoped (Phil. 2:24). He wishes to help Timothy meet the problems of doctrine (against the Gnostics), discipline, and church training which are increasingly urgent. There are personal touches of a natural kind about Timothy's own growth and leadership. There are wise words here from the greatest of all preachers to a young minister whom Paul loved.

CHAPTER I

1. *According to the commandment (kat' epitagēn).* A late
Koiné word (Polybius, Diodorus), but a Pauline word also
in N.T. This very idiom ("by way of command") in I Cor.
7:6; II Cor. 8:8; Rom. 16:26; I Tim. 1:1; Titus 1:3. Paul
means to say that he is an apostle under orders. *Of God our
Saviour (theou sōtēros hēmōn).* Genitive case with *epitagēn.*
In the LXX *sōtēr* (old word from *sōzō* for agent in saving,
applied to deities, princes, kings, etc.) occurs 20 times, all
but two to God. The Romans called the emperor "Saviour
God." In the N.T. the designation of God as Saviour is
peculiar to Luke 1:47; Jude 25; I Tim. 1:3; 2:3; 4:10; Titus
1:3; 2:10; 3:4. In the other Epistles Paul uses it of Christ
(Phil. 3:20; Eph. 5:23) as in II Tim. 1:10. In II Pet. 1:1
we have "our God and Saviour Jesus Christ" as in Titus
2:13. *Our hope (tēs elpidos hēmōn).* Like Col. 1:27. More
than the author and object of hope, "its very substance and
foundation" (Ellicott).

2. *True (gnēsiōi).* Legitimate, not spurious. Old word
from *ginomai,* but Pauline only in N.T. (Phil. 4:3; II Cor.
8:9; Titus 1:3; 2). In Phil. 2:20 the adverb *gnēsiōs* occurs
and of Timothy again. *Christ Jesus (Christou Iēsou).* So
twice already in verse 1 and as usual in the later Epistles
(Col. 1:1; Eph. 1:1).

3. *As I exhorted (kathōs parekalesa).* There is an ellipse
of the principal clause in verse 4 (*so do I now* not being in
the Greek). *To tarry (prosmeinai).* First aorist active infinitive of *prosmenō,* old verb, attributed by Luke to Paul
in Acts 13:43. *That thou mightest charge (hina paraggeileis).*
Subfinal clause with *hina* and the first aorist active subjunctive of *paraggellō,* old verb, to transmit a message along
(*para*) from one to another. See II Thess. 3:4, 6, 10. Lock
considers this idiom here an elliptical imperative like Eph.
4:29; 5:33. *Certain men (tisin).* Dative case. Expressly
vague (no names as in 1:20), though Paul doubtless has
certain persons in Ephesus in mind. *Not to teach a different*

doctrine (*mē heterodidaskalein*). Earliest known use of this compound like *kakodidaskalein* of Clement of Rome. Only other N.T. example in 6:3. Eusebius has *heterodidaskalos*. Same idea in Gal. 1:6; II Cor. 11:4; Rom. 16:17. Perhaps coined by Paul.

4. *To give heed* (*prosechein*). With *noun* understood. Old and common idiom in N.T. especially in Luke and Acts (8:10ff.). Not in Paul's earlier Epistles. I Tim. 3:8; 4:1, 13; Titus 1:14. *To fables* (*muthois*). Dative case of old word for speech, narrative, story, fiction, falsehood. In N.T. only II Peter 1:16; I Tim. 1:4; 4:7; Titus 1:14; II Tim. 4:4. *Genealogies* (*genealogiais*). Dative of old word, in LXX, in N.T. only here and Titus 3:9. *Endless* (*aperantois*). Old verbal compound (from *a* privative and *perainō*, to go through), in LXX, only here in N.T. Excellent examples there for old words used only in the Pastorals because of the subject matter, describing the Gnostic emphasis on aeons. *Questionings* (*ekzēteseis*). "Seekings out." Late and rare compound from *ekzēteō* (itself *Koiné* word, Rom. 3:11 from LXX and in papyri). Here only in N.T. Simplex *zētēsis* in Acts 15:2; I Tim. 6:4; Titus 3:9; II Tim. 2:23. *A dispensation* (*oikonomian*). Pauline word (I Cor. 9:17; Col. 1:25; Eph. 1:9; 3:9; I Tim. 1:4), Luke 16:2–4 only other N.T. examples. *In faith* (*en pistei*). Pauline use of *pistis*.

5. *The end* (*to telos*). See Rom. 6:21; 10:4 for *telos* (the good aimed at, reached, result, end). *Love* (*agapē*). Not "questionings." Rom. 13:9. "Three conditions for the growth of love" (Parry): "Out of a pure heart" (*ek katharas kardias*, O.T. conception), "and a good conscience" (*kai suneidēseōs agathēs*, for which see Rom. 2:25), "and faith unfeigned" (*kai pisteōs anupokritou*, late compound verbal in II Cor. 6:6; Rom. 12:9).

6. *Having swerved* (*astochēsantes*). First aorist active participle of *astocheō*, compound *Koiné* verb (Polybius, Plutarch) from *astochos* (*a* privative and *stochos*, a mark), "having missed the mark." In N.T. only here, 6:21; II Tim. 2:18. With the ablative case *hōn* (which). *Have turned aside* (*exetrapēsan*). Second aorist passive indicative of *ektrepō*, old and common verb, to turn or twist out or aside. In medical sense in Heb. 12:13. As metaphor in I Tim. 1:6;

6:20; II Tim. 4:4. *Vain talking (mataiologian)*. Late word from *mataiologos*, only here in N.T., in the literary *Koiné*.

7. *Teachers of the law (nomodidaskaloi)*. Compound only in N.T. (here, Luke 5:17; Acts 5:34) and ecclesiastical writers. *Though they understand (noountes)*. Concessive participle of *noeō*, old verb (Eph. 3:4, 20). *Neither what (mēte ha)*. Relative *ha* (which things). *Nor whereof (mēte peri tinōn)*. Here the interrogative *tinōn* used in sense of relative *hōn*. It may be regarded as the use of an indirect question for variety (Parry). *They confidently affirm (diabebaiountai)*. Present middle indicative of the common *Koiné* compound, in N.T. only here and Titus 3:8.

8. *If a man use it lawfully (ean tis autōi chrētai)*. Condition of third class with *ean* and present middle subjunctive of *chraomai* with instrumental case.

9. *Is not made for (ou keitai)*. The use of *keitai* for *tetheitai* (perfect passive of *tithēmi*) is a common enough idiom. See the same point about law in Gal. 18–23; Rom. 13:13. For "knowing this" *(eidōs touto)* see Eph. 5:5. *Unruly (anupotaktois)*. Dative (like all these words) of the late verbal (*a* privative and *hupotassō*). In N.T. only here, Titus 1:6, 10; Heb. 2:8. *Ungodly (asebesi)*. See Rom. 4:5; 5:6. *Sinners (hamartōlois)*. See Rom. 3:7. *Unholy (anosiois)*. Common word (*a* privative and *hosios*. In N.T. only here and II Tim. 3:2. *Profane (bebēlois)*. Old word from *bainō*, to go, and *bēlos*, threshold. See Heb. 12:16. *Murderers of fathers (patrolōiais)*. Late form for common Attic *patralōiais* (from *patēr*, father, and *aloiaō*, to smite) only here in N.T. *Murderers of mothers (mētrolōiais)*. Late form Attic *mētralōiais*. Only here in N.T. *Manslayers (andraphonois)*. Old compound (*anēr*, man, *phonos*, murder). Only here in N.T.

10. *For abusers of themselves with men (arsenokoitais)*. Late compound for sodomites. In N.T. only here and I Cor. 6:9. *Men-stealers (andrapodistais)*. Old word from *andrapodizō* (from *anēr*, man, *pous*, foot, to catch by the foot), to enslave. So enslavers, whether kidnappers (men-stealers) of free men or stealers of the slaves of other men. So slave-dealers. By the use of this word Paul deals a blow at the slave-trade (cf. Philemon). *Liars (pseustais)*. Old word, see Rom. 3:4. *False swearers (epiorkois)*. Old word (*epi*, *orkos*, oath). Perjurers. Only here in N.T. For similar lists,

see I Cor. 5:11; 6:9f.; Gal. 5:19f.; Rom. 1:28f.; 13:13; Col. 3:5; Eph. 5:5; II Tim. 3:2f. *The sound doctrine (tēi hugiain-ousēi didaskaliāi)*. Dative case after *antikeitai*, for which verb see Gal. 5:17 for the conflict between the Spirit and the flesh. "The healthful (*hugiainō*, old word for being well, as Luke 5:31; III John 2, in figurative sense in N.T. only in the Pastorals) teaching." See Titus 1:9; II Tim. 4:3.

11. *Of the blessed God (tou makariou theou)*. Applied to God only here and 6:15, but in Titus 2:13 *makarios* occurs with *elpis* (hope) of the "epiphany of our great God and Saviour Jesus Christ." *Which was committed to my trust (ho episteuthēn egō)*. "with which (*ho* accusative retained with first aorist passive verb *episteuthēn*) I was entrusted."

12. *I thank (charin echō)*. "I have gratitude to." Common phrase (Luke 17:9), not elsewhere in Paul. *That enabled me (tōi endunamōsanti me)*. First aorist active articular participle of *endunamoō*. Late verb, but regular Pauline idiom (Rom. 4:20; Phil. 4:13; Eph. 6:10; I Tim. 1:12; II Tim. 4:17). *Appointing me to his service (themenos eis diakonian)*. Second aorist middle participle. Pauline phrase and atmosphere (Acts 20:24; I Cor. 3:5; 12:18, 28; II Cor. 3:6; 4:1; Col. 1:23; Eph. 3:7; I Tim. 4:6; II Tim. 4:5, 11).

13. *Before (to proteron)*. Accusative of general reference of the articular comparative, "as to the former-time," formerly, as in Gal. 4:13. *Though I was (onta)*. Concessive participle agreeing with *me*. *Blasphemer (blasphēmon)*. Old word either from *blax* (stupid) and *phēmē*, speech, or from *blaptō*, to injure. Rare in N.T. but Paul uses *blasphēmei*, to blaspheme in Rom. 2:24. *Persecutor (diōktēs)*. So far found only here. Probably made by Paul from *diōkō*, which he knew well enough (Acts 22:4, 7; 26:14f.; Gal. 1:13, 23; Phil. 3:6; II Tim. 3:12). *Injurious (hubristēn)*. Substantive, not adjective, "an insolent man." Old word from *hubrizō*, in N.T. only here and Rom. 1:30. *I obtained mercy (eleēthēn)*. First aorist passive indicative of *eleeō*, old verb. See II Cor. 4:1; Rom. 11:30f. *Ignorantly (agnoōn)*. Present active participle of *agnoeō*, "not knowing." Old verb (Rom. 2:4). In a blindness of heart. *In unbelief (en apistiāi)*. See Rom. 11:20, 25.

14. *Abounded exceedingly (huperepleonasen)*. Aorist active indicative of the late and rare (Ps. of Sol. 5:19 and in Herond.) compound *huperpleonazō* (here alone in N.T.), in

later ecclesiastical writers. The simplex *pleonazō* Paul used in Rom. 5:20; 6:1 and the kindred *hupereperisseusen* used also with *hē charis*. Paul is fond of compounds with *huper*. For "faith in Christ Jesus" see Gal. 3:26, for "faith and love in Christ Jesus" as here, see II Tim. 1:13.

15. *Faithful is the saying* (*pistos ho logos*). Five times in the Pastorals (I Tim. 1:15; 3:1; 4:9; Titus 3:8; II Tim. 2:11). It will pay to note carefully *pistis*, *pisteuō*, *pistos*. Same use of *pistos* (trustworthy) applied to *logos* in Titus 1:9; Rev. 21:5; 22:6. Here and probably in II Tim. 2:11 a definite saying seems to be referred to, possibly a quotation (*hoti*) of a current saying quite like the Johannine type of teaching. This very phrase (Christ coming into the world) occurs in John 9:37; 11:27; 16:28; 18:37. Paul, of course, had no access to the Johannine writings, but such "sayings" were current among the disciples. There is no formal quotation, but "the whole phrase implies a knowledge of Synoptic and Johannine language" (Lock) as in Luke 5:32; John 12:47. *Acceptation* (*apodochēs*). Genitive case with *axios* (worthy of). Late word (Polybius, Diod., Jos.) in N.T. only here and 4:9. *Chief* (*prōtos*). Not *ēn* (I was), but *eimi* (I am). "It is not easy to think of any one but St. Paul as penning these words" (White). In I Cor. 15:9 he had called himself "the least of the apostles" (*elachistos tōn apostolōn*). In Eph. 3:8 he refers to himself as "the less than the least of all saints" (*tōi elachistoterōi pantōn hagiōn*). On occasion Paul would defend himself as on a par with the twelve apostles (Gal. 2:6–10) and superior to the Judaizers (II Cor. 11:5f.; 12:11). It is not mock humility here, but sincere appreciation of the sins of his life (cf. Rom. 7:24) as a persecutor of the church of God (Gal. 1:13), of men and even women (Acts 22:4f.; 26:11). He had sad memories of those days.

16. *In me as chief* (*en emoi prōtōi*). Probably starts with the same sense of *prōtos* as in verse 15 (rank), but turns to order (first in line). Paul becomes the "specimen" sinner as an encouragement to all who come after him. *Might shew forth* (*endeixētai*). First aorist middle subjunctive (purpose with *hina*) of *endeiknumi*, to point out, for which see Eph. 2:7 (same form with *hina*). *Longsuffering* (*makrothumian*). Common Pauline word (II Cor. 6:6). *For an ensample* (*pros*

hupotupōsin). Late and rare word (in Galen, Sext. Emp., Diog. Laert., here only in N.T.) from late verb *hupotupoō* (in papyri) to outline. So substantive here is a sketch, rough outline. Paul is a sample of the kind of sinners that Jesus came to save. See *hupodeigma* in II Peter 2:6.

17. This noble doxology is a burst of gratitude for God's grace to Paul. For other doxologies see Gal. 1:5; Rom. 11:36; 16:27; Phil. 4:20; Eph. 3:21; I Tim. 6:16. White suggests that Paul may have often used this doxology in his prayers. Lock suggests "a Jewish liturgical formula" (a needless suggestion in view of Paul's wealth of doxologies seen above). For God's creative activity (King of the ages) see I Cor. 10:11; Eph. 2:7; 3:9, 11. *Incorruptible* (*aphthartōi*). As an epithet of God also in Rom. 1:23. *Invisible* (*aoratōi*). Epithet of God in Col. 1:15. *The only God* (*monōi theōi*). So Rom. 16:27; John 5:44; 17:3. *For ever and ever* (*eis tous aiōnas tōn aiōnōn*). "Unto the ages of ages." Cf. Eph. 3:21 "of the age of the ages."

18. *I commit* (*paratithemai*). Present middle indicative of old and common verb, to place beside (*para*) as food on table, in the middle to entrust (Luke 12:48) and used by Jesus as he was dying (Luke 23:46). Here it is a banking figure and repeated in II Tim. 2:2. *According to the prophecies which went before on thee* (*kata tas proagousas epi se prophēteias*). Intransitive use of *proagō*, to go before. When Timothy first comes before us (Acts 16:2) "he was testified to" (*emartureito*) by the brethren. He began his ministry rich in hopes, prayers, predictions. *That by them thou mayest war the good warfare* (*hina strateuēi en autais tēn kalēn strateian*). Cognate accusative (*strateian*, old word from *strateuō*, in N.T. only here and II Cor. 4:4) with *strateuēi* (second person singular middle present subjunctive of *strateuō*, old verb chiefly in Paul in N.T., I Cor. 9:7; II Cor. 10:3). As if in defensive armour.

19. *Holding faith and a good conscience* (*echōn pistin kai agathēn suneidēsin*). Possibly as a shield (Eph. 6:16) or at any rate possessing (Rom. 2:20) faith as trust and a good conscience. A leader expects them of his followers and must show them himself. *Having thrust from them* (*apōsamenoi*). First aorist indirect middle participle of *apōtheō*, to push away from one. Old verb (see Rom. 11:1f.). *Made ship-*

wreck (*enauagēsan*). First aorist active indicative of *nauageō*, old verb from *nauagos* (shipwrecked, *naus*, ship, *agnumi*, to break), to break a ship to pieces. In N.T. only here and II Cor. 11:25. *Concerning the faith* (*peri tēn pistin*). Rather, "concerning their faith" (the article here used as a possessive pronoun, a common Greek idiom).

20. *Hymenaeus* (*Humenaios*). The same heretic reappears in II Tim. 2:17. He and Alexander are the chief "wreckers" of faith in Ephesus. *Alexander* (*Alexandros*). Probably the same as the one in II Tim. 4:14, but not the Jew of that name in Acts 19:33, unless he had become a Christian since then. *I delivered unto Satan* (*paredōka tōi Satanāi*). See this very idiom (*paradounai tōi Satanāi*) in I Cor. 5:5. It is a severe discipline of apostolic authority, apparently exclusion and more than mere abandonment (I Thess. 2:18; I Cor. 5:11; II Cor. 2:11), though it is an obscure matter. *That they might be taught not to blaspheme* (*hina paideuthōsin mē blasphēmein*). Purpose clause with *hina* and first aorist passive subjunctive of *paideuō*. For this use of this common late verb, see I Cor. 11:32; II Cor. 6:9.

CHAPTER II

1. *First of all (prōton pantōn)*. Take with *parakalō*. My first request (first in importance). *Intercessions (enteuxeis)*. Late word (Polybius, Plutarch, etc.), only here in N.T. and 4:5, though the verb *entugchanō* in Rom. 8:27, 34; 11:2, 25. The other three words for prayer are common (Phil. 4:6). *For all men (huper pantōn anthrōpōn)*. The scope of prayer is universal including all kinds of sinners (and saints).

2. *For kings (huper basileōn)*. And this included Nero who had already set fire to Rome and laid it on the Christians whom he was also persecuting. *And all them that are in high place (kai pantōn tōn en huperochēi ontōn)*. *Huperochē* is old word (from *huperochos* and this from *huper* and *echō*), but in N.T. only here and I Cor. 2:1. *That we may lead (hina diagōmen)*. Purpose clause with present active subjunctive of *diagō*, an old and common verb, but in N.T. only here and Titus 3:3. *Tranquil (ēremon)*. Late adjective from the old adverb *ērema* (stilly, quietly). Here only in N.T. *Quiet (hēsuchion)*. Old adjective, once in LXX (Isa. 66:2), in N.T. only here and I Peter 3:4. *Life (bion)*. Old word for course of life (not *zōē*). So Luke 8:14. *Gravity (semnotēti)*. Old word from *semnos* (Phil. 4:8), in N.T. only here, 3:4; Titus 2:7.

3. *Acceptable (apodekton)*. Late verbal adjective from *apodechomai*. In inscriptions and papyri. In N.T. only here and 5:4.

4. *Willeth (thelei)*. God's wish and will in so far as he can influence men. *That all men should be saved (pantas anthrōpous sōthēnai)*. First aorist passive infinitive of *sōzō* with accusative of general reference. See I Cor. 10:33; II Cor. 5:18f. *To the knowledge (eis epignōsin)*. "The full knowledge" as in Col. 1:6; Eph. 4:13 (ten times in Paul). See II Tim. 3:7 for the whole phrase "full knowledge of the truth" (*alētheia* 14 times in the Pastorals). Paul is anxious as in Colossians and Ephesians that the Gnostics may not lead the people astray. They need the full intellectual apprehension of Christianity.

567

5. *One God* (*heis theos*). Regular Pauline argument for a universal gospel (Gal. 3:20; Rom. 3:30; Eph. 4:6). *One mediator* (*heis mesitēs*). Late word (Polybius, Philo) from *mesos* (middle), a middle man. In N.T. only here, Gal. 3:20; Heb. 8:6; 9:15; 12:24. *Between God and men* (*theou kai anthrōpōn*). Ablative case (though objective genitive may explain it) after *mesitēs* (notion of separation) as in Rom. 10:12; Heb. 5:14. *Himself man* (*anthrōpos*). No "himself" (*autos*) in the Greek.

6. *A ransom for all* (*antilutron huper pantōn*). "A reminiscence of the Lord's own saying" (Lock) in Matt. 20:28 (=Mark 10:45) where we have *lutron anti pollōn*. In the papyri *huper* is the ordinary preposition for the notion of substitution where benefit is involved as in this passage. *Anti* has more the idea of exchange and *antilutron huper* combines both ideas. *Lutron* is the common word for ransom for a slave or a prisoner. Paul may have coined *antilutron* with the saying of Christ in mind (only one MS. of Psa. 48:9 and Orph. *Litt.* 588). See Gal. 1:4 "who gave himself for our sins." *The testimony* (*to marturion*). Either the nominative absolute or the accusative absolute in apposition to the preceding clause like *to adunaton* in Rom. 8:3. *In its own times* (*kairois idiois*). Locative case as in 6:15; Titus 1:3. See Gal. 6:9 for "due season." There is no predicate or participle here, "the testimony in its due seasons" (plural).

7. *For which* (*eis ho*). The testimony of Jesus in his self-surrender (verse 6). See *eis ho* in II Tim. 1:11. *I was appointed* (*etethēn egō*). First aorist passive indicative of *tithēmi*. *Preacher and apostle* (*kērux kai apostolos*). In II Tim. 1:10 Paul adds *didaskalos* (herald, apostle, teacher) as he does here with emphasis. In Col. 1:23f. he has *diakonos* (minister). He frequently uses *kērussō* of himself (I Cor. 1:23; 9:27; Gal. 2:2; Rom. 10:8f.). *I speak the truth, I lie not* (*alētheian legō, ou pseudomai*). A Pauline touch (Rom. 9:1). Cf. Gal. 1:20; II Cor. 11:31. Here alone he calls himself "a teacher of the Gentiles," elsewhere apostle (Rom. 11:13), minister (Rom. 15:16), prisoner (Eph. 3:1).

8. *I desire* (*boulomai*). So Phil. 1:12. *The men* (*tous andras*). Accusative of general reference with the infinitive *proseuchesthai*. The men in contrast to "women" (*gunaikas*)

in 9. It is public worship, of course, and "in every place" (*en panti topōi*) for public worship. Many modern Christians feel that there were special conditions in Ephesus as in Corinth which called for strict regulations on the women that do not always apply now. *Lifting up holy hands* (*epairontas hosious cheiras*). Standing to pray. Note also *hosious* used as feminine (so in Plato) with *cheiras* instead of *hosias*. The point here is that only men should lead in public prayer who can lift up "clean hands" (morally and spiritually clean). See Luke 24:50. Adverb *hosiōs* in I Thess. 2:10 and *hosiotēs* in Eph. 4:24. *Without wrath and disputing* (*chōris orgēs kai dialogismou*). See Phil. 2:14.

9. *In like manner that women* (*hosautōs gunaikas*). *Boulomai* must be repeated from verse 8, involved in *hosautōs* (old adverb, as in Rom. 8:26). Parry insists that *proseuchomenas* (when they pray) must be supplied also. Grammatically that is possible (Lock), but it is hardly consonant with verses 11 to 15 (White). *Adorn themselves* (*kosmein heautas*). Present active infinitive after *boulomai* understood. Old word from *kosmos* (arrangement, ornament, order, world). See Luke 21:5; Titus 2:10. See I Cor. 11:5ff. for Paul's discussion of women's dress in public worship. *In modest apparel* (*en katastolēi kosmiōi*). *Katastolē* is a late word (a letting down, *katastellō*, of demeanour or dress, arrangement of dress). Only here in N.T. *Kosmios* is old adjective from *kosmos* and means well-arranged, becoming. W. H. have adverb in margin (*kosmiōs*). *With shamefastness* (*meta aidous*). Old word for shame, reverence, in N.T. only here and Heb. 12:28. *Sobriety* (*sōphrosunēs*). Old word, in N.T. only here, verse 15, and Acts 26:15 (Paul also). *Not with braided hair* (*mē en plegmasin*). Old word from *plekō*, to plait, to braid, for nets, baskets, here only in N.T. Cf. I Peter 3:1 (*emplokēs*). *And gold* (*en chrusiōi*). Locative case with *en* repeated. Some MSS. read *chrusōi*. Both used for gold ornaments. *Or pearls* (*ē margaritais*). See Matt. 7:6 for this word. *Or costly raiment* (*ē himatismōi polutelei*). *Himatismos* a common *Koiné* word from *himatizō*, to clothe. *Poluteles*, old word from *polus* and *telos* (great price). See Mark 14:3.

10. *Becometh* (*prepei*). Old word for seemly. Paul wishes women to wear "becoming" clothes, but *theosebeian* (god-

liness, from *theosebēs*, John 9:31, *theos, sebomai*, worship) is part of the "style" desired. Only here in N.T. Good dress and good works combined.

11. *In quietness* (*en hēsuchiāi*). Old word from *hēsuchios*. In N.T. only here, Acts 22:2; II Thess. 3:12. *In all subjection* (*en pasēi hupotagēi*). Late word (Dion. Hal., papyri), in N.T. only here, II Cor. 9:13; Gal. 2:5. See I Cor. 14:33–35.

12. *I permit not* (*ouk epitrepō*). Old word *epitrepō*, to permit, to allow (I Cor. 16:7). Paul speaks authoritatively. *To teach* (*didaskein*). In the public meeting clearly. And yet all modern Christians allow women to teach Sunday school classes. One feels somehow that something is not expressed here to make it all clear. *Nor to have dominion over a man* (*oude authentein andros*). The word *authenteō* is now cleared up by Kretschmer (*Glotta*, 1912, pp. 289ff.) and by Moulton and Milligan's *Vocabulary*. See also Nägeli, *Der Wortschatz des Apostels Paulus* and Deissmann, *Light*, etc., pp. 88f. *Autodikeō* was the literary word for playing the master while *authenteō* was the vernacular term. It comes from *aut-hentes*, a self-doer, a master, autocrat. It occurs in the papyri (substantive *authentēs*, master, verb *authenteō*, to domineer, adjective *authentikos*, authoritative, "authentic"). Modern Greek has *aphentes*=Effendi="Mr."

13. *Was first formed* (*prōtos eplasthē*). Note *prōtos*, not *prōton*, first before Eve. First aorist passive indicative of *plassō*, old verb, in N.T. only here and Rom. 9:20 (cf. Gen. 2:7f.).

14. *Being beguiled* (*exapatētheisa*). First aorist passive participle of *exapateō*, old compound verb, in N.T. only by Paul (II Thess. 2:3; I Cor. 3:18; II Cor. 11:3; Rom. 7:11; 16:18; I Tim. 2:14). Not certain that *ex-* here means "completely deceived" in contrast to simplex (*ouk ēpatēthē*) used of Adam, though possible. *Hath fallen* (*gegonen*). Second perfect indicative active, permanent state. See I Cor. 11:7.

15. *Through the child-bearing* (*dia tēs teknogonias*). Late and rare word (in Aristotle). Here alone in N.T. From *teknogonos* and this from *teknon* and root *genō*. This translation makes it refer to the birth of the Saviour as glorifying womanhood. That is true, but it is not clear that Paul does not have mostly in mind that child-bearing, not public

teaching, is the peculiar function of woman with a glory and dignity all its own. "She will be saved" (*sōthēsetai*) in this function, not by means of it. *If they continue* (*ean meinōsin*). Condition of third class, *ean* with first aorist active subjunctive of *menō*, to continue. Note change to plural from the singular (*sōthēsetai*).

CHAPTER III

1. *Faithful is the saying (pistos ho logos).* Here the phrase points to the preceding words (not like 1:15) and should close the preceding paragraph. *If a man seeketh (ei tis oregetai).* Condition of first class, assumed as true. Present middle indicative of *oregō,* old verb to reach out after something, governing the genitive. In N.T. only here, 6:10; Heb. 11:16. *The office of a bishop (episkopēs).* Genitive case after *oregetai.* Late and rare word outside of LXX and N.T. (in a Lycaonian inscription). From *episkopeō* and means "over-seership" as in Acts 1:20.

2. *The bishop (ton episkopon).* The overseer. Old word, in LXX, and inscriptions and papyri. Deissmann (*Bible Studies,* pp. 230f.) has shown it is applied to communal officials in Rhodes. See Acts 20:28 for its use for the elders (presbyters) in verse 17. So also in Titus 1:5, 7. See Phil. 1:1. The word does not in the N.T. have the monarchical sense found in Ignatius of a bishop over elders. *Without reproach (anepilēmpton).* Accusative case of general reference with *dei* and *einai.* Old and common verbal (*a* privative and *epilambanō,* not to be taken hold of), irreproachable. In N.T. only here, 5:7; 6:14. *Of one wife (mias gunaikos).* One at a time, clearly. *Temperate (nēphalion).* Old adjective. In N.T. only here, verse 11; Titus 2:2. But see *nēphō,* to be sober in I Thess. 5:6, 8. *Soberminded (sōphrona).* Another old adjective (from *saos* or *sōs,* sound, *phrēn,* mind) in N.T. only here, Titus 1:8; 2:2, 5. *Orderly (kosmion).* See on 2:9. Seemly, decent conduct. *Given to hospitality (philoxenon).* Old word (see *philoxenia* in Rom. 12:13), from *philos* and *xenos,* in N.T. only here, Titus 1:8; I Peter 4:9. *Apt to teach (didaktikon).* Late form for old *didaskalikos,* one qualified to teach. In Philo and N.T. only (I Tim. 3:2; II Tim. 2:24).

3. *No brawler (mē paroinon).* Later word for the earlier *paroinios,* one who sits long at (beside, *para*) his wine. In N.T. only here and Titus 1:3. *No striker (mē plēktēn).* Late word from *plēssō,* to strike. In N.T. only here and Titus

1:3. *Gentle* (*epieikē*). See on Phil. 4:5 for this interesting word. *Not contentious* (*amachon*). Old word (from *a* privative and *machē*), not a fighter. In N.T. only here and Titus 3:2. *No lover of money* (*aphilarguron*). Late word (*a* privative and compound *phil-arguros*) in inscriptions and papyri (Nägeli; also Deissmann, *Light*, etc., pp. 85f.). In N.T. only here and Heb. 13:5.

4. *Ruling* (*proistamenon*). Present middle participle of *proistēmi*, old word to place before and (intransitive as here) to stand before. See I Thess. 5:12; Rom. 12:8. *In subjection* (*en hupotagēi*). See verse 11.

5. *If a man knoweth not* (*ei tis ouk oiden*). Condition of first class, assumed as true. *How to rule* (*prostēnai*). Second aorist active infinitive of same verb *proistēmi* and with *oiden* means "know how to rule," not "know that he rules." *How* (*pōs*). Rhetorical question expecting negative answer. *Shall he take care of* (*epimelēsetai*). Future middle of *epimeleomai*, old compound (*epi*, direction of care towards) verb, in LXX, in N.T. only here and Luke 10:34f. *The church of God* (*ekklēsias theou*). Anarthrous as in verse 15, elsewhere with article (I Cor. 10:32; 15:9; II Cor. 1:1; Gal. 1:13). The local church described as belonging to God. No one in N.T. but Paul (Acts 20:28) so describes the church. This verse is a parenthesis in the characteristics of the bishop.

6. *Not a novice* (*mē neophuton*). Our "neophyte." Vernacular word from Aristophanes on, in LXX, and in papyri in the original sense of "newly-planted" (*neos, phuō*). Only here in N.T. *Lest* (*hina mē*). "That not." *Being puffed up* (*tuphōtheis*). First aorist passive participle of *tuphoō*, old word (from *tuphos*, smoke, pride), to raise a smoke or mist (a smoke-screen of pride). In N.T. only here; 6:4; II Tim. 3:4. *He fall into* (*empesēi eis*). Second aorist active subjunctive with *hina mē*, negative purpose, of *empiptō*, old verb, to fall into. Note both *en* and *eis* as in Matt. 12:11; Luke 10:36. *The condemnation of the devil* (*krima tou diabolou*). See Rom. 3:8 for *krima*. Best to take *tou diabolou* as objective genitive, though subjective in verse 7, "the condemnation passed on or received by the devil" (not just "the slanderer," any slanderer).

7. *From them that are without* (*apo tōn exōthen*). "From the outside (of the church) ones." Paul's care for the witness

of outsiders is seen in I Thess. 4:12; I Cor. 10:32; Col. 4:5.
There are, of course, two sides to this matter. *Reproach*
(*oneidismon*). Late word from *oneidizō*. See Rom. 15:3.
The snare of the devil (*pagida tou diabolou*). Here subjective
genitive, snare set by the devil. *Pagis*, old word from *pēgnumi*, to make fast. So a snare for birds (Luke 21:35), any
sudden trap (Rom. 11:9), of sin (I Tim. 6:9), of the devil
(I Tim. 3:7; II Tim. 2:26). Ancients used it of the snares of
love. The devil sets special snares for preachers (conceit
verse 6, money 6:9, women, ambition).

8. *Deacons* (*diakonous*). Accusative case of general reference like the preceding with *dei einai* understood. Technical sense of the word here as in Phil. 1:1 which see (two
classes of church officers, bishops or elders, deacons). *Grave*
(*semnous*). See Phil. 4:8. Repeated in verse 11; Titus 2:2.
Not double-tongued (*mē dilogous*). Rare word (*dis, legō*)
saying same thing twice. Xenophon has *dilogeō* and *dilogia*.
In Pollux, but LXX has *diglōssos* (double-tongued, Latin
bilinguis). Only here in N.T. One placed between two persons and saying one thing to one, another to the other. Like
Bunyan's Parson "Mr. Two-Tongues." *Not given to much
wine* (*mē oinōi pollōi prosechontas*). "Not holding the mind
(*ton noun* understood as usual with *prosechō*, I Tim. 1:4)
on much wine" (*oinōi*, dative case). That attitude leads to
over-indulgence. *Not greedy of filthy lucre* (*mē aischrokerdeis*).
Old word from *aischros* (Eph. 5:12) and *kerdos* (Phil 1:21).
"Making small gains in mean ways" (Parry). Not genuine
in verse 3. In N.T. only here and Titus 1:7 (of bishops).

9. *The mystery of the faith* (*to mustērion tēs pisteōs*). "The
inner secret of the faith," the revelation given in Christ.
See for *mustērion* in Paul (II Thess. 2:7; I Cor. 2:7; Rom.
16:25; Col. 1:26; Eph. 3:9). *In a pure conscience* (*en katharāi
suneidēsei*). See 1:19. "The casket in which the jewel is to
be kept" (Lock).

10. *First be proved* (*dokimazesthōsan prōton*). Present
passive imperative third plural of *dokimazō*, old and common
verb, to test as metals, etc. (I Thess. 2:4, and often in Paul).
How the proposed deacons are to be "first" tested before
approved Paul does not say. See Phil. 1:10 for the two senses
(test, approve) of the word. *Let them serve as deacons* (*dia-
koneitōsan*). Present active imperative of *diakoneō* (same

root as *diakonos*), common verb, to minister, here "to serve as deacons." Cf. *diakonein* in Acts 6:2. See also verse 13. *If they be blameless (anegklētoi ontes)*. "Being blameless" (conditional participle, *ontes*). See I Cor. 1:8; Col. 1:22 for *anegklētos*.

11. *Women (gunaikas)*. Accusative with *dei einai* understood (*hosautōs*, likewise) as in verse 8. Apparently "women as deacons" (Rom. 16:1 about Phoebe) and not women in general or just "wives of deacons." See Pliny (*Ep*. X. 97) *ministrae*. *Not slanderers (mē diabolous)*. Original meaning of *diabolos* (from *diaballō*, Luke 16:1), the devil being the chief slanderer (Eph. 6:11). "She-devils" in reality (Titus 2:3). "While men are more prone to be *dilogous*, doubletongued, women are more prone than men to be slanderers" (White). *Faithful in all things (pistas en pāsin)*. Perhaps as almoners (Ellicott) the deaconesses had special temptations.

12. *Of one wife (mias gunaikos)*. At a time as in verse 2. *Ruling well (proistamenoi kalōs)*. As in 4.

13. *Gain to themselves (heautois peripoiountai)*. Present middle indicative of *peripoieō*, old verb, to make besides (*peri*, around, over), to lay by. Reflexive (indirect) middle with reflexive pronoun (*heautois*) repeated as often happens in the *Koiné*. In N.T. only here, Luke 17:33; Acts 20:28 (Paul also, quoting Isa. 43:21). *A good standing (bathmon kalon)*. Late word from *bainō*, in LXX for steps at a door (I Sam. 5:5). In plural the steps of a stair. In the inscriptions it means a good foothold or standing. The ecclesiastical writers (Theodoret) take it to be a higher grade or rank, but it is doubtful if Paul means that here. *Much boldness (pollēn parrēsian)*. A Pauline phrase (II Cor. 3:12; 7:4; Phil. 1:20). *In the faith which is in Christ Jesus (en pistei tēi en Christōi Iēsou)*. Pauline phrase again (Acts 26:18; Gal. 3:26; Col. 1:4; Eph. 1:15; II Tim. 1:13; 3:15).

14. *Shortly (en tachei)*. Old idiom (locative case of *tachos*, quickness, speed). See Rom. 16:20. A pseudonymous writer would hardly have put in this phrase. Paul's hopes were not to be realized, but he did not know that.

15. *But if I tarry long (ean de bradunō)*. Condition of third class with *ean* and the present active subjunctive of *bradunō*, old verb, to be slow (usually intransitive), from *bradus* (slow, dull, Luke 24:25), in N.T. only here and

II Peter 3:9. *That thou mayest know (hina eideis)*. Final clause with *hina* and second perfect active subjunctive of *oida*, to know. *How men ought (pōs dei)*. "How it is necessary for thee" (supply *se* more naturally than *tina*, any one). Indirect question. *To behave themselves (anastrephesthai)*. Present middle (direct) infinitive of *anastrephō*, old verb, to turn up and down. See II Cor. 1:12; Eph. 2:3. *In the house of God (en oikōi theou)*. Probably here "household of God," that is "the family of God" rather than "the house (or temple) of God." Christians as yet had no separate houses of worship and *oikos* commonly means "household." Christians are the *naos* (sanctuary) of God (I Cor. 3:16f.; II Cor. 6:16), and Paul calls them *oikeioi tou theou* (Eph. 2:19) "members of God's family." It is conduct as members of God's family (*oikos*) that Paul has in mind. *Which (hētis)*. "Which very house of God," agreeing (feminine) with the predicate word *ekklēsia* (church). *The church of the living God (ekklēsia theou zōntos)*. Probably here the general church or kingdom as in Colossians and Ephesians, though the local church in verse 5. *The pillar and ground of the truth (stulos kai hedraiōma tēs alētheias)*. Paul changes the metaphor again as he often does. Those words are in apposition to *ekklēsia* and *oikos*. On *stulos*, old word for pillar, see Gal. 2:9 and Rev. 3:12 (only other N.T. examples). *Hedraiōma*, late and rare word (from *hedraioō*, to make stable) occurs here first and only in ecclesiastical writers later. Probably it means stay or support rather than foundation or ground. See Col. 1:23; II Tim. 2:19 for similar idea. See also Matt. 16:18f.

16. *Without controversy (homologoumenōs)*. Old adverb from the participle *homologoumenos* from *homologeō*. Here only in N.T. "Confessedly." *Great (mega)*. See Eph. 5:32. "A great mystery." *The mystery of godliness (to tēs eusebeias mustērion)*. See verse 9 "the mystery of the faith," and 2:2 for *eusebeia*. Here the phrase explains "a pillar and stay of the truth" (verse 15). See in particular Col. 1:27. "The revealed secret of true religion, the mystery of Christianity, the Person of Christ" (Lock). *He who (hos)*. The correct text, not *theos* (God) the reading of the Textus Receptus (Syrian text) nor *ho* (neuter relative, agreeing with *mustērion*) the reading of the Western documents. Westcott and Hort

print this relative clause as a fragment of a Christian hymn (like Eph. 5:14) in six strophes. That is probably correct. At any rate *hos* (who) is correct and there is asyndeton (no connective) in the verbs. Christ, to whom *hos* refers, is the mystery (Col. 1:27; 2:2). *Was manifested (ephanerōthē)*. First aorist passive indicative of *phaneroō*, to manifest. Here used to describe the incarnation (*en sarki*) of Christ (an answer also to the Docetic Gnostics). The verb is used by Paul elsewhere of the incarnation (Rom. 16:26; Col. 1:26) as well as of the second coming (Col. 3:4). *Justified in the spirit (edikaiōthē en pneumati)*. First aorist passive indicative of *dikaioō*, to declare righteous, to vindicate. Christ was vindicated in his own spirit (Heb. 9:14) before men by overcoming death and rising from the dead (Rom. 1:3f.). *Seen of angels (ōphthē aggelois)*. First aorist passive indicative of *horaō*, to see, with either the instrumental or the dative case of angels (*aggelois*). The words were probably suggested by the appearance of Jesus (*ōphthē*, the usual form for the resurrection appearances of Christ) of the angels at the tomb and at the ascension of Christ. See Phil. 2:10; I Peter 3:22 for the appearance of Jesus to the angels in heaven at the ascension. Some would take "angels" here to be "messengers" (the women). *Preached among the nations (ekēruchthē en ethnesin)*. First aorist passive indicative of *kērussō*, to proclaim. The word *ethnos* may mean "all creation" (Col. 1:23) and not just Gentiles as distinct from Jews. Paul had done more of this heralding of Christ among the Gentiles than any one else. It was his glory (Eph. 3:1, 8). Cf. 2:7. *Believed on in the world (episteuthē en kosmōi)*. First aorist indicative passive again of *pisteuō*, to believe (II Thess. 1:10). Cf. 1:15 and II Cor. 5:19. *Received up in glory (anelēmphthē en doxēi)*. First aorist passive again (six verbs in the same voice and tense in succession, a rhythmic arrangement like a hymn). Cf. Rom. 8:29f. This time the verb is *analambanō*, the verb used of the ascension (Acts 1:11, 22, which see). In a wonderful way this stanza of a hymn presents the outline of the life of Christ.

CHAPTER IV

1. *Expressly* (*rētōs*). Late adverb, here alone in N.T., from verbal adjective *rētos* (from root *reō*). The reference is to the Holy Spirit, but whether to O.T. prophecy (Acts 1:16) or to some Christian utterance (II Thess. 2:2; I Cor. 14:1ff.) we do not know. Parry recalls the words of Jesus in Matt. 24:10, 24. *In later times* (*en husterois kairois*). Old adjective (Matt. 21:31) usually as adverb, *husteron* (Matt. 4:2). Relative time from the prediction, now coming true (a present danger). *Some shall fall away* (*apostēsontai tines*). Future middle of *aphistēmi*, intransitive use, shall stand off from, to fall away, apostatize (II Cor. 12:8). *From the faith* (*tēs pisteōs*). Ablative case (separation). Not creed, but faith in God through Christ. *Giving heed* (*prosechontes*). Supply *ton noun* (the mind) as in 3:8. *Seducing spirits* (*pneumasin planois*). Old adjective (*planē*, wandering), here active sense (deceiving). As substantive in II Cor. 6:8. Probably some heathen or the worst of the Gnostics. *Doctrines of devils* (*didaskaliais daimoniōn*). "Teachings of *daimons*." Definite explanation of the preceding. Cf. I Cor. 10:20f.

2. *Through the hypocrisy of men that speak lies* (*en hupokrisei pseudologōn*). For *hupokrisis*, see Gal. 2:13. *Pseudologos* (*pseudēs, legō*) *Koiné* word from Aristophanes on. Here only in N.T. "A good classical word for liars on a large scale" (Parry). *Branded in their own conscience as with a hot iron* (*kekaustēriasmenōn tēn idian suneidēsin*). Accusative case *suneidēsin* retained with the perfect passive participle of *kaustēriazō*, a rare verb only here and once in Strabo. Branded with the mark of Satan (II Tim. 2:26) as Paul was with the marks of Christ (Gal. 6:17). Agreeing in case with *pseudologōn*.

3. *Forbidding to marry* (*kōluontōn gamein*). Present active participle of common verb *kōluō*, to hinder, genitive case agreeing with *pseudologōn*. See Col. 2:16, 21f., where Paul condemns the ascetic practices of the Gnostics. The Essenes, Therapeutae and other oriental sects forbade marriage. In I Cor. 7 Paul does not condemn marriage. *To abstain from meats* (*apechesthai brōmatōn*). Infinitive dependent, not on

578

kōluontōn, but on the positive idea *keleuontōn* (implied, not expressed). Ablative case of *brōmatōn* after *apechesthai* (present direct middle, to hold oneself away from). See I Cor. 8–10; Rom. 14 and 15 for disputes about "meats offered to idols" and Col. 1:22f. for the Gnostic asceticism. *Which God created* (*ha ho theos ektisen*). First active indicative of *ktizō* (Col. 1:16). Cf. I Cor. 10:25. *To be received* (*eis metalēmpsin*). "For reception." Old word, only here in N.T. *By them that believe and know* (*tois pistois kai epegnōkosi*). Dative case, "for the believers and those who (one article unites closely) have known fully" (perfect active participle of *epiginōskō*), a Pauline use of the word (Col. 1:6).

4. *Creature* (*ktisma*). Late word from *ktizō*, result of creating. See Gen. 1:31; Mark 7:15; Rom. 14:14 for the idea stated. *To be rejected* (*apoblēton*). Old verbal adjective in passive sense from *apoballō*, to throw away, here only in N.T. *If it be received* (*lambanomenon*). "Being received." Present passive participle of *lambanō*, in conditional sense, "with thanksgiving."

5. *It is sanctified* (*hagiazetai*). Present passive indicative of *hagiazō*, here "rendered holy" rather than "declared holy." Cf. verse 4. *Through the word of God and prayers* (*dia logou theou kai enteuxeōs*). See 2:1 for *enteuxis*. Paul seems to refer to Genesis 1. It is almost a hendiadys "by the use of Scripture in prayer."

6. *If thou put the brethren in mind of these things* (*tauta hupotithemenos tois adelphois*). Present middle participle of *hupotithēmi*, to place under, to suggest, old and common verb, here only in N.T., "suggesting these things to the brethren." *Thou shalt be a good minister of Christ Jesus* (*kalos esei diakonos Christou Iēsou*). This beautiful phrase covers one's whole service for Christ (3:1–7). *Nourished in* (*entrephomenos*). Present passive participle of *entrephō*, old verb, to nourish in, used by Plato of "nourished in the laws," here only in the N.T. *The words of the faith* (*tois logois tēs pisteōs*). Locative case. The right diet for babes in Christ. The Bolshevists in Russia are feeding the children on atheism to get rid of God. *Which thou hast followed* (*hēi parēkolouthēkas*). Perfect active indicative of *parakoloutheō*, old verb, to follow beside, of persons (often in old Greek) or of ideas and things (Luke 1:3; I Tim. 4:6; II Tim. 3:10). With associative instrumental case *hēi* (which).

7. *Refuse* (*paraitou*). Present middle imperative second person singular of *paraiteō*, old verb, to ask of one and then to beg off from one as in Luke 14:18f.; Acts 25:11; I Tim. 4:7; 5:11; Titus 3:10; II Tim. 2:23. *Profane* (*bebēlous*). See 1:9. *Old wives' fables* (*graōdeis muthous*). On *muthos*, see 1:4. *Graōdeis*, late word (Strabo, Galen) from *graus*, old woman, and *eidos* (look, appearance). Such as old women tell to children like the Gnostic aeons. *Exercise thyself* (*gumnaze seauton*). Present active imperative of *gumnazō*, originally to exercise naked (*gumnos*). Old and common verb, but in N.T. only here and Heb. 5:14; 12:11.

8. *Bodily exercise* (*hē sōmatikē gumnasia*). *Gumnasia* (from *gumnazō*), also a common old word, here only in N.T. So also *sōmatikē* (from *sōma*, body) in N.T. only here and Luke 3:22. *Profitable* (*ōphelimos*). Another old word (from *ōpheleō*, to help, to profit), in N.T. only here, Titus 3:8; II Tim. 3:16. *For a little* (*pros oligon*). "For little." Probably extent in contrast to *pros panta* (for all things), though in James 4:14 it is time "for a little while." *Which now is* (*tēs nun*). "The now life." *Of that which is to come* (*tēs mellousēs*). "Of the coming (future) life."

9. See 1:15 for these very words, but here the phrase points to the preceding words, not to the following as there.

10. *To this end* (*eis touto*). The godliness (*eusebeia*) of verse 8. See II Cor. 6:10 as Paul's own commentary. *We labour* (*kopiōmen*, Col. 1:29) *and strive* (*kai agōnizometha*, Col. 1:29). Both Pauline words. *Because we have set our hope* (*hoti elpikamen*). Perfect active indicative of *elpizō* (Rom. 15:12). *Saviour of all men* (*sōtēr pantōn anthrōpōn*). See 1:1 for *sōtēr* applied to God as here. Not that all men "are saved" in the full sense, but God gives life (6:13) to all (Acts 17:28). *Specially of them that believe* (*malista pistōn*). Making a distinction in the kinds of salvation meant. "While God is potentially Saviour of all, He is actually Saviour of the *pistoi*" (White). So Jesus is termed "Saviour of the World" (John 4:42). Cf. Gal. 6:10.

12. *Despise* (*kataphroneitō*). Imperative active third singular of *kataphroneō*, old verb, to think down on, to despise (Rom. 2:4). *Thy youth* (*sou tēs neotētos*). Genitive case of old word (from *neos*) as in Mark 10:20. *Be thou* (*ginou*). Present middle imperative of *ginomai*. "Keep on

becoming thou." *An ensample (tupos)*. Old word from *tuptō*, a type. Pauline use of the word (I Thess. 1:7; II Thess. 3:9; Phil. 3:17; Titus 2:7). *To them that believe (tōn pistōn)*. Objective genitive. *In word (en logōi)*. In conversation as well as in public speech. *In manner of life (en anastrophēi)*. "In bearing" (Gal. 1:13; Eph. 4:22). *In purity (en hagneiāi)*. Old word from *hagneuō (hagnos)*. Sinlessness of life. Used of a Nazirite (Numb. 6:2, 21). Only here and 5:2 in N.T.

13. *Till I come (heōs erchomai)*. "While I am coming" (present indicative with *heōs*), not "till I come" (*heōs elthō*). *Give heed (proseche)*. Present active imperative, supply *ton* noun, "keep on putting thy mind on." The reading (*tēi anagnōsei*). Old word from *anaginōskō*. See II Cor. 3:14. Probably in particular the public reading of the Scriptures (Acts 13:15), though surely private reading is not to be excluded. *To exhortation (tēi paraklēsei)*, *to teaching (tēi didaskaliāi)*. Two other public functions of the minister. Probably Paul does not mean for the exhortation to precede the instruction, but the reverse in actual public work. Exhortation needs teaching to rest it upon, a hint for preachers today.

14. *Neglect not (mē amelei)*. Present active imperative in prohibition of *ameleō*, old verb, rare in N.T. (Matt. 22:5; I Tim. 4:14; Heb. 2:3; 8:9). From *amelēs (a* privative and *melei*, not to care). Use with genitive. *The gift that is in thee (tou en soi charismatos)*. Late word of result from *charizomai*, in papyri (Preisigke), a regular Pauline word in N.T. (I Cor. 1:7; II Cor. 1:11; Rom. 1:11; etc.). Here it is God's gift to Timothy as in II Tim. 1:6. *By prophecy (dia prophēteias)*. Accompanied by prophecy (1:18), not bestowed by prophecy. *With the laying on of the hands of the presbytery (meta epitheseōs tōn cheirōn tou presbuteriou)*. In Acts 13:2f., when Barnabas and Saul were formally set apart to the mission campaign (not then ordained as ministers, for they were already that), there was the call of the Spirit and the laying on of hands with prayer. Here again *meta* does not express instrument or means, but merely accompaniment. In II Tim. 1:6 Paul speaks only of his own laying on of hands, but the rest of the presbytery no doubt did so at the same time and the reference is to this incident. There is no way to tell when and where it was done, whether at

Lystra when Timothy joined Paul's party or at Ephesus just before Paul left Timothy there (1:3). *Epithesis* (from *epitithēmi*, to lay upon) is an old word, in LXX, etc. In the N.T. we find it only here, II Tim. 1:16; Acts 8:18; Heb. 6:2, but the verb *epitithēmi* with *tas cheiras* more frequently (Acts 6:6 of the deacons; 8:19; 13:3; I Tim. 5:22, etc.). *Presbuterion* is a late word (ecclesiastical use also), first for the Jewish Sanhedrin (Luke 22:66; Acts 22:5), then (here only in N.T.) of Christian elders (common in Ignatius), though *presbuteros* (elder) for preachers (bishops) is common (Acts 11:30; 15:2; 20:17, etc.).

15. *Be diligent in these things* (*tauta meleta*). Old verb from *meletē* (care, practice), present active imperative, "keep on practising these things." In N.T. only here and Acts 4:25. *Give thyself wholly to them* (*en toutois isthi*). Present imperative second person singular of *eimi*, "keep on in these things." Note five uses of *en* in verse 12 and three datives in verse 14. Plutarch (*Pomp.* 656 B) says Caesar was *en toutois* ("in these things"). It is like our "up to his ears" in work (*in medias res*) and sticking to his task. *Thy progress* (*sou hē prokopē*). Koiné word from *prokoptō*, to cut forward, to blaze the way, in N.T. only here and Phil. 1:12, 25. Paul's concern (purpose, *hina* and present subjunctive *ēi* of *eimi*) is that Timothy's "progress" may be "manifest to all." It is inspiring to see a young preacher grow for then the church will grow with him.

16. *Take heed to thyself* (*epeche seautōi*). Present active imperative of old verb *epechō*, to hold upon (Phil. 2:1, 16), but here *ton noun* (the mind) must be supplied as in Acts 3:5 and as is common with *prosechō*. With dative case *seautōi*. "Keep on paying attention to thyself." Some young preachers are careless about their health and habits. Some are too finical. *And to thy teaching* (*kai tēi didaskaliāi*). This is important also. *Continue in these things* (*epimene autois*). Present active imperative of *epimenō*, old and common verb to stay by the side of a person or thing. See Rom. 6:1; Col. 1:23. "Stay by them," "stick to them," "see them through." "Stick to the business of framing your own life and your teaching on right lines" (Parry). *Thou shalt save* (*sōseis*). Future active of *sōzō*, effective future, finally save. Cf. I Cor. 9:27; John 10:9.

CHAPTER V

1. *Rebuke not an elder* (*presbuteroi mē epiplēxēis*). Dative case *presbuteroi* used in the usual sense of an older man, not a minister (bishop as in 3:2) as is shown by "as a father." First aorist (ingressive) active subjunctive with negative *mē* (prohibition against committing the act) of *epiplēssō*, to strike upon, old verb, but here only in N.T. and in figurative sense with words rather than with fists. Respect for age is what is here commanded, an item appropriate to the present time. *The younger men as brethren* (*neōterous hōs adelphous*). Comparative adjective *neōteros* from *neos* (young). No article, "younger men." Wise words for the young minister to know how to conduct himself with old men (reverence) and young men (fellowship, but not stooping to folly with them).

2. *The elder women as mothers* (*presbuteras hōs mēteras*). Anarthrous again, "older women as mothers." Respect and reverence once more. *The younger as sisters, in all purity* (*neōteras hōs adelphas en pasēi hagniāi*). Anarthrous also and comparative form as in verse 1. See 4:12 for *hagnia*. No sort of behavior will so easily make or mar the young preacher as his conduct with young women.

3. *That are widows indeed* (*tas ontōs chēras*). For *ontōs* (actually, really), see Luke 23:47; I Cor. 14:25; and verse 5. For widows (*chēra*) see Mark 12:40, 42; Acts 6:1; I Cor. 7:8. Parry notes that in verses 3 to 8 Paul discusses widows who are in distress and 9 to 16 those who are in the employment of the local church for certain work. Evidently, as in Acts 6:1–6, so here in Ephesus there had arisen some trouble over the widows in the church. Both for individual cases of need and as a class Timothy is to show proper respect (*timā*, keep on honouring) the widows.

4. *Grandchildren* (*ekgona*). Old word from *ekginomai*, here only in N.T. *Let them learn* (*manthanetōsan*). The children and grandchildren of a widow. Present active imperative third person plural of *manthanō*. "Let them keep

583

on learning." *First (prōton)*. Adverb, first before anything else. No "corban" business here. No acts of "piety" toward God will make up for impiety towards parents. *To shew piety (eusebein)*. Present active infinitive with *manthanetōsan* and old verb, in N.T. only here and Acts 17:23. From *eusebēs (eu, sebomai)*, pious, dutiful. *Their own family (ton idion oikon)*. "Their own household." Filial piety is primary unless parents interfere with duty to Christ (Luke 14:26). *To requite (amoibas apodidonai)*. Present active infinitive of *apodidōmi*, to give back, old and common verb (Rom. 2:6), to keep on giving back. *Amoibas* (from *ameibomai*, to requite like for like) is old and common word, but here only in N.T. *Their parents (tois progonois)*. Dative case of old and common word *progonos* (from *proginomai*, to come before), "ancestor." In N.T. only here and II Tim. 1:3. See 2:3 for "acceptable" *(apodekton)*.

5. *Desolate (memonōmenē)*. Perfect passive participle of *monoō* (from *monos*), "left alone," old verb, here alone in N.T. Without husband, children, or other close kin. *Hath her hope set on God (ēlpiken epi theon)*. Perfect active indicative of *elpizō*, "hath placed her hope (and keeps it) on God." Text doubtful whether God *(theon)* or Lord *(Kurion)*. *Continues (prosmenei)*. See on 1:3. With dative case here. *Night and day (nuktos kai hēmeras)*. "By night and by day" (genitive, not accusative). Paul does not say that she should pray "all night and day."

6. *She that giveth herself to pleasure (hē spatalōsa)*. Present active participle of *splatalaō*, late verb (Polybius) from *spatalē* (riotous, luxurious living). In N.T. only here and James 5:5.

7. *That they may be without reproach (hina anepilēmptoi ōsin)*. See 3:2 for *anepilēmptos*. Final clause with *hina* and present subjunctive.

8. *Provideth not for his own (tōn idiōn ou pronoei)*. Condition of first class with *ei* and present active (or middle *pronoeitai*) indicative of *pronoeō*, old verb, to think beforehand. Pauline word in N.T. only here, II Cor. 8:21; Rom. 12:7. With genitive case. *He hath denied the faith (tēn pistin ērnētai)*. Perfect middle indicative of old verb *arneomai*. His act of impiety belies (Titus 1:16) his claim to the faith (Rev. 2:13). *Worse than an unbeliever (apistou cheirōn)*.

Ablative case of *apistou* after the comparative *cheirōn*. Who makes no profession of piety.

9. *Let none be enrolled as a widow* (*chēra katalegesthō*). Present passive imperative of *katalegō*, old verb, to set down in an official list, only here in N.T. "Let a widow be enrolled," the negative coming later, "having become of no less than sixty years" (*mē elatton etōn hexēkonta gegonuia*). Second perfect active participle of *ginomai*. For the case of *etōn*, see Luke 2:42. This list of genuine widows (verses 3 and 5) apparently had some kind of church work to do (care for the sick, the orphans, etc.). *The wife of one man* (*henos andros gunē*). Widows on this list must not be married a second time. This interpretation is not so clear for 3:2, 12; Titus 1:6.

10. *If she hath brought up children* (*ei eteknotrophēsen*). Condition of first class. Late and rare word (Aristotle, Epictetus), first aorist active indicative of *teknotropheō* (*teknotrophos*, from *teknon*, *trephō*), here only in N.T. Qualification for her work as leader. *If she hath used hospitality to strangers* (*ei exenodochēsen*). First aorist again and same condition. Late form (Dio Cassius) of old verb *xenodokeō* (Herodotus), to welcome strangers (*xenous dechomai*). Only here in N.T. Hospitality another qualification for such leadership (3:2). *If she hath washed the saints' feet* (*ei hagiōn podas enipsen*). Same condition and tense of *niptō* (old form *nizō*), common in N.T. (John 13:5). Proof of her hospitality, not of its being a church ordinance. *If she hath relieved the afflicted* (*ei thlibomenois epērkesen*). Same condition and tense of *eparkeō*, to give sufficient aid, old word, in N.T. only here and verse 16. Experience that qualified her for eleemosynary work. *If she hath diligently followed* (*ei epēkolouthēsen*). Same condition and tense of *epakoloutheō*, old verb, to follow close upon (*epi*). So here, verse 24; I Peter 2:21. In a word such a widow• must show her qualifications for leadership as with bishops and deacons.

11. *But younger widows refuse* (*neōteras de chēras paraitou*). Present middle imperative as in 4:7. "Beg off from." They lack experience as above and they have other ambitions. *When they have waxed wanton* (*hotan katastrēniasōsin*). First aorist (ingressive) active subjunctive of *katastrēniaō*, late compound (only here and Ignatius), to feel the impulse of

sexual desire, but simplex *strēniaō* (Rev. 18:7, 9). Souter renders it here "exercise youthful vigour against Christ" (*tou Christou*, genitive case after *kata* in composition).
12. *Condemnation* (*krima*). See 3:6. *They have rejected* (*ēthetēsan*). First aorist passive of *atheteō*, late verb (first in LXX and Polybius), to reject, set aside (from *athetos*). See I Thess. 4:8; Gal. 2:21. *Their first faith* (*tēn prōtēn pistin*). "Their first pledge" (promise, contract) to Christ. It is like breaking the marriage contract. Evidently one of the pledges on joining the order of widows was not to marry. Parry suggests a kind of ordination as with deacons and bishops (technical use of *krima* and *pistis*).
13. *And withal* (*hama de kai*). See Philemon 22 for this very phrase, "and at the same time also." Such young enrolled widows have other perils also. *They learn to be idle* (*argai manthanousin*). There is no *einai* (to be) in the Greek. This very idiom without *einai* after *manthanō* occurs in Plato and Dio Chrysostom, though unusual. *Argai* (idle) is old adjective (*a* privative and *ergon*, without work). See Matt. 20:3; Titus 1:12. *Going about* (*perierchomenai*). Present middle participle of *perierchomai*, old compound verb. See Acts 19:13 of strollers. *From house to house* (*tas oikias*). Literally "the houses," "wandering around the houses." Vivid picture of idle tattlers and gossipers. *But tattlers also* (*alla kai phluaroi*). Old word from *phluō* (to boil up, to throw up bubbles, like blowing soap bubbles). Only here in N.T. *Phluareō* in III John 10 only in N.T. *And busybodies* (*kai periergoi*). Old word (from *peri*, *ergon*), busy about trifles to the neglect of important matters. In N.T. only here and Acts 19:19. See II Thess. 3:11 for *periergazomai*. *Things which they ought not* (*ta mē deonta*). "The not necessary things," and, as a result, often harmful. See Titus 1:11 *ha mē dei* (which things are not necessary).
14. *I desire* (*boulomai*). See 2:8. *The younger widows* (*neōteras*). No article and no word for widows, though that is clearly the idea. *Neōteras* is accusative of general reference with *gamein* (to marry) the object (present infinitive active) of *boulomai*. *Bear children* (*teknogonein*). A compound verb here only in N.T. and nowhere else save in Anthol. See *teknogonia* in 2:15. *Rule the household* (*oikodespotein*). Late verb from *oikodespotēs* (Mark 14:14), twice in the papyri,

only here in N.T. Note that the wife is here put as ruler of the household, proper recognition of her influence, "new and improved position" (Liddon). *Occasion (aphormēn)*. Old word (*apo, hormē*), a base to rush from, Pauline use in II Cor. 5:12; 11:12; Gal. 5:13. *To the adversary (tōi antikeimenōi)*. Dative case of the articular participle of *antikeimai*, a Pauline idiom (Phil. 1:28). *Reviling (loidorias)*. Old word (from *loidoreō*), in N.T. only here and I Peter 3:9. Genitive case with *charin*.

15. *Are turned aside (exetrapēsan)*. Second aorist (effective) passive indicative of *ektrepō*. See 1:6. *After Satan (opisō tou Satanā)*. "Behind Satan." Late use of *opisō* (behind) as a preposition. Used by Jesus of disciples coming behind (after) him (Matt. 16:24).

16. *That believeth (pistē)*. "Believing woman." *Hath widows (echei chēras)*. The "any believing woman" is one of the household-rulers of verse 14. The "widows" here are the widows dependent on her and who are considered as candidates to be enrolled in the list. *Let her relieve them (eparkeitō autais)*. For this verb (imperative present active) see verse 10. *Let not be burdened (mē bareisthō)*. Present passive imperative (in prohibition *mē*) of *bareō*, old verb (*baros*, burden), Pauline word (II Cor. 1:8). *That are widows indeed (tais ontōs chērais)*. Dative case with *eparkesei* (first aorist active subjunctive with *hina*, final clause). See verse 3 for this use of *ontōs* with *chērais* "the qualified and enrolled widows." Cf. verse 9.

17. *The elders that rule well (hoi kalōs proestōtes presbuteroi)*. See verse 1 for ordinary sense of *presbuteros* for "older man." But here of position in same sense as *episkopos* (3:2) as in Titus 1:5 = *episkopos* in verse 7. Cf. Luke's use of *presbuteros* (Acts 20:17) = Paul's *episkopous* (Acts 20:28). *Proestōtes* is second perfect active participle of *proistēmi* (intransitive use) for which see 3:4. *Let be counted worthy (axiousthōsan)*. Present passive imperative of *axioō*, to deem worthy (II Thess. 1:11). With genitive case here. *Of double honour (diplēs timēs)*. Old and common contract adjective (*diploos*, two-fold, in opposition to *haploos*, single fold). But why "of double honour"? See 6:1 for "of all honour." White suggests "remuneration" rather than "honour" for *timēs* (a common use for price or pay). Liddon proposes "honor-

arium" (both honour and pay and so "double"). Wetstein gives numerous examples of soldiers receiving double pay for unusual services. Some suggest twice the pay given the enrolled widows. *Especially those who labour in word and teaching (malista hoi kopiōntes en logōi kai didaskaliāi).* Either those who work hard or toil (usual meaning of *kopiaō*, II Tim. 2:6) in preaching and teaching (most probable meaning. See verse 18) or those who teach and preach and not merely preside (a doubtful distinction in "elders" at this time). See Titus 1:8f. See both *kopiaō* and *proistamai* used for same men (elders) in I Thess. 5:12 and the use of *kopiaō* in I Cor. 15:10; 16:16.

18. *Thou shalt not muzzle (ou phimōseis).* Prohibition by *ou* and future (volitive) indicative of *phimoō* (from *phimos*, muzzle), old word, quoted also in I Cor. 9:9 as here from Deut. 25:4, and for the same purpose, to show the preacher's right to pay for his work. See I Cor. 9:9 for *aloōnta (when he treadeth out the corn). The labourer is worthy of his hire (axios ho ergatēs tou misthou autou).* These words occur in precisely this form in Luke 10:7. It appears also in Matt. 10:10 with *tēs trophēs* (food) instead of *tou misthou*. In I Cor. 9:14 Paul has the sense of it and says: "so also the Lord ordained," clearly meaning that Jesus had so said. It only remains to tell whether Paul here is quoting an unwritten saying of Jesus as he did in Acts 20:35 or even the Gospel of Luke or Q (the Logia of Jesus). There is no way to decide this question. If Luke wrote his Gospel before A.D. 62 as is quite possible and Acts by A.D. 63, he could refer to the Gospel. It is not clear whether Scripture is here meant to apply to this quotation from the Lord Jesus. For *ergatēs* (labourer) see Phil. 3:2.

19. *Against an elder (kata presbuterou).* In the official sense of verses 17f. *Receive not (mē paradechou).* Present middle imperative with *mē* (prohibition) of *paradechomai*, to receive, to entertain. Old verb. See Acts 22:18. *Accusation (katēgorian).* Old word (from *katēgoros*). In N.T. only here, Titus 1:6; John 18:29 in critical text. *Except (ektos ei mē).* For this double construction see I Cor. 14:5; 15:2. *At the mouth of (epi).* Idiomatic use of *epi* (upon the basis of) as in II Cor. 13:1.

20. *Them that sin (tous hamartanontas).* The elders who

continue to sin (present active participle). *In the sight of all* (*enōpion pantōn*). "In the eye of (*ho en opi ōn*, the one who is in the eye of, then combined = *enōpion*) all" the elders (or even of the church). See next verse and Gal. 1:20. Public rebuke when a clear case, not promiscuous gossip. *May be in fear* (*phobon echōsin*). Present active subjunctive with *hina* (final clause), "may keep on having fear" (of exposure). Possibly, "the rest of the elders."

21. *The elect angels* (*tōn eklektōn aggelōn*). For this triad of God, Christ, angels, see Luke 9:26. "Elect" in the sense of the "holy" angels who kept their own principality (Jude 6) and who did not sin (II Peter 2:4). Paul shows his interest in angels in I Cor. 4:9; 11:10. *Observe* (*phulaxēis*). First aorist active subjunctive of *phulassō*, to guard, to keep (Rom. 2:26). Subfinal use of *hina*. *Without prejudice* (*chōris prokrimatos*). Late and rare word (from *prokinō*, to judge beforehand), three times in the papyri, here only in N.T. "Without prejudgment." *By partiality* (*kata prosklisin*). Late word from *prosklinō*, to incline towards one (Acts 5:36), only here in N.T.

22. *Lay hands hastily* (*cheiras tacheōs epitithei*). Present active imperative of *epitithēmi* in the sense of approval (ordination) as in Acts 6:6; 13:3. But it is not clear whether it is the case of ministers just ordained as in 4:14 (*epithesis*), or of warning against hasty ordination of untried men, or the recognition and restoration of deposed ministers (verse 20) as suits the context. The prohibition suits either situation, or both. *Be partakers of other men's sins* (*koinōnei hamartiais allotriais*). Present active imperative of *koinōneō* (from *koinōnos*, partner) with *mē* in prohibition with associative instrumental case as in II John 11; Rom. 12:13. On *allotrios* (belonging to another) see Rom. 14:4. *Keep thyself pure* (*seauton hagnon tērei*). "Keep on keeping thyself pure." Present active imperative of *tēreō*.

23. *Be no longer a drinker of water* (*mēketi hudropotei*). Present active imperative (prohibition) of *hudropoteō*, old verb (from *hudropotēs*, water drinker, *hudōr*, *pinō*), here only in N.T. Not complete asceticism, but only the need of some wine urged in Timothy's peculiar physical condition (a sort of medical prescription for this case). *But use a little wine* (*alla ainōi oligōi chrō*). Present middle imperative of *chraomai*

with instrumental case. The emphasis is on *oligōi* (a little). *For thy stomach's sake* (*dia ton stomachon*). Old word from *stoma* (mouth). In Homer throat, opening of the stomach (Aristotle), stomach in Plutarch. Here only in N.T. Our word "stomach." *Thine often infirmities* (*tas puknas sou astheneias*). *Puknos* is old word, dense, frequent. In N.T. only here, Luke 5:33; Acts 24:26. *Astheneias* = weaknesses, lack of strength (Rom. 8:26). Timothy was clearly a semi-invalid.

24. *Evident* (*prodēloi*). "Openly plain," "plain before all." Old word, in N.T. only here and Heb. 7:24. *Going before unto judgment* (*proagousai eis krisin*). See 1:18 for *proagō*. The sins are so plain that they receive instant condemnation. *And some men also they follow after* (*tisin de kai epakolouthousin*). Associative instrumental case *tisin* with *epakolouthousin* for which verb see verse 10, "dog their steps" (Parry) like I Peter 2:21, not clearly manifest at first, but come out plainly at last. How true that is of secret sins.

25. *Such as are otherwise* (*ta allōs echonta*). "Those (deeds, *erga*) which have it otherwise." That is good deeds not clearly manifest. *Cannot be hid* (*krubēnai ou dunantai*). Second aorist passive infinitive of *kruptō*. There is comfort here for modest preachers and other believers whose good deeds are not known and not blazoned forth. They will come out in the end. See Matt. 5:14-16.

CHAPTER VI

1. *Under the yoke* (*hupo zugon*). As slaves (*douloi*, bondsmen). Perhaps under heathen masters (I Peter 2:18). For the slave problem, see also Philemon; Col. 3:22; Eph. 6:5; Titus 2:9. See Matt. 11:29 for Christ's "yoke" (*zugon*, from *zeugnumi*, to join). *Their own masters* (*tous idious despotas*). That is always where the shoe pinches. Our "despot" is this very Greek word, the strict correlative of slave (*doulos*), while *kurios* has a wider outlook. Old word only here, Titus 2:9; II Tim. 2:21; I Peter 2:18 for human masters. Applied to God in Luke 2:29; Acts 4:24, 29 and to Christ in II Peter 2:1. *The name of God* (*to onoma tou theou*). See Rom. 2:24. If the heathen could say that Christian slaves were not as dependable as non-Christian slaves. Negative purpose with *hina mē* and present passive subjunctive (*blasphēmētai*).

2. *Let not despise them* (*mē kataphroneitōsan*). Negative imperative active third plural of *kataphroneō*, to think down on. See 4:12. He must not presume on the equality of Christian brotherhood not allowed by the state's laws. Some of these Christian slaves might be pastors of churches to which the master belonged. For the difficulty of the Christian master's position, see I Cor. 7:22; Philemon 16. *But rather* (*alla mallon*). Render the Christian Master better service. *They that partake of the benefit* (*hoi tēs energesias antilambanomenoi*). For *euergesias* (genitive case after participle) see Acts 4:9, only other N.T. example of this old word. Present middle participle of *antilambanō*, old verb, to take in turn, to lay fast hold of, in N.T. only here, Luke 1:54; Acts 20:35.

3. *Teacheth a different doctrine* (*heterodidaskalei*). See 1:3 for this verb, present active indicative here in condition of first class. *Consenteth not* (*mē proserchetai*). Also condition of first class with *mē* instead of *ou*. *Proserchomai* (old verb, to come to, to approach, with dative) is common enough in N.T. (Heb. 4:16; 7:25, etc.), but in the metaphorical sense of coming to one's ideas, assenting to, here only in N.T.,

but is so used in Philo and Irenaeus (Ellicott). *Sound words* (*hugiainousin logois*). See 1:10 for *hugiainō*. *The words of our Lord Jesus Christ* (*tois tou kuriou hēmōn Iēsou Christou*). Either subjective genitive (the words from the Lord Jesus, a collection of his sayings in Lock's opinion like 5:18 and Acts 20:35, at least in the Spirit of Jesus as Acts 16:7; I Cor. 11:23) or objective genitive about Jesus like II Tim. 1:8; I Cor. 1:18. *According to godliness* (*kata eusebeian*). Promoting (designed for) godliness as in Titus 1:1.

4. *He is puffed up* (*tetuphōtai*). Perfect passive indicative of *tuphoō*, for which see 3:6. *Knowing nothing* (*mēden epistamenos*). Present middle participle of *epistamai*. Ignorance is a frequent companion of conceit. *Doting* (*nosōn*). Present active participle of *noseō*, to be sick, to be morbid over, old word, only here in N.T. *Disputes of words* (*logomachias*). Our "logomachy." From *logomacheō* (II Tim. 2:14), and that from *logos* and *machomai*, to fight over words, late and rare word, here only in N.T. See Plato (*Tim.* 1085 F) for "wars in words" (*machas en logois*). *Whereof* (*ex hōn*). "From which things." *Surmisings* (*huponoiai*). Old word from *huponoeō*, to surmise, to suspect (Acts 25:18), only here in N.T. All these words are akin (envy, *phthonos*, strife, *eris*, railings or slanders, *blasphēmiai*), all products of an ignorant and conceited mind.

5. *Wranglings* (*diaparatribai*). Late and rare (Clem. of Alex.) double compound (*dia*, mutual or thorough, *paratribai*, irritations or rubbings alongside). "Mutual irritations" (Field). *Corrupted in mind* (*diephtharmenōn ton noun*). Perfect passive participle of *diaphtheirō*, to corrupt, genitive case agreeing with *anthrōpōn* (of men) and retaining the accusative *ton noun*. *Bereft of the truth* (*apesterēmenōn tēs alētheias*). Perfect passive participle of *apostereō*, old verb (I Cor. 6:8) with the ablative case after it (*alētheias*). *A way of gain* (*porismon*). Late word from *porizō*, to provide, to gain. Only here in N.T. "Rich Christians." Predicate accusative with *einai* (indirect assertion) in apposition with *eusebeian*, the accusative of general reference.

6. *With contentment* (*meta autarkeias*). Old word from *autarkēs* (*autos, arkeō*) as in Phil. 4:11. In N.T. only here and II Cor. 9:8. This attitude of mind is Paul's conception of "great gain."

7. *Brought into* (*eisēnegkamen*, second aorist active stem with first aorist ending, common in the *Koiné*), *carry out* (*exenegkein*, second aorist active infinitive). Note play on the prepositions *eis-* and *ex-*. 8. *Food* (*diatrophas*). Plural, supports or nourishments (from *diatrephō*, to support). Old word, here only in N.T. *Covering* (*skepasmata*). Plural, "coverings." Late word from *skepazō*, to cover. Here only in N.T. *We shall be content* (*arkesthēsometha*). First future passive of *arkeō*, to be content. Old word. See II Cor. 12:9. This is the *autarkeia* of verse 6. *There with* (*toutois*). Associative instrumental case, "with these."

9. *Desire to be rich* (*boulomenoi ploutein*). The will (*boulomai*) to be rich at any cost and in haste (Prov. 28:20). Some MSS. have "trust in riches" in Mark 10:24. Possibly Paul still has teachers and preachers in mind. *Fall into* (*empiptousin eis*). See on 3:6 for *en*—*eis* and 3:7 for *pagida* (snare). *Foolish* (*anoētous*). See Gal. 3:1, 3. *Hurtful* (*blaberas*). Old adjective from *blaptō*, to injure, here alone in N.T. *Drown* (*buthizousin*). Late word (literary *Koiné*) from *buthos* (bottom), to drag to the bottom. In N.T. only here and Luke 5:7 (of the boat). Drown in the lusts with the issue "in destruction and perdition" (*eis olethron kai apōleian*). Not annihilation, but eternal punishment. The combination only here, but for *olethros*, see I Thess. 5:3; II Thess. 1:9; I Cor. 5:5 and for *apōleia*, see II Thess. 2:3; Phil. 3:19.

10. *The love of money* (*hē philarguria*). Vulgate, *avaritia*. Common word (from *philarguros*, II Tim. 3:12, and that from *philos*, *arguros*), only here in N.T. Refers to verse 9 (*boulomenoi ploutein*). *A root of all kinds of evil* (*riza pantōn tōn kakōn*). A root (*riza*). Old word, common in literal (Matt. 3:10) and metaphorical sense (Rom. 11:11-18). Field (*Ot. Norv.*) argues for "the root" as the idea of this predicate without saying that it is the only root. Undoubtedly a proverb that Paul here quotes, attributed to Bion and to Democritus (*tēn philargurian einai mētropolin pantōn tōn kakōn*), where "metropolis" takes the place of "root." Surely men today need no proof of the fact that men and women will commit any sin or crime for money. *Reaching after* (*oregomenoi*). Present middle participle of *oregō* (see 3:1) with genitive

hēs (which). *Have been led astray* (*apeplanēthēsan*). First aorist passive indicative of *apoplanaō*, old compound verb, in N.T. only here and Mark 13:22. *Have pierced themselves through* (*heautous periepeiran*). First aorist active (with reflexive pronoun) of late compound *peripeirō*, only here in N.T. Perfective use of *peri* (around, completely to pierce). *With many sorrows* (*odunais pollais*). Instrumental case of *odunē* (consuming, eating grief). In N.T. only here and Rom. 9:2.

11. *O man of God* (*ō anthrōpe theou*). In N.T. only here and II Tim. 3:17, there general and here personal appeal to Timothy. Cf. Deut. 33:1; I Sam. 2:27. *Flee* (*pheuge*), *follow after* (*diōke*). Vivid verbs in present active imperative. The preacher can not afford to parley with such temptations. *Meekness* (*praüpathian*). Late compound from *praüpathēs*, in Philo about Abraham, here only in N.T.

12. *Fight the good fight* (*agōnizou ton kalon agōna*). Cognate accusative with present middle imperative of *agōnizō*, Pauline word (I Cor. 9:25; Col. 1:29). *Lay hold on* (*epilabou*). Second (ingressive) aorist middle imperative of *epilambanō*, "get a grip on." See same verb with genitive also in verse 19. *Thou wast called* (*eklēthēs*). First aorist passive of *kaleō* as in I Cor. 1:9; Col. 3:15. *The good confession* (*tēn kalēn homologian*). Cognate accusative with *homologēsas* (first aorist active indicative of *homologeō*, the public confession in baptism which many witnessed. See it also in verse 13 of Jesus.

13. *Who quickeneth all things* (*tou zōogonountos ta panta*). Present active participle of *zōogoneō* (*zōogonos*, from *zōos*, *genō*), late word to give life, to bring forth alive, in N.T. only here and Acts 7:19. See I Sam. 2:6. *Before Pontius Pilate* (*epi Pontiou Peilatou*). Not "in the time of," but "in the presence of." *Witnessed* (*marturēsantos*). Note *martureō*, not *homologeō* as in verse 12. Christ gave his evidence as a witness to the Kingdom of God. Evidently Paul knew some of the facts that appear in John 18.

14. *That thou keep* (*tērēsai se*). First aorist active infinitive of *tēreō*, with accusative of general reference (*se*) in indirect command after *paraggellō*. *Without spot* (*aspilon*). Late adjective (*a* privative, *spilos*, spot, Eph. 5:27). In inscription and papyri. *Without reproach* (*anepilēmpton*). See 3:2;

5:7. *Until the appearing (mechri tēs epiphaneias).* "Until the epiphany" (the second epiphany or coming of Christ). Late word in inscriptions for important event like the epiphany of Caligula, in the papyri as a medical term. In II Thess. 2:18 we have both *epiphaneia* and *parousia.* See Titus 2:13; II Tim. 1:10; 4:1, 8.

15. *In its own times (kairois idiois).* Locative case. Maybe "in his own times." See 2:6. Clearly not for us to figure out. *Who is the blessed and only Potentate (ho makarios kai monos dunastēs).* "The happy and alone Potentate." *Dunastēs,* old word, in N.T. only here, Luke 1:52; Acts 8:27 (the Eunuch). See 1:11 for *makarios. The King of kings (ho basileus tōn basileuontōn).* "The King of those who rule as kings." Oriental title. So with "Lord of lords." See Rev. 10:16.

16. *Who only hath immortality (ho monos echōn athanasian).* "The one who alone has immortality." *Athanasia (athanatos, a* privative and *thanatos),* old word, in N.T. only here and I Cor. 15:53f. Domitian demanded that he be addressed as "*Dominus et Deus noster.*" Emperor worship may be behind the use of *monos* (alone) here. *Unapproachable (aprositon).* See Psa. 104:2. Late compound verbal adjective (*a* privative, *pros, ienai,* to go). Here only in N.T. Literary *Koiné* word. *Nor can see (oude idein dunatai).* See *aoraton* in Col. 1:15 and also John 1:18; Matt. 11:27. The "amen" marks the close of the doxology as in 1:17.

17. *In this present world (en tōi nun aiōni).* "In the now age," in contrast with the future. *That they be not highminded (mē hupsēlophronein).* Present active infinitive with negative in indirect command after *paraggelle,* "not to be high-minded." Only instance of the word save some MSS. of Rom. 11:20 (for *mē hupsēlaphronei*) and a scholion on Pindar. *Have their hope set (ēlpikenai).* Perfect active infinitive of *elpizō. On the uncertainty of riches (epi ploutou adēlotēti).* Literary *Koiné* word (*adēlotēs*), only here in N.T. A "vigorous oxymoron" (White). Cf. Rom. 6:4. Riches have wings. *But on God (all' epi theōi).* He alone is stable, not wealth. *Richly all things to enjoy (panta plousiōs eis apolausin).* "A lavish emphasis to the generosity of God" (Parry). *Apolausis* is old word from *apolauō,* to enjoy, in N.T. only here and Heb. 11:25.

18. *That they do good (agathoergein).* Late word (*agathos,*
ergō), in N.T. only here and Acts 14:17. *Rich in good works*
(*ploutein en ergois kalois*). See Luke 12:21 "rich toward
God" and Matt. 6:19f. for "treasures in heaven." *Ready to*
distribute (eumetadotous). Late and rare verbal (*eu, meta,*
didōmi). Free to give, liberal. Only here in N.T. *Willing*
to communicate (koinōnikous). Old adjective, ready to share,
gracious, liberal again. Only here in N.T. See Gal. 6:6;
Phil. 4:15.

19. *Laying up in store (apothēsaurizontas).* Late literary
word (*apo* and *thēsaurizō*), only here in N.T. Same paradox
as in Matt. 6:19f., "laying up in store" by giving it away.
Which is life indeed (tēs ontōs zōēs). See 5:3 for *ontōs.* This
life is merely the shadow of the eternal reality to come.

20. *Guard that which is committed unto thee (tēn parathēkēn*
phulaxon). "Keep (aorist of urgency) the deposit." *Parathē-*
kēn (from *paratithēmi,* to place beside as a deposit, II Tim.
2:2), a banking figure, common in the papyri in this sense
for the Attic *parakatathēkē* (Textus Receptus here, II Tim.
1:12, 14). See substantive also in II Tim. 1:12, 14. *Turning*
away from (ektrepomenos). Present middle participle of
ektrepō, for which see 1:6; 5:15. *Babblings (kenophōnias).*
From *kenophōnos,* uttering emptiness. Late and rare compound, in N.T. only here and II Tim. 2:16. *Oppositions*
(antitheseis). Old word (*anti, thesis*), antithesis, only here
in N.T. *Of the knowledge which is falsely so called (tēs*
pseudōnumou gnōseōs). "Of the falsely named knowledge."
Old word (*pseudēs, onoma*). Our "pseudonymous." Only
here in N.T.

21. *Have erred (ēstochēsan).* First aorist active indicative
of *astocheō.* See 1:6 for this word.

EPISTLE TO TITUS
Probably 66 or 67

Apparently from Nicopolis

CHAPTER I

1. *According to the faith of God's elect (kata pistin eklektōn theou).* Here *kata* expresses the aim of Paul's apostleship, not the standard by which he was chosen as in Phil. 3:14; a classic idiom, repeated here with *epignōsin, eusebeian, epitagēn,* "with a view to" in each case. For "God's elect" see Rom. 8:33; Col. 3:12. *The knowledge (epignōsin).* "Full knowledge," one of Paul's favourite words. For the phrase see I Tim. 2:4. *Which is according to godliness (tēs kat' eusebeian).* "The (truth) with a view to godliness." The combination of faith and full knowledge of the truth is to bring godliness on the basis of the hope of life eternal.

2. *God who cannot lie (ho apseudēs theos).* "The non-lying God." Old adjective (*a* privative and *pseudēs*), here only in N.T. See II Tim. 2:13. In Polycarp's last prayer. *Promised (epēggeilato).* First aorist middle indicative of *epaggellō.* Antithesis in *ephanerōsen de* (manifested) in verse 3 (first aorist active indicative of *phaneroō*). Same contrast in Rom. 16:25; Col. 1:26. *Before times eternal (pro chronōn aiōnōn).* Not to God's purpose before time began (Eph. 1:4; II Tim. 1:9), but to definite promises (Rom. 9:4) made in time (Lock). "Long ages ago." See Rom. 16:25.

3. *In his own seasons (kairois idiois).* Locative case. See I Tim. 2:6; 6:15. *In the message (en kērugmati).* See I Cor. 1:21; 2:4 for this word, the human proclamation (preaching) of God's word. *Wherewith I was intrusted (ho episteuthēn).* Accusative relative *ho* retained with the first aorist passive indicative of *pisteuō* as in I Tim. 1:11. See I Tim. 2:7. *Of God our Saviour (tou sōtēros hēmōn theou).* In verse 4 he applies the words "*tou sōtēros hēmōn*" to Christ. In 2:13 he applies both *theou* and *sōtēros* to Christ.

597

4. *My true child* (*gnēsiōi teknōi*). See I Tim. 1:2 for this adjective with Timothy. Titus is not mentioned in Acts, possibly because he is Luke's brother. But one can get a clear picture of him by turning to II Cor. 2:13; 7:6–15; 8:6–24; 12:16–18; Gal. 2:1–3; Titus 1:4f.; 3:12; II Tim. 4:10. He had succeeded in Corinth where Timothy had failed. Paul had left him in Crete as superintendent of the work there. Now he writes him from Nicopolis (Titus 3:12). *After a common faith* (*kata koinēn pistin*). Here *kata* does mean standard, not aim, but it is a faith (*pistin*) common to a Gentile (a Greek) like Titus as well as to a Jew like Paul and so common to all races and classes (Jude 3). *Koinos* does not here have the notion of unclean as in Acts 10:14; 11:8.

5. *For this cause* (*toutou charin*). In N.T. only here and Eph. 3:1, 14. Paul may be supplementing oral instruction as in Timothy's case and may even be replying to a letter from Titus (Zahn). *Left I thee in Crete* (*apeleipon se en Krētēi*). This is the imperfect active of *apoleipō*, though MSS. give the aorist active also (*apelipon*) and some read *kateleipon* or *katelipon*. Both are common verbs, though Paul uses *kataleipō* only in I Thess. 3:1 except two quotations (Rom. 11:4; Eph. 5:31) and *apoleipō* only here and II Tim. 4:13, 20. Perhaps *apoleipō* suggests a more temporary stay than *kataleipō*. Paul had apparently stopped in Crete on his return from Spain about A.D. 65. *That thou shouldest set in order* (*hina epidiorthōsēi*). Late and rare double compound (inscriptions, here only in N.T.), first aorist middle subjunctive (final clause with *hina*) of *epidiorthoō*, to set straight (*orthoō*) thoroughly (*dia*) in addition (*epi*), a clean job of it. *The things that were wanting* (*ta leiponta*). "The things that remain." See 3:13; Luke 18:22. Either things left undone or things that survive. In both senses the new pastor faces problems after the tornado has passed. Parry takes it "of present defects" in Cretan character. *And appoint* (*kai katastēsēis*). Final clause still and first aorist active subjunctive of *kathistēmi*, the word used in Acts 6:13 about the deacons. The word does not preclude the choice by the churches (in every city, *kata polin*, distributive use of *kata*). This is a chief point in the *epidorthōsis* (White.) *Elders* (*presbuterous*). See I Tim. 3:2; 4:17. *As I gave thee charge*

THE EPISTLES OF PAUL 599

(*hōs egō soi dietaxamēn*). First aorist (constative) middle imperative of *diatassō*, clear reference to previous personal details given to Titus on previous occasions.

6. *Blameless* (*anegklētos*). In a condition of first class. Used in I Tim. 3:10 of deacons which see. *That believe* (*pista*). Added to what is in I Tim. 3:4. "Believing children." *Not accused of riot* (*mē en katēgoriāi asōtias*). See I Tim. 5:19 for *katēgoria* and Eph. 5:18 for *asōtia*. "Not in accusation of profligacy." *Unruly* (*anupotakta*). See I Tim. 1:9. Public disorder, out of doors. See also verse 10.

7. *The bishop* (*ton episkopon*). Same office as "elder" in 1:5. "Elder is the title, oversight is the function" (B. Weiss). *As God's steward* (*hōs theou oikonomon*). See I Cor. 4:1f. for Paul's idea of the bishop (elder) as God's steward (cf. I Cor. 9:17; Col. 1:25; Eph. 3:2; I Tim. 1:4). *Not self-willed* (*mē authadē*). Old word (from *autos*, *hēdomai*), self-pleasing, arrogant. In N.T. only here and II Peter 2:10. *Not soon angry* (*orgilon*). Old adjective from *orgē* (anger). Here only in N.T. Vulgate, *iracundum*. For "brawler" and "striker" see I Tim. 3:2. *Not greedy of filthy lucre* (*aischrokerdē*). "Not greedy of shameful gain." Used of deacons in I Tim. 3:8, *aphilarguron* used of elders in I Tim. 3:3.

8. *A lover of good* (*philagathon*). Late double compound (*philos, agathos*). See Wisdom 7:22. Here only in N.T. *Just* (*dikaion*), *holy* (*hosion*) not in I Tim. 3. *Temperate* (*egkratē*). Old and common adjective (*en, kratos*, strength), having power over, controlling, here only in N.T. Picture of self-control.

9. *Holding to* (*antechomenon*). Present middle participle of *antechō*, old verb, to hold back, in middle to hold oneself face to face with, to cling to, as in I Thess. 5:14. *The faithful word* (*tou pistou logou*). See I Tim. 1:15; 6:3; Rom. 16:17. Some would see a reference here to Christ as the Personal Logos. *That he may be able* (*hina dunatos ēi*). Final clause with present active subjunctive. Paul several times uses *dunatos eimi* in the sense of *dunamai*, with infinitive as here (Rom. 4:21; 11:23; II Tim. 1:12). *The gainsayers* (*tous antilegontas*). Present active participle of *antilegō*, old word, to answer back, as in Rom. 10:21. "The talkers back."

10. *Vain talkers* (*mataiologoi*). Late and rare compound, empty talkers, in Vett. Val. and here. See I Tim. 1:6 for

mataiologia. Deceivers (phrenapatai). Late and rare compound, in papyri, eccl. writers, here alone in N.T. "Mind-deceivers." See Gal. 6:3 for *phrenapatāin. Specially they of the circumcision (malista hoi ek tēs peritomēs).* Same phrase in Acts 11:2; Gal. 2:12; Col. 4:11. Jews are mentioned in Crete in Acts 2:11. Apparently Jewish Christians of the Pharisaic type tinged with Gnosticism.

11. *Whose mouths must be stopped (hous dei epistomizein).* Literally, "whom it is necessary to silence by stopping the mouth." Present active infinitive *epistomizein,* old and common verb (*epi, stoma,* mouth), here only in N.T. To stop the mouth either with bridle or muzzle or gag. *Overthrow (anatrepousin).* Old and common verb, to turn up, to overturn. In N.T. only here and II Tim. 2:18. In papyri to upset a family by perversion of one member. *Things which they ought not (ha mē dei).* Note subjective negative *mē* with indefinite relative and indicative mode. *For filthy lucre's sake (aischrou kerdous charin).* The Cretans are given a bad reputation for itinerating prophets for profit by Polybius, Livy, Plutarch. Paul's warnings in I Tim. 3:3, 8; 6:5 reveal it as "a besetting temptation of the professional teacher" (Parry). See verse 7 above. Disgraceful gain, made in shameful ways.

12. *A prophet of their own (idios autōn prophētēs).* "Their own prophet." Self-styled "prophet" (or poet), and so accepted by the Cretans and by Cicero and Apuleius, that is Epimenides who was born in Crete at Cnossos. It is a hexameter line and Callimachus quoted the first part of it in a Hymn to Zeus. It is said that Epimenides suggested to the Athenians the erection of statues to "unknown gods" (Acts 17:23). *Liars (pseustai).* See I Tim. 1:10 for the word. The Cretans had a bad reputation on this line, partly due to their claim to having the tomb of Zeus. *Evil beasts (kaka thēria).* "Wicked wild beasts." Lock asks if the Minotaur was partly responsible. *Idle gluttons (gasteres argai).* "Idle bellies." Blunt and forceful. See Phil. 3:19 "whose god is the belly" (*hē koilia).* Both words give the picture of the sensual gormandizer.

13. *Testimony (marturia).* Of the poet Epimenides. Paul endorses it from his recent knowledge. *Sharply (apotomōs).* Old adverb from *apotomos* (from *apotemnō,* to cut off), in

N.T. only here and II Cor. 13:10, "curtly," "abruptly." It is necessary to appear rude sometimes for safety, if the house is on fire and life is in danger. *That they may be sound* (*hina hugiainōsin*). Final clause with *hina* and present active subjunctive of *hugiainō*, for which verb see on I Tim. 1:10.

14. See I Tim. 1:4 for *prosechō* and *muthois*, only here we have *Jewish* (*Ioudaikois*) added. Perhaps a reference to the oral traditions condemned by Christ in Mark 7:2–8. See also Col. 2:22, apparently Pharisaic type of Gnostics. *Who turn away from the truth* (*apostrephomenōn*). Present middle (direct) participle of *apostrephō*, "men turning themselves away from the truth" (accusative according to regular idiom). "The truth" (I Tim. 4:3) is the gospel (Eph. 4:21).

15. *To them that are defiled* (*tois memiammenois*). Perfect passive articular participle of *miainō*, old verb, to dye with another colour, to stain, in N.T. only here, Jude 8; Heb. 12:15. See *memiantai* (perf. pass. indic.) in this verse. *Molunō* (I Cor. 8:7) is to smear. *Unbelieving* (*apistois*). As in I Cor. 7:12f.; I Tim. 5:8. The principle or proverb just quoted appears also in I Cor. 6:12; 10:23; Rom. 14:20. For the defilement of mind (*nous*) and conscience (*suneidēsis*) in both Gentile and Jew by sin, see Rom. 1:18–2:29.

16. *They profess* (*homologousin*). Present active indicative of *homologeō*, common verb (*homou, legō*) as in Rom. 10:10f. *Eidenai* (know) is second perfect active infinitive of *oida* in indirect assertion. *By their works* (*tois ergois*). Instrumental case. *They deny* (*arnountai*). Present middle of *arneomai*, old verb, common in the Gospels and the Pastoral Epistles (I Tim. 5:8; Titus 2:12; II Tim. 2:12). *Abominable* (*bdeluktoi*). Verbal adjective from *bdelussomai*. Only in LXX and here. *Disobedient* (*apeitheis*). See Rom. 1:30. *Reprobate* (*adokimoi*). See on I Cor. 9:27; Rom. 1:28.

CHAPTER II

1. *But speak thou* (*su de lalei*). In contrast to these Pharisaic Gnostics in Crete. *Befit* (*prepei*). Old verb to be becoming, seemly. See I Tim. 2:10; Eph. 5:3. With dative case *didaskaliāi*. *Sound* (*hugiainousēi*). Healthful as in 1:13; 2:2; I Tim. 1:10, common word in the Pastorals. 2. *Aged men* (*presbutas*). See Philemon 9 for this word. For discussion of family life see also Col. 3:18–4:1; Eph. 5:22–6:9; I Tim. 5:1–6:2. For the adjectives here see I Tim. 3:2, 8; for the substantives see I Tim. 6:11. 3. *Aged women* (*presbutidas*). Old word, feminine of *presbutēs*, only here in N.T. See *presbuteras* in I Tim. 5:2. *Reverent* (*hieroprepeis*). Old word (*heiros*, *prepei*). Only here in N.T. Same idea in I Tim. 2:10. Like people engaged in sacred duties (Lock). *In demeanour* (*en katastēmati*). Late and rare word (inscriptions) from *kathistēmi*, deportment, only here in N.T. *Not slanderers* (*mē diabolous*). See I Tim. 3:11; II Tim. 3:3. *Nor enslaved to much wine* (*mēde oinōi pollōi dedoulōmenas*). Perfect passive participle of *douloō*, with dative case *oinōi*. See I Tim. 3:8. "It is proved by experience that the reclamation of a woman drunkard is almost impossible" (White). But God can do the "impossible." *Teachers of that which is good* (*kalodidaskalous*). Compound word found here alone, *bona docentes* (teaching good and beautiful things). A sorely needed mission. 4. *That they may train* (*hina sōphronizōsin*). Purpose clause, *hina* and present active subjunctive of *sōphronizō*, old verb (from *sōphrōn*, sound in mind, *saos*, *phrēn*, as in this verse), to make sane, to restore to one's senses, to discipline, only here in N.T. *To love their husbands* (*philandrous einai*). Predicate accusative with *einai* of old adjective *philandros* (*philos*, *anēr*, fond of one's husband), only here in N.T. *Anēr* means man, of course, as well as husband, but only husband here, not "fond of men" (other men than their own). *To love their children* (*philoteknous*). Another old compound, here only in N.T. This exhortation

602

is still needed where some married women prefer poodle-dogs to children.

5. *Workers at home (oikourgous)*. So the oldest MSS. (from *oikos, ergou*) instead of *oikourous*, keepers at home (from *koiso, ouros*, keeper). Rare word, found in Soranus, a medical writer, Field says. Cf. I Tim. 5:13. "Keepers at home" are usually "workers at home." *Kind (agathas)*. See Rom. 5:7. See Col. 3:18; Eph. 5:22 for the same use of *hupotassomai*, to be in subjection. Note *idiois* (their own). See I Tim. 6:1 for the same negative purpose clause (*hina mē blasphēmētai*).

6. *The younger men (tous neōterous)*. Just one item, besides "likewise" (*hosautōs* as in 3 and I Tim. 2:9), "to be soberminded" (*sōphronein*, old verb as in Rom. 12:3). It is possible to take "in all things" (*peri panta*) with *sōphronein*, though the editors take it with verse 7.

7. *Shewing thyself (seauton parechomenos)*. Present middle (redundant middle) participle of *parechō* with the reflexive pronoun *seauton* as if the active voice *parechōn*. The *Koiné* shows an increasing number of such constructions (Robertson, *Grammar*, p. 811). See active in I Tim. 1:4. *An ensample (tupon)*. For this word see II Thess. 3:9; Phil. 3:17. *Uncorruptness (aphthorian)*. Only example, from late adjective *aphthoros* (*a* privative and *phtheirō*).

8. *Sound (hugiē*, Attic usually *hugiā* in accusative singular), elsewhere in Pastorals participle *hugianōn* (verse 1). *That cannot be condemned (akatagnōston)*. Only N.T. example (verbal, *a* privative and *katagnōstos*) and in IV Macc. 4:47. Deissmann (*Bible Studies*, p. 200) quotes it from an inscription and the adverb from a papyrus. *He that is of the contrary part (ho ex enantias)*. "The one on the opposite side" (your opponent). Cf. verse 9; I Tim. 5:14. *May be ashamed (hina entrapēi)*. Final clause with *hina* and second aorist passive subjunctive of *entrepō*, to turn, in middle and passive to turn one on himself and so be ashamed (to blush) as in II Thess. 3:14; I Cor. 4:14. This sense in the papyri. *Evil (phaulon)*. Old word, easy (easy morals), worthless, bad, as in II Cor. 5:10.

9. *Servants (doulous)*. "Slaves." Supply "exhort" (*parakalei*). See I Tim. 6:1 for "masters" (*despotais*). *Well-pleasing (euarestous)*. See on II Cor. 5:9. *Not gainsaying (mē antilegontas)*. "Not answer back." See Rom. 10:21.

10. *Not purloining* (*mē nosphizomenous*). Present middle participle of *nosphizō*, old verb (from *nosphi*, apart), in middle to set apart for oneself, to embezzle, in N.T. only here and Acts 5:2f. *Fidelity* (*pistin*). See Gal. 5:22; I Tim. 5:12 for *pistis* in the sense of faithfulness. Nowhere else in the N.T. do we have *agathē* with *pistis* as here, but an Oxyr. papyrus (iii. 494, 9) has this very phrase (*pāsan pistin endeiknumenēi*). Westcott and Hort put *agapēn* in the margin. See 3:2. *That they may adorn* (*hina kosmōsin*). Final clause with *hina* and present active subjunctive. See I Tim. 2:9 for *kosmeō*. Paul shows slaves how they may "adorn" the teaching of God.

11. *Hath appeared* (*epephanē*). "Did appear," the first Epiphany (the Incarnation). Second aorist passive indicative of *epiphainō*, old verb, in N.T. here, 3:4; Luke 1:79; Acts 27:20. *Bringing salvation* (*sōtērios*). Old adjective from *sōtēr* (Saviour), here alone in N.T. except *to sōtērion* (salvation, "the saving act") in Luke 2:30; 3:6; Eph. 6:17. *Instructing* (*paideuousa*). See I Tim. 1:20. *Ungodliness* (*asebeian*). See Rom. 1:18. *Worldly lusts* (*tas kosmikas epithumias*). Aristotle and Plutarch use *kosmikos* (from *kosmos*) about the universe as in Heb. 9:1 about the earthly. Here it has alone in N.T. the sense of evil "in this present age" as with *kosmos* in I John 2:16. The three adverbs set off the opposite (soberly *sōphronōs*, righteously *dikaiōs*, godly *eusebōs*).

13. *Looking for* (*prosdechomenoi*). Present middle participle of *prosdechomai*, old verb, the one used of Simeon (Luke 2:25) and others (Luke 2:38) who were looking for the Messiah. *The blessed hope and appearing of the glory* (*tēn makarian elpida kai epiphaneian tēs doxēs*). The word *epiphaneia* (used by the Greeks of the appearance of the gods, from *epiphanēs*, *epiphainō*) occurs in II Tim. 1:10 of the Incarnation of Christ, the first Epiphany (like the verb *epephanē*, Titus 2:11), but here of the second Epiphany of Christ or the second coming as in I Tim. 6:14; II Tim. 4:1, 8. In II Thess. 2:8 both *epiphaneia* and *parousia* (the usual word) occur together of the second coming. *Of our great God and Saviour Jesus Christ* (*tou megalou theou kai sōtēros Iēsou Christou*). This is the necessary meaning of the one article with *theou* and *sōtēros* just as in II Peter 1:1, 11. See

Robertson, *Grammar*, p. 786. Westcott and Hort read *Christou Iēsou*.

14. *Who gave himself for us* (*hos edōken heauton huper hēmōn*). Paul's great doctrine (Gal. 1:4; 2:20; I Tim. 2:6). *That he might redeem us* (*hina lutrōsētai*). Final clause, *hina* and the aorist middle subjunctive of *lutroō*, old verb from *lutron* (ransom), in N.T. only here, Luke 24:21; I Peter 1:18. *Purify to himself* (*katharisēi heautōi*). Final clause with first aorist active subjunctive of *katharizō*, for which verb see Eph. 5:26. *Lawlessness* (*anomias*). See II Thess. 2:3. *A people for his own possession* (*laon periousion*). A late word (from *perieimi*, to be over and above, in papyri as well as *periousia*), only in LXX and here, apparently made by the LXX, one's possession, and so God's chosen people. See I Peter 2:9 (*laos eis peripoiēsin*). *Zealous of good works* (*zēlōtēn kalōn ergōn*). "A zealot for good works." Substantive for which see I Cor. 14:12; Gal. 1:14. Objective genitive *ergōn*.

15. *With all authority* (*meta pasēs epitagēs*). See I Cor. 7:6; II Cor. 8:8. Assertion of authority is sometimes necessary. *Let no man despise thee* (*mēdeis sou periphroneitō*). Present active imperative in prohibition of *periphroneō*, old verb, only here in N.T., to think around (on all sides). Literally, "let no man think around thee" (and so despise thee). In I Tim. 4:12 it is *kataphroneitō* (think down on), a stronger word of scorn, but this one implies the possibility of one making mental circles around one and so "out-thinking" him. The best way for the modern minister to command respect for his "authority" is to do thinking that will deserve it.

CHAPTER III

1. *To be in subjection to rulers, to authorities, to be obedient* (*archais exousiais hupotassesthai peitharchein*). Remarkable double asyndeton, no *kai* (and) between the two substantives or the two verbs. *Peitharchein* (to obey), old verb (from *peithomai, archē*), in N.T. only here and Acts 27:21. *To be ready unto every good work* (*pros pan ergon agathon hetoimous einai*). Pauline phrase (II Cor. 9:8; II Tim. 2:21; 3:17), here adjective *hetoimos* (II Cor. 9:5), there verb.

2. *To speak evil* (*blasphēmein*). See Col. 3:8; I Tim. 6:4. *Not to be contentious* (*amachous einai*). "To be non-fighters" (I Tim. 3:3), originally "invincible." *Gentle* (*epieikeis*). See I Tim. 3:3. *Meekness* (*praütēta*). *Praotēta*. See Col. 3:12.

3. *Aforetime* (*pote*). "Once" in our unconverted state as in Eph. 2:3. *Foolish* (*anoētoi*). See Rom. 1:14, 21. *Disobedient* (*apeitheis*). See Rom. 1:30. *Deceived* (*planōmenoi*). Present passive participle of *planaō* though the middle is possible. *Divers lusts* (*hēdonais poikilais*). "Pleasures" (*hēdonais* from *hēdomai*, old word, in N.T. only here, Luke 8:14; James 4:1, 3; II Peter 2:13). *Poikilais* (old word) is many-coloured as in Mark 1:34; James 1:2; II Tim. 3:6, etc. *Living* (*diagontes*). See I Tim. 3:6 (supply *bion*). *In malice* (*en kakiāi*). See Rom. 1:29. *Envy* (*phthonōi*). See Rom. 1:29. *Hateful* (*stugētoi*). Late passive verbal from *stugeō*, to hate. In Philo, only here in N.T. *Hating one another* (*misountes allēlous*). Active sense and natural result of being "hateful."

4. *The kindness* (*hē chrēstotēs*). See Rom. 2:4 for this very word used of God as here. *His love toward man* (*hē philanthrōpia*). "The philanthrophy of God our Saviour." Old word from *philanthrōpos*, for love of mankind, in N.T. only here and Acts 28:2. *Appeared* (*epephanē*). See 2:11 and here as there the Incarnation of Christ. See I Tim. 1:1 for *sōtēr* with *theos* (God).

5. *Done* (not in the Greek, only the article *tōn*), "not as a result of works those in righteousness which we did." Same

idea as in Rom. 3:20f. *According to his mercy he saved us* (*kata to autou eleos esōsen*). See Psa. 109:26 and I Peter 1:3; Eph. 2:4. Effective aorist active indicative of *sōzō*. *Through the washing of regeneration* (*dia loutrou palingenesias*). Late and common word with the Stoics (Dibelius) and in the Mystery-religions (Angus), also in the papyri and Philo. Only twice in the N.T. (Matt. 19:28 with which compare *apokatastasia* in Acts 3:21, and here in personal sense of new birth). For *loutron*, see Eph. 5:26, here as there the laver or the bath. Probably in both cases there is a reference to baptism, but, as in Rom. 6:3–6, the immersion is the picture or the symbol of the new birth, not the means of securing it. *And renewing of the Holy Spirit* (*kai anakainōseōs pneumatos hagiou*). "And renewal by the Holy Spirit" (subjective genitive). For the late word *anakainōsis*, see Rom. 12:2. Here, as often, Paul has put the objective symbol before the reality. The Holy Spirit does the renewing, man submits to the baptism after the new birth to picture it forth to men.

6. *Which* (*hou*). Genitive case by attraction from *ho* (grammatical gender) to the case of *pneumatos hagiou*. We do not have grammatical gender (only natural) in English. Hence here we should say "whom," even if it does not go smoothly with *execheen* (he poured out, second aorist active indicative of *ekcheō*). The reference is to the great Pentecost (Acts 2:33) as foretold by Joel (2:28). *Richly* (*plousiōs*). Then and to each one in his own experience. See Rom. 10:12; I Tim. 6:17.

7. *Being justified by his grace* (*dikaiōthentes tēi ekeinou chariti*). First aorist passive participle of *dikaioō* and instrumental case of *charis* as in Rom. 3:24; 5:1. *That we might be made heirs* (*hina klēronomoi genēthōmen*). Purpose with *hina* and first aorist passive of *ginomai*. See Rom. 4:13; 8:17.

8. *The saying* (*ho logos*). In verses 4–7. *I will* (*boulomai*). See I Tim. 2:8. *That thou affirm confidently* (*se diabebaiousthai*). Indirect command. For the verb see I Tim. 1:7. *That they may be careful* (*hina phrontizōsin*). Sub-final use of *hina* with present active subjunctive of *phrontizō*, old verb, only here in N.T. *To maintain good works* (*kalōn ergōn proïstasthai*). Present middle infinitive of *proistēmi*, intransitive use, to stand before, to take the lead in, to care for.

Paul is anxious that "believers" may take the lead in good works.

9. *Fightings about the law* (*machas nomikas*). "Legal battles." See I Tim. 6:4; II Tim. 2:23. Wordy fights about Mosaic and Pharisaic and Gnostic regulations. *Shun* (*periistaso*). Present middle imperative of *periistēmi*, intransitive, step around, stand aside (II Tim. 2:16). Common in this sense in the literary *Koiné. Unprofitable* (*anōpheleis*). Old compound adjective (*a.* privative and *ophelos*), in N.T. only here and Heb. 7:18.

10. *Heretical* (*hairetikon*). Old adjective from *hairesis* (*haireomai*, to choose), a choosing of a party (sect, Acts 5:17) or of teaching (II Peter 2:1). Possibly a schism had been started here in Crete. *Refuse* (*paraitou*). Present middle imperative of *paraiteō*, to ask from, to beg off from. See same form in I Tim. 4:7; 5:11. Possibly an allusion here to Christ's directions in Matt. 18:15–17.

11. *Is perverted* (*exestraptai*). Perfect passive indicative of *ekstrephō*, old word to turn inside out, to twist, to pervert. Only here in N.T. *Self-condemned* (*autokatakritos*). Only known example of this double compound verbal adjective (*autos, kata, krinō*).

12. *When I shall send* (*hotan pempsō*). Indefinite temporal clause with *hotan* and the first aorist active subjunctive (or future indicative) of *pempō* (same form). *Artemas* (*Artemān*). Perhaps abbreviation of Artemidorus. Nothing more is known of him. *Or Tychicus* (*ē Tuchikon*). Paul's well-known disciple (Col. 4:7; Eph. 6:21; II Tim. 4:12). *To Nicopolis* (*eis Nikopolin*). Probably in Epirus, a good place for work in Dalmatia (II Tim. 4:10). *I have determined* (*kekrika*). Perfect active indicative. I have decided. *To winter there* (*ekei paracheimasai*). First aorist active infinitive of *paracheimazō*, a literary *Koiné* word for which see Acts 27:12; I Cor. 16:6.

13. *Zenas the lawyer* (*Zēnān ton nomikon*). Possibly abbreviation of Zenodorus and may be one of the bearers of the Epistle with Apollos. Probably an expert in the Mosaic law as the word means in the Gospels. A converted Jewish lawyer. The Latin term is *jurisconsultum* for *nomikon. Apollos* (*Apollōn*). Paul's friend (Acts 18:24–19:1; I Cor. 1:12ff.). *Set forward* (*propempson*). First aorist active im-

perative of *propempō*, old verb, to send on ahead (I Cor. 16:6, 11; Rom. 15:24). *That nothing be wanting unto them* (*hina mēden autois leipēi*). Purpose with *hina* and present (or second aorist *lipēi*, some MSS.) subjunctive of *leipō*, old verb to leave, to remain, to lack. With dative case here (*autois*). 14. *Our people* (*hoi hēmeteroi*). "Our folks." The Cretan converts, not just Paul's friends. *Let learn* (*manthanetōsan*). Present active imperative, keep on learning how. *To maintain* (*proïstasthai*). See verse 8. *For necessary uses* (*eis anagkaias chreias*). "For necessary wants." No idlers wanted. See I Thess. 4:12; II Thess. 3:10f. *Unfruitful* (*akarpoi*). See I Cor. 14:14; Eph. 5:11. 15. *That love us* (*tous philountas hēmās*). Paul craved the love of his friends as opposed to 2:8.

SECOND TIMOTHY
From Rome

Probably Early Autumn of 67 or Spring of 68

CHAPTER I

1. *According to the promise of the life which is in Christ Jesus (kat' epaggelian zōēs tēs en Christōi Iēsou).* "With a view to the fulfilment of the promise." See Titus 1:1 for this same use of *kata*. For *kat' epaggelian* see Gal. 3:29. See I Tim. 4:8 for the phrase "promise of life." Here or there "life that in Christ Jesus" includes the present as well as the future. 2. *Beloved (agapētoi).* Instead of *gnēsiōi* (genuine) in I Tim. 1:2. He had already called Timothy *agapēton* (verbal adjective of *agapaō*) in I Cor. 4:17, an incidental and strong proof that it is Paul who is writing here. This argument applies to each of the Pastorals for Paul is known by other sources (Acts and previous Pauline Epistles) to sustain precisely the affectionate relation toward Timothy and Titus shown in the Pastorals. 3. *I thank (charin echō).* "I have gratitude." As in I Tim. 1:12. Robinson cites examples of this phrase from the papyri. It occurs also in Luke 17:9; Acts 2:47. *Charis* in doxologies Paul uses (I Cor. 15:57; 2:14; 8:16; 9:15; Rom. 6:17; 7:25). His usual idiom is *eucharistō* (I Cor. 1:4; Rom. 1:8; Philemon 4; Phil. 1:3) or *eucharistoumen* (I Thess. 1:2; Col. 1:3) or *ou pauomai eucharistōn* (Eph. 1:16) or *eucharistein opheilomen* (II Thess. 1:3). *Whom I serve from my forefathers (hōi latreuō apo progonōn).* The relative *hōi* is the dative case with *latreuō* (see Rom. 1:9 for this verb), progressive present (I have been serving). For *progonōn* (forefathers) see I Tim. 5:4. Paul claims a pious ancestry as in Acts 24:14; Acts 26:5; Gal. 2:14; Phil. 3:4-7. *In a pure conscience (en katharāi suneidēsei).* See I Tim. 1:5 and Acts 23:1. *Unceasing (adia- leipton).* Late and rare compound, in N.T. only here and

Rom. 9:2 which see. The adverb *adialeiptōs* is more frequent (in the papyri, literary *Koiné*, I Thess. 1:2; Rom. 1:9). The adjective here is the predicate accusative, "how I hold the memory concerning thee unceasing." The use of *adialeiptōs* (adverb) is a sort of epistolary formula (papyri, I Thess. 1:2; 2:13; 5:17; Rom. 1:9). *Remembrance* (*mneian*). Old word, in N.T. only Pauline (seven times, I Thess. 1:2; Rom. 1:9; Phil. 1:3).

4. *Night and day* (*nuktos kai hēmeras*). Genitive of time, "by night and by day." As in I Thess. 2:9; 3:10. *Longing* (*epipothōn*). Present active participle of *epipotheō*, old word, eight times in Paul (I Thess. 3:6; Phil. 1:8, etc.). *Remembering thy tears* (*memnēmenos sou tōn dakruōn*). Perfect middle participle of *mimnēskō*, old and common verb with the genitive, only here in the Pastorals and elsewhere by Paul only in I Cor. 11:2. Probably an allusion to the scene at Miletus (Acts 20:37). Cf. Acts 20:19. *That I may be filled with joy* (*hina charas plērōthō*). Final clause with *hina* and first aorist passive subjunctive of *plēroō* (with genitive case *charas*), a verb common with Paul (Rom. 8:4; 13:8).

5. *Having been reminded* (*hupomnēsin labōn*). "Having received (second aorist active participle of *lambanō*) a reminder" (old word from *hupomimnēskō*, to remind, in N.T. only here and I Peter 1:13). For the idiom see Rom. 7:8, 11. A reminder by another while *anamnēsis* remembrance (I Cor. 11:24f.) is rather a recalling by oneself (Vincent). *Of the unfeigned faith* (*tēs anupokritou pisteōs*). Late compound for which see II Cor. 6:6; Rom. 12:9. *Dwelt* (*enōikēsen*). First aorist active indicative of *enoikeō*, old verb, in N.T. only in Paul (Rom. 8:11; Col. 3:16). *First* (*prōton*). Adverb, not adjective (*prōtē*). *In thy grandmother Lois* (*en tēi mammēi Lōidi*). Old word, originally the infantile word for *mētēr* (mother), then extended by writers to grandmother as here. Common for grandmother in the papyri. Lois is the mother of Eunice, Timothy's mother, since Timothy's father was a Greek (Acts 16:1). Probably both grandmother and mother became Christians. *I am persuaded* (*pepeismai*). Perfect passive indicative of *peithō*, "I stand persuaded." In the Pastorals only here and verse 12, common in Paul's other writings (Rom. 8:38, etc.).

6. *For the which cause* (*di' hēn aitian*). "For which cause,"

stronger than *dio*. So in verse 12; Titus 1:13. Only example of *aitia* by Paul save in Acts 28:20. *I put thee in remembrance* (*anamimnēskō*). Old compound to remind (I Cor. 4:17; II Cor. 7:15). *That thou stir up* (*se anazōpurein*). Present active infinitive of *anazōpureō*, old double compound (*ana* and *zōpuron*, live coal, *zōos* and *pur*, then the bellows for kindling), to rekindle, to stir into flame, to keep blazing (continuous action, present time), only here in N.T. See I Thess. 5:19 for the figure of fire concerning the Holy Spirit. See *anaptō* in Luke 12:49. *The gift of God* (*to charisma tou theou*). See I Tim. 4:14. Here Paul says *mou* (my), there he mentions the presbytery. Paul felt a deep personal interest in Timothy. See I Cor. 7:7; Rom. 6:23; 11:29 for the gift of God.

7. *A spirit of fearfulness* (*pneuma deilias*). Here *pneuma* is the *charisma* of verse 6, the human spirit as endowed by the Holy Spirit (Rom. 8:15). *Deilia* is an old word (*deilos*, *deidō*) and always in a bad sense of cowardice, only here in N.T. *Of power* (*dunameōs*). One of Paul's characteristic words (Rom. 1:16). *Of love* (*agapēs*). One of the gifts of the Spirit (Gal. 5:22). "Which drives out fear" (Lock) as in I John 4:18. *Of discipline* (*sōphronismou*). Late Koiné word (from *sōphronizō*, to control), self-control, here only in N.T. See I Tim. 2:9 for *sōphrosunē*.

8. *Be not ashamed of* (*mē epaischunthēis*). First aorist (ingressive) passive subjunctive (in prohibition) of *epaischunomai*, old word, to be ashamed. Again in verse 16 without augment (*epaischunthēn*), transitive use of the passive voice as often in the Koiné (Robertson, *Grammar*, p. 818). See Rom. 1:16; 6:21. "Do not become ashamed" (as he had not). *The testimony of our Lord* (*to marturion tou kuriou*). For the old word *marturion* see I Cor. 1:6; 2:1. Paul probably has in mind the saying of Jesus preserved in Mark 8:38 (= Luke 9:26). See also 2:12. *His prisoner* (*ton desmion autou*). As in Phil. 1:12; Philemon 1, 9; Eph. 3:1; 4:1 (the first Roman captivity). Paul is in his last captivity and refers to it again in verse 16 and 2:9. *Suffer hardship with* (*sunkakopathēson*). First aorist active imperative of the double compound *sunkakopatheō*, first known use and in N.T. only here and 2:3 (in eccles. writers). But *kakopatheō*, to suffer evil, is old verb (2:9; 4:5). Paul is fond of com-

pounds of *sun*. Paul challenges Timothy by this verb which he apparently coins for the purpose to a joint (*sun*) suffering with the Lord Jesus and Paul "for the gospel" (*tōi euaggeliōi*, dative case rather than associative instrumental "with"). *According to the power of God* (*kata dunamin theou*). Given by God (II Cor. 6:7).

9. *Called us with a holy calling* (*kalesantos klēsei hagiāi*). Probably dative, "to a holy calling." *Klēsis* here apparently not the invitation, but the consecrated service, "the upward calling" (Phil. 3:14). See I Cor. 7:20; Eph. 4:1, 4 for the use of *kaleō* with *klēsis*. Paul often uses *kaleō* of God's calling men (I Thess. 2:12; I Cor. 1:9; Gal. 1:6; Rom. 8:20; 9:11. *Purpose* (*prothesin*). See Rom. 9:11; Eph. 1:11 for *prothesin*. *Which was given* (*tēn dotheisan*). First aorist passive articular participle agreeing with *charis* (grace), a thoroughly Pauline expression (I Cor. 3:10; Rom. 12:3, 6, etc.), only here in Pastoral Epistles. *Before times eternal* (*pro chronōn aiōniōn*). See Titus 1:2.

10. *But hath now been manifested* (*phanerōtheisan de nun*). First aorist passive participle of *phaneroō* agreeing with *charin*. See Titus 1:3; Col. 1:26; 3:4 for *phaneroō* and the contrast made. *By the appearing* (*dia tēs epiphaneias*). Only here of the Incarnation (except the verb, Titus 2:11; 3:4), but for the second coming see Titus 2:13. *Who abolished death* (*katargēsantos men ton thanaton*). First aorist active participle of *katargeō*, the very phrase in I Cor. 15:26 and Heb. 2:14. *Brought to light* (*phōtisantos de*). First aorist active participle of *phōtizō*, literary *Koiné* word for which see I Cor. 4:5; Eph. 1:18, to turn the light on. *Life and incorruption* (*zōēn kai aphtharsian*). The opposite of *thanatos*, "life and immortality" (unchangeable life).

11. *For which* (*eis ho*). For the gospel. See I Tim. 2:7 for this verse.

12. *These things* (*tauta*). His imprisonment in Rome. *Yet I am not ashamed* (*all' ouk epaischunomai*). Plain reference to the exhortation to Timothy in verse 8. *Him whom I have believed* (*hōi pepisteuka*). Dative case of the relative (*hōi*) with the perfect active of *pisteuō*, the antecedent to the relative not expressed. It is not an indirect question. Paul knows Jesus Christ whom he has trusted. *I am persuaded* (*pepeismai*). See verse 5. *To guard* (*phulaxai*). First aorist

active infinitive of *phulassō*, the very word used in I Tim.
6:20 with *parathēkēn* as here, to guard against robbery or
any loss. *That which I have committed unto him (tēn parathēkēn mou)*. Literally, "my deposit," as in a bank, the
bank of heaven which no burglar can break (Matt. 6:19f.).
See this word also in verse 14. Some MSS. have the more
common *parakatathēkē* (a sort of double deposit, *para*, beside,
down, *kata*). *Against that day (eis ekeinēn tēn hēmeran)*. The
day of Christ's second coming. See also 1:18; 4:8; II Thess.
1:10, and often in the Gospels. Elsewhere, the day of the
Lord (I Thess. 5:2; II Thess. 2:2; I Cor. 1:8; II Cor. 1:14),
the day of Christ or Jesus Christ (Phil. 1:6, 10; 2:16), the
day (I Thess. 5:4; I Cor. 3:13; Rom. 13:12), the day of redemption (Eph. 4:20), the day of judgment (Rom. 2:5, 16).

13. *The pattern of sound words (hupotupōsin hugiainontōn
logōn)*. See I Tim. 1:16 for *hupotupōsin* and I Tim. 1:10 for
hugiainō. *Which (hōn)*. Genitive plural with *ēkousas* (didst
hear) or attracted to case of *logōn* (*akouō* is used either with
the accusative or the genitive).

14. *That good thing which was committed unto thee (tēn
kalēn parathēkēn)*. Simply, "the good deposit." *Guard
(phulaxon)*. As in I Tim. 6:20. God has also made an in-
vestment in Timothy (cf. verse 12). Timothy must not
let that fail. *Which dwelleth in us (tou enoikountos en hēmin)*.
It is only through the Holy Spirit that Timothy or any of
us can guard God's deposit with us.

15. *Are turned away from me (apestraphēsan me)*. Second
aorist passive (still transitive here with *me*) of *apostrephō*,
for which verb see Titus 1:14. For the accusative with these
passive deponents see Robertson, *Grammar*, p. 484. It is
not known to what incident Paul refers, whether the refusal
of the Christians in the Roman province of Asia to help
Paul on his arrest (or in response to an appeal from Rome)
or whether the Asian Christians in Rome deserted Paul in
the first stage of the trial (4:16). Two of these Asian deserters
are mentioned by name, perhaps for reasons known to
Timothy. Nothing else is known of Phygelus and Hermogenes except this shameful item.

16. *Grant mercy (dōiē eleos)*. The phrase nowhere else in
the N.T. Second aorist active optative of *didōmi*, the usual
form being *doiē*. This is the usual construction in a wish

about the future. *Unto the house of Onesiphorus* (*tōi Onēsiphorou oikōi*). The same phrase in 4:19. Apparently Onesiphorus is now dead as is implied by the wish in 1:18. *For he oft refreshed me* (*hoti pollakis me anepsuxen*). First aorist active indicative of *anapsuchō*, old verb, to cool again, in LXX and *Koiné* often, here only in N.T., but *anapsuxis* in Acts 3:20. In the first imprisonment or the second. If he lost his life for coming to see Paul, it was probably recently during this imprisonment. *Was not ashamed of my chain* (*halusin mou ouk epaischunthē*). Passive deponent again (first aorist indicative) with accusative as in 1:8. For *halusin* (chain) see Eph. 6:20. Note absence of augment in *epaischunthē*.

17. *When he was in Rome* (*genomenos en Romēi*). Second aorist middle participle of *ginomai* (coming to Rome, happening in Rome). *He sought me diligently and found me* (*spoudaiōs ezētēsen me kai heuren*). Effective aorists both of them (first of *zēteō*, second of *heuriskō*). He did it at the risk of his own life apparently.

18. *Grant to him to find mercy* (*dōiē autōi heurein eleos*). Second aorist active optative in wish for the future again as in verse 16. Find mercy from the Lord (Jesus) as he found me. *Thou knowest very well* (*beltion su ginōskeis*). Literally, "thou knowest better (than I)," for he did those things in Ephesus where thou art. Only N.T. example of *beltion*, in D text of Acts 10:28.

CHAPTER II

1. *Be strengthened* (*endunamou*). Present passive imperative of *endunamoō*. See already I Tim. 1:12; Rom. 4:20; Phil. 4:13; Eph. 6:10. "Keep on being empowered," "keep in touch with the power." *In the grace that is in Christ Jesus* (*en tēi chariti tēi en Christōi Iēsou*). Where the power is located. Christ is the dynamo for power only when and while we keep in touch with him.

2. *From me* (*par' emou*). As in 1:13. Paul was Timothy's chief teacher of Christ. *Among many witnesses* (*dia pollōn marturōn*). Plutarch has *dia* in this sense and Field (*Ot. Norv.*) suggests that it is a legal phrase "supported by many witnesses." Not mere spectators, but testifiers. See Paul's use of *dia* I Thess. 4:2; II Cor. 2:4; Rom. 2:27; 14:20. Paul in I Cor. 15:1–8 gives many witnesses of the resurrection of Christ. *Commit thou* (*parathou*). Second aorist middle imperative of *paratithēmi* (I Tim. 1:18) to deposit, same metaphor as *parathēkē* in 1:12, 14. "Deposit thou." *Faithful* (*pistois*). "Trustworthy," "reliable," as in I Tim. 1:12 of Paul himself. *Able* (*hikanoi*). Capable, qualified, as in I Cor. 15:9; II Cor. 2:16; 3:5. *Others also* (*kai heterous*). Not necessarily "different," but "others in addition." This is the way to pass on the torch of the light of the knowledge of God in Christ. Paul taught Timothy who will teach others who will teach still others, an endless chain of teacher-training and gospel propaganda.

3. *Suffer hardship with me* (*sunkakopathēson*). See 1:8 for this verb. The old preacher challenges the young one to share hardship with him for Christ. *As a good soldier* (*hōs kalos stratiōtēs*). Paul does not hesitate to use this military metaphor (this word only here for a servant of Christ) with which he is so familiar. He had already used the metaphor in I Cor. 9:7; II Cor. 10:3f.; I Tim. 1:18. In Phil. 2:25 he called Epaphroditus "my fellow-soldier" (*sunstratiōtēn mou*) as he did Archippus in Philemon 2.

4. *No soldier on service* (*oudeis strateuomenos*). "No one serving as a soldier." See I Cor. 9:7 for this old verb and

616

II Cor. 10:3; I Tim. 1:18 for the metaphorical use. *Entangleth himself* (*empleketai*). Old compound, to inweave (see Matt. 27:29 for *plekō*), in N.T. only here and II Peter 2:20. Present middle (direct) indicative. *In the affairs* (*tais pragmateiais*). Old word (from *pragmateuomai*, Luke 19:13), business, occupation, only here in N.T. *Of this life* (*tou biou*). No "this" in the Greek, "of life" (course of life as in I Tim. 2:2, not existence *zōē*). *Him who enrolled him as a soldier* (*tōi stratologēsanti*). Dative case after *aresēi* (first aorist active subjunctive of *areskō*, to please, I Thess. 2:4, purpose clause with *hina*) of the articular first aorist active participle of *stratologeō*, literary *Koiné* word (*stratologos*, from *stratos* and *legō*), only here in N.T.

5. *If also a man contend in the games* (*ean de kai athlēi tis*). Condition of third class with present (linear) active subjunctive of *athleō*, old and common verb (from *athlos*, a contest), only this verse in N.T., but *sunathleō* in Phil. 1:27. Note sharp distinction between *athlēi* (present subjunctive, engage in a contest in general) and *athlēsēi* (first aorist active subjunctive, engage in a particular contest). Not "except he have contended," but simply "unless he contend" (in any given case) "lawfully" (*nomimōs*). Old adverb, agreeably to the law, in N.T. only here and I Tim. 1:8. *Is not crowned* (*ou stephanoutai*). Present passive indicative of *stephanoō*, old verb (from *stephanos*, crown); in N.T. only here and Heb. 2:7, 9. One apodosis for two protases. The victor in the athletic contests was crowned with a garland.

6. *The husbandman that laboureth* (*ton kopiōnta geōrgon*). "The toiling tiller of the soil" (*geōrgon*, from *gē* and *ergō*, worker of the earth). See *geōrgion* (field) in I Cor. 3:9 and also I Cor. 9:7. *First* (*prōton*). As is natural and right. *To partake* (*metalambanein*). Old word as in Acts 2:46 to share in. Paul elsewhere uses *metechō* as in I Cor. 9:12.

7. *Consider* (*noei*). Present active imperative of *noeō*, old verb, to put your mind (*nous*) on. See Eph. 3:4 and like command in I Cor. 10:15. *Understanding* (*sunesin*). "Comprehension" (from *suniēmi*, to send together, to grasp). See Col. 1:9; 2:2. This is a blessed promise that calls for application.

8. *Risen from the dead* (*egēgermenon ek nekrōn*). Perfect passive participle of *egeirō*, still risen as the perfect tense

shows in I Cor. 15:4, 12–20. Predicate accusative. "Remember Jesus Christ as risen from the dead." This is the cardinal fact about Christ that proves his claim to be the Messiah, the Son of God. Christ is central for Paul here as in Phil. 2:5–11. *Of the seed of David (ek spermatos Daueid).* The humanity of Christ as in Rom. 1:3; Phil. 2:7f. *According to my gospel (kata to euaggelion mou).* Paul's very phrase in Rom. 2:16; 16:25. Not a written gospel, but my message. See also I Cor. 15:1; II Cor. 11:7; Gal. 1:11; 2:2; I Tim. 1:11.

9. *Wherein (en hōi).* In my gospel. *I suffer hardship (kakopathō).* "I suffer evil." Old compound (*kakon, paschō*), elsewhere in N.T., 4:5; James 5:13. *Unto bonds (mechri desmōn).* "Up to bonds." A common experience with Paul (II Cor. 11:23; Phil. 1:7, 13, 14; Col. 4:18). *As a malefactor (hōs kakourgos),* old compound (*kakon, ergō,* doer of evil), in N.T. only here and Luke 23:32ff. (of the robbers). One of the charges made against Paul. *Is not bound (ou dedetai).* Perfect passive indicative of *deō,* to bind. Old verb. See I Cor. 7:27, 39; Rom. 7:2. I am bound with a chain, but no fetters are on the word of God (Pauline phrase; I Thess. 2:13; I Cor. 14:36; II Cor. 2:17; Phil. 1:14; Titus 2:5).

10. *For the elect's sake (dia tous eklektous).* "Because of the elect." God's elect (Rom. 8:33; Col. 3:12; Titus 1:1) for whom Paul suffered so much (Col. 1:6; 12:15; Phil. 2:17; Eph. 3:1, 13). *That they also may obtain (hina kai autoi tuchōsin).* Purpose clause with second aorist (effective) active subjunctive of *tugchanō* with genitive. "They as well as I," Paul means. *The salvation (tēs sōtērias).* The final salvation "with eternal glory" (*meta doxēs aiōniou).* This phrase only here and I Peter 5:10, but in II Cor. 4:17 we have "eternal weight of glory."

11. *Faithful is the saying (pistos ho logos).* The saying which follows here though it can refer to the preceding as in I Tim. 4:9. See I Tim. 1:15. It is possible that from here to the end of 13 we have the fragment of an early hymn. There are four conditions in these verses (11 to 13), all of the first class, assumed to be true. Parallels to the ideas here expressed are found in II Thess. 1:5; I Cor. 4:8; II Cor. 7:3; Rom. 6:3–8; Col. 3:1–4. Note the compounds with *sun (sunapethanomen, we died with,* from *sunapothnesko* as in II Cor. 7:3; *sunzēsomen, we shall live with,* from *sunzaō*

as in II Cor. 7:3; *sumbasileusomen, we shall reign with*, from *sumbasileuō* as in I Cor. 4:8). For *hupomenomen* (we endure) see I Cor. 13:7 and for *apistoumen* (we are faithless) see Rom. 3:3. The verb *arneomai*, to deny (*arnēsometha*, we shall deny, *arnēsetai*, he will deny, *arnēsasthai*, deny, first aorist middle infinitive) is an old word, common in the Gospels in the sayings of Jesus (Matt. 10:33; Luke 12:9), used of Peter (Mark 14:70), and is common in the Pastorals (I Tim. 5:8; Titus 2:12; II Tim. 3:5). Here in verse 13 it has the notion of proving false to oneself, a thing that Christ "cannot" (*ou dunatai*) do.

14. *That they strive not about words* (*mē logomachein*). Word apparently coined by Paul from *logomachia* (I Tim. 6:4 which see), a back formation in that case. A mere war of words displeases Paul. (Titus 3:9.) *Useful* (*chrēsimon*). Late and rare word from *chraomai*, here only in N.T. *To the subverting* (*epi katastrophēi*). Old word (from *katastrephō*, to turn down or over), here only in N.T. (except II Peter 2:6 in some MSS., not in Westcott and Hort). "Because of the overthrow" (result *epi*, not aim), useless for this reason. Such war of words merely upsets the hearers.

15. *Give diligence* (*spoudason*). First aorist active imperative of *spoudazō*, old word, as in I Thess. 2:17; Gal. 2:10. *To present* (*parastēsai*). First aorist active infinitive of *paristēmi* as in Col. 1:22, 28. *Approved unto God* (*dokimon tōi theōi*). Dative case *theōi* with *dokimon*, predicate accusative, old adjective (from *dechomai*), for which see I Cor. 11:19; II Cor. 10:18. *A workman* (*ergatēn*). See II Cor. 11:3; Phil. 3:2. *That needeth not to be ashamed* (*anepaischunton*). Late double compound verbal adjective (*a* privative, *epaischunō*), in Josephus and here alone. *Handling aright* (*orthotomounta*). Present active participle of *orthotomeō*, late and rare compound (*orthotomos*, cutting straight, *orthos* and *temnō*), here only in N.T. It occurs in Proverbs 3:6; 11:5 for making straight paths (*hodous*) with which compare Heb. 12:13 and "the Way" in Acts 9:2. Theodoret explains it to mean ploughing a straight furrow. Parry argues that the metaphor is the stone mason cutting the stones straight since *temnō* and *orthos* are so used. Since Paul was a tent-maker and knew how to cut straight the rough camel-hair cloth, why not let that be the metaphor? Certainly plenty of exegesis

is crooked enough (crazy-quilt patterns) to call for careful cutting to set it straight.

16. *Shun* (*periistaso*). See Titus 3:9. *Babblings* (*kenophōnias*). See I Tim. 6:20. *Will proceed* (*prokopsousin*). Future active of *prokoptō*, "will cut forward." See Gal. 1:14; Rom. 13:12. *Further in ungodliness* (*epi pleion asebeias*). "To more of ungodliness." See Rom. 1:18; I Tim. 2:2.

17. *Will eat* (*nomēn hexei*). "Will have (future active of *echō*) pasturage or increase" (*nomē*, old word from *nemō*, to pasture, in N.T. only here and John 10:9). *As doth gangrene* (*hōs gaggraina*). Late word (medical writers and Plutarch), only here in N.T. From *graō* or *grainō*, to gnaw, to eat, an eating, spreading disease. Hymenaeus is probably the one mentioned in I Tim. 1:20. Nothing is known of Philetus.

18. *Men who* (*hoitines*). "The very ones who." *Have erred* (*ēstochēsan*). "Missed the mark." First aorist active indicative of *astocheō*, for which see I Tim. 1:6; 6:21. *That the resurrection is past already* (*anastasin ēdē gegonenai*). Second perfect active infinitive of *ginomai* in indirect assertion after *legontes* (saying) with the accusative of general reference (*anastasin*). *Overthrow* (*anatrepousin*). See Titus 1:11.

19. *Howbeit* (*mentoi*). Strong adversative, "however." *Firm* (*stereos*). Old adjective, solid, compact, in N.T. only here, I Peter 5:9; Heb. 5:12, 14. See *stereōma* in Col. 2:5. For *themelios* see I Cor. 3:11; Rom. 15:20; I Tim. 6:19. Cf. *hedraiōma* in I Tim. 3:15. *Seal* (*sphragis*). See I Cor. 9:2; Rom. 4:11. *Knoweth* (*egnō*). Timeless aorist active indicative of *ginōskō*. Quotation from Numb. 16:5. *Let every one depart* (*apostētō pās*). Paraphrase of Numb. 16:27; Isa. 26:13; 52:11; Jer. 20:9. Second aorist active imperative of *aphistēmi* (intransitive use), "Let every one stand off from." Probably another echo of the rebellion of Korah.

20. *In a great house* (*en megalēi oikiāi*). Metaphor of a palace. He doubtless has the Kingdom of God in mind, but he works out the metaphor of a great house of the rich and mighty. *Vessels* (*skeuē*). Old word *skeuos*. See Rom. 9:21 for the same double use as here. *Of gold* (*chrusā*). Old contracted adjective *chruseos*, only here by Paul. *Of silver* (*argurā*). Old contracted adjective *argureos*, in N.T. here, Acts 19:24; Rev. 9:20. *Of wood* (*xulina*). Old adjective, in

N.T. only here and Rev. 9:20. *Of earth (ostrakina)*. Late adjective, from *ostrakon*, baked clay, in LXX, in N.T. only here and II Cor. 4:7.

21. *If a man purge himself (ean tis ekkatharēi)*. Paul drops the metaphor of the house and takes up the individual as one of the "vessels." Condition of third class with first aorist active subjunctive of *ekkathairō*, old verb, to cleanse out, in LXX, in N.T. only here and I Cor. 5:7. *From these (apo toutōn)*. From the vessels for dishonour of verse 20. *Sanctified (hēgiasmenon)*. Perfect passive participle of *hagiazō*, for which verb see I Cor. 6:11. *Meet for the master's use (euchrēston tōi despotōi)*. Dative case *despotēi* (for which word see I Tim. 6:1) with *euchrēston*, neuter singular like *hēgiasmenon* agreeing with *skeuos*. Old verbal adjective (*eu* and *chraomai*, to use well), useful or usable for the master. In N.T. only here and 4:11. See *achrēston* in Philemon 11. *Prepared (hētoimasmenon)*. Perfect passive participle of *hetoimazō*, in a state of readiness, old and common word, elsewhere by Paul only I Cor. 2:9 (LXX).

22. *Youthful (neōterikas)*. Literary *Koiné* word (Polybius, Josephus), only here in N.T. There are lusts peculiar to flaming youth. *Flee (pheuge)*. Present active imperative of *pheugō*, old and common verb. In this sense see I Cor. 6:18. *Follow after (diōke)*. Present active imperative of *diōkō* as if in a chase for which sense see I Thess. 5:15. Steady pursuit of these virtues like those in Gal. 5:22. *Call on the Lord (epikaloumenon ton kurion)*. See I Cor. 1:2; Rom. 10:12–14.

23. *Ignorant (apaideutous)*. Old verbal, here only in N.T. (*a* privative and *paideuō*). Untrained, uneducated, "speculations of a half-educated mind" (Parry). *Refuse (paraitou)*. See I Tim. 4:7. *They gender strifes (gennōsin machas)*. Present active indicative of old and common verb *gennaō* (Rom. 9:11). "They beget battles." See 2:14.

24. *Must not strive (ou dei machesthai)*. Rather, "it is not necessary for him to fight" (in such verbal quibbles). The negative *ou* goes with *dei*, not with the infinitive *machesthai*. *Gentle (ēpion)*. Old word (from *epos*, speech), affable, mild, in N.T. only here (and I Thess. 2:7 in some MSS.; W. H. have *nēpios*). *Teachable (didaktikon)*. See I Tim. 3:2. *Forbearing (anexikakon)*. Late compound (from future of *anechō*, *anexō*, and *kakon*, putting up with evil). Here only in N.T.

25. *Correcting* (*paideuonta*). See Titus 2:12. "Schooling" (Parry). *Oppose themselves* (*antidiatithemenous*). Present middle (direct) participle of *antidiatithēmi*, late double compound (Diodorus, Philo) to place oneself in opposition, here only in N.T. *If peradventure God may give* (*mē pote dōiē ho theos*). Here Westcott and Hort read the late form of the second aorist active optative of *didōmi* for the usual *doiē* as they do in 1:18. But there it is a wish for the future and so regular, while here the optative with *mē pote* in a sort of indirect question is used with a primary tense *dei* (present) and parallel with an undoubted subjunctive *ananēpsōsin*, while in Luke 3:15 *mē pote eie* is with a secondary tense. Examples of such an optative do occur in the papyri (Robertson, *Grammar*, p. 989) so that we cannot go as far as Moulton does and say that we "must" read the subjunctive *dōēi* here (*Prolegomena*, pp. 55, 193). *Repentance* (*metanoian*). "Change of mind" (II Cor. 7:10; Rom. 2:4). *Unto the knowledge of the truth* (*eis epignōsin alētheias*). Paul's word "full knowledge" (Col. 1:9).

26. *They may recover themselves* (*ananēpsōsin*). First aorist active subjunctive of *ananēphō*, late and rare word, to be sober again, only here in N.T., though *nēphō* is in I Thess. 5:6. *Out of the snare of the devil* (*ek tēs tou diabolou pagidos*). They have been caught while mentally intoxicated in the devil's snare (I Tim. 3:7). See Rom. 11:9 for *pagis*. *Taken captive* (*ezōgrēmenoi*). Perfect passive participle of *zōgreō*, old verb, to take alive (*zōos, agreō*), in N.T. only here and Luke 5:10 (of Peter). "Taken captive alive." *By him unto his will* (*hup' autou eis to ekeinou thelēma*). This difficult phrase is understood variously. One way is to take both *autou* and *ekeinou*, to refer to the devil. Another way is to take both of them to refer to God. Another way is to take *autou* of the devil and *ekeinou*, of God. This is probably best, "taken captive by the devil" "that they may come back to soberness to do the will of God." There are difficulties in either view.

CHAPTER III

1. *Know this* (*touto ginōske*). See I Cor. 11:3; Phil. 1:12. *In the last days* (*en eschatais hēmerais*). See James 5:3 and I Tim. 4:1. *Grievous* (*chalepoi*). Hard. See Eph. 5:16. *Shall come* (*enstēsontai*). Future middle of *enistēmi* (intransitive use), old verb, to stand on or be at hand, as in II Thess. 2:2. 2. *Lovers of self* (*philautoi*). Old compound adjective (*philos, autos*), here only in N.T. *Lovers of money* (*philarguroi*). Old compound adjective, in N.T. only here and Luke 16:14. See I Tim. 6:10. *Boastful* (*alazones*). Old word for empty pretender, in N.T. only here and Rom. 1:30. *Haughty* (*huperēphanoi*). See also Rom. 1:30 for this old word. *Railers* (*blasphēmoi*). See I Tim. 1:13. *Disobedient to parents* (*goneusin apeitheis*). See Rom. 1:30. *Unthankful* (*acharistoi*). Old word, in N.T. only here and Luke 6:35. *Unholy* (*anosioi*). See I Tim. 1:9. *Without natural affection* (*astorgoi*). See Rom. 1:31. 3. *Implacable* (*aspondoi*). Truce-breakers. Old word, only here in N.T. though in MSS. in Rom. 1:31 (from *a* privative and *spondē*, a libation). 3. *Slanderers* (*diaboloi*). See I Tim. 3:11; Titus 2:3. *Without self-control* (*akrateis*). Old word (*a* privative and *kratos*), here only in N.T. *Fierce* (*anēmeroi*). Old word (*a* privative and *hēmeros*, tame), only here in N.T. *No lovers of good* (*aphilagathoi*). Found only here (*a* privative and *philagathos*, for which see Titus 1:8). See also Phil. 4:8. A papyrus describes Antoninus as *philagathos* and has *aphilokagathia*. 4. *Traitors* (*prodotai*). Old word (from *prodidōmi*), in N.T. only here, Luke 6:16; Acts 7:52. *Headstrong* (*propeteis*). Old word (from *pro* and *piptō*), falling forward, in N.T. only here and Acts 19:36. *Puffed up* (*tetuphōmenoi*). Perfect passive participle of *tuphoō*. See I Tim. 3:6. *Lovers of pleasure* (*philēdonoi*). Literary *Koiné* word (*philos, hēdonē*), only here in N.T. *Lovers of God* (*philotheoi*). Old word (*philos, theos*), only here in N.T. 5. *A form of godliness* (*morphōsin eusebeias*). For *morphōsin*, see Rom. 2:20. The outward shape without the reality.

Having denied (*ērnēmenoi*). Perfect middle participle of *arneomai* (see 2:12f.). *Power* (*dunamin*). See I Cor. 4:20. See Rom. 1:29–31 for similar description. *Turn away* (*apotrepou*). Present middle (direct) imperative of *apotrepō*, "turn thyself away from." Old verb, only here in N.T. See IV Macc. 1:33. **6.** *That creep* (*hoi endunontes*). Old and common verb (also *enduō*) either to put on (I Thess. 5:8) or to enter (to slip in by insinuation, as here). See same idea in Jude 4 (*pareiseduēsan*), II Peter 2:1 (*pareisaxousin*), Gal. 2:4 (*pareisēlthon* and *pareisaktous*). These stealthy "creepers" are pictured also in Titus 1:11. *Take captive* (*aichmalōtizontes*). "Taking captive." Present active participle of *aichmalōtizō*, for which see II Cor. 10:5; Rom. 7:23. *Silly women* (*gunaikaria*). Literally, "little women" (diminutive of *gunē*), found in Diocles (comedian of 5 century B.C.) and in Epictetus. The word here is neuter (grammatical gender) plural. Used contemptuously here (only N.T. example). Ramsay suggests "society ladies." It is amazing how gullible some women are with religious charlatans who pose as exponents of "new thought." *Laden with sins* (*sesōreumena hamartiais*). Perfect passive participle of *sōreuō*, old word from Aristotle down (from *sōros*, a heap) to heap up. In N.T. only here and Rom. 12:20. Associative instrumental case *hamartiais*. *Divers* (*poikilais*). Many coloured. See Titus 3:3. One has only to recall Schweinfurth, the false Messiah of forty odd years ago with his "heavenly harem" in Illinois and the recent infamous "House of David" in Michigan to understand how these Gnostic cults led women into licentiousness under the guise of religion or of liberty. The priestesses of Aphrodite and of Isis were illustrations ready to hand. *Agomena* (present passive participle) means "continually led astray or from time to time."

7. *Never able to come to the knowledge of the truth* (*mēdepote eis epignōsin alētheias elthein dunamena*). Pathetic picture of these hypnotized women without intellectual power to cut through the fog of words and, though always learning scraps of things, they never come into the full knowledge (*epignōsin*) of the truth in Christ. And yet they even pride themselves on belonging to the intelligentsia!

8. *Like as* (*hon tropon*). "In which manner." Adverbial accusative and incorporation of the antecedent *tropon* into the relative clause. *Jannes and Jambres* (*Iannēs kai Iambrēs*). Traditional names of the magicians who withstood Moses (*Targum of Jonathan* on Ex. 7:11). *Withstood* (*antestēsan*). Second aorist active (intransitive) of *anthistēmi*, to stand against, "they stood against" (with dative *Mōusei*). Same word used of Elymas in Acts 13:8 and repeated here *anthistantai* (present middle indicative). Paul here pictures the seducers of the *gunaikaria* above. *Corrupted in mind* (*katephtharmenoi ton noun*). Perfect passive participle of *kataphtheirō*, old compound, in N.T. only here in critical text. See II Cor. 11:3 and I Tim. 6:5 for *diaphtheirō*. The accusative *noun* is retained in the passive. *Reprobate* (*adokimoi*). See I Cor. 9:27; Titus 1:16. They had renounced their trust (*pistin*) in Christ.

9. *They shall proceed no further* (*ou prokopsousin epi pleion*). Future active of *prokoptō*. See 2:16. *Folly* (*anoia*). Old word (from *anoos*, *a* privative and *nous*), want of sense, here only in N.T. *Evident* (*ekdēlos*). Old word (*ek*, *dēlos*, outstanding), here only in N.T. *Theirs* (*ekeinōn*). Of Jannes and Jambres (Ex. 7:12).

10. *Didst follow* (*parēkolouthēsas*). First aorist active indicative of *parakoloutheō*, for which see I Tim. 4:6. Some MSS. have perfect active *parēkolouthēkas* (thou hast followed). Nine associative-instrumental cases here after the verb (*teaching*, *didaskaliāi*, Rom. 12:7; *conduct*, *agōgēi*, old word here only in N.T.; *purpose*, *prothesei*, Rom. 8:28; *faith*, *pistei*, I Thess. 3:6; *longsuffering*, *makrothumiāi*, Col. 1:11; *persecutions*, *diōgmois*, II Thess 1:4; *sufferings*, *pathēmasin*, II Cor. 1:6f.). The two last items belong to verse 11.

11. *What things befell me* (*hoia moi egeneto*). Qualitative relative (*hoia*) referring to actual experiences of Paul (*egeneto*, second aorist middle indicative of *ginomai*) more fully described in II Cor. 11:30–33. The Acts of the Apostles tell of his experiences in Antioch in Pisidia (13:14, 45, 50), in Iconium (14:1–5), in Lystra (14:6–19). See also Gal. 2:11. *What persecutions I endured* (*hoious diōgmous hupēnegka*). Qualitative relative again with *diōgmous*. The verb is first aorist active indicative of *hupopherō*, old verb, to bear under as in I Cor. 10:13. *Delivered me* (*me erusato*). First aorist

middle of *ruomai*, old verb, with *ek* here as in I Thess. 1:10. Used again of the Lord Jesus in 4:18.

12. *That would live godly (hoi thelontes zēin eusebōs)*. "Those who desire (will, determine) to live godly." Paul does not regard his experience as peculiar, but only part of the price of loyal service to Christ. *Shall suffer persecution (diōchthēsontai)*. Future passive of *diōkō*, "shall be persecuted" (shall be hunted as wild beasts).

13. *Impostors (goētes)*. Old word from wailers (*goaō*, to bewail), professional mourners, deceivers, jugglers. Here only in the N.T. Modern impostors know all the tricks of the trade. *Shall wax worse and worse (prokopsousin epi to cheiron)*. "Shall cut forward to the worse stage." See 2:16 for *prokoptō*. *Cheiron* is comparative of *kakos*, "to the worse than now." *Deceiving and being deceived (planōntes kai planōmenoi)*. Present active and present passive participles of *planaō*. The tragedy of it all is that these seducers are able to deceive others as well as themselves.

14. *But abide thou (su de mene)*. Emphatic contrast (*su de*), "But thou." Present active imperative of *menō*, common verb, to remain. *In the things which (en hois)*. The antecedent to *hois* is not expressed ("in which things") and the relative is attracted from *ha* accusative with *emathes* (didst learn, second aorist active indicative of *manthanō*) to the case of the unexpressed antecedent (locative with *en*). *Hast been assured of (epistōthēs)*. First aorist passive indicative of *pistoō*, old verb (from *pistos*, faithful), to make reliable, only here in N.T. *Knowing from whom (eidōs para tinōn)*. Second perfect active participle of *oida*. Note *tinōn* (ablative case after *para* in an indirect question). The list included the O.T. prophets, Paul, Eunice, Lois. There ought to be moral authority in such personages.

15. *From a babe (apo brephous)*. Only here in the Pastorals. This teaching from the fifth year, covering the whole of Timothy's recollections. See Mark 9:21 *ek paidiothen*, from a child. *Thou has known (oidas)*. Present active indicative, progressive perfect reaching from a babe till now. Would that Christian parents took like pains today. *The sacred writings (hiera grammata)*. "Sacred writings" or "Holy Scriptures." Here alone in N.T., though in Josephus (Proem to *Ant.* 3; *Apion* 1, etc.) and in Philo. The adjective *hieros*

occurs in I Cor. 9:13 of the temple worship, and *gramma* in contrast to *pneuma* in II Cor. 3:6f.; Rom. 2:29 and in John 5:47 of Moses' writings, in Acts 28:21 of an epistle, in Gal. 6:11 of letters (characters). In Ephesus there were *Ephesia grammata* that were *bebēla* (Acts 19:19), not *hiera*. *To make thee wise* (*se sophisai*). First aorist active infinitive of *sophizō*, old verb (from *sophos*), in N.T. only here, and II Peter 1:16. *Which is in* (*tēs en*). Common idiom with the article, "the in." The use of the Scriptures was not magic, but of value when used "through faith that is in Christ Jesus."

16. *Every scripture inspired of God is also profitable* (*pāsa graphē theopneustos kai ōphelimos*). There are two matters of doubt in this clause. One is the absence of the article *hē* before *graphē*, whether that makes it mean "every scripture" or "all scripture" as of necessity if present. Unfortunately, there are examples both ways with both *pās* and *graphē*. Twice we find *graphē* in the singular without the article and yet definite (I Peter 2:6; II Peter 1:20). We have *pās Israēl* (Rom. 11:26) for all Israel (Robertson, *Grammar*, p. 772). So far as the grammatical usage goes, one can render here either "all scripture" or "every scripture." There is no copula (*estin*) in the Greek and so one has to insert it either before the *kai* or after it. If before, as is more natural, then the meaning is: "All scripture (or every scripture) is inspired of God and profitable." In this form there is a definite assertion of inspiration. That can be true also of the second way, making "inspired of God" descriptive of "every scripture," and putting *estin* (is) after *kai*: "All scripture (or every scripture), inspired of God, is also profitable." *Inspired of God* (*theopneustos*). "God-breathed." Late word (Plutarch) here only in N.T. Perhaps in contrast to the commandments of men in Titus 1:14. *Profitable* (*ōphelimos*). See I Tim. 4:8. See Rom. 15:4. Four examples of *pros* (facing, with a view to, for): *didaskalian*, teaching; *elegmon*, reproof, in LXX and here only in N.T.; *epanorthōsin*, correction, old word, from *epanorthoō*, to set up straight in addition, here only in N.T., with which compare *epidiorthoō* in Titus 1:5; *paideian*, instruction, with which compare Eph. 6:4.

17. *The man of God* (*ho tou theou anthrōpos*). See I Tim.

6:11. *May be complete* (*hina ēi artios*). Final clause with *hina* and present subjunctive of *eimi*. *Artios* is old word (from root *arō*, to fit), specially adapted, here only in N.T. *Furnished completely* (*exērtismenos*). Perfect passive participle of *exartizō*, rare verb, to furnish (fit) fully (perfective use of *ex*), in N.T. only here and Acts 21:5. In Josephus. For *katartizō*, see Luke 6:40; II Cor. 13:11.

CHAPTER IV

1. *I charge thee* (*diamarturomai*). Rather, "I testify."
See I Thess. 4:6. See I Tim. 5:21 for this verb and appeal
to God and Christ. *Who shall judge* (*tou mellontos krinein*).
"The one going or about to judge" (regular idiom with
mellō). *The quick and the dead* (*zōntas kai nekrous*). "Living
and dead." See I Thess. 4:16f. *And by his appearing* (*kai
tēn epiphaneian*). Accusative of conjuration (verbs of swear-
ing), after *diamarturomai* as is *basileian* (by his kingdom).
See I Thess. 5:27. For *epiphaneian*, see 1:10; Titus 2:13;
I Tim. 6:14; II Thess. 2:8.
2. *Preach the word* (*kēruxon ton logon*). First aorist active
imperative of *kērussō*. For "the word" used absolutely,
see I Thess. 1:6; Gal. 6:6. *Be instant in season, out of season*
(*epistēthi eukairōs akairōs*). Second aorist (ingressive) active
imperative of *ephistēmi* (intransitive use), "take a stand,"
"stand upon it or up to it," "carry on," "stick to it." The
Vulgate has "*insta*." The two adverbs are like a proverb
or a play (pun) on the word *kairos*. There are all sorts of
seasons (*kairoi*), some difficult (*chalepoi*, 3:1), some easy
(*eukairei*, I Cor. 16:12). *Reprove* (*elegxon*). First aorist
active imperative of *elegchō*. "Bring to proof." Eph. 5:11.
Rebuke (*epitimēson*). First aorist active imperative of *epitimaō*, to give honour (or blame) to, to chide. Common in
the Gospels (Luke 17:3). *Exhort* (*parakaleson*). First aorist
active imperative of *parakaleō*, common Pauline word.
3. *A time when* (*kairos hote*). One of the *akairōs* (out of
season) times. *Will not endure* (*ouk anexontai*). Future
middle (direct) of *anechō*. "Will not hold themselves back
from" (Col. 3:13). *Having itching ears* (*knēthomenoi tēn
akoēn*). Present middle (causative) participle of *knēthō*, late
and rare form of the Attic *knaō*, to scratch, to tickle, here
only in N.T. "Getting the ears (the hearing, *tēn akoēn*)
tickled." The Vulgate has *prurientes*. Cf. the Athenians
(Acts 17:21). Clement of Alexandria tells of speakers tickling
(*knēthontes*) the ears of those who want to be tickled. This

is the temptation of the merely "popular" preacher, to furnish the latest tickle.

4. *Will turn away their ears* (*tēn akoēn apostrepsousin*). Future active of old verb *apostrephō*. See I Cor. 12:17 for this use of *akoē*. The people stopped their ears and rushed at Stephen in Acts 7:57. *Will turn aside* (*ektrapēsontai*). Second future passive of *ektrepō*. They prefer "myths" to "the truth" as some today turn away to "humanism," "bolshevism," "new thought" or any other fad that will give a new momentary thrill to their itching ears and morbid minds.

5. *But be thou sober* (*su de nēphe*). Present active imperative of *nēphō*, for which see I Thess. 5:6, 8. "Be sober in thy head." *Suffer hardship* (*kakopathēson*). See 2:9. *Do the work of an evangelist* (*ergon poiēson euaggelistou*). See I Cor. 1:17; Eph. 4:11 for *euaggelistēs*, gospelizer. *Fulfil* (*plērophorēson*). First aorist active imperative of *plērophoreō*, for which see Col. 4:12. In Col. 4:17 Paul uses *plēroō* to Archippus about his ministry as he here employs *plērophoreō*. Both verbs mean to fill full.

6. *I am already being offered* (*ēdē spendomai*). Present (progressive) passive indicative of *spendō*, old verb, to pour out a libation or drink offering. In N.T. only here and Phil. 2:17. "What was then a possibility is now a certainty" (Parry). The sacrifice of Paul's life-blood has begun. *Of my departure* (*tēs analuseōs mou*). Our very word "analysis." Old word from *analuō*, to loosen up or back, to unloose. Only here in N.T., though *analusai* for death is used by Paul in Phil. 1:23 which see for the metaphor. *Is come* (*ephestēken*). Perfect active indicative of *ephistēmi* (intransitive use). See I Thess. 5:3 and Luke 21:34. The hour has struck. The time has come.

7. *I have fought the good fight* (*ton kalon agōna ēgōnismai*). Perfect middle indicative of *agōnizomai*, a favourite figure with Paul (I Cor. 9:25; Col. 1:29), with the cognate accusative *agōna* (Phil. 1:27, 30, etc.). The "fight" is the athletic contest of his struggle for Christ. *I have finished the course* (*ton dromon teteleka*). Perfect active indicative of *teleō*. He had used this metaphor also of himself to the elders at Ephesus (Acts 20:24). Then the "course" was ahead of him. Now it is behind him. *I have kept the faith* (*tēn pistin*

tetēreka). Perfect active indicative again of *tēreō*. Paul has not deserted. He has kept faith with Christ. For this phrase, see Rev. 14:12. Deissmann (*Light*, etc., p. 309) gives inscriptions in Ephesus of a man who says: "I have kept faith" (*tēn pistin etērēsa*) and another of a man of whom it is said: "He fought three fights, and twice was crowned." 8. *Henceforth* (*loipon*). Accusative case, "for the rest." *There is laid up for me* (*apokeitai moi*). Present passive of *apokeimai*, old verb, to be laid away. See Col. 1:5 for the hope laid away. Paul's "crown of righteousness" (*ho tēs dikaiosunēs stephanos*, genitive of apposition, the crown that consists in righteousness and is also the reward for righteousness, the victor's crown as in I Cor. 9:25 which see) "is laid away" for him. *At that day* (*en ekeinēi tēi hēmerāi*). That great and blessed day (1:12, 18). *The righteous judge* (*ho dikaios kritēs*). "The just judge," the umpire who makes no mistakes who judges us all (II Cor. 5:10). *Shall give me* (*apodōsei moi*). Future active of *apodidōmi*. "Will give back" as in Rom. 2:6 and in full. *But also to all them that have loved his appearing* (*alla pāsin tois ēgapēkosin tēn epiphaneian autou*). Dative case of the perfect active participle of *agapaō*, to love, who have loved and still love his second coming. *Epiphaneia* here can as in 1:10 be interpreted of Christ's Incarnation. 9. *Shortly* (*tacheōs*). In verse 21 he more definitely says "before winter." Apparently the trial might drag on through its various stages. 10. *Forsook me* (*me egkateleipen*). Imperfect (MSS. also have aorist, *egkatelipen*) active of the old double compound verb *egkataleipō*, for which see Rom. 9:29. Clearly in contrast to verse 9 and in the sense of I Tim. 6:17, wilful desertion. Only mentioned elsewhere in Col. 4:14. *Crescens* (*Krēskēs*). No other mention of him. *Titus to Dalmatia* (*Titos eis Dalmatian*). Titus had been asked to rejoin Paul in Nicopolis where he was to winter, probably the winter previous to this one (Titus 3:12). He came and has been with Paul. 11. *Only Luke is with me* (*Loukas estin monos met' emou*). Luke is with Paul now in Rome as during the first Roman imprisonment (Philemon 24; Col. 4:14). *Take Mark* (*Markon analabōn*). Second aorist active participle of *analambanō*,

old verb, to pick up, as in Eph. 6:13, 16. "Pick up Mark."
He is useful to me (estin moi euchrēstos). See 2:21 for *eu-chrēstos.* Paul had long ago changed his opinion of Mark
(Col. 4:10) because Mark had changed his conduct and had
made good in his ministry. Now Paul longs to have the
man that he once scornfully rejected (Acts 15:37ff.).
12. *Tychicus I sent to Ephesus (Tuchikon apesteila eis
Epheson).* Perhaps Paul had sent him on before he came
to Rome. He may have been still on the way to Ephesus.
13. *The cloke (tēn phelonēn).* More common form *pheilonē.*
By metathesis for *phainolē,* Latin *paenula,* though which
language transliterated the word into the other is not known.
The meaning is also uncertain, though probably "cloke"
as there are so many papyri examples in that sense (Moulton
and Milligan, *Vocabulary*). Milligan (*N.T. Documents,*
p. 20) had previously urged "book wrap" as probable but
he changed his mind and rightly so. *With Carpus (para
Karpōi).* "Beside Carpus," at his house. Not mentioned
elsewhere. Probably a visit to Troas after Paul's return
from Crete. *The books (ta biblia).* Probably papyrus rolls.
One can only guess what rolls the old preacher longs to have
with him, probably copies of Old Testament books, possibly
copies of his own letters, and other books used and loved.
The old preacher can be happy with his books. *Especially
the parchments (malista tas membranas).* Latin *membrana.*
The dressed skins were first made at Pergamum and so
termed "parchments." These in particular would likely be
copies of Old Testament books, parchment being more ex-
pensive than papyrus, possibly even copies of Christ's sayings (Luke 1:1-4). We recall that in Acts 26:24 Festus referred to Paul's learning (*ta grammata*). He would not waste
his time in prison.
14. *Alexander the coppersmith (Alexandros ho chalkeus).*
Old word, only here in N.T., for metal-worker (copper, iron,
gold, etc.). Possibly the one in 1:20, but not the one in
Acts 19:33f. unless he afterwards became a Christian. *Did
me much evil (moi kaka enedeixato).* Evidently he had some
personal dislike towards Paul and possibly also he was a
Gnostic. *Will render (apodōsei).* Future active of the same
verb used in verse 8, but with a very different atmosphere.
15. *Be thou ware also (kai su phulassou).* Present middle

(direct) imperative of *phulassō*, "from whom keep thyself away." *Withstood* (*antestē*). Second aorist active indicative of *anthistēmi*, "stood against my words." See 3:8; Gal. 2:11. 16. *At my first defence* (*en tēi prōtēi apologiāi*). Original sense of "apology" as in Phil. 1:7, 16. Either the first stage in this trial or the previous trial and acquittal at the end of the first Roman imprisonment. Probably the first view is correct, though really there is no way to decide. *No one took my part* (*oudeis moi paregeneto*). "No one came by my side" (second aorist middle indicative of *paraginomai*). See I Cor. 16:3. *But all forsook me* (*alla pantes me egkateleipon*). Same verb and tense used of Demas above (verse 10), "But all were forsaking me" (one by one) or, if aorist *egkatelipon*, "all at once left me." *May it not be laid to their account* (*mē autois logistheiē*). First aorist passive optative in future wish with negative *mē*. Common Pauline verb *logizomai* (I Cor. 13:5; Rom. 4:3, 5).

17. *But the Lord stood by me* (*ho de kurios moi parestē*). Second aorist active of *paristēmi* (intransitive use), "took his stand by my side." See Rom. 16:2. Clearly Jesus appeared to Paul now at this crisis and climax as he had done so many times before. *Strengthened me* (*enedunamōsen me*). "Poured power into me." See Phil. 4:13. *That through me the message might be fully proclaimed* (*hina di' emou to kērugma plērophorēthēi*). Final clause with *hina* and first aorist passive subjunctive of *plērophoreō* (see verse 5). Either to the rulers in Rome now or, if the first imprisonment, by his release and going to Spain. *And that all the Gentiles might hear* (*kai akousōsin panta ta ethnē*). Continuation of the purpose with the aorist active subjunctive of *akouō*. *I was delivered out of the mouth of the lion* (*erusthēn ek stomatos leontos*). First aorist passive indicative of *ruomai* (I Thess. 1:10). A proverb, but not certain what the application is whether to Nero or to Satan (I Thess. 2:18) or to the lion in the arena where Paul could not be sent because a Roman citizen.

18. *Will deliver me* (*rusetai me*). Future middle. Recall the Lord's Prayer. Paul is not afraid of death. He will find his triumph in death (Phil. 1:21f.). *Unto his heavenly kingdom* (*eis tēn basileian autou tēn epouranian*). The future life of glory as in I Cor. 15:24, 50. He will save (*sōsei*, effective future) me there finally and free from all evil. *To whom*

be the glory (*hōi hē doxa*). No verb in the Greek. Paul's final doxology, his Swan Song, to Christ as in Rom. 9:5; 16:27.

19. *Prisca and Aquila* (*Priscan kai Akulan*). Paul's friends now back in Ephesus, no longer in Rome (Rom. 16:3). See 1:16 for the house of Onesiphorus.

20. *Erastus* (*Erastos*). See Acts 19:22; Rom. 16:23. *Trophimus* (*Trophimon*). A native of Ephesus and with Paul in Jerusalem (Acts 20:4; 21:29). *At Miletus sick* (*en Milētōi asthenounta*). Present active participle of *astheneō*, to be weak. Probably on Paul's return from Crete.

21. *Before winter* (*pro cheimōnos*). Pathetic item if Paul was now in the Mamertine Dungeon in Rome with winter coming on and without his cloak for which he asked. How long he had been in prison this time we do not know. He may even have spent the previous winter or part of it here. Eubulus, Pudens, Linus, Claudia are all unknown otherwise. Irenaeus does speak of Linus. *The Lord be with thy Spirit* (*ho kurios meta tou pneumatos sou*). Let us hope that Timothy and Mark reached Paul before winter, before the end came, with the cloak and with the books. Our hero, we may be sure, met the end nobly. He is already more than conqueror in Christ who is by his side and who will welcome him to heaven and give him his crown. Luke, Timothy, Mark will do all that mortal hands can do to cheer the heart of Paul with human comfort. He already had the comfort of Christ in full measure.